One Gospel from Two

MARK'S USE OF MATTHEW AND LUKE

One Gospel from Two

MARK'S USE OF MATTHEW AND LUKE

A Demonstration by the Research Team of the
International Institute for Renewal of Gospel Studies

EDITED BY

DAVID B. PEABODY,

WITH LAMAR COPE AND ALLAN J. McNICOL

TRINITY PRESS INTERNATIONAL
A Continuum imprint
HARRISBURG • LONDON • NEW YORK

Trinity Press International
A Continuum imprint
P.O. Box 1321, Harrisburg, PA 17105

Cover design: Wesley Hoke

Library of Congress Cataloging-in-Publication Data

One Gospel From Two : Mark's Use of Matthew and Luke / edited by David B. Peabody; with Lamar Cope and Allan J. McNicol.

   p. cm.

Includes indexes.

ISBN 1-56338-352-7 (pbk.)

1. Bible. N.T. Mark—Criticism, interpretation, etc. 2. Bible. N.T. Mark—Relation to Matthew. 3. Bible. N.T. Mark—Relation to Luke. I. Peabody, David Barrett, 1946- . II. McNicol, Allan J. (Allan James), 1939- . III. Cope, Lamar. IV. International Institute for the Renewal of Gospel Studies.

BS2585.2 .O54   2002
226.3'066—dc21   2002009365

Printed in the United States of America

02 03 04 05 06 07   10 9 8 7 6 5 4 3 2 1

IN MEMORIAM — WILLIAM REUBEN FARMER
(1 FEBRUARY 1921 – 31 DECEMBER 2000)

We proudly dedicate this volume to our long-time mentor, colleague and friend, William R. Farmer. In 1982 Bill's commitment to careful, critical Biblical research, especially in the area of Gospel Studies, led him to found and initially to co-chair, along with Dom John Bernard Orchard, the International Institute for Renewal of Gospel Studies. Since its inception, the Institute has provided funding for research, travel grants, computer equipment, and many conferences on the gospels. One such conference occurred in Münster, Germany in 1976 that celebrated the bicentennial of the separate publication of Johann Jakob Griesbach's synopsis. Another conference was held in Jerusalem in 1984 that focused debate among three teams of experts, each representing and defending a different source critical view of the origins of the synoptic gospels. It was at this latter conference that most of the team members who eventually researched, wrote and published *Beyond the Q Impasse* began to collaborate. Bill Farmer contributed a great deal to that earlier, companion volume and now also to this one.

When Bill's health took its final turn for the worse in November of 2000, he had just finished facilitating a major conference on the Eucharist in the Gospels and Paul. He had also completed a monograph that was a summing-up of his ideas on the origins of the Gospels (still in preparation). In other words, in addition to working on this volume, Bill remained an active force in Biblical studies to the very end. It is, therefore, a pity he did not live to see the publication of this compositional analysis of Mark on the Two Gospel Hypothesis. *One Gospel from Two* includes many of his latest judgments on a variety of critical issues related to the Gospel of Mark.

In addition to his considerable contributions to Biblical studies, we also remember Bill for his lifelong commitment to social justice and his courageous stand, especially with people of color, in their struggle for equality. That which Bill Farmer learned in his study and taught in his classes, he exemplified in his life. Within the limits of human frailty, Bill strove for integrity.

Therefore, it only remains for me to say, on behalf of my colleagues in the International Institute for Renewal of Gospel Studies, how much we have treasured the months and years of close collaboration that we shared with Bill Farmer. He was unfailingly supportive, open-minded, hard working, and insightful. It was a joy to work with him, and without his resolute and creative leadership, none of us would have had half the fun we did in our years of working on the Gospels.

David L. Dungan
Executive Director
International Institute for Renewal of Gospel Studies
March 2002

CONTENTS

CONTENTS

CONTENTS

PREFACE

As advocates of the Two Gospel (formerly "Griesbach") Hypothesis, we have been asked for decades by colleagues who do not share our source theory to provide detailed discussions of how, prior to the composition of Mark, Luke first made use of Matthew and, then, how Mark, writing third, made use of both Matthew and Luke. With the release of *One Gospel from Two,* combined with *Beyond the Q Impasse,* we are now able to offer these two volumes as our considered and detailed responses to these long-standing requests.

Like its predecessor, this book is the product of close collaboration among members of the Research Team of the International Institute for Renewal of Gospel Studies. Shortly after the publication of *Beyond the Q Impasse* in 1996, a continuing research team composed of Lamar Cope, David L. Dungan, William R. Farmer, Allan J. McNicol, David B. Peabody, and Philip L. Shuler was joined by Thomas R. W. Longstaff. Tom came to the team with a research specialty in known examples of conflation, its characteristics and the Gospel of Mark. His expertise with computer technology and its applications enhanced the team's research capabilities. Tom is also primarily responsible for what others of us on the team judge to be an elegant, intuitive and "user friendly" interface for our recently published, color-coded, electronic synopsis of Mark and its parallels.

Dungan, Farmer, McNicol, Peabody, and Shuler were doing collaborative work on Mark's use of Matthew and Luke as early as 1982 as they prepared together to participate in the two-week Symposium on the Interrelations of the Gospels that was held in Jerusalem in April of 1984. These five colleagues, later joined by Cope, continued to do collaborative work on Mark after that conference, particularly under the auspices of the Society of Biblical Literature's Consultation (1988-1989) and Group (1990-1995) on "Redaction Criticism and the Two Gospel Hypothesis." By 1991, however, this research team had decided to turn its concentrated attention to the other major aspect of the Two Gospel Hypothesis, Luke's Use of Matthew, which eventually led to the publication of *Beyond the Q Impasse.*

Also by the early 1980s, many of us had rejected the name "Griesbach" as a label for our hypothesis and had come to call our source theory "the Two Gospel hypothesis" for several reasons. First, it brought the name of our theory into an intended contrast and tension with the dominant view among experts at that time, the Two Document or Two Source hypothesis (the priority of *the two documents/sources*, Mark and "Q," followed by the mutual, but independent, use of these sources by Matthew and Luke).

Second, this name change was intended to respond to some of our critics who seemed to assume that our theory focused on "Matthean priority." In response, we wished to make it clear on our theory that both of *the two gospels*, Matthew and Luke, were equally valuable, especially as sources for reconstructing the history and theology of the earliest Christian communities and, perhaps, also for reconstructing the life and teachings of Jesus.

Third, we also made this name change because of our discovery that Griesbach had predecessors, like Henry Owen in England and Friedrich Andreas Stroth in Germany, who advocated source theories of the gospels essentially the same as the one that eventually became associated with Griesbach's name. By the early 1980s, we had also discovered areas of disagreement with some of Griesbach's own views, such as his disdain for the value of any of the Patristic evidence and his claim that Mark contained nothing more than about twenty-four verses that were not found in Matthew, Luke or both.

Finally, in contrast to the work of Griesbach and his followers in eighteenth- and nineteenth-century Europe, our work is now grounded in extensive new research that has only been carried out over the last forty years. Here are some of the specifics of that research and its implications for our work on *One Gospel from Two*.

1. This book presupposes a completely new synopsis of Mark and its parallels, based for the first time upon an explicit theory of synopsis construction.

2. It utilizes a new set of paragraph/pericope and part divisions, with carefully articulated explanations of why we have divided the text in the ways we have. We have also provided new titles for these divisions that focus upon distinctive features of the text of Mark alone, rather than on one or more features that are common to two or three synoptic gospels in parallel.

3. It is based upon a re-evaluation of the critical texts of Mark and its parallels. Although we tend to agree with UBS[4] and Nestle-Aland[27], with aid from Reuben Swanson's horizontal-line synoptic displays of the full texts of many of the earliest and most important manuscripts of the Greek New Testament, we have sometimes preferred a reading that differs from the one offered by the distinguished committees who created these currently most utilized critical texts.

4. It is informed by a fresh and more nuanced reading of the patristic evidence, which turns out to be more unified on the questions of the sequence and interrelations of the gospels than we had previously thought.

5. It is founded on more than twenty years of detailed, critical re-examination of scholarship on the synoptic problem, back to the beginning of the modern period and, in selected instances, back beyond that time to the period of the earliest Church Fathers. We have certainly learned from our academic forebears, acknowledged and utilized what we have considered the best of their work, corrected it when necessary and, most importantly, tried not to repeat their errors, particularly in terms of research methods and some of their arguments in support of a source theory.

At the same time, we are acutely aware that the conclusions drawn in this volume go against the grain of more than one hundred and twenty years of general consensus with regard to the composition of the Gospel of Mark and most of the source material utilized by its author. The readers of this book will, therefore, need to read our work with particular sensitivity to significant differences between our views and those of many of our academic forebears and even many of our contemporary colleagues who have presupposed this popular consensus in their publications at least since the middle of the nineteenth century.

In fact, so indentured to the priority of Mark and "Q" are many of the most currently utilized tools for study of the gospels (the critical text, synopses, synoptic charts, many commentaries, etc.) that we have needed to construct and use some different instruments for our own study. Using these newly created instruments has led us to see and identify new evidence for our hypothesis and to present other, more widely recognized, evidence in a manner that better illustrates our source theory. Therefore, those who would check our work are asked to use the synopses and synoptic charts that we have constructed because those constructed by others were composed with other presuppositions, goals and purposes in mind.

Although some of the data and insights presented here about Mark's use of Matthew and Luke were published earlier by individual members of this team, they appear in this book not only in their most developed forms to date, but also as the building blocks of a more comprehensive and synthetic argument. Therefore, this book and its argument, especially when illustrated by our new synopsis of Mark and its parallels, enables the reader best to see the full force of the evidence that convinces us that Mark was not the earliest, primitive, foundational gospel of the Church, but rather a carefully composed, revision of its predecessors, Matthew and Luke.

ACKNOWLEDGEMENTS

This book had its beginnings in collaborative work done by the Research Team of the International Institute for the Renewal of Gospel Studies in the early 1980s. One of the first fruits of those initial collaborative efforts were the Team's contributions to the symposium on *The Interrelations of the Gospels* held in Jerusalem in 1984. A second was a "Narrative Outline of the Markan Composition According to the Two Gospel Hypothesis" that was peer reviewed within the SBL Group on "Redaction Criticism and the Two Gospel Hypothesis" (1988-1995) and published in the *SBL Seminar Papers* in 1990. A third was the article, signed by David L Dungan, on "The Two Gospel Hypothesis" that appeared in the *Anchor Bible Dictionary* in 1993.

At the Jerusalem Conference, direct responses to the Research Team's work on Mark's Use of Matthew and Luke were published by Frans Neirynck, Christopher M. Tuckett and Marie Émile Boismard. During the 1990 meeting of the Society of Biblical Literature, responses to our "Narrative Outline of the Markan Composition" were provided by Paul Coke, H. Edward Everding, Jr., and Frank E. Wheeler. We appreciate each of these respondents who, through careful and constructive criticism from a variety of source-critical perspectives, have helped us to sharpen our arguments for Mark's Use of Matthew and Luke that we now present in *One Gospel from Two*.

At the 1991 Annual Meeting of the Society of Biblical Literature, the Research Team temporarily turned its attention away from Mark's Use of Matthew and Luke and toward the other major aspect of the Two Gospel Hypothesis, Luke's Use of Matthew. Since the publication of our conclusions about this other aspect of our hypothesis in 1996 in *Beyond the Q Impasse*, we have benefited from a number of reviews of this book and other types of responses to our work. Here we take particular note of contributions by Steven C. Carlson, Robert A. Derrenbacker, Timothy A. Friedrichsen, Mark S. Goodacre, Peter Head, Christopher M. Tuckett, and John S Kloppenborg Verbin. (See the bibliography for full references.) We have learned from each of these colleagues and look forward to enjoying a continuing and constructive dialogue and debate with each of them in the future.

In addition to acknowledging our debts to these scholars and colleagues, we also express our appreciation to several of our benefactors . First, the Institute for the Renewal of Gospel Studies has supported our research and publications with grants for travel, computer equipment, subventions and scholarly conferences in North America and Europe. Second, we thank the institutions which support us as teachers and scholars – Carroll College, Waukesha, Wisconsin; Colby College, Waterville, Maine; the Institute for Christian Studies, Austin, Texas; McMurry University, Abilene, Texas; Nebraska Wesleyan University, Lincoln; Southern Methodist University and the University of Dallas in Texas and the University of Tennessee, Knoxville. In addition to our own, other institutions that have hosted our meetings and housed us during them have included the Episcopal Seminary of the

ACKNOWLEDGEMENTS

Southwest in Austin, Texas and Nashotah House, in Wisconsin. With support from these institutions we have been enabled to collaborate with one another face-to-face several times a year for many years and, through the computers and internet connections that have been provided by our home institutions, as well as the Institute, we have been able to continue our collaboration via e-mail between those indispensable face-to-face meetings.

Other technological aids that have contributed to our work include the electronic text of the Greek New Testament and the GraecaII font, made available by Philip Payne and Linguists Software, and the Accordance search engine and texts available from the Gramcord Institute. Floppy Copy in Salt Lake City, Utah produced multiple copies of our color-coded electronic synopsis of Mark and its parallels.

We also appreciate the support we have received over a long period of time from the staff of our publisher, Trinity Press International, especially Henry Carrigan, Editorial Director and Laura Hudson, Managing Editor. On 7 May 2002, The Morehouse Group, Inc., which included Trinity Press International, was wholly acquired by The Continuum International Publishing Group of London and New York.

Finally, we express our deepest appreciation to our wives and loved ones without whose support this book could not have been researched, written and published. To Jeri Brandt, Sandy Cope, Anne Dungan, Nell Farmer, Cindy Longstaff, Patricia McNicol and Anita Shuler, thanks is not enough. And to Patricia Gregory, "the cookie lady," thanks for sustenance through our many long meetings all over the country.

INTRODUCTION

The Next Step

In the conclusion to our volume, *Beyond the Q Impasse: Luke's Use of Matthew,*[1] we stated that we had provided a plausible account of the composition of Luke on the assumption that canonical Matthew was his main source. As far as we knew, it was an entirely new contribution to the field of Lukan Studies. Such an analysis of Luke was never attempted by Griesbach or any of his followers in the nineteenth century. In the conclusion, we stated that our next step would be to provide a pericope-by-pericope compositional analysis of the Gospel of Mark showing that a plausible account could be given of it, assuming that it was written after and on the basis of Matthew and Luke. After some forty years of painstaking research, going back beyond William R. Farmer's ground-breaking book, *The Synoptic Problem: A Critical Analysis,*[2] and after several preliminary attempts,[3] we now present *One Gospel from Two: Mark's Use of Matthew and Luke,* the necessary complement to *Beyond the Q Impasse,* to our peers and colleagues for their consideration and critical response.

In the following detailed compositional analysis, we do not posit the existence of lost versions of Mark (such as UrMarkus, Secret Mark or DeuteroMarkus), or lost recensions either of Luke (e.g., ProtoLuke) or of Matthew (Aramaic Matthew) to help make sense out of the text of Mark. The number of such hypothetical sources continues to grow in the scholarly literature on the Synoptic Problem for one fundamental reason: to defend the idea that Mark was written first. That task, however, in our view, is unnecessary. As we seek to demonstrate in this volume, Mark's secondary character vis-à-vis Matthew and Luke can be demonstrated at many different levels and in many different ways.

Problems with the Consensus Supporting the Two Document Hypothesis

Today, a strong consensus remains among scholars of the NT who are not experts in the Synoptic Problem that Mark was the first of the canonical Gospels to be composed. We do not need to rehearse

---

[1] Allan J. McNicol with David L. Dungan and David B. Peabody, eds. *Beyond the Q Impasse: Luke's Use of Matthew.* A Demonstration by the Research Team of the International Institute for [Renewal] of Gospel Studies (Valley Forge, Pa.: Trinity Press International, 1996).

[2] William R. Farmer, *The Synoptic Problem: A Critical Analysis* (New York: MacMillan, 1964; 2d ed.; Dillsboro, NC: Western North Carolina Press, 1976).

[3] One of these "preliminary attempts" was William R. Farmer, et al., "Narrative Outline of the Markan Composition According to the Two Gospel Hypothesis," *SBL 1990 Seminar Papers* (SBLSP 29; ed. David J. Lull; Atlanta, Ga.: Society of Biblical Literature, 1990), 212-39.

how this current consensus came to be. That history has been thoroughly documented elsewhere by proponents and opponents of the hypothesis.[4]

This form of the "Markan" hypothesis, that canonical Mark was the source of Matthew and Luke, from its inception in Germany in the latter part of the nineteenth century and during its subsequent elaboration by B. H. Streeter and others in England in the twentieth, was constantly confronted by a whole range of serious objections. Experts made repeated attempts, even then, to demonstrate that the priority of Mark was a questionable hypothesis.

THE SAYINGS GOSPEL, Q: ONE NECESSARY SUPPLEMENT TO MARKAN PRIORITY

For instance, there was the problem of the other source material used by Matthew and Luke besides Mark, that eventually came to be considered a single, written document by most of its advocates and named "Q." From whence did the idea for Q come in the first place? If Mark was the first Gospel and the source for the overall structure and much of the material in Matthew and Luke,

---

[4] For the classic study of this question, see Farmer, *Synoptic Problem*. For a summary of the development of the Two Document Hypothesis from a supporter's viewpoint see W. G. Kummel, *The New Testament: The History of the Investigation of Its Problems,* (trans. H. C. Kee; Nashville: Abingdon, 1972), 144-61. For a critique of the Markan hypothesis within the circle of German scholarship, see Hans-Herbert Stoldt, *Geschichte und Kritik der Markus-hypothese* (Göttingen: Vandenhoeck & Ruprecht, 1977; 2d rev. ed. Giessen: Brunen, 1986); ET of first edition, *History and Criticism of the Marcan Hypothesis* (trans. and ed. by Donald J. Niewyk, Macon, Ga.: Mercer University Press; Edinburgh: T & T Clark, 1980). A detailed analysis of methodological errors made by some of the leading nineteenth-century German advocates of the Markan hypothesis is given in David B. Peabody, "Chapters in the History of the Linguistic Argument for Solving the Synoptic Problem: the Nineteenth Century in Context," in *Jesus, the Gospels, and the Church: Essays in Honor of William R. Farmer* (ed. E. P. Sanders, Macon, Ga.: Mercer University Press, 1987), 47-68. For an almost contemporary critique of work done by the leading founders of the Marcan Hypothesis, see the doctoral dissertation by the distinguished Dutch scholar of early church history, H. U. Meijboom, *A History and Critique of the Origin of the Marcan Hypothesis 1835-1866* (trans. John J. Kiwiet; New Gospel Studies 8; Leuven: Peeters; Macon: Mercer University Press, 1992). On the argument that the Prussian government influenced nineteenth-century German Universities in their support of the Markan Hypothesis prior to and during the *Kulturkampf,* see William R. Farmer, "State Interesse and Marcan Primacy," in *Biblical Studies and the Shifting of Paradigms 1850-1914* (ed. Henning Graf Reventlow and William Farmer; Sheffield: Sheffield Academic Press, 1995), 15-49. For an analysis of other factors that may have led to the demise of the Griesbach Hypothesis and the subsequent ascendancy of the theory of Markan Priority in nineteenth-century Europe, see David Barrett Peabody, "H. J. Holtzmann and His European Colleagues: Aspects of the Nineteenth-Century European Discussion of Gospel Origins," in Farmer, ed., *Biblical Studies and the Shifting of Paradigms,* 50-131. For an overview of the state of the discussion of the Synoptic Problem by 1998, see William R. Farmer, "The Present State of the Synoptic Problem," in *Literary Studies in Luke-Acts: Essays in Honor of Joseph B. Tyson* (ed. Richard P. Thompson and Thomas E. Phillips; Macon, Ga.: Mercer University Press, 1998), 11-36. The most recent history of the debate over the Synoptic Problem is that by David L. Dungan, *A History of the Synoptic Problem: The Canon, the Text, the Composition, and the Interpretation of the Gospels* (Anchor Bible Reference Library; New York: Doubleday, 1999), esp. 302-91. Yet another rehearsal of the history of the discussion of the Synoptic Problem may be found in D. B. Peabody and B. Reicke, "Synoptic Problem," in *Dictionary of Biblical Interpretation* (2 vols.; ed. John H. Hayes, Nashville: Abingdon, 1999), 2:517-24. For the most complete bibliography of works related to the Synoptic Problem through 1988, see Thomas R. W. Longstaff and Page A. Thomas, *The Synoptic Problem: A Bibliography, 1716–1988* (Leuven: Peeters and Macon, Ga.: Mercer University Press, 1988).

then from whence came all of the similar material in Matthew and Luke not found in Mark (e.g., the Lord's Prayer, Beatitudes, etc.)? Answer: another source—which was inexplicably lost already in the first century. However, advocates of the "Logia/Λ/Ur-Matthäus/Spruchquelle/Q" hypothesis postulated that this source was so important and valuable that two different evangelists, Matthew and Luke, and their communities made extensive and painstaking use of it. Yet both communities allegedly lost it almost immediately and so completely that not even a fragment of a manuscript of Q can now be found. Furthermore, the "Q community," which is now said to have cradled the oldest "Sayings Gospel Q," also disappeared quite early in Christian history, so that no record of it can be now be found in the currently extant ancient sources. For the text of Q and descriptions of the community that produced and cherished it, scholars do often provide informed and skillful, yet necessarily creative and imaginative reconstructions.[5]

But the problems with Q do not end with its illusive nature. Another serious question quickly surfaced, "What was in Q?" Scholars in earlier generations produced significantly divergent reconstructions of Q, so that, when James Moffatt surveyed the seventeen most important reconstructions known to him by 1918 (e.g., those by Wellhausen, Holtzmann, Harnack, Réville, J. Weiss, B. Weiss, Stanton, Hawkins, et al.), he discovered that *not a single verse* of Matthew was common to all seventeen reconstructions.[6] How could such an astonishing lack of agreement arise? Weren't these scholars using the same two Gospels, Matthew and Luke, to reconstruct "Q"? Already in 1915, E. Lummis claimed,

> Q cannot be determined because, in order to work at all, Q must remain indeterminate. Each critic…must be able to apply a specially adapted conception of this purely hypothetical document.[7]

In recent years, understanding of Q has been compounded by additional proposed recensions of it: e.g., Q^1, Q^2, Q^3, Q^{Mt}, Q^{Lk}, etc. It remains to be seen what the impact will be of the recently published, definitive reconstruction of "the Sayings Gospel Q."[8] Note that it is no longer described by its advocates merely as one of the sources of Matthew and Luke. It has now been upgraded to the status of a "gospel" by the International Q Project.[9]

---

[5] The most recent and substantial work on the history of Q research, reconstructions of Q, its alleged community, theology, and ideology, is that by John S. Kloppenborg Verbin, *Excavating Q: The History and Setting of the Sayings Gospel* (Minneapolis: Augsburg Fortress; Edinburgh: T. & T. Clark, 2000).

[6] See James Moffatt, *Introduction to the New Testament* (Edinburgh: T & T Clark, 1918), 197-202.

[7] E. Lummis, *How Luke Was Written* (Cambridge: University Press, 1915), 31.

[8] James M. Robinson, Paul Hoffmann, John S. Kloppenborg, eds., The critical edition of Q: Synopsis Including the Gospels of Matthew and Luke, Mark and Thomas with English, German and French Translations of Q and Thomas (Minneapolis: Fortress; Leuven: Peeters, 2000).

[9] On the development of the name, "Q," to "Sayings Gospel Q," John S. Kloppenborg (now John Kloppenborg Verbin), once explained, "The successes of redaction criticism on the canonical Gospels encouraged its application to other documents, including one of the sources of Matthew and Luke, the so-called Q source, now called the Sayings Gospel Q. The change in nomenclature, indeed, is indicative of a shift in focus, for it

INTRODUCTION

A hypothesis is no better than the validity of its basic assumptions. In our previous volume, *Beyond the Q Impasse,* we provided objectively defensible evidence that one of Luke's major sources was Matthew—hence, we do not believe there is a need for Q in any form in order adequately to explain the literary history of the material now shared by Matthew and Luke. In this book, we present evidence that is most consistent with the view that Mark was the third Gospel to be written, based upon a conflation of Matthew and Luke.

The So-called "Minor Agreements" of Matthew and Luke against Mark: A Second Problem for Markan Priority

An additional problem dogging belief in the priority of Mark has been the seemingly ever increasing list of so-called "minor agreements" of Matthew and Luke against Mark within the material shared by all three of the Synoptic Gospels. Conceded from the beginning by its own adherents as a difficulty for the Two Document Hypothesis, the positive "minor agreements;" are the numerous words or phrases that are identical in Matthew and Luke, but are unlike the parallel word or phrase in Mark—even though these words and phrases appear in contexts where, on the Two Document Hypothesis, both Matthew and Luke have allegedly made independent use of Mark. On the Two Document Hypothesis, there are also the so-called negative "minor agreements," i.e., those words, phrases, and sometimes even whole pericopae in Mark that have no parallel in either Matthew or Luke.

How many of these positive and negative "minor agreements" are there? The list seems to get longer each time these agreements are counted. In 1909, Oxford's John Hawkins said he knew of some 218 cases, but that he believed only 21 of them needed any explanation; the rest were too trivial to merit attention.[10] A few years later, his colleague, B. H. Streeter, apparently disagreed, producing a

---

implies that Q is of interest not merely because it offers a solution to the source-critical problems of other (later) documents (Matthew and Luke), but because it is of intrinsic interest as one of the earliest expressions — perhaps the earliest expression — of Christianity in Palestine." In his footnote to the opening sentence of this material, Kloppenborg added, "The SBL Q Seminar has introduced 'Sayings Gospel,' in part to avoid the term source, which inevitably obscures Q as a document of intrinsic interest in its own right (much like calling the second Gospel "the Markan source"). And in part, this designation is intended to convey the notion that Q represents a "gospel" as much as do the narrative Gospels." John S. Kloppenborg, *The Shape of Q: Signal Essays on the Sayings Source* (ed. John S. Kloppenborg, Minneapolis: Fortress, 1994), 1-2 and 1-2n1. Cf. John S. Kloppenborg, "The Sayings Gospel Q and the Quest of the Historical Jesus," *HTR* 89/4 (1996): 307-44. For the most recent and authoritative statement on the current state of research on "the Sayings Gospel, Q," see Kloppenborg Verbin, *Excavating Q.* Others who refer to "Q" as a "gospel" would include, e.g., James M. Robinson, "The Sayings Gospel 'Q'," in *The Four Gospels: 1992 Festschrift Frans Neirynck* (3 vols.; ed. F. van Segbroeck et al., Louvain: Leuven University Press, 1992), 1:361-88; Arland Jacobsen, *The First Gospel* (Missoula, Mont.: Polebridge, 1992); Burton Mack, *Q — The Lost Gospel* (San Francisco: Harper-San Francisco, 1993). For a history of the term "Sayings Gospel Q," see Frans Neirynck, "Q: From Source to Gospel," *ETL* 71 (1995): 421-30.

[10] Rev. Sir John C. Hawkins, "Appendix B to Part III. The Alterations and Small Additions in Which Matthew and Luke Agree Against Mark," in *Horae Synopticae: Contributions to the Study of the Synoptic Problem,* (2d

thirty-six page discussion of these agreements that drew upon the investigations of his colleagues, Abbott, Hawkins, Burkitt and others.[11]

There is a common style of argumentation and the same dismissive tone in the works of all these scholars.[12] Namely, these problematic agreements are first grouped into categories. This technique, that attempts to "divide and conquer," of course, reduces the impact that might be made by the great number of such agreements. Streeter himself chose to divide these agreements and to use categories such as: "irrelevant agreements" (over 100), "deceptive agreements" (more than 50 more), "illusory agreements," and the like. After dismissing the import of these agreements, Streeter, like Hawkins before him, could then concentrate his attack only on those agreements even he had to admit were real problem cases.

Streeter dealt with some of these agreements in 1924 by claiming that these had been caused by an "overlap" between Mark and Q (as evidenced, e.g., in the Beelzebul controversy, the mission instructions, etc.). That is, Mark and Q had recorded some of the same stories.[13] In these cases, there are all sorts of agreements between Matthew and Luke against Mark—large and small (dozens of longer phrases and even whole verses)— because Matthew and Luke had allegedly followed Q, as well as Mark, in some pericopae. Where this mixture of sources did not prove convincing, even to Streeter, he resorted to amending the text of Mark (several dozen cases, including the alteration of whole phrases). Obviously, for a person of Streeter's training, sensitivity, and acumen to appeal to so many serious conjectures to solve this problem, these agreements can hardly be considered "minor" or "illusory."

---

ed.; Oxford: At the Clarendon Press, 1909, repr. 1968), 208-12; cf. "Pt IIIA. Section I. Passages [in Mk] Which May Have Been Omitted or Altered [by Matthew and Luke] as Being Liable to Be Misunderstood, or to Give Offence, or to Suggest Difficulties," 117-25, "Section II. Enlargements of the Narrative, Which Add Nothing to the Information Conveyed by It, Because They are Expressed Again, or are Directly Involved, in the Context," 125-26; "Section III. Minor Additions to the Narrative," 127-31; "Section IV. Rude, Harsh, Obscure or Unusual Words or Expressions, Which May Therefore Have Been Omitted or Replaced by Others," 131-38, "Section V. Duplicate Expressions in Mark, of Which One or Both of the Other Synoptists Use One Part, or Its Equivalent," 139-42, "Section VI. The Historic Present in Mark," 143-49; "Section VII. The Conjunction Καί Preferred to Δέ in Mark," 150-53. The preceding list calls attention to the fact that Hawkins, like Streeter, argued for the Two Document Hypothesis by atomizing the phenomena of the minor agreements. That is, he divided the so-called minor agreements of Matthew and Luke against Mark into several categories and provided different explanations for the evidence in each category, thus decreasing the impact of the number of these phenomena and lessening the chance that a network composed of some or all of these data could be noted.

[11] B.H. Streeter, *The Four Gospels* (London: Macmillan 1924), 295-331.

[12] See n 10 above.

[13] In 1911, however, Streeter had explained much of this same evidence by postulating "St. Mark's Knowledge and Use of Q" in *Oxford Studies in the Synoptic Problem* (ed. W. Sanday; Oxford: Clarendon, 1911), 165-83.

Fifty years later, the noted Flemish defender of the Two Document Hypothesis, Frans Neirynck, devoted an entire book to this issue. His list of these "Minor Agreements" increased to 750 cases.[14] In the most recent discussion by the Swiss scholar, Andreas Ennulat, there are more than 1000 cases of "minor agreement." Why is Ennulat's total so high? The number of such agreements depends on what one is willing to count. Neirynck and Ennulat included in their counts not only the hundreds of positive agreements, but also the hundreds of significant agreements in omission—where Matthew and Luke omit precisely the same words or phrases found in the text they are supposedly following in Mark. Ennulat further noted that these negative agreements were frequently part of a larger pattern that included both negative and positive agreements within a single distinguishable literary context.[15]

Even though Ennulat still defends the priority of Mark, his discussion broke with the custom of dividing up the agreements into a number of categories and providing different explanations for each category by means of scores of separate conjectures, as Streeter and Hawkins had done previously. Ennulat said the approach of Streeter and others required one to "believe too many happy coincidences." Instead, Ennulat insisted that a more comprehensive approach should keep in view various patterns of agreement, and that these could be found throughout the Triple Tradition.[16] Ennulat concluded from this that the version of Mark used by Matthew and Luke was different from the version of Mark that was later canonized.[17]

It is not difficult to see how these two problem areas, the appeal to Q, now including its several strata, and the so-called "minor agreements," have combined to raise questions about the adequacy of the theory of Markan priority, even among some of its advocates. If the hundreds of "minor agreements" scattered throughout the Triple Tradition are seen to merge with and form a pattern with the scores of "major agreements" (which had been split off from these "minor" agreements and given a different label, namely "Q"), then it becomes increasingly apparent that Luke was primarily dependent on Matthew and not Mark, and there is no need for Q or the priority of Mark.

Many subsequent attempts to defend the priority of Mark despite these difficulties have only tended to exacerbate the problem. If one postulates "Mark-Q overlaps" to get rid of some of this kind

---

[14] Frans Neirynck, The Minor Agreements of Matthew and Luke against Mark with a Cumulative List, BETL 37 (Leuven: Leuven University Press, 1974).

[15] Andreas Ennulat, Die "Minor Agreements": Untersuchungen zu einer offenen Frage des synoptischen Problems (Tübingen: Mohr/Siebeck 1994).

[16] If one refuses to split the evidence into two types: major agreements (now called Q) and "minor agreements" and instead look at their interconnections, the situation becomes even more difficult to explain on the Two Document Hypothesis.

[17] Ennulat, Minor Agreements, 418. For an excellent example of this hypothesis, see the report by Albert Fuchs in the symposium on the minor agreements held at Göttingen in 1991, "Die 'Seesturmperikope' Mk 4,35-41 parr im Wandel der urkirchlichen Verkündigung," in Minor Agreements: Symposium Göttingen 1991 (ed. Georg Strecker; Göttingen: Vandenhoeck & Ruprecht, 1993), 65-92.

of evidence, then it appears that Luke used a version of Q that had Matthean-like passages in it (such as John's preaching, the mission instructions, etc.) and combined them with passages from Mark which are also largely similar to Matthew. From this evidence it is not difficult to conclude that Luke's source material was very much like the Gospel of Matthew, plain and simple.[18]

Prominent Alternatives to the Two Document Hypothesis

The number of early opponents to the Two Document Hypothesis, in both Germany and England, tended to dwindle as the theory became more solidly entrenched in the leading universities of those countries. It should be noted, however, that French biblical scholars were never particularly attracted to this hypothesis, partly because it was so deeply identified with the Protestant cause. But it took nearly a century for some of the more significant challenges to the Two Document Hypothesis and alternative proposals to reemerge in Great Britain, the United States and, finally, in Germany.

The Traditional "Augustinian" Hypothesis

BISHOP BASIL CHRISTOPHER BUTLER IN GREAT BRITAIN

In 1951, the Abbot of the Roman Catholic Benedictine abbey at Downside, England, Bishop Basil Christopher Butler, published *The Originality of St. Matthew: A Critique of the Two Document Hypothesis*.[19] There, he took up and challenged each of the five main arguments put forward by B. H.

---

[18] G. Styler practically said as much in his article on "The Priority of Mark" in C. F. D. Moule's *The Birth of the New Testament* (2d ed.; San Francisco: Harper & Row, 1962), 223: "It was not necessary to maintain that Mk's version must at every point be older than Matt.'s parallel version since it was possible to say that anything in Matt. which seemed more original than Mk could have been derived from Q."

[19] B. C. Butler, *The Originality of St. Matthew* (Cambridge: Cambridge University Press, 1951). For some of his arguments in this work, Butler was indebted to two earlier advocates of the traditional "Augustinian" hypothesis, H. G. Jameson, *The Origin of the Synoptic Gospels: A Revision of the Synoptic Problem* (Oxford: Blackwell, 1922) and Dom John Chapman [1865-1933], *Matthew, Mark and Luke: A Study in the Order and Interrelation of the Synoptic Gospels* (ed. with an intro. and some additional matter by John M. T. Barton: London: Longmans, Green, 1937), published posthumously. In his editor's preface to Chapman's book, John M. T. Barton reports, "There is a note in the Abbot's handwriting at the top of the first page [of his manuscript] of Ch. 1: 'Begun 12th (or 13th) Jan. 1926' . . ." Chapman certainly knew and responded to Streeter's work of 1925 (cf., e.g., *Matthew, Mark and Luke*, 157, et al.). Did he, perhaps, even begin work on this monograph in response to Streeter's book of 1925? As do many authors, Butler also utilized some of his own previously published material in the composition of this book. See, e.g., "St. Luke's Debt to St. Matthew," *HTR* 32 (October 1939): 237-308 and the Preface to *Originality* (vi) where Butler acknowledges his use of this earlier article in what follows.

For Butler's most direct response to Streeter's first three arguments (based on common content, wording, and pericope order), see especially, "Chapter V. The Lachmann Fallacy" (62-71). Butler also introduces his response to Streeter's fourth argument in this chapter (67-71), but postpones a more detailed response to that argument on the relative roughness and Semitic character of Markan style until "Chapter XI. St. Mark's Gospel," 157-69. Butler finds that Streeter's fifth "argument" is not really an argument at all, but "a series of simple deductions from his hypothesis" and, therefore, dismisses it without much further ado (67-68).

Streeter for the priority of Mark.[20] The first argument, that Matthew contains 90% of the content of Mark, Luke, 50%, is not a valid argument, said Butler. As stated, it is merely a biased statement of certain facts that assumes the hypothesis it is seeking to prove. The percentages of agreement in content (which are correct in themselves) establish nothing more than that some kind of literary relationship probably obtains among Matthew, Mark, and Luke.

Streeter's second argument, that in any given passage most of the words in Mark are also found in Matthew or Luke or both, is another biased statement of certain facts that demonstrates nothing more than the first of Streeter's alleged arguments for Markan priority.

As for the third argument, "the relative order of incidents and sections in Mark is in general supported by both Matthew and Luke; where either of them deserts Mark the other is usually found supporting him,"[21] is no proof either. To believe that this statement of the evidence proves the priority of Mark, said Butler, involves "a schoolboyish error of elementary reasoning lying at the very base of the Two Document Hypothesis."[22] All it demonstrates is that Mark is some sort of middle term between Matthew and Luke.

Butler's book rocked the Markan Hypothesis in England to its foundations. Ten years later, the prominent Cambridge NT scholar, C. F. D. Moule, reissued his influential *Birth of the New Testament* with an Appendix by Geoffrey Styler acknowledging that Butler had indeed destroyed the traditional "argument from order of pericopae" for establishing Markan priority.[23]

The Modern Revival of the Griesbach Hypothesis

WILLIAM R. FARMER IN THE UNITED STATES

Butler's book prompted a young American scholar at the time, William R. Farmer, to look again at the history of the development of the Two Document Hypothesis. If Streeter could be so mistaken, were other scholars before him involved in this and, perhaps, other mistakes? Starting with the

---

[20] For Streeter's arguments for his Four Document Hypothesis (M, Mark, Q, and L), see "Part II. The Synoptic Problem," in his *The Four Gospels*, 149-364, which includes Streeter's Chapters VII-XII. Streeter's summary of his arguments is found on 151-54. His "five reasons for accepting the Markan Priority" are conveniently summarized on 151-52. Of particular note here are also "Chapter X. The Reconstruction of Q," 271-94, and "Chapter XI. The Minor Agreements of Matthew and Luke," 293-332. It is also revealing that Streeter placed "Chapter XII. The Lost End of Mark" in Part II, which deals with "The Synoptic Problem," rather than in his "Part I. The Manuscript Tradition," 26-148.

[21] Butler, *Originality*, cf. Streeter, *The Four Gospels*, 151.

[22] Butler, *Originality*, 63.

[23] Moule, Birth of the New Testament, 223-32.

earliest advocates of the Two Document Hypothesis in Germany in the 1830s,[24] and continuing on through Sanday's Oxford Seminar in the first decades of the twentieth century, Farmer published his results in 1964 in *The Synoptic Problem: A Critical Analysis*. His main conclusion: the arguments utilized in the entire history of the rise and establishment of Markan Priority were marked by faulty reasoning, lack of evidence, and extra-scientific factors.[25]

HANS-HERBERT STOLDT IN GERMANY

While Farmer focused on English scholarship, thirteen years later, in 1977, a second critique was published, this time concentrating on German scholars, from C. G. Wilke (1838) down through Johannes Weiss (1903). In *History and Criticism of the Marcan Hypothesis,* Stoldt first presented his findings in three parts. Part one was an historical survey, scholar by scholar, of the rise and proliferation of the Two Document Hypothesis. In this part, Stoldt documented case after case of flawed logic and tendentious use of evidence. Part two set out a systematic and synthetic refutation of every argument that had been advanced for the priority of Mark by these same scholars. Part three detailed numerous examples of "extra-scientific" factors that helped make the Markan hypothesis the favorite among members of the theological faculties of German Protestant Universities. His conclusion: Griesbach's arguments for the posteriority of Mark were never faced honestly or directly and remain to this day the best solution to the Synoptic Problem.

Whereas Farmer's book was greeted by cries of outrage and derision on both sides of the Atlantic,[26] Stoldt's book was dismissed under a ban of silence. In all of the possible venues in the German theological press, there was only one short review of Stoldt's work, by Hans Conzelmann.[27]

---

[24] Gottloh C. Storr and Johann Gottfried Herder, however, had already published work advocating Markan Priority as early as the closing decades of the eighteenth century. See Storr's *Ueber den Zweck der evangelischen Geschichte und der Briefe Johannis* (Tübingen, J. F. Heerbrandt, 1786) and Johann Gottfried Herder, "Regel der Zusammenstimmung unser Evangelien, aus ihrer Entstehung und Ordnung," in his *Sammtliche Werke zur Religion und Theologie* (Stuttgart; Tübingen: J. G. Cotta, 1830), 17:169-232. Even Johann Jakob Griesbach was, thereby, in a position to respond to the views of advocates of Markan priority, and did so in his famous *Commentatio*, in which he demonstrates that Mark is a conflation of Matthew and Luke. This work is now conveniently made available in *Griesbach Studies 1776-1976* (ed. Bernard Orchard and Thomas R. W. Longstaff; Cambridge University Press, 1978), 74-102 (Latin original) and 103-35 (ET by Bernard Orchard).

[25] W. R. Farmer, *The Synoptic Problem*, esp. 184-190. Farmer's conclusions were generally confirmed in the literature by the much earlier research of Hajo Uden Meijboom (first published in Dutch in 1866) and by the later, mostly independent, research of Stoldt.

[26] For a description of the earliest reactions to Farmer's book, see D. Dungan, "Mark—the Abridgement of Matthew and Luke," in *Jesus and Man's Hope* (2 vols.; ed. Donald Miller; Pittsburgh: Perspective Books 1970), 1:52; cf. Reginald H. Fuller, E. P. Sanders, and Thomas R. W. Longstaff, "The Synoptic Problem: After Ten Years," *PSThJ* 28/2 (1975): 63-74.

[27] For a critique of Conzelmann's review, see the Introduction to the ET of Stoldt's book (n. 4 above), xiv-xvii. An unedited version of Stoldt's reply to Conzelmann is also available in, "Reflections on Legitimacy and Limits of Theological Criticism by Hans-Herbert Stoldt, translated by Virgil Howard," *PSTJ* (Summer, 1980):

In other words, the Germans have never substantially answered Stoldt—heightening the impression among outsiders that, in Germany, the Markan hypothesis is no longer a scientific hypothesis but a *theologoumenon.*[28]

R e s p o n s e   a n d   D e f e n s e   o f   t h e   T w o   D o c u m e n t   H y p o t h e s i s

Fortunately, such is not the case with some contemporary defenders of Markan priority elsewhere. For instance, the Flemish scholar, Frans Neirynck, and the English scholar, Christopher Tuckett, have provided superb examples of aggressive, prolific, and scholarly engagement with opponents of the Two Document Hypothesis. Especially noteworthy is the fact that both of these defenders of the Two Document Hypothesis have conceded the validity of Butler's and Farmer's critiques of Streeter's main arguments and no longer use them.[29]

In fact, there is a striking gap between these leading defenders of the Two Document Hypothesis and such scholars as Raymond Brown, Robert Funk, and even Robert Stein who, as of the year 2001, continue to use Streeter's classic arguments as if they were still valid and had not been explicitly abandoned by Tuckett, Neirynck and other expert defenders of the Two Document Hypothesis.[30]

The Two Document Hypothesis arose in the midst of numerous alternative hypotheses, including those of Henry Owen and Johann Jakob Griesbach, whose source-critical view was later utilized by members of the Tübingen School. James Moffatt's *Introduction to the Literature of the New Testament* gives an excellent survey of the field up to turn of the century.[31] A later overview was

---

49-54. Also see William R. Farmer, "The Stoldt-Conzelmann Controversy: A Review Article," *PRST* 7 (1980): 152-62, and Farmer's own review of Stoldt's book, "Kritik der Markushypothese," *ThZ* 34 (1978): 172-74.

[28] Eta Linnemann argues that German seminary students have been "brain-washed" (her term) to accept this hypothesis unquestioningly Cf. her book, *Is There a Synoptic Problem? Rethinking the Literary Dependence of the First Three Gospels* (trans. Robert W. Yarbrough, Grand Rapids, Mich.: Baker, 1992).

[29] For Neirynck's general position, see his articles on the "Synoptic Problem" in *The Interpreter's Dictionary of the Bible* (Nashville, Abingdon, 1976), Supp.: 845-48, and in *The New Jerome Biblical Commentary* (ed. Raymond E. Brown, Joseph A. Fitzmyer, and Roland E. Murphy; Englewood Cliffs, N.J.: Prentice-Hall, 1990), 587-95 and in *Evanglica II* (Leuven:Leuven University Press, 1981). Compare his reference to the "post-Butlerian era" in "The Griesbach Hypothesis: The Phenomenon of Order," *ETL* 58 (1982): 114. For Tuckett, out of many examples, see most recently the concessions at the beginning of his discussion of "Jesus and the Gospels" in *The New Interpreter's Bible* (12 proposed vols.; ed. Leander Keck, et al.; Nashville: Abingdon Press, 1995), 8:71-86, esp. his section on "Source Criticism," 8:75-77.

[30] Robert H. Stein, *The Synoptic Problem: An Introduction* (Grand Rapids, Mich.: Baker, 1987), 67-70; R. E. Brown, *An Introduction to the New Testament* (New York, Doubleday, 1997), 111-122; Robert Funk, Roy Hoover, and the Jesus Seminar, *The Five Gospels: The Search for the Authentic Words of Jesus* (Polebridge Press and New York: Macmillan 1993), 10-11. Here Funk et al. reproduce Streeter's first four arguments almost verbatim, although they make no mention of Streeter's name in this context.

[31] James Moffatt, *Introduction to the Literature of the New Testament* (New York: Scribner's; Edinburgh: T. & T. Clark, 1911).

published by Xavier Léon-Dufour in a general introduction to the Bible edited by André Robert and André Feuillet.[32]

Gospel Origins and the Oral Tradition

One of the common early views about the sources of the Synoptic Gospels was that there must have been a large body of tradition, probably in Aramaic, probably oral, upon which the canonical Gospel writers drew independently for their accounts. Such were the views of Johann Gottfried Herder[33] and Johann Carl Ludwig Gieseler.[34] Similar views were advocated by J. B. Koppe[35] and Friedrich Schleiermacher,[36] although these last two authors were more sympathetic to the evangelists' use of written sources.

The importance of oral tradition for a complete understanding of the history of the development of the Synoptic Gospels has been emphasized more recently in works by Harald Riesenfeld, Birger Gerhardsson, Werner Kelber, and Bo Reicke.[37] Oral Tradition and its influence on the development of

---

[32] Xavier Léon-Dufour, "Les évangiles synoptiques," in *Introduction à la Bible* (2 vols.; ed. André Robert and André Feuillet; Tournai: Desclée, 1957; 2d ed.; 1959), 2:143-334, *Introduction to the New Testament* (trans. Patrick W. Skehan; New York: Desclée, 1965), 139-324. For a second French perspective, see the lengthy discussion in Léon Vaganay, *Le problème synoptique—une hypothèse de travail Bibliothèque de théologie* (série 3: Théologie biblique 1; Tournai: Desclée, 1954), 1-32. The main German introduction is that in the many editions of P. Feine, J. Behm, rev. W. G. Kümmel, *Introduction to the New Testament* (ET of 14th German ed. by H. C. Kee; Nashville: Abingdon 1966).

[33] Johann Gottfried Herder, "Regel der Zusammenstimmung unser Evangelien, aus ihrer Entstehung und Ordnung," in idem, *Sämmtliche Werke zur Religion und Theologie* (Stuttgart; Tübingen, J. G. Cotta, 1830), 17:169-232; *Vom Erlöser der Menschen, nach unsern drei ersten Evangelien* (Riga: J. F. Hartknoch, 1796) = *Herder's Christliche Schriften* 2; *Von gotes Sohn, der Welt Heiland, nach Johannes Evangelium. Nebst einer Regel der Zusammenstimmung unserer Evangelien aus ihrer Entstehung und Ordnung* (Riga: J. F. Hartknoch, 1797) = Herder's *Christliche Schriften* 3.

[34] Johann Carl Ludwig Gieseler, Historisch-kritischer Versuch über die Entstehung und die frühesten Schicksale der schriftlichen Evangelien (Leipzig: W. Engleman, 1818).

[35] J. B. Koppe, *Marcus non epitomator Matthaei* (Programme University of Göttingen: Helmstadii, 1782) repr. in *Sylloge commentationum theologicarum* (8 vols.; ed. D. J. Pott and G. A. Ruperti; Helmstadii [i. e. Helmstadt, Germany]: C. G. Fleckeisen, 1800-1807), 1(1800):35-69.

[36] Friedrich Daniel Ernst Schleiermacher, A Critical Essay on the Gospel of St. Luke. With an Introduction by the Translator, Containing an Account of the Controversy Respecting the Origin of the Three First Gospels since Bishop Marsh's Dissertation, ET of Über die Schriften des Lucas, ein kritischer Versuch (Berlin: G. Riemer, 1817), by Connop Thirwall (London: J. Taylor, 1825)

[37] Harald Riesenfeld, The Gospel Tradition and Its Beginnings: A Study in the Limits of "Formgeschichte." An Address Delivered at the Opening Session of the Congress on the Four Gospels in 1957, in the Examination Schools, Oxford, on 16 September 1957 (London: A. R. Mowbray, 1957; repr., 1961); Birger Gerhardsson, Memory and Manuscript: Oral Tradition and Written Transmission in Rabbinic Judaism and Early Christianity (Acta Seminarii Neotestamentici Upsaliensis 22; trans. Eric J. Sharpe; Lund: C. W. K. Gleerup, 1964); idem, Tradition and Transmission in Early Christianity (Coniectanea Neotestamentica 20; Lund: C. W. K. Gleerup, 1964); Werner Kelber, The Oral and Written Gospel. The Hermeneutics of Speaking and Writing in the Synoptic Tradition, Mark, Paul, and Q (Philadelphia: Fortress, 1983); Bo Reicke, The Roots of the Synoptic Gospels (Philadelphia: Fortress, 1986).

the Gospels also became the focus of two major conferences on the gospel traditions held in Dublin, Ireland and Varese (Gazada), Italy in 1989 and 1990, respectively,[38]

Most critical scholars today would accept the view that continuing oral tradition most likely influenced not only the traditions about Jesus prior to the composition of the synoptics, but also, most likely, the texts of the written Gospels as they were being composed and the transmission of their manuscripts afterward. However, few experts on the Synoptic Gospels today would explain all of the similarities and differences among the Gospels solely on the basis of oral tradition.[39] Most critical scholars find the evidence within the synoptics more than sufficient to warrant positing some kind of literary relationship among them, be it direct, indirect, or both.

Multiple Source Hypotheses

Marie-Émile Boismard of the Ecole Biblique in Jerusalem,[40] and his students, Arnaud Lamouille and Philippe Rolland,[41] stress multiple stages in the development of the canonical Gospels. These theories explain the variants between and among the Gospels by postulating the evangelists' use of several hypothetical sources. The strength of this source theory to explain every difference among the Synoptic Gospels is, however, also its weakness. That is, the ability to provide comprehensive explanations of all the minute similarities and differences among the Synoptic Gospels is possible only by postulating several more than two hypothetical sources.

Most scholars of the Gospels, therefore, find these hypotheses too complex to be convincing. Another virtue of such hypotheses, however, is the ability to take into account and explain all of the variants within the manuscript tradition, rather than simply those readings that are adopted into the

---

[38] Selected papers from those conferences now appear in Henry Wansborough, ed., *Jesus and the Oral Gospel Tradition* (JSNTSS 64; Sheffield: JSOT Press, 1991).

[39] Exceptions to these general statements, however, may be found in the relatively recent work by Linnemann, *Is There a Synoptic Problem?*, and John M. Rist, *On the Independence of Matthew and Mark* (SNTSMS 32; Cambridge: Cambridge University Press, 1978).

[40] Boismard's classic explanation of the sources of the Gospels appears in Pierre Benoit and Marie-Émile Boismard, *Synopse des quatre évangiles en français avec paralleles des apocryphes et de Peres* (Paris: Les Editions du Cerf 1972), Tome II "Commentaire." For Boismard's detailed exposition of his favorite passage for demonstrating the superiority of his Multiple Source Hypothesis (i.e., the introduction to the Feeding of the 5000), see D. Dungan, ed., *The Interrelations of the Gospels* (Leuven: University Press/Peeters 1990), 244-53. The exchange of views between Neirynck and Boismard about the significance of this passage for source-criticism of the Gospels has become rather extensive, given the limited literary context involved, Mk 6:30-34 and parallels. Cf. M. É. Boismard, *L'Evangile de Marc sa prehistoire* (Etudes bibliques, ns 26; Paris: Librairie Lecoffre 1994).

[41] Philippe Rolland, *Les premiers évangiles. un nouveau regard sur le probléme synoptique* (Lectio Divina 116; Paris: Cerf, 1984). An English outline summary of his work, sometimes relating it to that of his teacher, Boismard, has now been provided by Rolland in "A New Look at the Synoptic Question," *EuroJTh* 8/2 (1999): 133-44.

eclectically constructed critical text of the Greek NT, which, when taken as a reconstructed whole, has no representative at all among the extant manuscripts.

The Farrer-Goulder Hypothesis

Among alternatives to the Two Document Hypothesis today, the most popular one in England is the hypothesis most often associated with the name of Austin Farrer.[42] This hypothesis, which was most fully advanced by Farrer in an article in 1955, sustains Markan priority, but dispenses with Q by allowing that Luke utilized both Mark and Matthew. This way of dealing with the synoptic phenomena more easily explains the so-called "minor agreements" of Matthew and Luke against Mark than does the classical statement of the Two Document Hypothesis, which postulates the independent use of Mark and Q by Matthew and Luke. Recently, Michael Goulder and Mark Goodacre have led the charge against Q from this perspective.[43]

This hypothesis has its advocates in North America, some predating Farrer's essay of 1955. For instance, already in 1934, James Hardy Ropes of Harvard had published his own views about "dispensing with 'Q'." He was followed in this view by his student, Morton Scott Enslin.[44]

In an oral review of our earlier work, *Beyond the Q Impasse,* Mark Goodacre commented that he thought we were at least "half right."[45] That is, although he could agree with our arguments for dispensing with "Q" and in favor of Luke's direct use of Matthew, he could not support our views on the priority of Matthew and Luke to Mark. However, another current advocate of "Goulder's

---

[42] See, e. g., Austin Farrer, "On Dispensing with Q," in *Studies in the Gospels: Essays in Memory of R. H. Lightfoot* (ed. Dennis E. Nineham; Oxford: Basil Blackwell, 1955), 55-88, reprinted in *The Two Source Hypothesis: A Critical Appraisal* (ed. Arthur J. Bellinzoni, Jr.; Macon, Ga.: Mercer University Press, 1985), 321-56. Although Farrer's name is still most often associated with modern advocacy of this hypothesis, Farrer, like Griesbach, had precursors who advocated a similar source theory. See, e.g., James Hardy Ropes, *The Synoptic Gospels* (Cambridge, Mass.: Harvard University Press, 1934).

[43] Michael D. Goulder, *Luke: A New Paradigm* (2 vols.; JSNTSS 20, Sheffield: Sheffield Academic Press, 1989); Mark S. Goodacre, *Goulder and the Gospels: An Examination of a New Paradigm* (JSNTSS 133; Sheffield: Sheffield Academic Press, 1996); idem, *The Case Against Q: Studies in Markan Priority and the Synoptic Problem* (Harrisburg, Pa.: Trinity Press International, 2002). Other advocates of the Austin Farrer hypothesis in the United Kingdom would include Eric Franklin, Studies Director at St. Stephen's House, Oxford, (*Luke: Interpreter of Paul, Critic of Matthew* [JSNTSup 92; Sheffield: Sheffield Academic Press, 1994]); John H. Drury, Dean of the College and Cathedral, Oxford, (*Luke* [The J. B. Phillips' Commentaries; London & Glasgow: Collins, 1973], *Tradition and Design in Luke's Gospel* [London: Darton, Longman, and Todd, 1976], and *The Parables in the Gospels: A History and Allegory* [London: SPCK, 1985]), and H. Benedict Green, College of the Resurrection, Milfield, West Yorkshire ("The Credibility of Luke's Transformation of Matthew," in *Synoptic Studies: The Ampleforth Conferences of 1982 and 1983* [ed. C. M. Tuckett; JSNTSup 7; Sheffield: JSOT Press, 1984]).

[44] James Hardy Ropes, *The Synoptic Gospels* (Cambridge, MA: Harvard University Press, 1934; reprinted with a new preface by David E. Nineham, London: Oxford University Press, 1960); Morton Scott Enslin, *Christian Beginnings* Harper Torchbooks: Cloister Library TB 6, 2 vols. (New York: Harper & Brothers, 1938).

[45] Cf. Mark S. Goodacre, "*Beyond the Q Impasse* or Down a Blind Alley?" *JSNT* 76 (1999): 35-52.

hypothesis (Markan Priority without Q)," E. P. Sanders, has noted the following in a concluding chapter on the Synoptic Problem in a more general introduction to synoptic studies that he co-authored with Margaret Davies and published in 1989.

All the other proposed solutions [to the Synoptic Problem] have their own merits. The two-source hypothesis is the best solution to the arrangement of Luke, and the Griesbach the best explanation of why Mark is the middle term. But, it seems to us, they both break down. The two-source solution must deny what is very probable: that Luke knew Matthew. The Griesbach proposal attributes an inexplicable procedure to Mark. Further, it has some difficulty with many of the passages in which Matthew is the middle term. At first these seem to support Matthew's priority, but they make Mark's editorial procedure even harder to understand, since in some of these cases he preferred the parts of Matthew not already chosen by Luke.[46]

We should review the theories discussed:

1. The two-source theory — when complicated by the addition of Proto- and Deutero-Mark, further sources, two versions of Q, Mark-Q overlaps and Proto-Luke — can handle most of the material. Yet even with these complications difficulties remain. The two fatal ones are (1) the evidence that Luke knew Matthew (which not even the theories of Proto-Mark and Mark-Q overlaps entirely meet) and (2) the verbatim agreement between Mark and 'Q' in supposed overlap passages. Of all the solutions, this one, which remains the dominant hypothesis, is least satisfactory.

2. The Griesbach hypothesis (Matthew was copied by Luke, and Mark conflated them both) is technically possible. It suffers from the inability to explain Mark. It may be that here we face only a failure of imagination: why would anyone carefully conflate parts of Matthew and Luke, while omitting so much of both? Nevertheless, scholarship cannot accept a theory of literary relationship which it cannot comprehend. Moreover, what is known of ancient authors who conflated indicates that they did so by incorporating their sources in blocks, rather than by switching back and forth from phrase to phrase.

[3.] Goulder's hypothesis (Mark without Q) is also technically possible. Accepting it depends on being able to explain how Matthew and Luke were composed if the only sources were (in Matthew's case) Mark, Scripture and imagination; and (in Luke's case) Mark, Matthew, Scripture and imagination. Thus far Goulder has not persuaded us that one can give up sources for the sayings material. With this rather substantial modification, however, we accept Goulder's theory: Matthew used Mark and Luke used them both.

4. Boismard's multiple source theory is also technically possible. What is dubious is that such fine detail in the reconstruction of hypothetical documents can be correct. It certainly cannot be validated. We have noted, however, that his theory of crisscross copying has much to commend it in general.

It is, of course, gratifying to find a distinguished and respected advocate of another source theory, like E. P. Sanders, granting that the Griesbach hypothesis is, at least among the four hypotheses he considers, "the best explanation of why Mark is the middle term." And we provided evidence in *Beyond the Q Impasse* that, in our view, makes it "very probable that Luke knew Matthew."

---

[46] E. P. Sanders and Margaret Davies, *Studying the Synoptic Gospels* (London: SCM; Philadelphia: Trinity Press International, 1989), 112.

The essential difference between the Two Gospel (neo-Griesbach) Hypothesis and the Farrer-Goulder Hypothesis is whether or not Matthew and Luke knew Mark. The evidence discussed below leads us to conclude that Matthew and Luke's knowledge of Mark is both unnecessary to explain the data and unlikely, given the nature of the data. If, as both the advocates of the Farrer-Goulder Hypothesis and the Two Gospel Hypotheses claim, Luke knew and used Matthew and not the hypothetical "Sayings Gospel Q," then the following seem to us to be unlikely consequences of the Farrer-Goulder position.

1. Although Luke and Matthew share many of the pericopae in Mark in Mark's order, on the Farrer-Goulder Hypothesis, Luke would have consciously chosen to support the Markan sequence of pericopae virtually everywhere that Matthew had departed from it.

2. Although Luke and Matthew share much of the wording within Markan pericopae, on the Farrer-Goulder hypothesis, Luke has managed to support the wording of Mark within pericopae in innumerable places where Matthew had departed from it. If Luke did this unconsciously, then the "appearance" of alternating agreement in wording between Mark, on the one hand, and Matthew or Luke, on the other, displayed in our new synopsis of Mark, is an astounding accident. If Luke did this consciously, that seems to us to "attribute an inexplicable procedure to Luke."[47]

3. Since about twice as many elements of demonstrably Lukan and/or Matthean literary style appear in parallel contexts in Mark than do elements of Markan style in parallel contexts in Matthew or Luke, how is this seemingly anomalous evidence for the Farrer-Goulder hypothesis to be explained? Of course, "It may be that here we face only a failure of imagination."[48]

4. On the Farrer-Goulder hypothesis, Luke has managed to follow Matthew in eliminating altogether or diminishing the impact of a great deal of that network of integrated material in Mark that can best be attributed to the author. Why and how did he manage to do this?

5. On any hypothesis that posits Markan priority, why would one think that a less Jewish and less Palestinian form of the Jesus tradition was the source for a more Jewish and more Palestinian form of the same tradition, unless one were convinced, on other grounds, that Mark was the earliest Gospel? And, as a subcategory of this kind of consideration, why would one posit that a better and more clearly structured, Jewish style of argumentation that makes sophisticated and integral use of scripture was formulated from a comparable text where such features are, relatively speaking, diminished, blurred, or absent?

---

[47] Ibid., 16.
[48] Ibid.

6. Why is there no evidence in any ancient source that suggests that Mark was the first of the Synoptic Gospels to be written?

Furthermore, even granting the full measure of the work of Downing and others on ancient texts roughly contemporary with the Gospels that suggests that some "ancient authors who conflated . . . did so by incorporating their sources in blocks, rather than by switching back and forth from phrase to phrase,"[49] we do know of at least one ancient author, Tatian, who did precisely what Downing and others deny as the norm. As our new synopsis will also indicate more clearly than any other, in many pericopae, but certainly not all, Mark also did his work by carefully combining the wording of Matthew and Luke. At the very least, one would have to conclude that his text "appears to be" the result of such a method of conflation for some reason. The evidence that Mark is a careful blending of Matthew and Luke will not go away, even if some scholars choose to chart the shared order of pericopae within the synoptics in just two, distinct pairs, Matthew-Mark and Luke-Mark. Our new synopsis provides a clear alternative to that type of presentation of the relevant evidence and it will, hopefully, help others to see what we see among the three synoptics.

Finally, in what follows, we hope to make "explicable" what Sanders believed, presumably from his reading of the literature prior to 1989, to be "an inexplicable procedure for Mark." Below we also hope to answer all of Sanders' other questions about the composition of Mark on the Two Gospel Hypothesis, including those having to do with Matthew as the middle term at times, Mark's use of material in Matthew not previously adopted by Luke, Mark's careful conflation of the wording of his sources combined with so many Markan omissions, the comprehensibility of our hypothesis, and more.

---

[49] F. Gerald Downing, "Redaction Criticism: Josephus' *Antiquities* and the Synoptic Problem I," *JSNT* 8 (1980): 46-65; "Redaction Criticism: Josephus' *Antiquities* and the Synoptic Problem II," *JSNT* 9 (1980): 29-48. Cf. idem, "Compositional Conventions and the Synoptic Problem," *JBL* 107 (1988): 69-85.

THE TWO GOSPEL HYPOTHESIS

Since the Second World War, this hypothesis has been called the "Griesbach Hypothesis" after Johann Jakob Griesbach, because scholars in the nineteenth century thought he had invented it. However, we now know that, while still a young man of 23, in 1769, Griesbach visited London where he probably met an English scholar, Henry Owen. Owen had already published a book titled *Observations on the Four Gospels* (London 1764).[1] In fact, this book by Owen appeared in the catalog of Griesbach's library that was prepared prior to its sale, following Griesbach's death in 1812. Owen's views about the sources of the gospels, as set forth in this book, are essentially the same as those that became associated with Griesbach's name. Consequently, some Neo-Griesbachians in more recent times have renamed their hypothesis the "Owen-Griesbach Hypothesis."[2]

In 1982, David Barrett Peabody showed that the basic concept of Mark's dependence upon *both* Matthew and Luke goes back all the way to St. Augustine.[3] This realization, combined with urging from Bernard Orchard on other grounds, prompted yet another shift in nomenclature so that the hypothesis is now known as the "Two Gospel Hypothesis," highlighting the claim that Mark is dependent upon the two earlier gospels of Matthew and Luke.[4]

---

[1] For a discussion of what is known about the relationship between Owen and Griesbach, see David L. Dungan, *A History of the Synoptic Problem: The Canon, the Text, the Composition, and the Interpretation of the Gospels* (New York: Doubleday, 1999), 314-18.

[2] This was first done at the Cambridge Conference on the Synoptic Gospels, August 1979, sponsored by the International Institute for Renewal of Gospel Studies. For an account of this conference and the papers delivered there, see W. R. Farmer, ed., *New Synoptic Studies; Cambridge and Beyond* (Macon, Ga.: Mercer University Press 1983). In addition to Henry Owen, Friedrich Andreas Stroth preceded Griesbach in publishing source-critical views like Griesbach's on the Synoptic Problem. Stroth, however, first published his source-critical approach to the gospels in an article that did not carry his name, "Von Interpolationem im Evangelium Matthaei," in *Repertorium für biblische und morgenlandische Literatur* 9 (1781) 99-156. J. G. Eichhorn, then publisher of the journal, eventually identified Stroth as the author, in *Einleitung in das Neue Testament* (2 vols.; Leipzig: Weidmann, 1820), 1:465n1. Another pre-Griesbach author to assert that Mark was the third of the synoptics to be written was Anton Friedrich Büsching, *Die vier Evangelisten mit ihren eigenen Worten zusammengesetzt und mit Erklärungen versehen* (Hamburg, 1766), esp. 109-119. Büsching, unlike Owen, Stroth, and Griesbach, believed that Luke was the first of the synoptics to be written. A few years after Griesbach published his source-critical views, Edward Evanson published views similar to those of Büsching in *The Dissonance of the Four Generally Received Evangelists and the Evidence of Their Respective Authenticity Examined* (Ipswich: G. Jermyn, 1792).

[3] An early form of Peabody's work was published in 1983, along with selected papers that were presented at the Owen-Griesbach conference held at Cambridge in 1979. See D. B. Peabody, "Augustine and the Augustinian Hypothesis: A Reexamination of Augustine's Thought in *de consensu evangelistarum*," in W. R. Farmer, ed., *New Synoptic Studies*, 37-66. A shorter, more developed, but yet unpublished form of this report was presented in the Section on the Synoptic Gospels of the Annual Meeting of the Society of Biblical Literature in New York City in 1982.

[4] This term has understandably irritated some members of the Farrer School, notably Michael Goulder, who rightly points out that his theory, Luke is dependent upon the two gospels of Mark and Matthew, and that there was no "Q," is also a two gospel hypothesis. The authors of this book regret this point of irritation between us and our colleagues who advocate the Farrer-Goulder Hypothesis, but fear that we have published too much under this new label for us to turn away from it now. Furthermore, we are unsatisfied when we are identified too closely with Griesbach's views because our views differ significantly from those of Griesbach on several critical points, some of which we will enumerate and discuss further below.

INTRODUCTION

As contemporary advocates of the Two Gospel Hypothesis continue to discover, uncover, and recover evidence that the author of the Gospel according to Mark used the Gospels of Matthew and Luke as his main sources, they have moved a considerable distance beyond the methods and conclusions of Johann Jakob Griesbach and Henry Owen. They have created new technical tools for research (new synopses, comparative displays of the complete texts of some of the oldest and best manuscripts of the Gospels, computerized databases, etc.). These areas of scholarly research have been thoroughly reinvestigated. New evidence has been compiled in systematic form and much of it has been published. As a result, our updated view of the sources and composition of the Synoptic Gospels now rests upon a new foundation. The hypothesis is, therefore, worthy of a name that is less tied to Griesbach. For these reasons and others, the research team responsible for this volume has decided to continue to use the new label for our hypothesis, The Two Gospel Hypothesis.

Not only do twenty-first century advocates of the Two Gospel Hypothesis have better resources for research along the lines once pursued by Owen and Griesbach, but our approach and many of our critical judgments also differ in significant ways from those of our predecessors. For instance, like many scholars of the Enlightenment, particularly among Protestants, Griesbach himself discounted the value of the entire Patristic tradition. Advocates of the Two Gospel Hypothesis, on the contrary, are more appreciative of that tradition and believe that, when critically evaluated, some testimonies from the Patristic period provide interesting, valuable, and reliable information.

Unlike Griesbach, who diminished Mark's value by claiming that it contained no more than 24 verses that were not drawn from Matthew or Luke, advocates of the Two Gospel hypothesis are more impressed with the considerable amount of material in Mark that is not found in Matthew or Luke, even though such Markan supplements are usually shorter than the distinguishable pericopae that led Griesbach to his more limited verse count of such material.

Finally, by pursuing insights first published by Griesbach's followers, we have found an integrated network of material in Mark that is composed primarily of supplementary or edited material when Mark's text is understood to be dependent upon both Matthew and Luke. Such work most probably reflects the activity of the author of Mark because only that author (rather than one of his sources or some previous editor) would have been in a position to create such a network within the Gospel. One example of such a network may be seen in the retrospective use of πάλιν throughout the Gospel.

Before we move to the detailed presentation of our reasons for advocating Mark's use of Matthew and Luke, we alert the reader to the fact that the evidence we will be presenting will be difficult to see using any of the previously composed synopses, particularly those of Huck or Aland. They are biased, either intentionally (e.g., the early Huck, as an illustration of Holtzmann's source theory) or unintentionally (Aland, et al.), toward the Two Document Hypothesis. Other synopses make it more difficult to see the literary phenomena we will be discussing.[5] Instead, one is advised to use the charts and color-coded synopses that we have created to illustrate the analyses offered in this book.[6] We have included a few relatively simple synoptic charts and synopses in the book, but printing all of the complex, color-coded synopses that support our discussions would have made this book prohibitively expensive. The reader will, therefore, find our new synopses for all of Mark on the companion CD titled *A Synopsis of Mark: A Synopsis of the First Three Gospels Showing the Parallels to the Markan Text*.[7]

In our view, following the composition of the Gospel of Matthew, the next stage was Luke's use of Matthew to compose his gospel, a process that we discussed in detail in *Beyond the Q Impasse*. Subsequently, Mark made use of both Matthew and Luke when composing his Gospel. Six categories of evidence support this last stage of the Two Gospel hypothesis. However, as will be apparent below, some of these categories contain subcategories as well. These categories of evidence are not listed in order of importance. Rather, we believe that these several sets of literary phenomena, when taken together, support our conclusions in a synthetic and cumulative manner.

---

[5] For a discussion of the presentation of the literary phenomena in the synopses of Huck and Aland, see D. Dungan, "Theory of Synopsis Construction," in *Biblica* 61 (1980). 305-29; further, idem, "Synopses of the Future," in *Biblica* 66 (1985): 457-92. These two articles have been reprinted in a new hypertext format provided by Tom Longstaff on the CD, *A Synopsis of Mark*.

[6] Our search of the history of scholarship by those who once advocated the so called "Griesbach Hypothesis" has also recently brought to light a series of synopses previously unknown to us. These are the three editions of a "Griesbach" synopsis composed by Colin Campbell [1848-1931], M.A., D.D., one-time minister of the Parish of Dundee, former scholar and fellow of Glasgow University, Gunning Lecturer, 1916-1919, at the University of Edinburgh Campbell originally published his Griesbach Synopsis as *The First Three Gospels in Greek: Arranged in Parallel Columns*, (Glasgow: Hugh Hopkins, 1882), xxii + 222pp. A second edition revised followed in 1899, and a third edition revised in 1918. In the preface to the third edition of his Synopsis, dated September 1918, Campbell reveals that he was a former student of then "Emeritus Professor William Stewart, D.D. LL.D." [15 August 1835 - 1919]. Campbell also notes that "[t]he idea of development which 'Mark' illustrates in so many different directions on the materials presented by the other two synoptists seems alone to warrant the posteriority of his work --- an idea which Dr. William Stewart presented to his pupils in Glasgow University more than forty years ago [ca. 1868 or before], and which is conspicuous, especially in 'Mark's' manipulation of Matthean and Lucan passages into statements which are either pure combinations or of a neutral or alternative character." There is a brief paragraph on the life and work of William Stewart in *The New Schaff-Herzog Encyclopedia of Religious Knowledge* (ed. Samuel Macauley Jackson, et al.; 13 vols.; New York, London: Funk & Wagnalls, 1908-1914; reprint edition, Grand Rapids: Baker Book House, 1950), 11:91, s. v. "Stewart, William."

[7] As a companion to this book, Trinity Press International is distributing this new color-coded electronic synopsis of Mark on CD-ROM. The synopsis created by our friend and colleague, Bernard Orchard, used compositional assumptions that differ from those underlying *Beyond the Q Impasse—Luke's Use of Matthew* (Harrisburg, Pa.: Trinity Press International, 1996) and this book. Consequently and unfortunately, Orchard's synopsis does not illustrate the arguments in this book as well as our newer, and now also electronic and color-coded, synopsis. For a detailed critique of Orchard's synoptic arrangement, see David L. Dungan's review of Orchard's synopsis in *Biblica* 59 (1978): 584-87.

INTRODUCTION

Categories of Evidence Summarized

1. In the order of pericopae, except for those instances where Mark does not agree with *both* Matthew and Luke or where Mark contains a unique literary unit, *Mark alternately agrees* with Matthew and Luke. (See the "Chart" that illustrates this alternating agreement in pericope order on our separately published CD).

2. Within pericopae, *Mark also often alternately agrees* with Matthew and Luke *in wording.* (This can be seen in many of the individual synopses on the CD and in the examples provided in the analyses below).

3. Characteristic words and phrases of Matthew or Luke appear at least twice as often in parallel pericopae Mark than do characteristic words and phrases of Mark in parallel pericope in Matthew or Luke. (See the discussion of the methods of Zeller and Farmer below and the Appendix 2 on Zeller's results at the end of this volume.)

4. The network of repeated words and phrases that are both characteristic of the author of Mark and unique or distinctive within that gospel reflects a literary, historical, theological and/or ethical integrity that is consistent with the work of a single author. We have chosen to call this "The Markan Overlay.")

5. In several pericopae, Matthew presents well-organized argumentation, based upon the interpretation of Scripture. The parallels in Mark, on the other hand, are often fragmented, losing or obscuring the carefully structured logic of the Matthean text. Therefore, we see them as revisions of Matthew.

6. A significant body of "external evidence" from the patristic and later periods complements these categories of "internal evidence" and supports our conclusion about Mark's use of Matthew and Luke. *All* of the patristic evidence affirms that Matthew was the first Gospel to be composed and that John was the last. Much of this evidence also supports the view that Mark was composed after Matthew and Luke and that Mark drew some of his material from them.

The Six Categories of Evidence Elaborated and/or Illustrated.

1. The Evidence of Mark's Alternating Agreement with Matthew and Luke in Order of Pericopae

The traditional statement of the order of the content of the Synoptic Gospels, and the conclusion drawn from it, was fundamental to the development of the "consensus" that Mark was the earliest Gospel and that there was a second source, Q, for the common material in Matthew and Luke not found in Mark. The argument runs as follows: the three Gospels exhibit a common order. When either Mathew or Luke depart from that order, the other usually continues to agree with Mark. Matthew and Luke rarely agree in order against Mark and rarely place their common material in the same place in the order of Mark. Therefore, it follows that Matthew and Luke used Mark when writing their

Gospels and did so without knowledge of one another. If this is so, then there must have been another source for the common material found in Matthew and Luke but not in Mark.

B. C. Butler called this conclusion a "schoolboyish error" (see above, p. XXX), because elementary logic reveals that the data are explicable by either of two solutions. Consider the following oversimplified chart:

Mt	Mk	Lk
1	1	1
2	2	2
x	3	3
4	4	4
5	5	y
6	6	6
(x= an element of the Mt/Lk tradition not in Mk)		(y=an element of the Mt/Lk tradition not in Mk)

This can be explained by saying that Matthew and Luke followed Mark independently, since they do not agree in those places where they depart from Mark's order or where they insert their common material, not found in Mark, into the Markan outline. But this can equally well be explained by the proposal that Mark conflated material from Matthew and Luke. Where they agree, Mark copied. Where they differed, Mark chose one or the other.

From the perspective of the Two Gospel Hypothesis, the basic statement of this phenomenon is as follows: where Matthew and Luke have similar pericopae in the same order, relative to each other, Mark usually has a similar pericope in that same order. Where Matthew and Luke have pericopae that are not similar to each other, Mark's order of pericopae is usually similar to one or the other. Mark rarely has a pericope that is not in an order similar to that of either Matthew or Luke.[8] This striking alternation of Mark's agreement, now with Matthew and now with Luke, is easily explained as a conflation of Matthew and Luke. The Two Document Hypothesis requires the more difficult conclusion that Matthew and Luke, working independently, somehow managed to divide the text of Mark between them in such a precisely alternating fashion.

---

[8] This description of the phenomena used to function as one of the main arguments (e.g., in B. H. Streeter's discussion) for Markan priority until B. C. Butler pointed out the logical fallacy involved. Once Markan priorists were forced to give it up, however, they—principally F. Neirynck and C. Tuckett—had recourse to Lachmann's approach which *begins* by splitting the Gospels into two pairs: Mt//Mk and Lk//Mk and proceeding to analyze them separately. This approach was correctly opposed by D. Neville, who pointed out in *Arguments from Order in Synoptic Source Criticism: A History and Critique* (New Gospel Studies 7; Macon: Mercer University Press, 1994), 234, that "Lachmann's method disallows any literary connection between Matthew's and Luke's Gospels and thereby discounts Griesbach's hypothesis without having to argue against it on its own terms." See further the discussion in D. Dungan, *A History of the Synoptic Problem* (New York: Doubleday, 1999), 386-91.

An Illustration of the Order of Mk 1:1-6:6a		
Matthew	Mark	Luke
From John the Baptist Through the Call of the First Four Disciples Up to the Introduction to Jesus' First Sermon on the Mount Mt 3:1-4:22, 7:28-29 ==>	Beginning From John the Baptist Through the Call of the First Four Disciples and through Jesus' First Sermon in Capernaum Mk 1:1-22	From John the Baptist Through Jesus' First Sermon in Nazareth Lk 3:1-4:30
From the Conclusion of Jesus' First Sermon on the Mount Through the Gathering of Crowds Mt 8:1-12:16	From the Conclusion of Jesus' First Sermon in Capernaum Through the Gathering of Crowds and the Commissioning of 12 Disciples Mk 1:23-3:19	From the Conclusion of Jesus' First Sermon in Nazareth Through the Gathering of Crowds and the Commissioning of 12 Disciples Up to the Introduction to Jesus' Sermon on the Plain <=====Lk 4:31-6:19
Old Testament Proof Text Mt 12:17-21		
Jesus' True Relatives As the Beginning of Jesus' Wisdom Mt 12:22-13:53=====>	Jesus' True Relatives As the Beginning of Jesus' Wisdom Mk 3:20-4:34	Jesus' Wisdom Lk 6:20 – 8:18 Jesus' True Relatives Lk 8:19-21
Jesus' Power (Mt 9:10-17, 12:1-14)	Jesus' Power Mk 4:35-5:43	Jesus' Power <=====Lk 8:22-56
Retrospective Reflection on Jesus' Wisdom and Power Mt 13:54-54=====>	Retrospective Reflection on Jesus' Wisdom and Power Mk 6:1-6a	

The argument from the order of pericopae, as formulated by Streeter et al., is inconclusive because it is reversible. However, we believe that Mark's alternating agreement with Matthew and Luke in the order of pericopae, as illustrated above, is more easily explained as Mark's careful conflation of Matthew and Luke than as the accidental result of Matthew's and Luke's independent use of Mark.

As important as it is, this abstract description of the phenomena of order is only the beginning of our demonstration. Once the points in Mark's story where Mark shifts from agreement in order with Matthew to agreement in order with Luke and vice versa are identified, explanations of why Mark used his sources as he did must be provided. One thing is immediately obvious. Mark's "copying" was by no means a mechanical combination of sources. What theological, moral, and ecclesiological concerns guided his compositional activity? We begin to answer these questions in the chapter of this introduction entitled "The Provenance and Purpose of Mark." More detailed explanations are provided in the compositional analysis below, especially the opening sentences of the "General Observations" for each pericope.[9]

2. The Evidence of Mark's Alternating Agreement with Matthew and Luke in Wording Within Pericopae.

The way in which Mark alternately utilized his sources at the level of whole pericopae (the "macro-structure") is complemented by the way in which Mark combined words and phrases within individual pericopae (the "micro-structure"). In other words, these two sets of related phenomena represent two aspects of a consistent editorial policy on the part of the author of Mark.

As our discussions of individual pericopae reveal, Mark's wording is generally more similar to the Gospel whose order is currently being followed. However, words from the other source are usually combined with it to produce "blended phrases."[10]

---

[9] The reader will begin to get an overall picture of our understanding of Mark's alternating use of his sources, Matthew and Luke, along with those theological, moral, and ecclesiological concerns that guided his compositional activity, by isolating and reading all of our "General Observations" in sequence straight through this book.

[10] This phenomenon has attracted considerable attention. T. R. W. Longstaff has studied the nature of conflated texts from known examples, both ancient and medieval. As two of his six conclusions he writes, "the conflation of two or more sources which themselves exhibit a considerable degree of verbal similarity will frequently (although not always) result in small agreements (of a single word or a brief phrase) with one source against the other(s). These agreements may interrupt the use of a single source or may occur alternately in a single section." And again, "[R]edundancy and duplication, caused by the copying of similar words or phrases from two (or more) sources, may be present in a conflated account. The presence of this phenomenon, however, is more probable when an author is copying everything (or nearly everything) found in his sources than when he is using his sources with greater freedom." See Thomas R. W. Longstaff, *Evidence of Conflation in Mark? A Study in the Synoptic Problem* (SBLDS 28; Missoula, Mont · Scholars Press, 1977), 110-11 and 112. In an independent study of known examples of conflation, Roland Mushat Frye, a professor of English and an expert in Shakespeare, also once concluded, "In terms of conflation, the procedure postulated for Mark in the Griesbach Hypothesis conforms closely to what can be seen wherever I have found a literary work in which conflation is demonstrable beyond a shadow of a doubt. There are probably exceptions of which I am unaware, but the following characteristics are widespread enough to be regarded as highly typical: alternation between or among *Vorlagen*, condensation of overall or total length of the *Vorlagen*, frequent expansion within pericopae, and addition of lively details to provide a fresher and more circumstantial narrative. Here conformity to general literary patterns that we find in the Griesbach explanation of Synoptic order is not only very impressive, but telling evidence in its favor." Frans Neirynck also devoted an entire volume to Markan duality: *Duality in Mark: Contributions to the Study of the Markan Redaction* (BETL 31; Leuven University Press, 1972; 2d ed. with supplementary notes 1988). Although one may conclude from Neirynck's work that "duality" is characteristic of the style of the author of Mark, that need not provide a defense of Markan priority. If "duality" is, in fact, a characteristic of the style of the author of Mark, and Neirynck's work makes that highly probable, then an advocate of the Two Gospel hypothesis may respond to his work by noting that Mark would have found ample opportunities to compose such "dualisms" in the process of conflating Matthew with Luke.

Perhaps the context where this phenomenon is most easily seen is Mk 1:32-34, although attention is sometimes drawn only to the opening dualism rather than to all of the dualisms that permeate this short pericope. Here we present this Markan context with the aid of an English synopsis.[11]

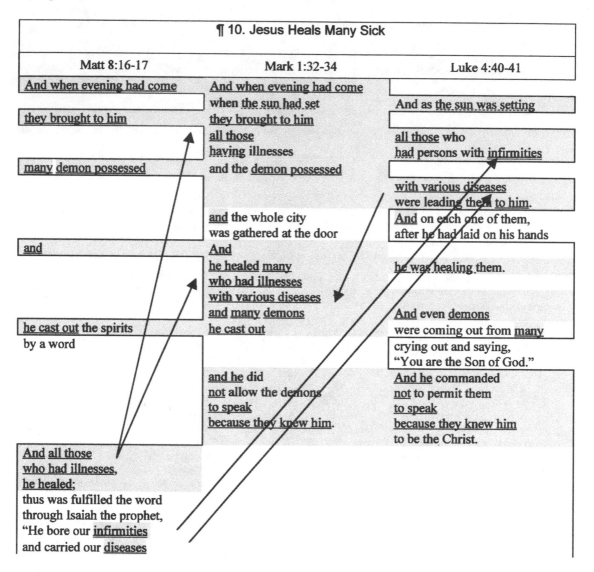

¶ 10. Jesus Heals Many Sick		
Matt 8:16-17	Mark 1:32-34	Luke 4:40-41
And when evening had come	And when evening had come when the sun had set	And as the sun was setting
they brought to him	they brought to him	
	all those having illnesses	all those who had persons with infirmities
many demon possessed	and the demon possessed	
		with various diseases were leading them to him.
	and the whole city was gathered at the door	And on each one of them, after he had laid on his hands
and	And he healed many who had illnesses with various diseases and many demons	he was healing them.
he cast out the spirits by a word	he cast out	And even demons were coming out from many crying out and saying, "You are the Son of God."
	and he did not allow the demons to speak because they knew him.	And he commanded not to permit them to speak because they knew him to be the Christ.
And all those who had illnesses, he healed; thus was fulfilled the word through Isaiah the prophet, "He bore our infirmities and carried our diseases		

[11] A similar display may be found in Longstaff, *Evidence of Conflation in Mark?*, 142-43. Also see Longstaff's discussion of this Markan passage (140-52) in light of the demonstrable characteristics of known conflated documents he collected in the first part of his dissertation (1-125). Other Markan contexts, discussed by Longstaff, where the characteristics of conflation he deduced from known examples are demonstrable include Mk 1:29-31, Mk 3:1-6, Mk 9:38-41, Mk 11:15-19, and Mk 14:12-21.

This example is hardly unique. In fact, there are numerous examples of such Markan blending of the words from his two sources, Matthew and Luke. However, in this introduction we present just three further examples in "abstract," as opposed to synoptic, display. The first abstracts Mk 1:40-45 and parallels where Jesus heals a leper. The second abstracts Mk 10:46-52 and parallels where Jesus heals Bar Timaeus. The third abstracts Mk 2:15-17 and parallels where Jesus eats with toll collectors and sinners who follow him. Each of these abstracts shows the choices of synonymous expressions that Mark had available to him in Matthew and Luke. The shading indicates the choice Mark preferred between these alternatives.[12]

EXAMPLE ONE

Mk 1:40-45. Jesus Heals a Leper An Abstract of Alternating Markan Agreements with Matthew and Luke Shading Indicates Mark's Choices or Edited Preferences from Synonymous Expressions That Were Available in His Sources, Matthew and Luke	
Mt 8:1-4, 4:24-25, 9:30-34	Lk 5:12-16
1. Mt 8:2, λεπρός	1. Lk 5:12, ἀνὴρ πλήρης λέπρας
2. Mt 8:3, ἐκθαρίσθη αὐτοῦ ἡ λέπρα	2. Lk 5:13, ἡ λέπρα ἀπῆλθεν ἀπ' αὐτοῦ
3. Mt 8:4, καὶ λέγει αὐτῷ	3. Lk 5:14, καὶ αὐτὸς παρήγγειλεν αὐτῷ
4. Mt 8:4, ὅρα μηδενὶ εἴπῃς,	4. Lk 5:14, μηδενὶ εἰπεῖν,
5. Mt 8:4, ἀλλὰ ὕπαγε	5. Lk 5:14, ἀλλὰ ἀπελθών
6. Mt 8:4, τὸ δῶρον	6. Lk 5:14, περὶ τοῦ καθαρισμοῦ σου
7a. Mt 9:31, a form of διαφημίζω 7b. Contrast Mt 4:24, ἀπῆλθεν	7. Lk 5:15, διήρχετο
8. Mt 4:24, ἡ ἀκοή	8. Lk 5:15, a form of ὁ λόγος
9. Mt 4:24, ὅλην τὴν Συρίαν	9. Lk 5:16, ἐρήμοις

---

[12] Other contexts that display an impressive amount of such alternating Markan agreement in wording with Matthew and Luke would include: Mk 1:29-31 (synopsis 9), Mk 2:18-22 (synopsis 16), Mk 3:1-6 (synopsis 18), Mk 3:7-12 (synopsis 19), Mk 5:1-20 (synopsis 31), Mk 5:21-43 (synopsis 32), Mk 6:14-16 (synopsis 35), Mk 6:30-44 (synopsis 37), Mk 8:11-13 (synopsis 44), Mk 8:27-30 (synopsis 47), Mk 8:31-33 (synopsis 48), Mk 8:34-9:1 (synopsis 49), Mk 9:14-29 (synopsis 51), Mk 9:30-32 (synopsis 52), Mk 9:33-41 (synopsis 53), Mk 10:13-16 (synopsis 56), Mk 10:17-31 (synopsis 57), Mk 10:32-34 (synopsis 58), Mk 11:1-10 (synopsis 61), Mk 12:18-27 (synopsis 66), Mk 14:1-11 (synopsis 77), Mk 15:33-41 (synopsis 88), Mk 16:1-8 (synopsis 90), and Mk 16:9-20 (synopsis 91). At Mk 9:42-50 (synopsis 54) Mark has blended the wording of the Matthean doublet "On Moral Surgery" from Mt 5:29-30//Mt 18:6-9 in the way that he often blends the wording of parallels in Matthew and Luke.

EXAMPLE TWO

Mk 10:46-52. Blind Bartimaeus Sees Again and Follows Jesus "In the Way"	
An Abstract of Alternating Markan Agreements with Matthew and Luke Shading Indicates Mark's Choices or Edited Preferences from Synonymous Expressions That Were Available in His Sources, Matthew and Luke	
Mt 20:29-34//Mt 9:26-31	Lk 18:35-43
1. Mt 20:29, καί + genitive absolute of ἐκπορεύομαι and αὐτός + ἀπό Ἰεριχώ	1. Lk 18:35, εἰς Ἰεριχώ
2. Mt 20:29, "two blind men" (cf. Mt 9:26-31)	2. Lk 18:35, "a certain blind man" + a compound αἰτῆς
3. Mt 20:30, "Jesus"	3. Lk 18:38, "Jesus the Nazarene"
4. Mt 20:30, a form of κράζω	4. Lk 18:38, ἐβόησεν.
5. Mt 20:30, [κύριε], υἱὸς Δαυίδ	5. Lk 18:38, Ἰησοῦ υἱὲ Δαυίδ
6. Mt 20:31, ἵνα + a Form of σιωπάω	6. Lk 18:39, ἵνα + a Form of σιγάω
7. Mt 20:31, μεῖζον	7. Lk 18:39, πολλῷ μᾶλλον
8. Mt 20:32, καὶ στάς	8. Lk 18:40, σταθεὶς δέ
9. Mt 20:32, a form of φωνέω	9. Lk 18:40, a form of κελεύω
10. Mt 20:33, ἵνα ἀνοιγῶσιν οἱ ὀφθαλμοὶ ἡμῶν	10. Lk 18:41, ἵνα ἀναβλέψω
11. Mt 20:34, δὲ ὁ Ἰησοῦς	11. Lk 18:42, καὶ ὁ Ἰησοῦς
12. Mt 9:29, κατὰ τὴν πίστιν ὑμῶν γενηθήτω ὑμῖν	12. Lk 18:42, ἡ πίστις σου σέσωκέν σε.
13. Mt 20:34, καὶ εὐθέως/εὐθύς	13. Lk 18:43, καὶ παραχρῆμα

EXAMPLE THREE

Mk 2:15-17. Jesus Eats with Toll Collectors and Sinners Who Follow Him	
An Abstract of Alternating Markan Agreements with Matthew and Luke Shading Indicates Mark's Choices or Edited Preferences from Synonymous Expressions That Were Available in His Sources, Matthew and Luke	
Mt 9:10-13	Lk 5:29-32
1. Mt 9:10, Καί + 3rd singular of γίνομαι	1. Lk 5:29 Καὶ ἐποίησεν
2. Mt 9:10, a form of ἀνακείμαι	2. Lk 5:29, a form of κατακείμαι
3. Mt 9:10, ἐν τῇ οἰκίᾳ.	3. Lk 5:29 ἐν τῇ οἰκίᾳ αὐτοῦ.
4. Mt 9:10, πολλοὶ τελῶναι καὶ ἁμαρτωλοί	4. Lk 5:29, ὄχλος πολὺς τελωνῶν καὶ ἄλλων
5. Mt 9:11, ἔλεγον	5. Lk 5:30, ἐγόγγυζον
6. Mt 9:11, ἐσθίει	6. Lk 5:30, ἐσθίετε καὶ πίνετε
7. Mt 9:12, ἀκούσας	7. Lk 5:31 ἀποκριθείς
8. Mt 9:12, ὁ δέ	8. Lk 5:31, ὁ Ἰησοῦς
9. Mt 9:12, οἱ ἰσχύοντες ἰατροῦ	9. Lk 5:31, οἱ ὑγιαίνοντες ἰατροῦ
10. Mt 9:13, ἦλθον	10. Lk 5:32, ἐλήλυθα

These combinations often reveal an alternating structure which leads us to make the following claim. The presence of such structured parallels in Mark — now with Matthew, then with Luke, then with Matthew again, etc. — is readily explainable on the hypothesis that Mark combined words from his sources. To argue the opposite, that Matthew and Luke, independently and accidentally, alternately used precisely the wording that the other did not in so many pericopae is a practical impossibility. This blending of words within a pericope is, in our view, strong evidence of Mark's dependence upon Matthew and Luke and not the reverse. It is difficult to understand how Streeter could ever have taken the first two of Griesbach's main arguments about the alternating order of pericopae in Mark with Matthew and Luke and the alternating order of wording of Mark with Matthew and Luke within pericopae so that they somehow supported the simple priority of Mark.

3. The Evidence from Shared Linguistic Characteristics.

In the discussion of the Synoptic Problem since the Enlightenment, nothing has exhibited more methodological confusion and produced fewer results than misuse of the so-called "linguistic argument." Scholars often confuse two related but clearly distinct stages of research: (1) the process of isolating the linguistic characteristics of each of the synoptic evangelists, and (2) the use of the linguistic characteristics and their patterns of shared or distinct usage to suggest the direction of literary dependence among the Gospels.

Such arguments for identifying the work of authors is at least as old as the text-critical work on Homer that was done in Alexandria in the two or three centuries prior to the common era. Students attempted to correct and perfect the text of Homer as preserved in the various manuscripts by appealing to "the style of the author" as one criterion for choosing among variant readings. This criterion is still utilized by text critics of ancient manuscripts including, of course, contemporary text critics of the New Testament. Text critics often choose *the reading that most conforms to the style of the author*. However, in order to apply that criterion to the work of an author, or to distinguish his or her work from that of another author, one must already know and be able to describe the style of the author or authors whose work or works are being analyzed.

Since that same period in Alexandria, scholars have recognized that every author's literary style, like the personality of the author who manifests it, is a composite of many isolatable elements. As such, literary style may be broken down into a collection of *literary characteristics* such as favorite or habitual expressions, preferred vocabulary, repeated grammatical and syntactical constructions, etc.

In deciding whether a particular linguistic feature should be included among the linguistic characteristics that make up an author's style, critics have appealed to the criterion of "frequency." Repeated usage is one sign of an author's linguistic preference. But in the case of the Synoptic Gospels, because there are three texts to be considered, it has been enticing to scholars to apply a more complex criterion of "comparative frequency," rather than the simpler criterion of "internal frequency" (i.e., a frequency that is determined by simply counting the number of times recurrent words, phrases, etc. appear in a text). Unfortunately, the use of "comparative frequency" (i.e., noting how often one synoptic evangelist uses a literary feature in comparison to another to establish whether that feature is characteristic of that author) is a methodological mistake that has had grave consequences for the Synoptic Problem.

INTRODUCTION

If a scholar is to employ patterns of shared and distinctive usage between any two synoptic evangelists as evidence for the direction of literary dependence between them, it is important not to presuppose anything about the direction of dependence when identifying the linguistic characteristics of each synoptic evangelist in the first place. But scholar after scholar who has used a linguistic argument to help resolve the synoptic problem has done exactly that, either by explicitly presupposing one solution or by implicitly doing so through the use of the criterion of comparative frequency when isolating the linguistic characteristics of an author. [13]

But when David Barrett Peabody began to collect potentially redactional features of the text of Mark, he took into consideration the text of the gospel of Mark alone and employed the simple criterion of internal frequency, rather than comparative frequency, to isolate potentially redactional features of the text of Mark. In addition, Peabody chose to focus on repeated phraseology, rather than just repeated vocabulary items, grammatical and/or syntactical constructions. This required the application of a second criterion, the "number of elements" that compose a phrase, for identifying linguistic characteristics of Mark.

Peabody then applied these two criteria, "internal frequency" and "number of elements," in a complementary, balanced, and synthetic way. He gave similar weight to a shorter phrase that occurred with greater frequency in the text of Mark as to a longer phrase that occurred less frequently to decide whether either phrase should be labeled characteristic of the text of Mark.

Peabody then moved from isolating recurrent literary features of the text of Mark to a refining process that sought to identify those phrases and selected words which are used in special ways in Mark and may, therefore, be judged to have the highest probability of coming from the hand of the author. In order to identify those linguistic characteristics that most probably came from the author of Mark, Peabody applied three further criteria. These were: (1) the "compositional function" of the literary feature, (2) the "distribution" of the literary feature within the text of Mark, and (3) the "interlacing" of literary features, i.e., the combination or concentration of two or more distinguishable literary features of the text of Mark within a relatively limited literary context, usually within a single verse or sentence or a brief paragraph.

Peabody also subdivided "distribution," into three "factors;" (1) "The Factor of Distribution throughout the Gospel," (2) "The Factor of Appearance in Different Types of Material as Defined by the Form Critics," and (3) "The Factor of Appearance in *Passages* that Function Compositionally." It

---

[13] Support for this claim may be found in David Barrett Peabody, "Chapters in the History of the Linguistic Argument for Solving the Synoptic Problem: The Nineteenth Century in Context," in *Jesus, the Gospels, and the Church: Essays in Honor of William R. Farmer* (ed. E. P. Sanders; Macon, Ga.: Mercer University Press, 1987), 47-68. Cf. idem, "H. J. Holtzmann and His European Colleagues: Aspects of the Nineteenth-Century European Discussion of Gospel Origins," in *Biblical Studies and the Shifting of Paradigms. 1850-1914* (JSOTSS 192: ed. Henning Graf Reventlow and William Farmer; Sheffield: Sheffield Academic Press, 1995), 50-131, and David Peabody, *Mark as Composer* (New Gospel Studies 1; Macon, Ga.: Mercer University Press, 1987), 168-71.

is important to recognize and maintain the distinction between the third *factor* under the criterion of "distribution" and the *criterion* of "compositional function" of the literary *feature*. For instance, "πάλιν used retrospectively uniting two or more separated literary contexts" functions compositionally as a literary feature by "uniting two or more separated literary contexts" whether or not the literary context in which this instance of πάλιν appears would otherwise be considered "compositional." Literary contexts that have typically been considered "compositional," "editorial," or "redactional" would include glosses or asides in the text, prospective or retrospective passages, transitional passages, introductory or concluding passages, and at least some indicators of time, place, and/or geography.

Because Peabody did not utilize a criterion of "comparative frequency" in producing the 252 tables of linguistic characteristics in the text of Mark which he collected, the research team has drawn upon *Mark as Composer* to contribute to a solution to the Synoptic Problem. But our argumentation is not subject to a charge of circularity in the ways that many earlier arguments were.

Arguments for using linguistic characteristics of the Synoptic Gospels in solving the Synoptic Problem as outlined by Eduard Zeller (1843) and by William R. Farmer (1972, cf. 1964) surpass all others that have appeared in the scholarly literature.[14] Nevertheless, the discussion about these kinds of arguments remains at a stalemate in the literature.[15] The issue of method certainly needs further discussion. However, while acknowledging this, we have used what we believe to be a sound method that allows us to weigh relevant literary evidence and to draw conclusions from it about the more probable direction of literary dependence among the Gospels.

In the introduction to his Anchor Bible commentary on Mark, C. S. Mann included a section entitled, "Word Usage in Mark Compared with Matthew."[16] There Mann presented a comparative display of selected, shared vocabulary in Matthew and Mark. Mann limited his comparison to the shared vocabulary in Matthew and Mark that meet two further criteria: (1) Each word or phrase in these lists appears in one Gospel, when compared to the other, in a ratio of no less than 3:1, and (2) each of these shared words or phrases appears in the Gospel which makes less frequent use of it *only* in passages where the same word or phrase also appears in the parallel. By definition then, (3) the

---

[14] Eduard Zeller, "Studien zur neutestamentlichen theologie 4: Vergleichende Übersicht über den Wörtervorrath der neutestamentlichen Schriftsteller," *Theologische Jahrbücher* 2 (1843): 443-543; William R. Farmer, "Redaction Criticism and the Synoptic Problem," in *The Society of Biblical Literature One Hundred Seventh Annual Meeting Seminar Papers* (2 vols.; Society of Biblical Literature, 1971), 1:239-50.

[15] This stalemate/impasse is well reflected in the exchange between W. R. Farmer and Michael Goulder at the Ampleforth Conferences on the Gospels held in 1982 and 1983. See W. R. Farmer, "Certain Results Reached by Sir John C. Hawkins and C. F. Burney which make more sense if Luke knew Matthew, and Mark knew Matthew and Luke," in *Synoptic Studies*. JSNTSS 7, ed. C. M. Tuckett (Sheffield: JSOT Press, 1984), 75-98; M. D. Goulder, "Some Observations on Professor Farmer's 'Certain Results...'," in idem, 99-104; and W. R. Farmer, "Reply to Michael Goulder," in idem, 105-9.

[16] C. S. Mann, *Mark: A New Translation with Introduction and Commentary* (AB 27; Garden City, N.Y.: Doubleday, 1986), 165-72.

author of the Gospel in which a particular word or phrase occurs more frequently makes use of it *both* in passages where the other contains it and in contexts independent of a parallel in the other Gospel. Mann, thereby, avoids the mistake often made by other scholars who have presupposed that a simple analysis of comparative frequency of usage in two gospels, without also taking into consideration the presence or absence of parallel usages, has probative value for solving the Synoptic Problem.[17]

In this comparative chart, C. S. Mann presented 17 words that could provide evidence of Matthew's literary dependence upon Mark and 82 words that could provide comparable evidence of Mark's literary dependence on Matthew. The weight of the evidence heavily favors Matthew's priority to Mark.[18]

In 1843 Eduard Zeller published the results of his comparable research on all three pairs of Synoptic Gospels, Matthew/Luke, Matthew/Mark, and Luke/Mark. Zeller's work, therefore, may be used as a check on Mann's more limited analysis (see the appendix). Here we can only summarize some of that work in graphic form.

Like Mann's list, Zeller's lists were not based upon simple comparisons of the relative frequency of shared vocabulary in Mark//Matthew or Mark//Luke or Matthew//Luke, but on a more refined selection of words and phrases drawn from preliminary lists. In order to qualify for Mann's or Zeller's lists, each linguistic feature had to meet four criteria. First, the linguistic feature had to appear frequently enough in at least one Gospel to be considered "characteristic" of the text of at least one Gospel (*internal frequency*). Second, the linguistic feature had to appear in at least one parallel context in the two Gospels to be compared (*parallel contexts*). Third, Zeller also required that the linguistic feature appear in one Gospel more frequently than in the other (*comparative frequency*). Here it is important to note that these three initial criteria were necessary, but not sufficient, for making Mann's or Zeller's lists. A fourth criterion finally determined those words and phrases that appear in one of the lists. *Every* occurrence of a linguistic feature in the Gospel which included the feature less frequently must appear *only* in passages for which the Gospel with more frequent occurrences provides a parallel usage (*only parallels in that gospel where a literary feature is used less frequently*).

Zeller's work demonstrates that the use of these indicators shows the direction of literary dependence moving in opposite directions. That is, when one applies such a test to lists of the shared words and phrases in two of the synoptic Gospels, one discovers that some literary features suggest

---

[17] Scholars who have carefully examined, for instance, Holtzmann's form of the linguistic argument have reasonably concluded that his work is susceptible to charges of lack of sufficient refinement and, therefore, circularity.

[18] The comparative vocabulary chart in Mann's commentary on Mark of 1986 is quite similar to, if it is not actually part of, some work done over the summer of 1961 by E. P. Sanders, under the direction of William R. Farmer. At the time, Sanders was still a seminary student at the Perkins School of Theology, S. M. U., Dallas. Farmer's reflections on the development of this work by Sanders can now be found in "Certain Results," 73-85, esp. 82-83.

that the direction of literary dependence goes from Matthew to Mark while others suggest the reverse. The same thing is true for every possible relationship between any two of the three Synoptic Gospels: Matthew to Luke, Luke to Matthew, Mark to Matthew, Matthew to Mark, Mark to Luke, and Luke to Mark. At this point, the argument appears to be "reversible." However, Zeller suggested that the argument still had probative value if the evidence is weighed in the balance (e.g., eighty-two words weigh much more than seventeen words).[19]

On the basis of this kind of evidence alone Zeller concluded, like Mann a century and a half after him, that on balance it was more likely that Mark was literarily dependent upon Matthew, than the reverse. Zeller also concluded that on balance it was more likely that Mark was dependent upon Luke than the reverse. Here is a graphic summary of Zeller's balanced analyses of the direction of the literary dependence between Matthew and Mark as well as between Luke and Mark.

Zeller's Scale	
The Lighter Side of Zeller's Scale	The Heavier Side of Zeller's Scale
82 Words that Support the Conclusion that Matthew Depends on Mark	194 Words that Support the Conclusion that Mark Depends on Matthew
51 Words that Support the Conclusion that Luke Depends on Mark	134 Words that Support the Conclusion that Mark Depends on Luke

For comparative purposes, we provide here a graphic display of Mann's analysis.

Mann's Scale	
The Lighter Side of Mann's Scale	The Heavier Side of Mann's Scale
17 Words that Support the Conclusion that Matthew Depends on Mark	82 Words that Support the Conclusion that Mark Depends on Matthew

The reason for the significant reduction in the size of the numbers in Mann's balance scale which compares Matthew to Mark (17 versus 82) from those in Zeller's comparable scale (82 versus 194) is that Mann limited the items in his list to words that occurred in a ratio of no less than 3:1. Zeller had included all of the words that appeared more frequently in one Gospel than the other, in any ratio, no matter how small, *if* those words also met his and Mann's fourth criterion of appearing in the Gospel with the less frequent occurrences *only* in passages where the other Gospel writer provided a parallel.

---

[19] In *Beyond the Q Impasse* we utilized the term "one way indicator" to describe literary features that met these criteria. However, in light of some critical responses, particularly to that aspect of our earlier work, we have chosen not to utilize that particular language again in this book. This, however, should not be understood as a retreat from the conclusions we drew from such evidence there, but, simply as a more nuanced use of language to describe what we believe to be the more probable literary history of the synoptics based upon this kind of evidence.

Mann probably realized that a 2:1 ratio was too low to convince most scholars it was valuable. Whatever Mann's reason for imposing this limit on his analyses, his results are entirely consistent with those of Zeller and the conclusions of both scholars strongly support the priority of Matthew relative to Mark. Zeller's work goes farther and demonstrates that, on balance, Mark was probably literarily dependent upon Luke rather than Luke dependent upon Mark. Such results are consistent with the Two Gospel Hypothesis.[20]

Several concerns and counter arguments, however, keep some scholars from accepting the probative value of such a method of argumentation and the conclusions to be drawn from it. The first concern is that individual words do not comprise the best type of evidence upon which to build such a linguistic argument for solving the Synoptic Problem.

With this concern, all the members of the Research Team agree. Therefore, we give more weight to evidence provided by shared phrases and/or shared literary structures within the gospels than to evidence provided by simple vocabulary. We also give greater weight to the evidence provided when elements of the editorial work of one author show up in fragmentary form in the text of another gospel and only in parallel passages.

Furthermore, since the editorial work of the third synoptic evangelist could not possibly show up in the texts of the first and second evangelists, we would also conclude that the evangelist whose linguistic characteristics tend to be concentrated in material that is distinctive in that Gospel is most likely the third of the synoptic evangelists to have written.

This leads to another concern and a complication. It isn't always true that favorite characteristics show the direction of dependency. Favorite expressions may not have appealed to a copyist/editor; indeed they may be classified as favorite expressions of the earlier author *because* they did not appeal to the later writer. It is probably true that, sometimes, the later writer will copy favorite expressions from the earlier document inadvertently; however, sometimes a casual expression of the earlier writer

---

[20] In addition to the works cited above in footnotes 13-15, members of this research team have marshaled this type of linguistic evidence in the service of solving the Synoptic Problem in the following works: David Peabody, "A Pre-Markan Prophetic Sayings Tradition and the Synoptic Problem," *JBL* 97 (1978): 391-409; idem, "The Late Secondary Redaction of Mark's Gospel and the Griesbach Hypothesis: A Response to Helmut Koester," in *Colloquy on New Testament Studies: A Time for Reappraisal and Fresh Approaches* (ed. Bruce C. Corley; Macon, Ga.: Mercer University Press, 1983), 87-132; idem, "Response to the Multi-Stage Hypothesis," in *The Interrelations of the Gospels,* (ed. David L. Dungan; Louvain: Leuven University Press, 1990), 217-30; A. J. McNicol, "The Composition of the Synoptic Eschatological Discourse," in Dungan, ed., *Interrelations,* 157-300; David B. Peabody, "Repeated Language in Matthew: Clues to the Order and Composition of Luke and Mark," in *Society of Biblical Literature 1991 Seminar Papers* (SBLSP 30; ed. Eugene H. Lovering, Jr.; Atlanta, Ga.: Scholars, 1991), 647-86; William R. Farmer, "The Minor Agreements of Matthew and Luke against Mark and the Two-Gospel Hypothesis" in *Minor Agreements,* (ed. Georg Strecker; Göttingen: Vandenhoeck & Ruprecht, 1993), 163-208; Allan J. McNicol *Jesus' Directions for the Future: A Source and Redaction-History Study of the Use of the Eschatological Traditions in Paul and in the Synoptic Accounts of Jesus' Last Eschatological Discourse* (New Gospel Studies 9; Macon, Ga.: Mercer University Press, 1996); McNicol, *Beyond the Q Impasse.*

may have appealed so strongly to the latter that he utilized it more often and, therefore, it appears not only in contexts paralleled in his source, but also in contexts independent of the earlier Gospel.[21]

Again, we must grant that it is possible for one author to know and even to make use of the work of another author and not incorporate his source's favorite expressions. But the closer an author copies the text of a source, the more likely it is that the later author will inadvertently include some expressions from that source *at least in fragmentary form*. And it is unlikely that these two literary phenomena — (1) inadvertent copying, and (2) adopting another's casual phrases and making further use of them in independent literary contexts — are *equally* possible. The second is a far less frequent phenomenon when a later author is utilizing the work of an earlier author. In fact, it is hardly possible to conclude that the second phenomenon would take place at all, unless the dependent author thought that a particular expression in his or her source was "just the thing." The presence of a fragmentary form of a "favorite expression" of the earlier writer would mean that for the later writer it was not "just the thing." It would, rather, be "*almost* just the thing" which the later writer knew how to edit in such a way that it would become "just the thing" for him.

But it is unlikely that anyone would resort to this second explanation of such literary phenomena unless one wanted to exclude the phenomenon of "inadvertent copying" as the more likely explanation.[22] That would be necessary, for instance, if one wished to explain the evidence on the lighter side of Mann's and Zeller's scales from the perspective of the Two Gospel Hypothesis. However, to explain those words and phrases from the heavier side of Mann's and Zeller's scales on the basis of this second, less likely, reconstruction of the literary history of two Gospels is, to use the words of Eduard Zeller in English dress, "a reversal of the natural connection between cause and effect and a forced labeling of something as earlier which shows off its [literary] dependence in all places."[23]

In order to elaborate on the above points and principles, we turn now to an illustrative example that makes use of phrases, rather than vocabulary items, and highlights the importance of taking into consideration how a secondary evangelist may adopt the editorial work of an earlier evangelist *in fragmentary form*.

---

[21] Goulder, "Some Observations," 100.

[22] Cf. Farmer, "Reply," 105.

[23] Zeller, "Wortervorrath," 531-32.

Matthean Redaction in Mt 4:23, 9:35 and 10:1.	
Matthew 4:23	Matthew 9:35,10:1
‹4:23› <u>Καὶ περιῆγεν</u> ἐν ὅλῃ τῇ Γαλιλαίᾳ, <u>διδάσκων ἐν ταῖς συναγωγαῖς αὐτῶν</u> <u>καὶ κηρύσσων</u> <u>τὸ εὐαγγέλιον τῆς βασιλείας</u> <u>καὶ θεραπεύων πᾶσαν νόσον</u> <u>καὶ πᾶσαν μαλακίαν</u> ἐν τῷ λαῷ.	‹9:35› <u>Καὶ περιῆγεν</u> ὁ ᾿Ιησοῦς τὰς πόλεις πάσας καὶ τὰς κώμας, <u>διδάσκων ἐν ταῖς συναγωγαῖς αὐτῶν</u> <u>καὶ κηρύσσων</u> <u>τὸ εὐαγγέλιον τῆς βασιλειάς</u> <u>καὶ θεραπεύων πᾶσαν νόσον</u> <u>καὶ πᾶσαν μαλακίαν.</u> Matt 9:36-38 ‹10:1› Καὶ προσκαλεσάμενος τοὺς δώδεκα μαθητὰς αὐτοῦ ἔδωκεν αὐτοῖς ἐξουσίαν πνευμάτων ἀκαθάρτων ὥστε ἐκβάλλειν αὐτὰ <u>καὶ θεραπεύειν πᾶσαν νόσον</u> <u>καὶ πᾶσαν μαλακίαν</u>

Most critical scholars would agree that Matthew 4:23, 9:35 and 10:1 are the work of the author of Matthew. Not only is there considerable verbatim agreement among these three Matthean units, but Mt 4:23-5:2 and Mt 9:35-10:1 serve as summary, transitional statements that introduce the Sermon on the Mount (Mt 5:3-7:29) and the Missionary Discourse (Mt 10:2-11:1). There would also be consensus that at least one, if not the closest, verbal parallel to Mt 4:23 in Mark would be Mk 1:39. Mark 1:39, therefore, represents the fragmentary preservation of the editorial work of Matthew in a parallel context.

Something similar may be said about the parallel to Mt 9:35 at Mk 6:6b. Mark 6:6b is the only appearance in the Gospel of Mark of the word, περιῆγεν. In fact, it is the only occurrence in Mark of any form of the word, περιάγω. This sole appearance of περιῆγεν in Mark and only in a context parallel to Mt 9:35 represents the fragmentary preservation in Mark of a redactional formula that most likely derives from the author of Matthew and it is most easily explained as the result of Mark's accidental incorporation of this word from the redactional material in his source, Matthew.

The reverse is highly unlikely. One would have to suggest that Matthew saw the word περιῆγεν in his source, Mk 6:6b, and adopted that word into the parallel context at Mt 9:35 because it was "Matthew pleasing." But then Matthew must have expanded his use of this word into a major, redactional passage at 9:35 and then, earlier in his gospel at Mt 4:23 (cf. Mt 10:1), Matthew would have repeated essentially the same redactional passage which he created from this one word in Mk 6:6b. Such a procedure is incredible.[24]

---

[24] Frans Neirynck explains this literary evidence and other like it as Matthean "anticipations," but this rationalization is incredible, at least for scholars who have yet to find any of the arguments or rationalizations

4. The Evidence of the Markan Overlay

In our detailed discussions of the 91 Markan pericopae in this book, we often utilize the term, "Markan Overlay." We coined this term to describe a network of repeated words, phrases, grammatical constructions, themes, literary structures, and theological motifs that, primarily by their reoccurrence within the gospel, may be described as *characteristic of Mark*. In some cases, none of the members of an entire category of literary evidence ever appears in the parallels in Matthew or Luke. These literary features are, therefore, *unique to Mark* among the synoptics.[25] Other categories of this kind of evidence represent either repeated and consistent Markan alterations of the texts of Matthew or Luke or some combination of Markan supplements and modifications. These literary features are, therefore, not unique to Mark, but may be said to be *distinctive in Mark* among the synoptics.[26] Furthermore, within this network of material that is both *characteristic of* and *unique or distinctive to* Mark we find the literary unity one might expect in the work of a single author.

On the basis of our assessment of all of the relevant evidence known to us, much of which is presented and discussed in this book,[27] we have concluded that the author of Mark most probably composed his Gospel on the basis of a conflation of the texts of Matthew and Luke. We, therefore, expect that the hand behind these integrated and interrelated features in Mark was most likely that of the author. Hence, we describe all of the categories of evidence that make up this network as *Markan,* intending to give credit for it to the author of this Gospel, whatever the name of that person might have been.

Since many of the literary features within these networked sets of evidence are unique to or distinctive in Mark, we have described the network as *overlay*. Having composed his Gospel primarily from a blend of materials drawn from Matthew and Luke, *Mark* created this *overlay,* giving his Gospel that sense of unity that many of the leading advocates of Markan priority in the nineteenth century also noted, but utilized as evidence for the priority of Mark.[28]

THE IDEA OF A MARKAN OVERLAY IN RECENT STUDY

As early as the opening decades of the nineteenth century, Johann Daniel Schulze was arguing that the Gospel of Mark contained a unified layer of tradition concentrated in and sometimes even

---

for Markan priority convincing. cf. Frans Neirynck, "The Two-Source Hypothesis Textual Discussion. Matthew 4:23-5:2 and the Matthean Composition of 4:23-11:1," in Dungan, ed, *Interrelations*, 23-46, esp. 46.

[25] See, e.g., "πάλιν Used Retrospectively Uniting Two or More Separated Pericopae," *Mark as Composer*, pages 56-57, Table 70.

[26] See, e.g., τὸ εὐαγγέλιον used absolutely at Mk 1:15 (Markan supplement to Mt 4:17) Mk 8:35 (suppl. to Mt 16:24//Lk 9:24), Mk 10:29 (suppl. to Mt 19:29, different from Lk 18:29), Mk 13:10 (different from Mt 24:14, suppl. to Mt 10:18 and Lk 21:13), Mk 14:9 (different from Mt 26:13), Mt 16:15 (suppl. to Mt 28:19//Lk 24:47); cf. Peabody, *Mark as Composer*, 14, 38.

[27] See the summary of the six categories of evidence in support of the Two Gospel Hypothesis discussed earlier in this introduction.

[28] See Hans-Herbert Stoldt, *History and Criticism* (Macon, Ga.: Mercer University Press, 1980), esp. "Chapter VII. The Proof from Uniformity," 155-58.

confined to those parts of the Gospel that represented Markan supplements or alterations of the texts of Matthew or Luke or both.[29] This is, in fact, what one would anticipate if Mark was the third of the Synoptic Gospels to be written and its author made use of the texts of Matthew and Luke as the basis for that Gospel's composition.[30] Not surprisingly, advocates of the Two Gospel (Owen-Griesbach, neo-Griesbach) hypothesis in recent decades have come to concur with Schulze's judgment. What one might not expect, however, is that some scholars working from other hypotheses have more recently come to similar judgments. For instance Helmut Koester, in a 1983 article, isolated a layer of material in Mark that is not found in either Matthew or Luke. In his judgment this material had the unity of historical and theological perspective characteristic of the work of a single author, editor, or redactor. Koester further argued that this layer within the Gospel of Mark was added after the Gospels of Matthew and Luke had been composed and that, at least at points, this layer of tradition shared some features and perspectives with either the Deuteropauline epistles or the *Secret Gospel of Mark* discovered by Morton Smith.[31]

Coming from yet a third perspective, some advocates of a Deutero-Markus hypothesis, such as Albert Fuchs of Linz, Austria, also see a unified perspective in Mark emanating from an isolated network of material within the Gospel that has few, if any, parallels in the Gospels of Matthew and Luke.[32] Fuchs differs most from Koester, however, in that Fuchs believes that his network extends not only through many passages in Mark that are not found in Matthew and Luke, but also into an

---

[29] Johann Daniel Schulze, "Über den schriftstellerischen Charakter und Werth des Evangelisten Markus. Ein Beitrag zur Specialhermeneutik des N. T.," in *Analekten für das Studium der exegetischen und systematischen Theologie* (ed. Carl August Gottlieb Keil und Heinrich Gottlieb Tzschirner; Leipzig: J. A. Barth, 1812-22); "Erster Abschnitt," 2/2 (1814): 104-51; "Zweiter Abschnitt. Erster Halfte," 2/3 (1815): 69-132; and "Zweiter Abschnitt. Zweiter Halfte," 3/1 (1816): 88-127. Schulze was an advocate of a modified form of the Griesbach hypothesis. Specifically, Schulze believed that Mark utilized Ur-Schriften of the Gospels of Matthew and Luke, rather than the texts of these Gospels as now preserved in the NT.

[30] As appendices, Stoldt provided a number of interesting lists that include: (1) 180 instances of "minor additional details in Mark that extend beyond the text of Matthew and Luke, including passages where either Matthew or Luke is lacking," (2) 35 instances of "minor additional details in both Matthew and Luke that extend beyond Mark," (3) 35 instances of "concurrence of Matthew and Luke in expressions and wordings contrary to Mark," and (4) 22 instances of "concurrence of Matthew and Luke in diverging from Mark's word form; see Stoldt, *History and Criticism*. Of these four lists, numbers 1, 3, and 4 provide synoptic contexts where elements of "the Markan Overlay" may be found. With the aid of William R. Farmer's *Synopticon: The Verbal Agreement Between the Greek texts of Matthew, Mark, and Luke Contextually Exhibited* (London: Cambridge University Press, 1969) and Frans Neirynck's *The Minor Agreements of Matthew and Luke against Mark* (Louvain: Leuven University Press, 1974), Robert Paul Howard refined and expanded Stoldt's first list into "a listing of [383] Markan idiographs," i.e., those Markan contexts where Mark has provided something in addition to what both Matthew and Luke have contributed. A refinement of Howard's work was eventually submitted and approved as an MA Thesis in Religion at the University of Miami in Ohio; Robert Paul Howard, *The Markan Idiographs: What Do They Imply?* (MA Thesis, Oxford, Ohio: Miami University, 1984), vi + 217

[31] Helmut Koester, "History and Development of Mark's Gospel (From Mark to *Secret Mark* and "Canonical Mark") in Corley, ed., *Colloquy,* 35-57.

[32] As examples of Fuchs's approach, see his article entitled, "Die 'Seesturmperikope'" in Strecker, ed., *Minor Agreements,* 65-92 and his other selected publications listed on p. 233 of that volume.

extension of what he believes to be this same network, composed of common supplements or changes to the text of Mark, contained in the texts of Matthew and Luke.[33]

Fuchs argues that, by combining certain words, phrases, and passages unique to Mark with similar kinds of linguistic evidence within the triple tradition where Matthew and Luke agree on a reading different from Mark, one can isolate the text of a "Deutero-Markus." In Fuchs' view, this reconstructed text reflects a "second edition" of Mark that was independently utilized by Matthew and Luke in composing their Gospels. However, once so utilized, "Deutero-Markus" was lost. "Canonical Mark," therefore, represents a form of Mark earlier than that which was independently utilized by Matthew and Luke. Here is another significant difference between Koester and Fuchs. For Koester, "canonical Mark" represents a later version of Mark that was composed after Matthew and Luke made use of an earlier version of Mark, an "Ur-Marcus."[34]

It is not surprising to find careful students coming to different conclusions about the literary history of the Synoptic Gospels based upon similar evidence. This is one of the reasons that the Synoptic Problem is still a problem. It is very complex. At the same time, although the literary evidence that impressed scholars like Schulze, Koester, Fuchs and contemporary advocates of the Two Gospel hypothesis is not understood in the same way, it is interesting that these advocates of at least three different source theories (Two Gospel, Two Document, and Deutero-Markus) all agree that "canonical Mark" was not utilized by either Matthew or Luke in composing their Gospels.

The most striking structural evidence in the Markan Overlay is the use of "πάλιν ("again") Used Retrospectively Uniting Two or More Separated Pericopae." Mark carefully uses this editorial feature to link important sections of the gospel together. *Not one of these fifteen uses of πάλιν which provide basic structure for Mk 1:16-13:1, and which integrate separated literary contexts within it, ever appears in the parallels in either Mt or Lk.*[35] It seems impossible that the authors of Mt and Lk, if they were making independent use of Mk, as most advocates of the Two Document Hypothesis claim, could have omitted all fifteen instances of this important structural feature of Mk while adopting many, if not all, of the elements that Mark uses in conjunction with πάλιν to paint his literary picture of Jesus and his ministry.

---

[33] Compare the approach of Andreas Ennulat, *Die "Minor Agreements"* (Tübingen: Mohr/Siebeck, 1994).

[34] In fact, Koester is open to the possibility that Matthew and Luke made use of two different versions of Ur-Marcus, one that included Mk 6:45-8:21, used by Matthew and one that did not include that section of Mark, used by Luke. See, e.g., Koester, "History and Development," in Corley, ed., *Colloquy.*

[35] See the uniquely Markan uses of πάλιν at Mk 2:1, 13; 3:1, 20; 4:1, 5:21; 7:14, 31; 8:1, 13; 10:1bis, 10, 32; 11:27. C. Clifton Black fundamentally misrepresented Peabody's claims about this recurrent, literary feature of Mark's text in *The Disciples according to Mark: Markan Redaction in Current Debate* JSNTSS 27 (Sheffield: JSOT, 1989), 212-18. For instance, on p. 213, Black claims that this Markan usage occurs 52 times in Mk, rather than the 15 times it actually does occur. In fact, the simple vocabulary item, πάλιν, only occurs 28 times in Mk. Black compounded this and other mistakes in his reading of *Mark as Composer* by repeating some of them in his review of *Mark as Composer* for the *JAAR* 57 (Winter 1989): 421. A more accurate review of *Mark as Composer* that includes a number of corrections to Black's reading was subsequently provided by S. Johnson Samuel in the *Bangalore Theological Forum* 22 (1990): 45-63.

The Markan overlay consists primarily of sets of Markan supplements to Mt and Lk, combined with sets of Markan changes to the common testimony of Mt and Lk. We do not consider these supplements and changes isolated "minor agreements," but, in an approach somewhat similar to that of Koester and Fuchs, suggest that the overlay is a network of materials that reflects a single, unified, literary, historical, and theological perspective.[36] On the other hand, in our view, this network of material is not the work of an earlier or later redactor of canonical Mark, but rather, in accord with the work of Schulze, is a network that comes from the hand of the author of Mark. It is this network of material that convinced most scholars, particularly those in nineteenth-century Europe, that Mark's gospel was more "unified" than the gospels of Mt and Lk.[37]

One of the important arguments for the priority of Mark among those nineteenth-century scholars was "the proof from uniformity."[38] This is ironic because most of those critics did not recognize how much of the material that provides the impression of "unity" in Mark derives from either distinctive or unique material in Mark when Mark is compared with the parallel texts of Matthew and Luke. What provided the "sweet smell of a fresh flower, bursting with the pure life of the subject," in the views of some nineteenth-century gospel critics, was not the product of originality or eyewitness testimony, but elements of what we call the Markan Overlay.[39]

THEOLOGICALLY COHERENT ELEMENTS OF THE MARKAN OVERLAY

Mark repeatedly utilized a number of sets of words and phrases in the service of his theological agenda. Collectively, these words and phrases represent the lacquer or finish that binds together the pieces of Mark's narrative, drawn from Matthew and Luke, into a new and artful decoupage. Like lacquer, the elements of the Markan Overlay are also the aesthetic enhancements that Mark provided as he creatively revised his account of Jesus' life, ministry, death, and resurrection on the basis of a conflation of material in these earlier Gospels.

As an introduction to more detailed discussions of these linguistic features and the role they play (see Parts 1-7 and Appendix 3), we provide a preliminary sketch of Mark's overlay. In this sketch, we highlight several of the themes that contribute to the distinctive dramatic and theological perspective of Mark's Gospel.

---

[36] Compare the approach taken by William R. Farmer in "The Minor Agreements of Matthew and Luke against Mark and the Two-Gospel Hypothesis: A Study of These Agreements in their Compositional Contexts," in Strecker, ed., *Minor Agreements,* 163-208.

[37] In an oral review of *Beyond the Q Impasse,* Mark Goodacre once remarked that he could not see any obvious "seams" in that book nor was he able to reconstruct its editorial history, in spite of its authorship by a team of six scholars. That may be because one of our team gave our previous, truly coauthored book a final editorial "overlay" of his own that helped to provide that book with just the kind of "unity" that Goodacre observed.

[38] See Stoldt, *History and Criticism,* esp. chapter 7, "The Proof from Uniformity," 154-58. Cf. H. U. Meijboom, *A History and Critique* (Macon, Ga.: Mercer University Press, 1993), 97-130.

[39] Compare Stoldt's related chapter 8, "The Proof from Originality," in *History and Criticism,* 159-68.

As a first example we note that, from the beginning of Jesus' public ministry, Mark chose to depict him as a *teacher* who provided *new teaching*.[40] From *the beginning of the Gospel* (Mk 1:1), it is clear that one example of this new teaching was Jesus' healing work, also understood as an example of the nearness of the kingdom of God which Jesus proclaimed (Mk 1:15, 21, 27). For Mark, Jesus' announcement of the coming of the kingdom was *the gospel*,[41] i.e., *the Word* of God's saving power (Mk 1:14). Jesus stressed to his disciples the impact that *the Word*[42] would have (e.g., in the interpretation of the Parable of the Sower). Jesus noted that *the time*[43] for *the Gospel* had been fulfilled and even revealed to an inner core of disciples. A bit later in the Markan narrative, *the Mystery* of the Kingdom (Mk 4:12), which turns out to be Jesus' own life and destiny, is the essential clue to how the kingdom comes. This *secret/mystery*[44] would be available to all who could *see* and *hear* (Mk 4:24) but, in the total scheme of things, some would be prevented from seeing (Mk 4:12) and fall away (interpretation of the Parable of the Sower).[45] One fundamental issue that was raised by *the gospel* was whether the disciples would *see, hear, and understand*[46] or fall into the category of those who do not *understand* because *their hearts* remain *hardened* (Mk 6:52, etc.).[47]

As a method of self-revelation, Jesus himself took *the way* from Galilee to Jerusalem (Mk 8:27, 9:33-34, 10:33, 52). While *on the way,*[48] both *in a house to a select group*[49] and in a more open manner (Mk 8:32), Jesus *was teaching*[50] about his coming suffering, death, burial, and resurrection (Mk 8:31, 9:30-32, 10:32-43),[51] but the disciples failed to *understand* (Mk 9:32, cf. Mk 6:52, 8.17, 21).[52]

Finally, upon arriving in Jerusalem, Jesus fulfilled to the letter what he had said earlier about his fate. Peter denied him three times before the cock crowed *twice* (Mk 14:30, 72).[53] During his suffering he was *spit upon*.[54] The disciples who fled away when Jesus was arrested are, nevertheless, called upon to *follow him in the way,* as did the former *blind* man, Bar Timaeus (Mk 10:46-52). They

---

[40] Peabody, *Mark as Composer,* 29 (table number), 43 (page number); 84, 62; 111, 70; 115, 71; 116, 72; 117, 72; 184, 96; 238, 109. On this feature of the Markan overlay, cf. Koester, "History and Development," in Corley, ed., *Colloquy,* 44-47, and Peabody's response to Koester in the same volume, 120-25.

[41] Peabody, *Mark as Composer,* 14, 38, cf. 11, 38; 193, 98; 242, 110. Cf. Koester, "History and Development," in Corley, ed., *Colloquy,* 43-44, and Peabody's response, 116-20.

[42] Peabody, *Mark as Composer,* 69, 55.

[43] Ibid., 12, 38.

[44] Cf. Koester, "History and Development," in Corley, ed., *Colloquy,* 47-49, and Peabody's response, 125-28.

[45] Peabody, *Mark as Composer,* 118, 73.

[46] Ibid., 121, 75; cf. 117, 72, 119, 74.

[47] Ibid., 166, 91.

[48] Ibid., 178, 93.

[49] Ibid., table M, 158; cf. 120, 75; 170, 92.

[50] Ibid., 84, 62; cf. 115, 71.

[51] Ibid., 184, 96.

[52] Ibid., 121, 75; 166, 81.

[53] Ibid., 233, 108.

[54] Ibid., 175, 93. See Mk 10:34//Lk 18:32, no parallel in Mt 20:19, Mk 15:19//Mt 27:30, Luke absent.

are to be *baptized* with his *baptism* (Mk 38-39) and *drink from his cup* (Mk 10:39-40, cf. the Last Supper and Jesus' suffering prayer in Gethsemane).

Since the writing of Mark, Jesus' last week has been continually remembered in the Christian community in the way that Mark distinctively provided for such memory; i.e., as a full eight-day Holy Week, beginning with Palm Sunday and running through Easter Sunday. Furthermore, members of the historic Christian community of faith have continued to take up their crosses and follow Jesus by losing their lives in mission *for the sake of the gospel* (Mk 8:35, 10:29, et al.)[55] and by continuing to *watch*[56] for the culmination of God's plan, proclaiming *the gospel* to all nations (Mk 13).[57]

Thus, from beginning to end, Mark paints an overlay on his source material that depicts his own theological perspective while letting the traditions he inherited and adopted from Matthew and Luke shine through. We now briefly treat some of the key elements in the Markan overlay.

"THE GOSPEL" AND "THE WORD" USED ABSOLUTELY

An example of this theological overlay can be seen in the repeated occurrence of τὸ εὐαγγέλιον used absolutely.[58] Nowhere in the other canonical Gospels is the term, "the gospel" utilized absolutely, as it frequently is in Paul. Like Paul, the author of Mark equates "the gospel" with the proclamation of the saving significance of Jesus himself, as the suffering, dying, and rising Son of God.[59]

In Mark's Gospel there is also a distinctive but, in this case, not unique recurrence of "the Word," ὁ λόγος, used absolutely.[60] This is particularly prominent in Mark's version of the interpretation of the Parable of the Sower. However, in this case, the source for this Markan emphasis may have been the parallels in Matthew and Luke. Nevertheless, though the idea was already present in Mark's sources, Mark has heightened and extended it even in this context where the usage is shared. For instance, at Mk 4:14, Mark changes Matthew's initial "word of the kingdom" (Mt 13:19) and Luke's initial, characteristic and comparable "word of God" (Lk 8:11) to simply "the word" used absolutely. By utilizing his own preference here, Mark achieved a compromising conflation of Matthew and Luke. For Mark, "the word" used absolutely is probably the equivalent of "the gospel" used

---

[55] Peabody, *Mark as Composer,* 193, 98.

[56] Ibid., 121, 75.

[57] Perhaps even "to all the world, to all creation" (Mk 16:15).

[58] The evidence and the import of this distinctive literary and theological feature of Mark's Gospel for the source-critical debate between advocates of the Two Document Hypothesis and advocates of the Two Gospel Hypothesis is discussed in detail in David Peabody's article, "The Late Secondary Redaction of Mark's Gospel and the Griesbach Hypothesis: A Response to Helmut Koester," in Corley, ed., *Colloquy,* 86-132, esp. 116-20.

[59] See our fuller discussion of "the gospel" used absolutely in Mark at the beginning of part 1, in the notes to Mk 1:1 below. See also Peabody, *Mark as Composer,* 14, 38.

[60] Peabody, *Mark as Composer* 69, 55.

absolutely, and again refers to the saving significance of Jesus as Isaiah's Suffering Servant and God's savior of all humankind through his death and resurrection.

"THE MYSTERY" USED ABSOLUTELY

A third term that Mark utilizes absolutely but, in this case, only once in his Gospel, is "the mystery" (Mk 4:11, contra Mt 13:11 and Lk 8:1, "to know the mysteries"). For Mark, the one important "mystery" that is revealed only to those "inside" is that of the saving significance of the suffering, dying, rising Son of God. Although it is used this way only once in Mark, as a change from the common testimony of Matthew and Luke, "the mystery" used absolutely is also part of the Markan overlay. It is part of the layer of tradition that Koester claimed was added to the text of Mark after Matthew and Luke had been composed. It is also a feature of Koester's overlay that had a theological perspective similar to that found in some of the Deuteropauline Letters (Eph 6:19, cf. Eph 3:1-7). It was, of course, also an important element of the "messianic secret" motif that Wilhelm Wrede also believed was imposed on earlier tradition by the author of Mark.[61]

PASSION, DEATH AND RESURRECTION MOTIFS

The Markan emphasis on the saving power of the passion, death, and resurrection of Jesus is, of course, particularly clear in Mark's three Passion Predictions. Here the Markan overlay affirms that the resurrection will take place following the death of Jesus "after three days."[62] In their parallels, Matthew and Luke predict the resurrection "on the third day." The latter, of course, is in accord with the earliest extant pre-Pauline tradition about the resurrection, preserved in 1 Cor 15:3-7.

Mark's emphasis on Jesus' passion, death, and resurrection can also be detected in his editing of some of the miracle stories, where a "death and resurrection motif" has either been introduced or emphasized. For example, in Mk 1:31 Jesus is said to have "raised" the woman by grasping her hand.[63] Mark's point seems to be that her "resurrection" is made possible by Jesus' touch. Compare this to Mt 8:15, where Matthew utilizes the passive ἠγέρθη, "she was raised," presumably to give credit to God for her recovery. Luke, on the other hand, utilized the feminine participle, ἀναστάσα

---

[61] William Wrede, *Das Messiasgeheimnis in den Evangelien: Zugleich ein Beitrag zum Verständnis des Markusevangeliums* (Göttingen: Vandenhoeck & Ruprecht, 1963); English trans. J. C. G. Grieg, *The Messianic Secret* (Cambridge: James Clark & Co., 1971).

[62] Peabody, *Mark as Composer*, 188, 98. The root of Mark's language, "after three days," in the Passion Predictions, where Mark stands alone against Matthew and Luke, may nevertheless have its roots in the wording of Mt 27:63, "after three days," and in the Matthean use of the Jonah story as a parallel to the burial of the Son of Man (Mt 12:40, "For just as Jonah was three days and three nights in the belly of the sea monster, so for three days and three nights the Son of Man will be in the heart of the earth."). Cf. Koester, "History and Development," in Corley, ed., *Colloquy*, 52.

[63] See the similar Markan modification of Matthew and Luke at Mk 5:41 and 9:27. Cf. Peabody, *Mark as Composer*, 44, 47.

(Lk 4:39) in his parallel context, presumably describing the woman herself as "rising up" to serve her guests, after Jesus cured her by rebuking her fever.

Mark's modification of the texts of Matthew and Luke to introduce "a resurrection motif" into the story of the healing/raising of Peter's mother-in-law (Mk 1:29-31), is fairly subtle compared to his more extensive editing and supplementing of the story of the raising of an epileptic boy (Mt 17:14-20//Lk 9:37-43a) at Mk 9:14-29.[64] Numerous extensive Markan supplements to Matthew and Luke serve to emphasize the seriousness of the boy's health problem. Only Mark adds that, in the course of a convulsion, the boy "became like a dead man, so that many people said, 'He's dead'" (Mk 9:26). Then, as in Mk 1:29-31, Mark does not simply edit Matthew and Luke, but supplements their narratives with, "But, Jesus, grasping his hand, raised (ἤγειρεν) him, and he was raised (ἀνέστη)." Mark has again introduced a death and resurrection motif into his form of the story.

JESUS TEACHES PRIVATELY

Immediately following Mk 9:27, Mark modifies Mt 17:19 in ways that bring the parallel passage in Mk into conformity with three other passages in Mk where Jesus delivers esoteric teaching to his questioning disciples in a private setting, usually a house. Here Mark supplements Matthew's text by adding that this teaching was done, not simply "privately" (Mt//Mk), but "in a house" (Mk 9:28, cf. Mk 4:10, 7:17, and 10:10).[65]

A LITURGICAL MOTIF

Related to the death and resurrection motif of the Markan Overlay is another motif that could be generally described as "liturgical." The most notable way that Mark expressed his interest in the church's liturgy was by editing the Passion Narrative in Matthew and in Luke in ways that allow one to trace a full eight-day Passion Week in Mark, beginning with Palm Sunday and running through Easter Sunday. One cannot identify such a full eight-day week in either Matthew or Luke.[66]

SACRAMENTAL MOTIFS

Mark also heightened a "sacramental" motif by adding a saying about "baptism" to the saying about "the cup" that he found in Jesus' answer to the request that came from the sons of Zebedee (Mt 20:21-23//Mk 10:37-39; cf. the contextual parallel in Lk 22:24-30 and, perhaps, the non-contextual "parallel" at Lk 12:50). In Mt, it is the mother of the sons of Zebedee who requests special treatment for her sons, James and John. Mark's understanding of baptism as "dying and rising with Christ" is also in accord with Pauline tradition (Rom 6:4), as is Mark's preference for "the gospel" used

---

[64] See our discussion of Mk 9:14-29 in Part 5 below. Cf. Koester, "History and Development," in Corley, ed., *Colloquy,* 50-52, and Peabody's response, 129-30.

[65] Peabody, *Mark as Composer,* table M, 158; cf. 42, 47.

[66] See our chart of this eight-day Passion Week at the beginning of our discussion of Part 6 below.

absolutely, discussed above. Of course, "the cup" is also utilized by all three of the synoptic evangelists in the context of Jesus' prayer in the garden of Gethsemane as a metaphor for Jesus' suffering and death (Mt 26:39//Mk 14:36//Lk 22:42), but even here Mark's text looks like a careful conflation of Matthew and Luke (see synopsis 81).

All of the synoptic gospels include one or two feeding stories in language that is similar to the story of Jesus' Last Supper with his disciples.[67] However, in his editing of Mt 16:9-12 at Mk 8:19-21, Mark not only altered the Matthean version in significant ways (see the discussion below) to make rather different points, but also supplemented Matthew's version of this story with even more strongly eucharistic language, drawn from the feeding stories.[68]

BLINDNESS OF THE DISCIPLES

Mark also heightens his depiction of "the blindness of the disciples" when compared to Matthew and Luke by supplementing their versions of the story of the stilling of the storm with the words, "For they did not understand about the loaves, but their heart was hardened." (Mk 6:52). One finds similar Markan supplements at Mk 3:5 and Mk 8:14-21, esp. 8:17.[69]

JESUS AS TEACHER AND HEALER

Mark utilizes the vocative of the title "teacher" ($\delta\iota\delta\acute{\alpha}\sigma\kappa\alpha\lambda\epsilon$) for Jesus more often than either Matthew or Luke. This may suggests that Mark understood Jesus' teaching activity as just as important, no less so than did Matthew or Luke, even though Mark records less of the *content* of that teaching than do either Matthew or Luke.[70] Nevertheless, Mark seems to have thought of Jesus' miracles and healings as constituting some of his most important "teachings." In his parallel to the widely differing Sermon on the Mount in Matthew (Mt 4:23-7:29) and the Sermon in Nazareth in Luke (Lk 4:16-30), Mark chose merely to indicate that Jesus gave a sermon in a synagogue in Capernaum, recording only its effects, not its content (Mk 1:21-22).

Having thus acknowledged the minimal agreement between Matthew and Luke in the parallel contexts, Mark then follows Luke's content and order of events in the story of the healing of the man with an unclean spirit (Mk 1:23-28//Lk 4:33-37). Jesus' healing of this man by exorcism is the first healing, exorcism, or any other type of miracle in the Gospel of Mark. After the healing, Mark alone

---

[67] On the language of the feeding stories see Peabody, *Mark as Composer*, 161-64, 88-90.

[68] Peabody, *Mark as Composer*, 164, 90. Cf. Synopsis 45.

[69] Peabody, *Mark as Composer*, 166, 91.

[70] Helmut Koester includes a number of Markan literary contexts, like the one discussed in this paragraph, where Mark's supplements and differences from Matthew and Luke include some form of the words $\delta\iota\delta\acute{\alpha}\sigma\kappa\omega$ or $\delta\iota\delta\alpha\chi\acute{\eta}$. These passages are included in Koester's version of the Markan overlay that was added to the text of Mark after Matthew and Luke had been composed and that reflected some of the same theology as the Deuteropauline Letters and the *Secret Gospel of Mark*. See Koester, "History and Development," esp. 44-47, and Peabody's response in the same volume, esp. 120-25.

has the crowds exclaim, "What is this, *a new teaching?*" (Mk 1:27; cf. Lk 4:36, "Who/What is this word?"). If Mark did think of miracles as important teaching from Jesus, as the preceding suggests, that may also help to explain why Mark includes every miracle story common to Matthew and Luke but one, the healing of the centurion's servant (Mt 8:5-13//Lk 7:1-10). To this almost totally inclusive collection of miracle stories from Matthew and Luke, Mark *adds two more* (Mk 7:32-37, Mk 8:22-26, cf. the shared language in these two distinctive miracle stories with that in Mk 5:21-24, 35-43, which does have parallels in Mt 9:18-19, 23-26 and Lk 8:40-42, 49-56).[71]

Another set of details composed of just two members is related to Mark's interest in miracle stories, particularly as an expression of Jesus' most important teaching. Both members, however, are Markan supplements to the text of Matthew and Luke. Specifically, only Mark records (twice) that Jesus used spittle as a means of healing (Mk 7:33 and 8:23).[72] This small set of Markan linguistic features is found only in the two miracle stories with which Mark supplements the narratives of Matthew and Luke (Mk 7:32-37, cf. Mt 15:30-31; Mk 8:22-26).[73]

USE OF FOREIGN WORDS

Mark also often supplements the texts of Matthew and Luke by inserting Aramaic-sounding words. These sometimes appear in Mark's versions of healing stories as something like magic formulae (Mk 5:41, 7:34). However, Mark always provides translations of these Aramaic-sounding words, and some Latin loanwords. The translations are introduced by certain fixed formulae, such as ὅ ἐστιν or ὅ ἐστιν μεθερμηνευόμενον.[74]

---

[71] Peabody, *Mark as Composer,* 135, 80.

[72] Ibid., 175, 93.

[73] These two stories alone contain 16 of the mere 24 verses that Griesbach claimed were unique to Mark over against Matthew and Luke. "Marcus totum libellum suum, si viginti et quatuor circiter commata, quae de sua penu addidit, excipias, de quibus posthaec dicetur, e Matthaei et Lucae commentariis," *Io. Iac. Griesbachii theol. D. et Prof Primar in academia Jenensi commentatio qua Marci Evangelium totum e Matthaei et Lucae commentariis decerptum esse monstratur, scripta nomine Academiae Jenensis (1789, 1790) jam recognita multisque augmentis locupletata;* reprinted in *J. J. Griesbach: Synoptic and text-critical studies 1776-1976* (ed. Bernard Orchard and Thomas R. W. Longstaff; Cambridge: Cambridge University Press, 1978), 74-102. The quotation is drawn from p. 78 = ET, p. 108, "Mark compiled his whole work (apart from about twenty-four verses which he added from his own sources, of which we shall speak later) from the works of Matthew and Luke." Note that, as Schulze indicated early in the nineteenth century, and Stoldt, *History and Criticism,* and Ennulat, *The Minor Agreements,* confirmed in detail, there are far more than 24 verses of unique material in Mark.

[74] See Peabody, *Mark as Composer,* 103, 68, and Mk 5:41, 15:22, 15:34; Mk 3:17, 7:11, 7:34, 12:42, 15:16, and 15:42. Such evidence is hardly consistent with the view that the author of Mark was a Jewish Christian, living in Galilee, writing prior to the first Jewish revolt against Rome in 70 CE. On such a reconstruction, what need would Mark's probable community of readers have for such translations? Similarly, what need would there be for such Markan supplements as his very lengthy characterization of Jewish practice in Mk 7:2-4? On the basis of such textual evidence, Pierson Parker has demonstrated that such a reconstruction of the background of the author and his readership is highly unlikely. Cf. "The Posteriority of Mark," in Farmer, ed., *New Synoptic Studies,* 143-59.

These theological features of the overlay are grounded in a mass of linguistic details, many of which are unique to Mark (see Appendix 3). Together, these features paint a coherent picture of Jesus' life and affirm Mark's own theological perspective. These will be discussed in more detail in the next chapter on "The Provenance and Purpose of Mark."

5. The Evidence for the Fragmentary Preservation in Luke and Mark of a Jewish Style of Argumentation in Matthew

At several points in the Synoptic Gospels we encounter an important phenomenon which has not often been taken into account, particularly in the discussion of the Synoptic Problem. On a number of occasions the Gospel of Matthew presents material in a precisely organized and logical way, often centered around an interpretation of the Hebrew Scriptures. In several of those cases, the parallel passages in Luke and/or Mark break up or reorder the material so that the internal logic of the unit is lost. When that happens, the question that arises is, "Did Matthew create the structure of the unit and then Luke and/or Mark fail to see it or ignore it?" Or, "Did Matthew find just the elements he needed in Mark or Q to construct his carefully organized passage?" There is no clear a priori answer.

In many cases vestiges of key pieces of the Matthean structure remain in Mark or Luke, strongly suggesting that Luke and Mark were rewriting Matthew's Christian-Jewish work for a very different, largely Gentile audience. Either failing to grasp the structure of Matthew's argument or finding it irrelevant, they freely rearranged the material to suit the structure and purpose of their own gospels. The reverse is almost impossible! That Matthew could have found in the very different structures of Mark or Q just the right pieces to create his tightly structured argument, replete with details that reflect an intimate knowledge of Jewish tradition, is difficult to envision. Although one might argue that Matthew was so fortunate in one or two cases, when the phenomenon occurs with regularity that line of reasoning becomes untenable. The key Matthean logical and structural patterns that both Luke and Mark exhibit in broken and/or fragmentary form strongly suggest their literary dependence on Matthew. As we will show in the commentary below, such broken patterns dramatically appear in Mark within the following shared literary contexts, among others.

Pericopae 19-22 (Mk 3:7-35//Mt 12:15-50//Mt 9:32-34, cf. Lk 6:12-19, 11:14-23 and 12:10)

Pericopae 23-24 (Mk 4:1-12//Mt 13:1-17//Lk 8:4-10)

Pericope 40 (Mk 7:1-23//Mt 15:1-20, Lk NP)

Pericope 57 (Mk 10:17-31//Mt 19:16-30//Lk 18:18-30)

Similarly, Longstaff has suggested that in Matthew's gospel the narratives about women at the tomb of Jesus, and at his resurrection, reflect Jewish practices with respect to burial and mourning which might not have been well understood by Mark and his readers.[75]

---

[75] Thomas R. W. Longstaff, "The Women at the Tomb: Matthew 28:1 Re-Examined," *NTS* 27/2 (1981) 277-82. A revised and expanded version of this essay appeared as "What Are Those Women Doing at the Tomb of

6. Supplementary Evidence from Patristic Testimony

In 1977, at a conference in San Antonio, Texas, George Kennedy, a classics scholar, encouraged New Testament scholars to reexamine and to take more seriously the patristic evidence bearing on the question of the origins and interrelationships among the canonical gospels.[76] Three years later, at a follow-up conference in Cambridge, England, William R. Farmer presented a paper intended to do just that. Subsequently, a patristics scholar in residence in Rome, Giuseppe Giovanni Gamba, responded to Farmer's presentation with full documentation of all relevant patristic texts. Both papers were then published in 1983 as the opening essays of *New Synoptic Studies*.[77] The survey of the patristic evidence which follows is drawn from these essays. This is supplemented by an essay in the same volume by David Peabody that reevaluates Augustine's views on the sequence and interrelationships among the Gospels, especially as those views may be derived from a re-reading of Augustine's *De consensu Evangelistarum*.[78]

PAPIAS

Papias produced an exegetical work on the Gospels consisting of five books. This work has not been preserved, but it was known and cited by Eusebius, Bishop of Caesarea, in his famous and indispensable *Ecclesiastical History*.

Eusebius gave three citations. The first is of value in clarifying the exact place of Papias in the history of the transmission of the gospel tradition. Eusebius is concerned that Irenaeus had written that Papias was a "hearer of John." He wants it understood that this cannot mean that Papias knew John the apostle. And, therefore, to make clear that Papias in no way had been a hearer and eyewitness of any of the apostles, Eusebius quotes at length from the preface of Papias's work as follows:

And I shall not hesitate to set down for your benefit, along with the interpretations, all that I ever carefully

---

Jesus?" in *A Feminist Companion to Matthew* ed. Amy-Jill Levine with Marianne Blickenstaff (Sheffield: Sheffield Academic Press, 2001), 196-204.

[76]"Classical and Christian Source Criticism," in *The Relationship Among the Gospels: An Interdisciplinary Dialogue* (ed. William O. Walker, Jr., San Antonio: Trinity University Press, 1978), 147-52. Among Kennedy's observations on New Testament scholarship from the perspective of a classical scholar was the following: "…'scientific' skepticism can easily be carried too far. Ancient traditions have sometimes been confirmed by archaeology; ancient writers sometimes meant what they said and occasionally even knew what they were talking about. Skepticism about skepticism is especially appropriate in the period from the first century B. C. to the second century of the Christian era, because this is the most learned, best informed, and most securely datable period in history before modern times. . . . The New Testament could not have been written at a time of greater literacy, education, or understanding" (pp. 126-27).

[77] William R. Farmer, "The Patristic Evidence Reexamined: A Response to George Kennedy," and Giuseppe Giovanni Gamba, "A Further Reexamination of Evidence from Early Tradition," in Farmer, ed., *New Synoptic Studies, ,* 3-15 and 17–35, respectively.

[78]"Augustine and the Augustinian Hypothesis: A Reexamination of Augustine's Thought in *De Consensu Evangelistarum*," in Farmer, ed., *New Synoptic Studies,* 37–64.

learnt and remember from the elders, for of their truth I am confident. For, unlike most, I did not take delight in those who have much to say, but rather in those who teach what is true; nor in those who recount the commandments of others, but rather in those who recall the commandments given to the faith by the Lord and derived from the truth itself. And if ever anyone chanced to come who had actually been a follower of the elders, I would inquire as to the discourses of the elders, what [the elders reported that] Andrew or Peter had said, or what Philip, or what Thomas or James, or what John or Matthew or any other of the Lord's disciples had said, and what [the elders reported that] Ariston and John the Elder, disciples of the Lord are saying. For, I did not suppose that information out of books would be nearly so helpful to me as the words of an abiding and living voice.[79]

Since Ariston and John the Elder were not of the Twelve, they would presumably belong to a wider circle of transmitters of tradition, and would have (at least in the eyes of Papias) stood in some authoritative relationship to the living oral tradition going back to Jesus and his original followers. Eusebius reports that Papias included in his work accounts of the words of the Lord from Ariston and traditions from John the Elder.

What Eusebius later cites from Papias about the Gospels has been studied with the greatest interest. The citation is as follows:

And the Elder used to say this: "Mark, indeed, having been the interpreter of Peter wrote down accurately all that he could recall of what [Peter had said] was either said or done by the Lord—although not in the correct order. For he [himself—i.e., Mark] had not heard the Lord, nor had he followed him, but later on, as I said, he followed Peter who used to adapt his teaching to the needs [of his hearers], but not with a view to putting together the Lord's oracles in orderly fashion: So that Mark was not off target in thus writing down things as he recalled them [i.e., from his memory of what he had heard Peter say]. For he kept a single aim in view, namely to omit nothing of what he had heard [Peter say], and to include no false statements in his account.[80]

This is a remarkable passage in several respects. First, Papias is referring to a matter on which the Elder apparently commented repeatedly. He "used" to say it in the sense that he did not say it on one particular occasion, but whenever the matter came up.

The issue, which came up repeatedly, clearly had to do with Mark's arrangement of topics. This arrangement the Elder admits is faulty, but this fault is not fatal. For Mark's purpose was simply to put down in writing everything he could recall of what he had heard Peter say and to be careful to state these matters truthfully. Since Peter himself adapted what he had to say in accordance with the varying needs of his hearers, and not in accordance with any need for these reports to be arranged in a continuous written narrative, Mark did not have from Peter any set arrangement for the topics in his

---

[79] Eusebius, *Hist. eccl.*, 3.39.34.
[80] Eusebius, *Hist. eccl.*, 3.39.15.

Gospel. His work then can best be judged in terms of his own purpose and it is wrong to fault him for something he could not have been expected to do correctly. Mark himself, who had not been a follower of Jesus, was dependent on Peter, who never wrote a gospel and who, therefore, never undertook the task of giving his reports an order that would fit them into a continuous narrative. Taking this into consideration, Mark had done quite well and can be best appreciated when it is known that he has preserved the witness of Peter fully and truthfully. This is how the Elder, John, reasoned whenever he heard Mark's Gospel criticized—according to Papias as recorded by Eusebius. Eusebius continues in these words:

> Such then is Papias's account of Mark, and about Matthew this was said, "Matthew collected *ta logia* in the Hebrew language, but each interpreted them as he was able."[81]

These words of Papias have never been satisfactorily explained. They have been variously understood to mean that Matthew wrote his Gospel in Hebrew; that he compiled the words of Jesus in Hebrew; that he wrote his Gospel in Greek, though in Jewish style; and so forth. One can safely conclude little, if anything, about the sequence in which the Gospels were composed from the words of Papias as cited by Eusebius. It is quite otherwise, however, when we come to the next piece of external evidence.

CLEMENT OF ALEXANDRIA

Clement of Alexandria lived in the second half of the second century and was in personal contact with a number of elders from different parts of the Mediterranean world. Eusebius cites Clement as follows:

> Now this work is not a writing composed for show; but notes stored up for my old age, a remedy against forgetfulness, an artless image, and a sketch of those clear and vital words which I was privileged to hear from blessed and truly notable men. Of these, one, the Ionian, I met in Greece, another in south Italy, a third in Coele-Syria, another was from Egypt, and there were others in the east, one of them an Assyrian, another in Palestine of Hebrew origin. But when I met the last, and in power he was, indeed, the first, I hunted him out from his concealment in Egypt and found rest.[82]

The last Elder mentioned refers undoubtedly to Clement's famous teacher, Pantaenus, whom he met in Alexandria in the early eighties of the second century. This means that most of the contacts that Clement established with the various teachers he met were made during the previous decade. Thus, the testimony which these elders passed on to Clement from an earlier period carries us in a reliable way well back into the first half of the second century. Eusebius, in the sixth book of his *Ecclesiastical History,* writes as follows:

---

[81] Eusebius, *Hist. eccl.,* 3.39.16.
[82] Eusebius, *Hist. eccl.,* 5.11.34.

And, again in the same books [*Hypotyposeis*], Clement has inserted a tradition of the primitive elders with regard to the order of the Gospels as follows. He used to say that those Gospels were written first which include the genealogies, and that the Gospel according to Mark came into being in this manner: When Peter had publicly preached the word at Rome, and by the Spirit had proclaimed the gospel, that those present, who were many, exhorted Mark (as one who had followed him [i.e., Peter] for a long time, and remembered what had been spoken), to make a record of what was said; and that he did this, and distributed [copies of] the Gospel among those that asked him. And that when the matter came to Peter's knowledge, he neither strongly forbade it nor urged it forward. But that John, last of all, conscious that the outward facts had been set forth in the Gospels [i.e., those with genealogies and Mark], was urged on by his disciples [as Mark had been urged on by the Christians in Rome], and, divinely moved by the Spirit, composed a spiritual gospel. This is Clement's account.[83]

It is difficult to know to what extent Eusebius is closely citing Clement and to what extent he may be paraphrasing him. If the whole of his account is drawn from the tradition of the primitive elders we can reason as follows. Since the Gospels with genealogies are clearly Matthew and Luke, they were written first.[84] Nothing is said as to which of them was actually first. But both Mark and John were clearly written after Matthew and Luke, John's being the last of the four.

The tradition that Clement says he received from the primitive elders bearing on the question of whether Matthew and Luke were written before Mark and John, or whether John has written last of all, is generally accepted. Nothing in what Papias reports conflicts with or causes any difficulty for accepting this tradition. It appears to be quite unmotivated and, so far as is known, it constitutes the earliest extant reliable external evidence bearing on the question of the sequence of the Gospels. Both Farmer and Gamba concur on this point.

---

[83] Eusebius, *Hist. eccl.*, 6.14.5-7; Clement, *Hypotyposeis*, 6. It is possible that when this point about the earlier date for Gospels with genealogies was first made, it was to counter Marcion's claims for originality of his gospel—which had no genealogy. But the observation itself counts in favor of Matthew and Luke being earlier than Mark and John in any case, for they also, like Marcion's gospel and the *Gospel of the Ebionites*, did not have genealogies.

[84] For another interpretation of Clement's testimony, see Stephen C. Carlson, "Clement of Alexandria on the 'Order' of the Gospels," *NTS* 47/1 (January 2001): 118-25. Here Carlson not only demonstrates skill in analyzing the Greek texts of relevant primary source material, but also an intimate knowledge of the scholarly discussion of this testimony by Clement, particularly as that has been published in the most recent literature. One group of Carlson's acknowledged colleagues and dialogue partners, each of whom advocates a different source hypothesis about the synoptic gospels, has also enriched Carlson's work. Leonard Maluf advocates a form of the Griesbach or Two Gospel hypothesis; Mark S. Goodacre, the Farrer-Goulder hypothesis; and Peter Head, the Two Document hypothesis. This article by Carlson, therefore, deserves a more substantial and detailed response than can be provided in a footnote. Preliminarily, however, we would respond that Carlson has made a plausible case for rendering προγεγράφθαι in this particular literary context as "writing publicly" (Matthew and Luke) as opposed to "publishing more privately," at least originally (Mark). However, this does not necessarily mean that Carlson's reading of this testimony is the more correct reading. It is just as plausible to continue to render this word temporally because this alternate meaning is well attested in ancient Greek literature. Whether this temporal reading does any injustice to this particular literary context will have to remain, for now, the subject of later debate and discussion.

The reference to the plural, "elders," should be noted. Apparently Clement's source was not limited to just one elder. Rather, the tradition was known and received in different places in the second century church.

Alternatively, Clement's account may be a composite, drawn together from all that he could recall of what various elders had said. In this case, one item would have concerned the temporal relationship of Matthew and Luke, which had genealogies, to the Gospels that did not: "Those with genealogies were written first." Another item would have concerned the Elder, John. John was written after the others and intended to complement them in a "spiritual manner." If Clement knew from the other traditions that Matthew and Luke were written first and that John came last of all, it would have been for him a simple deduction to place Mark after Matthew and Luke, and before John. This would fully explain what Clement says about the order of the Gospels. But, here again, there is no apparent motive for the item about Matthew and Luke. So the very least that can be said is that Clement's tradition supports the view that Mark and John were written after Matthew and Luke. And, unless there is some reason to doubt the tradition concerning John, we should also conclude that Clement's account supports the view that John was written last. If we grant these conclusions it follows that Clement's account supports the view that Mark was written third. And it would appear that this deduction is unaffected by any doubt that might be cast upon the reliability of the details Clement relates concerning the circumstances under which Mark was written. In other words, the reliability of Clement's tradition concerning the circumstances under which Mark was written can be considered independently of the question as to the position of Mark in the sequence in which the Gospels were written. Mark's being third can be logically deduced solely from the tradition Clement records concerning the other three.

IRENAEUS

Irenaeus of Lyons, an older contemporary of Clement of Alexandria, was also a widely traveled man. He was especially well acquainted with the churches of Asia Minor, the churches of the Rhone valley in southern France, and the church in Rome. At about the time Clement ended his extensive travels and settled in Alexandria, Irenaeus, who had become the Bishop of Lyons, wrote his famous work, *Against Heresies.*

In the third book of that work Irenaeus adduced proof from the scriptures to combat the heresies of his day. In the first chapter of this book, there is a passage referring to the Gospels. Eusebius, in Book Five of his *Ecclesiastical History,* has preserved the original Greek text of this important passage:

> Matthew published a written gospel among the Hebrews composed in their own language [or dialect, or style], while Peter and Paul were preaching the gospel in Rome and founding the church there. After their decease, Mark, the disciple and interpreter of Peter, did also hand down to us in writing the things that

used to be preached by Peter. And Luke, as well, the companion of Paul, set down in a book the gospel which Paul used to preach. Afterwards, John, the disciple of the Lord, the one who had leaned upon his breast, also set forth [in writing] the gospel, while residing at Ephesus in Asia.[85]

This statement by Irenaeus, though including information bearing on the question of sequence, does not purport to treat the four Gospels in the strict order of their composition. But some pertinent data can be deduced from his words. First, he writes that Matthew wrote his Gospel while Peter and Paul were active in Rome.

It seems most natural to understand Irenaeus to imply that Luke, as well as Mark, composed his Gospel after the death of Peter and Paul. However, he does not specify the relationship between Mark and Luke. Matthew was written while Peter and Paul were active in Rome; that is one period of time. Mark and Luke were written after the death of Peter and Paul. Their deaths mark the end of one and the beginning of another period of time. With John, however, Irenaeus clearly includes a sequential reference: John wrote "afterwards," that is, after Mark and Luke had written their Gospels.

Hans von Campenhausen has noted that the order of the Gospels followed by Irenaeus is generally Matthew, Luke, Mark, and John and he observes that this order would seem to be "the order most familiar to Irenaeus himself."[86] The evidence for this view is drawn from the same work of Irenaeus, *Against Heresies,* and relates to the order in which Irenaeus cites the Gospels as he builds his case against heresy. For example, in defending his thesis that the creator God is one and the same as the God declared by the gospel, he takes up proof first from Matthew (3.9.1-3); second, from Luke (3.10.1-5); third, from Mark (3.10.6); and fourth, from John (3.11.1-6). So, also in discussing the Gospels in relation to the different heretical groups, he treats them in the same order, associating Matthew with Ebionites, Luke with Marcionites, Mark with Docetists, and John with Valentinians (3.11.7).

Finally, in refuting the view that God was not the Father of Christ, Irenaeus again refers to the Gospels in the order, Matthew, Luke, Mark, and John (4.6.1).

ORIGEN

Origen almost certainly knew the work of Irenaeus, and Clement was his predecessor in Alexandria. It is with no little interest, therefore, that we turn to Origen's statement on this matter. His statement has been preserved by Eusebius in Book Six of his *Ecclesiastical History.* Eusebius writes as follows:

In the first of his [commentaries] on the Gospel [i.e., that] according to Matthew, defending the canon of the church, he gives his testimony that he recognizes only four Gospels, writing somewhat as follows:

---

[85] Eusebius, *Hist, eccl.,* 5.8.14.
[86] Hans von Campenhausen, *The Formation of the Christian Bible* (Philadelphia: Fortress Press, 1972), 195.

"Having learnt by tradition concerning the four Gospels (which alone are unchallenged in the church of God under heaven), the first [Gospel] written was that according to Matthew, who was once a toll-collector, but afterwards an apostle of Jesus Christ, who published it for those who, from Judaism, came to believe, composed as it was in the Hebrew language. And second, was that according to Mark who wrote it in accordance with Peter's instructions, whom also Peter acknowledged as his son in the catholic epistle, speaking in these terms: She that is in Babylon, elect together with thou, saluteth thou; and so doth Mark my son (I Peter 5:13). And third, that according to Luke, who wrote the Gospel that was praised by Paul, for those who from the Gentiles [came to believe]. After them all, that according to John."[87]

It appears most likely that, by the time of Origen, on some common ground of ecclesiastical authority located between the church in the Rhone valley and Alexandria in Egypt, the four-fold Gospel canon had gained acceptance. From that center it was promulgated by teachers like Origen as if it had always been so.

There is no reason to think that Origen had evidence to support the order Matthew, Mark, Luke, and John that he does not mention. And, in fact, it is possible that when he systematically moves from first to second to third, and last of all, he does not himself think of this order as the historical order in which these Gospels were composed. It should be noted that only with reference to Matthew is it explicitly said that this Gospel was written first. The subsequent references to Mark being "second" and Luke being "third" presumably are also to be understood "chronologically," but that is not certain. In any case, Eusebius includes Origen's statement because of its bearing on the *number* (not the *order)* of the Gospels in the canon of the church. He probably accepted Origen's order as the canonical order. But there is *no* unambiguous patristic evidence that this order was the chronological order of composition. By contrast, it is to be emphasized that Eusebius included *Clement's* statement because of its bearing on the *order* of the Gospels. Eusebius adds nothing to our knowledge about the order of the Gospels. What he writes about order corresponds to what he knew from Origen and Irenaeus. Nor does he actually say that Mark and Luke were composed in that sequential order. That is left ambiguous as well it might be, since Eusebius knew the tradition from Clement that places Mark after Luke.

Summary

Eusebius neither contradicts nor confirms either the order Luke-Mark or the order Mark-Luke. His statements are compatible with either, and/or both, as well as with anything that is said about order by Clement, Irenaeus, or Origen. All, including Eusebius, agree that John is fourth. No one denies that Matthew was the first to write a Gospel, though Clement merely implies that Matthew was before Mark and John, not that he was first. Papias, Irenaeus, Origen, and Eusebius all appear to speak of a Hebrew Matthew. The order Luke-Mark is supported by Clement, and, on balance, by Irenaeus, when

---

[87] Eusebius, *Hist. eccl.,* 6.25.36.

his overall witness is carefully examined. Origen has probably followed the ecclesiastical order fixed in the four-fold Gospel canon. He may also have thought that that was the order in which the Gospels were composed.

If the order of the four-fold Gospel canon was known to Irenaeus, why is it that he generally does not follow it? On the other hand, if the four-fold Gospel canon emerged in Rome under the influence of Irenaeus' "history of salvation" theme, then both the comprehensive theological conceptualization and the canonical order would be explained. "First to the Jews and then to the Gentiles" places the more Jewish Matthew before the other three. Mark comes next because it represents the apostle Peter, who had close ties to Jewish Christianity yet eventually favored admitting Gentiles into the church and was martyred for that faith in Rome, the foremost Gentile city. Then comes Luke, which represents Paul, the apostle to the Gentiles. And finally comes the work of John, who was regarded as the author of both the Fourth Gospel and the Book of Revelation. The canonical order of the Gospels and the order of Origen are the same, and that order is readily susceptible to a theological explanation. On the other hand, the order Matthew, Luke, Mark, and John, supported by the witness of Clement and Irenaeus and clearly contradicted by no one, unless it be Origen, is *not* readily susceptible to any such theological explanation. It is an enigma unless it is what it is purported to be, a historical order supported by the earliest and most explicit, external evidence available.

It is sometimes asserted that little weight should be given to the testimony of the Fathers because they are not interested in the "Synoptic Problem" as it was studied in the nineteenth and twentieth centuries, and because even when these authors speak of the order of the Gospels it is not certain that it is the *chronological* order with which they are concerned. In response to this mistaken conclusion it can be said that the fact that these authors are disinterested in the "Synoptic Problem" (in the *chronological order of the composition* of the Gospels) provides no critical ground for discounting the importance of their evidence. On the contrary, their testimony is all the more trustworthy because, on the point at issue, they are disinterested witnesses. As can be seen from this survey, the patristic evidence clearly weighs in favor of the Two Gospel Hypothesis, and offers no support for the Two Document Hypothesis.

But what about the so-called Augustinian Hypothesis, i.e., that Mark used Matthew, and Luke used Matthew and Mark? Is there any patristic evidence to support this hypothesis?

As late as the ninth century, the Irish monk Sedulius Scottus was still giving credence to the view set forth in Eusebius' *Ecclesiastical History* that Matthew and Luke wrote their Gospels before Mark. But by the end of the Middle Ages, this view appears to have given way to what came to be viewed as the traditional view of the church—that Mark was written second and was the "epitomizer" of Matthew. John Calvin rejected this traditional view on the grounds that Mark generally takes more words to tell the same Gospel story than does Matthew. Therefore it doesn't make sense to say that Mark produced a shorter version of Matthew. This observation gained ground during the

Enlightenment and eventually opened the way for reversing the traditional relationship. It was Matthew who was dependent on Mark, and who expanded Mark, rather than the other way around. Thus came into being the idea that Mark could be the earliest Gospel, an idea, however, which has no support among the Fathers. It is rather an idea that emerged from an enlightenment "jettisoning" of a late medieval misconception.

The idea that Mark's Gospel was second and epitomized that of Matthew is referred to in all previous histories of the Synoptic Problem as the "Augustinian Hypothesis,"[88] and can be traced to certain remarks of his in book one of his *Harmony of the Gospels.*

But in 1983 David Peabody published his essay on Augustine. He discovered in book four of the *Harmony of the Gospels* that Augustine eventually reversed himself on this very important point. What Augustine wrote in this context, which had been overlooked by all students of the Synoptic Problem, is clear. He contrasts what he said in book one (quod in primo libro) with what he came to regard as the more probable view (quod probabilius intelligitur), namely that Mark accompanies not only Matthew, but both Matthew *and* Luke (cum ambobus incedit). This is the essence of the Two Gospel Hypothesis.

Until recent decades, the patristic evidence appeared to be essentially divided. In light of recent research it can be said that, on balance, the patristic evidence strongly supports the Two Gospel Hypothesis with regard to the order of the composition of the Gospels.[89]

---

[88] This, of course, does not apply to David Dungan's *A History of the Synoptic Problem.*

[89] Researchers are now fortunate to be able to consult all the relevant patristic texts in the original Greek or Latin brought together and translated by Dom Bernard Orchard in "The Historical Tradition," part two of *The Order of the Synoptics: Why Three Synoptic Gospels?* (ed. by Bernard Orchard and Harold Riley, Macon, Ga.: Mercer University Press, 1987), 111-226.

THE PROVENANCE AND PURPOSE OF MARK

During the past several decades a major debate has emerged over whether the purpose of Mark can be determined primarily by studying the literary structure of the text or whether it is necessary to reconstruct the socio-historical world behind the text, thereby throwing light on its referentiality. Our position is that these two approaches must work together, hand-in-glove: the text itself and the world behind the text should both be used to discover Mark's purpose and provenance. Our discussion will utilize both perspectives. We will start with a remark about the socio-historical world behind the text of Mark.

A BEGINNING POINT

We find no compelling evidence to reject the patristic assertion that Mark was written in Rome. We believe that this would have been no more than a few decades after the martyrdoms of Peter and Paul in 65-68 CE.

This view presumes that the intended readership is aware of persecution for the faith (Mk 10:30; 13:13). A credible historical account of the origin of this persecution can be constructed. Tacitus (*Ann.* 15.38-44) gives a lengthy description of the fire at Rome in July of 64, and its aftermath. One consequence was that some members of the sect of the Christians in Rome were persecuted and martyred (*Ann.* 15.44). Pliny's letter to Trajan offers confirmatory evidence that hostility expressed toward the Christians in Rome resulted in sporadic trials in the ensuing decades. Presuming Trajan's knowledge of such trials, Pliny inquired about such legal details as the process of conviction and punishment (Pliny *Ep.* 10.96). For some time it has been noted that the description of Peter's denial of Jesus in the Gospel tradition (including Mark) seems to echo a knowledge of such procedures (Mk 14:66-72).[1] Additional evidence that these were turbulent times for the church in Rome is found in the First Epistle of Clement to the Corinthians 5:1-6:2. This writing not only records the deaths of Peter and Paul in Rome but cryptically notes that there were other persecutions that followed. Another wave of persecution is associated with the reign of Domitian (80-96 CE) and such persecutions may have continued until the early 4th century. In summary, what the evidence suggests is that starting from 65-68 the church at Rome encountered persecution and certain extraordinary legal difficulties with the authorities. Although these problems would ebb and flow, it appears that from this time onward there was always the possibility that Christians could be hauled into court to face dire consequences because of their loyalty to Jesus.

It is not clear what effect this persecution had on the Roman Christians. Various outcomes ranging from apostasy, internal squabbling and quarreling, to struggles between Jewish and Gentile factions,

---

[1] G. W. H. Lampe, "St. Peter's Denial and the Treatment of the *Lapsi*," in *The Heritage of the Early Church: Essays in Honor of G. V. Florovsky (Orientalia Christiana Analecta* 195 (ed. D. Neiman and M. Schatkin: Rome: Pontifical Oriental Institute, 1973). 113-121. Cf. *Mart. Pol.* 9-10.

or other negative consequences may have followed in the wake of these events. The paucity of the literary sources renders it impossible to recover precisely what was going on in the church in those decades, but it is not hard to imagine that demoralization must have set in among various circles within the Christian community because of their marginalization. The case would be stronger if Hebrews could be shown to be addressed to the Christians at Rome during this period, as many believe.

MARK'S BASIC RHETORIC: THE TRIAL OF JESUS AND HIS DISCIPLES

Moving away from socio-historical issues, we now turn to evidence yielded by the text itself. Scholars reading Mark on the macro-level have long noted that essential to its structure is a basic tension among the three groups who dominate the action in the narrative: Jesus, the disciples, and the religious and political authorities. The issue of faithfulness is central. Throughout Mark Jesus is faithful to his initial proclamation of the gospel of God (Mk 1:14). The political authorities (both Jewish and Roman) stand at the other end of the spectrum in opposition to him. In the middle are the disciples. They teeter on the line between belief and unbelief. Much of the drama in Mark results from the developing crises of the disciples' ultimate allegiance. One way to perceive this is to look more closely at how Jesus and the disciples act vis-à-vis those in the wider sector who are openly hostile to them.

Trial of Jesus

From the outset, the trial theme looms large in the account of Jesus' life. After being addressed as Son of God at his baptism (Mk 1:11), immediately Jesus is cast out into the desert (Mk 1:12-13). He is tested by Satan in a scene that echoes Israel's struggle in the wilderness. He gains an initial victory; but this encounter only foreshadows the trials that he, the suffering just one, will have to pass through later. Mark also ominously notes the arrest of John the Baptist (Mk 1:14). Thus, from the beginning, the fates of both John and Jesus are connected inextricably with struggle and violence.

Despite the fact that Jesus is declared to be the Son of God at the baptism, and is recognized grudgingly as such by the demonic powers and their agents, his mission and true identity remains disconcertingly hidden to humans. This is a critical point with regard to the Markan account of Jesus' ministry. Although he commences his ministry by announcing the nearness of the kingdom, and supports that message with displays of great power in healings and exorcisms, it is evident that the kingdom remains veiled and hidden to many throughout his ministry (Mk 1:15, cf. 4:11b-12). Even if he is the Son of God he is dreadfully misunderstood and treated shamefully by the controlling authorities. The mystery of the kingdom is that (despite all the evidence to the contrary) there is a direct link between what was taking place in Jesus' obscure and marginalized mission and the emergence of God's new world, where the promise of Jesus' life will ultimately be manifested. And as it was in Jesus' case, so it is for the Christian community at the time of the writing of Mark.

Jesus confronts enemies of the kingdom both among his own people, who reject him as a blasphemer (Mk 2:7; 14:64), and the Roman authorities, who ultimately put him on trial (Mk 15:1-20). Jesus predicts his confrontation with the might of Rome, and subsequently experiences its savage power in his execution. Without question he remains faithful to his commitments. In keeping with Israel's traditional hope for the triumph of their faithful martyrs, God manifests greater power than the human authorities and vindicates Jesus by raising him from the dead. This has to be the meaning of the empty tomb no matter what we think about the issue of the longer ending. The later follower, Mark's ideal reader, cannot hope to fully replicate Jesus. But as he awaits Jesus' appearance as the heavenly Son of Man, this disciple, if only he has eyes to see and ears to hear, can understand that just as the kingdom was a hidden power and presence in Jesus' ministry, so it may still be in his time (Mk 4:23). Jesus anticipated his ultimate vindication, despite God's apparent absence at critical moments. Likewise, buoyed by faith and hope based on Jesus' life, the later disciple also looks beyond appearances and awaits similar vindication.

In this context, Mark holds up the vindication of the Son of God despite incredible debasement as a heroic model for emulation. During his ministry Jesus' true nature and destiny were veiled to his followers. It was only open to understanding when one shows great faith (Mk 11:23-24). As such, the total spectrum of Jesus' life represents the true paradigm for the coming of the kingdom. It functioned as a transcendent word to a church self-absorbed with its marginalization and the internal struggles that placed it in danger of overlooking the truth about the workings of the reign of God. Jesus embraced the truth that the secret power of the kingdom is working toward a favorable resolution even when one is undergoing brutal rejection and marginalization. The setting forth of this insight is essential to the purpose of Mark.

Trial of Disciples

The disciples, with Peter as their most visible representative, often represent a counter-point to Jesus' faithfulness. As far as narrative development is concerned, they play a critical role in the Markan story. Whereas the course of Jesus' life consistently unveils the true nature of the kingdom, the disciples, as transparencies of leaders of the later Christian community, represent not ideal but "real life" responses to various crises that arise as one awaits full realization of God's purposes. Their actions do not function as an archetypal model for believers to follow. Through their connection with the fate of Jesus, in both their successes and failures, the disciples project how the values of the gospel play out in real life. Thus readers are able to identify with the disciples and recognize correspondences in their own life situation.

Not surprisingly, then, the role of the disciples functions as a highlight in the structure of Mark. Immediately after the announcement of the kingdom, before Jesus begins his early Galilean mission of preaching and casting out of demons (Mk 1:20-3:19), he selects an inner core group of followers to accompany him (Mk 1:16-20). The initial impression of the disciples is favorable; the reader wants them to succeed in their vocation. By the end of the early Galilean mission Jesus extends his call to the Twelve (Mk 3:7-19). They constitute a new family committed to doing the will of the Father (Mk 3:31-34 cf. 3:20-21).

However, as the Galilean ministry proceeds we begin to hear of disciples who will hear and receive the word joyfully but will only endure for a while, eventually giving up under the stress of tribulation and persecution (Mk 4:17). Consequently, it is not much of a surprise to discover that when the twelve are commissioned to preach and to cast out demons they prove inadequate to the task (Mk 6:7b-13). By the end of the Galilean ministry, in the face of opposition from the political powers (Herodians and Pharisees), they exhibit confusion and are without full understanding (Mk 8:14-21).

Matters do not improve in the following section of Mark (Mk 8:27-10:52). Peter, perhaps like the first stage of the healing of the blind man at Bethsaida (Mk 8:24), glimpses Jesus' true glory only in a distorted fashion (Mk 8:27-33). The request of James and John for chief positions of power (Mk 10:37) indicates that spiritual arrogance and self-seeking ambition still maintains a hold on the future leaders of the kingdom. Indeed, we have to wait to the end of this unit, in an apparent counter-point, to see at last a positive example of one who worthily models the way of discipleship (Mk 10:46-52)—and he comes from outside the circle of the twelve!

Arriving in Jerusalem, the disciples are privy to Jesus' extensive critiques of the Jerusalem leadership (Mk 11:1-14:11). They are warned that the day is coming when they too will have to face a test of their allegiance to the way of the gospel. This they will do before representatives of the power structures of the time (Mk 13:9-13). And then, in the concluding segment of Mark's narrative (Mk 14:12-16:8), the first of these tests comes suddenly. It focuses upon Peter's personal crisis, which mirrors that of many later followers of Jesus. Peter had boldly confessed total allegiance (Mk 14:29), affirming *not I* (οὐκ ἐγώ = Mk 14:29) will betray him. But when figures even loosely related to the authorities suspect him of being a follower of Jesus, Peter quickly wilts and states that he (ἐγώ) does not know Jesus (Mk 14:68, 71). In a riveting account of a man being tested; despite warnings that he will deny Christ, Peter is deaf to the call for absolute allegiance (Mk 14:29, 68, 71-72).An ancient Christian reader could not have been presented with a more vivid portrayal of what is at stake in holding firm to the way of the kingdom. As John Donahue has noted, "Peter's craven apostasy before a maidservant and a mocking crowd are a virtual 'antimyth' of martyrdom."[2] Peter's conduct was in direct contrast to the claims of the gospel (Mk 8:34-38) which summons people to carry their crosses and give up all to follow him.

---

[2] John Donahue, "Windows and Mirrors: The Setting of Mark's Gospel," *CBQ* 57 (1995): 25. The often noted fact that Peter was remorseful and later became a martyr himself may be meaningful for later apostates who repent, but it is not likely to be as central to Mark's message as some make it out to be. Cf. Lampe, "St. Peter's Denial," 113-33.

To a challenged church of the latter decades of the first century this all too realistic description of what could happen even to a great leader must have come to Christian communities like a splash of cold water over one's face on a brisk morning. No one is immune from apostasy. In another text (Acts 14:22) Barnabas and Paul teach that "through many tribulations we must enter the Kingdom of God." For Mark, these tribulations even involved problems occurring within the church. They would include acts of cowardice, defections of leaders under pressure, and even betrayal within the faith community; all of which were epitomized by Peter or another of the disciples. But despite this disheartening state of affairs, paradoxically, Jesus' promise of the coming of God's new world is made even more sure. Jesus clearly foretold that betrayal and treachery would raise its ugly head in the course of the disciples' journey (Mk 14:18, 27, 30), and it did. He also promised that their life of discipleship would finally end in reconciliation and victory (Mk 14:28; 16:7). Despite the disputed nature of the longer ending, Mark leaves us in little doubt that the disciples would eventually come to faith and understanding. This would only be precipitated by Jesus' death and resurrection. Accepting Jesus' death and resurrection as God's plan for his Son was essential, a sine qua non of coming within reach of the mystery of the kingdom. As it would take the death and resurrection of Jesus to bring the disciples to insight concerning the nature of the kingdom, so all later disciples must accept the reality that at the heart of their faith is the story of the crucified Son of God.

In the meanwhile, as Mark's readers awaited the full realization of God's purposes for his creation, the story of Jesus and his disciples would remind those who had eyes to see and ears to hear that the way of the kingdom always stands in conflict with the claims of the power-brokers who worship the gods of the age. Sometimes, as with Peter's capitulation, these forces gain temporary victories, but they cannot ultimately triumph. For Mark, it was only a matter of time before these forces would be fully put to rout, upon the return of the Son of man (Mk 13:24-27).

MARK'S PURPOSE AND THE TWO GOSPEL HYPOTHESIS

These conclusions are essentially congruent with some previous theological analyses of Mark. We have arrived at such conclusions primarily on the basis of a methodology not dependent on any particular theory of sources . Now it is time to recall a comment made a generation ago by Nils Dahl with respect to the sayings of Jesus in Mark. "Since Mark has chosen some sayings and excluded others, the selection must be determined by the evangelist's intention."[3]

Dahl spoke these words from the perspective of a Markan priorist. Since most exegetes have worked on Mark from similar source-dependent presuppositions, it has proven difficult to carry out the task Dahl recommended. But in light of the Two-Gospel Hypothesis—the presupposition that Mark utilized as sources both Matthew and Luke—Dahl's challenge to determine Mark's compositional intentions ought to be taken up afresh. If Mark used Matthew and Luke, we could give

---

[3] Nils Dahl, "The Purpose of Mark's Gospel," in *Jesus in the Memory of the Early Church* (Minneapolis: Augsburg Publishing House, 1976), 53.

greater precision to observations made about the purpose of this Gospel than would be possible if Mark is assumed to be the first Gospel. We should be able to look more closely at those places where Mark makes major editorial changes in his use of Matthew and Luke, and suggest reasons for his selection and editing of material. Indeed, we plan to demonstrate in this book that engagement with such passages does prove especially fruitful.

MARK UNDERSCORES ONE GOSPEL
DRAWN FROM TWO, MATTHEW AND LUKE

Matthew and Luke both emerged amid major concerns about the *identity of Israel* in light of the belief that Jesus the Messiah had come and inaugurated the kingdom of heaven/God.

Matthew stressed that by fulfilling the law and the prophets through his obedient life Jesus did not set aside the law's demands but enhanced them. Indeed, obedience to the law and the prophets, although understood differently than it was by most Pharisees and Sadducees, was normative for the disciple of Jesus (Mt 5:17-20; 7:12; 28:16-20). With the advent of Jesus, what changed was the hermeneutical application of the law. All of the commandments of the law were to be viewed in dependence upon Jesus' interpretation of the two love commandments (Mt 22:34-40). This hermeneutical principle undergirded and guided the eschatological assembly of restored Israel: the immediate readership of the first Gospel. And it was to be taught to all future followers of Jesus, even Gentiles (Mt 28:16-20). Given the normative nature of the law for Matthew it should come as no surprise that a certain degree of interpretive tension exists in any Christian Gentile appropriation of this work.

Luke also was intensely interested in the impact of Jesus' coming for Israel. For Luke, Jesus was the one who came to announce the good news that the kingdom of God was coming to Israel (Lk 4:18, 43; 7:22; 8:1; 9:6; 16:16; 20:1). The question of Israel's acceptance or rejection of this proclamation was foundational for both Luke and Acts. For Luke, many in Israel received Jesus as the Messiah and thus fulfilled the prophetic promises for the restoration of Israel (Acts 1:6; 2:30-36). Throughout Acts, restored Israel was synonymous with the people of God. Gentiles, still maintaining their ethnic identity, were added to "the tabernacle of David" in keeping with the promises of the messianic era (Acts 15:14-18). Conceptually, these two groups maintained their separate identities until the very end of Acts (Acts 28:17-28).[4] Luke accounted for the incorporation of the Gentiles into the people of God through an understanding of prophecy and fulfillment. The restoration of Israel remained a major focus, starting with his first two chapters and continuing throughout the two volumes.

---

[4] Jacob Jervell, *The Theology of the Acts of the Apostles* (NTT; New York: Cambridge University Press, 1996), 34-43.

In contrast to Matthew and Luke, the status of Israel is not a central concern for Mark. Those debates are in the past. Mark, we would argue, emerges in a context where the church is primarily Gentile in composition and orientation. Although Mark is historically faithful in recording that Jesus' ministry took place within Israel, Mark's story of Jesus is the "good news" or gospel for all of humankind who are prepared to accept Jesus' call (Mk 16:15-16).

Consequently Mark's message is not Matthew's "gospel of the Kingdom" nor even Luke's announcement of Jesus' preaching good news that the time of fulfillment of the prophets for the restoration of Israel is at hand. Rather, for Mark, the story of Jesus' life expresses how God's saving power (gospel) was manifested and exercised a claim over the world. This gospel was first promised in Isaiah (Mk 1:1-2), came to light when Jesus began to preach (Mk 1:14-15), and is accepted by following a particular course of life (Mk 8:35; 10:29). Mark's Gentile-Christian readers are called to be loyal (Mk 14:9) to this gospel and to announce it to all creation (Mk 13:10; [16:15]).

In making this argument, Mark develops a clear compositional strategy. First, Mark adopts the traditional Petrine and Pauline kerygma as set forth in Luke-Acts as the basic framework for his narrative account of Jesus' life (Acts 1:21-22; 2:22-36; 10:37-42; 13:24-41).[5]

Second, Mark carefully drew material from both Matthew and Luke to provide the content of his account of Jesus' life as an embodiment of the one gospel. In blending his two main sources into one narrative, Mark lays out an effective arrangement for telling the story of Jesus' life in keeping with his theological agenda. At its core Mark's structural arrangement is disarmingly straightforward.[6] Starting with a clever blending of both Matthew and Luke, Mark condenses into just twenty verses the crucial elements of Jesus' early ministry up until the Sermon on the Mount (cf. Mk 1:21/Mt 4:23). Then, after carefully noting that Jesus taught (Mk 1:20-21), Mark supplements his account of the early Galilean ministry by incorporating the Lukan order of Jesus' activity from his initial Sermon in Nazareth to the Sermon on the Plain (Lk 4:31-6:19/Mk 1:20-3:19). Mark omits the Sermon on the Plain, as he had the Sermon on the Mount. He then presents the heart of Jesus' Galilean ministry as an account of the demonstration of Jesus' wisdom and power (Mk 3:20-6:6a). The pericopae in this unit alternate between a segment drawn from Matthew (Mt 12:22-13:35/Mk 3:20-4:34) and one from Luke (Lk 8:22-56/Mk 4:35-5:43).[7] After this massive demonstration of wisdom and power, Mark presents the mission of the Twelve, carefully delineating their going out and return (Mk 6:6b-30).

---

[5] David L. Dungan, "The Purpose and Provenance of the Gospel of Mark According to the "Two-Gospel" (Griesbach) Hypothesis," in *Colloquy on New Testament Studies,* (ed. Bruce C. Corley; Macon, Ga.: Mercer University Press, 1983), 151-52.

[6] See our outline for the details of this arrangement pericope by pericope. It must be remembered that as well as making a selection of pericopae from Matthew and Luke, Mark regularly blended material within these pericopae from his two main sources.

[7] Mk 6:1-6a is a retrospective summary of Mk 3:20-5:43 incorporating some material mainly from Mt 13:53-58 and echoes of Lk 4:16-30.

Then comes the climax of the Galilean ministry in the majestic account of the Feeding of the 5000, in which Mark agrees with the order of both Matthew and Luke (Mk 6:31-44).

Thereafter Mark basically follows the order of Matthew until the end of his account. First, Mark creates a tour of Jesus from Bethsaida to Bethsaida (Mk 6:45-8:22). The order of pericopae for the content of this unit is drawn exclusively from Matthew. Similarly, the trip to Jerusalem and the Passion Narrative (Mk 8:27-16:20) is primarily dependent on the Matthean order of pericopae. But Mark will occasionally utilize a pericope from Luke when warranted by his theological agenda. Such is the disarming simplicity of Mark's compositional procedure. The net result is that Mark has presented the one gospel/kerygma in the form of a biographical account of Jesus' ministry.

Third, through blending both Matthew and Luke into one account, on the basis of the kerygma, Mark presented a Jesus whose life functioned as a model for direct instruction (catechesis) of wavering believers in the Christian-Gentile communities, especially at Rome.[8] The Christian-Jewish Matthew had a following in Greater Syria, and Luke was probably dispersed among the churches of Paul throughout the Diaspora. Both of these accounts of Jesus' life had their constituencies and were rapidly becoming entrenched in the church. Nevertheless, to discerning readers discrepancies between the two accounts were plainly visible. To teachers who wished to present the basic story of Jesus this must have been troublesome and annoying.

One might not venture to replace Matthew and Luke. One could, however, write a gospel that diminished the differences between these two foundational accounts. This new form of the gospel would serve two purposes. One, it would defend Christianity against the charge that its philosophy was false because its foundational documents were inconsistent. Two, it would serve a theological agenda. This is precisely what Mark did. Mark's Jesus was an epiphany of the Son of God whose ministry of power was encapsulated in a massive mystery, namely, as the paradigm of the coming kingdom, he had to be crucified before his ultimate vindication. Everything in Mark's account, from its initial intimations of violence, through the announcement of the mystery of the kingdom and the misunderstanding of the disciples, to its culmination with the revelation of the crucified Son of God at the cross was pressed into the mold of this unified theological vision. This was the word that the church needed to hear.

Understanding that Mark's writing was guided by a particular theological vision also explains Mark's omissions of much of Matthew and Luke. In order to present his theological vision with clarity Mark omitted from his sources freely. Mark's editorial activity reflects two fundamental points. (1) Mark would only use material that would contribute to his theological vision of narrating Jesus' life as an expression of the one gospel. (2) Since Matthew and Luke could never be replaced,

---

[8] Examples of how Mark has incorporated a focus on the Gentiles into his message can be found throughout our Commentary sections below. Cf. Pierson Parker, "The Posteriority of Mark," in *New Synoptic Studies* (ed. William R. Farmer; Macon, Ga.: Mercer University Press, 1983), 79-103.

the reader could attain additional details about what Jesus said and did by reading them. Thus, the two foundational memoirs of Jesus' life, Matthew and Luke, were not to be replaced but to have a capstone, Mark.

CONCLUSION

We have argued that Mark was written in the context of Christianity in Rome toward the end of the first century. Although we cannot be too specific about the particular situation of the churches in Rome at the time, external and internal evidence combine to indicate that Mark was written to a community that was preoccupied with internal struggles and marginalization at the hands of the wider culture. Consequently, it had difficulty seeing that Jesus' announcement of the kingdom was fulfilled. As such it was in need of a word that would function as a midpoint correction and bring the church to a clearer understanding.

Mark, drawing upon the Lukan representation of the kerygma of Peter and Paul, recounts the well known story of Jesus' life as "the word" or gospel. Jesus' opponents function as transparencies of those who marginalized the church in Mark's time. And, likewise, the disciples function as transparencies of church leaders and believers in the local Christian communities toward the end of the first century. In such a situation Mark retells the story of Jesus to show that Jesus' life embodied the true nature of the kingdom. After tremendous humiliation as the crucified Son of God he was vindicated. The disciples, facing similar difficulties to those encountered by Jesus, wavered in their faith but, on the basis of Jesus' death and resurrection, eventually understood the mystery of Jesus' life and came to insight about the kingdom (assuming Mark did not originally end at 16:8). Mark's purpose was to remind the wavering believers of his time that in their marginalization they follow the path of Jesus.

HOW TO READ THIS BOOK, WITH A KEY TO ITS FORMAT

This book is designed so that it may be of use to several different types of readers. The ideal reader will work through the book with the electronic synopses of Mark and its parallels on our companion CD open. Our argument is often dependent upon viewing the synoptic relationships more precisely than most, if not all, previous synopses have displayed them. It may also prove helpful to have David Peabody's *Mark as Composer* available in order to refer to the tables there. In references to this work, Peabody's table number has been cited first; then, the page number.

Readers interested in the Synoptic Problem will find source-critical comments at the beginning of each section of **General Observations** which immediately follow the narrative paraphrase of each pericope in Mark. A reading of these observations in order will provide . an overview of the evidence that Mark did indeed use Matthew and Luke.

A less technically interested reader may choose first to read though all the narrative paraphrases in order, as a way of sensing the flow of the Gospel. Then, such a reader may wish to read through the *Overview* and *Summary* of each part in order, before turning to our pericope by pericope discussions that include our most technical, critical comments.

Of course, the reader who wishes to consult our treatment of a specific passage may do so either by using the indices or by turning directly to the main body of this book where our discussions of individual pericopae appear in the Markan order.

Parts

We have organized our compositional analysis of Mark in three basic ways, as we did in *Beyond the Q Impasse: Luke's Use of Matthew*. The largest division, the part, coincides with our understanding of the major segments of Mark's story. Each part begins with an *Overview* and concludes with a brief *Summary*. These are printed in larger type and, thus, provide something of an inclusio around the series of pericopae that constitute each part. Each *Overview* highlights prominent features of the part and, thus, the evidence that led to our decision to delimit each part in the way we did. Each *Summary* is retrospective by summarizing many of those same prominent features of the part, but is also prospective by alluding to literary elements and themes that will follow in subsequent parts of Mark's gospel.

Sections

Within some of these parts we found it necessary to provide subdivisions which we have called sections. These are each made up of two or more pericopae. Some sections are given a brief introduction, setting forth our reasons for seeing the pericopae within that section as belonging to a distinct literary unit, larger than a pericope, but smaller than a part.

Pericopae

Finally, we deal with Mark's text pericope by pericope. Our discussion of each pericope includes: a pericope header, a narrative paraphrase, general observations, and a series of verse-by-verse critical comments. Other elements that occasionally appear include synopses, excurses and charts.

The Pericope Header.

➤ **The number of the pericope.** The pericopae identified on literary-critical grounds have been assigned numbers running consecutively through Mark, beginning with pericope 1 [Mk 1:1] and ending with pericope 92 [Mk 16:9-20; note that the assigning of a number to this pericope is not necessarily meant to affirm its authenticity].

➤ **The title of the pericope.** In formulating these titles we have attempted to focus the reader's attention exclusively on Mark's version of the teaching or story contained in the pericope. We have made no attempt to produce titles that might apply equally well to parallels in the other Gospels, as other synopses have done.

Compare, for example, the title, often given to Mk 10:17-31, "The Rich, Young Ruler." This character is described as "rich" in all three of the synoptics (Mt 19:22/Mk 10:22/Lk 18:23), but as "a ruler" only in Lk 18:18 and as "young," only in Mt 19:19

By way of contrast, we entitled this same pericope, "Jesus Teaches on Wealth," thereby concentrating on Mark's version of the story and eliminating features unique to Matthew or Luke. Of course, if Mark were conflating, harmonizing, or blending Matthew and Luke, as the Two Gospel Hypothesis maintains, then this pericope provides important evidence of how Mark might have gone about those tasks.

➤ **Chapter and verse references in Mark with parallels in Matthew and/or Luke**

We have centered all of the references to Mark under the title in the pericope header. References to chapters and verses in Matthew and Luke are flush left and right, respectively.

We have placed chapter and verse references in Matthew or Luke that we consider "primary" parallels to Mark on the same line with the chapter and verse references to Mark. These are usually contextual parallels (i.e., passages in Luke or Matthew that appear in the same relative order as in Mark), as well as verbal parallels to Mark, but there are some exceptions. For instance, on the basis of a higher concentration of verbatim agreements and verbal similarities, we have judged Mt 10:17-22 to be the primary parallel to Mk 13:9-16, rather than the contextual parallel at Mt 24:9-14.

However, because Mt 10:17-22 is not the contextual parallel, we have placed this reference to Matthew in parentheses, as we always do for non-contextual parallels. We have, therefore, also left Mt 24:9-14 without parentheses, as we always do for contextual parallels.

"Secondary" parallels to Mk are dropped down a line or two from the Markan reference, depending upon how many we believe need to be noted.

Between the references to Matthew and Mark on the left and to Luke and Mark on the right, we have also utilized a system of arrow and line coding that indicates different levels of verbal and, usually, contextual agreement between Mark, on the one hand, and Matthew or Luke on the other. Specifically:

- ➢ A double lined arrow =====>) indicates the highest level of agreement, both in terms of shared, relative order of pericopae and in terms of shared wording.

- ➢ A single lined arrow (———>), indicates a reduced level of agreement.

- ➢ A single line without an arrow head (-----------) indicates an even more reduced level of agreement.

- ➢ The absence of either an arrow or a line indicates that we find only minimal evidence of a literary relationship.

The Narrative Paraphrase

Directly under each pericope header is found an interpretive paraphrase of the contents of the pericope. It has three purposes. As in *Beyond the Q Impasse,* an effort has been made to provide a fresh restatement of what is said in the pericope, without depending directly on any previous English translation. However, we encountered a classic Markan dilemma in working with these narrative paraphrases. If we translated Mark in a literal way, however fresh and lively, we encountered elements of Mark's style which grate on the ear and eye of an English reader. For example, the frequent use of the historic present is a colloquial style in Greek and in English. We found, however, after a serious attempt to follow Mark's usage, that the reading was too rough for the average reader of English, so we chose, instead, to render the Markan historic present, oftentimes, as a simple past tense. Similarly, in some cases, Mark's repetition of καί becomes too cumbersome. Nevertheless, the narrative paraphrases attempt to present the text of Mark in a lively English idiom, while avoiding some of the elements of Markan style that would make the reading of a particular narrative paraphrase distracting rather than helpful. These representations of the text will, we hope, give the reader a sense of the flow of the Gospel, but we do not claim that they are technical translations.

General Observations

The analysis of each pericope in Mark continues with a set of general observations, beginning with source-critical comments. This paragraph first relates Mark to Matthew and Luke in the general order of pericopae and makes some comments on his method of composition within the pericope and/or the section or part in which it is found. Next we provide an overview of the main issues raised by the passage. That prepares the way for the immediately following detailed analysis of verses.

Critical Comments

The body of the Compositional Analysis is comprised of verse by verse annotations introduced by the chapter and verse number in Mark in **bold text**. If we provide more than one, distinct annotation within a verse or group of verses, second and subsequent annotations within those verses are introduced with a •.

Synopses, Excurses and *Charts*

While we feel strongly that the best way to follow the argument of this book is to consult our complete, color-coded synopsis of Mark on CD-ROM, there are a few places in this book where we have felt that it was sufficiently important for our argument and presentation also to provide a synopsis. These occasional synopses have been given descriptive titles and are numbered consecutively throughout the book.

Occasionally, we have also elaborated upon our argumentation by inserting some excurses. These may explain some important literary features of Mark's text that go beyond individual pericopae or elaborate upon some central themes or concepts related to Mark and its composition.

Finally, we have also inserted some charts into our discussion that typically illustrate some structural features of Mark when compared to the parallels in Matthew or Luke. Like the synopses, these excurses are numbered consecutively throughout the book. The charts, however, have been assigned consecutive letters of the alphabet. The name and the contextual placement of each Synopsis, Excursus or Chart within this book may be found in the Table of Contents.

THE BEGINNING OF THE GOSPEL OF JESUS CHRIST

Overview

Mark opens his account by informing the reader that he is presenting an account of the gospel (good news) of Jesus Christ, [the Son of God].

This gospel had its origin in promises given to Isaiah and the prophets (Mk 1:2-3). Its fulfillment began when John the Baptist appeared, preaching in the wilderness (Mk 1:4-8), and culminated in the life and work of Jesus of Nazareth (Mk 1:8-15).

Although this part functions as a preface to Mark's story of Jesus' ministry, several themes crucial for understanding the Markan portrait of Jesus already emerge. First, the part is bordered by an *inclusio* on the theme of the gospel (Mk 1:1, 14b-15). This indicates that the theme of Jesus' life as gospel is important for Mark.

Second, although Mark's account of Jesus has its origin in the promises of scripture, it comes to fruition with the announcement by both John and Jesus of a new *way* emerging in the *wilderness* (Mk 1:2-4; 1:12). This *way* may have overtones of the recapitulation of Israel's original entrance into the land, but it is much more. It is an anticipation that the center of life for the people of God will no longer be in Jerusalem. To follow Jesus along this *way* will be to follow a path of discipleship different from that offered by the temple leadership (see Mk 8:27-14:11).

Third, at his baptism, when the heavens are rent apart, Jesus is addressed as the Son of God. Already his testing in the wilderness (Mk 1:12-13) and the announcement of the fate of John (Mk 1:14) hint that Jesus' sonship will be defined by humiliation and suffering on behalf of others.

Thus, through this terse introductory narrative about John and his baptizing activity in the wilderness (Mk 1:2-8), Jesus' baptism by John (Mk 1:9-11), Jesus' testing in the wilderness (Mk 1:12-13), and the brief summary of Jesus' initial message (Mk 1:14-15), Mark provides a succinct overture to his account of Jesus' *way* as gospel.

¶1. The Beginning of the Gospel

Mt 1:1-14 ---------------------   **Mk 1: 1**   ------------Lk 1:1-4, 3:23-38

The "beginning of the gospel," the good news about Jesus the Messiah, the Son of God was like this.

> *General Observations.* The opening of Mark's Gospel combines elements from both Matthew and Luke. Specifically, Mark opens with a note about "the beginning" (cf. Lk 1:2) of "the gospel of Jesus Christ," (cf. Mt 1:1) "[the Son of God]" (cf. Lk 3:38).
>
> • If Mark composed an *inclusio* from the beginning of Jesus' genealogy in Matthew and the end of Jesus' genealogy in Luke, that may help to explain Mark's omission of the differing birth and infancy narratives in Mt 1:18-2:23 and Lk 1:5-2:40[52], which fall between the two different literary contexts for the genealogies in Mt 1:1-17 and Lk 3:23-38. Furthermore, presuming that the author of Mark had read Acts, paying particular attention to the details of the kerygma, Mark could not omit all of the material prior to Luke's genealogy (Lk 1:1-3:27) because "the Gospel of Jesus Christ, the Son of God," must "begin with the baptism of John" (cf. Acts 1:21-22, 10:37; Lk 3:1-22//Mt 3:1-17//Mk 1:4-11).
>
> **Mk 1:1.** Mark's opening verse, "The beginning of the gospel of Jesus Christ [the Son of God]," may have parallels both to Luke's opening verses ("beginning," ἀρχή, Lk 1:2) and to Matthew's ("Jesus Christ," Ἰησοῦ Χριστοῦ, Mt 1:1). Compare the similar wording of Clement of Rome's statement (ca. 95 CE) in reference to an earlier letter to the church at Corinth: "Take up the epistle of the blessed Paul the Apostle. What did he write first to you *in the beginning of the Gospel?*" (1 Clem 47:1-2).
>
> • Matthew's work begins by identifying Jesus as "son of Abraham and son of David" (Mt 1:1). Luke's genealogy of Jesus (Lk 3:23-38 cf. Mt 1:1-17) includes both Abraham and David as two of Jesus' ancestors (Lk 3:34, 32), but significantly concludes by designating Jesus as "Son of God." Both Matthew's opening designation of Jesus as "Messiah/Christ" (Mt 1:1) and Luke's closing designation of Jesus as "son of God" (Lk 3:38) may have influenced Mark to designate the central figure of his Gospel, in his opening verse, as both "Jesus Christ" (Mk 1:1//Mt 1:1) and "the son of God" (Mk 1:1//Lk 3:38).
>
> • The noun "gospel" never appears in Luke's narrative about Jesus, but only its verbal cognate, "to evangelize." The noun "gospel/evangel," however, does appear in Acts. But nowhere in Matthew's book or even in Luke's two volume work is "the gospel" ever identified with a specific writing, as it seems to be here in Mark's introduction/superscription. Matthew refers to Jesus himself "preaching the gospel of

the Kingdom" (Mt 4:23, 9:35, 24:14) and he uses the term, "this gospel," once (Mt 26:13). Luke, in the Acts of the Apostles, refers to "the word of the gospel" (Acts 15:7) and to "the gospel of the grace of God" (Acts 20:24), but neither Matthew nor Luke ever simply refers to "the gospel" in an absolute sense, as Mark does frequently. Except for the two phrases that delimit Mark's opening *inclusio*, "the gospel of Jesus Christ [the Son of God]" (Mk 1:1) and "the Gospel of God" (Mk 1:14), Mark consistently uses the term "the gospel" absolutely (Mk 1:15, 8:35, 10:29, 13:10, 14:9 [16:15], as does Paul in numerous contexts (cf. Rom 1:9, 16; 10:16, 1 Cor 4:15; 9:14, 18; 15:1; Gal 1:11; 2:2; Phil 1:5, 7, 12, 27; 1 Thess 2:4, 8, 9; Phlm 13). The unique appearance of "the gospel" used absolutely in Mark when compared with the parallel texts of Matthew and Luke supports the view that Mark wrote later than Matthew and Luke and added this distinctively Markan and Pauline term to a text created primarily from Matthew and Luke. On the Two Document Hypothesis, one has to imagine Matthew and Luke, independently of one another, either omitting or modifying all five or six of these distinctively Markan uses of "the gospel."

Excursus 1: "The Gospel" and the "Gospels"

This Markan emphasis on "the gospel" probably contributed to the development of an early tradition according to which the name "gospel" was attached to works on the life and teachings of Jesus. Matthew had referred to his work as a "book" (Mt 1:1), while Luke seems to have described his treatise as a "narrative" (Lk 1:1). However, Mark's word "gospel" became the predominant designation for this type of early Christian literature while the other evangelists' descriptions of their works have been subsumed under Mark's more distinctively Christian title. Justin Martyr seems to have preferred the Greek term, ἀπομνημονεύματα, "memoirs," in referring to Matthew, Mark, Luke and John.[1] Like Paul and Mark before him, Justin could also refer to "the gospel" (cf. *Dialogue with Trypho*, 10:2).

Justin did make less extensive use of the plural, "gospels," when referring to this type of early Christian literature (cf. Justin, *1 Apol* 66.3). However, in spite of this relatively early use of the plural in Justin, the church generally agreed with Paul (and implicitly also with Mark who never uses the plural) that there is "no other gospel" (Gal 1:6-9).[2] Hence, the one and only gospel has

---

[1] For the term, "memoirs" as a designation for the gospels see Justin Martyr, *1 Apol.*, 67.4-5; 66.3; *Dialogue with Trypho*, 100.4; 101.3; 102.5; 103.6; 104.1; 105.1, 5, 6; 106.1, 3, 4; 106.1. Cf. the discussion of Justin and Tatian in D. L. Dungan, *A History of the Synoptic Problem: The Canon, the Text, the Composition, and the Interpretation of the Gospels* (New York: Doubleday, 1999), 28-43.

[2] For other absolute uses of "the gospel" in some of the earliest non-canonical Christian literature, see *1 Clement*, 42:1-2; Ignatius, *To the Philadelphians*, 9, *To the Smyrnaeans*, 5, 7; Polycarp, *To the Philippians*, 6:3; *Martyrdom of Polycarp*, 1:1, 4:1, 22:1; *Didache*, 11:3 , 15:3 and *Barnabas*, 8:3. Justin only rarely makes use of the plural, "gospels," (*1 Apol.*, 66:3), but Irenaeus frequently utilizes the plural when he is referring to all four of the Gospels commonly received by his time (cf., e.g., Irenaeus, *Adv. haer.*, 3.1.1, 3.11.7-9).

emerged in the manuscript tradition only as "The Gospel" which is "According to Matthew," "According to Mark," "According to Luke," and "According to John."[3]

• Unlike Mt 3:2 and 4:17, where the author depicts the content of the preaching of John and that of Jesus as identical, the author of Mark is careful to distinguish the essence of Jesus' message from that of John. According to Mark, John had appeared in the wilderness preaching "a baptism of repentance for the forgiveness of sins" (Mk 1:4; contrast Mk 1:14-15), but Mark's summary of Jesus' proclamation of "the Gospel of God" (Mk 1:14) is provided by Jesus' words, "The time is fulfilled and the kingdom of God is at hand. Repent and believe in the Gospel" (Mk 1:15). Some of the language in this Markan summary of the preaching of John is Lukan,[4] but the language Mark utilizes to summarize and distinguish the preaching of Jesus from that of John is Mark's own. According to Mark, Jesus even calls people to "repent and believe in the gospel [about himself]." Such use of language by Mark does not fit the life situation of Jesus, but would have quickly become normative in the life situation of the early church, particularly in those churches influenced by Paul's proclamation of "the gospel."

¶ 2. The Prophecy About John

Mt 3:3 cf. Isa 40:3 ===>	Mk 1:2-3	<=Lk 3:4-6; cf. Isa 40:3-5
(Mt 11:10, cf. Mal 3:1, Ex 23:20)	cf. Mal 3:1 and Isa 40:3	(Lk 7:27; cf. Mal 3:1)

As the prophet Isaiah wrote, "Behold, I will send my messenger before you to prepare your way. He is a voice crying in the wilderness saying, 'Prepare the way of the Lord. Make His paths straight.'"

General Observations. On the Two Gospel Hypothesis, Mark has added the quotation from Mal 3:1 (that was applied to John the Baptist at Mt 11:10//Lk 7:27) to the quotation from Isa 40:3 (that was applied to John at Mt 3:3//Lk 3:4-6) on the principle that both of these prophecies are about John. Thus, the very opening words of Mark reveal that this author is capable of conflating sources himself or, less probably, of using a conflated text as a source. This conclusion would be true even if Mark conflated texts

---

[3] Cf. Martin Hengel, *Studies in the Gospel of Mark* (tr. John Bowden, Philadelphia: Fortress, 1985), esp. ch. 3, "The Titles of the Gospels and the Gospel of Mark," pp. 64-84.

[4] As M. É. Boismard has written, "The activity of John the Baptist is formulated in identical terms by Mark 1:4 and Luke 3:3: 'preaching a baptism of repentance for the forgiveness of sins.' This way of speaking is not Markan but Lukan: the word 'repentance' is nowhere else read in Mk, but eleven times in Luke/Acts. The expression 'baptism of repentance' is not read elsewhere in the NT except Acts 13:24 and 19:4. If the formula 'for the forgiveness of sins' belongs to primitive theology (Matt 26:28, Col 1:14, Eph 1:7) this forgiveness of sins is not linked with 'repentance' except in Luke 24:47, Acts 2:38, 3:19, 5:31, 8:22, 26:18-20" See P. Benoit and M. -É. Boismard, *Synopses des quatre evangiles en francais.* II (Paris, 1972), 25. An English translation may be found in Orchard-Riley, *The Order of the Synoptics* (Macon, Ga.: Mercer University Press. 1987), 36.

directly from the scriptures (Isa 40:3, Mal 3:1 and perhaps also Ex 23:20), rather than by way of Matthew and Luke. Synopsis ¶ 2 shows the quotations of these scriptures in Greek as Matthew and Luke distinctively rendered them, comparing them to critical texts of these same passages from the LXX (Mt 11:10//Lk 7:27 cf. Mal 3:1 and Mt 3:3//Lk 3:4 cf. Isa 40:3).

Mk 1:2. By using a conflated text of OT testimonia or, by conflating texts himself, Mark differed from Matthew and Luke on the location of the quotation from Mal 3:1 (Mk 1:2, cf. Mt 11:10//Lk 7:27).

• Most manuscripts have Mark omitting ἐμπροσθέν σου (Mt 11:10/Lk 7:27) although these words appear in A and the Byzantine witnesses. Given the uncertainty of the textual tradition it is difficult to determine whether there is an agreement of Matthew and Luke against Mark here.

• Mark, of course, also causes a discrepancy in his text since Mal 3:1 is clearly not a quotation from Isaiah, as Mark's text claims (Mk 1:2) and as later scribes have tried to correct (K, Π*, P, A, 𝔐, G^sup, M, U, W, Π^c, 118, f^{13}, 2, 28, 579, 1424). Matthew and Luke only say that these words from Mal 3:1 were "written," i.e., they were from the scriptures, but they don't attribute these words to Isaiah, as does Mark. If the reference to "in the prophets" in the variant reading is not correct, it is most likely that the attribution of Malachi 3:1 (and Ex 23:20?) to Isaiah in Mark resulted from Mark's literary procedure of removing this quotation of Mal 3:1 from its original literary context (Mt 11:10//Lk 7:27) and conflating it with another citation that was correctly attributed to Isaiah (Mt 3:3//Lk 3:4).

Mk 1:3. A second, perhaps less noticed, agreement of Matthew and Luke against Mark in this context is the location of the quotation from Isa 40:3 (Mt 3:3//Lk 3:4//Isa 40:3 cf. Mk 1:3). Both Matthew and Luke include it *after* a temporal reference to John and the nature of his baptizing activity (Mt 3:1-2//Lk 3:1-3, cf. Mk 1:4), but Mark records it *before* his parallel reference to John (Mk 1:3//Isa 40:3). Mark's movement of this quotation is less difficult to explain than the independent movement of this quotation to the same location by both Matthew and Luke. Mark's arrangement results in the reference to "the way" in Isaiah following directly a reference to "the way" in Malachi. This allows Mark to highlight "the way in the wilderness," which will function as an important theme in his account.

• Mark omits that part of Luke's quotation from Isa 40 that extends beyond the text quoted by Matthew (Lk 3:5-6//Isa 40:4-5, cf. Mt 3:3//Isa 40:3) in order to follow the common testimony of Matthew and Luke (Mk 1:3//Mt 3:3//Lk 3:4). See "Synopses," ¶ 2 and ¶ 3.

Excursus 2: The Early Church Fathers' Identification of Each of the Four Beasts of Rev 4:7 and Ezek 1:10 with Each of the Four Gospels

Irenaeus (*Adv. haer.*, 3.11.8) was one of the early fathers of the church who utilized the lofty prophetic beginning of Mark's Gospel to justify his attribution of the eagle, a creature of the heavens, to the Gospel of Mark. Irenaeus attributed one creature each from the list of four found in Rev 4:7 (Lion, Ox, Man, and Eagle) to each of the four Gospels accepted by him (John, Luke, Matthew, Mark). Irenaeus's system of attribution (Man=Matthew, Lion=John, Ox=Luke, Eagle=Mark) probably reflects the order in which these creatures appear in Ezek 1:10 (Man, Lion, Ox, Eagle) correlated with the order in which the Gospels appeared in pre-Vulgate Latin versions of the Christian canon which he knew (Matthew, John, Luke, Mark). This canonical order of the Gospels may combine an order of dignity --- the apostles (Matthew, John) preceding the apostolic men (Luke, Mark) --- with the order of composition that was assumed at the time (Matthew before John and Luke before Mark).

Augustine [*De consensu evangelistarum* esp. 1.2.4, 1.3.6, 1.6.9 and 4.10.11] later disagreed with Irenaeus and others before him when he applied the figure of the man to Mark and justified his decision by noting (1) that the entire text of a Gospel should be considered when making such an assignment, rather than just the opening sentences that Irenaeus and others had utilized, and (2) it was more appropriate to assign the figure of the man to Mark because the text of Mark revealed that the theme of Christ's regal human nature (Matthew/Lion/King of Beasts) had been combined with the theme of Christ's sacerdotal human nature (Luke/ox/sacrificial animal) in Mark's unified theme of "Christ's one human nature" (Mark/man/human).

Jerome, an older contemporary of Augustine, made yet another assignment of these four creatures: Matthew=Man, Luke=Ox, Mark=Lion, John=Eagle (*Prologus quattuor evangeliorum* [*praefatio in Comm. in Mattheum*]). His arrangement has tended to be reflected in Christian art from his time to the present. Note, for instance, the prominence of the lion motif in St. Mark's square and basilica in Venice where the Venetians claim to have lain St. Mark's body.

¶ 3. John Preaches and Baptizes

Mt 3:4-6, 11-12 ========>   Mk 1:4-8   <===Lk 3:3b, 3a, 15-18

So it was that John the baptizer appeared in the wilderness of Judea, preaching repentance for the forgiveness of sins, and everyone was coming out to be baptized by him. And he said to them, "He who comes after me is mightier than I. I baptize you with water, but he will baptize you with the Holy Spirit."

> *General Observations.* After Mark brought together the two quotations applied to John the Baptist, one from Mal 3:1 in a relatively remote context (Mt 11:10//Lk 7:27) and one

from Isaiah (see the discussion above) in the more immediate parallel literary context (Mt 3:1//Lk 3:1), he then encountered conflicting temporal references in his two major sources. Matthew made a very general reference, "And in those days," while Luke dated the subsequent events to a precise time in the Roman Empire. Faced with this considerable discrepancy in his source materials, Mark moved past these detailed statements in Luke to the story of John [the Baptist] appearing in the wilderness, preaching repentance (Mk 1:4//Mt 3:1-2//Lk 3:2-3). This leap forward allowed Mark to follow his conflated prophecy, which had made reference to "a voice crying in the wilderness," with the temporal reference to John the Baptist appearing "in the wilderness." Both John and Jesus begin their "way" in the wilderness (Mk 1:4-6; 12-13). In both cases this way will lead to martyrdom.

Mk 1:4. After beginning Mk 1:4 with wording resembling Mt 3:1, Mark turned to Luke's account to describe John's preaching as "a baptism of repentance for the forgiveness of sins" (Lk 3:3). Thus, in contrast to Matthew, where the summary of the content of the preaching of John and Jesus was identical (Mt 3:2; 4:17), Mark clearly distinguished the two.

Mk 1:5. Omitting Mt 3:3//Lk 3:4, which he had already used (cf. Mk 1:2-3), Mark next narrates the gathering of all Judea and all of the citizens of Jerusalem around John for baptism in the Jordan River (Mk 1:5//Mt 3:5-6). Compare Mark's even more geographically inclusive collection of crowds at Mk 3:7-8 (cf. Mt 12:15, 4:25, and Lk 6:17-18, and Synopsis ¶ 19).

• Mark also brings the reference to "confessing sins" in relationship to baptism at Mk 1:5 (cf. Mt 3:6) closer to the summary note about John's baptism as one of "repentance for the forgiveness of sins" (Mk 1:4//Lk 3:3, cf. Mt 3:2) by delaying the description of John's clothing. On the Two Source Hypothesis, only Luke borrowed the reference in Mark to "forgiveness of sins" (Mk 1:4//Lk 3:3) while only Matthew borrowed the reference to "confessing their sins" (Mk 1:5//Mt 3:6). This would seem to be an odd coincidence for two authors independently making use of a common source, as required by the Two Document Hypothesis.. Mark's combination of "confessing sins" and "forgiveness of sins," one from each of his sources, is a simpler explanation.

• The connection between "confession," "forgiveness of sins," and "baptism" anticipates the importance of the connection between baptism and the Lord's Supper for Mark (cf. Mk 10:38-39; 16:16).

Mk 1:6. John is depicted as dressed like Elijah (2 Kings 1:8), the prophet whose return was sometimes expected among Jewish people as one of the signs of the end times (cf. Mal 4:5-6). The details of John's clothing most likely came to Mark from Matthew, not simply because Luke does not record them, but because it is only in Matthew that John the Baptist is explicitly identified as Elijah (Mt 11:14; 17:12-13). Later in Mark's gospel (in agreement with both Matthew and Luke) people explicitly compare Jesus, not only with John the Baptist, but also with Elijah or another of the prophets (Mk 6:14-16; 8:27-28).

Mk 1:7-8. John and Jesus both begin their way in the wilderness. John proclaims (ἐκήρυσσεν) that the one coming after him will be greater. Jesus proclaims (κηρύσσων) the gospel (Mk 1:14-15).

• In Matthew, John the Baptist plays the important role of Elijah, finally come to usher in the last days. In Luke, John's role as Elijah is implicitly denied because Luke omits the key verses in Matthew where the identification of John and Elijah is made explicit (Mt 11:14, no parallel in Mark; cf. Lk 7:30 and 16:16; Mt 17:10-13, no parallel in Luke). Mark has a parallel to Mt 17:10-12a, but, like Luke, also omits Mt 17:12b-13 where the identification of John with Elijah is made most explicit. For Luke, *Jesus* is "the prophet" par excellence, not John. For Mark, John is just the forerunner of Jesus, one who points to the greater one. It is, therefore, unnecessary for Mark to include the specific details of John's proclamation (Mt 3:7-10//Lk 3:7-9) or Luke's additional dialogue between John and a series of inquirers (Lk 3:10-16a). Rather Mark can pick up the narrative at precisely the point where John is comparing himself with Jesus who is greater, and whose baptism with the Holy Spirit [and fire? The text is uncertain] is to be distinguished from John's simple water baptism (Mk 1:7-8//Mt 3:11//Lk 3:16). Mark can also omit Jesus' eschatological preaching about judgment with fire (Mt 3:12//Lk 3:17), just as he omitted similar preaching from John earlier (Mt 3:7-10//Lk 3:7-9). Also, Mark passes over Luke's relatively brief, early account of the imprisonment of John (Luke 3:18-20). He chooses rather to include, and even to expand, the more detailed account from Matthew later (Mt 14:3-12, cf. Mk 6:17-29). In sum, the preceding evidence supports our view that the Gospel of Mark represents a stage on a trajectory of distancing the relationship between Jesus and John that is later than that reflected in Matthew and Luke.

¶ 4. John Baptizes Jesus

Mt 3:13-17 =======>   Mk 1:9-11   <======= Lk 3:21-22

One day, Jesus of Nazareth came from Galilee to be baptized by John in the Jordan River. When Jesus came up out of the water, immediately he saw the heavens torn apart and the Holy Spirit descending upon him like a dove. A voice came from heaven saying to Jesus, "You are my beloved son. I am well pleased with you."

General Observations. On the Two Gospel hypothesis, Mark follows Luke's lead in moving directly to the baptism scene and avoiding Matthew's complicated dialogue between John and Jesus over whether Jesus needed to be baptized by John (Mt 3:14-15). Mark prefers to narrate the simple fact of Jesus' baptism by John. For Mark, this is the quintessential announcement of Jesus' divine sonship, already proclaimed in the opening verse of the Gospel. (cf. Mk 1:1 and Acts 1:22,10:37, et al.).

Mk 1:9. Mark introduces this story with a vague temporal reference, "in those days" (Mk 1:9, cf. Mt 3:1) and notes that Jesus came from Nazareth in Galilee (Mk 1:9, cf. Mt 4:13//Lk 4:16) in order to be baptized in the Jordan by John.

Mk 1:10. Mark is not content with the relatively simple statement that the heavens "opened," either after Jesus was baptized (Luke) or after he came up from the water (Matthew). Instead Mark depicts the heavens as "ripped apart" (σκιζομένους) so that Jesus sees the Spirit come down from the heavens like a dove *into* him ("*on* him" in Matthew and Luke). Mark may depart from the common text of Mt//Lk here because he intentionally paralleled this event with the story of the rending of the temple curtain at the time of Jesus' crucifixion (Mt 27:51/Lk 23:45; cf. Mk 15:38). At Jesus' baptism the heavenly dome ("firmament" in the KJV, cf. Gen 1:6) separating the divine world from the human world is "ripped asunder" by the inauguration of Jesus' public ministry. In a similar way, the curtain in the temple in Jerusalem, which separated the exclusive domain of the High Priest in the Holy of Holies from the more generally accessible holy places of the temple precincts, was "ripped apart" by the culminating event of Jesus' public ministry, his crucifixion and death. On the Two Gospel Hypothesis Mark read about the "ripping apart" (ἐσχίσθη) of the temple curtain in both Matthew and Luke (Mt 27:51//Lk 23:45). In order to draw this explicit parallel between the first event in Jesus' public ministry and his last one he simply changed the common text of Matthew and Luke at the baptism scene.

Mk 1:11. If the longer reading of Mk 1:1 is accepted, then readers of Mark would have known about the claim that Jesus was "the Son of God" from the very "beginning of the gospel of Jesus Christ, [the Son of God]" (Mk 1:1). However, no matter how one reconstructs the text of Mk 1:1, a reader would definitely know that Mark affirmed Jesus as "the Son of God" no later than Mk 1:11. As in Lk 3:22, Mark has the divine voice address Jesus at his baptism in the second person (privately?, Mk 1:11//Lk 3:22), rather than having the heavenly voice address everyone present with a third person, in reference to Jesus, "This man" (Mt 3:17). The use of the third person in Matthew conforms more with the Greek text of Isa 42:1-4 (later cited in full at Mt 12:17-21) which clearly provides the necessary background for understanding both the words from heaven at Jesus' baptism (Mt 3:17//Lk 3:22//Mk 1:11) and the words from heaven at

Jesus' "transfiguration" (Mt 17:5//Lk 9:35//Mk 9:7). The use of the second person address by Luke and Mark, which blurs the connection with the Isaiah text but still depends upon it to make sense of these words from heaven, probably indicates that the second person usage in Lk/Mk here is secondary. Furthermore, this aspect of our argument remains valid, even if one adopts the reading of D, Justin, et al., at Lk 3:22, Υἱός μου εἶ σύ, ἐγὼ σήμερον γεγέννηκά σε, is adopted, as we did in *Beyond the Q Impasse* in light of Luke's certain retrospective use of Ps 2:7 at Acts 13:33.[5] Thus, the tradition history of the story of Jesus' baptism can be readily explained as a movement from Mt 3:17 through Lk 3:22 to the conflated text of Mk 1:11.

Synopsis 1: Illustrating Mark's Conflation of Mt 3:17 and Lk 3:22b [D, Justin, et al.]		
Mt 3:17	Mk 1:11	Lk 3:22b
⟨3:17⟩ καὶ ἰδοὺ φωνή	⟨1:11⟩ καὶ φωνή	⟨3:22⟩ καὶ φωνὴν ἐκ τοῦ οὐρανοῦ
	ἐγένετο	γενέσθαι,
ἐκ τῶν οὐρανῶν λέγουσα,	ἐκ τῶν οὐρανῶν,	
Οὗτός ἐστιν	Σὺ εἶ	
ὁ υἱός μου	ὁ υἱός μου	Υἱός μου εἶ σύ,
ὁ ἀγαπητός.	ὁ ἀγαπητός.	ἐγὼ σήμερον γεγέννηκά
ἐν ᾧ εὐδόκησα.	ἐν σοὶ εὐδόκησα.	σε.

¶ 5. Satan Tempts Jesus

Mt 4:1-11 ---------------------- Mk 1:12-13 ---------------------- Lk 4:1-13

Immediately after that, the Holy Spirit drove Jesus out into the wilderness where he was tempted by Satan for forty days in the midst of wild beasts, and angels were serving him.

General Observations. At this point Mark comes to Luke's version of Jesus' genealogy (Lk 3:23-38, cf. Mt 1:2-17). Since Mark has already utilized the minimal amount of material he intends to utilize from this Lukan genealogy at Mk 1:1, where he blended it with an equally limited number of elements drawn from Matthew's version of Jesus' genealogy, Mark moves forward to the next unit in the common order of Matthew and

---

[5] McNicol et al., *Beyond the Q Impasse,* 76.

Luke, the story of Jesus' temptation in the wilderness. However, Mark's version of this story is severely apocopated (Mt 4:1-11//Lk 4:1-13; cf. Mk 1:12-13).

• Advocates of the Two Source Hypothesis suggest an "overlap" between the text of Mark here and the text of the hypothetical source, "Q," since it is unthinkable that Matthew and Luke, making independent use of Mark at this point, could possibly have constructed their very similar and extensive versions of this story from the text of Mark alone. Mark's abbreviation of Matthew and Luke here, according to the Two Gospel Hypothesis, is certainly a better explanation of the literary history of these synoptic contexts than is the theory that Matthew and Luke have managed, independently of one another, to make such extensive, similar, sometimes identical expansions of Mark's story. If Mark was working with Matthew and Luke, he was faced with an irreconcilable difference in the order of the temptations. That problem, combined with his preference to record demonstrations of Jesus' power rather than discourses, led him to omit the account of the contest with Satan. As John begins his ministry in the wilderness (Mk 1:4-6), so with a similar economy of wording, Mark narrates how Jesus begins his ministry in the wilderness to bring prophecy to completion (Mk 1:2-3).

Mk 1:12. Mark begins his brief version of Jesus' temptation by substituting a typical Markan introduction, καὶ εὐθύς (Peabody, *Mark as Composer,* 5, 36) for Matthew's equally distinctive introductory τότε (Mt=90, Mk=6, Lk=15, Jn=10, Acts=21).

• In this verse, Mark has inadvertently avoided Matthew's characteristic use of ἀναχωρέω as well as Luke's equally characteristic use of ὑποστρέφω[6] (Collison, p. 67) by substituting ἐκβάλλω (cf. Peabody, *Mark as Composer,* 49, 48; 62, 52; 211, 102).

Mk 1:13. In conformity with his earlier editorial work emphasizing John the Baptist preaching "in the wilderness," Mark adopts both εἰς τὴν ἔρημον from Mt 4:1 and ἐν τῇ ἐρήμῳ from Lk 4:1 into Mk 1:12-13. Mark thereby creates one of his characteristic "dual" expressions.[7]

• Mark has altered the common text of Mt 4:1//Lk 4:2 from "devil" to "Satan." This alteration may reveal Mark's knowledge of the longer version of the temptation story common to Matthew and Luke where the term, "Satan" was used, but which Mark otherwise omitted (Ὕπαγε, Σατανᾶ in Mt 4:10 was also omitted by Luke at Lk 4:8). Mark uses "Satan" six times and never uses διάβολος which may suggest that this is a Markan linguistic preference.

---

[6] Cf. Goulder, *Luke,* vol. 2, 809.

[7] Category 10, double statement: temporal or local; Frans Neirynck, "Duality in Mark," *ETL* 47/3-4 (Dec. 1971): 414-16

• Mark's additional reference to "wild beasts" may be an attempt to depict Jesus as an exemplary prototype in a scene that would have been familiar to Roman Christians who were themselves led to face "wild beasts," θηρία, in that city's circuses and arenas as early as the time of Nero (cf. Tacitus, *Ann.*, 15.44.2).[8] Already in 1 Cor 15:32, Paul wrote, "If, humanly speaking, I fought with wild beasts at Ephesus, what gain is that for me?" (εἰ κατὰ ἄνθρωπον ἐθηριομάχησα ἐν Ἐφέσῳ, τί μοι τὸ ὄφελος) Although Paul utilizes a conditional clause here and may be using figurative language, he has chosen the image of "fighting with wild beasts" as an impressive example of human action, even of self sacrifice, which amounts to nothing if there is no resurrection of the dead. As is also well-known, the author of Revelation commonly uses images of wild beasts, θηρία, as symbols for Rome, the Roman Emperor, and the priesthood of the imperial cult whose authority led to the martyrdom of Christians first in Rome itself and later throughout the empire (Rev 11:7; 13:1-18; 14:9-11; 15:2, 16:2, 10, 13; 17:1-17; 19:19-20; 20:4, 10). In the writings of Josephus and many of the apostolic fathers, reference to "fighting with wild beasts" was also common (Josephus, *War*, 7:38; Ignatius, *To the Romans*, 4:1, 5:3; *To the Smyrnaeans*, 4:2; *Martyrdom of Polycarp*, 2:4, 3ff.; 11:1ff.; *Diognetus*, 7:7; Shepherd of Hermas, *Vision* 3.2.1).

• Mark has also omitted the common reference in Matthew and Luke to Jesus' hunger at the end of his temptations. Mark does, however, conclude his account with a reference to (table?) service by angels which would be an appropriate response to Jesus' hunger, at the conclusion of his story, in agreement with Mt 4:11 (cf. Mk 1:13). Luke has nothing similar in his version of this story. Mark's omission of any reference to Jesus' hunger while including a reference to table service by angels as a response to that hunger may be an example of what Ernest DeWitt Burton once described as "clear omission from one document of matter which was in the other, the omission of which destroys the connection." Burton considered this evidence of the secondary character of one text to another.[9] In this case, it would be evidence for the secondary nature of the text of Mark to the text of Matthew.

---

[8] With reference to the note in Mk 1:13, "he was with the wild beasts," Bas M. F. van Iersel comments, "Because there is nothing about how Jesus behaves among the wild beasts or how they react to his presence, it is somewhat arbitrary to picture the scene as an idyllic or eschatological paradise." *Mark: A Reader-Response Commentary* (JSNTSS 164; Sheffield: Sheffield Academic Press, 1998), 102. Van Iersel's remark is probably in reply to the critical judgments of scholars like Joachim Jeremias *New Testament Theology. The Proclamation of Jesus* (New York: Scribner's, 1971), 68-75; and R. Bauckham, "Jesus and the Wild Animals (Mark 1.13): A Christological Image for an Ecological Age," in Joel B. Green and Max Turner, eds., *Jesus of Nazareth, Lord and Christ: Essays on the Historical Jesus and New Testament Christology* (Grand Rapids, Mich.: Eerdmans, 1994), 3-21.

[9] Ernest DeWitt Burton, *Some Principles of Literary Criticism and their Application to the Synoptic Problem.* (The Decennial Publications, vol. 5; Chicago: University of Chicago Press, 1904), 198.

¶ 6. John is Arrested/Jesus Begins to Preach

Mt 4:12-17 =======>   Mk 1:14-15   <------------------Lk 4:14-15

                                                           (cf. Lk 3:18-20)

Suddenly, John the Baptist is arrested and put in jail. Then Jesus came up to Galilee and began to preach the gospel of God, saying, "The time is fulfilled and the kingdom of God is at hand. Repent and believe in the gospel."

General Observations. Mark continues to follow the order of Matthew for this and the next story.

• Luke retrospectively refers to the arrest of John immediately before the baptism scene (Lk 3:18-20). Matthew refers to the arrest of John not only following the baptism scene (Mt 3:13-17//Lk 3:21-22), but also in the next story, the temptation scene (Mt 4:1-11). Luke's genealogy (Lk 3:23-38) falls between his versions of the baptism and temptation scenes. Mark had already echoed the two different genealogies of Matthew and Luke at Mk 1:1, in agreement with Matthew's order (Mk 1:1//Mt 1:2-17, cf. Lk 3:23-38). Mark, therefore, makes no mention of Jesus' genealogy here and agrees with the wording and order of Matthew in making retrospective reference to the arrest of John immediately following the temptation scene (Mk 1:14//Mt 4:12).

• Mark's opening reference to "the gospel" is repeated here at the conclusion to part one, forming an *inclusio*.

Mk 1:14. It was not only important to Mark to describe John's preaching and baptism as preparatory for the "gospel" of Jesus Christ, but also to introduce John so that his arrest (in agreement with both Mt 4:12 and Lk 3:19-20) could be used as the context for the actual beginning of Jesus' ministry. With John's way ending in his arrest, Mark also creates anticipation of what will happen to Jesus.

• Again, Mark avoided the characteristically Matthean ἀναχωρέω and the similarly Lukan use of ὑποστρέφω by going his own way with a use of ἔρχομαι. See Mark's comparable technique at Mk 1:12//Mt 4:1//Lk 4:1.

Mk 1:15. The phrase "the time is fulfilled," (Mk 1:15; cf. 13:33) functions similarly to "*the* gospel" (Mk 1:15, 8:35, 10:29, 13:10, 14:9, [16:9], cf. Mk 1:1 and 14) and "*the* word" (Mk 1:45; 2:2; 4:14-20, 33; 8:32, 9:10, 10:22, [16:20]). The Greek word Mark uses for "time" here is not chronological time; i.e., clock or "sundial" time, but something more like "the auspicious moment," which has been recognized and observed in religious communities in many places, times, and cultures. It is "the time" when the "word" goes forth.

• The words in Mark's text, ἤγγικεν ἡ βασιλεία . . . μετανοεῖτε [the kingdom is at hand . . . repent] represent Mark's fragmentary preservation of a formula clearly traceable to Matthew (see Mt 3:2 and 4:17). As such, it reflects the secondary nature of the text of Mark to the parallel text of Matthew. In a complementary fashion, in several places where Mk 1:15 differs from the text of Mt 4:17, one finds clear evidence of the interests of Mark. Compare, for instance, Mark's use of *"the* time," and *"the* gospel," and the alteration of the more Jewish "kingdom of the heavens" in Matthew to "kingdom of God," a term more suitable for a predominantly Gentile Christian community. In sum, Markan composition in this verse is consistent with the Two Gospel Hypothesis.

Summary

Mark has shown in his opening part that, in keeping with the promise of the prophets, both John the Baptist and Jesus came from the wilderness preaching a message that God's new world was near. John was imprisoned. This alerts the reader that Jesus' announcement of the gospel will also take him down a treacherous road.

JESUS CALLS DISCIPLES,
PREACHES, AND CASTS OUT DEMONS

Overview

Part two of Mark begins with the call of the first four disciples (Mk 1:16-20) and concludes with the call of "the twelve" (Mk 3:7-19). The call of a fifth disciple comes about two-thirds of the way through the part (Mk 2:13-14). This part may, therefore, be seen as delimited by an *inclusio*, the opening and closing members of which include stories of the call of Jesus' disciples. Consequently, the calling of the disciples is a major theme of this part, but a second is related to it: Jesus' own pattern of ministry, "preaching and casting out demons" (Mk 1:39), is depicted as the design for the ministry of his disciples (Mk 3:7-19). The twelve will emulate this pattern during their later missionary activities, first described in Mk 6:6b-13 and later given full expression in Mk 16:16-20 (in the disputed longer ending).

In Mk 1:21-45, Jesus begins his mission, which is based in Capernaum. He performs several exorcisms and healings as demonstrations of God's power. Favorable reports that God was active in his ministry spread throughout the region (Mk 1:28, 45). However, this activity provokes the opposition described in Mk 2:1-3:6. In Mk 2:1-3:6 Jesus engages in conflict with a series of opponents. Two of the most significant encounters come at the beginning and end of this unit of material. In the story of the healing of the paralytic Jesus is accused of blasphemy because of his pronouncement that the man's sins had been forgiven (Mk 2:5, 7). According to Mark, the scribes properly argue that only God can forgive sins, but they fail to reach the conclusion that Mark intends his readers to draw, namely, that Jesus is God's Son acting directly on his behalf. Ominously, the charge of blasphemy by the scribes anticipates one of the charges that will be made against Jesus at his trial (Mk 14:64). At the conclusion of this part the Pharisees and Herodians seek to destroy Jesus (Mk 3:6). This is a clear anticipation of one of Mark's central themes: the Son of God must suffer. In the midst of this hostility Jesus begins to gather his true family (Mk 1:16-20; 2:13-14; 3:7-19). Thus, by the end of this part, the key protagonists in Mark's story (Jesus, his opponents, and the disciples) are clearly identified.

Although Mark is primarily dependent upon the order of Lk for his arrangement of pericopae in this unit, he refashions the material in keeping with his own literary interests. Chief among these is Mark's introduction of πάλιν used retrospectively to unite two or more separated pericopae (see Markan overlay, above). The net result is that Mark's narrative of Jesus' early ministry in Galilee has a definite sense of unity; various expressions of the power of the Son of God occur in this Part, but they provoke a gathering storm of opposition.

¶ 7. Jesus Calls the First Four Disciples

Mt 4:18-22==========>   Mk 1:16-20   (cf. Lk 5:1-11)

Going along by the Sea of Galilee, Jesus saw Simon Peter and his brother Andrew fishing with nets. Jesus said, "Follow me. I will make you fishers of men." Immediately they dropped their nets and followed him. A little further on, Jesus saw James and John, the sons of Zebedee. At once he called them, and they followed him immediately, leaving their father and their employees behind.

General Observations. Mark continues to follow the order of Matthew.

Mk 1:16-20. The four disciples whom Jesus calls first --- Simon, Andrew, James, and John --- become, in Mark's gospel, an inner core of Jesus' closest disciples (Mk 1:16-20, 29; 3:16-18, 13:3). Jesus will even give symbolic names to three of them. Simon is given the additional name, "Peter/Rock," while James and John are called "Sons of Thunder" (Mk 3:16-17). Later, at Mk 1:29, Mark connects these four --- Simon, Andrew, James, and John --- to the story about the healing of Simon's mother-in-law in Simon's house (cf. Mt 8:14//Lk 4:38). Also, Mark specifies all four of these members of the inner circle at Mk 13:3, where no names are present in his sources (contrast Mt 24:3 and Lk 21:5-7).

Excursus 3: Mark's Omission of the Sermon on the Mount

As David Dungan and others have noted elsewhere, scholars who have composed synopses of the Gospels of Matthew, Mark, and Luke have made at least three different editorial decisions about where the Sermon on the Mount should be placed in relationship to the text of Mark (Mk 3:19-20, Mk 1:39-40, and Mk 1:21-22).[1]

---

[1] David L. Dungan, "Synopses of the Future," *Biblica* 66 (1985): 457-92; "Theory of Synopsis Construction," *Biblica* 61 (1980): 305-29.

• Mk 3:19-20.[2] Kurt Aland, Marie Émile Boismard, and John Bernard Orchard, for instance, place Matthew's Sermon on the Mount immediately following Mk 3:19, which is where Luke's Sermon on the Plain would best be placed in the Markan outline.

• Mk 1:39-40.[3] Other scholars, like Albert Huck and all his translators, placed the Sermon on the Mount between Mk 1:39 and Mk 1:40 on the basis of a few linguistic agreements among all three of the Synoptic Gospels at that point.

• Mk 1:21-22.[4] Griesbach and others have placed the Sermon on the Mount between Mk 1:20 and Mk 1:21. In recent years, Frans Neirynck, who shares few of Griesbach's views when it comes to source-critical analysis of the Gospels, has come to agree. This decision was also made recently in the new Flemish synopsis.

A decision about the placement of Matthew's Sermon on the Mount and Luke's Sermon on the Plain in relation to the text of Mark has been especially influenced by the obvious agreements in structure, content, and language between the two sermons. A second major consideration has been a tendency by some synopsis creators to increase the number of shared pericopae in order between[5] and among the three synoptics. Among those who display all three of the Synoptic Gospels, Tischendorf has the

---

[2] Mk 3:19-20 is the boundary between the call of the twelve in Mk (Lk 6:12-19//Mk 3:7-19) and his version of the Beelzebul controversy (Mk 3:20ff.). In Luke, the Sermon on the Plain immediately follows the call of the twelve (Lk 6:20-7:1.)

[3] Mark 1:39, "and he went preaching throughout Galilee preaching in their synagogues and casting out the demons," is similar to Mt 4:23, the introduction to the Sermon on the Mount, "and he went about in the whole of Galilee teaching in their synagogues and preaching the gospel of the kingdom and healing every disease and every sickness among the people," and to Lk 4:44, "and he was preaching in the synagogues of Judea." The next verse in Luke begins his version of the call of the first *three* disciples (Lk 5:1-11, cf. the call of the first *four* in Mt 4:18-22//Mk 1:16-20, which in Matthew immediately precedes the Sermon on the Mount, Mt 4:23-7:29). Luke 5:1-11 is, in turn, immediately followed by the story of the Healing of the Leper in Luke and Mark (Lk 5:12-16//Mk 1:40-45). This story immediately follows the Sermon on the Mount (Mt 4:23-7:29) in Mt 8:1-4.

[4] Mk 1:20-21 falls between the call of the first four disciples (Mt 4:18-22//Mk 1:16-20) and the Sermon on the Mount (Mt 4:23-7:29). Words found in Mk 1:22//Lk 4:32 significantly parallel the narration in Mt that concludes the Sermon on the Mount (Mt 7:28-29//Mk 1:22//Lk 4:32).

[5] Frans Neirynck, in seeking to illustrate and defend his views on Markan priority and the independent redaction of Mark by Matthew and Luke, has chosen to display the shared pericope order in Matthew and Mark and, in a separate display, the shared pericope order in Mark and Luke. In choosing these two of three possible pairs of Synoptic Gospels for display, Neirynck is able to reduce the total number of transpositions in pericope order that need explanation. However, in doing this, Neirynck does not display a fundamental datum among the synoptics, i.e., the alternating agreement in pericope order of Mark; now with Matthew, now with Luke, often with both. Since this is the datum of synoptic relationships that most influenced Griesbach to alter the reigning source theory of his day; i.e., the so-called "Augustinian" hypothesis, to a source theory that came to bear Griesbach's name, advocates of the Two-Gospel (neo-Griesbach) Hypothesis find Neirynck's displays of the evidence of pericope order inadequate, confined as they are to two separated pairs: Matthew-Mark, and Luke-Mark. Cf. Neville, "Arguments from Order," in *Synoptic Source Criticism: A History and Critique* (New Gospel Studies 7; Macon, Ga.: Mercer University Press, 1997), esp. 232-37.

fewest number of pericopae in parallel; advocates of the neo-Griesbach hypothesis (not including Orchard) have the most. Aland, Huck, and others fall in between. These different results are partially the consequence of decisions about the size and number of pericopae. Smaller pericopae allow for a greater degree of sequential parallelism.

There are three basic assumptions leading this research team to display in its synopsis the Sermon on the Mount inserted after Mk 1:20. The first is that Matthew composed the first of the Gospels that later came to be canonized. In his Gospel, Matthew chose to narrate Jesus' inaugural sermon (the Sermon on the Mount) immediately following the call of only four of Jesus' disciples (cf. Mt 4:18-22). Matthew 4:23-7:29 then presents the introduction to and body of the Sermon on the Mount.

The second fundamental assumption is that Luke made use of Matthew in composing his Gospel. Mark had not yet been written. In contrast to Matthew, Luke decided not to narrate a sermon with content similar to the Sermon on the Mount until all twelve of the Jesus' disciples had been called and were present for it. In conjunction with this decision, however, Luke also decided to agree with Matthew and to narrate an inaugural sermon at the beginning of Jesus' ministry. Luke's version of Jesus' inaugural sermon comes at precisely the same point in his narrative as does Matthew's Sermon on the Mount (Mt 4:23-7:29//Lk 4:16-32). Luke's version of Jesus' inaugural sermon better served the narrative concerns of Luke by introducing many of the major themes and emphases (e.g., concern for the poor, Elijah and Elisha themes, etc.) of Jesus' ministry that would unfold throughout Luke's Gospel.

The third basic assumption is that Mark wrote the third of the Synoptic Gospels on the basis of source material he drew primarily from Matthew and Luke. On this hypothesis, when confronted by two very different versions of Jesus' inaugural sermon, at the same point in the common narrative order of Matthew and Luke, Mark chose simply to note the fact that Jesus engaged in teaching at that point in his narrative, in agreement with both of his sources (Mk 1:21-22). Mark may have followed this literary strategy because the content of Matthew's version of Jesus' inaugural Sermon on the Mount (Mt 4:23-7:29) differed so much from Luke's version of Jesus' Inaugural Sermon in Nazareth (Lk 4:16-30[32]) that he simply could not harmonize them.

¶ 8. Jesus Teaches and Heals in a Synagogue

Mt 4:23-7:29	Mk 1:21-28	Lk 4:16b-37
(Mt 4:13 8:5, 9:26, 31)		

While in the synagogue in Capernaum on the Sabbath, Jesus delivers his first sermon. Those gathered there are amazed at Jesus' manner of teaching because he teaches on his own authority and not like the scribes, who presumably teach on the basis of the authority of the Hebrew scriptures and Jewish traditions. While Jesus is teaching and preaching, a man confronts him with an unclean spirit. The demons possessing him inquire whether Jesus, whom they recognize as "the Holy One of God," wants to destroy them. Jesus silences the demons and exorcises them. Everyone marvels and asks, "What is this? A new teaching according to authority? He even commands the unclean spirits and they obey him." Because of these events, Jesus' fame begins to spread throughout the whole of Galilee.

General Observations. On the Two Gospel Hypothesis, Mark is following the text of Mt 4:12-22//Lk 4:14-15, which concludes in Matthew with the call of the first four disciples (Mt 4:18-22//Mk 1:16-20). Mark would have come next to the introduction to Jesus' first sermon in Matthew, the Sermon on the Mount (Mt 4:23-7:29), and to Luke's very different version of Jesus' inaugural sermon, in Nazareth (Lk 4:16-30). In keeping with his focus on Jesus continuing "on the way" (Mk 8:27-10:52) to the cross, Mark has omitted the content of both of these very different inaugural sermons of Jesus and continued the movement of Jesus' ministry by inserting into his narrative Luke's dramatic series of healings (Lk 4:31-5:26) which immediately follows Jesus' inaugural sermon in Lk 4:16-30. Although he omits the content of both inaugural sermons in Matthew and Luke, Mark does provide a note about the people's reaction to Jesus' inaugural sermon (Mk 1:22) in language that is very similar to that recorded in both Mt 7:28-29 and Lk 4:31-32. Despite the omission of both sermons, Mark does his best to agree otherwise with both Matthew and Luke by placing the reaction to Jesus' inaugural sermon (1) in a synagogue (Mk 1:21//Lk 4:16 cf. Mt 4:23), (2) on the Sabbath (Mk 1:21//Lk 4:16 and 4:31), and (3) in Capernaum (Mk 1:21, Mt 4:13, 8:5 [cf. Lk 7:1], and Lk 4:16).

Chart A: Elements Influencing the Composition of Mk 1:21-28		
Mt 4:13	Mk 1:21	Lk 4:16-30
From Nazareth		Sermon in Nazareth
to Capernaum =========>	Capernaum	<===== Lk 4:31 Capernaum
		Lk 4:16, 31
	on the Sabbath	<======== on the Sabbath
cf. Mt 4:23		Lk 4:16
in their synagogues	in the synagogue	<======= in the synagogue
Mt 4:23-7:27		
Sermon on Mount	Sermon	
Mt 7:28-29	Mk 1:22	Lk 4:32
Response to the Sermon ===>	Response to the Sermon	<=== Response to the Sermon
Mt 8:5 Capernaum		
	Mk 1:22-28	Lk 4:33-37
	Healing of Unclean	<===== Healing of Unclean

Matthew's characteristic redactional summary passage (Mt 4:23-25, cf. Mt 9:35 and 10.1) that *immediately precedes* his version of Jesus' inaugural sermon (Mt 5:1-7:29) includes the note that Jesus "went around the whole of Galilee, teaching in their synagogues and preaching the gospel of the kingdom and healing every disease and every sickness among the people." (Mt 4:23, cf. Mk 1:21-2:12//Lk 4:16-5:26). In conformity with this summary passage in Matthew, Luke's version of Jesus' inaugural sermon is set in a synagogue and, more specifically than Matthew's summary here, occurs on the Sabbath (Lk 4:16//Mk 1:21). Further, the Healing of the Man with the Unclean Demon that *immediately follows* Jesus' inaugural sermon in Luke takes place on another Sabbath in another synagogue (Lk 4:31, 33, cf. Mk 1:21). On the Two Gospel Hypothesis, Mark has collapsed these two contiguous stories in Luke into a single Sabbath synagogue scene in at least partial agreement with Matthew's summary passage in Mt 4:23 and with this summary writ large in Lk 4:16-5:26//Mk 1:21-2:12.

Excursus 4. Mark's Choice of Capernaum as the Center of Jesus' Galilean Ministry

Mark has Jesus' inaugural sermon take place in Capernaum, rather than Nazareth, as Luke has recorded it. Such an editorial and historical decision by Mark appears to be based upon two notes, one each in Luke and in Matthew. First, Luke reports that the Healing of the Man with an Unclean Demon (Lk 4:31-37) that immediately follows Luke's version of Jesus' inaugural sermon (Lk 4:16-30) took place in Capernaum (Lk 4:31). Second, Matthew reports that the Healing of the Centurion's Servant (Mt 8:5-13), the second story to follow Matthew's version of Jesus' inaugural Sermon (Mt 5:1-7:29), also took place in Capernaum (Mt 8:5). Given the impressive similarities in structure, content, and wording between Matthew's Sermon on the Mount (Mt 5:1-7:29) and Luke's Sermon on the Plain (Lk 6:20-7:1), it is worthy of note that the Healing of the Centurion's Servant, the *second* story (Mt 8:5-13) following the Sermon on the Mount (Mt 5:1-7:29) is Luke's *first* story (Lk 7:2-10) immediately following the Sermon on the Plain in Lk 6:20-7:1. In accord with Matthew, Luke reports that this healing took place in Capernaum. Of course, one cannot know whether Mark would have taken note of all of these references to Capernaum in Mt 4:13, Lk 4:31 and Mt 8:5//Lk 7:2, but it is a fact that Mark does report that the reaction to Jesus' inaugural sermon and the first healing following that sermon both took place in a synagogue, on the Sabbath, in Capernaum. With the inclusion of these facts, Mark's account comes into basic conformity with details that could have been drawn from Lk 4:16-30//Mt 5:1-79//Mk 1:21-22 (inaugural sermon); Mt 4:13-17//Mk 1:21 (in Capernaum); Mt 4:18-22//Mk 1:16-20 (call of first four disciples); Mt 4:23//Lk 4:16-5:26//Mk 1:21-2:12 (preaching and healing in synagogue[s]); and Lk 6:20-7:10//Mt 5:1- 8:13//Mk 1:21-28 (an impressive sermon followed [almost, in the case of Matthew] immediately by a healing in Capernaum).

If the network of agreements observed here is accidental, it involves a remarkable series of coincidences. On the other hand, if this network is the result of the work of the author of Mark, it is a very impressive example of composition. We believe that this is an important example both of the care Mark took in the utilization of his source material and his skill at conflation.

• Between Mk 1:21 and Mk 3:5, Mark follows the order of pericopae in Luke, omitting only Luke's version of the call of the first three disciples (Lk 5:1-11), since Mark had already chosen to narrate Matthew's version of that story at Mk 1:16-20//Mt 4:18-22. As one might expect, Mark is more influenced by the wording of the Gospel whose order of pericopae he is following. In this case, of course, that means that Mark's text is closer to the wording of Luke than that of Matthew.

Mk 1:21-22. Mark will later tie a number of events to this pivotal passage: "going to Capernaum" becomes the previous referent for the πάλιν retrospective at Mk 2:1; "into a synagogue" becomes the previous referent for the πάλιν retrospective at Mk 3:1; "was teaching" becomes the previous referent for πάλιν retrospective at Mk 2:13, 4:1-2, and 10:1b. This network of passages using πάλιν is powerful compositional evidence of Mark's editorial hand.

Mk 1:23-26. While Jesus is teaching and preaching, a man with an unclean spirit confronts him. Compare the similar wording of Mk 5:2 (cf. Peabody, *Mark as Composer,* 32-33, 44). Although Mark is not averse to using various linguistic forms of δαίμων, it is noteworthy that here, just as in Mk 5:2, Mark alters Lk 4:33 at Mk 1:23 with similar wording.

Mk 1:27. It is significant that this healing of a man with an unclean spirit is labeled "new teaching" (διδαχὴ καινή) by the synagogue congregation, according to Mark's version of this story. Although Mark's Gospel contains fewer of Jesus' didactic instructions than do either Matthew or Luke, it does include all of the miracle stories in both Matthew and Luke except Mt 8:5-13//Lk 7:2-10. Mark also has two miracle stories that neither Matthew nor Luke include (Mk 7:31-37 and Mk 8:22-26). Mark seems to have thought of miracles, healings, and exorcisms as an important part of the "teaching" of Jesus. If this is so, then the author of Mark has announced this to his readers through this, the first of Jesus' healings in his Gospel. It is worth noting that Asclepius, one of the most popular healing gods of the ancient Mediterranean world, was also considered a teacher (διδάσκαλος).[6] Jesus' exorcism underscores the fact that his teaching accompanied by the actual demonstration of power had authority (cf. Mk 1:22).

• The questions and comments in Mk 1:27 are similar to the question that will be raised by Jesus' disciples following the story of Jesus stilling a storm. There the disciples ask, "Who then *is this*, that both the wind *and* the sea *obey him*?" (Mk 4:41) In both Mark and Luke, Jesus commands obedience both from unclean spirits; i.e., from demonic and debilitating spiritual powers, and from the potentially destructive powers of nature.

• In this story, Jesus is clearly modeling what the disciples will be called to do: preach and cast out demons (Mk 3:13-19, cf. Mk 1:39 and Mk 6:7-13). Also this functions as a link to the previous pericope, where Jesus calls the four to "come after me" (Mk 1:17).

---

[6] See, for instance, the preface to "The Sacred History of Asklepios" included in *Documents for the Study of the Gospels,* ed. David R. Carlidge and David L. Dungan (2d ed., rev. and enl.; Minneapolis: Fortress, 1994), 121-24, esp. 124, where the author addresses Asclepius directly as "Greatest of Gods and Teacher."

¶ 9. Jesus Heals Simon's Mother-in-law

(Mt 8:14-15)   Mk 1:29-31   <===========Lk 4:38-39

Immediately Jesus left the synagogue and entered the house of Simon and Andrew along with James and John. Now Peter's mother-in-law was sick and immediately Jesus came and took her hand and helped her stand up. Her fever left her so that she was able to serve her guests.

> *General Observations.* Although Mark continues to follow the order of Luke for this narrative, several close verbal agreements with Matthew 8:14-15 against Luke suggest Mark's knowledge of Matthew and his conflation of these two sources. Mark begins by preferring Lukan language in Mk 1:29-30//Lk 4:38 and ends the unit more in agreement with Mt 8:15//Mk 1:31. Mark's additional material is characteristic of the author. For example,

> ➢ The addition of εὐθύς at Mk 1:29 and 1:30 (Peabody, *Mark as Composer,* 5, 36)

> ➢ A set of four disciples (Simon and Andrew, James and John) constituting an inner core of Jesus' disciples twice in Mark (Peabody, *Mark as Composer,* 21, 41).

> ➢ The resurrection imagery utilized in Mk 1:31, "grasping the hand and raising (ἐγειρεῖν)" (cf. Peabody, *Mark as Composer,* 44, 47).

This is strong evidence in support of the view that Mark composed his narrative by conflating material from Matthew and Luke and supplementing his version of the story in accord with his own literary style. Advocates of the Two Document Hypothesis would have to explain how Matthew and Luke, while *independently* editing this pericope in Mark, have managed both to eliminate all of Mark's literary characteristics and to split the remaining words within the pericope between them.

• One of the ways that Mark typically ties a narrative to the material that precedes it is by the use of the simple copula, καί. Thirty-five times in the Gospel Mark adds εὐθύς to this connective. The repeated use of "and immediately" (25 occurrences without any intervening word[s]) gives a certain urgency or fast paced quality to the Markan narrative. Of these twenty-five occurrences of καὶ εὐθύς, almost half (11/25) appear in the first two chapters of Mark. This is clearly a striking element of Mark's characteristic literary style and vocabulary.

Mk 1:29. The setting in "a house" is typical of Mark (Peabody, *Mark as Composer,* 42, 47).

• Jesus' inner core of *four* disciples make their first appearance since their call (Mk 1:16-20) here in Mk 1:29. They will be highlighted by Mark again in a scene on the Mount of Olives (Mk 13:3; versus "his/the disciples" at Mt 24:1, 3, and "some" at Lk 21:5). Jesus giving instruction to an inner core of disciples is typical of the Markan overlay.

Mk 1:30. Peter's wife does not appear in Mark's Gospel or any other, but this story presupposes her existence (cf. 1 Cor 9:5).

Mk 1:31. Jesus' technique of "raising" this woman by "grasping her hand" is typical of the Markan description of Jesus as healer. Jesus uses the same technique later to "raise" (ἐγείρειν) the apparently dead daughter of Jairus (Mk 5:21-24a, 35-43, esp. 5:41-42), and to revive an epileptic boy who also appeared to be dead (Mk 9:14-29, esp. 9:26-27). By utilizing this language, Mark enriches his narrative with a "resurrection motif" that is often absent or less obvious in the parallel narratives.

10. Jesus Heals Many Sick

(Mt 8:16-17)   Mk 1:32-34   <========Lk 4:40-41

That evening at sundown, all who were sick or possessed by demons were brought to Jesus. Soon the whole city had gathered in front of Peter's house. Jesus healed many of the sick and cast out many demons. Moreover, he would not allow the demons to speak since they knew who he was.

General Observations. At this point Mark continues to follow Luke as his major source. However, this Markan summary passage exhibits remarkable evidence of conflation. Mark 1:32 begins with a famous duplicate expression composed of "halves," consisting of "when evening came" ('Οψίας δὲ γενομένης) from Matthew and "when the sun went down" (Δύνοντος δὲ τοῦ ἡλίου) from Luke. However, this is only one of several Markan combinations of elements from Matthew and Luke that may be noted in this context (see the synopsis in the introduction above, as well as the synoptic display and discussion of this pericope in Longstaff, *Evidence of Conflation,* 140-152).

Mk 1:32-34. While Matthew refers to the sick who are brought to Jesus as δαιμονιζομένους πολλούς . . . τοὺς κακῶς ἔχοντας (Mt 8:16) and Luke refers to these persons as ποικίλαις νόσοις . . . καὶ δαιμόνια (Lk 4:40), Mark refers both to τοὺς κακῶς ἔχοντας καὶ τοὺς δαιμονιζομένους (Mk 1:32) and to the ποικίλαις νόσοις καὶ δαιμόνια (Mk 1:34). This pattern of alternating agreement in wording with

Matthew and Luke within a pericope, coming as it does immediately after a duplicate expression referring to evening, is particularly strong evidence that Mark has conflated Matthew and Luke. On the Two Document Hypothesis this neat division of Mark's text by Matthew and Luke is more difficult to explain.

Mk 1:33. The pressing of crowds "before the door" is a distinctively Markan additional detail (Mk 1:33 cf. Mk 2:2; Peabody, *Mark as Composer,* 47-48, 48)

• On the Two Gospel Hypothesis, Mark blends together similar amounts of distinctive material, some from Matthew and some from Luke, while adding or modifying his text in conformity with his own distinctive literary style. Advocates of the Two Document Hypothesis need to explain how Matthew and Luke, while *independently* editing this pericope in Mark, have managed both to eliminate all of Mark's literary characteristics and to split the remaining words within the pericope between them.

Excursus 5. On Conflation

In the analyses below we frequently suggest that a passage in Mark's Gospel is a conflation of material taken from Matthew and Luke. It is important to be clear about how we are using the term "conflation" in this volume. The term is, of course, frequently used in textual criticism where its meaning is quite clear. In that context it refers to the process or result of bringing together and combining readings from two or more texts in order to produce a single, composite text. A clear example of such conflation, in its simplest form, can be seen at Acts 6:8. The variant readings πλήρης χάριτος and πλήρης πίστεως are each to be found in several manuscripts. One manuscript (E) gives the conflated reading πλήρης χάριτος καὶ πίστεως.

The definition of conflation as the process or result of bringing together and combining readings from two or more texts in order to produce a single, composite text is satisfactory. However, recognition of this process becomes increasingly complex and difficult as progressively larger units of material are considered. The analyses must be done cautiously and carefully. Additions, deletions, and other modifications made during the process of conflation must be taken into account. This complexity has led some scholars to conclude that "there are no certain tests to distinguish true from apparent conflation."[7] While it may be true that there are no tests that will enable us to distinguish true from apparent conflation with absolute certainty, a careful study of known examples of conflation will enable us to identify characteristics of this compositional method which can be seen in a conflated text.

---

[7] See E. P. Sanders, *The Tendencies of the Synoptic Tradition* (Cambridge: The University Press, 1969), 264.

The presence of these characteristics certainly adds credibility to the proposal that a given text was produced by combining material taken from two or more sources.

Unfortunately much of the discussion of conflation relies too heavily on speculation and often on rhetorical questions, about what an author may or may not be expected to do. Thus it is often argued that, if Mark were the third of the Synoptic Gospels and conflating material taken from Matthew and Luke, he would have had no reason for omitting as much as he does. Examples of such omissions include the birth narratives, the Sermon on the Mount/Sermon on the Plain, many of the parables and teachings of Jesus, and the accounts of the appearances of the Risen Jesus. The list could, of course, be extended to include other "inexplicable omissions." As Longstaff has pointed out,[8] however, such reasoning seems to be based upon an unfounded and perhaps illegitimate assumption. There are, after all, many *possible* reasons why an author would write again something that has already been written. The later author might wish to supplement the earlier works by the addition of greater detail or by the addition of entirely new material. The author might wish to refine or correct them in some substantive way. In these and similar cases the later author would probably intend the new document to replace the earlier documents used as sources with the expectation that they would subsequently disappear from general use. It is also possible, however, that the later author would write, not to replace, but rather to summarize or interpret the earlier works by setting the material in a different context or by focusing upon different aspects or concerns. In these cases the later author might well intend that the new document be used along with the earlier documents. Since in such cases the omission of materials would not imply their loss, there would be no compelling reason to include all of the material found in the source documents. Indeed, if Mark is the latest of the Synoptic Gospels, given the respect that he affords his sources, it seems far more likely that he writes for an audience that will continue to have access to these Gospels as well as to his new composition.[9]

In *Evidence of Conflation in Mark? A Study in the Synoptic Problem,* Longstaff analyzed several documents where both the sources and the conflated documents were available for comparison. His purpose was to identify the literary characteristics that result from the use of this compositional method and thus to provide a more objective basis for examining the question of whether Mark's gospel could be understood as a conflation of material taken from Matthew and Luke. His observations about this method of composition are, of course, more widely applicable. It is important to recognize that the characteristics of conflation that he identifies must be understood to be descriptions of what is observed frequently to occur and not statements about normative "rules" governing the process. As we have acknowledged, conflation can be, and often is, a very complex and widely diverse phenomenon.

---

[8] Thomas R. W. Longstaff, *Evidence of Conflation in Mark? A Study in the Synoptic Problem* (SBLDS 28, Missoula, Mont.: Scholars Press, 1977).

[9] See Thomas R. W. Longstaff, "Crisis and Christology: The Theology of Mark," in Farmer, ed., *New Synoptic Studies,* 373ff, where reasons are offered for a number of the Markan omissions.

In addition to the different purposes for which people write again something that has already been written, some of the variables to be kept in mind are these: the individual differences among authors that cause them to write in very different styles, the different situations in which authors live and work (which are frequently reflected in their compositions), and the differences in the relationship among an author's sources (*i.e.,* a conflator may incorporate documents that are themselves related or that are quite independent of each other). While these (and other) limitations must be kept in mind, it is possible to identify several features that are characteristic of known examples of conflation. These characteristics may then be used to evaluate suggestions about what an author would or would not do and to assess the probability that a particular document was produced by this editorial method. Based upon his analyses, Longstaff describes several characteristics of a conflated document.[10]

1. The first characteristic of conflation is implicit in the definition of the term itself. Since conflation is defined as the process or result of bringing together and combining readings from two or more texts in order to produce a single, composite text, it follows that at least part of the content and vocabulary of each of the sources will appear in the conflated document. It is important to note, however, that while this is a characteristic of conflation that will always appear, it does not constitute proof that conflation has, in fact, taken place. Other explanations must also be considered. In the case of the Synoptic Problem this would include the suggestion that Matthew and Luke have each made use of Mark, copying different portions of their source.

2. The second characteristic of conflation is the observation that often, but not always, authors who conflate carefully compare and then meticulously combine their sources. When an author is combining sources which themselves exhibit a considerable degree of word-for-word agreement (as well as differences) the comparison of the sources can be quite detailed, resulting in small agreements with one source against the other or leaving small agreements between the source documents where a change has been introduced. Indeed, in the work of each of the authors whose conflated works Longstaff analyzed, there were numerous places where the author who conflates was closely copying from one source but who interrupted that careful copying to include some small detail from another of his sources. To give only two examples of this phenomenon it can be noted that in lines 5 and 6 of the Greek fragment of the *Diatessaron* Tatian has copied the phrase ΟΨΙΑΣ ΔΕ ΓΕΝΟΜΕΝΗΣ ΕΠΙ ΤΗ ΠΑΡΑΣΚΕΥΗ Ο ΕΣΤΙΝ ΠΡΟΣΑΒΒΑΤΟΝ from Mark but while doing so has preferred Matthew's ΔΕ to Mark's ΚΑΙ ΗΔΗ. Similarly, at the end of his description of Thomas Becket's behavior upon his return to Canterbury, Roger of Hovedon (who conflates narratives from Benedict of Peterboro's account with that in the *Passio Sancti Thomae*) interrupts his exact copying of Benedict of Peterboro's text to take three words (et exhortationis

---

[10] Supporting evidence for these statements can be found in the detailed analyses in Longstaff, *Evidence of Conflation in Mark?* Seven statements there have been combined into six for this review.

verbo) from the *Passio*. There are even times when such small agreements occur alternately in the same section demonstrating that the conflator has carefully compared his sources and woven them together skillfully into the composite account. For example, the opening words of the Greek fragment of the *Diatessaron* are taken from Matthew (ΖΕΒΕΔΑΙΟΥ), Mark (ΚΑΙ CΛΛΩΜΗ), and Luke (ΚΑΙ ΑΙ ΓΥΝΑΙΚΕC). Further, although the same precision cannot be obtained when dealing with a document in translation, it appears that the list of commandments in Tatian's version of the story of the Rich Young Ruler (*Diatessaron* 28:42-29:11 where Tatian combines Matthew 19:16-30, Mark 10:17-31 and Luke 18:18-30) has been taken from Luke but with the additions of "Do not defraud" from Mark and "Love thy neighbor as thyself" from Matthew. Such "weaving together" of fine detail from a plurality of sources was evident in each of the examples of conflation studied.

This evidence challenges a widely held assumption about conflation, namely that authors who conflate follow one source at a time. Indeed the contrary seems often to be the case. The conflation of two or more sources that themselves exhibit a considerable degree of verbal similarity will often (although not always) result in small agreements (of a single word or brief phrase) with one source against the other(s). These agreements may interrupt the use of a single source or may occur alternately within a single sentence.

3. Another observed characteristic of conflation is a tendency for an author to make the transition from one source to another at a place where the two sources are in verbal agreement. While this characteristic of conflation does not describe every transition from one source to another, it does occur frequently enough to warrant mention as a characteristic of this editorial method. Of course this phenomenon will be limited to instances in which the conflator is combining sources which are themselves closely similar. It is, however, significant that this phenomenon was observed in the work of every one of the authors whose methods of conflation were analyzed. It may, therefore, be taken to be a characteristic of this compositional method.

4. It has often been suggested that redundancy and duplication will appear as evidence of conflation. While this phenomenon was observed in the text of the *Diatessaron*, it was not observed as characteristic of the other conflated documents analyzed. This suggests that when examining documents for evidence consistent with the suggestion that the work is the result of conflation the author's purpose must be considered. Authors who intend their work to be inclusive (without significant omission) are more likely to produce documents with redundancy and duplication than are authors who more freely omit material found in their sources.

5. One of the more important observations is that conflation is not a mechanical process. The detailed analyses of several examples of conflation showed clearly that each author had left the mark of his

own perspective on the final product. Sometimes the changes are <u>major</u> and immediately obvious. This is the case with Roger of Hovedon's revision of the section reporting Henry II's claim that the archbishopric of Bourges belonged to Aquitaine, his march to Berry, his truce with Louis VII of France, and his presence in Bur on Christmas Day, 1170. His alteration of his sources here is quite clear. More interesting, though, are the small changes in wording that provide a significant change in the meaning of the text. Thus (in lines 1 and 2 of the Greek fragment of the *Diatessaron*) Tatian's substitution of ΑΙ ΓΥΝΑΙΚΕϹ ΤΩΝ ϹΥΝΑΚΟΛΟΥΘΗϹΑΝΤΩΝ for Luke's ΑΙ ΓΥΝΑΙΚΕϹ ΑΙ ϹΥΝΑΚΟΛΟΥΘΟΥϹΑΙ seems, with a simple change of case, to transform the phrase "the women who followed him" to "the wives of those who followed him," thus removing women from the category of those who followed Jesus. This is not unlike the difference that Cope observes between Matthew 19:17 (τί με ἐρωτᾷς περὶ τοῦ ἀγαθοῦ; εἷς ἐστιν ὁ ἀγαθός. Why do you ask me about the good? The good; *i.e.*, the Torah, is one) and Mark 10:18 (τί με λέγεις ἀγαθόν; οὐδεὶς ἀγαθός εἰ μὴ ὁ θεός. Why do you call me good? No one is good except God.). Cope's suggestion is that a question about the Torah has been transformed into a Christological question about Jesus.[11] In any case a significant change in meaning has been introduced into this narrative by the secondary author.

It is also important to observe that an author who conflates need not always treat a given source in the same way. This was particularly obvious in the work of Roger of Hovedon who sometimes follows his sources very closely and at other times substantially rewrites an entire section.

6. Finally in the analyses of conflation undertaken by Longstaff it was clear that authors who conflate sometimes condense and sometimes expand the works that they copy. Therefore (perhaps constituting a negative characteristic of conflation) despite frequent assumptions to the contrary neither abbreviation nor expansion of the source material can be considered a clear characteristic of this editorial method.

While none of these observed characteristics of conflation can be used as proof for the claim that a particular document has been produced using this editorial method, they can be used to assess the probability of such a proposal and to show whether or not the proposed conflation displays characteristics consistent with what is known about this method of composition.

---

[11] See the analysis in Lamar Cope, *Matthew: A Scribe Trained for the Kingdom of Heaven* (Catholic Biblical Quarterly Monograph Series 5; Washington: The Catholic Biblical Association of America, 1976), 111-19.

¶ 11. Jesus Goes On a Tour, Preaching and Casting Out Demons

(Mt 4:23)   Mk 1:35-39   <==========Lk 4:42-44

Very early the next morning, Jesus went out to a lonely place to pray. Later Simon and the others followed him and when they found him they said, "Everyone wants to know where you are." He said, "Let us leave and go to other towns to preach and heal, for that is why I came out." With that, he began a journey throughout Galilee.

General Observations. Mark continues to follow Luke's order of pericopae. For this story, Mark mainly utilizes Luke's account of a "preaching" tour (Lk 4:42-44). However, Luke's story of the call of the first *three* disciples immediately follows this summary passage (Lk 5:1-11), and Mark has already narrated the call of the first *four* disciples, in agreement with the order and wording of Matthew (Mk 1:16-20//Mt 4:18-22). The last verse in this pericope, Mk 1:39, provides evidence of Mark's conflation of Lk 4:44, the verse that immediately precedes the call of the first disciples in Lk 5:1-11, with Mt 4:23, the verse that immediately follows the call of the first disciples in Mt 4:18-22 (see Synopsis). By conflating Mt 4:23 with Lk 4:44, Mark is able to describe this tour as including both "preaching," (derived from Mt 4:23//Lk 4:44) and "casting out demons," in accord with Mark's own repeated depiction of the pattern of Jesus' ministry and that of his closest disciples (See also Mk 3:13-15, 6:7, 12-13). The addition of "casting out demons" may be Markan terminology for the references to Jesus "healing every disease and every malady" in the two most obvious redactional summaries in the text of Matthew (Mt 4:23//Mt 9:35). This evidence of Mark's conflation of redactional passages from Matthew and Luke, in accord with Mark's own perspective, is strong compositional evidence in support of the Two Gospel Hypothesis.

Mk 1:35. Mark's temporal reference here, "extremely early in the morning," is similar to the one at Mk 16:2 (Peabody, *Mark as Composer*, 52, 49), which describes the time the women arrived at Jesus' tomb following Jesus' death. These two similar temporal references represent Markan supplements to his source material and, by their similarity, may also be said to conform with Mark's literary style. Such evidence is more easily explained as Markan addition than as omission by Matthew and Luke.

• The motif of "Jesus at prayer" is Lukan (Lk 3:21, 5:16, 6:12, 9:18, 9:28-29, 11:1, 22:41, and 44-45). Mark shares this motif with Luke here (Mk 1:35//Lk 5:16) and everywhere else it is found in Mark (Mk 6:46//Lk 9:18; Mk 14:32, 35, 38//Lk 22:41, 44-45). On the other hand, Luke can utilize this motif in contexts independent of Mark (Lk

3:21, 6:12, 9:28-29 and 11:1). This linguistic evidence would point to Mark's literary dependence upon Luke on the basis of fragmentary preservation of a Lukan characteristic.

Mk 1:36. For the description of Jesus' disciples as "those with him," compare part of the purpose of the call of the disciples at Mk 3:14; i.e., "in order to be with him." The disciples are called "those with him" again at Mk 5:40 [see also 5:37 and 14:33 and 16:10]. It seems to be characteristic of Markan composition.

Mk 1:39. Jesus sets the pattern for ministry in this context: "to preach and cast out demons"(Mk 1:39). Jesus will later call (Mk 3:14-15) and, subsequently, commission "the twelve" for these same tasks (Mk 6:12-13).

• Though Jesus is "teacher" for Mark, his summaries of Jesus' activity always involve both teaching and healing. Mark chooses to use "preaching" (κηρύσσων) instead of "teaching" (διδάσκων) from Matthew because it conforms with his own terminology about the activity of Jesus and the disciples (see Synopsis).

• The phrase, "in their synagogues" is Matthean (Mt 4:23, 9:35, 10:17, 13:54). Mark uses this term only here, where he shares it with Mt 4:23. The close verbatim agreement and the use of this Matthean phrase is strong evidence of Mark's literary dependence upon Matthew (see Synopsis).

• Although Mark is currently drawing his order of events from Luke, Mark probably shares "throughout the whole of Galilee" with Mt 4:23 here, although "Galilee" in A Δ Θ φ it vg sy^p may be original at Luke 4:44.[12]

¶ 12. Jesus Heals a Leper

Mt 8:1-4 ----------------------> Mk 1:40-45   <==========Lk 5:12-16
(Mt 4:23-25, 9:30-34)

One day a leper meets Jesus and begs him to heal him. Moved with pity, Jesus immediately heals him, warning him to speak of it to no one, but to go to the priest and make the offering Moses commanded for such a healing. Instead, the man spreads the word far and wide so that Jesus can no longer openly come into any city. Nevertheless, people flock to him from everywhere.

---

[12] See McNicol et al., *Beyond the Q Impasse*, 93-94 for a discussion of this variant.

General Observations. Since Mark has already narrated the call of the first four disciples (Mt 4:18-22//Mk 1:16-20, cf. Lk 5:1-11), Mark moves ahead to the next literary unit in Luke, the Cleansing of the Leper (Lk 5:12-16), which Matthew also narrated (Mt 8:1-4), but placed immediately after the Sermon on the Mount (Mt 5:2-7:29).

• Our views on the order of pericopae in Mk 1:35-45 and any purported connection with the Sermon on the Mount have already been explained in the excursus on Mark's omission of the Sermon on the Mount, above. Mark continues to share Luke's order of events with this story of the Healing of the Leper. The story contains classic evidence of Mark's blending of Matthew and Luke. Words and phrases seem to be woven together within this Markan story into a number of "duplicate expressions." In the process, Mark adds or omits numerous tiny details. Note, for instance, the Markan addition of "moved with pity" at Mk 1:41a[13] and the addition of the motif of Jesus not being able to carry on normal human activity because of crowds around him in Mk 1:45 (cf. Peabody, *Mark as Composer,* 68, 54). Mark agrees with Luke's form of the story, but also agrees with Matthew in numerous details.

Mk 1:41. The Markan additional detail about Jesus "being moved with pity" is a characteristically Markan supplement to the narratives of Matthew and Luke concerning the emotions of characters, especially the emotions of Jesus (cf. Mk 6:34, 8:2 for other uses of σπλαχνίζομαι in Mk).[14]

Mk 1:42. While Matthew refers to the leprosy being cleansed (Mt 8:3, ἐκαθαρίσθη) and Luke describes the leprosy leaving the leper (Lk 5:13, ἀπῆλθεν), Mark records both that "the leprosy left him" and that the leper "was cleansed." Here is another instance of alternating agreement in wording with Matthew and Luke within a pericope.

Mk 1:43. While no single piece of the following evidence is decisive, the concatenation of evidence suggests that the text of Mk 1:43-45 has been influenced not only by Lk 5:12-16 and Mt 8:1-4, but also by Mt 9:30-35. In support of this claim we note: The appearance of the word, ἐμβριμάομαι (Mk 1:43, καὶ ἐμβριμησάμενος αὐτῷ, no parallels in either Mt 8:3 or Lk 5:13). ἐμβριμάομαι appears a total of 5 times in the NT. Mark uses the term twice, here and in Mk 14:5. Matthew uses the term once (Mt 9:30 //Mk 1:43), and John uses the term twice, with a different connotation.

---

[13] If the text of D, which reads "having become angry" for "being moved with pity" in the vast majority of MSS is accepted at Mk 1:41, that would not materially affect our line of argumentation here.

[14] Meijboom, *A History and Critique,* 108-10.

• The shared usage of διαφήμιζω (Mk 1:45//Mt 9:31). There are 3 usages of this term in the NT; the parallel here and once without parallel in Mt 28:15.

• The significant Matthean doublet in Mt 4:23//Mt 9:35 that might help to link these two broader literary contexts in Matthew.

• The distinctively Markan double negative in Mk 1:44 may have resulted from the combination of single negatives from Mt 8:4//Lk 5:14 and Mt 9:30.

• All told, this evidence supports the conclusion that Mark has conflated not only Mt 8:1-4 and Lk 5:12-16, but has also made use of Mt 9:30-35 in composing this unit.

Mk 1:45. This is the first appearance in Mark's text of "the Word" used absolutely (13 times, plus one at 16:20; Peabody, *Mark as Composer,* 69, 55). Compare similar absolute uses of "the Gospel" and "the time" in Mark. This is a critical piece of the Markan overlay and a clear indication of Markan editorial activity.

• The reference in Mk 1:45 to "crowds gathering" is the first previous referent for numerous later πάλιν passages where "crowds gather again" (Mk 2:1, 2:13, 3:20, 4:1-2, 8:1, and 10:1, cf. Peabody, *Mark as Composer,* 70, 56-57)

¶ 13. Jesus Preaches and Heals a Paralytic by Forgiving His Sins

Mt 9:1-8 ----------------------->   Mk 2:1-12   <=========Lk 5:17-26

After some days, Jesus comes to Capernaum again. People hear that he is at home and many gather, so that there is no longer even room before the door. Jesus takes the occasion to speak the word to them. Some people carry a paralytic to Jesus, but they cannot get near because of the crowd. So they remove the roof over Jesus' head and let the paralytic down on a pallet. Seeing their faith, Jesus says to the paralytic, "My son, your sins are forgiven." The scribes see this and say to themselves, "This is blasphemy! Only God forgives sins!" Jesus immediately perceives their thoughts and says, "Is it any easier to say, your sins are forgiven, or to say, rise, take up your pallet and walk?" The Pharisees don't say anything. Jesus goes on, "So that you may know that the Son of Man has authority on earth to forgive sins, I say (and he turns to the paralytic) rise, take up your pallet and go home." Immediately the paralytic got up and went out, to everyone's amazement, so that they glorify God and say, "We never saw anything like this!"

General Observations. Following an incident in which Jesus touches a leper, Mark narrates a series of conflict stories between Jesus and his opponents (Mk 2:1-3:6). Mark continues to follow the order of Luke. He shares most of this text with Luke, but blends in details from Matthew. Mark 2:1-4 is more closely parallel to Luke than to Matthew; Mark 2:5-6a is much closer to Matthew 9:2 than to Luke 5:20; Mark 2:6bff. is closer to Luke 5:21ff. Once again this illustrates the phenomenon of alternating agreement within pericopae, a characteristic which results from Markan conflation, as illustrated especially well above at Mk 1:32-34 and 1:40-45.

• Markan additions to and changes of Matthew and Luke in this story result in a number of agreements of Matthew and Luke against Mark (the so-called minor agreements of the Two Document Hypothesis).[15] The most striking of these is the fact that, when confronted with a variety of terms in Matthew and Luke for the "bed," Mark imposes uniformity by using the Latin loanword, κράβαττος (stretcher?).

At Mk 2:9, Mark adds κράβαττον.

At Mk 2:4, Mark changes Luke's κλινίδιον to κράβαττον (cf. Lk 5:19)

At Mk 2:11, Mark changes Matthew's κλίνη and Luke's κλινίδιον to κράβαττον (cf. Mt 9:6//Lk 5:24)

At Mk 2:12, Mark changes Luke's ἐφ' ὃ κατέκειτο to κράβαττον (cf. Lk 5:25).

Κράβαττος appears once more in Mark at Mk 6:55, nowhere in Matthew or Luke, four times in John, twice in Acts, and nowhere else in the NT. Other NT authors, including Matthew and Luke as we have seen here, use other words for "bed," such as κλίνη, κλινίδιον or κλινάριον. It is easier to explain these data as the result of Mark's imposing a unity on his text with the use of the Latin loanword, κράβαττος, than it is to explain them as the result of Matthew and Luke independently editing Mark's text in different ways but agreeing to omit or change every single usage of κράβαττος.

Mk 2:1. The statement, "Jesus comes into Capernaum *again* (πάλιν)," refers the reader back to Mk 1:21, where Jesus first came into Capernaum.

---

[15] Cf. Farmer, "The Minor Agreements of Matthew and Luke Against Mark and the Two Gospel Hypothesis: A Study of These Agreements in Their Compositional Contexts," in Strecker, ed., *Minor Agreements,* 163-208.

Mk 2:2. Jesus draws a crowd about the door of the house where he is staying (Mk 2:2, cf. Mk 1:33, Peabody, *Mark as Composer,* 47, 48). The detail of "gathering before the door" is a Markan addition to his source material in the two places where it occurs. It functions as a small feature of the Markan overlay.

• Jesus takes this occasion to "speak the word" to these crowds. The phrase, "speaking of the word," is customary for Jesus according to the author of Mark (Mk 2:2, 4:33, 8:32; Peabody, *Mark as Composer,* 69, 55). At first, Jesus will "speak the word" only in parables (Mk 4:33), but later, when he begins to predict the coming events relating to his arrest, suffering, death, and resurrection, he will "speak the word quite openly" (Mk 8:31-32, cf. Mk 9:30-32, 10:32-34).

Mk 2:2-4. The author of Mark depicts normal activity as being curtailed by the large crowds pressing on Jesus. Such a motif is characteristic of Mark (Mk 1:45, 2:2 and 3:30, Peabody, *Mark as Composer,* 68, 54).

• Because of the crowd, the people carrying the paralytic must find an unusual way through the roof of the house in order to bring the paralytic to Jesus for healing. In a similar way, Jesus must later make special arrangements for a boat (Mk 3:9) from which to teach the crowds, lest they crush him (Mk 4:1).

• The addition of a specific number to Mark's account of this story (cf., e.g., the addition of the number, 2000, to the reference to the swine at Mk 5:13) is characteristic of the author of Mark. Commentators have often referred to this as Mark's penchant for vivid detail.

Mk 2:5-12. Note the similarity of language on the lips of Jesus' opponents here, εἰ μὴ εἰς ὁ θεός (Mk 2:7, cf. Lk 5:21, εἰ μὴ μόνος ὁ θεός) and that of Jesus later at Mk 10:18//Lk 18:19. See also Mark's expanded quotation of the Shema at Mk 12:29//Deut 6:4 LXX (Peabody, *Mark as Composer,* 76, 59). On the Two Gospel Hypothesis, Luke has clarified the charge of blasphemy against Jesus in Mt 9:3 by adding the comment, "No one can forgive sins, except God alone (μόνος)." Mark, in the later context, Mk 10:18//Lk 18:19, will adopt Luke's phrasing, εἰ μὴ εἰς ὁ θεός, and, even later, in Mk 12:29, Mark will expand the text of the Shema to include the words, κύριος εἰς ἐστιν. In both of these later contexts εἰς is appropriate, but it is not appropriate here. Nevertheless, Mark seems to have been so interested in the concept of "the one God" that it has influenced his editorial work in this context, as it did in the other two.

• Mark is more careful than Luke to make the initial statement by Jesus, "Stand up, take up your mat, and walk" (Mk 2:9), parallel the final command, "Stand up, take up your mat, and go home" (Mk 2:12). Luke's initial statement is simply, "Stand up and walk" (Lk 5:23). It is more likely that Mark, knowing the Lukan story, produced the closer parallel than that Luke deliberately eliminated it. Whether or not this story is but a different version of the similar story in Jn 5:2-9 and, if so, whether the Synoptic or Johannine story is more original is a form-critical problem beyond the scope of our inquiry. It is worth noting that neither the forgiveness of sins issue in Mark and Luke's story nor the healing on the sabbath issue of the ensuing Johannine debate is at all present in the simple Johannine healing story.

• A close connection between healing and forgiveness of sins is posited by Mark. For the first time in the narrative Jesus is accused of blasphemy. The charge of blasphemy will also be pivotal in Jesus' confrontation with the high priest (Mk 14:64). Here we have another clear anticipation that Jesus' way will end in tragedy.

¶ 14. Jesus Calls Levi, the Tax Collector

Mt 9:9 ----------------------->   Mk 2:13-14   <=========Lk 5:27-28

Again by the sea, the crowd comes and Jesus teaches them. Moving along, Jesus encounters a tax-collector named Levi, the son of Alphaeus, seated at his tax collecting desk. Jesus calls and Levi stands up and follows.

General Observations. Mark continues to follow the order of Luke. This part of Mark is framed by stories of the calling of disciples (Mk 1:16-20 and 3:13-19). An additional call motif is present in this intermediate story about the call of a fifth disciple.

Mk 2:13. Mark introduces the call of Levi with a verse replete with Markan redactional characteristics that are completely missing in the two parallel accounts of Matthew and Luke.

Jesus goes out "again" (Peabody, *Mark as Composer,* 70, 56-57)

"by the sea" (cf. Mk 1:16; Peabody, *Mark as Composer,* 15, 39)

"all the crowd comes to him" (Peabody, *Mark as Composer,* 85, 62) "and he was teaching them" (Peabody, *Mark as Composer,* 84, 62; cf. Mk 10:1b for another verse that is almost as densely filled with Markan literary characteristics).

The setting, "by the sea," provides the context for the call of the fifth disciple as it did for the call of the first four disciples (Mk 4:16-20). Just as Simon, Andrew, James, and John did earlier, so now Levi responds immediately when called by Jesus.

Every word or phrase in this verse that does not stand in verbatim agreement with either Matthew, Luke, or both is characteristic of Mark, and none of the words and phrases in Mark that are paralleled in the other Gospels is characteristic of Mark. What other explanation is there for such a consistent pattern of positive and negative correlations than that Mark has freely recomposed the loosely parallel texts of Matthew and Luke and, in doing so, overlaid the whole text with many of his own characteristic words and phrases? On the Two Document Hypothesis, one would have to conclude that Matthew and Luke managed to omit only what is characteristic of Mark, each independently taking from Mark only what is not characteristic of Mark.

Mk 2:14. Mark has drawn the name Levi from Luke. The additional Markan description of this fifth disciple as "the son of Alphaeus" (Mk 2:14) has given rise to textual variants for this disciple's name, Levi or James. The Markan addition of "the son of Alphaeus" is consistent with Markan supplements elsewhere in that Gospel. See, for instance, the Markan additions of "when Abiathar was high priest" at Mk 2:26, "the son of Timaeus, Bar Timaeus" at Mk 10:46, the name "Salome" at Mk 15:40 and 16:1, "the mother of Joses" at Mk 15:47, and "the father of Alexander and Rufus" at Mk 15:21.

• Mark makes it clear that Jesus' call to discipleship involved not only an invitation to the morally upright but even to those "toll collectors" reckoned as sinners. As such it served as a fitting introduction to the next pericope.

¶ 15. Jesus Eats with Tax Collectors and Sinners Who Follow Him

Mt 9:10-13 --------------------	Mk 2:15-17	<=========Lk 5:29-32
(Mt 9:13 = Hos 6:6)		(cf. Lk 15:1-2)

Then Jesus went to his home where his presence attracts many "toll collectors and sinners" who had chosen to follow him. The scribes of the Pharisees who saw Jesus eating with these persons challenged Jesus' disciples, asking why their teacher did this. Jesus overhears and responds with a proverb, "Those who are strong have no need of a doctor, but those who have illnesses," which Jesus then interprets for this particular situation with the words, "I did not come to call righteous people, but sinners."

General Observations. Mark continues to follow the order of Luke for the next four stories. These constitute a series of debates between Jesus and his opponents. Throughout this section Mark follows the order of Luke 5:17-6:11, where Luke has collected a number of controversy stories found in the same order in Mt 9:1-17 and 12:1-14. Mark's use of Luke's structure explains the text of Mark here at least as well the common notion that Mark 2:1 3:6 is either a Markan composition or a Markan editing of a pre-synoptic collection. On the Two Gospel Hypothesis, Mark follows Luke for the structure of this section, but close verbal agreements with Matthew and the familiar pattern of alternating agreement with Matthew and Luke in a single pericope indicate that Mark has made use of both of his sources when incorporating this material into his Gospel.

These debates gradually intensify until Jesus' opponents begin a plot to destroy him, a note that Mark adopts from the parallel context in Mt 12:14 to conclude this section (Mt 12:15//Mk 3:6). Following Luke, the debates fall into two pairs. The first pair focuses on issues about eating, the second, on Sabbath observance. Jesus first debates with the Pharisees about eating with toll collectors (Mk 2:15-17); second, about not eating; i.e., fasting (Mk 2:18-22); third, about working on the Sabbath in order to eat (Mk 2:23-28), and fourth, about healing on the Sabbath (Mk 3:1-5).

• This is the first of four interrelated controversies that immediately follow Levi's call. This story shares a significant feature with the story that immediately precedes it, i.e., "toll collectors" (Mt 9:9-13//Lk 5:27-32//Mk 2:13-17). Mark enhances the linkage between the previous story to highlight the theme of the call of all to discipleship by adding, "there were many and they were following him" in Mk 2:15 and "he eats with toll collectors and sinners" in Mk 2:16 (cf. Mk 2:14)

• This story is a particularly good example of close conflation in Mark, as that is best seen in the companion synopsis ¶15.

Mk 2:15. The motif of Jesus in the house, although in his sources, is typical for Mark.

• The use of ἦσαν/ἦν γάρ to introduce a parenthetical comment is characteristic of Markan composition (Peabody, *Mark as Composer*, 18, 40). The comment conforms with both Mark's penchant for duality (πολλοί) and for the addition of colorful detail.

Mk 2:16. Note the repetition of the words, "he eats with toll collectors and sinners," in Mk 2:16. The threefold usage of "toll collectors and sinners" (cf. Mk 2:15) is striking. It underscores the irrefutable fact that Jesus openly welcomed those of ill repute into his fellowship.

• In keeping with Mt 9:13 Mark omits Luke's reference to repentance (Lk 5:32).

¶ 16. When to Eat and not to Eat

Mt 9:14-17 --------------------	Mk 2:18-22	<=========Lk 5:33-39
		(cf. Lk 15:3)

At that time, the disciples of the Pharisees and the disciples of John the Baptist are fasting, but the disciples of Jesus are not. People ask him, "Why don't your disciples fast like they do?" Jesus answered, "Do the guests fast at a wedding festival? Of course not! However, the days are coming when the bridegroom won't be here; then the guests will fast. No one uses a piece of new cloth to patch an old garment because it will tear out. Likewise, no one puts new wine into old wineskins; they will burst and the wine be lost." Thus, the new order is incompatible with the old.

General Observations. For the second debate over issues surrounding eating Mark continues to follow the Lukan order. But the unit itself displays a remarkable pattern of alternating agreement in Mark, first with Matthew, then with Luke, alternating back and forth throughout the pericope. Only eleven of the 123 words (9 %) that Mark uses are absent from the parallel text of Matthew, Luke, or both. It is difficult to explain on the Two Document Hypothesis how Matthew and Luke could have divided the Markan material between them so neatly. This is a striking example of one type of Markan conflation, in which Mark alternately incorporates blocks of material from Matthew and Luke (see Synopsis ¶ 16).[16]

• According to Mark, Jesus' disciples do not observe the practice of fasting as the disciples of John the Baptist and of the Pharisees do. Jesus' response is predicated on the presupposition that since the time of salvation was present it was not appropriate to fast. Attached to this observation is the comment on the patch and wineskins. Mark underscores the incompatibility of the new with the old (cf. Mk 1:27). This emphasis on breaking with the tradition of Israel is characteristic of Mark.

---

[16] Cf. Longstaff, *Evidence of Conflation in Mark?*, 223-32.

Mk 2:18. Mark never refers to "The disciples of John" apart from this context (Mt 9:14//Lk 5:33) but they play larger roles in Matthew, Luke and John (cf. Mt 11:2//Lk 7:18, Lk 11:1; Jn 1:35, 3:25 and 4:1). It is historically probable that some competition arose between the disciples of John and those of Jesus either during their lifetimes or, as seems more likely, following their deaths. Perhaps the conflict between the followers of John and the followers of Jesus was not as important in the community for which Mark was written. This may be a fragmentary preservation in Mark of a prominent theme in other Gospels.

Mk 2:19. The additional material in Mk 2:19 underscores Mark's understanding of these teachings. By closely conflating Mt 9:15 with Lk 5:34, Mark is able first to repeat a question similar to the one in Matthew and follow it by a statement derived from Luke, with explanatory expansions. Mark's supplement emphasizes the duration of the time (χρόνος) when fasting is not appropriate, i.e., while Jesus lives.

Mk 2:21. Mark alters the common testimony of Matthew and Luke, "throw on" (ἐπιβάλλω) to the more precise "sews" (ἐπιράπτω). In the process, however, Mark destroys the poetic alliteration (ἐπιβάλλει + ἐπίβλημα) of the Greek version of this saying of Jesus in Matthew and Luke.

¶ 17. Jesus' Teaching on Eating/Feeding Even on the Sabbath

Mt 12:1-8 ---------------------->   Mk 2:23-28   <=============Lk 6:1-5
(Mt 12:7 = Hos 6:6)

It is the Sabbath and Jesus and his disciples are walking through grain fields, picking sufficient grain even to make a path through the field. The Pharisees complain that Jesus and his disciples are doing what is forbidden on the Sabbath. Jesus responds to this critique by calling attention to a precedent set by King David. Specifically, when David and those with him had need and were hungry, David and his entourage entered "the house of God" and David ate the special showbread that was set aside for ritual use and which only priests were allowed to eat. David then gave some to those who were with him. According to Mark, all this took place "when Abiathar was high priest." To conclude this teaching, Jesus again makes use of proverbial material and links two proverbs together, one as a rationale for the other. The first proverb, "God provided the Sabbath for the sake of humans, not humans for the sake of the Sabbath," provides the rationale for the second, "the Son of Man [i.e., Jesus as God's representative] is Lord even/also of the Sabbath."

General Observations. Mark still follows the order of pericopae in Luke for this third debate. Probably for this reason, Mark omits the explicit reference to "hunger" in Mt 12:1, but he also omits the reference to "eating" in Mt 12:1//Lk 6:1. He has also added to his source material a note about the disciples "making their way" (Mk 2:23), the reference to "the high priest, Abiathar" (Mk 2:26), and the additional logion, "The Sabbath came to be on account of the human being, not the human being on account of the Sabbath" (Mk 2:27). On the other hand, the Markan omissions blur the connection, already somewhat blurred by Luke, between "hunger," "eating," and Jesus' reply to those who criticized him. Mark's emphasis comes at the end of the unit with his creation of the double logia about the Sabbath. This emphasis on the Sabbath sayings may have distracted Mark from various narrative details that had brought coherence to the debate, especially in Matthew.[17] It is generally recognized that the Matthean version of Mt 12:1-8 reflects the nuanced subtleties of an inner-Jewish debate over observance of the Sabbath.Mark represents a fragmentary preservation of that discussion. Indeed, the second saying on the Sabbath (Mk 2:27) comes close to providing a rationale for dropping the Sabbath altogether. A trajectory of Sabbath observance in the early church which gradually moved toward liberalization is more plausible than the idea of a radical "rejudaization" by Matthew, as Markan priority would require here.

• Since for Mark Jesus' healings are some of his most important "teachings," this and the next conflict story focus on Jesus' authoritative teaching on the Sabbath. In most forms of the Judaism of Jesus' day neither eating nor performing acts of mercy were prohibited on the Sabbath, but certain kinds of work were. According to Matthew, Jesus' disciples were innocent of the charges raised against them by the Pharisees because their work was related to the relieving of hunger (Mt 12:5-7). Whether "rubbing grain with one's hands" (Lk 6:10) would be prohibited work on the Sabbath might be debated, but certainly "making a path" (ὁδὸν ποιεῖν, Mk 2:23, contrast Mt 12:1 and Lk 6:1) through a grain field would appear to be prohibited work on the Sabbath. Therefore, the disciples of Jesus in Mark are more likely to be guilty of breaking the requirements of Sabbath observance than are the disciples in Matthew and Luke. Thus, Mark's additional comment that Jesus and his disciples "began to make a path" makes Jesus' appeal to a precedent set by David about hungering and eating (Mt 12:3-4//Lk 6:3-4//Mk 2:25-26) beside the point. In fact, Mark omits Matthew's second precedent about the priests who are required to carry out worship duties on the Sabbath, but this

---

[17] Mark's editorial activity here has been noted by some who do not hold the Griesbach hypothesis. For instance, Helmut Koester has argued that the additional logion on the Sabbath at Mk 2:27 was an expansion of the text of Mark after Matthew and Luke were composed. Koester, "History and Development," 35-57.

precedent is precisely to the point that some work was allowed on the Sabbath (Mt 12:5-6). In other words, Mark's editing results in a somewhat awkward version of the story.

Mk 2:26. Mark's additional note that David's actions took place during the high priesthood of Abiathar (Mk 2:26), if the text is correct, contradicts the biblical record, which dates these events during the high priesthood of Abiathar's father, Ahimelech (1 Sam 21:1-6; cf. 1 Sam 22:20). This is one of several problems in Mark's text with regard to Jewish history, Judaism, and Palestinian geography.[18] Such inaccuracies create a problem for those who hold that the Gospel of Mark was composed in Galilee. One would expect the Gospel of Mark to contain more accurate information about Judaism, Jewish customs, and Palestinian geography if it were composed there.[19] Since Sepphoris and Tiberias, the most important cities in Galilee, 40-100 C.E., were centers of Judaism, it is hard to imagine a population there that would not have been familiar with Jewish custom and practice. This kind of literary evidence indicates that Mark was written outside of Syria, primarily for Gentile-Christian readers.

Mk 2:27. A substantial addition to this story when compared to the versions in Matthew and Luke is found in Mk 2:27. This addition, asserting that the creation, Sabbath included, was for people, is Mark's attempt to underscore the subsequent Son of Man saying, which Mark does share with Matthew and Luke, that the Son of Man has authority to determine whatever may take place on the Sabbath (Mt 12:8//Lk 6:5//Mk 2:28).

¶ 18. Jesus Heals on the Sabbath

Mt 12:9-14=========>   **Mk 3:1-6**   <==========Lk 6:6-11

The same Sabbath, Jesus went into a synagogue again where he met a man with a crippled hand. People were watching to see whether he would heal him, so they would be able to accuse him of breaking the Sabbath. Aware of their spiteful intentions, Jesus says to the man, "Come here." Then turning to those watching him he asks, "Is it legal to do good on the Sabbath or to do harm, to save a life or to kill?" They don't answer. Angered and saddened by their hardness of heart, Jesus says to the man, "Stretch out your hand," and

---

[18] See Pierson Parker, "The Posteriority of Mark," in Farmer, ed., *New Synoptic Studies,* 67-142, for long lists of alleged Marcan errors and infelicities, including those about Judaism, Jewish customs, and Palestinian geography. The significant textual tradition of D, W, it, and sy^S omits Abiathar.

[19] Some advocates of Markan priority have wanted the earliest gospel to have closer ties to Judaism and Palestine than a gospel that tradition has affirmed as written in Rome would have had. See W. Marxsen, *Mark the Evangelist,* (trans. R. Harrisville, Nashville: Abingdon Press, 1969), 92-95, 151-89, 204-206. On the Two Gospel Hypothesis such evidence of the secondary character of Mark is easier to explain. In fact, a later date and provenance in Rome or Italy goes a long way toward accounting for such data.

immediately the hand is healed. The Pharisees immediately walk out and confer with the Herodians how to destroy Jesus.

General Observations. The series of four controversy stories shared by Luke and Mark concludes here. At the beginning of this story, Mark shares with Luke alone the desire of Jesus' opponents to find some accusation against him (Mk 3:2//Lk 6:7 cf. Lk 6:11). At the end of this story, Mark shares with Matthew alone a very clear reference to a desire of some to destroy Jesus (Mk 3:6//Mt 12:14, cf. Lk 6:11). Thus the series of conflict accounts (Mk 2:1-3:6) which began with the accusation of blasphemy (Mk 2:7) comes to a crescendo with a plot to kill Jesus. A major signpost on the way to Jesus' martyrdom has been passed. Again, this blending of elements from Matthew and Luke is easier to explain on the Two Gospel hypothesis, as Markan editorial activity, than as the independent redaction of Mark by Matthew and Luke. At Mk 3:6 Mark turns again to Matthew for the note about the reaction of the Pharisees, to which Mark adds a reference to the Herodians. Mark will continue to follow Matthew's order for the next few verses.

Mk 3:1. Jesus' going "into a synagogue again" recalls Jesus' earlier entry into a synagogue at Mk 1:21. The πάλιν at Mk 3:1 reflects back to Mk 1:21 in this way while the immediately previous use of πάλιν at Mk 2:1 reflects back to Mk 1:21 in another way, coming into Capernaum. With this distinctive literary characteristic, the author of Mark weaves a network of relationships among separated pericopae throughout his Gospel as a fundamental organizing principle for his narrative account.

Mk 3:4. Certain acts of mercy and the saving of a life were permitted by the Sabbath law of the period. Jesus' questions about the permissibility of doing evil and killing on the Sabbath are rhetorical. They provide a contrast between Jesus' act of mercy in healing the man with the withered hand and the hardness of heart, the evil intent, of those around Jesus who were watching him to accuse him.

• The note that "they were silent," (οἱ δὲ ἐσιώπων) is unique to Mark in this story, as it is again in Mk 9:34 (Peabody, *Mark as Composer,* 90, 65; cf. the singular in Mk 14:61).

Mk 3:5-6. According to the Two Document Hypothesis the distinctive Markan addition μετ᾽ ὀργῆς συλλυπούμενος ἐπὶ τῇ πωρώσει τῆς καρδίας αὐτῶν represents an agreement of omission by Matthew and Luke. However, the detail of the "hardness of heart" is characteristic of the author of Mark and, on the Two Gospel Hypothesis, this phrase is a supplement to the story provided by the author (Peabody, *Mark as*

Composer, 166, 91). Further, it is precisely at this point, where Mark is composing and supplementing Matthew and Luke, that Mark shifts from following Luke (Lk 6:8b-10a//Mk 3:3-5) to following Matthew (Mt 12:13-14//Mk 3:5b-6). Mark's move to Mt 12:13 anticipates his inclusion of the note about the harsh reaction to Jesus (Mk 3:6//Mt 12:14) which is of critical importance for Mark's theology. This web of literary evidence is entirely consistent with the Two Gospel Hypothesis.

Mk 3:6. Mark's additional comment that the Pharisees gave counsel "immediately with the Herodians" at the *end* of this Lukan/Markan series of four controversy stories (Mk 2:15-3:5//Lk 5:29-6:11; against Mt 9:10-17 and 12:1-14) may be compared with Mark's comment about the plot of Pharisees and Herodians at the *beginning* (Mk 12:13) of a later series of four controversies (Mk 12:13-37). Luke never mentions "the Herodians" in his narrative about Jesus, but Matthew shares the second of the two Markan references to "the Herodians" (Mk 12:13//Mt 22:15). There are no other NT references to this group of Jesus' opponents. It may be assumed that they were thought to be supporters of Herod Antipas and perhaps others in the Herodian line. We have no other information about such a group.[20] With Mk 3:6, this series of controversies between Jesus and his opponents ends.

¶ 19 Jesus' Fame Spreads and a Huge Crowd Gathers

Mt 12:15-16=======>	Mk 3:7-12	(Lk 6:17-19)
(cf. Mt 4:23-25)		(cf. Lk 4:41)

Jesus withdrew with his disciples to the Sea of Galilee, but a huge crowd followed, having been attracted from Galilee, Judea and Jerusalem, Idumea, from beyond the Jordan, and even from the region of Tyre and Sidon. Worried that such a large crowd might crush him, Jesus ordered his disciples to get a boat ready, for he had healed many and those who were sick were trying to touch him and get well. And whenever the unclean spirits would see him, they would fall down before him crying, "You are the Son of God!" but he would order them not to make him manifest.

General Observations. Since Mark was in agreement with Matthew and not Luke at the end of the previous pericope (Mk 3:6//Mt 12:14), it is not surprising to find Mark continuing to agree with Mt 12:15-16 for the brief healing summary that follows. A similar healing summary is also found in Lk 6:17-19. Within Mk 3:7-12, therefore, Mark conflated Mt 12:15-16 with Lk 6:17-19, utilizing Mt 12:15 to open the unit (Mk 3:7//Mt 12:15) and Mt 12:16 to close it (Mk 3:12//Mt 12:16). In addition to these

---

[20] John Meier, "The Historical Jesus and the Historical Herodians," *JBL* 119.4 (2000): 740-46.

contextual parallels to Mk 3:7-12 (Mt 12:15-16//Lk 6:17-19), Mark also utilized the list of crowds from various locales that Matthew had provided as part of his introduction to the Sermon on the Mount (Mt 4:23-5:2; cf. Mk 3:7-8). Mark's use of Mt 4:24-25 in this context may initially appear to be difficult to explain, but there are at least three possibilities. First, on the Two Gospel Hypothesis, Luke had already combined Mt 12:15 with Mt 4:24-25 to compose Lk 6:17, so it may have been possible for Mark to make this connection and to expand on Luke's earlier conflation (Mk 3:7-8). Second, Lk 6:17-19 introduces the Sermon on the Plain (Lk 6:20-7:1) which, of course, has striking parallels in content to Matthew's Sermon on the Mount (Mt 5:3-7:29). This also might have encouraged Mark to combine material from the introduction to Matthew's Sermon on the Mount (Mt 4:23-5:2) with material from Luke's introduction to the Sermon on the Plain (Lk 6:17-19). Third, Mark drew a connection between Mt 12:15-16, the contextual parallel to Mk 3:7-12, and the introduction to the Sermon on the Mount by means of the duplicated language found in Mt 12:15 and Mt 4:24-25, i.e., καὶ ἠκολούθησαν αὐτῷ ὄχλοι πολλοί + καὶ ἐθεράπευσεν αὐτούς. Both of these phrases are linguistic characteristics of the author of Matthew that are found not only in these two contexts (Mt 12:15-16 and Mt 4:23-5:2), but also elsewhere in Matthew. And if ἠκολούθησεν in Mk 3:7 is original to the text of Mark, it represents a fragmentary preservation of a formulaic expression in Matthew in the parallel text of Mark, even as ἀνεχώρησεν in Mk 3:7 represents another. Almost all of the remaining wording in Mk 3:7-12 that is not found in Matthew, Luke, or both can be attributed to Mark (see the detailed notes below). Therefore, virtually all of the literary evidence to be found in Mk 3:7-12 can be readily explained by the Two Gospel Hypothesis.

• On the Two Gospel Hypothesis, Luke got the list of names of the twelve apostles from Mt 10:1-4. We have also demonstrated in *Beyond the Q Impasse* (100-102) that Luke connected the list of cities in Mt 4:24-25 with the names of the apostles in Mt 10:1-4, at least in part via the doublet in Mt 4:23 and Mt 9:35. In Lk 6:12-19, if Luke did make use of the list of crowds from Mt 4:25 at Lk 6:17 and the names of the twelve disciples from Mt 10:1-4 at Lk 6:12-16, then Mark's editorial work in Mk 3:7-19 would have been facilitated by Luke's previous combination of a number of separated literary contexts in Matthew. By combining terminology from Mt 12:15-16, Mt 4:23-5:2 and Mt 9:35-10:4 Mark simply expanded on the connections that had already been made by Luke (Mk 3:7-19).

• Jesus' early healing and teaching (Mk 3:14) ministry in Galilee now comes to a climax in this summary unit. Despite the call to silence, news about Jesus' epiphanic glory spreads far and wide.

Mk 3:7. Mark has provided a typical Markan location: πρὸς τὴν θάλασσαν; (Peabody, *Mark as Composer, 95, 66); cf.* παρὰ τὴν θάλασσαν (Peabody, *Mark as Composer,* 15, 39).

• References to the "withdrawal" (ἀνεχώρησεν) of Jesus and others is typical of Matthew; it occurs ten times there, once in Mark in this parallel passage (Mt 12:15//Mk 3:7), and nowhere else in the Synoptic Gospels. This is a strong piece of linguistic evidence of Mark's direct literary dependence upon the text of Matthew.

• At the same time, the Greek words Mark uses for a "great multitude" (πολύ + πλῆθος) appear only six times in the NT: four times in Luke-Acts and twice in this Markan parallel (Lk 6:17//Mk 3:7-8). This is almost as strong a piece of literary evidence of Mark's direct literary dependence upon Luke.

Mk 3:7-8. Mark's text also appears to be a combination of the list of cities and regions in Lk 6:17 ("a great multitude" from Judea, Jerusalem, Tyre, and Sidon) with others taken from Mt 4:25 ("many crowds" from Galilee, Jerusalem, and "across the Jordan"). To these, Mark probably adds a unique reference to Idumea (Mk 3:8, absent in several manuscripts including W, Θ, f^l), but even without this Markan addition, the Markan list of places of origin of the crowds that followed Jesus is the most impressive such list in the Synoptics (cf. Mt 12:15, Mt 4:25, Lk 6:17, and Mk 3:7-8).

• But Mark, in agreement with Luke, does not share the continuation of Matthew's summary; i.e., a lengthy quotation from scripture introduced by a fulfillment of prophecy formula so typical of Matthew (Mt. 12:17-21).

Mk 3:9. The verse is a Markan composition that functions to anticipate the boat that is supplied to Jesus on account of the crowds at Mk 4:1//Mt 13:2. (Peabody, *Mark as Composer,* 96, 67) The diminutive (in this case, "little boat") is characteristic of Mark.[21] The phrase διὰ τὸν ὄχλον meaning "on account of the crowd" is also characteristic of Mark (Peabody, *Mark as Composer,* 73, 58)

Mk 3:10. The word μάστιξ appears three times in Mark (3:10, 5:29, 34), once in Luke (7:21), once in Acts (22:24), and once in Hebrews (11:36), but nowhere else in the NT. The appearance of this vocabulary item here may indicate Markan composition.

---

[21] Neirynck, *Minor Agreements,* 285.

Mk 3:11. This verse reflects some interesting verbal parallels to Lk 4:41, although the Lukan literary context for these words is different (cf. Mk 1:32-34//Mt 8:16-17//Lk 4:40-41). However, when Mark made use of Lk 4:40-41 at Mk 1:32, he omitted the words, "crying out and saying 'You are the Son of God.'" These are precisely the words from Luke 4:41 that now appear at Mk 3:11. Mark seems to have moved this affirmation of Jesus as the Son of God to the present context to explain Jesus' command of silence to the unclean spirits, and to prepare for the call and commissioning of the twelve.

Mk 3:12. Mark concludes this pericope with the same charge to silence as in Mt 12:16 with one major exception, the addition of πολλά adverbial, which is characteristic of Mark (Peabody, *Mark as Composer,* 100, 67).

¶ 20. Jesus Makes Twelve Disciples to Be with Him to Preach and Cast Out Demons
(Mt 10:1-4) =========>   **Mk 3:13-19**   **<=========Lk 6:12-16**
    (Mt 5:1)

And Jesus goes up on a mountain and calls those whom he wanted and they came to him. And he made a company of twelve men who would be with him and whom he could send out to preach and to cast out demons. And the twelve he made his disciples were named: Simon whom he called Peter, and the brothers James and John, the sons of Zebedee, and he called them Boanerges which means sons of thunder, and Andrew and Philip and Bartholomew and Matthew and Thomas and James the son of Alphaeus, and Thaddeus and Simon the Canaanite and Judas Iscariot, who betrayed him.

General Observations. After the Markan version of the gathering of crowds and the healing of many in Mk 3:7-12, Mark narrated the call and commissioning of "the twelve" closest followers [apostles] of Jesus. For Mark's use of Matthew and Luke in this pericope, consult the general observations for the previous pericope, (cf. Synopsis 19). Mark here conflates Lk 6:12-16 with Mt 10:1-4. In addition, there are a few echoes of Mt 5:1. Mark's use of the opening words of the Sermon on the Mount in Matthew would be appropriate here since Mark's slightly earlier use of Lk 6:19 at Mk 3:11 brought Mark to the opening of Luke's comparable Sermon on the Plain (Lk 6:20-7:1).

• If Mark used Mt 4:24-25 from the introduction to the Sermon on the Mount (Mt 4:23-5:2) at Mk 3:7-8, then it is reasonable to assume that Mark also knew the setting for this sermon. If so, Mk 3:13 reflects the setting of Jesus "going up into the mountain" at Mt 5:1. Mark's account also reflects Luke's setting "on the mountain" (Lk 6:12) which, as in Mark, introduces his version of the call of the twelve apostles (Lk 6:12-16).

Mk 3:13-14. Using very carefully chosen terminology Mark emphasizes that Jesus called those whom he desired, made twelve disciples/apostles to be with him (cf. Mk 5:18), and sent them out to preach and to cast out demons (cf. Mk 1:32-39, 6:7-13).

• The reference to how Jesus "made" (ἐποίησεν) the Twelve is striking (cf. Mk 1:17 and 1:3). The formation of the Twelve is a product of divine action, and thus their potential failure raises the stakes not only for the outcome of the story but also for the fulfillment of God's promises.

• The designation, "apostles," for the Twelve disciples is Lukan (Lk 6:13, 9:10, 11:49, 17:5, 22:14 and 24:10). The two times Mark uses the designation "apostles" for "the Twelve" are both taken over from Luke (Lk 6:13//Mk 3:14, Lk 9:10//Mk 6:30). This is further evidence of Mark's literary dependence upon the text of Luke.

• From this point on, Mark will regularly portray Jesus as giving this group of disciples esoteric instruction—a key element of the Markan overlay (Mk 4:10-12, 7:17-23, 9:28-29, 10:10-12) although this motif is not entirely unique to Mark (Mt 13:10-17, Lk 8:8-10).

Mk 3:16-19. For his list of the names of Jesus' "apostles" in Mk 3:14-19, Mark prefers Matthew's order and list of names, but recounts them in the accusative in agreement with Luke (against the nominative in Matthew).[22]

• Only Mark says that Jesus designated the two sons of Zebedee as "sons of thunder" (Mk 3:17). Interestingly, this unique Markan detail allows scholars to recognize a reference to Mk 3:17 in the work of Justin Martyr (*Dial. Tryph.*, 106.9-10), who more frequently quotes Matthew and Luke than Mark and who often actually quotes conflated texts of Matthew and Luke.[23] This is the earliest clear reference to Mark in the church fathers. Justin lived from approximately 100 to approximately 165 CE.

---

[22] Cf. Meijboom, *A History and Critique,* 178.

[23] Arthur J. Bellinzoni, *The Sayings of Jesus in the Writings of Justin Martyr* (Supplements to Novum Testamentum 17; Leiden: E. J. Brill, 1967).

Summary

With the selection of the Twelve Mark has concluded a part of his Gospel that focuses on the call to discipleship. As well as being called to be exemplars of the pattern of Jesus' ministry ("preaching and casting out demons"), the Twelve will become the beneficiaries of special esoteric teaching, usually in a house. Despite these privileges the disciples will not be immune from colossal failures.

PART THREE

JESUS' WISDOM AND POWER

Overview

Jesus has constituted his true family through the selection of the Twelve. Now Mark proceeds to narrate the heart of the Galilean ministry of Jesus. A central focus of Mark's narrative is the repeated emphasis that only Jesus' true family, the disciples, are given the capacity to understand his wisdom and power (cf. Mk 3:31-35).

This part stands between the call of the Twelve (Mk 3:13-19) and their commissioning (Mk 6:7-13). The part consists of two major sections, one characterized by an emphasis on Jesus' wisdom (Mk 4:1-4:34), the other by an emphasis on his power (Mk 4:35-5:43). The retrospective questions in the concluding story of this part focus precisely on these two features of Jesus and his ministry.

The introduction to the part sharpens the distinction between Jesus' true family and his opponents (Mk 3:20-35). Jesus' true family are those who do God's will, while his opponents are those who claim he is possessed by an unclean spirit. The dialogue also introduces the major themes of wisdom and power. In section one of the part, the Parables Discourse, Jesus' wisdom is emphasized (Mk 4:1-34). Section two illustrates Jesus' power over the creation, the unseen world, sickness, and death (Mk 4:35-5:43). For the conclusion of the part, Mark uses Matthew's story of Jesus' rejection at Nazareth as a retrospective narrative on Jesus' wisdom and power (Mk 6:1-6a).

The structure of the part may be conveniently viewed with the following diagram:

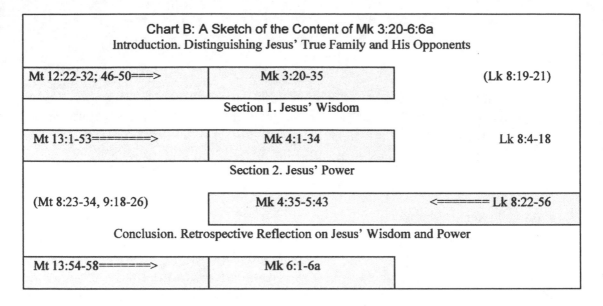

Chart B: A Sketch of the Content of Mk 3:20-6:6a		
Introduction. Distinguishing Jesus' True Family and His Opponents		
Mt 12:22-32; 46-50===>	Mk 3:20-35	(Lk 8:19-21)
Section 1. Jesus' Wisdom		
Mt 13:1-53=======>	Mk 4:1-34	Lk 8:4-18
Section 2. Jesus' Power		
(Mt 8:23-34, 9:18-26)	Mk 4:35-5:43	<======= Lk 8:22-56
Conclusion. Retrospective Reflection on Jesus' Wisdom and Power		
Mt 13:54-58=======>	Mk 6:1-6a	

Central to the development of Mark's Story of Jesus in this part is Jesus' announcement to the Twelve, "To you has been given the secret of the kingdom of God." (Mk 4:10-11). The story about Jesus' true family (Mk 3:13-35) prepares for this announcement. The Parable of the Sower and its interpretation, which surround this announcement (Mk 4:1-9; 13-20), help to interpret it. In the Parable of the Sower, Mark emphasizes that the hearers are to hear the message of the fate of the seed sown on different soils. And in the interpretation Mark tells his readers what they are to hear. They are to hear "the Word," which for Mark is equivalent to "the Gospel."

Once the assertion is made that the disciples are the ones who see and hear, a question comes to the fore: "Will the disciples indeed be among those who see, hear, and understand, or will they be overcome by the desire of other things and not bear fruit?" (cf. Mk 4:1-20). They hear Jesus' wisdom, but fail to understand. They see the great acts of Jesus' power (Mk 4:35-5:43), but they are afraid (cf. Mk 4:41). Even the homefolks of Jesus did not see or understand (cf. Mk 6:6). The reader of Mark's story is led to wonder, "Will the disciples ever come to understand the nature of the kingdom?"

Throughout the part, the impression grows that Jesus is in a momentous confrontation with Satan (Mk 3:27), and the Evil One is not prepared to relinquish easily. Nevertheless, the parables of growth (Mk 4:1-34) give assurances that despite present ambiguity and endangerment to the harvest, in the end the kingdom will come. Evil will be defeated. God's promises will come to fulfillment.

INTRODUCTION: JESUS' TRUE FAMILY AND HIS OPPONENTS. MK 3:20-35

¶ 21. Jesus Responds to Accusations That He Is Possessed

Matt 12:22-32=>	Mk 3:20-30	Luke 11:14-23
(Matt 9:32-34)		(Luke 12:10)

Jesus comes home and again the crowd gathers, keeping Jesus so busy he can't even eat. And when close associates heard he was back, they came to get him, for there was talk that, "He is beside himself." However, the scribes who had come down from Jerusalem were saying, "He is possessed by Beelzebul. He casts demons out because he obeys their leader." Summoning them to him he began to say, "How can Satan cast out Satan? If a kingdom or a family is divided against itself, it can't last. And if Satan is divided against himself, he won't last, but will come to an end. No one can enter the home of a strong man and steal his belongings without first tying him up. Now listen closely: every sin and every blasphemy will be forgiven the sons of men except one — whoever blasphemes against the Holy Spirit remains unforgiven forever, being guilty of an eternal sin (for some were saying "Jesus is possessed by an unclean spirit!")."

General Observations. At the end of his version of the section on the gathering of the crowds, the healing of many (Mk 3:7-12//Lk 6:17-19), and the call of the twelve disciples (Mk 3:13-19//Lk 6:12-16), which Mark has reordered vis-à-vis Luke by conflating Lk 6:6-19 with Mt 12:15-16 and the similar Matthean unit at Mt 4:23-5:1, Mark encounters the beginning of Luke's Sermon on the Plain (Lk 6:20-7:1). Having already passed over the similar Sermon on the Mount in Matthew (Mt 4:23-7:29, cf. Lk 4:31-32//Mk 1:21-22), Mark also omits the Sermon on the Plain, but moves from Luke back to Matthew at the point where he last made use of Matthew (Mk 12:16//Mk 3:12). From there, omitting the Matthean "proof from prophecy" (Mt 12:17-21) as is customary for Mark, he follows Matthew's order for the next pericope, the Beelzebul Controversy (Mt 12:22ff.//Mk 3:20ff.) .

• Most of the wording is taken from Matthew, with only slight blending with Luke.

• Mark has composed this literary unit by constructing an *inclusio* that focuses attention on the charge that an unclean spirit possesses Jesus. The opening and closing members of the *inclusio*, as well as a similarly constructed interim statement, contain uses of ἔλεγον + ὅτι + an accusation of demon possession leveled against Jesus (Mk 3:21, 3:30; cf. Mk 3:22).

Synopsis 2: Three Similar Accusations Against Jesus at Mk 3:21, 22, and 30.		
Mark 3:21	Mark 3:22	Mark 3:30
‹3:21› καὶ ἀκούσαντες οἱ παρ᾽ αὐτοῦ ἐξῆλθον κρατῆσαι αὐτόν· ἔλεγον γὰρ ὅτι ἐξέστη.	‹3:22› καὶ οἱ γραμματεῖς οἱ ἀπὸ Ἱεροσολύμων καταβάντες ἔλεγον ὅτι Βεελζεβοὺλ ἔχει καὶ ὅτι ἐν τῷ ἄρχοντι τῶν δαιμονίων ἐκβάλλει τὰ δαιμόνια.	‹3:30› ὅτι ἔλεγον, Πνεῦμα ἀκάθαρτον ἔχει.

Thus Mark has focused the unit on the demon possession charge: Jesus is accused, first by some close to him of being beside himself, and then by the scribes who came down from Jerusalem, of being possessed. In the course of the story, as Mark narrates it, Jesus is not *only* accused of healing by the agency of Beelzebul, the prince of demons (in agreement with Matthew and Luke), but even of "having Beelzebul" dwelling within. This contrasts with the scene at Jesus' baptism where the *Spirit* is said to have come down "into him" (Mk 1:10). In this Markan context, Jesus is accused of a demon possession more extreme than any other recorded in the NT.

Mk 3:20. Opening this literary unit is a scene change, "then he went into a house." This is a Markan compositional device (Peabody, *Mark as Composer,* 42, 47).

• The verse also includes another Markan πάλιν retrospective that refers to "crowds coming together again," looking back to Mk 1:45, 2:1-2, and 2:13. Later contexts where similar motifs appear include Mk 4:1-2, 8:1, 10:1.

• A third Markan compositional feature within the verse is the phrase, "so that they could not even eat" (Mk 3:20, cf. Mk 6:31; Peabody, *Mark as Composer,* 105, 69). All of these Markan redactional features are absent from the parallel contexts in Matthew and Luke, suggesting that the entire verse is a Markan composition added to the tradition received from Matthew and Luke. On the Two Document Hypothesis the verse is a remarkable "minor agreement" in omission. It is one of the features of this story that has often caused advocates of the Two Document Hypothesis to resort to theories of "Mark-Q" overlaps.

Mk 3:21-22. Pericope 22 (Mk 3:31-35) may suggest that "those around him" (οἱ παρ' αὐτοῦ) in Mk 3:21 means Jesus' family. If so, at this point in the Markan narrative Jesus' family or his relatives came out to get him. Arguing against the view that οἱ παρ' αὐτοῦ are Jesus' relatives is the fact that, in Mark's narrative, the family of Jesus is not actually said to arrive outside the house where Jesus has gone until Mk 3:31. The Greek phrase οἱ παρ'αὐτοῦ is ambiguous. It could refer to the people around Jesus observing the proceedings or it may refer to the Twelve. Given this ambiguity, it is questionable to claim that this verse is evidence for the hypothesis that Mark has a *Tendenz* to demean Jesus' earthly family.[1]

• As noted above, Mark creates an *inclusio* around the Beelzebul controversy that focuses the reader's attention on three accusations made against Jesus: (1) he is beside himself (Mk 3:21, the opening member of the *inclusio*), (2) he is possessed by Beelzebul (Mk 3:22), and (3) he is possessed by an unclean spirit (Mk 3:30). The first and third accusations have no parallels at all in Matthew or Luke. The second is a Markan modification of the shared text (Mt 12:24/9:24/Lk 11:15) which says that "Jesus cast out demons by Beelzebul, the prince of demons." Mark's modification here results in an intensification of the charge, "he has Beelzebul." Mark goes on to explain this with the phrase already present in the parallels in Matthew and Luke. Thus Mark, building on what was present in Matthew and Luke, has heightened the level of accusations against Jesus, thereby underscoring the gravity of the charge of possession.

• The first accusation, that Jesus is beside himself (ἐξέστη) seems to have its origin in the verb ἐξίσταντο in Mt 12:23. However, this verb no longer carries the idea of "amazement," but something more critical, like the charges in Mk 3:22 and 3:30. Note also the further agreements, καί and ἔλεγον, in Mt 12:23//Mk 3:21.

Mk 3:23. By having Jesus call to *them* (i.e., either the crowd, those around Jesus, or the scribes from Jerusalem) "in parables," Mark may already anticipate "the parables

---

[1] Contra J. S. Kloppenborg, "The Theological Stakes in the Synoptic Problem," in F. Van Segbroeck, et al., eds., *The Four Gospels: Festschrift Frans Neirynck* (Leuven: Leuven University Press, 1992), 93-120, esp. 97-104. For another perspective see John Painter, "When Is a House Not Home? Disciples and Family in Mark 3.13-35," *NTS* 45/4 (October 1999): 498-513.

chapter" (Mk 4:1-34). But here he is primarily referring to the parabolic teachings that follow in Mk 3:24-30.

Mk 3:24-30. From Mt 12:24ff., Mark narrates the Pharisees' slander about Satan, and Jesus' riddling reply. Matthew's version had been carefully structured. He had expanded the Beelzebul story from Mt 9 to prove that Jesus possesses the Spirit as promised in the formula citation of Isa 42. Matthew has Jesus say that divided things do not stand. If Jesus is Satan's agent, then his kingdom is divided and will not stand. The Pharisees' argument would then be patently absurd. Mark expands upon the absurdity of the charge by adding that, if true, it would mean that Satan's kingdom was breaking up and coming to an end (ἀλλὰ τέλος ἔχει, Mk 3:26). But of course it did not. The only way to defeat Satan is to do what Jesus is doing: invade his household (Mk 3:27). Thus it is nothing short of blasphemy to say that Jesus is possessed of Satan (Mk 3:22, 28-30). But by following Luke, who had displaced Mt 12:28, Mark loses the fundamental thread of the Beelzebul argument; that is, Jesus possesses the Holy Spirit and the accusation is a calumny against God himself.[2] Thus the closing lines, Mk 3:28-30, require the assertion that Jesus possesses the Holy Spirit and not Beelzebul in order to make sense. In Matthew it is clear that they have called the Holy Spirit Beelzebul, but in Mark that is not clear at all.

• Mark's version of the Beelzebul controversy has posed considerable difficulty for the Two Source Hypothesis because it contains a massive network of agreements of Matthew and Luke against Mark. B. H. Streeter even felt compelled once to postulate a "Mk - Q" overlap here.[3] The way Mk 3:20-30 has been viewed here is not clear from the displays of the parallels in other synopses. It is crucial that the reader consult our synopsis closely with respect to this passage. It attempts to display this evidence more helpfully, particularly from the perspective of the Two Gospel Hypothesis. There is, in fact, a need for a variety of new synopses based upon other source theories because earlier synopses, constructed for different purposes, have displayed the relevant evidence in an atomistic and fragmentary way.

---

[2] It is, of course, well known that "blasphemy" in Judaism was limited to accusation against God, directly or indirectly, so it is appropriate in the Beelzebul context but disputable in the trial of Jesus context. See G. Kittel and G. Friedrich, eds., *Theological Dictionary of the New Testament*, (trans. G. Bromiley; Grand Rapids: Eerdmans, 1985), 107-8.

[3] B. H. Streeter, "V. St. Mark's Knowledge and Use of Q," in W. Sanday, ed., *Studies in the Synoptic Problem* (Oxford: Clarendon Press, 1911), 166-83. Contrast Streeter, *The Four Gospels* (London: Macmillan, 1924), 186-91, 209-11, 305-6. This is one of Fuchs' passages that requires a Deutero-Marcus.

Mk 3:30. We divide the text here because Jesus' answer to the scribes is one thing (Mk 3:23-30); his answer to his family, another (Mk 3:31-35).

¶ 22. Who is Jesus' True Family?

Mt 12:46-50=======>   Mk 3:31-35   (Lk 8:19-21)

Jesus' mother and brothers were standing outside calling to him to come outside. The crowd around Jesus was saying, "Your mother and brothers are outside and they are seeking you." Answering, Jesus says to them, "Who are my mother and brothers?" After he had looked around at everyone seated there, he answered his question, "Behold *here* are my mother and my brothers! Whoever would do the will of God is my brother and my sister and my mother!"

General Observations. Mark continues to follow the order and language of Matthew, showing his knowledge of Luke only by the inclusion of a few small but sometimes telling details. The introduction to this part, which Mark began in Mk 3:20, comes to a climax here in the story about Jesus' true family (Mt 12:46-40//Mk 3:31-35, cf. Lk 8:19-21 and Lk 11:27-28). Mark omits the teachings in Mt 12:33-45 that were, like the Beelzebul controversy, linked by Matthew to the Isaiah 42 text in Mt 12:17-21. These same sayings appear in a different order and in at least two separated literary contexts in Luke (Lk 6:43-45, 11:29-32, and 11:24-26).

The effect of the Markan omission of Mt 12:33-45 is that Mark is able to attach the story of Jesus' true family directly to the end of the so-called "Beelzebul controversy." In Mk 3:22-30 Jesus is seen as actively destroying Satan's household. Now he speaks about the household of his family that will be characterized, not by filial or ethnic connections, but by dedicated discipleship.

Mk 3:31. In contrast to both Matthew and Luke, Mark begins this story by telling his readers that members of Jesus' family, standing outside, "sent to him summoning him" (cf. Mt 12:46, where members of the family are said to be "seeking to speak with him," and Lk 8:19, where they are "not able to reach him").

Mk 3:32-34. With a typically Markan addition of graphic detail, Mark says that Jesus "looked around the circle of those seated around him" (καὶ περιβλεψάμενος τοὺς κύκλῳ καθημένους, Mk 3:34). In accord with Mark's stylistic penchant for repeating language within a relatively short literary context, these people would seem to be members of the same crowd mentioned at Mk 3:32 (καὶ ἐκάθητο περὶ αὐτὸν ὄχλος).

Mark 3:32 and Mk 3:34 both include a form of κάθημαι + περὶ αὐτόν. Both also represent Markan supplements to Matthew and Luke.

• If the words καὶ αἱ ἀδελφαί σου are accepted as the more original text of Mk 3:32, one would conclude that they are also a Markan supplement, intended to lay the groundwork for the conclusion at Mk 3:35 where "sister" is included, along with brother and mother, in agreement with Mt 12:50.

Mk 3:35. On the Two Gospel Hypothesis, Mark's version of this teaching, "whoever should do *the will of God*," is a conflation of Matthew's "*will of* my father" (Mt 12:50) with Luke's "*word of God*." (Lk 8:21 and Lk 11:28). By means of this conflation, Mark included only those words or very similar words that are found in Mt 12:50, or Lk 8:21, or both. Although Mark stresses the theme of doing God's will via Jesus' teaching much less than Matthew, it is still important to him and his compressed version of this section of Matthew does highlight the concept.

SECTION ONE: JESUS WISDOM. MK 4:1-34

¶ 23. Jesus Teaches the Parable of the Sower
Mt 13:1-9==========>   **Mk 4:1-9**   **<============Lk 8:4-8**

Again Jesus began to teach beside the sea and such a large crowd came to him he got into a boat, and the crowd was gathered along the edge of the water. And he began teaching them in many parables, saying, "Listen! There was once a farmer who sowed his seed. Some of the seed fell on a path and the birds came and ate it. Other seed fell on rocky ground where there wasn't much soil. It sprang up quickly but the sun burned it out since it had shallow roots. Other seed landed among weeds and the weeds prevented the new plants from growing. However, other seed fell on good soil and bore a great harvest, thirty- and sixty- and a hundred-fold. He who has ears to hear, let him hear!"

General Observations. To open this new section Mark continues to follow the order and the language of Matthew for the Parable of the Sower.

• Following a typical Markan πάλιν scene change ("again he began to teach them beside the sea"; Mk 4:1-2, against Mt 13:1), Mark begins his teaching parables unit with the story of the sower who sowed the seed. For all three evangelists this parable is an exemplar parable, which may suggest that it was treated as a model parable for instruction in widespread areas of the church. Mark has kept close to the wording of both Matthew and Luke in his composition of this parable. However, in blending together Matthew and Luke, Mark has managed to articulate a fundamental theological idea which also comes out in the interpretation (Mk 4:13-20); the seed sown by the Sower is "the word," which for Mark is the fundamental equivalent of "the Gospel." "The Word" which Jesus and the twelve are proclaiming, like the production of the different soils on which the seed falls, will meet with widely varied results.

Mk 4:1-2. The project of the sower is endangered by the lack of productivity of three kinds of soil. But, surprisingly, a bountiful harvest still ensues because in God's mysterious purpose there is some good soil. Although faithlessness and betrayal put God's promises in jeopardy, the kingdom will come. Mark has set the scene for his parables chapter with language that is typical of the author. For instance, Mark says that:

Jesus "began to teach by the sea again (πάλιν)" (Mk 4:1 [cf. Mk 2:13; 1:16, 1:21, 3:7], Peabody, *Mark as Composer,* introduction and 84, 62; 67, 54). In fact, Mark supplemented the texts of Matthew and Luke in Mk 4:1-2 with three references to Jesus' teaching: (1) "And again he began to teach," (2) "and he was teaching them," and (3) "and he was saying to them in his teaching". On the Two Document Hypothesis, how is one to explain how Matthew and Luke, independently of one another, systematically stripped the introduction to this "parables chapter" in Mark of its most characteristic feature, a "teaching motif"? All three of these phrases that represent Markan supplements in this Markan context are also characteristics of Mark's text (Peabody, *Mark as Composer,* 111, 70; 84, 62; 117, 72). In fact, the first two of these three phrases have the highest probability of coming from the hand of the author (Peabody, *Mark as Composer,* 161-66)

"A great crowd gathers to him" (Mk 4:1 [cf. Mk 1:45, 2:2, 2:13, 3:7-8, 3:20; Peabody, *Mark as Composer,* Table I, 155, and Table K, 157).

Then Jesus gets into "the boat" that was held in readiness for him earlier in order to protect him from the crowd (Mk 4:1 [cf. Mk 3:9], Peabody, *Mark as Composer,* 96, 67).

• The reference to Jesus "sitting by the sea and teaching" may echo Luke 5:3 where Jesus is said to have "sat out of the boat and was teaching." (cf. the synopsis for ¶ 7).

• Although "speaking in parables" occurs already at Mk 3:23, the words, "And he taught them many things in parables" in Mk 4:2 also serves as the opening of an *inclusio* that concludes with Mk 4:33-34.

Mk 4:3. Only Mark prefaces the Parable of the Sower with the imperative, Ἀκούετε, constructing a frame around the parable that is completed by Mk 4:9//Mt 13:9//Lk 8:9, "Let him who has ears to hear (ἀκούειν), let him hear (ἀκουέτω)."

• The sentence Καὶ ἐδίδασκεν αὐτοὺς ἐν παραβολαῖς πολλὰ καὶ ἔλεγεν αὐτοῖς ἐν τῇ διδαχῇ αὐτοῦ, Ἀκούετε also serves as a theme in Mark's Gospel that is repeated almost verbatim at Mk 12:38 by the comparable phrase, Καὶ ἐν τῇ διδαχῇ αὐτοῦ ἔλεγεν· Βλέπετε . . . (cf. Peabody, *Mark as Composer,* 117, 72). The first of these comparable phrases appears just prior to the first of Mark's story parables, and the second appears at Mk 12:38 at the end of a series of four controversy stories (Mk 11:27-12:37). That series includes the last story parable in Mark's Gospel, the Parable of the Tenants in the Vineyard (Mk 12:1-12). Could these comparable thematic expressions which admonish the disciples of Jesus both to "hear/listen" and to "see/watch out" delimit an even larger *inclusio* around all of the parables that Mark chose to include in his Gospel? If so, Mark has stressed the "see" and "hear" themes in a very different way than Matthew did in Mt 13.

Mk 4:4-7. After the initial ὃ μέν construction (Mk 4:4), Mark uses the singular ἄλλο to describe the sowing of seed, but for the last in the series Mark uses a plural in accord with Matthew's consistent use of the plural, ἄλλα. On the other hand, in telling this same parable, Luke consistently utilizes ἕτερον in the singular, and connects the various sowings with the simple copula, καί. Mark, therefore, agrees with Matthew on the use of a form of ἄλλος, but with Luke on use of the singular (cf. Luke's ἕτερος). In a complementary fashion, Mark agrees with Luke on the use of καί, thereby also disagreeing with Matthew's use of δέ. The final appearance of ἄλλα in the plural in Mk 4:8, in verbatim agreement with Mt 13:8, may be an example of what Mark Goodacre and others have come to identify as evidence of "fatigue" on the part of one evangelist and, thereby, a clear indication of Mark's dependence on Matthew in this context.[4] That is, Mark failed to make his usage of ἄλλο consistent because he inadvertently followed Matthew in this case.

---

[4] Mark Goodacre, "Fatigue in the Synoptics," *NTS* 44 (1998): 45-58.

• Note also the repeated use of ἐν in Mk 4:8, again differing from Matthew.

Mk 4:8. Mark's additional comment here about the seed ἀναβαίνοντα καὶ αὐξανόμενα helps to emphasize his theme of growth in the collection of three parables of the "growing seed." Compare a similar Markan change and expansion of αὐξάνω in Mt 13:32//Lk 13:19 to ἀναβαίνει καὶ γίνεται in Mk 4:32.

• Mark also reverses the numbers in Matthew's ending of the Parable of the Sower (100-60-30) to bring out the steadily increasing process of growth of the Kingdom (30-60-100).

¶ 24. Jesus Explains Why He Teaches Outsiders in Parables
Mt 13:10-11, 13-17 ====>   Mk 4:10-12   <------------------- Lk 8:9-10

Later, when he was alone, those around him with the twelve asked him about the parables. And he said, "To you is given the mystery of the kingdom of God, but to those outside all teachings are in riddles in order that seeing they might see but not perceive and hearing might hear but not understand lest they should repent and God forgive them their sins."

General Observations. Mark continues to follow Matthew's order of pericopae. However, he carefully conflates the wording of Mt 13:10-11 with that of Lk 8:9-10a in composing Mk 4:10-11. At that point, Mark comes to Mt 13:12, which Luke had already moved to Lk 8:18. Intending to utilize Lk 8:18 later, Mark omits the parallel at Mt 13:12 and draws from the language of Mt 13:13 in composing Mk 4:12.

Mk 4:10. As usual, Mark adds detail to the tradition he received from Matthew and Luke, Καὶ ὅτε ἐγένετο κατὰ μόνας and οἱ περὶ αὐτὸν σὺν τοῖς δώδεκα.

• Mark's familiar scene-change is typical of his overlay: public teaching followed by secret interpretation to his disciples.

• The phrase οἱ περὶ αὐτοῦ is a typical Markan alteration of οἱ μαθηταί in Mt 13:10/Lk 8:9 (cf. Mk 3:34 note above).

• Mark presents Jesus as intentionally concealing the message of salvation from "those outside" by speaking to them only "in parables." In his theory of parable interpretation Mark enunciates the major theme of mysterious election that will run through all of these parables, viz., the hardening of "those outside" while "you," i.e., those inside, are given the "secret of the kingdom of God" clearly and plainly.

Mk 4:11-12. In contrast to both of his sources (Mt 13:11//Lk 8:10), which refer to the "mysteries" (plural) of the kingdom, Mark discusses the single "mystery." Mark appears to use the singular "mystery" in the same way he utilizes "the gospel," "the word," and "the time" absolutely. Mark's usage has some affinities with the Deuteropauline tradition, and this has led even advocates of Markan priority such as Helmut Koester to affirm the secondary nature of Mark's text, in this case, to the parallels in Matthew and Luke.[5]

• In Mt 13 the theory of parable interpretation is very similar to the interpretative use of the prophets by members of the Qumran community. That is, one can read the parables for clues about what will happen in the impending judgment.[6] Matthew uses this theory for every interpretation of a parable in his Gospel. Luke retained Matthew's language here even though he did not share the theory. Nor did he consider the connection of Mt 13:16-17 to what immediately precedes it to be important, but removed those verses to another context (Lk 10:23-24). Given this difference in his sources, Mark is creative in developing his own theory of parable interpretation to produce a different emphasis. He assumes that there is a deep divide between those inside, who are given the secret, and those outside, for whom everything happens in riddles. His emphasis is that without the work of God one will never come to see the connection between Jesus' mission and the kingdom of God.

• Mark concludes the statement on parable interpretation with the line, "lest they should turn and be forgiven," which is not found in either the Matthean allusion to the Isaiah 6 text in Mt 13:13 nor in the Lukan parallel, Lk 8:10. There is serious dispute over whether the original text of Matthew included vss. 14-15. If Mark's version of Matthew did include the full citation and LXX text, then he has abbreviated it considerably. If his version of Matthew only included Mt 13:13,16-17, then Mark has added the line about turning and being forgiven, probably from memory of this popular early Christian testimonium (Jn 12:40, Acts 28:26-27).[7] In either case, the Markan addition (or revision)

---

[5] Helmut Koester, "History and Development of Mark's Gospel (From Mark to *Secret Mark* and "Canonical" Mark)," in Corley, ed., *Colloquy,* 35-57.

[6] See L. Cope, *Matthew: A Scribe* (Washington: The Catholic Biblical Association of America, 1976), 16-18.

[7] See K. Stendahl, *The School of St. Matthew* (Philadelphia: Fortress Press, 1968), 129-32.

highlights his view that Jesus' use of mysterious teaching was part of the divine plan for Jesus' career.

¶ 25. Jesus Explains the Secret Meaning of the Parable of the Sower
Mt 13:18-23==========>   Mk 4:13-20   <===========Lk 8:11-15

And Jesus says to them, "You don't understand *this* parable? How will you understand all of the others? The "farmer" sows the word everywhere. Some people are like the path where the seed fell. Satan sees them and comes immediately and takes the word sown in them. Other people are like rocky ground. When they hear the word, they react immediately with joy, but then they give up, especially if they are persecuted because of the word. Still others hear the word, but are more interested in wealth and the pleasures of this world, and these stifle the word. However, those who hear the word and accept it bear fruit thirty- and sixty- and a hundred-fold.

General Observations. After omitting Mt 13:16-17, as had Luke previously, Mark next incorporates the interpretation of the Parable of the Sower (Mt 13:18-23//Mk 4:13-20//Lk 8:11-15) in general agreement with both of his sources.

• In his version of the interpretation, Mark does not concentrate on "the word of the kingdom" (Mt 13:19) or "the word of God" (Lk 8:11), but simply on "the Word" used absolutely (Mk 4:14, 15bis, 16, 17, 18, 19, 20). This conforms with Mark's preference for "the gospel," "the time," and, as we just observed in Mk 4:11, "the mystery," all used absolutely. Nevertheless, the Markan interpretation of the parable has some awkwardness about it. The focus of the parable is on the sower's random sowing in different kinds of soil and the resulting differences in the harvest. The interpretation shifts attention to the reception of the seed (="the Word") by the various kinds of soil, which allegorically become different kinds of people. That is, the emphasis shifts from the action of the sower to the reception of the seed by the soils in this interpretation. The shift was already present in his sources, but Mark's focus on *the word* has intensified it.

• In general, Mark follows the common wording of Matthew and Luke. But where they differ, at least four times, Mark goes his own way. First, when Matthew says, "the word of the kingdom" and Luke says, "the word of God," Mark simply writes "the word." Second, where Matthew utilizes "the evil one" and Luke, "the devil," Mark writes "Satan." Third, when Matthew emphasizes "understanding" and Luke "faithfulness," Mark omits any reference to either. Fourth, at the conclusion, when Matthew continues with his theme of "understanding" and Luke modifies this to "holding fast," Mark has "accepts" (Mk 4:20//Mt 13:23//Lk 8:15).

Mk 4:13. The verse is a Markan composition and represents a compromising general statement which agrees with Matthew in referring to several parables (Mt 13:1-53), but also with Luke in making reference to but one parable (cf. Lk 8:4-15). This verse also includes two uses of verbs meaning "to know," precisely the word that was omitted by Mark at Mk 4:10//Mt 13:11//Lk 8:10. This is a strong indication that the author of Mark knew the wording of Matthew and Luke's phrase about knowing the secrets of the kingdom.

• Matthew's use of ἀκούω in Mt 13:18 is influenced by the allusion to Isa 6:9-10 in Mt 13:13,16-17. Mark's use of οἴδατε breaks this connection between the theory of parable interpretation and the interpretation of the Parable of the Sower. Mark's fragmentary preservation of Matthew's careful exegetical interpretation of the parables is evidence of Mark's secondary character. The same is true of Matthew's use of "understand" in Mt 13:19 and 23, derived from the allusion to Isaiah 6 in Mt 13:13 and omitted by Mark (and Luke) in both cases.

Mk 4:20. Mark's reversal of the sequence of numbers in the Parable of the Sower is maintained here at the end of the interpretation. Mark continues to emphasize the theme of growth that characterizes his entire parables chapter.

¶ 26. A Lamp Is for a Lamp Stand; The Hidden Is to Be Manifested; Equal Measure and Future Gifts for the "Haves" and the "Have Nots"

(Mt 5:14-16, 10:26-27, 13:12)	Mk 4:21-25	<===========Lk 8:16-18
(Mt 6:22-23, 7:1-2) ====>		(Lk 6:37-38, Lk 11:33-36, Lk 12:2-3)

And he went on to say, "Nobody lights a lamp and then puts it under the bed or under a measuring vessel, does he? Isn't it to be placed on a stand? Likewise, God will not permit anything to remain hidden that will not be made manifest! So, take care. The way you treat others is the way you will be treated, and even more will be added. To him who has shall more be given, while to him who has not, even what he has will be taken away."

General Observations. Matthew next has the Parable of the Tares, which is not a parable of growth but the first in the series of six twinned kingdom parables in Mt 13. Mark, who wants to focus on growth parables, moves therefore to the collection of sayings in Lk 8:16-18 which immediately follow Luke's version of the interpretation of the Parable of the Sower (Lk 8:11b-15). We argued earlier in *Beyond the Q Impasse* that Lk 8:16-18 is a Lukan redactional construction made up of one excerpt from each of Matthew's first three discourses, in Matthew's order (Lk 8:16//Mt 5:15; Lk 8:17//Mt 10:26 and Lk 8:18//Mt 13:12 (cf. Mt 13:13). If that argument is sound, then most of Mk 4:21-25 represents a fragmentary preservation of a clearly Lukan compositional passage within the parallel passage in Mark. If so, this is clear evidence of Mark's literary dependence upon Luke in this context. The beginning of the concluding saying in Lk 8:18, "For whoever has, *it shall be given* to him, and whoever does not have, even what he seems to have, shall be taken from him" shares a common theme of "giving" with the collection of sayings in Lk 6:37-38. Within that context of the Sermon on the Plain, which Mark recently passed over (Mk 3:19-20), we read, "Do not judge, and you will not be judged; do not condemn, and you will not be condemned. Forgive, and you will be forgiven; *give, and it will be given to you.* A good measure, pressed down, shaken together, running over, will be put into your lap; for the measure you give will be the measure you get back" (cf. Mt 7:2, 7). Making a connection based on the term measuring, Mark inserts this last saying into his parallel to Lk 8:16-18 at Mk 4:24. Certainly this collection of sayings in Mark is cryptic, but they seem to make the same point as the parables of growth. Understanding the purposes of God in Jesus' ministry only develops from inauspicious beginnings. But, eventually, those who persevere will receive insight (cf. Mk 13:33-37).

• Mark has edited Lk 8:16-18 by inserting his characteristic phrase καὶ ἔλεγεν αὐτοῖς as an introduction (Mk 4:21a) and by breaking the Lukan unit into two parts by inserting a second καὶ ἔλεγεν αὐτοῖς at Mk 4:24 (Peabody, *Mark as Composer*, 89, 64). To conclude the first of his two-part unit, Mark also added the phrase εἴ τις ἔχει ὦτα ἀκούειν ἀκουέτω (concluding the ending of the sower parable in all three Gospels and thus emphasizing the theme of "hearing" that permeates Mark's entire unit on parables (Mk[3:20-21] 4:1-34).

Mk 4:21. Mark seems to have conflated a saying about a lamp "under a measuring vessel" (either from Mt 5:15, the Matthean contextual parallel to Lk 8:16, or from Lk 11:33, if the words ὑπὸ τὸν μόδιον are authentic there) with one about a lamp "under a cot" (which is found only in Lk 8:16).[8] If Mark conflated Lk 8:16 with Lk 11:33 at Mk

---

[8] Lk 11:33-36, like Lk 8:16-18 and Lk 11:53-12:2, on the Two Gospel Hypothesis, are Lukan redactional constructions based upon verses from Matthew that appear in separated literary contexts (Lk 8:16-18= Mt 5:15 + Mt 10:26 + Mt 13:12; Lk 11:33-36 = Mt 5:15-16 + Mt 6:22-23; Lk 11:53-12:3 = Mt 10:26(-27?) + Mt 16:1,

4:21, then he has not only demonstrated his tendency to conflate, but has also conflated two obviously Lukan redactional passages (See especially ἵνα οἱ εἰσπορευόμενοι + τὸ φῶς + βλέπωσιν in both Lukan verses) and, thereby, again clearly demonstrated his literary dependence not only upon the *text* of Luke, but upon the hand of the *author* of Luke.

¶ 27. God's "Harvest" Will Take Place

cf. Mt 13:24-30   Mk 4:26-29
Parable of Tares

And he said, "The Kingdom of God is like a farmer who scatters seed upon the ground and then goes to sleep and rises again, day and night. Soon the young shoots appear, then the growing stalk, then the first buds of grain, and finally the ripe, full heads of grain. Immediately, the farmer gets out his sickle because harvest time has come."

General Observations. Mark next includes a second parable of growing seed that is not in either of his sources. Although Matthew's Parable of the Tares is about seed and has a number of verbal similarities to Mk 4:26-29, Matthew's kingdom parable focuses primarily on the final separation of two types of plants that have grown from two types of seed, not on the growth of one kind of seed, as do the other two parables Mark utilizes in this series.

Mark generally does not include apocalyptic, judgment-oriented parables, but the linguistic similarities between the Parable of the Tares and the Parable of the Seed Growing Automatically may have prompted Mark to choose this parable from his special source material at this point. Certain striking linguistic similarities between Mt 13:24-30 and Mk 4:26-29 include the following:

> ➤ a form of λέγω (Mt 13:24//Mk 4:26)

> ➤ ἡ βασιλεία (Mt 13:24//Mk 4:26)

> ➤ a form of ἄνθρωπος (Mt 13:24//Mk 4:26)

> ➤ a form of καθεύδω (Mt 13:35//Mk 4:27)

> ➤ a form of σῖτος (Mt 13:25//Mk 4:28)

---

6 + Mt 23:1 and perhaps other fragments of Matthew). See David B. Peabody, "Luke's Sequential Use of the Sayings of Jesus from Matthew's Great Discourses: A Chapter in the Source-Critical Analaysis of Luke on the Two-Gospel (Neo-Griesbach) Hypothesis," in *Literary Studies in Luke-Acts* (ed. Richard P. Thompson and Thomas E. Phillips; Macon, Ga.: Mercer University Press, 1998), 37-58, esp. extended fn. 32 on pp. 47-48.

> a form of βλαστάνω (Mt 13:26//Mk 4:27) and

> a form of ὁ θερισμός (Mt 13:30//Mk 4:29).

• However, it does not appear that Mk 4:26-29 is a creation of the author of Mark. The general absence of linguistic characteristics typical of the author of Mark within Mk 4:26-28 suggests that the author is utilizing source material rather than composing. Perhaps the parallel to the tares in Mt above prompted Mark to choose the parable of the seed growing automatically from his own source tradition and insert it here.

Mk 4:26. Mark introduces this distinctive parable with the introductory formula that is typical of Mk 4:1-34, καὶ ἔλεγεν (Peabody, *Mark as Composer*, 89, 64).

• Mark's change of Matthew's ἡ βασιλεία τῶν οὐρανῶν to ἡ βασιλεία τοῦ θεοῦ is typical, and lessens the Semitic character of Mark's text in comparison with Matthew (Peabody, *Mark as Composer*, 13, 38).

• The substitution of the phrase, ἐπὶ τῆς γῆς for Matthew's ἐν τῷ ἀγρῷ αὐτοῦ (Mt 13:24) conforms with repeated usage of this phrase elsewhere in the text of Mark (Peabody, *Mark as Composer*, 82, 62; 118, 73; 201, 100).

Mk 4:27. The inclusion of καὶ ἐγείρηται contributes to the "resurrection motif," a key part of the overlay with which the author of Mark often enriches his narrative.

• Mark's use of the opposites "day and night" and "sleeping and rising" (καὶ καθεύδη καὶ ἐγείρηται) reflects common eschatological terminology similar to that used in Paul's argumentation in 1 Thess 5:1 10 and 1 Cor 15. It is not clear whether this is an echo of Paul's letter or if these terms are simply standard Christian metaphors in this milieu.

Mk 4:28. Matthew utilizes σῖτος four times, but Mark uses it only here (in rough parallel with one of Matthew's usages; Mt 13:25). This evidence would be consistent with the view that Mark is literarily dependent upon Matthew for the story.

Mk 4:29. Matthew utilizes the word harvest (θερισμός) six times. Mark uses this word only here (in parallel with one of Matthew's six usages [Mt 13:30]). This evidence would also be consistent with Mark's literary dependence upon Matthew.

• The use of εὐθύς is characteristic of Mark (Peabody, *Mark as Composer*, 5, 36) although the author usually prefers καὶ εὐθύς.

¶ 28. The Parable of the Mustard Seed
Mt. 13:31-32 =====>   Mk 4:30-32   (Lk. 13:18-19)

And he continued, saying, "With what parable shall we compare the kingdom of God? It is like a grain of mustard seed, the smallest of all the seeds when it is sown. But then it grows up and becomes the greatest of all shrubs, putting forth large branches so that birds of the air can make nests in its shade."

General Observations. Mark returns to Matthew for another "seed" parable to complete his collection of parables of growth. He makes some minor changes in this last seed parable and thus creates a series of agreements against Mt//Lk .

➤ πῶς ὁμοιώσωμεν at Mk 4:30 in contrast to ὁμοία ἐστίν at Mt 13:31//Lk 13:18.

➤ the relative pronoun alone in Mk 4:32 in contrast to ὅν λαβὼν ἄνθρωπος at Mt 13:31//Lk 13:19.

➤ ἀναβαίνει at Mk 4:32 in contrast to a form of αὐξάνω at Mt 13:32//Lk 13:19.

➤ ὑπὸ τὴν σκιὰν αὐτοῦ at Mk 4:32 in contrast to ἐν τοῖς κλάδοις αὐτοῦ at Mt 13:32//Lk 13:19.

➤ the Parable of the Leaven follows the Parable of the Mustard Seed immediately in Matthew and Luke but is absent altogether from Mark, probably because it is not a seed parable.

• Mark's additions are hints that reveal his particular understanding of this parable. For Mark, it is a miniature scenario which predicts the mysterious growth of Jesus' mission from "the smallest 'seed' on the earth" to its becoming "the greatest of all shrubs on the earth," "putting forth large branches" so the birds of the air (Gentiles?) can make nests in its "shade."

Mk 4:30. Mark again introduces this parable with καὶ ἔλεγεν (cf. *Composer* 89, 68 but see ἔλεγεν οὖν also in Lk 13:18).

• Mark, as usual, prefers Luke's "kingdom of God" to Matthew's circumlocution, "kingdom of the heavens."

Mk 4:31. The phrase, ἐπὶ τῆς γῆς, which appears as a Markan dualistic expression in this verse, is a frequent Markan supplement. (Peabody, *Mark as Composer,* 82, 62).

• Mark's change of Matthew's ἐν τῷ ἀγρῷ and Lk's εἰς κῆπον ἑαυτοῦ to ἐπὶ τῆς γῆς and the addition of the same phrase at the end of this verse are consistent with editorial changes found throughout Mark (cf. the note at Mk 4:26 in the discussion of the previous seed parable).

Mk 4:32. The more inclusive "under its shade" (ὑπὸ τὴν σκιὰν αὐτοῦ), which Mark has substituted for ἐν τοῖς κλάδοις αὐτοῦ, common to Matthew and Luke (cf. Dan 4:21 LXX, Theodotion), brings the language of the parable closer to that of Dan 4:12 LXX, Ezek 17:23 and Ezek 31:6.

¶ 29. Jesus Speaks Only in Parables to the Crowd
Mt 13:34-35==========>   Mk 4:33-34
(cf. Mk 4:2)

And with many similar parables Jesus was speaking the word to the crowd as they were able to hear it. Apart from parables, he wasn't saying anything to them. But when he was alone with his disciples, he would explain everything.

General Observations. Mark omits Matthew's Parable of the Leaven (Mt 13:33, cf. Lk 13:20-21). It is not a parable of growth, which is the focus of Mark's version of the parables. However, immediately following the Parable of the Leaven in Matthew, Mark finds a summary transition in Mt 13:34-35 which he reformulates into the conclusion of his unit and the closing member of the *inclusio* that began at Mk 4:1-2. With this, Mark concludes his description of Jesus' teaching "the Word" to the crowd only in parables, which are followed by private explanation to his disciples.

Mk 4:33. The addition of ὁ λόγος used absolutely to the text of Mt 13:34 to describe the content of the Christian message conforms with Markan literary style (cf. Peabody, *Mark as Composer,* 69, 55). This usage is particularly prominent in Mark's version of the interpretation of the Parable of the Sower (Mk 4:14//Mt 13:19, τὸν λόγον τῆς βασιλείας//Lk 8:11, ὁ λόγος τοῦ θεοῦ; Mk 4:15a, no parallels; Mk 4:15b//Lk 8:12; Mk 4:16//Mk 13:20//Lk 8:13; Mk 4:17//Mt 13:21; Mk 4:18//Mt 13:22a; Mk 4:19//Mt 13:22b; Mk 4:20//Mt 13:23//Lk 8:15). On the Two Gospel Hypothesis, in conformity with his preference for "the Word" used absolutely, Mark first changed Matthew's "word of the kingdom" (Mt 13:19) and Luke's "word of God" (Lk 8:11), which clarify their subsequent uses of "the Word" used absolutely in this literary context. Mark then adopted every occurrence of "the Word" used absolutely from Matthew, Luke, or both, and even added this usage to his version of the interpretation of the Parable of the Sower (cf. Mk 4:15a).

Mk 4:34. The motif of Jesus providing esoteric teaching to his disciples in private is a well known characteristic of the text of Mark (cf. Peabody, *Mark as Composer,* Table M, 158). Mark's use of this motif to conclude his parables chapter, however, may have been prompted by the quotation from Ps 78:2 in the parallel at Mt 13:35, particularly the note about "things hidden from the foundation of the world," a formulation which he omits.

SECTION TWO. JESUS' POWER. MK 4:35-5:43

¶ 30. Jesus Stills the Storm; The Disciples Still Do not Have Faith
(Mt 8:23-27)   **Mk 4:35-41**   **<===========Lk 8:22-25**

And he says to them in the evening of that same day, "Let's cross over to the other side." So, they get into a boat and head for the far side of the Sea of Galilee. A number of other boats accompany them. And a great windstorm comes up and begins to beat upon the little boat so that it began to fill with water. Now Jesus was asleep in the stern, lying on a cushion. The disciples wake him and say, "Teacher! Don't you care if we are destroyed?" Jesus then gets up, rebukes the wind and says to the sea, "Be still!" And the wind stops and there is a great calm. And he says to them, "Why are you so afraid? How is it you still do not have faith?" However, they were overwhelmed by great fear, saying to one another, "Who in the world is he? Both the wind and the sea obey him!"

General Observations. Mark has utilized only the parables of growth from Matthew's parable chapter. Mark omits the rest of Matthew's parables (tares, leaven, treasure, pearl, and dragnet—all part of a set of six paired kingdom parables probably taken from a source by Matthew). Instead of utilizing Mt 13:54-58, the story of Jesus' rejection in his hometown, Mark moves back to where he had been in Luke, Lk 8:18//Mk 4:25. The next story in Luke is Jesus' True Family (Lk 8:19-21), which Mark has already used in agreement with Matthew (Matt 12:46-50//Mk 3:31-35), so Mark moves forward to the next story in Luke, the Stilling the Storm (Lk 8:22-25). He then follows Luke's order in the presentation of four demonstrations of power in Mk 4:35-5:43//Lk 8:22-56. By doing this, Mark is able to follow-up his depiction of Jesus' wisdom in Mk 3:20-4:34 with a section that emphasizes Jesus' power over creation, the unseen world, sickness and death. To conclude this part of the Gospel, Mark goes back to the Matthean story of Jesus' rejection in his hometown (Mt 13:54-58) in accord with his demonstrable interest in retrospective passages.

• In general, Mark elaborates upon each of the four miracle stories he has adopted in order from Luke with numerous picturesque details, which also is a feature of his compositional technique. Some of the details contributed by Mark would include the following:

➤ Mk 4:36, "and other boats were with him;"

➤ Mk 4:38, "in the bow of the boat on a cushion;"

➤ Mk 5:3, "and no one could restrain him, even with a chain;"

➤ Mk 5:5, "night and day among the tombs and on the mountains he was always howling and bruising himself with stones;"

➤ Mk 5:13, "about two thousand" pigs;

➤ Mk 5:20, "and everyone marveled;"

➤ Mk 5:26, "She endured much under many physicians and had spent all that she had; and she was no better, but rather grew worse;"

➤ Mk 5:32, "and he was looking around to see the woman who had done this."

➤ Mk 5:41, "and he says to her, 'Talitha koum,' which, being translated means 'Little girl, I say to you, Arise.'"

• These data suggest that it is a mistake to claim that there is little in Mark that is not in Matthew and Luke in this story.

• "Fear" on the part of Jesus' disciples (and the crowd around him) is another distinctive, but certainly not unique, Markan theme that appears in all four of the miracle stories in this section. For "fear" on the part of Jesus' disciples, see especially:

➤ Mk 4:41//Lk 8:25;

➤ Mk 5:33, cf. Lk 8:47;

➤ Mk 5:36//Lk 8:50;

➤ Mk 6:50//Mt 14:27;

➤ Mk 9:6//Mt 17:6//Lk 9:34;

➤ Mk 10:32, cf. Mt 20:17 and Lk 19:31;

> ➤ Mk 16:8//Mt 28:8 for "fear" on the part of the disciples.

> ➤ And see Mk 5:15//Lk 8:35 for "fear" on the part of the crowd around Jesus.

Within the section Mark has heightened the theme of "fear," which was already prominent in Luke's parallel literary unit (Lk 8:22-56), by his modification of Lk 8:47 at Mk 5:33. For Mark, expressions of fear seem to be synonymous with misunderstanding of Jesus' mission (cf. Mk 16:8).

• The story of the stilling of the storm in Mark shares a number of literary features with the story of Jesus walking on the water (Mk 6:45-52, cf. Peabody, *Mark as Composer,* 124, 77).

Mk 4:35. "To the other side" is *one* of the referents for the πάλιν retrospective at Mk 5:21.

• Mark modifies Lk 8:22, Ἐγένετο δὲ ἐν μιᾷ τῶν ἡμερῶν, with the use of ἐν ἐκείνῃ τῇ ἡμέρᾳ in the same way that he had modified Lk 5:35 earlier at Mk 2:20 (cf. Peabody, *Mark as Composer,* 4, 35).

• Mark's omission of τῆς λίμνης from Lk 8:22 also conforms with Markan style. In contrast to Luke, but in agreement with Matthew, Mark prefers ἡ θάλασσα to ἡ λίμνη to describe the "sea" of Galilee. Luke is the only canonical gospel writer who utilizes the word λίμνη (Lk 5:1, 2, 8:22-23, 33; the only other NT usages are in Revelation; Rev 19:20, 20:10, 14, 15, 21:8).

Mk 4:36. The narrator's aside that other boats were with the one containing Jesus is another example of the kind of detail with which the author of Mark frequently supplements his version of a story taken from Matthew or Luke. This may be compared with Mk 1:18-20 where Mark also supplemented Matthew. While Mt 4:22 says that the sons of Zebedee left their father alone in the boat when they chose to follow Jesus, Mark's supplement says that the father of the sons of Zebedee was not left alone in the boat, but rather "was in the boat with hired servants."

Mk 4:37. On the Two Gospel Hypothesis, Mark's expression, καὶ γίνεται λαῖλαψ μεγάλη ἀνέμου, is an alternating word by word conflation of Mt 8:24 with Lk 8:23.

Synopsis 3: Close Alternating Conflation of Mt 8:24 and Lk 8:23 at Mk 4:37		
Matthew 8:24	Mark 4:37	Luke 8:23
καὶ ἰδού	καὶ γίνεται	καὶ κατέβη
σεισμὸς	λαῖλαψ	λαῖλαψ
μέγας	μεγάλη	
	ἀνέμου	ἀνέμου
ἐγένετο		

Mk 4:38. Mark's additional detail about Jesus sleeping "in the stern of the boat on a pillow" is a typical Markan supplementary detail that heightens the contrast between the fear of the disciples and the calm that characterizes Jesus throughout this stormy situation. The phrase, "on a pillow," is verisimilitude. It is the kind of detail a preacher may add to a text from scripture to make it more life-like.

• Mark's change of the title, Κύριε, in Mt 8:25 and the typically Lukan ἐπιστάτα in Lk 8:24 to διδάσκαλε at Mk 4:38 conforms with a distinctive, but again not unique, Markan preference for having Jesus addressed in the Greek vocative as "teacher."[9] This Markan preference for διδάσκαλος as an address to Jesus is consistent with this author's view that Jesus' actions (wonders) are some of his most important "teachings" (cf. Mk 1:21-28 and our discussion above). While Mark's Jesus is not depicted as doing much actual teaching, διδάσκαλος functions as an important Christological title for Mark.

Mk 4:40. Mark's text is a careful conflation of Mt 8:26 with Lk 8:25.

Synopsis 4: Close Alternating Conflation of Mt 8:26 and Lk 8:25 at Mk 4:40		
Matthew 8:26	Mark 4:40	Luke 8:25
καὶ	καὶ	
λέγει αὐτοῖς,	εἶπεν αὐτοῖς,	εἶπεν δὲ αὐτοῖς,
Τί δειλοί ἐστε,	Τί δειλοί ἐστε;	
ὀλιγόπιστοι;	οὔπω ἔχετε πίστιν;	Ποῦ ἡ πίστις ὑμῶν;

Again, Mark chooses a term from Matthew, a phrase from Luke, a phrase from Matthew and a phrase from Luke. This is another striking instance of patterns of alternating Markan agreement with Matthew or Luke within pericopae. Independent editorial work on Mark by Matthew and Luke to produce this phenomenon is quite difficult to conceive, especially since it occurs so frequently.

---

[9] Neirynck, *Minor Agreements*, Display 30, 280.

Mk 4:41. Mark's addition of the cognate noun φόβος to the verb φοβέομαι that he adopted from Lk 8:25 conforms to an element of Markan literary style, i.e., the use of a verb with a cognate accusative or dative, such as ἐφοβήθησαν φόβον.[10] See above the bullet on "fear" under general observations to Mk 4:35-41.

¶ 31. Jesus Heals a Foreign Demoniac; He Wants to Be Jesus' Disciple
(Mt 8:28-34)   Mk 5:1-20   <==========Lk 8:26-39

They came to the other side of the sea to the land of the Gerasenes. And after he had gotten out of the boat, immediately a man with an unclean spirit met him. He was living among the tombs there and was so strong no one could bind him, even with chains. Night and day among the tombs and on the mountains he would rant and rave and beat himself with stones. When he saw Jesus from afar, he ran and bowed down to him, crying out in a loud voice, "What have I got to do with you, Jesus, Son of the Most High God? I conjure you by that God, do not torment me!"—for Jesus was saying, "Come out of the man you unclean spirit!" And Jesus asked him, "What is your name?" And he says, "My name is Legion, for we are many." And he was pleading wildly with him not to send them out of that country. Now there happened to be a large herd of pigs nearby, grazing on the hillside. They begged Jesus, "Send us into the pigs!" Jesus did so and the unclean spirits came out of the man and flew into the herd of pigs, about 2000 in all. Immediately they jumped up and rushed down the hill into the sea and were drowned. As soon as the herdsmen saw this, they fled and announced it in the city and in the country round about. People came to see what had happened. So they came to Jesus and saw the man formerly possessed by demons seated, clothed, and calm, and they were terrified. They began to plead with Jesus to leave their country. However, the healed man begged him to let him go with him as a disciple. Instead, Jesus told him, "Go home and tell your friends how much mercy the Lord has shown you today!" And he left and began to announce in the Decapolis what Jesus had done for him. And all were astonished.

General Observations. Mark continues to follow Luke, using his change in place name and heavily depending upon Luke's wording. Mark blends in some terminology from Matthew, such as ἦλθον εἰς τὸ πέραν, Mk 5:1; μνημείων, Mk 5:2, and adds numerous details which heighten the story's dramatic vividness. See, for example, the statement that "no one was any longer able to bind the demon possessed man" (Mk 5:3), and most of the balance of the text of Mk 5:3-5.

---

[10] Neirynck, "Duality in Mark," 396-97.

• In this pericope Jesus encounters the forces of the unclean spirits and puts them to rout. The overall thrust of the pericope highlights Jesus' tremendous power as the Son of God. A man under the control of demonic powers who could not be kept in chains becomes totally impotent in the presence of the power of the Son of God. The demons that possess the man are reduced to *begging* to enter swine.

• Much of the Gentile motif which is pronounced in this unit, (e.g., unclean region, reference to the divine as "Most High God," a common Gentile expression) comes from Luke. However, the fact that the man becomes a missionary in the Decapolis (Mk 5:20) may be Mark's anticipation of the later Gentile mission.

Mk 5:1. "To the other side" (Mk 5:1 cf. Mk 4:35) is a referent for the πάλιν retrospective at Mk 5:21 (see the introduction, Appendix 3 and Peabody, *Mark as Composer,* 123, 76).

Mk 5:2. This verse contains a number of words that are peculiar to Mark. Similar language is found in Mk 6:53-54 (Peabody, *Mark as Composer,* 129, 78). Here is another example of how Mark introduces changes or supplements to the texts of Matthew and/or Luke. Those changes also conform with the style of the author of Mark.

• Mark, having described Jesus as "in the boat" at Mk 4:36, is careful to have him "get out of the boat" at Mk 5:2, once he has crossed over "to the other side." Similarly, at Mk 6:45, in agreement with Mt 14:22, Jesus is described as embarking in the boat, but only Mark is careful to describe Jesus as disembarking later (Mk 6:54, contrast Mt 14:34-35).

• The description of the ἄνθρωπος ἐν πνεύματι ἀκαθάρτῳ in Mk 5:2 is identical to the language used to describe the possessed man at Mk 1:23. These words have no synoptic parallel at Mk 5:2. The language of Lk 4:33 is also slightly different in the parallel to Mk 1:23. This could be Markan phraseology. It differs from the common testimony of Mt 8:28, δαιμονιζόμενοι, and Lk 8:27, δαιμόνια. In general, Mark prefers to describe demon-possessed people as having "an unclean spirit" (Peabody, *Mark as Composer,* 33, 44).

Mk 5:3-5. Most of these three verses constitute material unique to Mark. These Markan additions illustrate how Jesus "is able to bind the strong man and plunder his house" (cf. Mk 3:27), thereby strengthening the tie between this story and Mark's version of the "Beelzebul controversy" in Mk 3:20-30.

For Mark, the "house" of the demon-possessed, strong man is not only "among the tombs" (with Mt//Lk), but also "in the mountains" (against Mt//Lk). With this additional reference to "the mountains" as a place where Jesus is challenged by the demonic, could Mark be reflecting more knowledge of the story of Jesus' temptation (Mt 4:1-13//Lk 4:1-13), than he exhibited in his earlier abbreviation (Mk 1:12-13)? Compare not only the reference to "a very high mountain" where "all the kingdoms of the world may be seen" in Mt 4:8 (cf. Lk 4:5) with the reference to "the mountains" in Mk 5:5, but also the common references to "days *and nights*" spent in the mountains (Mt 4:2, cf. Mk 5:5).

Mk 5:6. Here Mark describes a man who "ran to Jesus from afar" (Mk 5:6) and "did obeisance to him" (cf. Lk 8:28, "fell toward" Jesus). There are seven examples of people "running" to Jesus in Mark. Only Mk 15:36//Mt 27:48 has a parallel in the text of either Matthew or Luke, although *all of the stories* in which people run to Jesus in Mark do have parallels in either Matthew or in both Matthew and Luke. Again, it seems more likely that Mark added this motif to his text than that Matthew and Luke, working independently, consistently omitted it.

Mk 5:9. The unclean spirit is also named "Legion" (λεγιών = the Latin, legio) in Lk 8:30. If Mark were written for an audience that understood Latin loanwords, it would also be appropriate for Mark to adopt this word from Luke. Here it seems to function as an explanation that Jesus is dealing, not with one unclean spirit, but a whole host of them (cf. Mk 5:13, 15).

Excursus 6: Latin Loanwords and Latin-style phrasing in Mark

In addition to λεγιών (Mk 5:9, 15), probable Latin loanwords in Mk would include κράβαττος (Latin "grabatus," Mk 2:4, 9, 11, 12, 6:55), μόδιος (Latin "modius," Mk 4:21), σπεκουλάτωρ , δηνάριον (Latin "denarius," Mk 6:37, 12:15, 14:5), ξέστης (Latin "sextarius," ? Mk 7:4), κῆνσος (Latin "census," Mk 12:14), Καῖσαρ (Latin "Caesar," Mk 12:14, 16, 17), κοδράντης (Latin "quadrans," Mk 12:42), φραγελλόω (Latin "flagello," Mk 15:15), πραιτώριον (Latin "praetorium," Mk 15:16), κεντυρίων (Latin, "centurio," Mk 15:39, 44, 45). Latin loanwords do not appear in the parallels to Mk 2:4, 2:9, 2:11, 2:12, 5:15, 6:27, 6:37, 6:55, 7:4, 12:42, 14:5, 15:39, 15:44 or 15:45. That is, more than half (14/23) of the occurrences of Latin loanwords in Mark are not found in the parallel in either Matthew or Luke. Verses where a Latin ioanword appears in Mark but not in the parallels in either Matthew or Luke are indicated by underlining above. Such evidence would be consistent with a provenance for Mark where Latin was known, including, of course, the city of Rome itself.

Possible Latin phraseology in Mk might include ἐπέθηκεν ὄνομα (Latin, "imposuit nomen," Mk 3:16, 17), ὅ ἐστίν (Latin "id est" or "hoc est," Mk 3:17, 7:11, 7:34, 12:42, 15:16, 15:42), ἐσχάτως ἔχειν (Latin "in extremis esse," Mk 5:23), ὥρας πολλῆς γενομένης (Latin "multus dies," Mk 6:35), ἱκανὸν ποιεῖν (Latin "satis facere," Mk 15:15), and ἐξ ἐναντίας αὐτοῦ (Latin, "coram" or "ex adverso eius," Mk 15:39). Not one of these potential Latin loan phrases in Mark has a parallel in Matthew or Luke.[11]

Mk 5:13. Mark's estimate of the number of swine as ὡς δισχίλιοι is an example of Mark adding specific numbers to his conflated text of Matthew and Luke. Other examples would include the Markan additions of δίς at Mk 14:30 and ἐκ δευτέρου and δίς within Mk 14:72.

Mk 5:18. At Mk 3:14, the author described one of Jesus' purposes in calling "the twelve" with the words, "that they might be with him," ἵνα ὦσιν μετ' αὐτοῦ. Therefore, it seems likely that Mark takes the petition of the former demoniac; i.e., "that he might be with him," ἵνα μετ' αὐτοῦ ᾖ as a petition to become a disciple. Jesus allows the man to become a disciple, but not one of the Twelve who, in Mark, are close "with him."

Mk 5:19. On the Two Document Hypothesis, it is claimed that Luke has changed Mark's "Lord = Jesus" to "God," thereby heightening the Christology from Mark to Luke. On the Two Gospel Hypothesis, one may counter that Mark has altered Luke's "God" to κύριος, probably the Greek equivalent of the divine name in Greek translations of the scriptures by this time. Mark thereby makes clear which God is being given credit for the healing of the former demoniac; i. e., the God of Abraham, Isaac, and Jacob. Or, it may be argued that Luke believes that Jesus' healing acts are by God's power working in Jesus, but Mark attributes the healing entirely to Jesus, the Lord (κύριος).

Mk 5:20. The theme of people "wondering" or "marveling" over Jesus is also common in Mark (Mk 1:27, ἐθαμβήθησαν; 5:20, ἐθαύμαζον; 9:15, ἐξεθαμβήθησαν; 10:24, ἐθαμβοῦντο; 10:32, ἐθαμβοῦντο; 12:17, ἐξεθαύμαζον; 15:5, θαυμάζειν; 15:44,

---

[11] See also Benjamin Wisner Bacon, *Is Mark a Roman Gospel?* (Harvard Theological Studies 7; Cambridge: Harvard, 1919; New York: Kraus Reprint Co., 1969). For a recent survey of the evidence see R. H. Gundry, *Mark: A Commentary on His Apology for the Cross* (Grand Rapids: Eerdmans, 1993), 1043-45.

ἐθαύμασεν; 16:5, ἐξεθαμβήθησαν; 16:6, ἐκθαμβεῖσθε). There are no parallels to these expressions at Mk 5:20, 9:15, 10:24, 10:32, 15:44, 16:5, and 16:6 (7/10). Therefore, this motif appears to be a recurring Markan supplement to the text of Matthew and Luke.

• The use of ἤρξατο plus the infinitive, which differs from Matthew and Luke at Mk 5:20, is consistent with Markan literary style.[12]

¶ 32. Mk 5:21-43. Jesus Heals Jairus' Daughter and Another Woman
(Mt 9:18-26)   Mk 5:21-43   <==========Lk 8:40-56

And when Jesus had crossed again in the boat to the other side, a great crowd was gathered around him and he was beside the sea. And a ruler of the synagogue named Jairus comes to him and seeing him falls at his feet and begs him fervently, saying, "My daughter is almost dead. Would you come and touch her so that she may be saved and live?" And Jesus went with him. And a great crowd was following him and was pressing upon him. And there was a woman who had an issue of blood nonstop for twelve years and she had suffered much from many physicians and spent all that she had and benefited nothing but rather got worse—when she saw Jesus, coming in from the crowd behind him, she touched his cloak, for she was saying, "If I can touch even his cloak, I will be healed." And immediately the fountain of her blood dried up and she knew in her body that she was healed from the disease. And knowing within himself that power had gone out of him, turning into the crowd, Jesus said, "Who touched my cloak?" And his disciples said to him, "You can see the crowd pressing upon you and you ask, 'Who touched me?'" And he was looking around to see who had done it. But the woman, filled with fear and trembling, knowing what had happened to her, came and bowed to him and told him the whole truth. And he said to her, "Daughter, your faith has saved you. Go in peace. And be healed of your disease."

While he was still speaking, some people came from the house of the synagogue ruler saying, "Your daughter has died. Why bother the teacher any longer?" But Jesus heard the word that was spoken and said to the synagogue ruler, "Don't be afraid; only believe." And he did not permit anyone to follow him except Peter and James and John, the brother of James. And when they arrived at the house of the synagogue ruler and he saw a commotion and many crying and wailing, when he had entered he said, "Why are you weeping and wailing? The child is not dead but sleeping." And they began to laugh at him, but he cast them all outside. Then he took the father of the child and the mother

---

[12] Neirynck, *Minor Agreements,* Display 13, 242-44.

and those with him and went in where the child was. Taking the child's hand he said, "Talitha cumi," which means when translated, "Little girl, I say to you, get up." And immediately the little girl got up and walked, for she was twelve years old. And there was a great amazement and he commanded them strictly that no one should know this, and he said "Give her something to eat."

General Observations. Mark continues to follow the order of Luke's miracle story unit (Lk 8:22-56//Mk 4:35-5:43, cf. Mt 8:23-34 and Mt 9:18-26) through the Healing of Jairus' Daughter (Mk 5:21-24a and 5:35-43) with its interpolated story of the Healing of the Woman with the Issue of Blood (Mk 5:24b-34). These two stories were already combined in Matthew, from whence Luke got them, but Mark has added numerous details and created a whole pattern of Markan supplements to the texts of Matthew and Luke (especially evident in Mk 5:21, 26, 29, 32-33, 36-40). Mark has also made a number of alterations to the common text of Mt/Lk (see the synopsis.) These Markan alterations to the common text of his sources include:

> ἰδού in Mt 9:18//Lk 8:41, cf. Mk 5:22.

> "she died" in Mt 9:18//Lk 8:42, against Mk 5:23, ἐσχάτως ἔχει

> προσελθοῦσα in Mt 9:20//Lk 8:44, against ἐλθοῦσα in Mk 5:27.

> τοῦ κρασπέδου in Mt 9:20//Lk 8:44, no parallel in Mk 5:27.

> οἰκία in Mt 9:23//Lk 8:51, against οἶκος in Mk 5:38.

> γάρ in Mt 9:24//Lk 8:52, no parallel in Mk 5:39.

> αὐτῆς in Mt 9:25//Lk 8:54, against τοῦ παιδίου in Mk 5:41.

> φήμη in Mt 9:26//Lk 4:14b, against ἀκοή in Mk 1:28.

• Mark has carefully conflated the texts of Matthew and Luke while, at the same time, considerably expanding them. These stories provide excellent examples of how Mark's version of most of the stories preserved in all three of the Synoptic Gospels is usually the longest of the three, even though Mark's Gospel is shorter than either Matthew or Luke.

• These two intercalated/sandwiched[13] stories were probably already related as healings of females, or more specifically "daughters," in the tradition from which Matthew

---

[13] Tom Shepherd, *Markan Sandwich Stories: Narration, Definition and Function* (AUSDDS 18; Grand Rapids, Mich.: Eerdmans, 1993).

received them. Luke considerably expanded both stories, probably owing to his generally recognized interest in stories about women. In this process, Luke also supplied an additional relationship between the stories by inserting a reference to "twelve years" into the story of the Healing of Jairus' Daughter (Lk 8:42). In the Healing of Jairus' Daughter, the twelve years refers to the age of the young woman, and in the Healing of the Woman with the Issue of Blood, to the duration of the woman's illness (cf. Lk 8:43, also noted in Mt 9:20). This linkage of the two stories is even more obvious in Luke because the references to "twelve years" appear in adjacent verses (Lk 8:42-43). Perhaps without noticing the use to which Luke had put this phrase, Mark moved the reference to "twelve years" as the age of Jairus' daughter to a later and more dramatic context in the second half of his version of this story (Mk 5:42). This separation of the two references to "twelve years" (Mk 5:25 and 5:42) also made the link between the two stories less obvious in Mark than it was in Luke.

• Mark borrows from Luke (Lk 8:51//Mk 5:37) the reference to Peter, James, and John being a privileged group who see the raising of Jairus' daughter. This incident is part of a wider pattern of the three being privileged to be present at esoteric events (Mk 1:29-31 and 13:3 [with Andrew]; Mk 9:2-8 and 14:32-42). Nevertheless, these privileged events do not insulate these three against gross misunderstanding and betrayal (Mk 10:35-45; 14:66-72). Jesus' greatest acts of power are of no effect without the faith that can endure hardship and accept the cross.

Mk 5:21. Mark begins this story with another use of πάλιν in a retrospective manner. The phrase, "to the other side *again*" refers back to Mk 5:1 and probably also to Mk 4:35, which say that "Jesus crossed over to the other side of the Sea [of Galilee]". (Peabody, *Mark as Composer,* 123, 76, and 126-30).

• The Markan compositions, "gathering of a great crowd" and "by the sea" (Mk 5:21), are consistent with the style of the author of Mark (Peabody, *Mark as Composer,* 163-164).

Mk 5:22. Matthew describes the father of the girl who "just died" as "one ruler." Luke expands this to "a man by the name of Jairus who was a ruler of the synagogue." Mark conflates the two, describing this person as "one," (in agreement with Mt 9:18) "of the rulers of the synagogue, by the name of Jairus" (in agreement with Lk 8:41).

Mk 5:23. The addition of πολλά adverbial is consistent with the style of the author of Mark (Peabody, *Mark as Composer,* 100, 67).

• In the first part of this story, Matthew reports that this man's daughter "just died" (Mt 9:18) while Luke reports that she "was dying" (Lk 8:42; in support of this translation, cf. Lk 8:49 where her death is subsequently reported). With this apparent inconsistency between Matthew and Luke, Mark awkwardly says that the girl ἐσχάτως ἔχει ("she is at an end"). Mark prefers to highlight the dramatic healing at the close of the story by stating there, just before Jesus' arrival at Jairus' home, that the daughter is dead (Mk 5:35//Lk 8:49).

• In Mt 9:18, the girl's father begged Jesus to "come and lay his hands upon her and she will *live*." Later, in the story of the Woman with the Issue of Blood, Matthew and Mark record that this other woman wanted to be *saved* (Mt 9:21//Mk 5:28) from her illness. And all three of the Synoptics report that she was, in fact, so *saved*, although Matthew is more emphatic about this than Luke or Mark (see ἐσώθη in Matthew in addition to ἡ πίστις σου σέσωκέν σε, Mt 9:22//Lk 8:48//Mk 5:34). Even though Luke's version of the story anticipates the "salvation" of Jairus' daughter in the second part of his version of this story (Lk 8:50), Mark moved this reference forward into the first part of his version. As a result, Mk 5:23 is a conflation of the contextual parallel at Mt 9:18, "she will live," with the later reference in Lk 8:50, "she will be saved." The resultant text of Mk 5:23, therefore, reads "she may be saved *and* she may live."

Mk 5:26-27. Although Luke had already considerably expanded the text of Matthew in describing the serious nature of the illness of the woman with the issue of blood, Mark has further heightened the seriousness of her condition, especially with the addition of the note that "she was getting no better, but rather becoming worse." Although the concentration of participles in Mk 5:26-27 (παθοῦσα, δαπανήσασα, ὠφεληθεῖσα, ἐλθοῦσα, ἀκούσασα, ἐλθοῦσα), does not conform with the demonstrable style of the author of Mark elsewhere, which rarely includes such periodization, this supplementary material is not unprecedented in Markan composition (cf. Mk 7:25).

Mk 5:29-30. Mark's alteration of the typically Lukan παραχρῆμα into the typically Markan εὐθύς is in accord with Markan stylistic preference. Also see the additions of εὐθύς at Mk 5:30 and 5:42(bis?).[14] The phrase, καὶ εὐθύς, at the beginning of both Mk 5:29 and 5:30 may serve as an example of a Markan "dualism." However, these duplicated phrases may also serve as members of an *inclusio*, embracing Mark's additional comment about the woman "knowing in her body that she had been healed

---

[14] Neirynck, *Minor Agreements*, Display 26, 274-76.

from her illness." This note, in turn, anticipates the comparable note about Jesus "knowing in himself" that power had gone out from him when the woman touched his garments. Special internal knowledge of what is happening or being said around him seems to be a characteristic of Mark's picture of Jesus (cf. the Markan supplements at Mk 2:8, 5:30, and 8:17; Peabody, *Mark as Composer,* 77-78 and 80, 60).

• The phrase ἀπὸ τῆς μάστιγος is confined to this story in Mark. The word, μάστιξ, appears in Mk 3:10, 5:29, 5:34; and in Lk 7:21 without parallel in Mark, and in Acts 22:24 and Heb 11:36, but nowhere else in the NT.

Mk 5:31. Mark never adopts the characteristically Lukan address to Jesus, ἐπιστάτα (Luke: six times, twice with no comparable parallel).

Mk 5:38-39. When Jesus is depicted in Mt 9:23 as entering the house of the ruler, he sees a crowd "groaning." In the comparable context in Lk 8:52, Jesus observes people "crying." In Mk 5:38, Jesus is depicted as observing both "groaning," in agreement with Mt 9:23, and "crying" in agreement with Lk 8:52. As is characteristic of him, Mark then repeats these narrative details in the subsequent dialogue (Mk 5:39). Mark heightens the gravity of this scene with his supplemental note about "much wailing" in the house.

Mk 5:41-42. Mark (in parallel with Lk 8:54-56) next depicts the "resurrection" of this apparently dead girl in language reminiscent of the "resurrection motif" with which Mark supplemented his narrative at Mk 1:31. (cf. Mk 9:27; Peabody, *Mark as Composer,* 44, 47). The connection between Jesus' esoteric teaching and resurrection appears to be a characteristic theme of Mark and a vital part of the overlay. When these anticipations are linked with the passion predictions they highlight the centrality of Jesus' resurrection as the vindication of his ministry. Without the resurrection of Jesus, faith in God's promises would be without foundation.

• In addition to the "grasping of the hand," Mark adds a "magic word" in Aramaic to Jesus' healing technique in this story. Pierson Parker has argued that wherever Mark makes use of Aramaic or Hebrew, something seems amiss[15] and, as usual, whenever Mark includes Aramaic words in his text, he always attempts to translate them for the

---

[15] See Pierson Parker, "1. The Posteriority of Mark," in Farmer, ed., *New Synoptic Studies,* 67-142. Parker's discussion of Mark's apparent lack of knowledge of Hebrew and Aramaic is found on pp. 70-73. Compare Roland Mushat Frye, "The Synoptic Problems and Analogies in Other Literatures," in *The Relationships Among the Gospels* (ed. William O. Walker; San Antonio, Tx.: Trinity University Press, 1978), 261-302, esp. on the criterion of language, pp. 264-71.

benefit of his (predominantly Gentile?) readers (cf. Peabody, *Mark as Composer,* 103, 68). The problematic character of the Aramaic wording and translation is attested by the wide variation in the textual tradition. Under these circumstances, the appearance of this Aramaic terminology can just as easily count for the secondary nature of Mark rather than Markan priority on the grounds of primitiveness.

• Glosses beginning with ἦν γάρ or ἦσαν γάρ as well as the use of a verb with a cognate accusative or dative, both of which appear as supplements to the text of Mk 5:42 (cf. Lk 8:55-56) frequently occur within the text of Mark (Peabody, *Mark as Composer,* 18, 40; 169, 91).

Mk 5:43. Mark's change of παρήγγειλεν in Lk 8:42 to διεστείλατο conforms with Markan stylistic preference (Peabody, *Mark as Composer,* 147, 85). With the exception of a variant at Mt 16:20//Mk 8:30 that reads ἐπιτιμάω, the verb διαστέλλομαι is found in the NT only in the Gospel of Mark (5:43, 7:36, 8:15, 9:9), Acts 15:24, and Heb 12:20. On the hypothesis of Markan priority, this evidence represents agreement on the part of Matthew and Luke to avoid the verb διαστέλλομαι. As such, the evidence represents an anomaly for Markan priority. On the other hand, this evidence is consistent with the Two Gospel Hypothesis, since Mark's literary characteristics are most likely to appear wherever Mark's text represents a change from or supplement to his sources, Matthew and/or Luke.

¶ 33. Jesus' Wisdom and Power Amaze His Hometown.

Mt 13:54-58 =========>   Mk 6:1-6a   (Lk 4:16-30, esp. 16, 22, 24)

And he went away from there and came to his own home town and his disciples were following him. And when it was the Sabbath he began to teach in the synagogue and many listening were astonished saying, "Whence does this man get all this? And what is the wisdom given to him? And what acts of power occur by his hands! Is he not the child of the carpenter, the son of Mary and brother of James and Joses and Jude and Simon? And are not his sisters here with us?" He offended them. And Jesus said to them, "A prophet is not without honor except in his home town and among his relatives and in his own home." Consequently he was not able to do any miracles there, except that he laid his hands upon a few sick people and healed them. He marveled because of their unbelief.

General Observations. Mark has just completed his use of Luke's miracle story unit (Lk 8:22-56//Mk 4:35-5:43). He is now ready to return to Mt 13:53 where he was last following Matthew's order of pericopae. As noted under general observations for ¶ 30, Mark makes use of Matthew's story of Jesus' rejection in his hometown as a retrospective passage looking back on the whole of Mk 3:20-5:43. This story highlights the theme of blindness and unbelief all around Jesus, themes that reoccur in both parts 4 and 5 of Mark's Gospel. Indeed, they will be highlighted by stories of blind men that conclude both parts.

• Mk 6:1-6a concludes this part of Mark (Mk 3:20-6:6a) by recounting Jesus' return to his own country. During Jesus' teaching in the local synagogue, the crowds ask, "From whence [do] these things [come] to this man? What is the wisdom that has been given to this one? [From whence are] such acts of power that have come to be through his hands (Mk 6:2)?" For Mark, the first question serves as a retrospective query about the source of the wisdom conveyed by Jesus in Mark's parable chapter, Mk 3:20-4:34. The second serves as a retrospective query about the source of Jesus' power in Mark's miracle chapter, Mk 4:35- 5:43. Thus Mark is able to summarize the previous two major literary units by means of these two retrospective questions (Mk 6:1-6).

Mk 6:1. Mark's addition of "his disciples were following him" to the texts of Matthew and Luke prepares the reader for the commissioning of the twelve that follows immediately.

Mk 6:2. In this verse, Mark may have conflated the detail about Jesus' teaching from Mt 13:54 with the detail that this happened on a Sabbath from Lk 4:16. The scenes recorded in both Matthew and Luke occur in Jesus' homeland (Nazareth). However, since Mark has already viewed Jesus' inaugural sermon as having taken place (cf. our discussion at Mk 1:20) it is probable that Mark simply adds the detail about the Sabbath because Jesus is going to the synagogue.

Mk 6:3. With some minimal editorial work, Mark has changed the question on the lips of those in the synagogue from Matthew's, "Is this not the son of the carpenter?" to his own, "Is this not the carpenter, the son of Mary?" Compare Lk 4:22, "Is this one not the son of Joseph?" which agrees more with Matthew's question than with Mark's. Note, however, that in a few manuscripts, including $\mathfrak{P}^{45}$, Mark agrees here with Matthew. If this represents scribal harmonization to the text of Matthew, it occurred quite early, as the evidence from $\mathfrak{P}^{45}$ would indicate. It does seem odd that the Gospel that doesn't recount the birth narrative would be reluctant to call Jesus a son of Joseph. On the other hand, if Mark knows Matthew and Luke well, the statement that Jesus was a son of Joseph may seem impious and not in accord with the text.

• Mark adopts the verb, σκανδαλίζομαι, from Mt 13:57. Matthew utilizes this verb 16 times in his gospel. Mark has it 8 times. All of the Markan occurrences have parallels to Matthew. Therefore, Mark repeats the language of Mt 18:8 in both Mk 9:43 and 9:45 (see the synopsis, 54, of Mk 9:43, 45, 47-48). This Markan usage of a basic linguistic characteristic of Matthew is consistent with Mark's literary dependence upon Matthew.

Mk 6:4. Mark's insertion of καὶ ἐν τοῖς συγγενεῦσιν αὐτοῦ to the saying in Mt 13:57, "A prophet is not without honor except in his homeland and in his home," at the end of this part underscores the discussion on family in the introduction to the part in Mk 3:31-35. Jesus' true family is not necessarily his earthly relatives. It consists of those who understand the secret of the kingdom (Mk 4:11; cf. Jn 7:1-5).

Mk 6:5. Mark's expansion of Mt 13:58 adds detail to Matthew's comment, "Jesus did not do there many miracles on account of their lack of faith." The expansion says that Jesus "was not able to do there any miracle, *except*, after placing his hands on a few sick people, he healed them. And [Jesus] marveled . . . ."[16] But there is no indication of dependence here, as is often argued; Mark and Matthew simply say the same thing in two different ways.

---

[16] Only by editing his presentation of the literary evidence in Mk 6:5-6 was Sir John C. Hawkins able to use the parallels between Mt 13:58 and Mk 6:5-6 to support the cause of Markan priority. In a section of John C. Hawkins' *Horae Synopticae* (Oxford: Clarendon Press, 1909) entitled, "A. St. Mark's Gospel. Section I. Passages which may have been omitted or altered as being liable to be misunderstood, or to give offence, or to suggest difficulties," Hawkins argued, "Mk vi.5 'He could (ἐδύνατο) there do no mighty work, save, &c.', compared with Mt xiii.58 'He did not many mighty works there because of their unbelief. . .'" 118. Jesus' power is not depicted as more limited in Mk 6:5-6 in comparison to Jesus' depiction in Mt 13:58 when the entirety of these verses is presented. Hawkins rather seriously misrepresented the data here. And these same misrepresented data presumably influenced B. H. Streeter, one of Hawkins' colleagues in William Sanday's Oxford Seminar on the Synoptic Problem when he fashioned the opening part of his fourth argument for Markan priority, "(4) The primitive character of Mark is further shown by (a) the use of phrases likely to cause offence, which are omitted or toned down in the other Gospels..." and used this same misrepresentation of the data as an example; B. H. Streeter, *The Four Gospels* (London: Macmillan, 1924) 151-52, 162.

Summary

Sandwiched between the call of the disciples and their commission (Mk 3:13-19 and 6:7-13) Mark has narrated his account of the heart of Jesus' Galilean ministry. The Twelve are blessed not only because they are witnesses of great teaching and acts of power, but also they are reckoned to be part of Jesus' true family (Mk 3:31-35) and given the secrets of the kingdom (Mk 4:11). Beyond this, Peter, James, and John are even privileged to see someone raised from the dead (Mk 5:37-42).

Yet, during these astonishing times, an ominous tone of increasing opposition grows ever more prominent. Jesus' enemies claim he is possessed (Mk 3:20-30). He is rejected in his own home town (Mk 6:1-6). Most of the soil on which his word falls is unproductive (Mk 4:7-9). There are many impediments to the arrival of the harvest. Indeed, it is still an open question whether the disciples will be able to overcome these impediments.

JESUS FEEDS MANY, BUT FEW UNDERSTAND

Overview

Following his rejection at Nazareth (Mk 6:1-6a), Jesus gives the Twelve authority over the unclean spirits and sends them forth on a mission tour of preaching and healing (Mk 6:7-13). This is the first of two tours that establish the basic structure of this part (Mk 6:7-30 and 6:45-8:26). The second tour is clearly delineated by the references to going out of Bethsaida (Mk 6:45) and returning there (Mk 8:22). Between the two tours, Mark narrates the amazing incident of the Feeding of the Five Thousand (Mk 6:31-44). This pericope is of pivotal significance for Mark because it is conspicuously echoed in later segments of the part (Mk 6:52; 8:17, 21). With this part Mark brings the first half of his narrative to a close and also concludes his account of the Galilean ministry of Jesus.

As part 3 ended, the people in Jesus' home town, because of their incapacity to hear or see, clearly stood outside of Jesus' spiritual family. As Mark's narrative progresses to the end of Jesus' Galilean ministry, an increasing number of people who play an important role in the story are identified as spiritual outsiders.

In the narrative, Herod, the Pharisees and the disciples all show strong opposition to Jesus or failure to understand him. While the disciples are on their mission, Mark utilizes an aside to describe Herod's reaction to Jesus' fame (Mk 6:14-29). This aside not only provides an account of John the Baptist's fate that foreshadows Jesus' death, but continues the theme of Herodian opposition to Jesus (cf. Mk 3:6).

During the second tour of this part, the Pharisees oppose Jesus (Mk 7:1-23). A retrospective passage later in the part Mark has Jesus warn the disciples to beware of the leaven (evil influence) of both Herod and the Pharisees (Mk 8:15). Clearly, from the Markan standpoint, these opponents do not understand the mystery of the kingdom and are thus marked as outsiders (cf. Mk 4:12 and 3:6).

Perhaps more surprising is the conduct of the disciples. After returning from their mission of preaching and casting out demons they witness two astonishing acts of power, the Feeding of the Five Thousand and the Walking on the Water (Mk 6:31-52). Yet they respond, not with faith, but with terror and astonishment (Mk 6:50,

52). In fact, Mark alone says that the disciples did not understand because their hearts were hardened (Mk 6:52). In an especially poignant and related episode, after the Feeding of the Four Thousand Mark has Jesus ask the disciples, "Why do you debate about the loaves? Do you neither know nor understand? Are your hearts hardened? Having eyes do you not see and having ears do you not hear and do you not remember?" (Mk 8:17-18). Here Mark's reader discovers that the disciples who have been given the secret of the kingdom nevertheless fail to see, hear, or understand because of the hardness of their hearts. The disciples' failure to understand becomes even more disturbing in Mark's narrative because the author has surrounded Mk 8:1-21 with two accounts of healing, one about a person who can neither hear nor speak and one about a person who can not see (Mk 7:31-37 and 8:22-26). Both of these healing narratives are unique to Mark. Thus, when one arrives at the end of the Galilean ministry in Mark's Gospel, the early promise aroused by the announcements of Jesus' divine sonship comes to fruition, but much remains clouded in mystery and misunderstanding.

¶ 34. Jesus Sends Out the Twelve to Preach and Cast Out Demons
(Mt 9:35-10:1, 5-16)   **Mk 6:6b-13**   **<==============Lk 9:1-6**
(cf. Lk 10:1-16)

And he went around the villages teaching. And he called the Twelve and began to send them out two by two and he gave them authority to cast out unclean spirits. And he commanded them to take nothing for the road except a staff only; no bread, no bag, no money in their belts, but to wear sandals and not to wear two tunics. And he began to say to them, "Wherever you enter a house, remain there until you leave that place. And whatever place will not receive you, nor listen to you, depart from there shaking off the dust from your feet as a witness to them." When they had left, they preached that people should repent and they cast out many demons and anointed with oil many that were sick and healed them.

General Observations. Upon concluding his use of Mt 13:53-58 at Mk 6:1-6a, Mark had to decide how to proceed. His progress through Matthew had brought him to Mt 14:1-2, Herod's ruminations about who Jesus was said to be by others. His progress through Luke, on the other hand, had brought him to Lk 9:1-6, Luke's version of the commissioning of all twelve disciples. Mark chose to narrate his version of Lk 9:1-6 (Mk 6:6b-13) before his version of Mt 14:1-2. However, while following the pericope order of Lk for the commissioning story, the linguistic evidence indicates that Mark also consulted the parallel in Mt 9:35-10:16. Since he had already made use of the list of names of the twelve apostles in narrating their "call" (See Mk 3:13-19 and the synopsis,

¶ 20), Mark now omits Mt 10:2-4, which includes this list of names. On the Two Gospel Hypothesis, Luke divided these two events into separate contexts, in distinction from Matthew, where Jesus is depicted as commissioning all twelve of his closest disciples at the same time that the final seven are called. The call of Jesus' twelve closest disciples is recorded at Lk 6:12-16, but their commissioning does not come until Lk 9:1-6. This allowed Luke to bring the commissioning of the twelve into closer proximity to his distinctive call and commissioning of 70 [72] "other" disciples. Since Mark, for the most part, does not record any episodes from Luke's "Travel Narrative," including Luke's story of the call and commissioning of the 70[72], Mark does not share Luke's need to separate the "call" from the "commissioning" of the Twelve. Mark's separation of these two events in his Gospel may be the result of his borrowing some, but not all, of the elements of Luke's editorial activity here. To this extent it provides further evidence of Mark's direct literary dependence upon the text of Luke.

Excursus 7: Mark's use of Mt 4:23 and 9:35

By this point in his narrative, Mark is thoroughly familiar with the two great redactional passages in Mt 4:23 and Mt 9:35. The following evidence is intended to support this claim.

Mark appears to have conflated elements of Mt 4:23 and 4:24 with some from Lk 4:37 in composing Mk 1:28 (see synopsis ¶ 8).

There is some evidence of Mark's use of Mt 4:23 at Mk 1:39 where Mark conflated it with Lk 4:44 (see synopsis ¶ 11). Luke 4:44 is the verse that immediately precedes Luke's version of the call of the first four disciples (Lk 5:1-11) and Mt 4:23 is the verse that immediately follows Matthew's version of the call of the first three disciples (Mt 4:18-22//Mk 1:16-20).

There is good linguistic evidence that Mark drew some of the geographical locations mentioned in Mk 3:7-8 from Mt 4:25 and some from the contextual parallel, Lk 6:17. Mark made his collection of regions from which people came out to see and engage Jesus more comprehensive than the comparable verses in either Matthew or Luke or even both combined. Mark even added "Idumea" to his conflated list of regions drawn from Mt 4:25 and Lk 6:17. Mark's link to Mt 4:25 at Mk 3:7-8 may well have been the contextual parallel in Mt 12:15, which repeats much of the language of Mt 4:25 (see synopsis ¶ 19).

Mark would have passed over Mt 9:35 as one of the verses omitted from Mt 9:18-11:10 while Mark was more faithfully following Luke's order of pericopae, Lk 4:16-6:11//Mk 1:21-3:5.

Having made a link between Mt 12:15 and Mt 4:25 at Mk 3:7-8 through the common language found in these two verses in Matthew, one may also easily note Mt 4:23 again, two verses earlier, and perhaps also Mt 9:35 again, which is a virtual doublet of Mt 4:23. Thus Mt 9:35 became the source for Mk 6:6b (see the discussion in the introduction.)

Mark, on the Two Gospel Hypothesis, did conflate the list of the names of the twelve apostles in Mt 10:1-4 with the list in Lk 6:12-16 to compose Mk 3:13-19. Mt 10:1-4, in turn, is only four verses away from Mt 9:35 (Mt 9:35-38), and it is, in fact, at Mt 9:35 that Mark begins composing Mk 6:6b-13, his version of the commissioning of the Twelve, rather than with the first verse of the contextual parallel at Lk 9:1-6 (see synopsis ¶ 34). These facts provide at least circumstantial evidence that Mark knew and reflected upon, although he did not fully incorporate, two clear and highly significant redactional passages in Mt 4:23-25 and Mt 9:35. Such evidence supports the view that Mark was literarily dependent not only upon a Matthean-like text, but upon that layer of Matthew that represents the work of the author/composer of that Gospel. By beginning at Mt 9:35 rather than Lk 9:1 in composing Mk 6:6b-13, Mark begins with the words καὶ περιῆγεν. This is source-critically significant because this is the only place where Mark makes use of περιάγω in the whole of his Gospel. Matthew, on the other hand, makes use of this vocabulary item three times. More significant, however, is the fact that the phrase καὶ περιῆγεν is precisely how the two most notable redactional passages in Matthew begin (Mt 4:23//Mt 9:35). Mark's usage here may be seen as parallel to Mt 9:35, but perhaps also to Mt 4:23. In this case, it is highly unlikely that this agreement between Matthew and Mark is the result of their use of a common source. Rather, Mark's text here probably represents a fragmentary preservation of a major structural and redactional feature of Matthew that was, most likely, contributed by the author of that Gospel, namely Mt 4:23. It represents the strongest kind of literary evidence for Mark's literary dependence upon the work of the author of Matthew.[1]

Mk 6:6b. Mark's addition of κυκλῷ may accord with his style. Mark uses this term three times (Mk 3:34, 6:6, and 6:36); Luke, once in parallel with a usage in Mark (Lk 9:12//Mk 6:36). Other NT usages are Rom 15:19, Rev 4:6, 5:11, and 7:11.

Mk 6:7. Here Mark begins his account of the mission journey of the disciples.

---

[1] Professor Neirynck's attempt to defend Markan priority and to explain this and other literary evidence that connect Mk 6:6b with Mt 4:23 and 9:35 on the basis of a "Matthean anticipation" is a noble, but finally unconvincing, effort. See, for instance, F. Neirynck, "Synoptic Problem," in *The New Jerome Biblical Commentary* (ed. Raymond E. Brown, Joseph A. Fitzmyer, Roland E. Murphy; Englewood Cliffs, N.J.: Prentice Hall 1990), 587-95, esp. 588-89; and idem, "The Two-Source Hypothesis Textual Discussion. Matthew 4:23-5:2 and the Matthean Composition of 4:23-11:1," in Dungan, ed., *The Interrelations of the Gospels,* 23-46.

•Mark's change of the simple aorist, ἀπέστειλεν in Mt//Lk, to ἤρξατο ἀποστελλεῖν also conforms with demonstrable Markan style (Peabody, *Mark as Composer,* 67, 54).

• Mark's choice of Matthew's "unclean spirits" (Mt 10:1) rather than Luke's "demons" (Lk 9:1) is also in accord with demonstrable Markan preferences (Peabody, *Mark as Composer,* 33, 44).

• Mark's specifying that the disciples were sent out "two by two" not only accords with his stylistic preferences (Peabody, *Mark as Composer,* 152, 86), but also may indicate his knowledge of Luke's distinctive story of the call and commissioning of the 70[72] (Lk 10:1-16, esp. Lk 10:1).

Mk 6:8-9. Mark's description of what the disciples are to take along on their missionary journey suggests that he does not appreciate either that the disciples were to rely on the good will of hosts in other cities and villages to provide completely for their needs (Matthew) or the extreme dangers they might face (Luke). Instead, Mark is even more accommodating to his Greco-Roman audience than Luke was. Unlike the Jesus of both Matthew and Luke, Mark's Jesus does allow his disciples to take along a staff (for protection?) and to wear sandals. The Jesus of Matthew and Luke does not allow the disciples to have two tunics, but the Jesus in Mark prohibits the disciples from *wearing* two tunics. Naturally, this would imply that they could *have* more than one. Otherwise, they could hardly be tempted to disregard such a prohibition. Mark's version of Jesus' commands to his disciples in commissioning them for their missionary work, therefore, depicts Jesus as less demanding than the Jesus of Matthew and Luke. At least, that is the conclusion one would draw on the Two Gospel Hypothesis about this particular set of Markan alterations to the common testimony of Matthew and Luke.

Mk 6:10. Mark breaks into Jesus' instructions here by adding one of his favorite introductory or transition formulae, καὶ ἔλεγεν αὐτοῖς. (Peabody, *Mark as Composer,* 89, 64).

Mk 6:12-13. Here, at last, the apostles perform in accordance with Jesus' previously established pattern of ministry and the purposes for which they were called: "preaching [repentance] and casting out demons," (Mk 3:14-16, cf. Mk 1:4//Lk 3:3 and Mk1:15//Mt 4:17), along with anointing the sick with oil (cf. James 5:13-16) and healing (cf. Mt 4:23, 9:35 and 10:1).

¶ 35. Herod Thinks John the Baptist Has Been Raised from the Dead

Mt 14:1-2 ------------------>   Mk 6:14-16   <============ Lk 9:7-9

King Herod heard about Jesus because his name had become well known and people were saying that John the Baptist was raised from the dead and this was why powers were at work through him. On the other hand, others were saying that Jesus was Elijah and still others that he was a prophet like one of the ancient prophets. When Herod heard this, he said, "No, John, whom I beheaded, has been raised."

General Observations. In the previous pericope Mark followed Luke 9:1-5 as his main source (Lk 9:1-5//Mk 6:6b-13). That pericope involved Jesus giving the disciples their instructions for a mission of preaching and healing. The next pericope in Luke is on the anxiety of Herod Antipas over Jesus' activity (Lk 9:7-9). Luke uses this material on the bewilderment of Herod as part of a wider plan to show that there is widespread puzzlement over Jesus' identity. The theme culminates in Peter's confession of Jesus' messianic identity a few verses later at Lk 9:18-20, and ultimately at the transfiguration in Lk 9:28-36. For Luke, the first mission of the disciples is practically a non-event. The disciples are dispatched in Lk 9:1-7 and are already back at Lk 9:10, after the brief note on Herod's concern. Mark, who has already shown a tendency to heighten the dramatic tone of his account in the unit on the raising of Jairus' daughter, allows for the passage of more time for the disciples' mission in his narrative. In Mark, the disciples will not return until Mk 6:30. In the meantime, Mark utilized Lk 9:7-9 to give his version of the story of Herod's anxiety, but he will also return to Matthew at exactly the place he left (Mt 13:58) and blend this Matthean text with the text of Luke to create his own version of this story (Mk 6:14-16). Mark continued to use Matthew's account, in order (Mt 14:3-12), for his description of the death of John the Baptist (Mk 6:14-29). After that lengthy narrative interlude, Mark narrated the return of the disciples. He then brought his account into harmony with Matthew and Luke with his narration of the Feeding of the Five Thousand (Mt 14:13-21//Lk 9:10-17//Mk 6:30-47).

Mk 6:14. At Mk 6:2, the people gathered in the synagogue ask, "Where did this man get all this? What is this wisdom that has been given to him? What deeds of power are being done by his hands? (cf. the similar, but much shorter questions in the parallel at Mt 13:54). Here in Mk 6:14 Herod is reported to have heard what others were saying about Jesus: "John the Baptist has been raised from the dead and, on account of this, the deeds of power are being energized in him." There is a similar report on the lips of Herod himself to his children/servants/slaves at Mt 14:2. That is, in both Matthew and Mark the question raised in the synagogue in Jesus' hometown (Mt 13:54//Mk 6:2) is, in turn, answered (if erroneously) by Herod in a later, but relatively close, literary context (Mt 14:2//Mk 6:14). Here Mark is closer to Luke in attributing these words about Jesus to others than Herod, but is closer to Matthew in the content of the report. However, at Mk 6:16, Herod himself also confesses that John has been raised, at least in partial agreement with the words on the lips of Herod at Mt 14:2.

• Mark utilizes βασιλεύς instead of τετράρχης (Mt 14:1//Lk 9:7) to describe Herod Antipas. This loose description may have been determined by the later narrative account at Mk 6:23 where he offers half of his kingdom to Herodias. Josephus (Ant., 18.240-56) narrates that Herod Antipas' desire to be remembered as a king ultimately led to his demise.

• Mark uses the perfect passive of ἐγείρω to describe what some were saying about Jesus, rather than the aorist passive in Matthew and Luke. The textual tradition is not unanimous. If the perfect is the correct text, then perhaps Mark is stressing that the story that Jesus was John raised from the dead was widespread and continued to be told for some time.

Mk 6:15. Mark's terminology in describing what Herod had heard from others about Jesus is similar to that found not only in Lk 9:8, the contextual parallel to Mk 6:15, but also Mt 16:14, part of the disciples' report to Jesus directly about what people were suggesting about him. Specifically, Mark follows Lk 9:8 closely down through the words, "others [were saying] that [he is] a prophet." Then Mark adds, in language similar to Mt 16:14, "[like] one of the prophets." On the Two Gospel Hypothesis, Luke had already compared the similar contexts in Mt 14:1-2 and Mt 16:13-16. Luke brought his versions of these two pericopae (Lk 9:4-9; 9:18-21) into even more striking agreement by adding "a certain prophet of the ancient ones was raised (Lk 9:8, 18)." With the two contexts in Luke even more similar than the parallels in Matthew, Mark followed Luke in making his two parallel contexts come in a similar place (cf Mk 6:15-16/Lk 9:8-9 and Mk 8:27-30/Lk 9:18-21). Nevertheless, Mark's use of "one of the prophets" (Mt 16:14) still indicates that Mark is blending in material from Matthew.

Mk 6:16. There is no parallel to this verse in Matthew. Mark could, therefore, only draw on Lk 9:9.

•Following Luke, Mark has chosen to adopt a form of ἀκούω for both Mk 6:14//Lk 9:7//Mt 14:1 and Mk 6:16//Lk 9:9. As noted above, Mark had altered the common testimony of Matthew and Luke on the use of ἠγέρθη at Mk 6:14 (cf. Mt 14:2//Lk 9:7) to the perfect tense. Now at Mark 6:16 Mark inserts the word ἠγέρθη into Herod's affirmation about John's relationship to Jesus, perhaps under the influence of Luke's redaction in Lk 9:8 (cf. Lk 9:19 where Luke added ἀνέστη as part of a longer additional clause in both contexts).

•Mark's rewriting of Lk 9:9 produces an awkward pericope. In Mark, Herod seems to have heard twice that Jesus was John the Baptist raised from the dead (Mk 6:14 and 6:16). Since the verbatim agreements between Mk 6:14-15 and Mt 14:1-2 are stronger than those between Mk 6:14-15 and Lk 9:7, and the only parallel to Mk 6:16 is Lk 9:9, it could well be that this awkwardness is the result of Mark copying one use of ἀκούω from Mt 14:1 and the other from Lk 9:9.

¶ 36. Why John the Baptist Was Murdered

Mt 14:3-12===========>   Mk 6:17-29   (cf. Lk 3:18-20)

Herod had recently sent men to seize John and bind him in prison because of what he had said about Herodias, who had been his brother Philip's wife, but now was Herod's. John had said to Herod, "It is not lawful for you to have your brother's wife." Herodias hated him for that, wanted to kill him, but was not able to because Herod feared John. Herod knew that John was a just and holy man; so he protected John and still listened to him eagerly. One day an opportune moment came for Herodias when Herod was celebrating his birthday with a banquet for his courtiers and officers and the leading men of Galilee. When Herodias' daughter came in and danced for everyone, she pleased Herod and his guests so much he said to her, "Ask for anything you want and I will give it to you!" Having left the guests she asked her mother, "What should I request?" Without hesitation she said, "The head of John the Baptist!" Immediately the daughter hurried back to the king and said, "I want you to give me John the Baptist's head on a platter right now." The king became very upset, but, because of his promise and his guests, he did not oppose her. So, without delay, the king sent a soldier with orders to bring his head. The soldier returned with John's head on a platter and he gave it to the girl and she gave it to her mother. When his disciples heard what had happened, they came and took his body away for burial.

General Observations. Mark has narrated his version of the "anxiety of Herod" (Mk 6:14-16) by blending material from Matthew and Luke (Mt 14:1-2//Lk 9:7-9). For the next episode, Mark chooses to utilize Mt 14:3-13 on the death of John (Mk 6:17-29). This pericope has no parallel in Luke. Mark chooses to use this material for the obvious reason of extending the interlude between the sending out of the Twelve and their return. It also functions as "filler" material to describe what happens while the disciples are on tour (see overview).

It has often been noted that this is the only significant unit in Mark where Jesus is not the major focus. However, that may be somewhat misleading. From at least as early as Mk 3:6, the reader has been alerted to the possibility that Jesus may suffer a violent death. The fate of John, reported as a device for creating suspense, functions to foreshadow the ultimate fate of Jesus.

• Mark is probably unaware of the precision of Matthew's γάρ . . . δέ parenthesis and so blurs it by adding the αὐτός (himself) to the introduction to the unit at Mk 6:17a to heighten Herod's blame and the certainty that John is dead. In Matthew 14, the γάρ . . . δέ construction of vss. 3 and 13 are the precise way one marks an extended parenthesis in Greek. Failure to read that construction correctly has greatly obscured both the Matthean story and the corresponding synoptic relationships.[2] Mark has added a number of colorful details to the sparse account in Matthew. Besides these picturesque details, there is nothing strongly characteristic of Mark in the story. The repeated use of καί is no more pronounced than in Matthew's version. However, Mark's repetition of γάρ at Mk 6:20 (cf. Mt 14:5) shows again that he is not aware of the parenthetical construction.

Mk 6:17-18. The addition of τοῦ ἀδελφοῦ αὐτοῦ/ σου in Mk 6:18 is an addition to the text of Mt 14.4. With this Mark produces a duplicate expression, typical of his composition.

Mk 6:20. The use of πολλά adverbial is characteristic of Markan composition (Peabody, *Mark as Composer*, 100, 67). This has no parallel in Matthew and appears to have been added by Mark.

Mk 6:29. The concluding construct of the unit, τὸ πτῶμα + καί + 3rd person aorist of τίθημι + pronoun + ἐν μνημείῳ, has a striking parallel in Mk 15:45-46, the scene of Jesus' burial (Peabody, *Mark as Composer*, 158, 87). The literary evidence that these phrases come from the hand of the author of Mark substantiates the view that Mark is making a deliberate connection here between the fate of John and that of Jesus.

---

[2] Lamar Cope, "The Death of John the Baptist in the Gospel of Matthew," CBQ 38,4 (1976): 515-19.

¶ 37. When the "Apostles" Return, Jesus Feeds Five Thousand
Mt 14:13-21==========>   Mk 6:30 - 44   <===========Lk 9:10-17

The apostles return to Jesus and tell all that they had done and taught. He says, "Come on, let's go to a deserted place where you can rest a bit," for so many people were milling around they couldn't even find time to eat. So they left in the boat for a deserted place where they would be alone. However, many saw them leaving and recognized them and began to run after them on foot to get there first. When he got out of the boat, he saw a great crowd and he felt pity for them, for they were "like sheep with no shepherd." He began to teach them many things. It was already late when his disciples came to him and said, "This is a deserted place; send the people away so they can go into the country and villages around to buy something to eat." Nevertheless, Jesus answered and said, "You give them something to eat." And they said to him, "You want us to go buy two thousand denarii worth of bread to give them to eat?" And he said to them, "How much bread do you have? Go and see." When they found out, they said, "Five, and two fish." Then he ordered everyone to sit down by companies on the green grass. And when they had sat down by groups, by hundreds and fifties, he took the five loaves and the two fish. After looking up to heaven he gave thanks and broke the loaves and started giving to his disciples to distribute bread to the crowd. He also divided up the two fish for everyone. And they all ate and were satisfied. And they gathered twelve baskets of bread fragments and pieces of fish. Five thousand males ate bread that day.

General Observations. Although Mark relies more on the language of Matthew here, he also makes use of Luke (cf. Lk 9:7-9//Mk 6:14-16; Lk 9:10-17//Mk 6:30-44, with Mt 14:3b-12//Mk 6:17-29 intervening). Mark's account is a skillful blend of details from both, with numerous expansions for purposes of vivid detail. See, for example, the comments below on Mk 6:34b, 37b-38, and 40.

• The return of the disciples (Mk 6:30-33) provides the occasion for Mark's version of the feeding of the five thousand (Mk 6:34-44). Mark returns to Luke for the account of their return. Mark emphasizes that the disciples reported "all that they had done *and taught,*" fulfilling their commission as outlined in Mk 6:12-13. His narrative is unique in that it accentuates "the Twelve" in a three-fold series: calling, sending, and return. It thus functions as a précis of later missionary activity in the church especially as recorded in the Acts of the Apostles.

• Few portions of the Synoptics are more intricate and complex than this one. Many commentators misread Mt 14:12-13. They claim that Matthew simply forgot that the death of John the Baptist was past news (cf. Mt 14:2 cf. Mk 6:14). Thus, they think Matthew has Jesus retreat in sorrow over John's death. However, as we noted above, Mt 14:3-12 is a true parenthesis, marked off as such by the appropriate Greek markers. Matthew had Jesus withdraw for fear of Herod, rather than out of sadness over John's death. Herod's earlier treatment of John the Baptist provided reason enough for Jesus to be fearful. From the Two Gospel perspective, Luke had eliminated the direct connection between the story of Herod's ruminations about Jesus' identity (Mt 14:1-2) and the immediately following story of Herod's murder of John (Mt 14:3-12). Luke achieved this, first, by moving a very abbreviated version of Mt 14:3-12 to the much earlier context, Lk 3:18-20. Then he made the unit about Herod's perplexity (Mt 14:1-2//Lk 9:7-9) an insertion, which provided for the passage of time between the sending and the return of the Twelve. Mark has chosen to follow Luke's order here, but he adds the story of the Baptist's death and the withdrawal to a lonely place from Mt 14:1-13. Thus, by supplementing Luke's story with this material from Matthew, Mark provides for a longer literary passage of time between Luke's distinctive sending and return of the Twelve. But other difficulties remain.

• Luke's urban setting for the feeding, in Bethsaida (Lk 9:10), produced internal inconsistencies with Matthew's statement that this feeding took place in a desert place, which Luke adopted without change (cf. Lk 9:12//Mt 14:15).[3] Mark sides with Matthew in leaving the Feeding of the 5000 in a desert place (Mk 6:36), but in deference to Luke's reference to Bethsaida, Mark sets the immediately following story in that city (Lk 9:10//Mk 6:45). In fact, Mark seems to utilize Bethsaida as the departure point for his second tour, that also ends in Bethsaida (Mk 6:45-8:26).

• Mark's use of the story of the return of the Twelve has broken the connection between the disciples' report to Jesus of the death of John (Mt 14:12//Mk 6:29) and Jesus' retreat (Mt 14:12//Mk 6:32). Two verses now intervene in Mark's version (Mk 6:30-31), one a Markan expansion of Lk 9:10, the other a Markan composition. In Mk 6:31 Mark provides his rationale for Jesus' withdrawal with his disciples to a desert place. They need to rest upon their return from their missionary activities and their return has brought so many people together, coming and going, that they did not even have sufficient time to eat.

• The feeding of the 5,000 by Jesus is very important for Mark, as it is for the other Gospels. As well as being a demonstration of great power, the unit underscores by

---

[3] McNicol et al., *Beyond the Q Impasse*, 136.

anticipation the importance of eucharistic meals for the Markan community (cf. Mk 6:41; 8:6; 14:23). This is consistent with a Markan interest in baptism and the Lord's supper.

Mk 6:31. This verse, like Mk 3:20, is unique to Mark. These two verses also share the uniquely Markan perspective that Jesus and the disciples were unable to eat. Other Markan features are the use of the historic present and of ἦσαν γάρ to begin a parenthetical comment (Peabody, *Mark as Composer,* 18, 40). The verse is clearly a Markan editorial construction, which does not appear in either Matthew or Luke. We believe it is far easier to explain this unique verse as a Markan supplement that provides an editorial comment than it is to explain it as an accidental agreement in omission by Matthew and Luke. The same is true of Mk 3:20.

Mk 6:32-33. Mark goes to more pains than Matthew to explain how the crowds got to the lonely place before Jesus and the disciples did. In Matthew, the crowds only hear of the departure and hurry to meet Jesus and the disciples in the desert. In Mark, the crowds actually see them depart and, therefore, have to run in order to arrive there first. Neither Matthew nor Mark explain how the crowd knew where Jesus and the disciples were going, but since one can see a boat anywhere on the lake from the shore, Mark's fuller explanation is at least credible.

• Mark again follows the text of Matthew fairly closely in these verses. For example, the phrase, ἐν τῷ πλοίῳ εἰς ἔρημον τόπον κατ᾽ ἰδίαν is almost identical to his source in Mt 14:13, ἐν πλοίῳ εἰς ἔρημον τόπον κατ᾽ ἰδίαν.

Mk 6:34. The "great crowd" in Mk 6:34 will become a previous referent for the πάλιν retrospective at Mk 8:1 and 10:1.

• A glance at our synopsis will show that Mark primarily followed Matthew for Mk 6:32-37a//Mt 14:13-17, then followed Luke more closely for Mk 6:37a-43a//Lk 9:13d-17. In Mk 6:34, however, where Mark is primarily following Matthew, Mark chooses to emphasize Jesus' teaching by substituting ἤρξατο διδάσκειν αὐτοὺς πολλά for ἐλάλει αὐτοῖς περὶ τῆς βασιλείας τοῦ θεοῦ, which is found only in Lk 9:11, rather than his healing, found in both Mt 14:14 (ἐθεράπευσεν) and Lk 9:11 (θεραπείας ἰᾶτο). Nevertheless, as noted in our comments on Mk 1:21-28, since Mark seems to identify Jesus' most important "teaching" with his healing ministry (Mk 1:27), Mark may not have consciously thought that the omission of any mention of Jesus' "healing" from the combined testimony of his sources (ἐθεράπευσεν/ θεραπείας ἰᾶτο) was significant.

• The explanation of Jesus' "pity" upon the crowd "because they were like sheep without a shepherd" is a Markan supplement. It has a significant parallel to an earlier literary context in Mt 9:36 (cf. synopsis ¶ 34, and our comments on Mk 6:6b-13). There Matthew used these same words to provide part of the rationale for the sending out of the Twelve (Mt 9:35-10:16). Mark does not utilize this comment in Mk 6:6b-13, the contextual parallel to Mt 9:35-10:16, but rather inserts it at this point in his narrative.

Mk 6:36. Mark's editing of this verse creates a remarkable web of relationships. He shares ἀπελθόντες with Mt 14:15 (cf. Lk 9:12; πορευθέντες), then κύκλῳ and ἀγρούς with Lk 9:12, then ἀγοράσωσιν ἑαυτοῖς with Mt 14:15. This is another example of the text of Mark alternating in agreement between Matthew and Luke within a pericope. Such literary evidence is most consistent with the view that Mark is conflating Matthew and Luke. The Two Document Hypothesis requires that independent copyists have divided the text of Mark between them in a coordinated manner---a very unlikely literary procedure.

Mk 6:37. ὁ δὲ ἀποκριθεὶς εἶπεν αὐτοῖς is a strong Markan literary characteristic (Peabody, *Mark as Composer,* 110, 70). Here these words are a Markan supplement. The disciples' question to Jesus about the need for them to go out and buy 200 denarii worth of loaves in order to feed such a crowd presents them as perplexed. However, for the reader, their reaction is understandable. Just a few verses earlier the disciples were commanded not to take any bread (Mk 6:8//Lk 9:3, no parallel in Mt) or even a copper coin with them in their belts on their missionary journey (Mk 6:8//Mt 10:9, no parallel in Lk). Mark's conflation of these two commands, one each from Matthew and Luke, serves Mark's literary purpose by highlighting the bewilderment of the disciples.

• Mark's parallel to βρώματα in Lk 9:13 (cf. Mt 14:15) is ἄρτους (Mk 6:37). Neither Matthew nor Luke refer to denarii here.

Mk 6:39-40. Mark's supplements, συμπόσια συμπόσια and πρασιαὶ πρασιαί, are in keeping with his preference for duplication used distributively (Peabody, *Mark as Composer,* 152, 86).

Mk 6:41-42. Twice Mark elaborates on the details about the fish used to feed the crowd. Only Mark indicates that the disciples were not only to distribute bread but also to divide the fish with everyone there. Moreover, he alone notes that the baskets filled with broken pieces not only included bread, but also fish. These additions are in keeping with the later church's increasing use of fish imagery in depictions of the Eucharist as well as the feeding stories. In fact, in many frescos found in the catacombs the art historian has difficulty distinguishing depictions of the feeding stories from those of the Eucharist. Here Mark's editing stands in a clear line of later church development.

¶ 38. Jesus Walks on the Water; The Disciples Don't Understand about the Loaves; Their Heart Is Hardened

Mt 14:22-33==========>   Mk 6:45-52

At once Jesus made his disciples get in the boat and cross to the other side to Bethsaida while he was dismissing the crowd. After he left them, he went up on the mountain to pray. At evening, the boat was in the middle of the sea and he was by himself on the land. Then he saw the disciples struggling to make headway because the wind was blowing against them. Toward dawn, Jesus came to them walking on the sea, meaning to pass them by. However, when the disciples saw him walking on the sea, they were terrified thinking that it was a ghost. They screamed out, for they all saw him and were scared to death. But he immediately began speaking to them and said, "Cheer up! It is I. Don't be afraid!" He got into the boat with them. The wind stopped. They were totally astonished (for they still did not understand about the bread, because their hearts were hardened).

General Observations. At this point, Luke omits a large section of Matthew and, therefore, rather than moving forward to the point were Luke rejoins Matthew (Mt 16:13//Lk 9:18), Mark chooses to follow the text of Matthew alone between Mk 6:45 and 8:21. This results in a relatively long section in which Mark is influenced only by Matthew (Mk 6:45-8:26, cf. Mt 14:22-16:12). As one might expect in such a section, Mark shares a great deal of verbal agreement with Matthew, yet Mark does some rewriting and supplementing of his Matthean source (esp. Mk 7:31-37 and 8:22-26), as well as some editing by omission (Mt 14:28-31 and 15:29-31).

• The most remarkable feature is Mark's omission of the details in Matthew's story about Peter walking on the water (Mt 14:28-31). Perhaps Mark saw this as a story about the disciples' fear and lack of faith and his Matthean source has too much about the disciples' faith (cf. Mt 14:28-29, 33). Certainly the idea of the disciples worshipping Jesus is not what Mark had in mind (Mt 14:33). Given Mark's closing statement, this story is clearly to be linked in the minds of Mark's readers with the story of the Feeding of the 5000; it is meant to underline the continuing lack of understanding that the disciples have about that incident. (Mk 6:52). On the Two Gospel Hypothesis, by omitting the story of Peter walking on the water, the reader of Mark's Gospel is led to focus more on the power of Jesus and, in contrast, the incapacity of the disciples to understand who he is.

Mk 6:45-47. Mark substitutes his characteristic καὶ εὐθύς for Matthew's καὶ εὐθέως.

• Mark specifies the location across the lake as "Bethsaida," having moved this detail from Lk 9:10, where it created internal problems for the story of the Feeding of the 5000. With this move, Mark also commences the second tour portion of this part. It is a journey from and a return to Bethsaida by Jesus and the disciples (Mk 6:45 and 8:22). This is a striking feature of the text of Mk, which is readily explainable as the result of Mark's editing of his source material.

Mk 6:48. Perhaps Mark's addition of καὶ ἤθελεν παρελθεῖν αὐτούς was Mark's attempt to link this episode with stories of divine epiphanies in the Jewish and Hellenistic religious tradition. Other elements, borrowed from Matthew, also link it to stories of divine epiphany. These would include control of the sea, the use of φαντάσμα, the use of the verb, ταράσσω and the statement of assurance, ἐγώ εἰμί.[4]

Mk 6:49-50. On the Two Gospel Hypothesis, Mark has omitted μαθηταί from Mt 14:26 at Mk 6.49 and added πάντες γὰρ αὐτὸν εἶδον to Mk 6:50 (cf. Mt 14:26-27). Although only the disciples are addressed by Jesus in Mk 6:50, Mark's modifications help to make the story apply to a wider audience.

Mk 6:52. Mark adds a final comment (vs. 52) that is extraordinarily revealing of his point of view: to Mark, this story is *a pictorial representation of the meaning of the feeding of the 5,000.* The disciples still do not understand "about the bread." Nor, Mark inserts, can they, "for their hearts were hardened." That is, they are caused *by God* to be incredibly uncomprehending. Only divine insight can heal this blindness and allow them (and succeeding generations of Christians) to grasp Jesus' miraculous power to "give bread" to the church, despite being surrounded by "howling seas at midnight" (i.e., terrifying danger). This verse is Markan editorial work. Mark's phrase ἦν αὐτῶν ἡ καρδία πεπωρωμένην is very similar to his comment at Mk 8:17 πεπωρωμένην ἔχετε τὴν καρδίαν. There are no parallels to any one of these three phrases in Matthew. Compare Mk 3:5, where the same theme is repeated, and where the relevant words are

---

[4] Cf. Gundry, *Mark*, 336-37.

again absent from the parallels. These three verses (Mk 6:51b-52, 8:17, and 3:5), therefore, represent a significant set of features that may be included in the Markan overlay (cf. Peabody, *Mark as Composer,* 166, 91).

¶ 39. Jesus Heals the Sick at Gennesaret.

Mt 14:34-36==========>   Mk 6:53-56

And after they had crossed over they landed at Gennesaret and tied up their boat. And when they got out of the boat immediately people recognized Jesus and ran around that whole neighborhood and began to bring sick people to wherever they heard he was. And whether he entered villages or cities or open fields, they would put those who were sick in the market places and call on him that they might touch even the fringe of his cloak and whoever touched it was healed.

General Observations. Mark continues to follow the text of Matthew, but greatly heightens the reaction of the people. In terms of structure, this part, Mk 6:45-56, in which a sea crossing and landing come at the beginning of a journey, is comparable to Mk 8:14-21, another sea crossing and landing which comes at the end of the tour.

• In contrast to the lack of faith shown by the disciples in the previous story, the people of Gennesaret recognize the power of Jesus and eagerly accept him.

Mk 6:53-54. Although Jesus and his disciples embarked for Bethsaida (according to Mk 6:45), they actually land in Gennesaret (Mk 6:53), which Mark may think of as a town or village but which was actually a region. Mark had attempted to solve a problem in Luke; i.e., the urban location of the feeding in Bethsaida (Lk 9:10), by moving the reference to Bethsaida to the opening of the subsequent pericope in his parallel (Mk 6:45). But he created a problem for his own text by indicating one destination at the time of embarkation (Bethsaida) but a different point of arrival (Gennesaret). This disparity is partly the result of Mark following Matthew's geography in Mk 6:53//Mt 14:34 while shifting to Luke's in Lk 9:10 (cf. Mk 6:45). In Mark's own larger literary context, Jesus does not actually arrive in Bethsaida until much later (Mk 8:22). Some commentators and advocates of Markan priority attempt to explain the discrepancy between the intended destination in Mk 6:45 and the actual one in Mk 6:53 by appealing to a shift in the boat's course by the strong winds mentioned in the text.[5]

---

[5] See, e.g., Vincent Taylor, *The Gospel According to Mark* (2d ed.; New York: Macmillan, 1966; repr. Grand Rapids, Mich.: Baker, 1981), 322; "the generally accepted opinion is that the wind prevented a landing at Bethsaida, and this view is probably correct."

• The added phrase about the mooring of the boat, καὶ προσωρμίσθησαν, contains the sole instance of this verb in the New Testament. Because it is unique, it cannot be explained as characteristic of Mark on the basis of the frequency of its reoccurrence within Mark's Gospel. On the other hand, given the relative brevity of each of the documents now contained in the NT canon and the relatively small sample of each author's work represented within it, it is not surprising that the vocabulary of each of the Synoptic evangelists includes words that are not found anywhere else in the NT.[6]

• The construction, Καὶ ἦλθον εἰς...καὶ ἐξελθόντος αὐτοῦ ἐκ τοῦ πλοίου εὐθύς, a significant Markan addition to Mt 14:35 in Mk 6:53-54, was found earlier at Mk 5:1-2 in the introduction to the Healing of the Gerasene Demoniac. There, however, these words were not all Markan additions to the text of Matthew and Luke, but the result of Mark's editing and expanding his conflated text of Mt 8:28 and Lk 8:26-27. The picture of Jesus with his disciples disembarking from the boat after a sea crossing is another element of the Markan overlay.

Mk 6:55. Mark heightens the drama of Mt 14:35 by using περιέδραμον, 'rushed about.' There are seven contexts in Mark where people are depicted as "running" to Jesus: Mk 5:6, τρέχω; 6:33, συντρέχω; 6:55, περιτρέχω; 9:15, προστρέχω; 9:25, ἐπισυντρέχω; 10:17, προστρέχω; 15:36, τρέχω. Only one of these has a parallel in either Matthew or Luke (Mt 15:36//Mt 27:48). There are two instances of τρέχω and its compounds in Matthew (Mt 27:48; 28:8). There are three in Luke (Lk 15:20; 19:4; and 24:12) without a parallel in either Matthew or Mark. There are also five occurring in Acts (Acts 3:11, 8:30, 12:14, 21:32 and 27:16). The image of people running to Jesus is characteristic of Mark. Both Matthew and Luke can utilize a verb for "running" where Mark has no parallel. But six of Mark's seven usages of a verb for "running" represent supplements to the texts of Matthew and Luke.

• Again Mark uses κραβάττος (cot), a word not found in Matthew or Luke (see the general observations above for ¶ 13, Mk 2:1-12).

Mk 6:56. Mark also expands the narrative by speaking of Jesus going around the area and the sick being brought to him wherever he was. Otherwise the verse is very similar to Mt 14:36. Among the similarities between Matthew and Mark here is the use of κρασπέδον, which Matthew uses three times, once in parallel with Mark (Mt

---

[6] For a list of all of the vocabulary items unique to Mark among NT authors, see the words marked with an * in Taylor, *Mark*, "Index of Greek Words Used in the Gospel," pp. 673-88.

14:36//Mk 6:56), once in parallel with Luke (Mt 9:20//Lk 8:44, against Mk 5:27), and once independently of both (Mt 23:5). This evidence, though very limited, lends support to Matthew's priority to both Luke and Mark.

¶ 40. Jesus Debates with Scribes and Pharisees over Eating with Unclean Hands
Mt 15:1-20============>   Mk 7:1-23

The Pharisees and some scribes from Jerusalem met him and saw some of his disciples eating bread with their hands defiled, that is, unwashed. For the Pharisees and all Jews do not eat unless they have washed their hands, and there are many other things they observe, such as washing cups and pots and bronze vessels. The Pharisees and scribes asked him, "Why do your disciples eat bread with defiled hands?" He said to them, "Well did Isaiah prophesy of you hypocrites, 'This people honors me with their lips, but their heart is far from me! In vain they worship me teaching people to observe the commandments of men!'" And he added, "You reject the commandment of God in order to keep your own tradition! For Moses said, 'Honor your father and your mother, and whoever speaks evil of father or mother will be put to death.' But you say, if any man says to his father or mother, "Qorban" (that is, given to God), then what he would have given his parents is no longer theirs but can be given to God instead. In this way, you permit him to avoid giving anything of value to his father or mother, thus nullifying the word of God."

And after he called the crowd to him again, he was saying, "Hear me all of you and understand. There is nothing outside you that is able to defile you, but the things which *come out of you* are what defile you." And after he entered the house apart from the crowd, his disciples asked him about the parable. And he said to them, "Are you blind too? Do you not see that whatever goes into a person from the outside cannot defile since it enters not your heart, but your stomach, and then goes on out again—so all foods are pure. But what comes out of a person's heart is what defiles you: evil thoughts, fornication, stealing, murder, adultery, envy, wickedness, lying, lust, pride. These are what really defile you."

General Observations: Mark, who began to follow Matthew's order again at Mt 6:34, continues for this pericope. However, here we encounter one of the most striking and controversial parallels between Mark and Matthew. Most of the elements of this unit are shared with Matthew except for the added explanation of Jewish customs, the relocation of the discussion into a house, and the omission of Jesus' criticism of the Pharisees. However, the elements of the unit are presented in a radically different order in Mark. This pericope is of vital importance to Mark for presenting a rationale for Christian abrogation of Jewish kosher practices and rites of purity. To do so Mark has significantly rearranged the Matthean controversy story and its explanation, and has carefully rewritten some of its key lines. This passage is famous for the Markan additions to the Matthean version that are obviously motivated by the need of his Gentile audience for fuller explanations of Jewish customs (see Mk 7:2-4, 13b, 19b, 22).

Chart C: A Comparative Abstract of the Structures of Mt 15:1-20 and Mk 7:1-23

Mt 15:1-20	**Mk 7:1-23**
	1-2 Setting: Pharisees and scribes see the disciples eat with unwashed hands.
	[Parenthesis: 3-5 An explanation of Jewish eating practices, cursory and vague.]
1-2 The Pharisees and scribes challenge Jesus on the disciples' behavior	5 The Pharisees and scribes question Jesus.
3-6 The Qorban counter-question as the reply.	
7-9 The Isaiah 29:13 citation	6-8 Jesus' reply (*part one*) - the Isaiah 29:13 text and an accusation.
	9-13 Jesus' reply (*part two*) - the Qorban retort.
	14 Jesus calls the people to him and calls for understanding.
10-11 A brief exegetical explanation to the crowd.	15 The general statement on clean and unclean.
12-14 Jesus responds to the Pharisees' criticism.	
	[16 *debated text:* If genuine, the call to assent is also found in Mk 4:9 and 23, cf. Mt 11:15, 13:9 and 43, Lk 8:8.]
	17 they go into a house and the disciples ask him about the parable.
12-20 Then a full exegesis is given to the disciples.	18-23 fuller explanation with a declaration about all foods made clean.

The original story in Mt 15:1-6 was a question-counter question debate. Matthew has expanded the story taken from the tradition by means of a fulfillment citation and subsequent explanation by Jesus. It is one of several examples of such use of the OT by Matthew.[7] As such, the Matthean structure is simple and direct. It is easily identifiable by the references to the key words from the Isaiah text that appear in the interpretation. Moreover, the change from lips to mouth in the Matthean interpretation strongly suggests that while Matthew quotes the LXX, as usual, he has in mind a Semitic V*orlage* (cf. Mt) where *both* lips and mouth occur. As we have seen above, not only does Mark's revision of his Matthean source make the structure confused, his omission of key elements of the exegetical allusions distorts the more original well-structured Matthean argument.

Mk 7:1-4. In contrast to Matthew's simple introduction to the *qorban* controversy, Mark chooses to amplify the introduction to the controversy in two ways. First, he has the visitors from Jerusalem observe the disciples' eating practice, so that the charge they are going to level later is supported; and, second, he explains to the readers that Jewish people have odd eating habits. This unit has always been an embarrassment to advocates of Markan priority. The comment about Jewish eating practices is clearly a parenthesis inserted in the middle of the sentence describing the opponents' observation of the disciples eating. The author explains to the reader that "the Pharisees and all the Jews" have special eating customs involving ritual washing and special utensils, etc. The explanation can only be for non-Jews, and it is put so awkwardly and so clearly in the tone of an outside observer, that it is difficult to envision the author as a Jew. Although there is no textual support for its omission, some scholars have argued that it is a late addition to the Markan text because it is so out of character with an early date and provenance for the Gospel. We take it to be characteristic of the author's limited knowledge of Judaism and his desire to explain to non-Jews the connections and disconnections with that tradition. The insertion of Mk 7:2-4, however, provides the reason for Mark's shift of the quotation from Isa (Mk 7:6-7) to a point prior to the qorban counterquestion and reply (Mk 7:9-13//Mt 15:3-6), in contrast to Matthew, who more appropriately placed it afterward (Mt 15:7-8). Mark views the Isaiah passage as the key to the argument and so moves directly to it. The result is Mark's awkward structure.

• The curious word πυγμῇ, which has caused much difficulty and textual confusion, means either to wash the hands "by rubbing with the fist" or to wash the hand "to the

---

[7] See L. Cope, *Matthew: A Scribe* (Washington: Catholic Biblical Association of America, 1976), 52-64.

wrist." Even some advocates of Markan priority, who might otherwise want to defend Mark's knowledge of Judaism and Jewish customs, have said that Mark seems to be unclear or even confused about these particular Jewish customs.[8]

Mk 7:5. The Pharisees and scribes challenge Jesus as to why his disciples eat with unwashed hands. From what we know of Halakic disputes, Jesus' answer, as depicted by Mark, is curious. There is no other example, even in Matthew, of a debate in which the initial answer is a formula quotation from the prophets, as here in Mark. Moreover, the final line of this section, "You abandon the commandment of God and hold to human tradition," draws a conclusion which has not been established. That is, it has not been said that the washing of hands before eating is not a Torah commandment, but only a long established social and ritual custom or a Pharisaic oral tradition. Since the qorban counter-argument has yet to be made, there is no support yet for the Markan assertion.

Mk 7:6. The word, ὑποκριτής, occurs in Mk 7:6, where it is paralleled in Mt 15:7, but nowhere else in Mark. Matthew, on the other hand, has this word not only here where it is parallel to Mark, but also in twelve other literary contexts with no Markan parallel (Mt 6:2, 5, 16; 7:5; 22:18; 23:13, 15, 23, 25, 27, 29 and Mt 24:51). This is strong linguistic evidence of Mark's literary dependence upon Matthew.

Mk 7:9-13. Mark signals a break in the argument here by inserting Καὶ ἔλεγεν αὐτοῖς (cf. the frequent insertions of this phrase in Mk 4:1-34).

• Mark now has Jesus respond to the Pharisees' question (Mk 7:5) with the qorban retort (Mk 7:9-13). Mark replaces Matthew's Διὰ τί καὶ ὑμεῖς παραβαίνετε with Καλῶς ἀθετεῖτε. What Mark failed to provide was any connection to the original question. That comes only in the final sentence about the tradition, Mk 7:13. Mark follows Matthew closely except for Mark's insertion of an Aramaic word, qorban, along with its translation into Greek introduced by a translation formula. This is characteristic of Mark's style (Peabody, *Mark as Composer,* 103, 68). The nine instances of ὅ ἐστιν used to introduce a translation represent yet another element of the Markan overlay (Mk 3:17; 5:41; 7:11, 34; 12:42, 15:16, 22, 34, 42), even though a few of these appear in the parallel(s).

---

[8] See, e.g., Morna Hooker, *The Gospel According to St. Mark* (Peabody, Mass.: Hendrickson Publishers, 1993),174-76; Samuel Tobias Lachs, *A Rabbinic Commentary on the New Testament: The Gospels of Matthew, Mark, and Luke* (Hoboken, N.J.; KTAV; N.Y.: Anti-Defamation league of B'Nai Brith, 1987), 246; cf. E. P. Sanders, *Jewish Law from Jesus to the Mishnah* (London: SCM; Philadelphia: Trinity Press International, 1990), 261-63.

• Mark again adds a gratuitous comment, "and you do many things like this" (Mk 7:13b).

Mk 7:14. In Mark, this unit is presented as a final statement to the crowd, "again." Although the context is very distant, the πάλιν here probably refers back to Mk 3:23.

Mk 7:15. Mark omits "into *the mouth*" and "out of *the mouth*" from both parts of the saying in Mt 15:11. This can hardly be considered an example of Mark's radical primitiveness. By omitting references to "the mouth," Mark not only disengages the comment from the Isaiah text upon which it is a comment, but renders the saying physiologically absurd. A Jewish audience might be prepared to give credence to a claim that what enters the mouth is not what defiles, but it would have been bewildered by a claim that everything that comes out of a man defiles him. Taken literally, for example, this saying would mean that one could not even exhale without defilement. The into and out of the mouth saying is difficult enough to envision in a strongly Jewish setting, but in the Matthean context of the Isaiah reference it is understandable. The removal of "mouth" from the saying does not represent radical authenticity, but unintelligibility. Those reading the Markan parallel must presuppose Matthew's exegesis of Isaiah here, although Mark's text does not contain all of the elements required to support such a reading. The question and qorban counterquestion may be primitive, but the use of the Isaiah reference as a mid-point proof text is characteristic of Matthew. Mark has blurred Matthew's precision regarding the technical use of scripture and Jewish attention to detail in matters of ritual cleanliness and purity.

Mk 7:17. Mark has the disciples go "into the house" for private discussion of the matter. This setting is repeated in Mk 9:28 and 10:10. Mk 7:17, therefore, may also be one of the previous referents for πάλιν at Mk 10:10, as Mk 9:28 most likely is. Virtually the same motif, without mention of a house, is also present in Mk 4:10-11a. These four examples (Mk 4:10, Mk 7:17, Mk 9:28, and Mk 10:10) represent yet another element of the Markan overlay (Peabody, *Mark as Composer,* M, 158). These four verses are without parallels. A more inclusive category; i.e., "οἶκος/οἰκία used to set the stage for the subsequent pericope," also typifies the text of Mark.

Mk 7:18-23. Since Mark has taken the entire pericope to be a discourse on *within* and *without*, he revises Matthew's text freely in this final, fuller explanation to the disciples. His first comment follows Matthew in saying that what goes into the mouth goes into the alimentary system and then is expelled. Mark also adds that these things from outside "don't go into the heart," perhaps under the influence of the words "out of the heart" in Mt 15:18 and 19. The quotation from Isaiah, which helps to formulate the whole of Mt 15:1-20, makes it clear that the central issue is what proceeds from the heart, not what goes into it. Mark has missed the point. Mark also concludes his version of these sayings of Jesus with the unparalleled note that "thus [Jesus] made all foods clean." A story with a similar point is found in Acts 10:9-15 where God is depicted as revealing to Peter the "clean" nature of many potential foods, presumably including some that were prohibited to Jews of this period, given Peter's response to this vision. This story in Acts, in fact, depicts God as affirming three times, with reference to certain potential sources of food, "What God has made clean, you must not call profane." On the Two Gospel Hypothesis, Mark would have had access to Luke and, most likely, also to Luke's second volume, the Acts of the Apostles. Therefore, Mark may have found in this story in Acts a warrant for the unique and extraordinary affirmation he places on the lips of Jesus here, "Thus he made all foods clean." This is a far cry from the perspective found in Matthew. It reveals the extent to which Mark, especially when compared to Matthew, has distanced himself from the conflict about Torah piety within Judaism and early Christianity.

• When Mark does shift to consideration of what defiles, he again stresses his inside and outside contrast, using ἔσωθεν ("from within," Mk 7:21, 23), which occurs only here in his Gospel.

• All of the evils cited in Mt 15:19 as the results of evil intentions of the heart are violations of the Ten Commandments except for the addition of *blasphemy*, which probably found its way here from the Beelzebul controversy in Mt 12. Mark, however, greatly expands the list into a typical Hellenistic vice list (cf. Rom 1:29; Gal 5:19-21; 1 Cor 5:9-10, 6:9; 2 Cor 12:20-21; *Test. Reu.*, 5:5) and thus further blurs the focus on halakic issues and interpretation.

• Our analysis of this pericope leads to the conclusion that Mk 7:1-23 is a secondary reordering of Mt 15:1-20. Mark has failed to follow the tight exegetical logic of the Matthean text and, thus produced a physiologically awkward revision of Matthew's interpretive section. Mark is decisively secondary in this passage.

¶ 41. A Greek Woman Asks for the "Crumbs" of Exorcism
Mt 15:21-28==========>   Mk 7:24-30

He arose and went to the region of Tyre. And he entered a house because he wanted no one to know he was there, but he was not able to remain hidden. Immediately, as soon as she heard of him, a woman whose daughter was possessed by an evil spirit came and fell at his feet. Now she was Greek, a Syrophoenician by birth, and she begged him to cast the demon out of her daughter. He responded to her, "Let the children be fed first, for it is not good to take bread intended for the children of Israel and throw it to dogs." But she answered, "Lord, sometimes puppies under the table eat crumbs from the children's bread!" And he said to her, "Go. On account of this saying, the demon has been cast out of your daughter!" And when she came to her home she found her child lying in bed and no sign of the demon.

General Observations. Mark continues to follow the text and order of Matthew. However, Mark makes a major editorial change in the Matthean structure of this story. Matthew uses his characteristic ἀναχωρεῖν to describe Jesus' strategic withdrawal after the confrontation with the Pharisees and scribes (Mt 15:21, cf. Mt 2:12, 14, 22; 4:12; 9:24; 12:15; 14:13; 27:5). Yet, in saying that Jesus retreats into the region of Tyre and Sidon, Matthew is vague about the nature of Jesus' travels in the territory; the general impression is that he is going into Gentile areas that give him cover. However, true to his earlier stated charge (Mt 10:5), Jesus is not anxious to meet Gentiles (cf. Mt 15:24). Mark, on the other hand, is much more deliberate about Jesus' intentions. The movement into Tyre is but another step on a journey starting at Bethsaida (Mk 6:45) that will take him to Sidon and back by the sea of Galilee into the Decapolis and surrounding areas. It will end at Bethsaida (Mk 8:21). Mark is much more explicit that the areas that Jesus visits are well-established Gentile communities and the reader is not given any substantive reason to conclude that Jesus did not mix with the Gentiles (cf. Mk 7:31).

• Mark uses πάλιν at Mk 7:31 to refer back to the opening of this unit, Mk 7:24 (Peabody, *Mark as Composer,* 132-33). In Mt 15:21 Jesus withdraws toward Tyre and Sidon. In Mk 7:24, Mark has Jesus depart into the regions of Tyre. Then he narrates the incident in the *home* of the Syrophoenician woman. Finally, in Mk 7:31, by another use of retrospective πάλιν, Mark has Jesus leave the regions of Tyre and pass through Sidon on his way back to the Sea of Galilee. This appears not only to be another instance of retrospective πάλιν, but also points to Mark's knowledge and use of Matthew (cf. the "parallel" references to "Sidon" in Mt 15:21 and Mk 7:31, and to "Tyre" in Mt 15:21, Mk 7:24, and Mk 7:31). Of course, Sidon is not on the way to Galilee from the region of Tyre. In fact, one would almost certainly have to go through the region of Tyre to get to Galilee from Sidon or its territory. The general reference in Matthew to the regions of Tyre and Sidon, which is made specific by Mark, is also thereby made geographically incorrect.

Mk 7:24. Mark makes several modifications to Mt 15:21, primarily for compositional reasons.

The use of ἀπῆλθεν ("went away)" indicates that Jesus is making a journey rather than withdrawing strategically in the face of hostility, as is suggested by the Matthean use ἀναχωρεῖν (cf. Peabody, *Mark as Composer,* 51, and 53, 49; 171, and 172, 92).

Mark cleverly splits in two (Mk 7:24, 31) Matthew's single use of Tyre and Sidon (cf. Mt 15:21). This striking difference points to a literary connection between the two.

The collocation of ἀναστάς + ἀπῆλθεν εἰς (see #51 above) appears to be Markan composition.

The reference to going into the house indicates that Mark has fewer problems with Jesus going into houses in Gentile areas than does Matthew. Mark may think that a house is a more appropriate setting for discussion about food under the table. In addition, Jesus entering a house, which sets the stage for the subsequent pericope, is typical of the Markan overlay (Peabody, *Mark as Composer,* 42, 47).

Καί + a negative + ἤθελεν + a form of γινώσκω is found not only here in Mk 7:24, but also in Mk 9:30 (Peabody, *Mark as Composer,* 173, 92, cf. Mk 5:43).

Although Mark borrowed several words and phrases from Mt 15:21 in composing both Mk 7:24 and Mk 7:31, the remaining elements of Mk 7:24 show a considerable concentration of demonstrable literary characteristics of the author of Mark. The author's hand is strikingly visible here wherever Mark's wording differs from Matthew.

Mk 7:25-26. Whereas Matthew has the woman approach Jesus a second time after being turned away by the disciples (Mt 15:22, 25), Mark has abbreviated the account by relating only one approach by the woman. These verses also exhibit Markan editorial activity.

Mark's use of εὐθύς (Mk 7:25) as a modification of Mt 15:22, is characteristic of Markan composition.

Mark omits the Matthean description of Jesus as the Son of David (cf. Mt 15:22). The title, "Son of David" is much more characteristic of Matthew than of Mark.

For Mark, the woman, described as a Greek, is further identified as Syrophoenician and not as Canaanite (cf. Mt 15:22). The latter is a Biblical term that might have been difficult for Mark's readers to understand.

Mark omits Mt 15:23-24. Compared to Matthew, Mark is much more open to Jesus' association with Gentiles during his earthly ministry. Mark omits all reference to such restrictive tradition.

Mk 7:27-28. Mark's πρῶτον, indicating the temporal priority of the mission to Israel, implies that later the Gentiles will also be able to participate in Jesus' offer of salvation; after the "first," there has to be a second.[9] Clearly, this is anticipated with Jesus' present trip through Gentile territories. This conforms to Paul's declaration in Rom 1:16, "to the Jew first, but also to the Gentile."

• Unlike Mt 15:26, Mark utilizes χορτάζειν (Mk 7:27) which he also used in both feeding accounts (Mk 6:42; 8:4, 8). This more explicitly links this story to the stories of the two feedings and helps to bring a unity to this part with its Markan focus on eating/feeding.

• More than Matthew, Mark highlights the boldness of the woman in claiming what she wants from God through Jesus; i.e., a share at the table of salvation. This seems to be the central point of the Markan redaction of this pericope.

• The ingratiating remark about the crumbs eaten by the dogs is a statement of great faith which clashes strongly with the attitude of the scribes and Pharisees shown in the previous pericope (Mk 7:1-23). As with the people of Gennesaret (Mk 6:53-56), Mark treats the marginalized here very favorably.

Mk 7:29-30. The reference to the child being found whole on the bed goes beyond the Matthean source (Mt 15:28). This is Markan verisimilitude. The setting of someone entering a house is also characteristic of Markan composition (Peabody, *Mark as Composer*, 42, 47).

---

[9] See Amy-Jill Levine, *The Social and Ethnic Dimensions of Matthean Salvation History* in Studies in the Bible and Early Christianity 14 (Lewiston: Edwin Mellen Press, 1988), 146.

¶ 42. Jesus Heals Another Foreigner in the Decapolis
Mt 15:29-31==========>   Mk 7:32-37

And Jesus returned from the regions of Tyre and went through Sidon to the Sea of Galilee up into the middle of the regions of the Decapolis. And they brought him a deaf and speech-impaired man to lay his hand upon him. And after taking him apart from the crowd, so that they were alone, he put his fingers into the man's ears and, spitting on his finger, touched the man's tongue and, looking up to heaven, sighed deeply and said, "Ephphatha," which means, "Be opened." The man's ears were opened and his tongue loosed, so he could speak plainly. Jesus ordered them to say nothing to anyone but instead they announced it eagerly. Astonished, they were saying, "He has done all things well! He makes even the deaf to hear and the speechless to speak."

General Observations. Mark continues to follow Matthew's order (Mt 15:29-31). Matthew's pericope here resembles Mt 4:23-5:1, a summary passage introducing the Sermon on the Mount. There people bring the sick and impaired to him in droves and Jesus heals them. After the crowds gather, Jesus goes up onto a mountain, sits down and delivers foundational teaching. Similarly, in Mt 15:29-31, Jesus goes onto a mountain and sits down, although here no major block of teaching follows.[10] The crowds come with the sick and impaired. Jesus heals them. The people are amazed.

Excursus 8: Mark's Composition of Mk 7:32-8:26

In Mt 15:31, Matthew first notes that the dumb speak and concludes with the observation that the blind see. Matthew has drawn his list of illnesses in Mt 15:30 from Isa 35:5-6 LXX. In fact, Matthew has already quoted this passage at Mt 11:5, introducing it with his typical fulfillment of prophecy formula. In the next pericope, with the nucleus of the new Israel gathered again, Matthew will depict Jesus as sharing a meal with this nucleus, (probably) in anticipation of the banquet of the Messianic age (Matt 15:32-39, the Feeding of the 4000). Mark has other interests. In Mark, Jesus is in the midst of a mission tour through Tyre, Sidon, and the outskirts of Galilee. In the earlier section, Mk 1:16-3:19, by both word and deed, Jesus preached the gospel to Israel. Most of the people, however, did not hear or see. Jesus is depicted as speaking parables and doing mighty works in the next part of Mark's Gospel (Mk 3:20-6:6a). But his fellow countrymen still do not *hear* nor *see* ("What is the wisdom given to him?" "What mighty works are done by his hands?" Mk 6:2). Now, toward the end

---

[10] Terence L. Donaldson, *Jesus on the Mountain: A Study in Matthean Theology* (JSNTSS 8; Sheffield: JSOT Press, 1985), 122-35, also notes carefully the parallels with Mt 4:23-5:1 and wonders whether the concern here is to show that Jesus teaches with deeds (Mt 15:32-39) as well as with words (Sermon on Mount). Mark misses the whole of the Matthean mountain theme and thus, again, gives an indication of secondariness.

of two mission tours (Mk 6:6b-30 and 6:45-8:26), the disciples themselves still have difficulty in understanding. Picking up on the imagery of Mt 15:31, Mark placed two healing stories around his disturbing account of the disciples' lack of understanding (Mk 8:1-21). The first is a story of a *deaf* man who is healed by Jesus so that he hears well and speaks cogently (Mk 7:31-37). The second is about a *blind* man to whom Jesus restores sight (Mk 8:22-26). These two stories serve as counterpoints to the profound misunderstanding of the disciples depicted in Mk 8:1-21. Just as the blind man can obtain physical sight only by God's power, the disciples are equally in need of God's power to provide insight into the gospel. Mk 8:22-26 is not found in Matthew or Luke, while Mk 7:31-37 has some echoes of Mt 15:29-31 but has been so heavily edited that it is also essentially a pericope unique to Mark.

Mark's compositional activity in this section (Mk 7:31-8:26) indicates the importance Mark places on the point demonstrated in the two healings; i.e., that it is Jesus who enables people to *hear* God's wisdom and to *see* his power, continuing the Markan emphasis on the Isaiah citation in Mk 4:12. In short, Mark's editorial work with Mt 15:30-16:12 in the Markan parallel strongly reveals demonstrable Markan thematic and theological interests in passages that are the supplements and alterations of the text of Matthew. Such evidence is perfectly consistent with the Two Gospel Hypothesis and, conversely, not what one would expect to be the case on the Two Document Hypothesis.

Mk 7:31. This verse is a Markan composition based on Mt 15:21 and 29. It begins with πάλιν used retrospectively. Although its characteristics are somewhat different from other examples, Mk 7:24 is probably the previous referent for the πάλιν in Mk 7:31 (Peabody, *Mark as Composer,* 132-33). The use of διὰ Σιδῶνος ("through Sidon") is awkward, but it is clearly Mark's attempt to combine elements of Matthew's geographical notes in both Mt 15:21 and 15:29.

• After leaving the regions of Tyre and Sidon, Mark has Jesus return from the west to the eastern bank of the lake. The reference to the Decapolis echoes the list of places in Mk 5:20. Morna Hooker makes the helpful observation that on the previous visit the inhabitants asked Jesus to leave (cf. Mk 5:1-20).[11] Now they beseech him for help (Mk 7:32). Note also that, when Mark was utilizing Lk 6:17-18 and Mt 4:25 to compose his most inclusive collection of the cities and regions from which people came out to see Jesus, the only region Mark did not adopt was "the Decapolis" (Mk 3:7-8, against Mt 4:25; see the synopsis ¶19). It is not unreasonable, therefore, to think that Mark preferred to depict Jesus going to the people in the Decapolis in Mk 5:1-20 and 7:24-31,

---

[11] Hooker, *Mark*, 185.

rather than having them come to Jesus from that region earlier. Mark's picture of Jesus' initiative in going out to the people could serve as a model for later missionary activity. Like Luke, Mark omits Jesus' harsh sayings about "being sent only to the lost sheep of the house of Israel" and, therefore, not going among the Gentiles (Mt 10:5 and Mt 15:24). On the other hand, Mark did not eliminate the story of the Healing of the "Greek, Syrophoenician" woman from his Gospel (Mt 15:21-28//Mk 7:24-30), as Luke did. Nevertheless, although Mark depicts Jesus in ministry in the Decapolis on at least two occasions (Mk 5:1-20 and 7:24-30), he does not specifically identify those whom Jesus engages as Gentiles.

Mk 7:32-33. Mark here goes his own way with his account of the healing of the deaf and speech impaired man. He replaces Matthew's summarizing account of Jesus' healing (Mt 15:30-31, which echoes Isa 35:5-6 LXX) and expands it with special features of his own creation. Also, Mark is interested in something else in the text of Isa 35:6: the appearance of the unusual word μογιλάλος ("speech impaired"). Mark uses this unusual word to elaborate on the man's condition.

• Notice the very close structural parallels between Mk 7:32-37 and 8:22-26. The parallels are conveniently displayed in Peabody, *Mark as Composer,* 135, 80-81. These parallels in language and structure seem to provide evidence that the stories were shaped by the same editor. In addition to the common linguistic features noted in this table, one may observe that in both units Jesus separates the one healed from the crowds.

Mk 7:36. The secrecy motif found at the conclusion of both of these stories (Mk 7:36 and 8:26) is perhaps Mark's way of indicating that Jesus' work is only capable of being comprehended by the action of God in keeping with his own purposes (see Appendix 1 on the messianic secret). Mark does use the verb ἐπιτιμάω but prefers διαστέλλομαι when composing Jesus' charges to secrecy (Peabody, *Mark as Composer,* 147, 85). This is further evidence of Mark's editorial activity within this pericope.

Mk 7:37. The reference here to Jesus "doing all things *well*" stands in contrast with Jesus' statement to the Pharisees in Mk 7.6-7; i.e., "*Well* did Isaiah prophesy against you."

¶ 43. Jesus Feeds the Four Thousand in the Decapolis

Mt 15:32-39===========>   Mk 8:1-10

In those days, a great crowd again came together and they had nothing to eat. He called his disciples and said, "I have compassion on this crowd because they have remained with me for three days now and they have nothing to eat. If I send them home hungry, they will faint on the way, for some came a long distance." And his disciples again said, "How can we feed them here in the desert?" He asked them, "How many loaves do you have?" They said, "Seven." He ordered the crowd to sit down on the ground and, taking the seven loaves, he gave thanks to God, broke, and gave bread to his disciples to give to the crowd. They had a few small fish and he blessed them and ordered them to be distributed as well. Everyone ate and was satisfied. They collected seven baskets full of leftovers. This time there were about four thousand men. He sent them away and immediately got into the boat with his disciples and headed back across the sea.

General Observations. The placement of this unit follows the Matthean order. Matthew seems to see this messianic Feeding of the 4000 as the climax of Jesus' mission to gather the scattered sheep of Israel, but Mark views it quite differently. For Mark, it functions as part of a wider unit providing another occasion to highlight the obduracy of the disciples. It prepares the readers for the critical dialogue between Jesus and the disciples in Mk 8:14-21. Several of Mark's editorial changes to Matthew's account emphasize the obduracy of the disciples.

Mk 8:1. Mark 8:1a is a Markan composition used to introduce Mark's use of Mt 15:32.

• After the opening phraseology ἐν ἐκείναις ταῖς ἡμέραις ("in those days"), Mark introduces a retrospective πάλιν to direct his readers back to the previous feeding story (Mk 6:34). This link, created by Mark, becomes even more important when Mark later rewrites Mt 16:5-12 so the focus shifts to reflection on the numbers of baskets full of broken pieces that were taken up at the end of each feeding (Peabody, *Mark as Composer,* 161, 88-89; 164, 90).

• The reference to the crowd may go back to Mk 7:33, or 7:14, or 6:34, or more than one of these earlier literary contexts (Peabody, *Mark as Composer,* 133-35).

Mk 8:2-3. By and large Mark follows the text of Mt 15:32b closely for the composition of Mk 8:2-3. However, the additional observation that the people have come from afar may not just be verisimilitude, but may indicate that quite different groups of people from different constituencies were present at this event. Is this another anticipation of the later outreach to the Gentiles?

• Mark takes ἐν τῇ ὁδῷ from Mt 15:32. This is an important anticipation of the repetition of this phrase that will help to provide thematic unity for part 5, Mk 8:27-10:52 ("'On the Way,' Jesus Reveals His Identity").

• The linguistic construction ἀπὸ μακρόθεν may indicate Markan composition (Peabody, *Mark as Composer,* 130, 79). Of the five times this phrase occurs in Mark, the first three have no parallel in Matthew and Luke (Mk 5:6, 8:3, 11:13). The two occurrences with parallels are confined to the passion narrative (Mk 14:54//Mt 26:58; Mk 15:40//Mt 27:55; cf. Lk 23:49).

Mk 8:4. Mark's text is relatively close to Mt 15:33. However, Mark highlights the anxiety of the disciples by having them ask, "Where could anyone (τις is not in Matthew) get bread in this wilderness to feed all of the people?" Normally such a response would seem reasonable, but in the context of Markan theology it sounds very much like the disciples are echoing the complaints of the children of Israel in the wilderness by questioning whether God will provide. In spite of having the Son of God (Mk 1:1) among them, the disciples' question reveals a major misunderstanding of his mission and work.

Mk 8:5-7. Matthew has Jesus take the bread and the fish and at the same time give thanks, break, and distribute them (Mt 15:34-36). Mark has Jesus distribute the bread and fish in two stages. There is a giving of thanks for each element and a distribution of each. Mark's editing makes this feeding story more similar in structure to the story of the institution of the Eucharist. By having two blessings, one over the bread and one over the fish, Mark is not only able to use εὐχαριστέω, but is also able to further the connection between the two feeding stories by introducing εὐλογέω into his version of the Feeding of the 4000---the word that was used for the blessing of both the bread and the fish in the Feeding of the 5000 .

Mk 8:8-9. For Matthew, the number of baskets full of broken pieces serves only to heighten the impression of the miraculous. Something similar could also be said about the comparable note at the end of Matthew's version of the Feeding of the 5000. For Mark, however, these notes provide previous referents for the retrospective passage that focuses on the numbers seven and twelve, a Markan composition from material that had a completely different focus in Mt 16:5-12 (cf. Mk 8:14-21).

• As in Mk 6:44/Mt 14:21, Mark omits Matthew's reference to the fact that a large number of men apart from women and children were fed (Mt 15:38). Luke had already omitted the reference to women and children from the Feeding of the 5000 (Mt 14:21/Lk 9:14a). Mark apparently sides with Luke by omitting.

Mk 8:10. Mark expands Mt 15:39 in several ways.

> The addition of καὶ εὐθύς.

> The reference to the departure μετὰ τῶν μαθητῶν αὐτοῦ ("with his disciples") is also characteristic of Mark (Peabody, *Mark as Composer,* 94, 66).

> In Mt 15:21/Mk 7:24, Matthew has τὰ μέρη and Mark, τὰ ὅρια. Here, the reverse takes place.

> The reference to Dalmanutha rather than Magadan (Mt 15:39) causes consternation on any source hypothesis. It is noticeable, however, that various forms of Magadan appear in the Western Text, Θ, *it*, and *syr*pal. Some influential text critics regard this as sufficient support for "Magadan" in the text of Mark in the late second century. If adopted, this reading would bring Mark into conformity with the text of Matthew.

> • Mk 6:45 is constructed in a similar way to Mk 8:10. Mark 6:45 immediately follows the Feeding of the 5000 (cf. Mt 14:22), just as Mk 8:10 immediately follows the Feeding of the 4000.

> • Both feeding stories are also followed by an account of a crossing of the sea and healings (Mk 6:45-56, cf. 8:10-26). This is a reminder that Jesus is on a journey. The conscious paralleling of the journey motif in Mk 6:45 and 8:10 is evidence of compositional design. Mark intended to draw attention to the parallel structures of the two journeys in this part (Mk 6:6b-6:30, and 6:45-8:26).

¶ 44. Pharisees Want Jesus to Prove Who He Is by a Sign from Heaven
Mt 16:1-4=============>   Mk 8:11-13   <--------------Lk 11:16, 29-30
(Mt 12:38-39)

Some Pharisees came out and began to argue with him demanding that he give them a sign from heaven. After he had groaned within himself he said, "Why does this generation want a sign? I tell you the truth, this generation will get no sign!" And he left them and disembarked again for the other shore.

General Observations. Mark continues to follow the order of Matthew, but makes a number of changes. Mark 8:11-13 is essentially a conflation of Mt 16:1-2a, 4-5 with Lk 11:29-30. Mark also omits the Matthean/Lukan unit on reading the signs (Mt 16:2b-3//Lk 12:54-56). Mark omitted the reference to "an evil and adulterous generation" in Mt 16:4a, but will insert it at Mk 8:38 so that it refers not to those seeking signs, but those who are ashamed of the Son of Man and his words.[12]

• Aside from his use of Mt 16:1-5, there is some indication that Mark also utilizes material from Lk 11:29-30. See, e.g., ἡ γενέα αὕτη in Lk 11:29//Mk 8:12, which is paralleled in Mt 16:4 by γενέα alone, and τῇ γενεᾷ ταύτῃ and σημεῖον in Lk 11:30//Mk 8:12, which have no exact parallels in either Mt 12:38-39 or Mt 16:1-4. In general, Mark begins with Mt 16:1-2a and concludes with Mt 16:4-5, inserting material from Lk 11:28-30 in between. This reconstruction of the literary history of Mk 8:11-13 is a pointed example of how different synoptic arrangements can lead to different conclusions about the literary history of particular passages. See electronic synopses ¶44 and top of ¶45 on CD-ROM.

• Beyond the source-critical issue, what is striking about the Markan composition of this pericope is his insistence on the absolute refusal of Jesus to provide professed skeptics a visual demonstration of his Messianic claims. To these people, *no sign* will be given (cf. Mk 4:11).[13] This is evident in Mark's omission of Mt 16:2-3 on reading the signs and the references to the "sign of Jonah" (Mt 16:4/Lk 11:29). This explanation of Mark's use of the parallels in Matthew and Luke on signs is preferable to the bewildering compositional procedures required by the Two-Source Hypothesis.[14]

Mk 8:11. Mark's use of ἤρξαντο followed by the infinitive is characteristic of his composition (Peabody, *Mark as Composer,* 67, 54).

• Mark's use of πειράζειν ("to test") is particularly striking. The first attempt to test Jesus comes from Satan (Mk 1:13). There, Jesus meets the test. His subsequent tests come from the Pharisees (8:11; 10:2; 12:15). Jesus also passes these tests.

---

[12] McNicol et al., *Beyond the Q Impasse,* 180-81. In *Beyond the Q Impasse* the research team has already addressed the Lukan editorial work on the teaching about a demand for a sign.

[13] McNicol et al., *Beyond the Q Impasse,* 177-78, 180-81.

[14] Compare the outline of the redaction history of this passage in Mark as reconstructed by advocates of the Two Source Hypothesis provided by C. S. Mann, *Mark* (Garden City, N.Y.: Doubleday, 1986), 330.

• Here Mark limits his attention to the Pharisees and omits any reference to the Sadducees (cf. Mt 16:1). Mark will substitute a reference to "Herod" for Matthew's "Sadducees" in Mk 8:15 (cf. Mt 16:6), and will eliminate any reference to the Sadducees in his parallels to Mt 16:11-12 (cf. Mk 8: 21). The only reference to the Sadducees anywhere in Mark's Gospel is at Mk 12:18 (parallel to Mt 22:23). Mark may have deleted references to Sadducees because this group had little or no significance in his Christian world. This is in keeping with the Two Gospel Hypothesis.

Mk 8:12. The unusual occurrence of ἀναστενάζειν, "to sigh deeply," is indicative of Jesus' strong resistance to providing a visible demonstration of divine power to skeptics. Jesus' resistance to giving a sign is further underscored by Mark's use of the emphatic denial (εἰ δοθήσεται) in which Jesus says no sign will be given.[15]

Mk 8:13. Once again this verse is dominated by Mark's use of πάλιν used retrospectively. Mark 8:10 is the previous referent.

¶ 45. The Meaning of the Baskets Left Over at the Two Feedings

Mt 16:5-12===========>   Mk 8:14-21   <--------------------Lk 12:1b
(Mt 12:40-42)   (Lk 11:30-32)

Now the disciples had forgotten to get bread and had only one loaf with them in the boat, but Jesus warned them saying, "Watch out. Keep away from the leaven of the Pharisees and the leaven of Herod." Worried, they began to discuss the matter with one another, for they did not have bread. Aware of what they were saying, Jesus said to them, "Why are you saying you have no bread? Do you still not know or understand? Are your hearts hardened? 'Having eyes do you not see and having ears do you not hear?' Don't you remember? When I broke the five loaves for the five thousand how many baskets full of broken pieces did you gather?" They said to him, "Twelve." "And when I broke the seven for the four thousand, how many baskets full of broken pieces did you gather then?" They said, "Seven." And he said to them, "Do you *not yet* understand?"

General Observations. Mark continues to follow the sequence of the Matthean narrative. But by means of several deft compositional moves he puts the unit to a far different use than Matthew. In Matthew, the unit constitutes a warning to the disciples to be wary of the pervasive influence and power of the Pharisaic and Sadducean authorities who played an important role in the power structure of first century Palestine. The

---

[15] For an analysis of Mark's grammatical construction here, see C. F. D. Moule, *An Idiom-Book of New Testament Greek* (2d ed.; Cambridge: Cambridge University Press, 1963), 179.

disciples are represented as people of "little faith" who have some trouble in immediately comprehending the lesson (Matt 16:9, 11). But when Jesus goes on to explain it to them they *understand* (Mt 16:12). Mark, however, highlights the obtuseness of the disciples. He will follow this unit with the healing of the blind man at Bethsaida, thus signaling a very different view of this story. Mark is bringing the part to a close. He has highlighted the absolute refusal of Herod (6:14) and the Pharisees (7:1-23 and 8:11-13) to acknowledge the activity of God in the mission of Jesus. Despite the extraordinary things that have taken place, according to Mark, Jesus still needs to warn his disciples not to fall into the same trap as Herod and the Pharisees (Mk 8:15). In response, the disciples manifest considerable confusion (Mk 8:16-17). This calls forth additional teaching from Jesus that is carefully structured by Mark (Mk 8:17-18). Jesus accuses the disciples of having a hardened heart and an incapacity to see or hear (spiritually). For Mark's readers, the references to hearing and seeing (Mk 8:18) echo Mk 7:31-37 (hearing) and Mk 4:10-12 (seeing) and anticipate Mk 8:22-26 (seeing). As a result of Jesus' mission, some people are hearing and seeing. The disciples ought to see the deeper meaning of this as evidence that the kingdom is present and working. Thus, the unit ends with Jesus walking the disciples carefully through the two recent feeding incidents. Despite difficult conditions, the disciples should receive insight, gain courage to persist, and not give up on their commitment to discipleship. For Mark, the focus of this pericope centers on the disciples' lack of understanding of the true meaning of the two feedings. That meaning is somehow symbolized in the numbers of the remaining baskets full of broken pieces, "12" and "7." Mark's omission or abbreviation of Matthew 16:11-12, however, makes the sentence even more enigmatic than it was in Matthew.

Mk 8:14. Mark moves εἰς τὸ πέραν from Mt 16:5 to Mk 8:13 and thus utilizes the phrase to refer to the departure of the disciples "to the other side." In Matthew this phrase was part of a description of the disciples' arrival on the opposite shore. Both the idea of Jesus and his disciples making frequent trips "to the other side" and doing so "in a boat" are recurring features of Mark (Peabody, *Mark as Composer*, 123, 76; 26, 42). Both of these motifs often overlap with Markan uses of πάλιν retrospective, and thus are characteristics of those portions of Mark that have the highest probability of originating with the author (Peabody, *Mark as Composer*, 163-64).

• In anticipation of the dispute among the disciples over bread, Mark introduces the otherwise odd detail that they had only one loaf in the boat.

Mk 8:15. Mark's change of Matthew's εἶπεν to διαστέλλετο conforms to a demonstrable Markan preference (Peabody, *Mark as Composer*, 147, 85).

• Again, Mark omits Matthew's reference to the Sadducees (see 8:11 above). The reference to the leaven of Herod is a direct echo of Mk 6:14-29.

Mk 8:16-17. The reference to the hardening of the heart is clearly Markan (cf. Mk 3:5; 6:52; Peabody, *Mark as Composer,* 166, 91). The earlier story about the walking on the water ends with similar terminology (Mk 6:52). That pericope in Mark immediately follows a feeding story (Mk 6:30-44) and a sea crossing (Mk 6:45-52). Here also the reference to the hardened heart of the disciples (Mk 8:17) comes immediately after a feeding episode (Mk 8:1-10) and a boat trip (Mk 8:11-13). The description of the spiritual condition of the disciples makes them appear more like "those on the outside" than Jesus' new spiritual family (Mk 3:31-35) who have special insight into the nature of the kingdom (cf. Mk 4:10-12).

Mk 8:18. The reference to not seeing or hearing is a Markan supplement to Mt 16:9. This terminology, which Mark utilized for the first time at Mk 4:12//Mt 13:13, was drawn originally from Isa 6:9-10. It is used here to describe the disciples as so overcome by "cares and anxieties" (cf. Mk 4:6-7) that they cannot appreciate the spiritual dimension of Jesus' ministry. The introduction of this theme reiterates the points made in the two incidents in which Jesus brought hearing and sight (Mk 7:31-37 and 8:22-26) and which Mark used to frame Mk 8:1-21. As the deaf and blind need God's power to see, the disciples need the same power for spiritual insight. It will take the death and resurrection of Jesus to enable the disciples to see, to hear, and to understand.

Mk 8:19-21. The careful rehearsal of the two earlier feeding stories was designed to show Jesus' followers that, despite the difficult situations that occur in the course of a life of discipleship, God (through his Son) more than adequately provides.

• Mark uses συνίημι (Mk 8:21) in questioning how it is that the disciples still "do not yet understand." Matthew had used the same verb to affirm that the disciples had, indeed, finally come to understand (Mt 16:12). What is to be understood, of course, differs considerably in these two Gospels. Mark's usage of συνίημι in Mk 8:17 directly echoes the use of the same verb in Mk 4:12 (Isa 6) and Mk 6:52. The occurrences of σύνιημι in Mk 6:52 and 8:17 lack parallels in Matthew or Luke. The idea of the disciples not understanding and their hearts being hardened is a key part of the Markan overlay.

• Some have understood that the number twelve may refer to Jesus' provision for the restored Israel (symbolized by being founded on the mission of the twelve apostles, cf.

Mk 6:30). In addition, the seven may be a reference to the seven Hellenists in Acts 6:1-7. Whatever symbolic significance is accorded to these numbers, one thing is clear. At this juncture in the Markan narrative account, the disciples still do not grasp the significance of Jesus' mission.

¶ 46. Jesus Makes a Blind Man See
Mk 8:22-26

And they arrive at Bethsaida and some people bring him a blind man and beg Jesus to touch him. Having taken the hand of the blind man, he left the village and after he had spit on his eyes and laid hands on him he asked, "Do you see anything?" And he looked up saying, "I see men who look like walking trees." Then Jesus laid his hands on the man's eyes again and the blind man saw everything clearly. Jesus sent him away to his house saying, "Don't go into the village."

General Observations. There are no Matthean or Lukan parallels to this pericope. In keeping with his compositional purposes outlined in the excursus on the composition of Mk 7:32-8:26 above, Mark seems to have used this story about a blind man to frame Mk 7:32-8:26 with a miracle story comparable to the one with which the unit began.

• The two stage healing process recorded in this pericope is unique. Nowhere else in any of the synoptic or Johannine traditions does one find an account of Jesus acting twice to bring about a healing. The initial contact of Jesus with the blind man brings about only partial sight; a second contact is required. The partial restoration of this man's sight may anticipate the next pericope in Mark's Gospel, where Peter sees only in part (cf. Mk 8:29, 32-33). More will be required for Peter to attain clear vision. This pericope, therefore, serves not only to conclude part 4, but also functions as a transition into part 5, which features the account of Jesus' journey *on the way* to Jerusalem. In this part the crowds and all of the disciples have demonstrated their blindness to Jesus' true identity.

Mk 8:22-26. There is a retrospective use of πάλιν in Mk 8:25 that unites two verses within the same pericope (Peabody, *Mark as Composer,* 183, 95). A network of significant compositional, structural, and verbal agreements connect this pericope and the healing of the deaf and speech impaired man (Mk 7:31-37) and the Healing of Jairus' Daughter (Mk 5:21-24, 35-43, Peabody, *Mark as Composer,* 135, 80-81). Notable in those two stories is πάλιν used retrospectively to unite two or more separated pericopae. Because of this usage of πάλιν and because of the extensive nature of the interrelationships among these three miracle stories, we are probably in touch with a major element of Mark's editorial work.

• Mark depicts Jesus as returning to Bethsaida, thus completing the tour that began in Bethsaida, as noted in Mk 6:45. Compare our comments on Mk 6:45-47.

• As we noted in the discussion of Mk 7:32-37, Mark's incentive to include a story about a blind man here may have come to him from Mt 15:31. There, Matthew's list of diseases that Jesus cured opens with a note about the healing of a speech challenged person (cf. Mk 7:32-37) and closes with a note about the blind receiving sight (cf. Mk 8:22-26). Mark's use of "Tyre and Sidon" in Mt 15:21 to open two separate pericopae in Mk 7:24 and Mk 7:31 is a comparable compositional technique.

• The use of saliva as a means of healing by Jesus is found in Mark only in the two miracle stories that Mk has used to frame Mk 8:1-21 (cf. Mk 7:33 and Mk 8:23). Although Jesus is depicted as utilizing this technique also in a miracle story in the Gospel of John (Jn 9:6), neither Matthew nor Luke ever depict Jesus as healing in this way. Since these miracle stories in Mk 7:32-37 and Mk 8:22-26 have virtually no parallels in either Matthew or Luke (but cf. Mt 15:30-31 with Mk 7:32-37), and there are relatively few whole pericope unique to Mark, the use of saliva in both of these stories becomes even more striking. At a minimum it suggests some connection between Mark and the Johannine "signs tradition." For a similar story from the second century CE, cf. Tacitus, *Histories,* 4,81.

• During Jesus' ministry of word and deed the Matthean account has a charge to silence after the healing of the two blind men (Mt 9:31). No such prohibition is placed after a similar incident immediately before Jesus enters Jerusalem (Mt 20:24-34). Mark's two famous accounts of the healing of blind men (Mk 8:22-26; 10:46-52) are similar in that the first account contains a call to silence while the second does not. From the perspective of the Two Gospel Hypothesis, Mark has structured his account of the healing of the blind man at Bethsaida to serve as the initial element of an *inclusio* around the "on the way" narrative of Mk 8:22-10:52.

Summary

Mark 6:6b-8:26 is a carefully constructed unit that develops the tension between belief and unbelief in Jesus' mission. Early in the part both Herod and the Pharisees (Mk 6:14-29; 7:1-23) are pictured as almost stereotypical opponents of the way of the gospel. Toward the end the disciples are warned, "Beware of the leaven of the Pharisees and the leaven of Herod (Mk 8:15)." On the other hand, various people, such as those from the area of Gennesaret (Mk 6:53-56) and the Syrophoenician woman (Mk 7:24-30), welcome Jesus as one who has extraordinary power. What is intriguing to the reader is the situation of the disciples. In spite of having been given "the secret of the kingdom" (Mk 4:11) and having special access to Jesus, their hearts become hardened (Mk 6:52; 8:17). The reader has good reason to wonder, after all that has happened, what will it take for them to understand?

"ON THE WAY," JESUS REVEALS HIS IDENTITY

Overview

Part 5 of Mark's account features Jesus' final journey to Jerusalem. In many ways this is one of his most carefully structured sections. It is framed by two stories which feature the healing of blind men (Mk 8:22-26; 10:46-52). The first story concludes part 4 but also functions as a transition to part 5. The second concludes part 5. Both stories emphasize the theme that while the blind come to see Jesus' true identity (cf. Mk 10:52) those who are sighted (i.e., the disciples) continue to struggle to understand his word about what would shortly take place.

Mark highlights Jesus' predictions that, before his ultimate vindication by the resurrection, he would be humiliated and killed (Mk 8:31; 9:30-31; 10:32-34). Each passion prediction is immediately followed by expressions of misunderstanding by the disciples (Mk 8:32-33; 9:32; 10:35-41). As if to underscore the seriousness of this misunderstanding the immediately following material focuses on the nature of true discipleship (Mk 8:34-38; 9:33-37; 10:42-45). The Markan addition to Mt 16:25 within Mk 8:35, "on behalf of the gospel," equates "the gospel" with suffering discipleship. Indeed, one could say that most of the material in Mark between the three passion predictions constitutes clarification by Jesus that true discipleship entails not quitting "on the way" to the cross.

This focus on suffering and death preceding vindication in resurrection is underscored elsewhere in this part of Mark. The emphasis is not only on the call to endure suffering, but on understanding that suffering, and even death, must precede vindication and glory. Hints of this had already appeared in Mark's version of the raising of Jairus' daughter (Mk 5:29-32). In addition to the three passion predictions this focus also occurs in Mk 9:9; 9:26-27; and 10:45. Here too Mark stresses the fact that death, burial, and resurrection will constitute the climax of Jesus' life. Yet, by the end of the part the disciples still fail to grasp this central feature of the gospel: the pathway to glory is the way of suffering.

Throughout this part Mark describes Jesus and his disciples as "on the way," using that phrase five times (Mk 8:27; 9:33, 34; 10:32, 52). Indeed, the first and last verses of this part include it. It should be remembered that Mark opens his Gospel with two references to "the way" (Mk 1:2-3; from Mal 3:1 and Isa 40:3). Now, before Jesus enters Jerusalem to give a stinging critique of the temple and announce the type of community that will replace it, he himself walks "in the way."

¶ 47. The Crowds as Well as the Disciples Are Blind to Who Jesus Is
Mt 16:13-20 =========>   Mk 8:27-30   <========= Lk 9:18-21

And Jesus left with his disciples for the villages of Caesarea Philippi in the hills northeast of the Sea of Galilee. On the way there, he began to ask his disciples, "Who do people say I am?" They answered, "Some say John the Baptist, others Elijah, others one of the ancient prophets." But he asked them, "Who do you say I am?" Peter answered, "You are the Messiah [the Son of God]." And he warned them to keep quiet about him.

General Observations. Mark's version is well balanced between Matthew and Luke. He begins by following Luke's shorter version, omitting Matthew's account of Jesus' approval of Peter's answer and his promise to Peter. He chooses Luke in relating Jesus' question in the first person: "Who do people say that I am?" He follows Matthew's account over Luke's at several points; most notably in the identification of place (villages in "Caesarea Philippi") and the omission of any reference to Jesus "praying" (Lk 9:18). After omitting Matthew's inclusion of Jeremiah, he prefers Matthew's "one of the prophets" to Luke's "one of the old prophets has risen." Clearly, on our hypothesis, Mark is working with both Matthew and Luke.

Mk 8:27-28. Although the reader has been aware of it from the beginning (Mk 1:1), this is the first time in Mark's narrative that Jesus is openly called "the Christ." Mark directly connects this title with the phraseology "on the way." This reflects the theme of part 5, the Christ is the one who will make the crucial journey that leads to the cross. Two things about Peter's confession are noteworthy: (1) its placement at the beginning of this part; and (2) the partial understanding (i.e., "partial sight," cf. Mk 8:33) that it demonstrates. It will only be at the end of Jesus' journey that the nature of the Christ will be revealed, and even then it will be the Roman centurion who recognizes it.

• The response of the disciples to Jesus' question closely parallels the wording of Herod's confusion about Jesus' identity just after the beheading of John the Baptist (Mk 6:14-29). In Mk 6:14-15, Herod hears that Jesus is a resurrected John, Elijah, or one of the prophets of old.

•There is not as much reason to reject υἱὸς τοῦ θεοῦ after "Christ," as is often assumed. It appears in the text of Sinaiticus and other textual traditions. The phrase is bracketed in Nestle at Mk 1:1 and is believed to be certain at Mk 3:11 and Mk 15:39 (all supported by Sinaiticus).

• Mark omits Mt. 16:17-19. Perhaps Mark did not think that, given the later conduct of Peter, it was appropriate to attribute his confession to revelation. Mark also finds no use for Matthew's characterization of the founding of the church using arguments intelligible only in a Semitic culture.

¶ 48. Jesus Predicts His Death and Resurrection; Peter Objects
Mt 16:21-23 ========>   Mk 8:31-33   <===========Lk 9:22

And he began to teach them that it was necessary for the Son of Man to suffer many things and be rejected by the elders and chief priests and scribes and be killed and after three days to rise again. Now he was speaking the word boldly and Peter grabbed Jesus and began to scold him. But Jesus looked around, saw his disciples and scolded Peter saying, "Get behind me Satan! You are not concerned for the things of God but men."

General Observations. Once again Mark utilizes both Matthew and Luke in his narrative. He follows Luke's reference to the υἱὸς τοῦ ἀνθρώπου and to the "rejection" by the leaders of his people. But Mark chooses to include the harsh rebuke of Peter, which Luke omitted (cf. Mt 16:32-33). While closely following Matthew's conclusion, Mark omits some of the content of Peter's rebuke of Jesus. Specifically, he omits the Matthean reference to Peter being a "hindrance" to him. Although it is important for Mark to show that Peter misunderstands, Mark's apparent softening of anti-Petrine tradition when compared with the parallel story in Matthew is important to note. This contradicts an alleged trajectory of increasing hostility toward the disciples posited on the Two Gospel Hypothesis, which John Kloppenborg Verbin has suggested is a problematic historical consequence of that hypothesis.[1]

•Mark's additional reference to Jesus having faced the disciples (Mk 8:33), while at the same time rebuking Peter, indicates that the rebuke is extended to all who would deny the suffering, rejection, and death of the "Christ."

---

[1] John S. Kloppenborg, "The Theological Stakes in the Synoptic Problem," in *The Four Gospels: Festschrift Frans Neirynck*, BETL 100 (ed. F. Van Segbroeck, et al.; (Leuven: Leuven University Press, 1992), 1:93-120, esp. 106-8.

• The fact that there are three such passion prediction passages and that all three occur in part 5 (Mk 8:31, Mk 9:30-32, 10:32-34) leads to the conclusion that a major focus throughout the whole unit is the teaching that suffering, rejection, and death belong to Jesus as "the Son of Man," a designation that, for Mark, is little more than Jesus' self-description.

Mk 8:31. The "teaching" "begins" immediately at Mk 8:31. ἤρξατο plus the infinitive –(here διδάσκειν) is one of the redactional features of Mark (Peabody, Mark as Composer, 67, 54; cf. also 142-43). Jesus' journey in part 5 begins with Jesus teaching, and the content of that teaching is that the Messiah will suffer before being vindicated.

• "And he began to teach them" is the referent for πάλιν retrospective at Mk 10:1b. Similarly, the entire first Passion prediction unit serves as a possible previous referent for the πάλιν at Mk 10:32.

Mk 8:32. Mark's addition of καὶ παρρησίᾳ τὸν λόγον ἐλάλει contains an example of "the Word" used absolutely, a characteristic of Markan composition (See Introduction and Peabody, Mark as Composer, 69, 55).

• The use of παρρησίᾳ ("plainly") further emphasizes the contrast between Jesus' teaching and Peter's (and the others') aggressive rebuke of Jesus. To the reader, in contrast with the partial sight of Peter (and the others), the teaching is clear.

¶ 49. Giving One's Life for the Gospel

Mt 16:24-28=============>   Mk 8:34-9:1   <-----------------------Lk 9:23-27
       (Mt 10:39)   (Lk 17:33)

And after he had called the crowd together with his disciples he said to them, "If anyone wants to follow me, let him deny himself and take up his cross and follow me. For whoever wishes to save his life will lose it and whoever loses his life for my sake and the gospel will save it. For what does it profit you to gain the whole world and forfeit your life? What can you give in return for your life? But whoever is ashamed of me and my words in this adulterous and sinful generation, the Son of Man will be ashamed of him when he comes in the glory of his Father with the holy angels. And some of you who are standing here will not taste death until they see the kingdom of God having come in power."

General Observations. Mark continues to follow the common order of Matthew and Luke. In wording, Mark shows a preference for Matthew, with a few significant exceptions taken from Luke, primarily at Lk 9:26//Mk 8:38.

• The pericope addresses the question of discipleship. It functions as Jesus' corrective to the misunderstanding of Peter expressed in Mk 8:32-33. To believe that Jesus is the Christ is to "deny" oneself, take up one's "cross" and "follow him" (Mk 8:34). After stating this thesis about discipleship, Mark reinforces its validity by including four γάρ statements in a concentric structure. The first and last statements begin with ὃ γὰρ ἐάν (Mk 8:35 and 38) while the two middle statements both begin with τί γάρ (Mk 8:36 and 37). The result is a concentric arrangement that yields an A-B-B-A pattern. The urgency of discipleship is then punctuated by the eschatological reference in Mk 8:38c to the time when Jesus (the Son of Man) "comes in the glory of his Father with the holy angels." This is a tightly woven pericope.

Mk 8:34. Matthew identifies Jesus' audience as the disciples (εἶπεν τοῖς μαθηταῖς, Mt 16:24). Luke uses πάντας (Lk 9:23-27), an ambiguous term, which may or may not mean the disciples are present. Mark eliminates ambiguity by specifying that the audience is "the crowd with his disciples" (τὸν ὄχλον σὺν τοῖς μαθηταῖς αὐτοῦ, Mk 8:34).

• The phrase, καὶ προσκαλεσάμενος τὸν ὄχλον σὺν τοῖς μαθηταῖς αὐτοῦ εἶπεν αὐτοῖς, is consistent with Markan style (cf. Mk 3:23; 7:14; 8:1; 10:42; and 12:43; see Peabody, Mark as Composer, 107, 69; cf. 163-64).

• Mark changes the common testimony of Matthew and Luke from a form of ἔρχομαι to ἀκολουθεῖν to increase the focus on discipleship (cf. Mark's supplement at the beginning of this verse, which also adds προσκαλεσάμενος). This addition also helps to focus the narrative on discipleship (cf. Mk 3:13 and 6:7).

• Mark provides two significant supplements, ἐν τῇ γενεᾷ ταύτῃ τῇ μοιχαλίδι καὶ ἁμαρτωλῷ in Mk 8:38 and the introductory Καὶ ἔλεγεν αὐτοῖς at the beginning of Mk 9:1. The second of these is typical of Mark (Peabody, Mark as Composer, 89, 64). The first may derive from the use of language Mark found in different literary contexts in Matthew and Luke (cf. Mt 16:4//Mt 12:39 and Lk 11:29).

Mk 8:35. Mark differs from Matthew/Luke by adding τὸ εὐαγγέλιον used absolutely (Peabody, Mark as Composer, 14, 38). The terminology of Mk 8:34-38 is, for Mark, a succinct statement of the essence of Jesus' life. Mark could not refrain from referring to this as gospel. As such, it is a critical part of the Markan overlay.

Mk 8:36-38. Mk 8:36-38 is a good example of the pattern of alternating Markan agreement with Matthew and Luke within a single pericope. This is to be distinguished from the compositional technique of word-by-word conflation that Mark also employs.

Synopsis 5: Illustrating Mark's Alternating Block Usage of Mt 16:26-27 and Lk 9:25

Matt 16:26-27	Mark 8:36-38	Luke 9:25-26
16:26 τί γὰρ ὠφεληθήσεται ἄνθρωπος	8:36 τί γὰρ ὠφελεῖ ἄνθρωπον κερδῆσαι	9:25 τί γὰρ ὠφελεῖται ἄνθρωπος κερδήσας
ἐὰν τὸν κόσμον ὅλον κερδήσῃ	τὸν κόσμον ὅλον	τὸν κόσμον ὅλον
		ἑαυτὸν δὲ ἀπολέσας
	καὶ ζημιωθῆναι	ἢ ζημιωθείς
τὴν δὲ ψυχὴν αὐτοῦ ζημιωθῇ	τὴν ψυχὴν αὐτοῦ	
ἢ τί δώσει ἄνθρωπος ἀντάλλαγμα τῆς ψυχῆς αὐτοῦ	‹8:37› τί γὰρ δοῖ ἄνθρωπος ἀντάλλαγμα τῆς ψυχῆς αὐτοῦ	
16:27 μέλλει γὰρ	8:38 ὃς γὰρ ἐὰν ἐπαισχυνθῇ με καὶ τοὺς ἐμοὺς λόγους ἐν τῇ γενεᾷ ταύτῃ	9:26 ὃς γὰρ ἂν ἐπαισχυνθῇ με καὶ τοὺς ἐμοὺς λόγους,
cf. Mt 16:4//Mt 12:39	τῇ μοιχαλίδι καὶ ἁμαρτωλῷ,	cf Lk 11:29
		τοῦτον
ὁ υἱὸς τοῦ ἀνθρώπου	καὶ ὁ υἱὸς τοῦ ἀνθρώπου ἐπαισχυνθήσεται αὐτόν, ὅταν	ὁ υἱὸς τοῦ ἀνθρώπου ἐπαισχυνθήσεται, ὅταν
ἔρχεσθαι ἐν τῇ δόξῃ τοῦ πατρὸς αὐτοῦ μετὰ τῶν ἀγγέλων αὐτοῦ,	ἔλθῃ ἐν τῇ δόξῃ τοῦ πατρὸς αὐτοῦ μετὰ τῶν ἀγγέλων τῶν ἁγίων	ἔλθῃ ἐν τῇ δόξῃ αὐτοῦ καὶ τοῦ πατρὸς καὶ τῶν ἁγίων ἀγγέλων
καὶ τότε ἀποδώσει ἑκάστῳ κατὰ τὴν πρᾶξιν αὐτοῦ.		

Mk 9:1. The introductory formula, καὶ ἔλεγεν αὐτοῖς, a Markan supplement to Matthew and Luke, indicates that Mark has added a new redactional introduction to this verse, thereby setting off the following logion of Jesus from what precedes it in the pericope and highlighting the content of Jesus' teaching within this verse (Peabody, Mark as Composer, 89, 64).

• In accord with his style, Mark has preferred Luke's βασιλεία τοῦ θεοῦ to Matthew's τὸν υἱὸν τοῦ ἀνθρώπου ἐρχόμενον ἐν τῇ βασιλείᾳ αὐτοῦ (cf. Peabody, Mark as Composer, 13, 38).

• Mark's distinctive reference to the kingdom of God having come "in power" results in part from Mark conflating "kingdom of God" from Luke with Matthew's "coming," where it was applied to the "coming" of "the Son of Man." Mark's addition of the prepositional phrase, "in power," modifying "the kingdom of God coming" has proved to be difficult for most commentators to interpret. On the Two Gospel Hypothesis, some progress toward an adequate interpretation of this verse may be provided by noting the possible influence on the author of Mark of themes characteristic of Luke-Acts. For instance, texts like Acts 2:22, "Jesus of Nazareth, a man attested to you by God and with deeds of power, wonders and signs that God did through him among you," Acts 10:38, "God anointed Jesus of Nazareth with the Holy Spirit and with power," as well as Acts 4:33 and 8:13, may have influenced the author of Mark here. See also the quotation of Isa 61:1 at Lk 4:18 for the affirmation of Jesus' "anointing" by God for his ministry, including the performance of acts of power such as restoring sight to the blind.

• Mark's deliberate change from the Matthean reference of the coming of the Son of Man to the Lukan kingdom of God also suggests an answer to the puzzling issue of Luke's use of the second perfect of ἔρχομαι in Mk 9:1. If Mark understands that the deeds of power done in early Christian mission (see above) were expressions of the coming of the kingdom of God then the Markan statement is understandable. Through the proclamation of the gospel the kingdom does come in the life-span of his hearers (cf. Mk 16:16-18). Mark, of course, by steering his composition away from the wording of Mt 16:28 does not have in mind the final consummation at the parousia, only its coming in the life of the community of faith. In the words of Vincent Taylor, "the kingdom is a visible manifestation of the Rule of God displayed in the life of an Elect Community."[2]

---

[2] Taylor, *The Gospel According to Mark* (London: Macmillan, 1963), 386.

¶ 50. The Transfiguration

Mt 17:1-13=========>   Mk 9:2-13   <-------------Lk 9:28-36

Six days later Jesus took Peter and James and John and climbed a high mountain where they could be apart by themselves. His appearance was changed before their eyes, so that his garments became glistening, brilliant white. Elijah and Moses appeared speaking with Jesus. Peter, afraid, responds, saying to Jesus, "Rabbi, it is a good thing we are here; let us make three canopies—one for you and one for Moses and one for Elijah." Then a cloud covered them and a voice from the cloud said, "This is my beloved Son, listen to him!" Quickly looking around they saw no one with them except Jesus.

As they were walking down the mountain, Jesus ordered them to tell no one what they had seen until after the Son of Man should be raised from the dead. So they kept the word to themselves, but they argued with each other over what resurrection from the dead meant. And they began to ask him, "Isn't it the case that the scribes say, 'Elijah must come first?'" But he said to them, "If Elijah really came first to restore everything, how is it written concerning the Son of Man that he must suffer many things and be treated with contempt? Yet, I say to you, Elijah has come and they did to him whatever they wanted to, just as it is written of him."

General Observations. Mark continues to follow the common order of Matthew and Luke, but generally prefers the language of Matthew.

• In this account one first notices the connection between the transfiguration of Jesus and the stories of what happened to Moses and Elijah at Sinai (cf. Exod 24, 1 Kgs 19:9-13). The references to the mountain, six days, Moses, and a cloud overshadowing Moses and his companions especially bring to mind the important theophany recorded in Exod 24. But there is also a direct connection with Mal 3-4. Mal 4:4-5 can be read as linking Moses and Elijah together as reappearing before the Day of the Lord. Apparently Mark sees the transfiguration as the fulfillment of that prediction (Mk 9:2-8). Mark omits any reference to a transformed face (Mt 17:2//Lk 9:29), expands on the dazzling white clothes (Mk 9:3, cf. Mal 3:2), and reverses the names of Moses and Elijah (Mt 17:3//Lk 9:30, cf. Mk 9:4). These changes may indicate a shift of emphasis away from Sinai theophanies to Elijah and the promise of his return, which is very prominent in Mal 4:5. For Matthew, the comparison between Jesus and Moses is paramount, and the fact that Moses and Elijah are the only persons to whom God spoke on the holy mountain is significant. For Mark, on the other hand, although Moses is prominent, Elijah plays the more important role (cf. Mk 9:9-13).

• Mark records a question raised by those with Jesus on the descent from the mountain: "What is the resurrection from the dead?" Although Matthew mentions Elijah and his coming to restore all things (Mt 17:11), Mark reconstructs the story by sandwiching the question about Elijah between two references to the passion of the Son of Man. This enables Mark to accent the similarity and difference between what happened to a returning Elijah (John) and the Son of Man (Jesus). See further below on Mk 9:9-13.

Mk 9:2. Mark follows Matthew's time designation ("six days") over against Luke's ("eight days"; Lk 9:28). The reference to "six days" and to a "mountain" produce echoes of God's revelation at Mt. Sinai (cf. Exod 24:16).[3]

• Mark highlights the experience of the three disciples with Jesus by adding μόνους to κατ᾽ ἰδίαν (cf. Mt 17:1; Exod 24:9). An adverb accompanied by further modification is a frequently recurring feature of the text of Mk (Peabody, Mark as Composer, 40, 46; 122, 76).

• Mark continues to follow Matthew closely, including the use of μετεμορφώθη with reference to the transfiguration, a word found in Phil 3:21 and 2 Cor 3:18 with reference to Jesus' resurrection (against Lk 9:29).

Mk 9:3. Mark adds στίλβοντα, to accent the "glistening" radiance of Jesus' clothing at the Transfiguration. In fact, according to Mark, the clothing is a whiter white than could be accomplished by a professional bleaching (also a Markan addition at Mk 9:3b, cf. Dan 7:9, Mal 3:2; 1 Enoch 62:15-16; 2 Enoch 22:8; Rev 3:5; 4:4; 7:9).

Mk 9:4. Following Matthew, Mark passes over Lk 9:31-33a, which has no parallel in Matthew.[4]

Mk 9:5. Mark had shifted the order of Moses and Elijah in Mk 9:4 to stress the comparison of Jesus with Elijah. But when Mark comes to Mk 9:5 he returns to the order he found in his sources; first, Jesus; second, Moses; and third, Elijah (Mt 17:4//Mk 9:5//Lk 9:33).

Mk 9:6. Mark describes the emotional state of the disciples with the term ἔκφοβοι, which means "having great fear" or "being exceedingly afraid." Outside of Mark, this

---

[3] See McNicol et al., *Beyond the Q Impasse*, 140, for comment on Luke's use of eight days.
[4] Ibid.

term only appears in Heb 12:21. This state of trembling attests to the disciples' partial vision; i.e., they simply do not yet understand, particularly in respect to the connection between Jesus' death and resurrection (cf. Mk 8:10, 21).

• Luke cites fear as the response of the disciples when they are enveloped in the cloud (Lk 9:34), while Matthew pointed to fear as the response of the disciples when they heard the voice from the cloud (Mt 17:6). Mark resolved the tension by moving the fear forward as an explanation for Peter's suggestion that three tents be built. The reference to Peter's not knowing what he was saying had already been supplied by Luke (Lk 9:33). Mark's moving this note about the fear of the disciples to a new context also helps to explain his omissions of Mt 17:6-7 and the details of Lk 9:34b.

Mk 9:7. Mark omits the Matthean reference to "in whom I do think well" (but note Mk 1:11) in favor of the emphasis on "hear him," which echoes Deut 18:15, 18, speaking of a future prophet like Moses. Jesus, the new Moses, is the one they are to hear now. For Mark this seems to be the function of the return of Moses.

Mk 9:8-9. The word ἐξάπινα appears in Mk 9:8, but nowhere else in the NT.

• The addition of περιβλεψάμενοι accords with Markan usage. περιβλέπω appears a total of seven times in the NT: six times in Mark, and once in Luke in a passage where the same vocabulary item is found in Mark (Mk 3:5//Lk 6:10; Mk 3:34; 5:32; 9:8; 10:23; and 11:11).

• The double negative is also characteristic of Mark.

• In general, Mark prefers ἀνίστημι when referring to the resurrection of Jesus. The two exceptions to this general principle are Mk 14:28 and 16:6, where he is dependent upon Matthew for ἐγείρω. Therefore, when Mark changes ἐγερθῇ in Mt 17:9 to ἀναστῇ in Mk 9:9 and supplements the text of Matthew in Mk 9:10, by including the use of ἀναστῆναι, Mark is simply demonstrating his typical vocabulary preference.

Mk 9:10-13. A form of συζητέω + πρὸς ἑαυτούς is consistent with Markan style (Peabody, Mark as Composer, 199, 100; cf. 37, 45), as is ὅταν + ἐκ νεκρῶν + a form of ἀνίστημι (Peabody, Mark as Composer, 198, 100). "The Word" used absolutely is also Markan. In short, Mk 9:10 is permeated with characteristics of the author of Mark. Such evidence suggests that Mark is composing his Gospel using material in Matthew and Luke, supplementing or altering that material in accord with his own style.

•The emphasis of Mk 9:10 is on resurrection. This is Markan composition preparing the reader for what follows in Mk 9:11-13, and integral to the Markan overlay. Mark, when discussing Elijah, does not reproduce the explicit Matthean connection (Mt 17:13) between John and Jesus, but bows to Luke in not saying explicitly that John was Elijah. Perhaps Mark may have been thinking of the rejection of Elijah himself in his prophetic mission in Israel (cf. 1 Kgs 19:2, 10).More likely, in light of the Elijah *redivivus* motif in the previous pericope (Mk 9:2-8) and Mal 4:4-5, together with the continuing importance of the Elijah motif in Mk 9:11-13, Mark is saying something more. The Elijah *redivivus* event has occurred (referring to John), but a restoration did not occur before he was killed (cf. Mk 9:13). Now the same fate of rejection will befall the Son of Man (Mk 9:12). But unlike John, the implication is that the Son of Man will finish the restoration by being raised from the dead (cf. Mk 9:10). That is the meaning of the reference to the resurrection of the dead that so bewildered the disciples (Mk 9:9b-10). Judging by what unfolds in the next pericope, when Jesus brings to life one that appears to be dead, the disciples are still unable to receive the full import of this saying (cf. Mk 9:14-29).

¶ 51. Raising an Epileptic Boy, Jesus Stresses the Power of Faith and Prayer
Mt 17:14-[21]=========>   Mk 9:14-29   <---------------Lk 9:37-43a
        Mt 21:21-22

When Jesus rejoins the rest of the disciples, he sees a large crowd gathered and scribes quarreling with them. Upon spying him the whole crowd ran up and greeted him. He asked, "What are you quarreling about?" And one of the persons in the crowd said, "Teacher, I brought my son to you because he has a speechless spirit. And whenever it seizes him it throws him down and he foams at the mouth and grinds his teeth and he has convulsions. I asked your disciples to cast it out and they were not strong enough." And he answered saying, "O faithless generation, how long will I be with you? Bring him to me." They brought the boy and Jesus asked the father how long his son had been sick. "Since childhood. If you can do anything, please have pity on us and do it." Amazed, Jesus replied, "If it is possible? All things are possible to anyone who believes." Immediately the child's father cried, "I believe! Help my unbelief!" When Jesus saw the crowd running over to watch, he reproved the evil spirit saying "You mute and deaf spirit, I command you to come out of him and leave him alone!" And after screaming and causing a terrible convulsion, it left and the boy was still as a corpse, so that many said, "He's dead!" But Jesus took him by the hand and lifted him and he arose. Later, after they had entered a house and were alone, his disciples asked him, "Why were we not able to cast it out?" And he said, "This kind cannot be cast out by anything except prayer."

General Observations. Mark continues to follow the common order of Matthew and Luke for this story, but greatly expands it. Markan expansion is more credible than an attempt to explain how both Matthew and Luke, working independently, omitted precisely the same material: (Mk 9:14b-16; 20b-25a; 25c-26a and 26b) and simultaneously added numerous similar details (cf. Mt 17:16-17//Lk 9:40-41).

• Mark enhances Matthew and Luke's account by adding many details and re-focusing the point of the story. Listed below are some of these Markan supplements and modifications.

Mark has expanded the opening of the story by introducing a debate between the disciples and the scribes (Mk 9:14) that is witnessed by a "great crowd."

The crowd is "amazed" upon seeing Jesus, "they run to him, and greet him" (Mk 9:15).

The symptoms and diagnosis of the boy are more extensively described (cf. Mk 9:18, 20b-21).

Jesus engages the father in a diagnosis, asking the length of the illness and receiving a response that further conveys the severity of the symptoms (Mk 9:21-22a).

Mark expands the father's supplication and Jesus' response (Mk 9:22b-24). Mark expands the rebuke by introducing direct speech: "You mute and deaf spirit, I command you to come out of him" (Mk 9:25b).

After the exorcism, Mark adds details in Mk 9:26-27 that introduce a death and resurrection motif (see the more detailed note to Mk 9:26-27 below).

Mark adds a characteristic motif of his overlay by having Jesus going into a house to deliver esoteric teaching to his disciples (Mk 9:28).

Mark concludes his version of the story by having Jesus explain that this kind of demon can only be exorcised by prayer (Mk 9:29, προσεύχη).

• Taking his lead from Mt 17:17; 17:20// 21:21-22, Mark considerably expands on the themes of faith and unfaith throughout the narrative. In Mark, the father becomes paradigmatic of the person who believes, but is still plagued with residual unbelief.

Mk 9:14-15. Markan redactional features include:

συζητεῖν (Peabody, Mark as Composer, 199, 100).

καὶ πᾶς ὁ ὄχλος (Peabody, Mark as Composer, 85, 62).

ὄχλος + πολύς (cf. Peabody, Mark as Composer, 112, 71).

forms of τρέχω (see note above).

Καί + εὐθύς is definitely Markan redaction.

καὶ εὐθὺς πᾶς ὁ ὄχλος (cf. Peabody, *Mark as Composer,* 85, 62).

Given Mark's expansion of this story, the presence of his redactional characteristics within those expansions is to be expected on the Two Gospel Hypothesis.

• Mark adds a second introduction to the story in which the scribes debate with the crowd, presumably about why the disciples had been unsuccessful in exorcising the boy's unclean spirit. This makes the subsequent story a public issue, rather than a private one between Jesus and the epileptic boy's father. Thus the story better conforms to Mark's motif of public teaching followed by private instruction to the disciples in a house (Peabody, *Mark as Composer,* 85, 158).

Mk 9:15-16. The animation or movement within Mk 9:15 is striking. The "great crowd" "saw him," and "were amazed" (before Jesus has done anything in this pericope). The word ἐκθαμβέομαι occurs in the NT only here and at Mk 14:33; 16:5, 6; and the verb "ran to him" (προστρέχω), only occurs at Mk 9:15; 10:17, and Acts 8:30 (cf. Mark's supplement in Mk 9:25 that includes ἐπισυντρέχει). These are clear indications of Markan composition.

• There are strong reasons to link Mk 9:14-16 with other Markan redactional passages, including Mk 2:6-8; 8:16-17; and Mk 9:33b-34 (cf. Peabody, Mark as Composer, 75, 59). The linkages involve the presence of the scribes, subsequent "discussions" or "questionings," and Jesus' asking them "why" they are speaking or asking about certain things.

Mk 9:18b-19. Within these two verses, there is an impressive network of "minor agreements" of Matthew and Luke against Mark.

Matthew and Luke agree that the disciples were not able to cast out the spirit (ἠδυνήθησαν), but Mark prefers the wording they were not strong [enough to do it] (ἴσχυσαν).

Matthew and Luke agree on the word order ἀποκριθεὶς δέ ὁ ᾽Ιησοῦς εἶπεν, against Mark's expression ὁ δὲ ἀποκριθεὶς αὐτοῖς λέγει...

Matthew and Luke agree on the addition of καὶ διεστραμμένη to ὦ γενεὰ ἄπιστος

Matthew and Luke agree on the addition of ὧδε.

This network is very complex and less likely to be the editorial work of two authors independently utilizing Mark than the result of Mark's editorial modifications of the common text of Matthew and Luke.

Mk 9:20. Again, Markan redaction is strong here. Examples are καί + εὐθύς (cf. the addition of εὐθύς at Mk 9:24) ἐπὶ τῆς γῆς and καί + a form of πίπτω + ἐπὶ τῆς γῆς (Peabody, Mark as Composer, 82, 62; 201, 100).

Mk 9:26-27. In keeping with the previous pericope, where it is underscored that in the death, burial, and resurrection of Jesus the restoration is taking place (cf. Mk 9:12), Jesus restores one "as dead" to life. The verses include a number of features that, taken together, could be described as a Markan overlay characterized by death and resurrection motifs. See, for instance, the Markan additions of καὶ ἐγένετο ὡσεὶ νεκρός and ὅτι ἀπέθανεν (Mk 9:26) and the two verbs, ἤγειρεν and ἀνέστη, that conclude Mk 9:27 (cf. the similar phraseology to describe the "raising" of Jairus' daughter in Mk 5:41-42). Sandwiched between an account that stresses death and resurrection (Mk 9:1-13, esp. Mk 9:9-13) and the second passion prediction (Mk 9:30-32), the death and resurrection motif here can hardly be accidental. As Jesus is moving on the way to Jerusalem, Mark is taking every opportunity to foreshadow the importance of what is to come. Although Matthew has the same sequence of pericopae, Mark has heightened this theme throughout his parallel sequence (see esp. Mk 9:10; 9:26-27).

Mk 9:28. Mark's hand is present in the phrase, "when he had entered the house" (καὶ εἰσελθόντος αὐτοῦ εἰς οἶκον), followed by his disciples questioning him. This is certainly Markan redaction. Furthermore, this verse serves as a previous referent for πάλιν at Mk 10:10 (cf. Mk 7:17 and 4:10 for similar contexts).

Mk 9:29. The introduction of "prayer" (προσευχή) by Mark is striking for two reasons. Prayer occurs in Mark only here and at Mk 11:17. Also, Mark's account did not depict Jesus using prayer in this exorcism.

•The reference to prayer is probably a recognition by Mark of the need for divine action in both the mission of Jesus and discipleship. The father with his cry, "I believe, help my unbelief," appealed to divine power and was vindicated. Now Jesus reaffirms that it is only on similar grounds that demonic powers can be defeated. On the Two Gospel Hypothesis, it is probable that Mark drew upon not only the contextual parallel to Mk

9:29 in Mt 17:20, but also the doublet to Mt 17:20 in Mt 21:21-22 for his composition. It is from that doublet, Mt 21:22, that Mark derives the reference to prayer.

¶ 52. Jesus Again Teaches about the Betrayal, Death, and Resurrection of the Son of Man

Mt 17:22-23 ==========>   Mk 9:30-32   <------------------Lk 9:43b-45

The journey continues as Jesus and those with him pass through Galilee, but he doesn't want anyone to know about it because he is now teaching his disciples. "The Son of Man is to be delivered into the hands of men who will kill him, but, after three days, he will be raised." As on several previous occasions, the disciples don't understand what Jesus is saying to them, but on this occasion they are afraid to question him.

General Observations. Mark continues to follow Matthew's order, but is influenced by the text of Luke. Mark 9:30 agrees with Mt 17:22 by naming Galilee. All three texts agree that the initial prediction of Jesus is that he will be "delivered," i.e., "handed over to the authorities." However, Mark follows Matthew in stating that "they will kill him" and "he will be raised." Mark then follows Luke in pointing out the lack of understanding on the part of the disciples, and on their being "afraid to ask him." This use of Luke provides the transition for Mark's shift to Luke in the next series of pericopae and is another example of alternating agreement between Matthew and Luke within one pericope.

• Mark's second prediction carries forward the themes of betrayal, death, and resurrection. The discussion takes place in a shroud of secrecy. The suffering messiah remains the barrier to the disciples' understanding, and they are now afraid to ask for further clarification. In spite of (or because of) this lack of understanding, Jesus continues to give more formal instruction on church regulations in the following pericopae.

• Passion prediction two is a possible referent for the πάλιν that introduces passion prediction three at Mk 10:32-34.

Mk 9:30. Mark has introduced this prediction by his Κἀκεῖθεν ἐξελθόντες παραπορεύοντο διὰ τῆς Γαλιλαίας, which is a characteristic Markan construction (Peabody, *Mark as Composer*, 9, 37).

Mk 9:31. The "Son of man" is Mark's preferred term for the suffering messiah. Mark's additional interpretive emphasis upon "teaching" probably reflects Markan redaction (Peabody, Mark as Composer, 84, 62).

• Also, one notes the use of καὶ ἔλεγεν αὐτοῖς, a strong Markan linguistic characteristic. Thus, despite the formulaic nature of these verses, Mark's editorial hand can still be detected.

• Mark replaces Matthew's "on the third day" with "after three days." On the Two Gospel Hypothesis Mark appears to correct his sources consistently on this point about time. He corrects Matthew and Luke in passion prediction one [Mk 8:31//Mt 16:21//Lk 9:22] and three [Mk 10:34//Mt 20:19//Lk 18:33]. He corrects Matthew in passion prediction two [Mk 9:32//Mt 17:23; cf. Lk 9:44, which has no time reference]).

Mk 9:32. Mark agrees with Luke in omitting the reference in Mt 17:23 to the disciples being "distressed,"[5] and shifts instead to Luke's reference (Lk 9:45) to their lack of understanding and to their being afraid to ask for clarification. This enables, or even prompts, Mark to shift smoothly to Luke for the next story. Although the unit constitutes a plea for communal unity, there is a clear transition in the manner of argumentation at Mk 9:42.

Excursus 9: Be at Peace with One Another: On the Composition of Mk 9:33-50

At this point Mark has Jesus come into Capernaum. Mark is constructing a unit where Jesus gives teaching to a select group of followers, the Twelve (Mk 9:35). After the interlude in the house (Mk 9:33-50), the journey to Jerusalem will resume again at Mk 10:1.

Scholars have noted that Mk 9:33-50 is one of three major blocks of Jesus' teaching in Mark (the other blocks are Mk 4:1-11 and 13:5-37). But beyond that, little source critical work has been done on the unit. At the end of the previous unit Mark was following Lk (Mk 9:32//Lk 9:45), and continues to do so (Mk 9:33-40//Lk 9:46-50). On the Two Gospel Hypothesis, Mark then expands the discourse by incorporating material from Mt 10:42 and 18:1-9 for Mk 9:41-48. Then, in Mk 9:41-50, Mark conflates and edits material from Mt 5:13 and 14:31-35, the only other contexts in the synoptics that contain the word, "salt," ἅλας.

---

[5] McNicol et al., *Beyond the Q Impasse*, 147.

Mk 9:33-50 is a plea for communal unity. As such, the summary in Mk 9:50 aptly states its theme, "Be at peace with one another." Given this form and context one may even say that it constitutes Mark's analog to Matthew's community regulations (Mt 18:1-19:1). Significantly Mk 9:33-50 occurs precisely at the same place in his narrative as Matthew's community regulations (Mt 18:1-19:1). Mark uses some material drawn directly from Matthew's community regulations (Mt 18:1-9), and other material that shares similar concerns. Mark's Jesus instructs the Twelve on issues such as: the greatest must be humble like children; avoid in-group arrogance; cause no offense; and, by use of poetic exaggeration, the disciple is urged to allow nothing (hand, foot, etc.) to prevent one from attaining the kingdom.

¶ 53. Acting in Jesus' Name

Mt 17:24-18:2, 4-5 ====>   Mk 9:33-41   <=========== Lk 9:46-50
(Mt 10:40-42)

They come to Capernaum and while he is in a house he asks them, "What were you discussing on the road?" They became silent, for they were arguing about who among them was the most important. He sits down, calls the Twelve to him, and says to them, "If someone wants to be first, that person will be last of all and a servant of everyone." Taking a child, he stood him in their midst and, putting his arms around him, he says, "Whoever receives one such child as this in my name receives me. And whoever receives me does not receive me, but the one who sent me."

John says to him, "Teacher, we saw someone casting out demons in your name and we stopped him because he was not following us." But Jesus disagrees, saying, "Don't stop him. No one who does a powerful act by means of my name will soon be able to speak evil of me. For he that is not against us is for us. Truly I tell you, whoever gives you a cup of water because you are followers of Christ will not lose his reward."

General Observations. At Mk 9:32, Mark was drawing upon Mt 17:23 and Lk 9:45. Mark's opening here comes from the place details in Mt 17:24-25 (in Capernaum, in a house). After making use of these geographical details, he omits the rest of Matthew's story about the temple toll because it would serve no purpose for his primarily Gentile readers. To proceed, Mark makes use of Lk 9:46-48 and certain parallel materials in Mt 18:1-6 and 10:40-42.

Mk 9:33-34. Καί + a verb of motion + εἰς Καφαρναούμ to introduce the setting of a passage appears in three Markan contexts (cf. Mk 1:21; 2:1; and 9:33-34; cf. Peabody, Mark as Composer, 27, 42). The use of οἰκία to set the stage for a teaching of Jesus is characteristic of Markan redaction (Peabody, *Mark as Composer*, 42, 47). Similarly, καί + the aorist of ἔρχομαι εἰς + the name of a place + καί is a characteristic Markan linguistic usage (Peabody, *Mark as Composer*, 34, 49). Any one of these usages would be significant in itself, but the combination is impressive. They indicate heavy Markan editing of this passage. The pericope has a number of structural similarities with Mk 2:6-8; 8:16-17; and 9:14, 16 (Peabody, *Mark as Composer*, 75, 59).

• The ἐν τῇ ὁδῷ that appears in both verses is a characteristic of Mark, particularly of part five. It is also likely that πρὸς ἀλλήλους . . . διελέχθησαν reflects the hand of this author (cf. Mk 2:6-8; 8:16-17; and 9:14, 16; see above). The repetition of the theme of "dialoguing in the way" is typical of Mark's style.

• The structure of the incident in Mt 18:1-5 is similar to Lk 9:46-48. Specifically, both of these versions of the incident with the child begin with a question and conclude with the answer. In Matthew, the story begins with, "Who then is greatest in the kingdom of heaven?" (Mt 18:1). In Luke, the comparable question is, "Who was the greatest of them?" (Lk 9:46). Matthew's answer is "Whoever therefore humbles himself like this child, this one is the greatest in the kingdom of heaven" (Mt 18:4). Luke's comparable answer is, "For the one who is really the least among all of you, this one is great!" (Lk 9:48b). For his composition, Mark includes a parallel introductory question, but it is expressed in indirect speech, unlike Matthew and Luke: "For they were dialoguing in the way about who is greater" (Mk 9:34). Mark has no answer. It is difficult to imagine two editors of Mk 9:34-35 coming up with the same structure while independently using a common source lacking that structure. On the Two Gospel Hypothesis, Mark encountered Matthew's placement of the answer immediately prior to the logion in Mt 18:5 and Luke's placement of his version of the answer immediately after the same logion (cf. Lk 9:48). He may have chosen to mediate by omitting both. Or, perhaps he provided his "answer" as a prelude to Mk 9:36 by using a logion in Mk 9:35 also found in Mt 20:27. Indeed, Mark's statement that "Whoever would be first, must be last of all and the servant of all (πάντων) conforms with Mark's editing of Mt 20:27 at Mk 10:44, where Mark changes Matthew's ὑμῶν to πάντων.

Mk 9:35. The phrase καὶ καθίσας ἐφώνησεν τοὺς δώδεκα καὶ λέγει αὐτοῖς functions as a referent for the πάλιν retrospective at Mk 10:32. Two similar Markan contexts (Mk 3:13-15 and 6:7) may also serve as referents for this use of πάλιν (cf. Peabody, *Mark as Composer*, 70, 57). This phrase at Mk 9:35, therefore, represents strong evidence of the hand of the author.

• "The Twelve" (δώδεκα) used absolutely to describe the inner core of the disciples is also Markan.

Mk 9:36. The detail of Jesus embracing the child is repeated at Mk 10:16. There Mark utilizes the same verb, ἐναγκαλίζομαι, found nowhere else in the NT and only twice in the LXX (cf. Prov 6:10; 24:33). On the Two Document Hypothesis, Matthew and Luke, using these two Markan stories featuring children, independently agree in all instances to omit the Markan terminology for "embracing."

• The Two Gospel Hypothesis posits that Luke omitted Mt 18:3 at Lk 9:48 and relocated a modified form of this verse at Lk 18:17. Later, Mark also omitted Mt 18:3 from his parallel at Mk 9:36, and copied Lk 18:17 at Mk 10:15.

Mk 9:37. Mark 9:37 closely follows Lk 9:48, itself a conflation of Mt 18:5 and Mt 10:40. Mark blends slightly with Mt 18:5 but for the most part he is still following Luke, as will become apparent in the next verse.

Mk 9:38. At this point Mark comes to a Lukan story without a Matthean parallel, and incorporates it. Mark will also utilize Mt 18:6 (Mk 9:42) after he has finished with Lk 9:49-50//Mk 9:38-40 and another saying that he modifies to relate to his theme of "acting in Jesus' name" (Mt 10:42//Mk 9:41).

•Mark seems to be attracted to the phraseology of "in my name" (Mk 9:37, 38, 41) that serves as a common link. A central theme of Jesus' speech in the house is warning his followers against those who have pretensions to power (cf. Mk 9:34, 50). To do something in Jesus' name is not a sign of proprietorship, but to be a servant.

• Mark changes Luke's favorite address to Jesus, ἐπιστάτα (Lk 9:49), to his own equally characteristic term, διδάσκαλε.

Mk 9:39-40. Mark supplements Luke 9:50 by depicting Jesus as affirming that any exorcism in his name is to be allowed.

• The themes of acting in the name of Jesus, power/miracle, and concern over the motivation to demonstrate acts of power are also present in Acts 8:9-24. This may be another point where Mark is familiar with the tradition in Acts, and perhaps indicates that the issue of who was authorized to do acts of power in Jesus' name was a widespread problem in the early church.

Mk 9:41. Mark returns to the use of the indefinite condition with the subjunctive (cf. Mk 10:37). Bearing the name of Christ means you belong to Christ (ὅτι Χριστοῦ ἐστε). This is one of the most striking instances of Mark's alternating use of Matthew and Luke in one pericope. Mark 9:38-40 follows Lk 9:49-50. Mark clearly shifts to Mt 10:42 before reverting to following Mt 18 (Mk 9:42). The similarity of Mt 10:42 and Mt 18:6 in content and wording facilitated Mark's shift.

• Mark's addition of γάρ brings the form of the subsequent saying into conformity with the previous saying in Mk 9:40//Lk 9:50b.

• Mark alters the words ἕνα τῶν μικρῶν τούτων in Mt 10:42 to ὑμᾶς in the parallel at Mk 9:41. Since Mark uses the phrase ἕνα τῶν μικρῶν τούτων in the immediately following verse (Mk 9:42//Mt 18:6) it is difficult to explain his alteration of this same phrase in Mk 9:41. However, the presence of ὑμᾶς in a comparable position in Mt 10:40 may have precipitated Mark's shift.

• Mark's change of εἰς ὄνομα μαθητοῦ in Mt 10:42 to ὀνόματι ὅτι χριστοῦ ἐστε, although somewhat awkward, is understandable. When this rewritten clause is placed in a reconstructed Markan context where "in my name," i.e., action in Jesus' name, has characterized each of the three previous logia, they fit the context better than "in the name of a disciple."

• "Truly I say to you that he will surely not lose his reward" (Mk 9:41) represents the fragmentary preservation of a larger unit in Matthew (prophet, righteous man, disciple: Mt 10:41-42) on the theme of "reward." This is good evidence of the dependence of Mk 9:41 on Mt 10:41-42.

¶ 54. Do Not Give Offense, But Be at Peace

Mt 18:6-9 =========>	Mk 9:42-50	<====(Lk 17:1-2, 14:31-35)
(Mt 5:29-30; 5:13)		

"But whoever is a cause of stumbling for one of these little ones who believes in me, it would be far better that they put a millstone around his neck and throw him into the sea. If your hand cause you to stumble, cut it off. It is better to go into eternal life maimed than to go to hell with both hands intact. If your foot does the same, cut it off. Similarly with your eye, pluck it out. Far better to enter the kingdom of God with only one eye than the fires of hell with both. Everyone is going to be salted with fire. Salt is good but if it has lost its flavor what use is it? Have salt among yourselves and be at peace with one another."

General Observations. Mark has now made the transition to Matthew. He quickly moves from Mt 10:42 back to the context of Mt 18 and the order he has been following before the brief move over to Luke. Perhaps the phrase ἕνα τῶν μικρῶν τούτων allowed Mark to make connections between Mt 10:40-42 and Mt 18:1-6. However, another characteristic Matthean word, σκανδαλίζω, clearly becomes the *Stichwort* for this unit (Mk 9:42, 45, 47). Moreover, that organizing term allows Mark to combine elements of Mt 5:29-30 with the material drawn from Mt 18 (Mk 9:42-48). Then, using the *Stichwort,* πῦρ, "fire" (Mk 9:49, cf. Mk 9:43 and 9:48), Mark composed a transitional logion, "Everyone shall be salted with fire" (Mk 9:49). Mark may have borrowed the verb, ἁλισθήσεται, from Mt 5:13. The concluding logion of Mark's unit thus focuses on salt. It appears that Mark utilizes the only passages in the Synoptic Gospels that discuss salt (Mt 5:13-14 and Lk 14:34-35). These two passages also include a note about "casting outside" which, of course, is similar to warnings that are repeated in Mt 18:8-9 and Mt 5:29-30 and are reflected in both Mk 9:45 and 9:47. Mark composed this unit carefully, and the process of summarizing evident here is similar to that at the end of the other two great discourse units in Mark (Mk 4:33-34; 13:33-37).

Mk 9:42. As we noted above, ἕνα τῶν μικρῶν τούτων may indicate Markan use of a Matthean expression. It occurs four times in Matthew 10:42, 18:6, 10, and 14 with only a single parallel here in Mk 9:42 (cf. Lk 17:2).

• Based upon this same reasoning, the shared uses of σκανδαλίσῃ also support Mark's use of Matthew. Matthew employs this verb 14 times in a variety of contexts. Mark's 8 instances all have Matthean parallels. This evidence supports the view that Mark utilized Matthew and, inadvertently adapted some Matthean vocabulary.

Mk 9:43-47. Mark 9:43, along with verses 45 and 47, presents an interesting source-critical puzzle. Matthew 18:8-9 consists of two sayings, one about the hand and foot and another about the eye. Matthew 5:29-30 also consists of two sayings, one about the right eye and one about the right hand. Perhaps Mark, taking Mt 18:8-9 as his basic guide, divided the first saying about hand and foot so that each part (hand and foot), received a separate treatment. Nevertheless, while following Mt 18:8-9, Mark fused / into his composition elements from the doublet at Mt 5:29-30. The most important and interesting data appears at the end of Mk 9:43 and Mk 9:45. At the end of Mk 9:43, Mark combined "he should go away into Gehenna" from Mt 5:30 with a slight modification of the note "into the eternal fire" from Mt 18:8. Mark's resultant conclusion conflates Mt 5:30 with Mt 18:8. Mark 9:43, therefore, reads "go away into

Gehenna, into the asbestos fire." There is related evidence of conflation at Mk 9:45, where βληθῆναι from Mt 18:8 is combined with εἰς τὴν γέενναν from Mt 5:30.

• In Mt 18:8-9, being cast into fire is contrasted with "coming into life." Mark uses a similar contrast in Mk 9:43 and Mk 9:45. However, in Mk 9:47, the contrast is with "the kingdom of God." In Mk 9:33-46, the term "kingdom of God" does not appear. In Mt 18:1-6, the term "kingdom of heaven" does appear three times (Mt 18:1, 3, and 4). Mark's use of "kingdom of God" at Mk 9:47 is probably a reflection of this repeated theme in the parallel Matthean context.

Mk 9:44, 46. Some manuscripts (A D K θ f^{13}, etc.) repeat the content of Mk 9:48, "where the worm does not die and the fire is not quenched," at Mk 9:44 and Mk 9:46. However, since other manuscripts (including the key Egyptian witnesses) omit both Mk 9:44 and 9:46, we have decided to adopt in our display of Mk 9:43-48, the critical text of UBS[4], which omits both Mk 9:44 and 46, with most modern critical editions.

Mk 9:49. This is a very difficult verse, as the textual variants show. The variants, however, appear to be interpretive efforts and the simplest reading is probably best. On any source hypothesis Mark has created the sentence. The connection between salt and fire may presume the requirement for salt in sacrifice in Lev 2:13 or it may simply be a cultural phenomenon that salt was associated with sacrificial fires generally in the Mediterranean world. There is too little data available to decide the question. What is clear is that the verb ἁλισθήσεται is found only here and in Mt 5:13 in the N T. It was clearly appropriate in the Matthean context of the salt parable. But Mark is almost certainly responsible for the linkage of fire and salt here. At any rate, it functions as a gnomic statement in Mark providing the basis for the concluding verse about salt.

Mk 9:50. The change from μωρανθῇ (Matthew and Luke) to ἄναλον γένηται is a striking example of Markan alteration of the shared testimony of Matthew and Luke. Here is another case where it is more difficult to see source dependency going in the other direction. It probably represents Mark's attempt to explain the more metaphorical expression found in his sources. The combination of having salt and peace may be drawn from Lk 14:31-34, which Mark echoes here.

• The metaphor of being salted with fire is as terse as it is oblique. In the biblical tradition both salt and fire function as agents in purifying sacrifices. Although this metaphor is hopelessly mixed, the admonition, "Be at peace with one another," not only functions as a conclusion to the entire section on communal unity, but also serves as a guide to interpret the metaphor. The struggles and difficulties of the community are purifying because they entail suffering (fire) and preserving because they advance the integrity of the community through faithful discipleship (salt). In a context of struggle, Jesus exhorts his community to be at peace with one another.

¶ 55. Do Not Get Divorced and Remarry

Mt 19:1-10 ==========>   Mk 10:1-12   (Lk 16:18)
(Mt 5:31-32)

Jesus leaves and goes to the region of Judea beyond the Jordan. Again crowds flock around him and he begins to teach them according to his custom. When some Pharisees drew near to see what he would say they asked him if it was legitimate for a man to divorce a woman. He answered and said to them, "What did Moses command you?" They said, "Moses permitted us to write a divorce document and put a woman away." But Jesus said, "He wrote you this commandment because you are so hard hearted! From the beginning of creation 'God made humans both male and female.' For this reason 'a man will leave his father and mother and be joined to his wife and the two will become one flesh.' The result is that they are no longer two, but one flesh. 'What God has joined, let no human divide.'" And when they were in the house again, his disciples asked him about this. And he said, "In God's eyes, whoever divorces his wife and marries another commits adultery against his first wife, and if she, having divorced her husband, marries another, she also commits adultery."

General Observations. Having completed his work with the Matthean unit on community regulations (Mt 18:1-19:1), Mark continues to follow Matthew's sequence of pericopae. At Lk 18:15//Mt 19:13 Mark will rejoin the sequence of Matthew/Luke. Although Mark is basically following Matthew here, he demonstrates some knowledge both of parallel traditions in Luke and Matthean doublets to material in Mt 18:1-19:12.

• The opening verse provides the setting for a continuation of Jesus' teaching. The focus is now on marriage and the family. Mark used the divorce/remarriage teaching in Mt 19:1-9 as his basic source, but he omitted Matthew's teaching on celibacy in Mt 19:10-12.

• Mark has restructured the Matthean controversy story to serve his purposes. It is an outstanding example of the literary phenomenon of "broken patterns" (see category of evidence 5 in the Introduction). The retreat to the house for private instruction to the disciples in Mk 10:10 is also a characteristic feature of the Markan overlay.

Chart D: Comparative Structures of Mt 19:1-12//Mk 10:1-12

Mt 19:1-12	Mk 10:1-12
Vs 3 Pharisees' question A: Is a man permitted to divorce his wife for any reason?	Vs 2 Pharisees question A: Is a man permitted to divorce his wife?
Vss 4-6 Jesus' answer A: the Genesis 2 background	
Vs 7 Pharisees' Question B: Why did Moses allow for divorce certificates?	Vs 3 Jesus' counter question B: What did Moses command?
Vs 8 Jesus' answer B: This was a concession because of your hardness of heart	Vs 4 Pharisees' answer B: Moses allowed for divorce with a certificate
	Vs 5 Jesus' retort C: This was a concession because of your hardness of heart
	Vs 6-9 Jesus continues: The Genesis 2 argument
Vs 9 Jesus continues: The prohibition of divorce and remarriage by the man, except on the grounds of adultery only	
Vs 10 The disciples' comment: If all this is so, it is better not to get married.	Vs 10 The disciples' question Jesus in the house again
	Vss 11-12 Jesus states the prohibition of divorce and remarriage for any reason initiated by either man or woman
Vss 11-12 Jesus' further comment on celibacy	

As this chart demonstrates, Mark has made two major transpositions. First, Mark chose the Genesis material to introduce Jesus' saying on divorce and remarriage rather than as the basis for discounting the Mosaic requirement for divorce certificates. Second, Mark made Jesus' statement on divorce and remarriage the conclusion and the focus of the dialogue, while Matthew's dialogue continues through the discussion of eunuchs/celibacy.

Mk 10:1. This verse provides strong evidence of Markan composition: There are several Markan linguistic characteristics:

This verse contains πάλιν used retrospectively to unite two or more separated pericopae. Mark 9:15 and 9:25 both describe the gathering of crowds and stand in the closest narrative proximity to Mk 10:1.

Mk 10:1 contains two uses of πάλιν, the second referring to the fact that Jesus, as was his custom, was teaching them again. The only previous literary contexts in which the motifs of gathering of crowds and Jesus teaching them are combined are Mk 2:13 and Mk 4:2, both of which also contain this particular usage of πάλιν.

• Mark's retention of εἰς τὰ ὅρια τῆς Ἰουδαίας [καὶ] πέραν τοῦ Ἰορδάνου strongly suggests that Mark has borrowed, with some modifications, an important element of Matthean redaction. In Matthew, these words are integral to the transition from the community regulations to the subsequent material. The words are part of the exegetical web of Matthew's claim that the prophecy cited in Mt 4:15 is fulfilled. As at Mk 3:8//Mt 4:25, Mark uses an important feature of Matthew's redaction without retaining the proof from prophecy from Isa (Mt 4:14-16) upon which it is based. This is good evidence of Mark' s literary dependence upon Matthew.[6]

• Mark changed Matthew's ἐθεράπευσεν to ἐδίδασκεν. Mark often characterizes Jesus' healing activity as teaching (cf. esp. Mk 1:27). Mark's change introduces Jesus' subsequent teaching activity more directly than does Matthew's parallel redactional summary. Further, Mt 19:2 is almost pure Matthean composition, including the plural ὄχλοι, "crowds". The parallel use of the plural in Mk 10:1 is its only occurrence in Mark. This is strong evidence for Mark's literary dependence upon a passage that probably derives from the hand of the author of Matthew.

Mk 10:2. There are a considerable number of manuscripts, primarily Egyptian witnesses but including representatives of the Western text, that omit Φαρισαῖοι in Mk 10:2. However, Φαρισαῖοι has been retained in UBS[4] and we assume its inclusion in our discussion.[7]

• Mark's use of ἀνδρί here instead of Matthew's ἀνθρώπῳ is probably caused by Mark looking ahead to the Genesis-based argument (see Mk 10:6//Mt 19:4). Mark uses ἀνήρ

---

[6] William R.Farmer, "The Minor Agreements of Matthew and Luke against Mark and the Two Gospel Hypothesis," in *Minor Agreements* ed. Georg Strecker, 189-93.

[7] See David L Dungan, *The Sayings of Jesus in the Churches of Paul* (Philadelphia: Fortress, 1971), 122-25.

only four times, two of them here, versus fifty-five instances of ἄνθρωπος. The term is accurate in this context since the issue is the husband/wife relationship.

Mk 10:3. The Markan structure of this controversy is curious. By having Jesus ask the opponents what Moses commanded, Jesus is placed at a disadvantage at the beginning of the story. That is, Mark's version requires the reader/hearer to see Jesus' final retort as a revision or a contradiction of the provision in the Torah at Deut 24:1ff. Matthew's version, on the other hand, sets up the Deuteronomy passage as a later concession by God (see the outlines above) to Israel's hard-heartedness. The Torah is not violated. Although the two stories are narrated in almost exactly the same words, their logic differs markedly. The Matthean form is clearly more at home in the realm of Torah debate within first century Judaism than is Mark's version. Despite the claims of many that the Matthean form represents "re-judaization," it seems more reasonable to the team to view the Markan text, with its appeal to a wider Greco-Roman audience, as secondary.

Mk 10:5-9. Other than the different order of some of the material, Mark follows Mt 19 very closely.

• The major Egyptian manuscripts omit καὶ προσκολληθήσεται πρὸς τὴν γυναῖκα αὐτοῦ. This reading may have come into some manuscripts by attraction to Mt 19:5. However, the use of a preposition and compound cognate verb is characteristic of Markan style (contrast Mt 19:5).

Mk 10:10. This verse is Markan composition. It contains the significant overlay of the disciples going into the house to have an esoteric discussion with Jesus. It also has an important use of the πάλιν construction echoing similar earlier situations (Mk 4:10, 7:17, and 9:28).

• The public questioning of Jesus on the topic of divorce and remarriage is introduced with ἐπηρώτων αὐτόν (Mk 10:2) Here at Mk 10:10 the private questioning of Jesus on this same subject by the disciples is introduced with the same words.

Mk 10:11-12. These verses are the focal point of the controversy for Mark. As such they represent not only the culminating point of Mark's argument, but the full development of the synoptic tradition on this issue. Mark's absolute prohibition of divorce and remarriage is a restatement of Lk 16:18. This tradition in Luke is, in turn, a conflation of Mt 5:32 and Mt 19:9.[8] And, as with Luke, this statement on the indissolubility of marriage is directly followed by a plea on behalf of children (Mk 10:13-16/Lk 18:15-17). Whereas all three of the traditions preserved in Matthew and Luke focus exclusively on male initiative in the divorce proceedings, Mark allows the woman to initiate a divorce. Both by saying that a man who divorces and remarries commits adultery against his first wife and by saying that a woman can initiate a divorce, the Markan tradition stands at some distance from common Jewish marriage and divorce customs and closer to the customs in the wider Greco-Roman world. It is the most developed of the synoptic traditions on marriage, divorce, and remarriage. For those who think that Mark represents the original teaching of Jesus, we suggest that even if Jesus had been more radical than Shammai on this issue, he would still have stated his position in Jewish legal terms, rather than Greco-Roman. On the other hand, in a Gentile Christian context where one of the attractions of the Christian movement was its call to sexual purity, a radical renunciation of divorce and remarriage may have been seen as positive.[9] The fact that such a position left marriage unprotected from adultery was either not considered or was thought a small price to pay.

¶ 56. Jesus Embraces the Children

Mt 19:13-15 =========>   **Mk 10:13-16**   **<========== Lk 18:15-17**
          (Mt 18:3)

People were bringing children to Jesus so that he might touch them, but the disciples forbade them. When Jesus saw it, he became angry and said to them, "Allow the children to come to me and do not forbid them, for of such is the kingdom of God. I tell you the truth, whoever does not receive the kingdom of God like a child will never enter it!" And having placed his arms around them and his hands upon them he blessed them.

General Observations. At this point Luke rejoins the order of Matthew, so Mark, who had been following the order of Matthew, is again able to follow the common order of Matthew and Luke. For Mk 10:13-14, Mark generally keeps to the common wording of both. But at Mk 10:15 Mark prefers the wording of Luke. And in Mk 10:16 Mark uses the text of Mt 19:15 as his conclusion, Luke having no parallel to these verses. Once again the reader is confronted with a pattern of alternating Markan agreement with Matthew and Luke in wording within a single pericope.

---

[8] See McNicol et al., *Beyond the Q Impasse*, 224-26.
[9] Elaine Pagels, *Adam, Eve, and the Serpent* (Random House, N.Y. 1988), 78-97.

• Although Mark, like Luke, has this pericope directly follow the divorce passage, the emphasis of the passage seems to be on receiving the kingdom as a child. This is an additional warning that God's kingdom does not come by the careful planning of humans but in more mysterious ways that are not susceptible to human calculation.

• When utilizing Mt 18:1-6, Luke had omitted Mt 18:3. Luke's modification of Mt 18:3 now appears at Lk 18:17, and Mark follows Luke's text at this point exactly.

Mk 10:13. Mark's version of this story begins in agreement with Lk 18:15//Mk 10:13. It ends, however, in Mk 10:16//Mt 19:15, with Mark's text agreeing with Matthew's wording for touching, τίθημι τὰς χεῖρας + a form of αὐτός. On the one hand, Mark chooses Matthew's παιδία rather than Luke's βρέφος, but Luke's ἅπτω rather than Matthew's "placing of the hands." This is a good case of Mark's blending of his sources.

• Although Mark omits the reference to Jesus' prayer in his parallel to Mt 19:13, he seems to reintroduce the motif with his additional comment that Jesus "blessed" the children (Mk 10:16).

Mk 10:14. The language of Mk 10:13-14, "seeing" and "rebuking," echoes the scene of Jesus "seeing" his disciples and "rebuking" Peter at Caesarea Philippi (Mk 8:33).

Mk 10:14-16. Mark's penchant for vivid descriptions is exemplified here in his additions of ἠγανάκτησεν in Mk 10:14 and ἐναγκαλισάμενος in Mk 10:16.

• Mark's addition of ἐναγκαλισάμενος in Mk 10:16 emphasizes the connection between this story and the note about children in Mk 9:33-37, esp. Mk 9:26. If Matthew and Luke are both following Mark, it is odd that in both of these pericopae they always omit the phrase about Jesus embracing the children.

¶ 57. Jesus Teaches on Wealth

Mt 19:16-30 ===========>   Mk 10:17-31   <=========== Lk 18:18-30

And while he was setting out on the way, a man ran up, knelt, and asked, "Good Teacher, what must I do to inherit eternal life?" Jesus said to him, "Why do you call me good? There is no one good except the one God. You know the commandments: do not kill, do not commit adultery, do not steal, do not bear false witness, do not defraud, honor your father and mother." But the man said to him, "Teacher, all these I have kept from my youth."

And Jesus looked at him with deep compassion and said, "You lack one thing: go and sell your possessions and give the money to the poor; you will have treasure in heaven. And then come, follow me." But dismayed at the word, he left sadly, for he had many possessions.

"To enter the kingdom of God! It is easier for a camel to go through the eye of a needle than for a rich man to enter the kingdom of God!" And they were even more amazed and said, "Then who can be saved?" Jesus looked at them and said, "With humans it is impossible but not with God because all things are possible with God."

Peter began to speak, "Look, we have left everything behind and we are following you!" Jesus said, "I tell you the truth, there is no one who has left a household or brothers or sisters or mother or father or children or lands for my sake and the sake of the gospel who will not receive one hundred fold, now in this age—houses and brothers and sisters and mothers and everything—but along with persecutions, and in the age to come, eternal life. But many who are first will be last and the last first."

General Observations. After Mark finished his unit on children in the last verse, following Mt 19:15/Mk 10:16, the next pericope is in sequence in Matthew and Luke. Mark follows their common order. Jesus' instructions for the community are full of details woven together from Matthew and Luke, focusing on the issue of wealth. Jesus required the man to separate himself from his wealth. But this was to a greater end, to gain eternal life. Indeed, just as Jesus himself will be vindicated at the end of the way, the sacrifice of the faithful will not go unrewarded (Mk 10:28-31).

Mk 10:17. Mark has heavily rewritten the introduction to this story. In typical fashion he dramatizes the arrival of the inquirer (προσδραμών, "ran up," see Mk 9:15, and γονυπετήσας, "knelt") far more than either Matthew or Luke. Mark's supplementary εἰς ὁδόν continues the theme of Jesus "on the way."

Mk 10:18. Luke had already been puzzled by εἷς ἐστιν ὁ ἀγαθός in Mt 19:17 because the substantive should call for a personal referent. Accordingly, he rewrote the entire exchange. Mt 19:17 had said, "Teacher, what good must I do to inherit life?" But Luke wrote, "Good Teacher, what must I do to inherit life?"[10] Then, instead of an answer to the question, as in Mt 19:18, Luke had Jesus challenge the appellation with, "Why do you call me good?" In so doing, Luke obscured the true topic of the unit, the kind of

---

[10] Lamar Cope, *A Scribe Trained for the Kingdom* (CBQMS 5; Washington: CBA 1976), 111-19.

behavior required for entrance into the kingdom. In Mt 19:16-22 the form is precise; question, counter question, answer, etc., and the topic is consistent: What is required to enter the kingdom? Keep the Torah. What else? If you would be perfect, give all and come follow. The fact that this exchange is built around allusions to Prov 3:35, 4:4, and 28:10, and that a similar but entirely independent exegesis is found in Pirke 'Abot, 6:3 makes it virtually certain that Matthew's form is the earlier one. This argument can be fortified if we read the controversial phrase in Mt 10:17, "The good (i.e., the Torah) is one."[11]

It would have been virtually impossible for Matthew to have created this structure from the awkwardly different version in Mark. Rather, Mark follows Luke's revision since it is important to him to assert that his mainly Gentile Christian readership worships the one God. Thus, although this text has long been used to argue that here Matthew changed Mark because he was embarrassed by Jesus' denial of personal goodness, it actually represents a powerful argument for the secondary character of the version found in Luke and Mark.[12]

Mk 10:19. Mark follows Mt 19:18 in the recitation of the commandments (the order of the first two is reversed in Lk 18:20). Mark adds, "do not defraud," which is not one of the Ten Commandments. It is not at all clear why Mark added this. Perhaps, if this is the genuine text, Mark has in mind Lev 19:13 (cf. Lev 19:11), which refers to fraud in paying wages and is thus a variant form of stealing.

Mk 10:20-21. Mark conflates material from Mt 19:21 and Lk 18:21-22 for this verse, but also adds the address of Jesus as "Teacher" (drawn from the beginning of the story) and his own note about Jesus looking at the man and having deep compassion for him. He follows Luke's lead in eliminating the command to be "perfect" in Mt 19:21. "Inherit," "Torah," "good," and "perfect" are key elements in the Proverbs passages which form the interpretive frame for this entire unit in Matthew and which are key elements of Pirke 'Abot, 6:3 where a similar discussion of "Torah" as "good" is

---

[11] Robert H. Gundry [*Mark. A Commentary on His Apology for the Cross* (Grand Rapids, Mich..: Eerdmans, 1992), 560] argues that the use of the nominative in Mt 19:17 has to be personal because the neuter is used in Prov 4:2 in the LXX. However, that fails to note that the exchange in Matthew requires a shift from *good thing* (τί ἀγαθόν) in 19:16 to *the good* (ὁ ἀγαθός) in 19:17. Since for Matthew the law is always masculine, the shift was natural and without it the retort would be unintelligible (which is precisely what happened in Luke's or Mark's reading of the verse in isolation from its logical context).

[12] Contrast the famous comment by F.W. Beare, "In fact, nothing is more certain, it is inconceivable that the Matthean form could arise except as a theologically motivated correction of the Markan text" (Review of W. R. Farmer's, *The Synoptic Problem*, in *JBL* 84 (1965): 297.

preserved. The revisions of the passage by both Luke and Mark leave only echoes of this structure. All that Luke and Mark wish to focus upon is the need to give to the poor.

Mk 10:22. Mark heightens the reaction of the young man from just hearing and being sorrowful (Mt//Lk) to being shocked or gloomy, στυγνάσας.

Mk 10:23-25. Mark's addition of the detail that Jesus "looked around" before starting this speech conforms to a Markan stylistic preference. Specifically, Mark uses καί + a form of περιβλέπω to describe an action of Jesus five times throughout his Gospel (cf. Mk 3:5, 3:34, 5:32, 10:23, 11:11). He uses a similar construction to describe Peter, James, and John "looking around" at Mk 9:8. Apart from these six Markan uses, περιβλέπω otherwise appears in the NT only at Lk 6:10, the Lukan parallel to Mk 3:5. This detail at Mk 10:23 definitely points to Markan composition.

• At Mk 10:23, Mark seems to have changed Luke's note that Jesus "saw" the rich man going away into a more general note that Jesus "looked around," presumably at his disciples. Mark now has Jesus address the disciples in words almost identical to the Lukan parallel (Mk 10:23//Lk 18:24). The only difference is that Mark adopts εἰσέρχομαι from Mt 19:23, rather than Luke's εἰσπορεύομαι. Mark probably does this as a first step in moving over to the text of Matthew as his primary source for the balance of this pericope, Mk 10:24-31//Mt 19:23-30.

• Matthew has Jesus introduce the saying about the camel with the words, "And again (πάλιν) I say to you." It is clear that Mark has a preference for the use of πάλιν and Matthew's usage of πάλιν here, though it is not retrospective but simply means "I repeat," may have prompted Mark to move from the text of Luke to Matthew at Mk 10:24ff.//Mt 19:24ff. Although Matthew does repeat the words, "rich man" and "enter the kingdom," in Mt 19:23 and 19:24, this does not seem to have been enough for Mark. Therefore, Mark supplements Matthew and Luke's narratives with an entirely new sentence, "Children, how difficult it is to enter into the kingdom of God," which provides more linkage between the similar statements in Mk 10:23 and Mk 10:25.

• Mark's expansion of the narrative in Mk 10:24 also includes the note that "the disciples marveled (ἐθαμβοῦντο) over his [Jesus'] words." Θαμβέω, and its compounds appear seven times in Mark but nowhere else in the NT. Mark uses this word to highlight again the confusion of the disciples. Without additional insight from God Jesus' statement in Mk 10:23b leaves the disciples bewildered.

Mk 10:26-27. The use of the adverb, περισσῶς, and its compounds is also characteristic of Markan style. (Peabody, Mark as Composer, 93, 176). Here it serves as Mark's substitute for the more Matthean σφόδρα (7 times in Matthew; rare elsewhere in the NT).

• Astonished, the disciples' respond to Jesus' teaching on wealth with the question, "And who is able (δύναται) to be saved?" For the reply, Mark carefully blends the texts of Matthew and Luke. Mark begins by slightly adapting Mt 19:26 to read, "Looking on them, Jesus says, 'With humans, [this is] impossible, but not with God. All things are possible . . . .'" To conclude, Mark adopts another "with God" from Luke 18:27. As a result, Mark's text parallel to Mt 19:26 and Lk 18:27, includes the phrases, "παρὰ θεῷ," from Matthew and "παρὰ τῷ θεῷ" from Luke. By utilizing both parallels, Mark composes a characteristic "dualistic expression."

• Again, with the statement on the astonishment of the disciples Mark underscores their incapacity to understand the situation. Mark 10:27 is very important because it not only represents Jesus' answer to this particular problem but is the missing piece in the riddle of Jesus' mission.

Mk 10:28. To begin Mk 10:28, Mark alters the verb, εἶπεν, common to Mt 19:27 and Lk 18:28, to ἤρξατο λέγειν, in accord with Markan stylistic preference (Peabody, Mark as Composer, 67, 54).

•Mark also prefers to include Matthew's πάντα in Peter's response, rather than Luke's τὰ ἴδια, as the more appropriate follow-up to the affirmation made in Mk 10:27, also depending upon Matthew, that "all things (πάντα) are possible with God." Mark continues to agree with Matthew in having Peter affirm to Jesus, "Behold, we have left everything and followed you."

Mk 10:29-30. Peter's implicit plea for assistance because he and the other disciples have left behind "everything" to follow Jesus elicits a word of hope, even though sacrifice may well characterize the lives of disciples in the immediate future. However, Jesus' message of hope in Mk 10:29 does not include the promise that the twelve disciples would sit upon twelve thrones, judging the twelve tribes of Israel. This Markan omission from the parallel in Mt 19:28 probably occurred because Luke had moved his parallel form of the logion to a much later context in Lk 22:28-30. Mark shows little concern about such specifically Jewish apocalyptic descriptions of glory.

• Like Luke before him, Mark also uses the ἀμὴν λέγω ὑμῖν formula. Matthew used it to introduce the saying about judging the twelve tribes of Israel (Mt 19:28). Mark, as Luke, uses it to introduce his statement about what the disciples have left and what they will later receive. Mark prefers the longer list of specific relatives, plus fields, from Mt 19:29, to Luke's more generalized listing in Lk 18:29.

• When Mark gives the purpose for the disciples leaving relatives and other possessions, he again mediates between Matthew and Luke. Matthew 19:29 says that the disciples left all these "on account of my [Jesus'] name," while Lk 18:29 says it is rather "on account of the kingdom of God." Mark's compromise includes something of both. In partial agreement with Matthew, Mark has Jesus say first that it is "on account of me." Then, in partial agreement with Luke, he says that it is also "on account of the gospel," in accord with Mark's preference for "the gospel" (Mk 10:29, cf. Mt 19:29 and Lk 18:29; cf. Mk 8:35).

• As he did in Mk 10:24, so also in concluding his form of the saying at Mk 10:30 Mark expands the parallels considerably. He repeats the statement that "everything that is lost for the gospel that will be returned now" (i.e., "in this time"), "houses and brothers and sisters and mothers and children and fields" (Mk 10:30, cf. the list in Mt 19:29//Mk 10:29). The father is not mentioned in Mk 10:30. Henceforth God will be their father.

• Mark adds, "along with persecutions." This signature statement must be an allusion to some contemporary or past experience(s) of persecution within the Markan world. It is also probably an anticipation of Mark's enhancement of the persecution motif in Mk 10:38-39. But even here the emphasis is that sufferings must be endured on the way to glory.

• Having turned to Luke for the note, "in this time," just prior to his detailed listing of things to be returned, Mark turned again to Luke for the conclusion to this saying, "and in the coming aeon, eternal life" (Mk 10:30//Lk 18:30, against Mt 19:29: "and will inherit eternal life").

Mk 10:31. But Mark also used the first of two Matthean versions of the generalizing logion, "Many who are first shall be last; and the last, first," to conclude this pericope (cf. Mt 19:30//Mk 10:31 and Mt 20:16 //Lk 13:30). These two forms of the same logion frame Matthew's parable of the laborers in the vineyard (Mt 20:1-15), which Mark omits. Again, we have an excellent example of the Markan pattern of alternately agreeing with the wording of Matthew and Luke.

¶ 58. Jesus Teaches for a Third Time about the Betrayal, Death and Resurrection of the Son of Man

Mt 20:17-19 ==========▶   Mk 10:32-34   ◀----------------- Lk 18:31-34
                                                                        (cf. Lk 13:30)

As they were going on the road up to Jerusalem, Jesus was walking well in front, causing both amazement and fear among those following. Once again, taking the Twelve aside, he began to tell them what was to happen to him. "Look, we are going up to Jerusalem and the Son of Man will be handed over to the chief priests and scribes. They will condemn him to death, hand him over to the Gentiles, and they will mock, spit on him, lash him, and kill him. After three days he will be raised."

General Observations. Since Mark had copied Matthew's first version of the saying, "The first shall be last and the last, first," at Mk 10:31//Mt 19:30, Mark chose not to include the second (Mt 20:16). Mark also omitted the intervening Parable of the Laborers in the Vineyard (Mt 20:1-15). Like Luke, Mark omits many Matthean parables. Immediately following the second saying on "first and last" in Matthew is a third passion prediction on the lips of Jesus. Following both Matthew and Luke, Mark composed his third version of the passion prediction.

• Mark's third passion prediction is an excellent illustration of a Markan pattern of alternating agreements with Matthew and Luke within a pericope. Mark first shares text with Matthew alone, then with both Matthew and Luke, then with Matthew alone, and finally with Luke. As a result, Mark has used almost everything that Matthew and Luke have in common and much of what they do not share. This pattern of composition results in the third becoming the longest of the Markan passion predictions.

• Although it is relatively easy to see how Mark could have conflated Matthew and Luke in Mk 10:32-34, it is much more difficult to account for the pattern of alternating agreement between Matthew and Luke on the reverse presupposition that they were using Mark independently.

Mk 10:32. Although the words, ἐν τῇ ὁδῷ, are found in Mt 20:17, Mark moved this expression forward in his account for emphasis. The theme of Jesus "on the way" to his destiny in Jerusalem characterizes part five of Mark's Gospel (Mk 8:27-10:52). The same phrase, ἐν τῇ ὁδῷ, appeared in the first verse of this part (Mk 8:27). It will also appear in the last (Mk 10:52).

• Although Luke is fond of periphrastic constructions, Mark also has a preference for them and supplies two in this verse in material that supplements the parallel text of Lk 18:31 and in a parallel to Matthew where none appear (Mt 20:17).

• This is the last of Mark's three passion predictions. At the same time, however, Mk 10:32-34 also contains the first two of six references to Jesus and his disciples "going to Jerusalem." The last of these references introduces six controversy stories in which Jesus engages a variety of opponents in Jerusalem during the last week of his life (Mk 11:27-12:37a). As Jesus now approaches the end of the road to his destiny, the author of Mark carefully prepares his readers for the climactic events that take place in Jerusalem.

• Mark supplements the common narrative of Matthew and Luke with notes that affirm that Jesus was preceding them and his companions marveled, and those who followed [Jesus] were also afraid. These Markan supplements prepare his readers for the challenging, life threatening, and life taking events that will take place in Jerusalem in a short time. Usually in Mark such expressions of fear and marveling by those following Jesus indicate lack of trust and belief.

• With another retrospective use of πάλιν, Mark reminds his readers that Jesus had already prophesied his passion on two other occasions with similar words. This πάλιν also serves as a reminder to Mark's readers that Jesus had also "taken his disciples aside" for instruction on earlier occasions (cf. e. g. Mk 9:35).

• The use of ἄρχομαι + the infinitive (as in ἤρξατο . . . λέγειν) is also characteristic of Mark (Peabody, Mark as Composer, 67, 54). Therefore, Mark's change of εἶπεν, shared by Matthew and Luke, to this construction is not surprising.

• The phrase τὰ μέλλοντα αὐτῷ συμβαίνειν in Mk 10:32 is reminiscent of a unique verse in Luke's version of the transfiguration story which also looks forward to some forthcoming events of Jesus' passion, οἳ ὀφθέντες ἐν δόξῃ ἔλεγον τὴν ἔξοδον αὐτοῦ, ἣν ἤμελλεν πληροῦν ἐν Ἰερουσαλήμ (Lk 9:31). Compare Lk 9:51-53, which opens Luke's distinctive travel narrative, most of which was omitted by Mark, just a few pericopae earlier, between Mk 9:41 and Mk 10:13.

Mk 10:33-34. The theme of Jesus "going up to Jerusalem," shared with the narrative of Mt 20:17 at Mk 10:32, is now repeated in the form of direct discourse in Mk 10:33 in agreement with both Mt 20:18 and Lk 18:31.

• Mark shares with Matthew alone the details that "chief priests and scribes" would "condemn [the Son of Man] to death and deliver him." Then Mark shares with Luke alone the details that his Gentile persecutors would "spit on him" and "kill him," but that he would be raised (ἀναστήσεται cf. ἐγερθήσεται in Mt 20:19).

• Mark concludes his third and final passion prediction passage by omitting the note about the misunderstanding of the disciples in Lk 18:34. This is just one piece of evidence that flies in the face of the claims of some advocates of the Two Document Hypothesis that Matthew and Luke only include elements of the so-called messianic secret where they share those elements with Mark. More fundamentally it calls into question the whole edifice of scholarly reconstruction on the messianic secret as set forth by Wrede and his successors (see the appendix on the messianic secret).

¶ 59. Two Want Places on the Right and Left; Ten Others Are to Be Servants
Mt 20:20-28 ===========>   Mk 10:35-45   (Lk 22:24-30)

James and John, the sons of Zebedee, come up to Jesus and say to him, "Teacher, we have a favor to ask of you." In response, Jesus says, "What do you want me to do for you?" They say, "Give us permission to sit, one on your right hand and one on your left hand when you enter into glory." Again Jesus responds, "You don't know what you are asking. Can you drink the cup I will drink or be baptized with the baptism with which I will be baptized?" They answered, "We can." "Well" he says, "The cup I drink you will drink and the baptism with which I am baptized you will be baptized; but sitting at my right hand or my left is not mine to grant but for those for whom it has been prepared."

Now the other ten disciples heard what James and John had asked Jesus and were angry at them. Nevertheless, Jesus called them all together and said, "You know the so-called rulers of the Gentiles act bossy and their 'big men' like to order everyone around. But I don't want you acting that way. Whoever wants to be the leader, let him be servant of all, and whoever wants to be number one, let him be the slave of all. For the Son of Man did not come to be served but to serve and to give his life as a ransom for many."

General Observations. Mark continues to follow the order of Matthew for the construction of this pericope. There is no direct Lukan parallel. Luke had incorporated material on who is the greatest at Lk 9:46-48 and again in the discourse after the Supper at Lk 22:25-27. For the most part, Mark closely follows the wording of Matthew. However, there are several striking editorial changes and additions that reflect Mark's theological agenda.

Mk 10:35. Mark adds the names of James and John to the phrase, "the sons of Zebedee," drawn from Mt 20:20, just as he will introduce these names at Mk 10:41 where the parallel in Matthew reads "two brothers." A reader of Matthew would have known these names from the earlier contexts, Mt 4:21 and Mt 10:2. Mark also had already paired James and John conveniently for his readers at Mk 1:19, 29; 3:17; 5:37.

• Mark inserts "Teacher" at Mk 10:35 (cf. Mt 20:21), one of Mark's preferred addresses for Jesus. (Peabody, Mark as Composer, 125, 78).

Mk 10:37. In Matthew, the mother asks that Jesus "speak" that her sons may have seats of authority in his kingdom. In Mark, the sons of Zebedee themselves ask (demand is probably too strong for αἰτέω here) that Jesus "give" them these seats. This heightens their audacity and misunderstanding and better explains the subsequent anger of the other ten disciples with James and John, not their mother.

• Mark's substitution of "glory" for "kingdom" in Mt 20:21 (cf. Mk 10:37) shifts the focus of the request for a place of the highest honor from the political realm to the religious. Mark may be avoiding any intimation that Jesus' kingdom could be compared in any way with Rome. This would be particularly necessary if Mark has a Roman provenance. It would be better that Jesus' kingdom be in a mythic world of "glory" only intelligible to insiders.

Mk 10:38-39. Mark adopts the metaphor of "cup" as "sacrifice" from Matthew (Mt 20:22-23; Mt 26:39//Mk 14:36//Lk 22:42) and supplements Matthew with a comparable image of baptism (cf. Lk 12:50 and Rom 6:3-5). The imagery clearly echoes the two great rites of baptism and the Lord's Supper that, in the early church, were both closely connected with the death of Jesus. As we have noted earlier there is a theme in Mk, going beyond Matthew and Luke, to underscore the importance of these rites (cf. Mk 6:30-43). But beyond this Mark may well be in possession of a tradition of the martyrdom of both the sons of Zebedee.[13]

Mk 10:41. Mark adds his characteristic ἤρξατο, "and he began," to Mt 20:24, and specifies the names of two disciples as he did in Mk 10:35. Having presented a particularly glaring instance of incomprehension by two key disciples, Mark now presents Jesus' response on the nature of true discipleship. To be a disciple is to be a servant. The teaching in Mk 10:42-45 brings to a crescendo the whole of part 5 (cf. Mk

---

[13] Martin Hengel, *Studies in the Gospel of Mark* (tr. John Bowden; Philadelphia: Fortress, 1985), 13, 126.

8:34-38; 9:33-37). It is only through servanthood that one receives the greatness of future glory.

Mk 10:42. Mark qualifies Matthew's note about the pagan rulers, writing instead about "those who seem to rule," perhaps introducing some sarcasm for his readers but also implicitly affirming that Caesar's power is not ultimate.

Mk 10:44. Even though it is only the change of a single word, it is probably important for Mark to say that a follower of Jesus must be a servant of all, rather than just "your" servant, as we find it in Mt 20:27. See Mark's earlier and similar supplement at Mk 9:35 and our note on that verse. Mark seems to avoid any implication that Christians must be servants of "the Twelve" or other church leaders, which the expression in Matthew might imply.

Mk 10:45. The famous "ransom" passage in this verse is almost identical to Mt 20:28. In Matthew the idea of Jesus' life being a ransom is connected with a larger network of servant themes in the Gospel. For Mark, however, the words of Mk 10:45 represent a commentary on the previous verses, Mk 10:42-45. True greatness is not seen as exalted personal status or position but as servanthood. As the representative of his people, Jesus came not to receive adoration but to give himself in service (Mk 10:45a). Likewise, in the second part of the couplet in Mk 10:45, Jesus giving his life as an "exchange" becomes the model of how through service one finds the kingdom. It may indicate the real answer to the question of James and John. In the full commitment of their discipleship they will find the kingdom.

¶ 60. Blind Bar Timaeus Sees Again and Follows Jesus "in the Way"
Mt 20:29-34 =======>   Mk 10:46-52   <========= Lk 18:35-43
(cf. Mt 9:26-31)

They come to Jericho. While Jesus, the disciples, and a considerable crowd were leaving, a blind beggar named Bar Timaeus sat by the road. Hearing that Jesus the Nazarene was there he began to call out saying, "Jesus, Son of David! Have mercy on me!" Many standing there scolded him and told him to be quiet. But he cried out all the more loudly, "Son of David! Have mercy on me!" Jesus stopped and said, "Call him," and they called him and said, "Be valiant! Get up and go to him. He is calling for you." Throwing aside his cloak he got up and went to Jesus. Jesus said, "What do you want me to do?" The blind man says, "Sir, I want to see!" Jesus says "Go! Your faith saved you." At that same time the man could see; and he began to follow Jesus "in the way."

General Observations. Having left the order of Matthew after the third passion prediction, Luke rejoined Mt for this story. Mark, therefore, is again able to draw upon parallel order and content in Matthew and Luke.

• This story returns to the blindness theme of the end of the preceding part (cf. Mk 8:22-26). Both of the stories that end what we have called parts 4 and 5 emphasize Mark's (Isaianic) theme of seeing/understanding in contrast with the incorrigible "blindness" of the Twelve. Here, an ironic contrast to the disciples' incomprehension of Jesus' way is provided by a "blind beggar" who instantly "sees" who Jesus is and identifies him --- from a distance! Bar Timaeus functions as a model for everything Jesus has been saying about discipleship on the journey to Jerusalem. His faith anticipates the faith that will be the essence of the new community (Mk 11:22-23). And so in the end, he follows Jesus in the way (Mk 10:52).

• There are important differences between Mk 10:46-52 and Matthew and Luke. For instance, Mark supplements his text with the famous: "the son of Timaeus, Bar Timaeus" in Mk 10:46. There is also a lengthy supplement in Mk 10:49-50. Mark changes the common wording of Matthew and Luke from κύριε to ῥαββουνί in Mk 10:51. Mark concludes with Luke's theme, "your faith has saved you" (Mk 10:52//Lk 18:42), and supplements the story significantly with the final words, "in the way." Thus, Mark ends where he began this part of his Gospel, with an emphasis on Jesus and his followers "in the way" (cf. Mk 8:27).

• After one removes the Markan supplements from this story, the remainder shows a careful blending that not only draws on the common text of Matthew and Luke, but also, alternately, on the distinctive phrasing of each. For instance, at the very beginning, Luke sets the story "when Jesus drew near to Jericho" while Matthew sets it, "when the disciples and Jesus came out of Jericho." By utilizing both of these introductions, one from Matthew and one from Luke, Mark produces the somewhat odd introduction, "And they came into Jericho" (cf. Lk), "and when he went out from Jericho" (cf. Mt.), but nothing happens in Jericho in between these two geographical settings. This opening double reference to Jericho is reminiscent of a similar opening double reference in Mk 1:32, "When evening had come" (cf. Mt) "and the sun had set" (cf. Lk). But here the doubling is much less appropriate. As this story and the one in Mk 1:32-34 progress, however, instead of continuing to produce such double references by adopting different notes from both Matthew and Luke, Mark chooses between alternatives presented by Matthew and Luke. For instance:

Excursus 10: Details of the Composition of Mark 10:46-52

At Mt 20:30, Matthew writes ἔκραξαν. In the parallel (Lk 18:38), Luke chooses ἐβόησεν. At Mk 10:47, Mark sides with Matthew and writes ἤρξατο κράζειν, formulating his expression in accord with the vocabulary item found in Matthew, but composing the Markan parallel in accord with his own style, ἄρχομαι + the infinitive (cf. Peabody, *Mark as Composer,* 67, 54).

Mark next sides with Luke's additional description of Jesus as "the Nazarene," although in a slightly different expression, against the simple reference to "Jesus" in Mt 20:30. Mark also agrees with Lk 18:38 by including the vocative, Ἰησοῦ, either as a supplement to the reference to "son of David" in Mt 20:30 or as a substitute for "Lord" there (the reading of κύριε in Mt 20:30 does not have conclusive attestation).

In Mk 10:48, Mark agrees with Luke's καί against the use of δέ in the parallel in Mt. Matthew also writes σιωπήσωσιν in Mt 20:31. In the parallel (Lk 18:39), Luke has the alternate verb, σιγήσῃ. Here, although Mark utilizes Matthew's vocabulary, he uses the singular, σιωπήσῃ, in agreement with Luke because Mark is following Luke's version of this story as the healing of one blind man, rather than two, as in both Mt 20:29-34 and Mt 9:26-31.

Next Mark moves in the other direction with Luke's expression, πολλῷ μᾶλλον, against Matthew's simpler μεῖζον.

Mark again agrees with Matthew (Mk 10:49), using καὶ στάς from Mt 20:32 against σταθεὶς δέ in Lk 18:40.

Mark also parallels Matthew in the use of φωνέω against Luke's alternative, κελεύω.

At Mk 10:51, Mark again adopts the simpler phrasing of Lk 18:41, ἵνα ἀναβλέψω, against the more elaborate formulation of Mt 20:33, ἵνα ἀνοιγῶσιν οἱ ὀφθαλμοὶ ἡμῶν.

Finally, at Mk 10:52, Mark shows his typical preference for καὶ εὐθύς, again in closer agreement with Mt 20:34, καὶ εὐθέως, than with the more Lukan καὶ παραχρῆμα at Lk 18:43.

These data indicate that Mark uses both Matthew and Luke as his sources. Mark usually accepts the common wording of both Matthew and Luke, and supplements that wording in keeping with his literary style and thematic interests (e.g., ἐν τῇ ὁδῷ). The evidence is entirely consistent with the Two Gospel Hypothesis. What is striking (and this has seldom been highlighted in the secondary literature) is the pattern of alternating Markan agreement between

Matthew and Luke in this pericope. The detail goes well beyond what is usually understood to be conflation. It seems to indicate a deliberate pattern of composition. This kind of composition is not some kind of mechanical piecing together of sources. The author knew both versions of the healing at Jericho. He wanted to combine them, and the result reflects the influence of both versions upon the new account. On the Two Document Hypothesis, however, one must explain how Matthew and Luke, independently, could have split the text of Mark between them so frequently.

Mk 10:46. Mark now rejoins Luke's order of events. However, he is presented at the outset with contradictory place references in his sources. Matthew 20:29 says, "And as they went out of Jericho," while Lk 18:35 says, "as he drew near to Jericho." Mark's solution is a classic example of conflation: "And they came to Jericho . . . and as he was leaving Jericho . . . ." Mark's addition of καὶ τῶν μαθητῶν αὐτοῦ possibly reflects his knowledge of the genitive absolute in Matthew 20:29 where the subject and the participle are plural, unlike Mark who uses singular equivalents in his rewritten parallel.

• The only other NT usage of προσαίτης is found in Jn 9:8, but the same verbal root with a different prefix is found in the Lukan parallel to Mk 10:46 (ἐπαιτῶν, Lk 18:35).

• Luke had already changed the reference to two blind men to a reference to only one, and Mark follows Luke in this strategy.

• Mark's odd supplement, ὁ υἱὸς Τιμαίου Βαρτιμαῖος, may represent a Greek translation, "the son of Timaeus," without a translation formula prior to a transliteration of an Aramaic original, "Son of Timaeus." Alternatively, Mark may not have recognized that "Bar Timaeus" is, in fact, the transliterated Aramaic equivalent for "the son of Timaeus." These explanations are, of course, not necessarily mutually exclusive.

Mk 10:48. Does Mark's supplement at Mk 10:32, καὶ ἦν προάγων αὐτοὺς ὁ Ἰησοῦς, represent a reversal of the scene recorded slightly later at Lk 18:39 (cf. Mk 10:48), where οἱ προάγοντες are reported to have rebuked Bar Timaeus for crying out to Jesus? If so, Mark would be affirming the real leadership of Jesus. It may also explain why Mark substituted the more general πολλοί for the substantive participle, οἱ προάγοντες, when he came to his parallel to Lk 18:39 at Mk 10:48.

Mk 10:49. Mark's supplement in Mk 10:49-50, which includes a use of ἔγειρε, may represent another instance of Mark introducing the resurrection motif where such a motif does not appear in the parallel(s). Such death and resurrection motifs which supplement the stories Mark used from Matthew and Luke are significant parts of what we have come to call the Markan overlay (cf. Mk 9:26-27).

Mk 10:51. The Gospel of John also includes an address to Jesus as "Rabbi" in the story of the healing of the blind man (Jn 9:1-12, esp. Jn 9:2), even as Mark utilizes "Rabbouni" in this context.

Mk 10:52. Three of the four versions of this story in the synoptics include an imperative from Jesus that prompts the healing of the blind man/men:

Matthew's imperative is γενεθήτω, "let it be," within the sentence, κατὰ τὴν πίστιν ὑμῶν γενηθήτω ὑμῖν, "According to your faith, let it be to you" (Mt 9:29) There is no comparable imperative in the doublet at Mt 20:34.

Luke's imperative is Ἀναβλέψον, "Receive your sight," to which Luke has added one of his favorite phrases, ἡ πίστις σου σέσωκέν σε, "Your faith has saved you." On the Two Gospel Hypothesis, Luke could have been prompted to make this addition under the influence of the word "faith," πίστις, in the doublet to the contextual parallel (Mt 9:29, cf. Mt 20:33//Lk 18:42).

Mark's version of Jesus' command to the blind man reads, "Go," ὕπαγε, to which Mark, like Luke, has added ἡ πίστις σου σέσωκέν σε. Mark makes use of the latter phrase twice within his Gospel, both times in parallel with Luke (Mt 9:22//Lk 8:48//Mk 5:34; Lk 18:42//Mk 10:52). Luke, on the other hand, utilizes this phrase not only in parallel with these two instances in Mark, but also in contexts where there is no Markan parallel (Lk 7:50; Mt 9:22//Lk 8:48//Mk 5:34; Lk 17:19; Lk 18:42//Mk 10:52; cf. Mt 9:29.).

We would argue that this is evidence in support of Mark's literary dependence upon Luke. Furthermore, we note that, of the four Lukan occurrences of the phrase, ἡ πίστις σου σέσωκέν σε, Luke twice follows it immediately with the additional phrase, πορεύου εἰς εἰρήνην (Lk 7:50 and 8:48) and precedes this phrase once with the same imperative, πορεύου (Lk 17:19). The characteristic Lukan phrase may, therefore, be described as ἡ πίστις σου σέσωκέν σε + πορεύου with the phrase, ἡ πίστις σου σέσωκέν σε, πορεύου εἰς εἰρήνην, being both the more common and the more extensive form. One time when Mark used the phrase, ἡ πίστις σου σέσωκέν σε, he also immediately appended a phrase similar to the fuller form of the Lukan formula (ὕπαγε εἰς εἰρήνην in Mk 5:34; cf. Lk 8:48). This Markan parallel to Luke, therefore, represents a clear example of the fragmentary preservation in Mk of a phrase that is characteristic of Luke (Lk 7:50NP; Lk 8:48//Mk 5:34//Mt 9:22) and strongly suggests Mark's dependence upon Luke. Both of the times that Mark utilized the phrase, ἡ πίστις σου σέσωκέν σε, in parallel with Luke, Mark precedes this phrase with the imperative, ὕπαγε (Mk 5:34//Lk 8:48 and Mk 10:52//Lk 18:42). One of these Markan uses of ὕπαγε serves as a substitute for the characteristically Lukan πορεύου (Lk 8:48//Mk 5:34). The other is a substitute for the contextually appropriate imperative, Ἀναβλέψον, here at Mk 10:52. Since the Lukan phrase is ἡ πίστις σου σέσωκέν σε + πορεύου, both of Mark's parallels, one at Mk 5:34//Lk 8:48 and one at Mk 10:52//Lk 18:42, not only demonstrate the fragmentary preservation in the text of Mark of a linguistic characteristic clearly traceable to the hand of Luke, but also represent Markan substitutions that conform with Markan style (Peabody, *Mark as Composer,* 143, 84). That is to say, in both Mk 5:34 and Mk 10:52, where Mark agrees with Luke (ἡ πίστις σου σέσωκέν σε) he demonstrates his literary dependence upon Luke. Where he differs (ὕπαγε), he uses a verb that conforms with Markan style. This is strong literary evidence that Mark copied Luke and poses a difficulty for the theory of Markan priority.

• Mark appropriately concludes the unit with a reference to ἐν τῇ ὁδῷ, which highlights a central motif of the part. In contrast to the befuddled disciples, Bar Timaeus grasps what it truly means to see: it means to follow Jesus in his way; i.e., to endure the suffering of the cross before receiving the glory of his vindication.

Summary

Jesus has now finished his final fateful journey to Jerusalem. He has stated forcefully that before his vindication as Son of Man he must suffer and die. He is fully prepared to walk the walk without quitting. But it is unclear, even after express teaching on what it means to follow his way, whether the disciples are prepared to do the same.

It will only be after Jesus has finished the course that the disciples will perceive the nature of the way and will understand that the gospel also entails suffering before vindication and not having the chief positions of power when they reach the holy city.

JESUS AND THE END OF THE TEMPLE ERA

Overview

After the long journey to Jerusalem, was narrated in part 5 (Mk 8:27-10:52), part 6 opens with an account of Jesus' entry into the city (Mk 11:1-10). The episode, which functions as a preface to the part, recounts Jesus' entry into the holy city and ends with cries from the people for a restoration of the kingdom of David. Earlier, in Mk 1:14-15, Jesus had announced the arrival of the kingdom of God. Later, he gave the disciples the secret of the kingdom. The basic theme of this part is re-focussing the people's expectation. The kingdom *will come,* but in a far different way than the crowds expect (Mk 11:9-10).

The main body of this part is divided into two sections, Mk 11:11-12:37a and Mk 12:37b-14:11. In the first section, Mark juxtaposes Jesus' cursing of the fig tree and its withering with his direct assault on the temple leadership. In the middle of Jesus' critique of the temple establishment, he announces that the leadership of the people of God will be given to those who will produce fruit (Mk 12:9). The crowds expected that the coming Son of David would inaugurate a new era of grandeur for Jerusalem (Mk 11:9-10 = Ps 118:25-26). Instead, Jesus announces that they will reject the coming Son of David. But mysteriously, the rejected one will become the cornerstone of the edifice of the new era (Mk 12:11-12 = Ps 118:23 34). The section ends with a return to the theme of David. The rejected but vindicated Son of David will be far greater than the earlier David (Mk 12:35-37a). The abased Messiah will be the glorious Messiah.

The second section (Mk 12:37b-14:11) concentrates on the nature of the kingdom which the Messiah (David's son) will bring. As the Messiah will be rejected by treacherous persons, so the Messiah's people will suffer a similar fate (Mk 13:9-13). Mark has Jesus give extensive instruction on what conduct is expected of the Messiah's people under these circumstances (Mk 13:5-37). In the Synoptic Gospels only Mark introduces and concludes these instructions (Mk 13:1-37) with accounts of extraordinary faithfulness that are juxtaposed to acts of treachery (Mk 12:38-44 and 14:1-11). Jesus commends faithfulness by word (Mk 13:5-37) and example (Mk 14:12-16:8) as the key that will bring into existence the kingdom that was announced at the outset of his ministry (Mk 1:14-15).

Excursus 11 with Chart E: Mark's Chronology of the Passion Week

All three Synoptic Gospels concur in describing the triumphal entry with a reference to Jesus drawing near to Jerusalem and Bethphage (Mt 21:1//Mk 11:1//Lk 19:28; Mark and Luke add a reference to Bethany). Matthew and Luke portray Jesus going on into the temple and driving out those who bought or sold there (Mt 21:10-17//Lk 19:45-46). Only Mark, however, seems to have provided the details of a full eight-day Passion Week for his readers. This may indicate that Mark was composed in a place where there was a growing liturgical concern, perhaps at a time when the liturgy had reached a somewhat later stage of development, (cf. Jn 20:26, Barn 15). The following chart assumes a blending of ancient Hebrew and Roman methods of reckoning time. On the Two Gospel Hypothesis, Mark was probably dependent upon his sources for the Hebrew method of reckoning of time, but at key points (see the chart below) he also utilizes Roman conventions. However, what is critical is that Mark has lengthened the Matthean account, and perhaps also that of Luke, by one day. Mark thus provides for a full eight-day passion week, Palm Sunday through Easter Sunday inclusive.

Temporal References in the Synoptics from the Day of Jesus' "Triumphal Entry" into Jerusalem to the Day of the First Report of Jesus' Resurrection

Matthew	Mark	Luke
Mt 21:10-16 Jesus enters Jerusalem, cleanses the temple and heals. "And leaving [the temple] he went out of the city to Bethany and lodged there" (Mt 21:17).	**Day 1**. Mk 11:11 Jesus enters Jerusalem, goes into the temple, looks around, and leaves Jerusalem, "as it was late," staying overnight in Bethany with the twelve.	In Luke, Jesus does not really enter Jerusalem, but cleanses the temple, nor does he leave Jerusalem. Nothing is said about where he spent the night.
Mt 21:18 "In the morning, as he was returning to the city, he was hungry." Curses fig tree; it withers at once (Mt 21:19).	**Day 2.** Mk 11:12 "On the following day, when they came from Bethany, he was hungry." Curses fig tree. "The disciples heard it."	Luke does not have the cursing of the fig tree episode.

236

Mt: no time referent.	Mk 11:15-19 Jesus cleanses the temple. Mk 11:19 "And when evening came they went out of the city," presumably back to Bethany.	Lk: no time referent except "one day."
Mt 21:20 "And when the disciples saw it, they marveled." Jesus explains his action as an example of the power of faith. (Here Mark has gained an extra day over Mt.)	**Day 3.** Mk 11:20 "As they passed by in the morning, they saw the fig tree withered away to its roots. Jesus encourages his disciples to trust God, pray, and forgive.	
Mt 26:1-5 "When Jesus had finished all these sayings, he said 'You know that after two days the Passover is coming.'"	**Day 4.** Mk 14:1-2 "It was now two days before the Passover and the Feast of Unleavened Bread."	Lk 22:1-2 "Now the Feast of Unleavened Bread drew near, which is called the Passover."
Mt 26:17-19 Preparation for Passover. "Now on the first day of Unleavened Bread the disciples of Jesus came to him . . ."	**Day 5.** Mk 14:12-16 (same). "And on the first day of Unleavened Bread, when they sacrificed the Passover lamb . . ."	Lk 22:7-13 (same). "Then came the day of Unleavened Bread, on which the Passover lamb had to be sacrificed . . ."
Mt 26:20-25 Last Supper. "When it was evening, he sat at table . . ."	Mk 14:17-21 (same). "And when it was evening he came with the Twelve . . ."	Lk 22:14-23 (same). "And when the hour came, he sat at table . . ."

	Day 6. Mk 15:1, "And . . . early in the morning. . ." Mk 15:25, "And it was at the third hour, they crucified him . . ." Mk 15:33, "Darkness over the land from the sixth to the ninth hour."	
Mt 27:57 "When it was evening"	Mk 15:42. "When evening had come, and since it was the day of Preparation, that is, the day before the Sabbath . . ."	Lk 23:54 "It was the day of Preparation and the Sabbath was beginning . . ."
Mt 27:62 "The next day, that is, after the day of Preparation . . ."	**Day 7.** [The Sabbath]	Lk 23:56b "On the Sabbath they rested . . ."
Mt 28:1 "After the Sabbath, as the first day of the week was dawning"	**Day 8.** Mk 16:1-2. "When the Sabbath was over..." "very early on the first day of the week."	Lk 24:1 "But on the first day of the week, at early dawn."

Chart F. The Hours of the Night of Jesus' Arrest

In a way similar to his handling of passion week, Mark also notes the timing of events during Jesus' final night, by making use of the names of each of the four Roman watches that Mark had specified for a different purpose at Mk 13:35-36.

Mk 13:35-36.	**Mk 14-15.**
Jesus commands his disciples not to be caught sleeping but to "watch"--- parallel the Roman reckoning of four watches of the night	Allusions to these four time references appear later in Mark.
1. **"at evening,"**	Mk 14:17, Jesus comes to the last supper **"at evening."**
2. **"middle of the night,"**	Mk 14:35-41, Then, in the garden, in the **middle of the night,** Jesus asks his disciples to "watch," prays "three" times, but the disciples are caught sleeping three times.
3. **"cock crow"**	Mk 14:72, And "the **cock crowed** a second time," cf. Mk 14:68 var., "first cock crow"
4. **"early."**	Mk 15:1, Jerusalem leadership takes counsel against Jesus **"early."**

¶ 61. Jesus Sends Two Disciples to Borrow a Colt

Mt 21:1-9 ==========>   Mk 11:1-10   <=========== Lk 19:28-40

And when they were drawing near to Jerusalem, to Bethphage and Bethany, by the Mount of Olives, he sent two disciples into the village with specific instructions as to what to do to get a colt on which no one had ever ridden. They found the colt and brought it back. Jesus mounted it and began his ride into Jerusalem. People spread their cloaks on the way and others placed leafy branches. And the crowd walked along with him, in front and in back, shouting, "Hosanna! Blessed is he who comes in the name of the Lord! Blessed is the coming time of the rule of the house of our father David! Hosanna in the highest!"

General Observations. Mark's account of the journey down the Mount of Olives depends primarily upon the text of Luke, but blends in key elements of the text of Matthew. This is particularly the case where Mark follows Luke in stating that the colt had never been ridden before and in giving additional details about the process of finding it (Mk 11:2/Lk 19:30; Mk 11:4-6/Lk 19:32-34). Mark, following Luke, also omits Matthew's citation of Zech 9:9 and the puzzling reference to the two animals (Mt 21:4-5, 7). On the other hand, Lk 19:37 is omitted and Mk 11:10 has the observers accent even more strongly than Mt 21:9 their expectation of the arrival of David's kingdom.

Mk 11:1. In this verse, Jesus and the disciples approach Jerusalem. Later, on two successive days (Mk 11:15, 27 [20 and 27 = the third day]) Jesus will enter into Jerusalem and into the temple. In all three cases (Mk 11:1, 15, 27) Mark uses a syntactical construction that sets up his πάλιν retrospective feature. Understandably, in the final occurrence of these visits to Jerusalem we find a πάλιν used retrospectively uniting the several literary contexts (cf. Mk 11:27, and Peabody, *Mark as Composer,* 70, 56-57; 221, 104).

Mk 11:2-6. These verses emphasize the theme of preparation. Nothing is accidental in the last week of Jesus' life, down to the last detail. Thematically, this passage has many similarities with Mk 14:12-16, where equally detailed attention to preparation for the Last Supper is emphasized (cf. Peabody, *Mark as Composer,* 229, 106)

• Characteristically, Mark omits Matthew's scriptural fulfillment statement (Mt 21:4-5). That fulfillment statement also has no parallel in Luke.

Mk 11:7-10. Mark's use of στιβάς, ("bed of leaves"[?]), seems to be his interpretation of Mt 21:8: "leafy branches from the trees". Luke omitted Matthew's reference to the throwing of the leafy branches on the way.[1]

• Jesus' party enters the city to the cries of the singing of the Hallel (Psalms 113-118). Hosannas as a call for future salvation ring out (cf. Ps 118:25 [Hebrew text]). Mark follows this with a quotation from the LXX of Ps 117:26. The quotation seems to function as a welcome to Jesus as the coming one who, in the view of those present, will reconstitute the Davidic kingdom (Mk 11:10, cf. Mk 10:44-48). In contrast to Matthew and Luke, who emphasize the personal acclaim directed to Jesus (Mt 21:4; Lk 19:34, 38), Mark focuses on the glory of the coming kingdom, which the people eagerly anticipate (Mk 11:10). We are left with the impression that the people expect the glorious kingdom to be realized at the arrival of Jesus. It is noticeable that this action takes place near the Mount of Olives where it was expected God would vindicate his

---

[1] McNicol et al., *Beyond the Q Impasse,* 247.

people against the nations (Mk 11:1). Eschatological expectations are running high. But the arrival of the kingdom will not take the course anticipated by many of the observers (see the textual discussion of Mk 12:35-37 below).

SECTION ONE: THE REPLACEMENT OF THE TEMPLE LEADERSHIP. MK 11:11-12:37A

¶ 62. The Time of the Temple's Usefulness Expires

Mt 21:10-22 ========>	Mk 11:11-[26]	<======= Lk 19:45-48
(Mt 17:20; 6:5, 14-15)		(Lk 17:5-6)

And he entered Jerusalem and the temple. And when he had scouted out everything, since it was already late, he departed for Bethany with the Twelve. The next day after they had returned, he was hungry and, seeing a fig tree in the distance that was good and leafy, he went to see what it had to eat. When he got to it, he found nothing but leaves, since it was not the season for figs. He says to it, "May no one ever eat fruit from you again!" His disciples heard him. And they went to Jerusalem and, once they were inside the temple, he began to cast out those who bought and sold in the temple. He knocked over the tables of the moneychangers and the stools of those who sold pigeons. He even would not allow anyone to carry a vessel through the temple. And he began to teach and say to them, "Is it not written that 'My house shall be called a house of prayer for all peoples and nations?' But you have made it into a den of thieves!" Now the chief priests and scribes heard and began to seek a way to destroy him, for they feared him because the whole crowd was amazed at his teaching. And when evening came, they left the city.

As they passed by early the next morning, they saw the fig tree withered away to its roots. Peter remembered and said to him, "Rabbi, look! the fig tree that you cursed has withered! And Jesus answered saying to them, "Put your trust in God! I tell you truly, whoever says to this mountain, 'Be taken up and cast into the sea!' and does not doubt in his heart but believes that what he says will come to pass, thus it will be for him. This is why I say to you: All things for which you pray and ask for, believing what you say, it will also be done for you. And whenever you all stand praying, forgive what you have against someone so that your father in heaven may forgive you your transgressions."

General Observations. On the Two Gospel Hypothesis there are several indicators that Mark has carefully utilized his sources to compose this unit in the service of his theological agenda.

There is the clear evidence in Mark that Jesus' actions symbolized a serious interruption of the normal activities in the outer precincts of the temple (Court of the Gentiles). Only

Mark mentions that Jesus did not allow anyone to carry a vessel through the temple (Mk 11:16).

The frantic activity that took place in the Court of the Gentiles is a Markan indicator that the temple was not functioning as an appropriate vehicle for the Gentiles. Only in Mk 11:17 are we told that God's house is a house of prayer for "all the Gentiles."

The careful composition of Mark 11:11-26 from different sources and separated pericopae in Matthew and Luke reveals a literary procedure whereby, in an *aba* construction (Markan intercalation), Mark deliberately frames the incident in the temple with the fig-tree story. This editorial framing is absent from Matthew, which has a different ordering of these incidents, and from Luke, which does not record this story at all. Furthermore, Mark not only frames the temple episode with the fig-tree incident, but uses the linguistic indicator, "Peter remembered" (Mk 11:21), as a way of making certain that the careful reader would see this connection. The way that Mark has utilized Matthew and Luke in the service of his composition may be seen in the four-part outline that follows.

Part 1: Jesus enters the temple and merely looks around one last time (Mk 11:11).

Part 2: On his way back from Bethany to the temple a second time, Jesus sees a fig tree with no figs and curses it (Mk 11:12-14).

Mark utilizes the Matthean account as the basis of his composition but reorders it by moving through the text of Mt 21:10-19 twice (see the synopsis). On the first pass through Mt 21:10-19 (Mk 11:11-14), Mark utilizes a few elements from Mt 21:10, 12, and 16-19. On the second pass (Mk 11:15-19), Mark first repeats his use of Mt 21:10, then picks up Mt 21:12-15, which he had skipped over during his first pass. During this pass, Mark also blends this section of Matthew with the parallel in Lk 19:45-48 and concludes with a second use of Mt 21:17. Mark, therefore, begins his two uses of Mt 20:10-19 at exactly the same place (Mt 20:10) and essentially concludes his second pass through Mt 21:10-19 at the same point where he began to copy the bulk of Matthew's text during the first pass (Mt 20:16-17). The "transitional verse," Mt 21:16, includes a citation of the scriptures, which Mark typically avoids. In reworking Mt 20:10-19, Mark divides the single Matthean account of the cursing and withering of the fig tree by placing the cursing (Mk 11:12-14) before the temple incident (Mk 11:15-19) and the withering afterward (Mk 11:20-[26]). This deliberate editorial reworking of Matthew, and the Markan reference to it "not being the season for figs," (Mk 11:13) indicate that, for Mark, time had run out on the viability of the temple in God's eschatological plan.

Part 3: This conclusion is reinforced in Mark's composition of Mk 11:15-19. Here, with the exception of a few details from Luke (primarily in Mk 11:18//Lk 19:47-48), Mark follows Matthew's text. At the same time, Mark does not change the order of Luke. Mark utilizes Lk 19:47-48 in its sequential order to show the intensity of the hatred of the temple authorities toward Jesus' actions in the Court of the Gentiles (ἐζήτουν αὐτὸν ἀπολέσαι). The characteristic Matthean emphasis (Mt 21:14-16) on the Messiah (Son of David) healing the blind and the lame is omitted. Despite the use of the title in the Bartimaeus incident (Mk 10:47,48), Mark, unlike Matthew, usually does not connect the title Son of David with healing.

Part 4: (Mk 11:20-26) After Jesus comes out of the temple, Peter says, "The fig tree you cursed has withered." Jesus' answer to Peter, "Have faith in God," seems to be a complete non sequitur unless it is interpreted in the context of the whole story, particularly the ending of this Markan pericope with Jesus' teachings on faith, prayer, and forgiveness. Where Matthew has treated the fig-tree curses as an expression of divine power, Mark treats it symbolically. Mark has linked the destruction of the fig tree with the confrontation in the temple. Mark has transformed both the fig tree story and the temple account and woven them into a unified section that serves to communicate in a dramatic and symbolic way. This section asserts that the bankrupt temple leadership of Jesus' day would wither away and that leadership would be placed in the hands of others who would bear the fruits of faith, prayer, and forgiveness. Such a reading accounts for the apparent non sequitur. This interpretation is also confirmed by Mark's unique conclusion to the Great Commandment (Mk 12:20-34), where Jesus indicates that similar expressions of the spiritual life will replace the function of temple sacrifices (cf. Mk 11:33). The "season" of the Temple has ended.

In fact, as the ongoing narrative will imply, the temple *shortly would be destroyed [by the Romans]* (cf. Mk 13:2, 14). That is presumed. What is important is the temple's replacement—a community of disciples characterized by trusting, forgiving, and praying. To compose this teaching of Jesus in Mk 11:25-26, Mark utilizes material from Matthew's Sermon on the Mount (Mt 6:5, 14-15). In short, Mark is saying it is not the "season" for animal sacrifices, but for a community characterized by spiritual sacrifices. Contrary to the expectations of the crowds who are calling for a restoration of Davidic rule (Mk 11:8-10), this will be the way the kingdom will arrive.

Mk 11:11. This verse is primarily Markan composition although it may echo Mt 21:10. It functions both to bring closure to the previous episode (Mk 11:1-10), but also to set the scene for the following unit on the sign of the end of the temple (Mk 11:11). Among the linguistic indicators of Markan composition are the following:

> ➢ the use of καί + aorist of ἔρχομαι or its compounds + εἰς + name of place + καί, which occurs sixteen times in Mark (Peabody, *Mark as Composer,* 54, 49; 61, 51).

> ➢ οἱ δώδεκα used absolutely to refer to the Twelve (Peabody, *Mark as Composer,* 102, 68).

• By having Jesus enter Jerusalem, look around, and leave *without entering the temple*, Mark has created a significant agreement of Matthew and Luke against Mark. Both Matthew and Luke can be read as having the first entrance of Jesus into the city and the incident in the temple (Matt 21:10-17/Lk 19:45-48) take place on the same day. Mark seeks to establish chronological markers in his organization of the passion account (see the chart above). To achieve this goal, and noting the imprecise chronology of events in his two major sources (viz., Mt 21:10, 12/ Lk 19:41, 45, and especially Lk 19:47), Mark gave the narrative more precision.

• Mark conflated several passages in Matthew on Jesus' approach to the city, entrance, and departure to lodge overnight at nearby Bethany (Mt 20:17; 21:10, 12). This enabled Mark to accent the link between the cursing of the fig tree and the temple incidents which, according to him, will take place over the next two days. That will provide the thematic context for additional teaching against the temple leaders (Mk 11:27-13:2). This procedure on the part of Mark is more plausible than that required on the Two Document Hypothesis where it must be argued that Matthew and Luke independently omitted Mk 11:11 in order to tidy up Mark's "clumsy" chronological account.

Mk 11:12-14. Mark enlivens the Matthean description of the cursing of the fig tree (Mt 21:18-19) with vividly detailed descriptions of Jesus' approach to the tree. According to Mk 11:13 Jesus spots the tree from afar (μακρόθεν). It has many leaves. He comes with great expectations of finding fruit (εἰ ἄρα τι εὑρήσει ἐν αὐτῇ).

• The reference to it being the wrong season for figs is puzzling (Mk 11:12). The image seems absurd if taken literally. Why would Jesus expect figs out of season? But metaphorically, the fig tree is a symbol for the temple leadership and Mark is anticipating that the temple leadership would be replaced shortly. The leadership of the coming kingdom would be placed in other hands that would produce fruit. Eschatologically speaking, it was the wrong season for the temple leadership of Jesus' time. Leadership of God's house would be given to others who will bear fruit (Mk 12:8).

Mk 11:15-16. In Mk 11:15 the construction ἤρξατο ἐκβάλλειν τοὺς πωλοῦντας is paralleled exactly in Lk 19:45. This is evidence in favor of Mark occasionally blending Matthew and Luke into one coherent narrative here. The use of ἤρξατο + the infinitive is, of course, characteristic of Markan composition (Peabody, *Mark as Composer,* 67, 54).

• The action of Jesus in Mk 11:15b-16 was meant to stop temporarily the normal operations of the temple (see above.) It was a symbolic gesture echoing Zech 14:21, which was read to say that at the appropriate eschatological day, "no trader should appear in the house of the Lord." In Mark's presentation, Jesus' actions indicate that day has come.

Mk 11:17. Mark extends the quotation from Isa 56:7 LXX to incorporate "all the Gentiles." The reference to the Gentiles does not occur in the parallels in Mt 21:13 or Lk 19:46. The quotation from Isaiah is part of a messianic promise that righteous Gentiles will participate in the blessings of the kingdom of God. When we take Jesus' oracle against the temple's leaders in its entirety (which describes the temple as a σπήλαιον λῃστῶν, "a den of bandits," cf. Jer 7:11) together with Mark's supplementary description of Jesus curtailing normal temple operations (Mk 11:16), we conclude that Mark thinks that the current temple leadership is about to be replaced by a radically different regime, one that would include both Jews and Gentiles (cf. Mk 7:19; 13:10; cf. Mk 16:15-16).

Mk 11:18-19. Mark uses the famous construction ἐφοβοῦντο γάρ to describe the response of the temple authorities in Jerusalem. For Mark, "fear" is usually the response of those who have not fully perceived Jesus' identity (cf. Mk 16:8). Here it is also an expression of deep concern about, and even hostility toward, Jesus

• The construction of third person imperfect of ἐκπλήσσω + ἐπὶ τῇ διδαχῇ αὐτοῦ (cf. Mt 22:23) is found also in Mk 1:22 // Mt 7:28 (Peabody, *Mark as Composer,* 31, 43). Perhaps Mark is using Mt 22:23 as a way of highlighting the crowds' astonishment that Jesus was both announcing and inaugurating the final eschatological era in a way that was far different than their expectations.

Mk 11:20-22. In these verses, Mark has the first of two similar constructions employing καί + a form of ἀναμιμνήσκω + ὁ Πετρός (cf. Peabody, *Mark as Composer,* 223, 104) to note that Peter remembered a previous saying (cf. Mk 14:29-31 and71-72). In this instance Peter remembered Jesus' earlier cursing of the fig tree (Mk 11:13-14). Could these verses be in part the source of the ancient tradition of the church that the Gospel of Mark was a collection of Peter's remembrances of sayings and events from Jesus' ministry?

• Mark introduces the theme of faith in Mk 11:22b. He draws the terminology from the parallel in Mt 21:20. What replaces the old era will be grounded in faith in God.

Mk 11:23-24. Mark utilizes tradition drawn from Mt 21:21-22 conflated with Mt 17:20 and Lk 17:6. In Mt 21:21-22 the sayings on faith have to do with the disciples' query with respect to Jesus' ability to cause the fig tree to wither. Jesus tells the disciples that if they have faith and persist in it they will even be able to command the mountain (viz., the Temple Mount?) to be picked up and hurled into the sea. Mark evidently perceives that this kind of faith ought to be characteristic of the life in the kingdom which will replace the order of the temple. He moralizes on its importance in Mk 11:23.

Mk 11:24-26. Mark drives home the claim that faith is the essential ingredient of discipleship. Mark now uses πιστεύειν ("to trust") in connection with prayer. Essentially Mk 11:24 is a Markan paraphrase of Mt 21:22 but it also echoes the introduction to Matthew's version of the Lord's Prayer (Mt 6:5) or the teaching on prayer in Mt 7:7-8 ("ask and receive").

Mk 11:25. Mark expands the teaching on prayer by going beyond the contextual parallel in Mt 21:22. He conflates it with other segments in Matthew on prayer to create additional teaching on the subject. Mark seems to have combined elements of the Lord's Prayer (Mt 6:12 and 14) with echoes of Mt 5:23-24. (εἰ τι ἔχετε κατά τινος Mk 11:25 // ὁ ἀδελφός σου ἔχει τι κατὰ σοῦ Mt 5:23). His purpose is to invoke the direct link found in Matthew between prayer and forgiveness. Mark picks up the characteristic Matthean phrase, ὁ πατὴρ ὑμῶν ὁ ἐν τοῖς οὐρανοῖς (Mk 11:25). Παράπτωμα occurs only in Mt 6:14-15 and in this Markan parallel (Mk 11:25, 26). Combined with the similar occurrence of ἀφίημι (Mt 6:14, 15; Mk 11:25, 26), this web of linguistic usages overwhelmingly points to a shared tradition. Mark appears to have partially preserved the characteristically Matthean phrase, "your Father who is in the heavens." This evidence points strongly to Mark's literary dependence on Matthew. This conclusion would be strengthened if Mk 11:26 is original. Although most of the

Egyptian evidence is united against it, there is strong support from D, A, Byzantine Witnesses, Vg, syr (p and h), and Cyprian.

• Mark's editorial activity in these verses seems to indicate that he is aware of some version of the Lord's Prayer. On the Two Gospel Hypothesis Mark does not have to repeat everything exactly as he finds it in Matthew and Luke. For Mark these two Gospels stand in their own right as reliable attestations of the Jesus tradition. Mark wrote to supplement them, not to replace them. In this instance, Mark echoes what is stated more fully in Matthew and Luke. Mark's fragmentary presentation of the Lord's Prayer is intended to underscore the theme he is developing: the need to connect prayer with forgiveness as a fundamental element of Jesus' new spiritual community. Those who reason that Mark had to be the first Gospel because, had he utilized Matthew or Luke, he would never have omitted the Lord's Prayer, should reexamine their logic. This passage (Mk 11:25-26), even if vs. 26 is eliminated on text-critical grounds, provides evidence that Mark did know the Lord's Prayer, or at least the most immediate context in which that prayer appears in Matthew. It would appear that Mark's community had reached a stage in the history of the tradition where it was possible simply to echo the Lord's Prayer in an exciting and creative new way.

¶ 63. Religious Leaders Question Jesus about His Authority

Mt 21:23-27 =========>   Mk 11:27-33   <-------------------Lk 20:1-8

They entered Jerusalem again and, as he was walking around the temple precincts, the chief priests and scribes and elders came to him and began to say, "By what authority do you do these things? Who gave you permission to do what you've done?" Jesus said to them, "I will ask you one question. If you answer me, then I will tell you by what authority I do these things. The baptism of John—was it sanctioned by the authority of heaven or by men? Tell me." And they began to argue among themselves saying, "If we say 'from heaven' he will ask 'Why did you not believe him?' We can't say 'by men'"—for they feared the crowd who all believed John really was a prophet. So they replied and said, "We don't know." And Jesus said to them, "Neither will I tell you by what authority I do these things."

General Observations. Matthew and Luke agree in sequence at this point (Mt 21:23-27; Lk 20:1-8). Mark follows their concurrent order and makes few editorial changes. Jesus' action in the temple precipitates a very vigorous response from his opponents. Jesus invokes the issue of the authority of John as part of his answer to his opponents (Mk 11:29-30). Perhaps it was more than a diversionary tactic. John set out to purify Israel but did not fulfill his mission completely. In contrast to John (cf. Mk 9:11-12), Jesus, as indicated by the previous pericope, will complete the mission.

Mk 11:27. Mark uses retrospective πάλιν to open this narrative account (cf. Mk 11:1, 11, 15). Here is another instance where Matthew and Luke do not share retrospective πάλιν. Again, this is significant evidence against Markan priority.

• The use of the historical present of ἔρχομαι is also a characteristic feature of Markan composition. This supports the view that Mk 11:27a is Markan redaction.

• Mark follows Luke in referring to the band of opponents who came out to encounter Jesus as the chief priests, teachers of the law, and elders (Mk 11:1; Lk 20:1). This incident seems to anticipate the hearing before the Sanhedrin where this three-fold group again encounters Jesus (Mk 15:1; Lk 22:66; cf. Mk 8:31; 14:43, 53).

Mk 11:28-33. Jesus' re-entry into debate with the religious authorities seems to echo the earlier round of debates in Mk 2:1-3:6. However, in this new cycle of discussions (Mk 11:27-12:40), Jesus is much more aggressive in challenging the sincerity of his opponents and in criticizing them. This is particularly evident in Mk 12:35-38 where he asks his interlocutors a question that really functions as the answer to the question they have raised about his identity (Mk 11:28-33). The Jerusalem leadership intend this exchange to be a critique of Jesus but Jesus turns it into a critique of them that will culminate ultimately in the announcement of the coming (or imminent) end of their temple.

¶ 64. Jesus Addresses Them in a Parable about Some Wicked Tenants

Mt 21:33-46 ==========>   Mk 12:1-12   <========== Lk 20:9-19

And he began to speak to them in parables. "Once upon a time there was a man who planted a vineyard and erected a hedge around it and dug a pit for the wine press and built a watchtower and gave it to tenants to care for while he went to another country. At the proper time, he sent a servant to the tenants to get some of the fruit of the vineyard. But they beat him and sent him away empty-handed. And again he sent them another servant and this one they hit over the head and humiliated. And another one they killed. And many others they beat or killed. He still had one left, a beloved son; he sent him last to them saying, 'They will respect my son!' However, those tenants said, 'This is the heir! Let's kill him and we will inherit the vineyard!' and they killed him and cast his body outside the vineyard. Well, what will the owner of the vineyard do? He will come and kill the tenants and give the vineyard to others. Haven't you read the scriptures?"

> The stone, which the builders rejected, has become the cornerstone. This was done by the Lord and is marvelous in our eyes.

Now the chief priests and the others really wanted to get rid of Jesus but they were afraid of the crowd; they knew he spoke the parable about them but they left him alone . . . for the moment.

General Observations. Mark continues to follow the order of both Matthew and Luke and edits the Parable of the Wicked Tenants accordingly (Mt 21:33-46; Lk 20:9-19; Mk 12:1-12). Luke had omitted Matthew's Parable of the Two Sons (Mt 21:28-32), and so does Mark. The coming of the owner to wreak vengeance on the rebellious tenants, which Mark finds in Mt 21:41 and Lk 20:16, provides Mark with an opportunity to highlight the disobedience of the temple leadership. By carefully blending Matthew and Luke, Mark produces his version of the Parable of the Wicked Tenants as a full scale attack on the temple leadership (Mk 12:1-12). Mark thus heightens the rhetoric of his anti-temple theme.

• Mark begins his narrative by first drawing from Lk 20:9 and then the balance of Mk 12:1 from Mt 21:33 (see Synopsis ¶ 64). As with an earlier parable (Mk 3:23 cf. Mk 4:2), this one has Jesus' opponents in mind. Mark accepts the construction ἤρξατο + infinitive that he finds in Lk 20:9, for it is one of his favorite linguistic expressions.

• Mark's use of the plural, "parables," in contrast to the singular in both Matthew and Luke, may reflect his knowledge of Mt 21:28-22:14 where Jesus is depicted as speaking three parables in a row. Compare Mark's similar use of the plural at Mk 3:23 as an anticipation of the forthcoming parables derived from Mt 13:1-53 (cf. Mk 4;1-34//Lk 8:4-18). There too Mark has considerably fewer parables than does Matthew in the parallel passage.

Mk 12:2-5. Mark recapitulates Mt 21:34-36, enabling him to utilize πάλιν again to unite two verses within the pericope (Mk 12:2, καὶ ἀπέστειλεν πρὸς τοὺς γεωργοὺς τῷ καιρῷ δοῦλον cf. Mk 12:4, καὶ πάλιν ἀπέστειλεν πρὸς αὐτοὺς ἄλλον δοῦλον Peabody, *Mark as Composer,* 183, 95).

• The verb, κεφαλιόω, in Mk 12:4 is a *hapax legomenon.* It may anticipate the later beating of Jesus on the head (κεφαλή) by the Roman soldiers (Mk 15:19).

• Mark's description of the sending of the messengers represents a blending of the divergent Matthean and Lukan accounts. Matthew's account is simply stated. Two groups of servants are sent (former and latter prophets?) and both are treated dishonorably. Afterward, the son is sent. He suffers a similar fate (Mt 21:34-39). Although the Lukan account of the sending of the messengers is internally consistent, its focus differs from Matthew's (Lk 20:10-15). Three servants are sent. They are received with increasing hostility although none are killed. Only the beloved son is killed. Mark sees the differences in these accounts and unites them, so that Mk 12:5b now says that, after the maltreatment of the first three servants (Luke), the owner sent "many others" (Matthew). Some were beaten and some were killed. With this "addition," the accounts of Matthew and Luke are combined, but the dramatic development of the story in the Matthean and Lukan versions is somewhat compromised. Mark has composed a third account that has a certain integrity of its own but presupposes the other two. It is more difficult to imagine Matthew and Luke independently drawing their accounts from Mark. Mark's account has no proper climax. The third man is killed, then many are killed, then the Son is killed. Where is the progression? Mark's appears to be a secondary composition.

• Mk 12:5b apparently represents Mark's effort to highlight the perfidy of the tenants (i.e., those in charge of the temple).

• A connection between this parable and the earlier cursing of the fig tree can now be seen. Jesus came seeking fruit on the fig tree, but found none (Mk 11:13). Similarly, the owner of the vineyard looked for the fruits from his vineyard, but found none (Mk 12:2-5). In both cases, there is an implicit criticism of the temple leadership. Thus, the Cursing of the Fig Tree (Mk 11:12-14) and the Parable of the Wicked Tenants (Mk 12:1-12) serve as the opening and closing members of an *inclusio* that surrounds this unit. It highlights Jesus' withering critique of the temple leadership in Jerusalem.

Mk 12:6. Note the agreement of Mark ("a beloved son") with Luke ("my beloved son") against Matthew ("his son").

Mk 12:8. Mark seems to have changed the common testimony of Mt/Lk that "the son" was thrown out of the vineyard first and then killed (Mt 21:39; Lk 20:15) to his being killed first and then thrown out (Mk 12:8). The textual tradition strongly favors this reading. If Mark saw "the son" as Jesus, did he think that Golgotha was inside the city?

Mk 12:9-12. Like Luke before him, Mark omitted Mt 21:43 (cf. Lk 20:18). Mark is not interested in the struggles within Judaism reflected in Matthew. Mark also omits Mt 21:44/Lk 20:18. Mark 12:10-11 focuses on Ps 117:22-23 LXX. He had already quoted this Psalm at Mk 11:9-10 to highlight the glory of the coming kingdom. Now Mark wishes to recapitulate the idea that the leadership of the kingdom has been taken from the current regime and invested in a rejected one who, ironically, will be the capstone or cornerstone of the new era. The authority of the son who had been rejected is now vindicated. This is driven home in Mk 12:12 where the temple leadership clearly perceives that this parable was spoken against them.

• The construction in Mk 12:12, καί + participle of ἀφίημι + object + aorist, is a Markan supplement and shows his linguistic characteristics (Peabody, *Mark as Composer,* 19, 40).

¶ **65. Jesus Is Asked, "Should We Pay Taxes to Caesar?"**

Mt 22:15-22 ==========>   Mk 12:13-17   <========= Lk 20:20-26

The chief priests and the scribes and the elders send some Pharisees and those partial to Herod Antipas to get him to say something incriminating. They come around and say soothingly, "Teacher, we know that you speak the truth with no bias toward anyone, but rightly teach the way of God. Tell us, is it right to pay the head tax to Caesar?" Perceiving their evil intentions, Jesus said, "Why are you testing me? Give me a denarius. They gave it to him and he said, "Whose image is on this?" They said, "Caesar." Jesus said, "Give back to Caesar the things that are his and to God what belongs to God." They were amazed at the adroitness of his answer.

General Observations Matthew follows his account of the Parable of the Wicked Tenants (Mt 21:33-45) with the Parable of the Marriage Feast (Mt 22:1-15). Luke utilized a similar parable in his travel account (Lk 14:16-24). Mark has omitted Matthew's account of the Parable of the Marriage Feast since it does not advance his theme. Matthew and Luke then come back into the same sequence with the unit on paying taxes to Caesar (Mt 22:15-22; Lk 20:20-26). Following Matthew and Luke, Mark presents several accounts of Jesus' final verdict on the religious leaders of Israel, which will conclude the first section of this part. As a development of this common testimony, Mark continues the discussion with the religious and political leaders of the people (Mk 11:27) by including the Pharisees and the Herodians as targets for critique (Mk 12:13). In so doing, Mark skillfully blends the accounts of Matthew and Luke. In Mt 22:15-16, the Pharisees send their disciples and the Herodians to engage Jesus. In Lk

20:19-20, the scribes and chief priests send spies to engage Jesus. Mark conflates the two accounts: the chief priests, scribes, and leaders of the people send the Pharisees and the Herodians to ask the question (Mk 11:27; 12:13). Seizing the moment, Jesus points to the image of Caesar and says that since Caesar's image is stamped upon the coin he exercises domain over that realm. But there is a more subtle point. Humans are made in God's image. God, through his spokesperson (his son Jesus), claims them.

Mk 12:13. As noted above, the subjects of ἀποστέλλουσιν are the scribes, chief priests, and leaders of the people (Mk 11:27). Mark draws ἀποστέλλουσιν from Mt 22:16. However, the use of καί + historic present of a verb of motion + πρὸς αὐτόν [= Ἰησοῦν] is characteristic of Mark (Peabody, *Mark as Composer,* 63, 53).

• The reference to the Pharisees and Herodians echoes Mk 3:6 where both groups react to a Sabbath healing with a plot to destroy him (see Peabody, *Mark as Composer,* 92, 65).

• Mark's use of ἀγρεύειν ("catch," as in an unguarded statement) varies from both the Matthean and Lukan parallels (Mt 22:15/Lk 20:20). However, the textual testimony is not unanimous, with D and Θ, having the Matthean reading, παγιδεύειν ("to entrap"). If ἀγρεύειν is the correct reading it is a Markan stylistic preference.[2] If the reading of the Western text is preferred, it indicates Mark's dependence on Matthew.

Mk 12:14. There is some debate whether κῆνσος ("poll tax") rather than ἐπικεφάλαιον, is the correct reading, mainly on the basis of the Egyptian manuscripts. If κῆνσος is read, Mark has followed Mt 22:17. However, D, Θ, and some Syrian manuscripts have ἐπικεφάλαιον ("tax upon the head"). The latter witnesses are usually taken as good evidence for the existence of a late second-century text. Mark, not having concurrent testimony in Matthew (κῆνσος) and Luke (φόρος) may have used the more colloquial terminology.

Mk 12:16-17. The use of ἐκθαύμαζειν now appears in Mk 13:17 as a *hapax legomenon*. Mann views the compound usage of this verb (against the simple form in Matthew and Luke) as evidence of a Markan linguistic preference.[3] The theme of "wondering" or "marveling" is a feature of the text of Mark (see our discussion at Mk 5:20.)

---

[2] Tuckett, *Revival of the Griesbach Hypothesis* (New York: Cambridge University Press, 1983), 123.
[3] C. S. Mann, *Mark* (Garden City, N.Y.: Doubleday, 1986), 471.

¶ 66. Sadducees Mock Jesus' Teaching on the Resurrection

Mt 22:23-33 ========>   Mk 12:18-27   <======== Lk 20:27-40

The Sadducees teach that there isn't going to be any resurrection of the dead. One day, some of them come up to Jesus and say, "Teacher, Moses' Law says that if a man's brother dies and leaves no heir, he must make the woman his wife and produce children for his brother. Now once there were seven brothers; the first got married and suddenly died leaving no heirs, so the next brother took her, but he also died before any children were born, so the third did likewise and *he* died, and all the rest also; *still* no children. Finally, after all the brothers were dead, the woman died. We know you teach that there will be a resurrection of the dead; which brother will be her husband then, all of them?"

Jesus said to them, "Can't you see how deceived you are? You know neither the scriptures nor the power of God. When they are raised from the dead, when there will be no more marrying nor giving in marriage, they will be like the angels of heaven. And as for the dead being raised, read in the book of Moses where God says to Moses from the burning bush, 'I am the God of Abraham, Isaac, and Jacob.' He is not the God of dead patriarchs but of living ones!"

General Observations. Mark continues to expand the groups of leaders in Judea who engage Jesus in controversy. The controversy with the leaders was inaugurated in Mk 2:1-3:6 and centered on Jesus' right to forgive sins. Following the common testimony of Matthew and Luke, Mark now has more groups debate with Jesus, and those debates grow more heated.

• Both Matthew and Luke record Jesus' debate with the Sadducees about the general resurrection following the debate with other opponents about whether it is appropriate to pay taxes to Caesar. Mark continues to blend Matthew and Luke, with one significant exception, which will be noted below.

Mk 12:18. Once again, Mark uses the historical present (ἔρχονται) with πρὸς αὐτόν to open a unit. This is Markan redaction and accounts for Mark's differences from Mt 22:23 and Lk 20:27.

Mk 12:19-23. The wording of Mark is relatively close to Matthew, with a blending of phraseology with Matthew and Luke.

• The clause, ὅταν ἀναστῶσιν (Mk 12:23, cf. Mk 12:25), is absent from many of the major textual witnesses (viz., ℵ B C* L Ψ and several major versions) as well from

Matthew and Luke. On the other hand, if this longer reading is correct, it would provide another example of Mark composing a duplicate expression.

Mk 12:24-27. Here the Matthean and Lukan accounts vary significantly. Advocates of the Two Source Hypothesis explain this by claiming that Lk 20:34-37a is based on a separate tradition independent of Mk.[4] The Two Gospel Research Team concluded that this was Lukan redaction of Matthew in keeping with Luke's ascetic *Tendenz* that believers are free to refrain from marriage because they have already entered into the same immortal life as the angels and, thus, no longer need to seek immortality through living on in their children.[5] Be that as it may, Mark sees that Matthew and Luke are not in harmony (Mt 20:30-33; Lk 20:34-38). Mark could have omitted the episode, but instead chose the Matthean theological perspective, but blended it with terminology drawn from Luke (viz., the reference to Moses and the bush: Mk 12:26; Lk 20:37; not in Matthew). By echoing Luke, perhaps Mark understands Lk 20:34-36 as positing a temporal duality of "now" and "then." Believers in this age may marry and be given in marriage, but in the age to come there is no need for either.

• At Mk 12:27 Mark omits Mt 22:33, because he had already recorded a similar note in an earlier context (cf. Mk 11:18).

• The unit ends with the claim that God has a living relationship with the faithful of all generations. Although Mark is only repeating what is in Matthew and Luke it is significant that once again he concludes a unit with a belief in resurrection.

¶ 67. A Scribe Asks Jesus about the Greatest Commandment

Mt 22:34-40, 46=======>　　　　Mk 12:28-34　　　　<========Lk 20:39-40

　　　　　　　　　　　　　　　　　　　　　　　　　　(Lk 10:25-28)

One of the scribes saw how skillfully Jesus debated and asked him this question, "Which commandment is the most important of all?" Jesus replied, "The first is: 'Hear O Israel, the Lord our God is One,' and 'you shall love the Lord your God with all your heart, soul, mind, and strength.' And the second is: 'You shall love your neighbor as yourself.'" There are no commandments greater than these. The scribe said to him, "Well done, teacher. You have spoken truly that he is one and there is no other; and to love him with all one's heart and mind and strength, and one's neighbor as oneself. These are more important than all

---

[4] Turid Karlsen Seim, *The Double Message: Patterns of Gender in Luke-Acts* (Edinburgh: T. & T. Clark/Nashville: Abingdon, 1994), 213.

[5] McNicol et al., *Beyond the Q Impasse*, 254.

commandments about burnt offerings and sacrifices." When Jesus saw that he had spoken wisely, he commended him: "You are not far from the Kingdom of God!" After that, no one dared to debate with him any further.

General Observations. Mark has been following the concurrent testimony of Matthew and Luke. When Mark composed his version of the question of the resurrection (Mk 12:18-27), following the order of Matthew he came next to the question of the greatest commandment (Mt 22:34-40). However, this is not the case with Luke, who had utilized Matthew's version of the greatest commandment episode as an introduction to his account of the Parable of the Good Samaritan (Lk 10:25-29). Luke had followed his version of the question of the resurrection (Lk 20:27-40) with the unit on David's son (Lk 20:41-44). So Matthew and Luke do not in agree in order. Mark determined to use the Matthean account to show that it is possible to stand in continuity with the heritage of Abraham and Moses without the worshipping in the temple. Procedurally, Mark followed Matthew's account of the greatest commandment episode (Mt 22:34-40). However, Mark expanded the pericope by emphasizing the importance of monotheism (Mk 12:29b, 32) and the need to construe the demand of Torah as a call to love God and neighbor.

• The emphasis on monotheism would be particularly important to Mark's predominantly Gentile audience. However, by shaping the pericope in this way, it also becomes a centerpiece of the anti-temple theme of this section. This is clear in the composition of Mk 12:33, where the validity of the temple operations appears to be undermined by remarks about sacrifices from a figure with impeccable credentials within Judaism. The words are no sooner out of the mouth of the scribe when Jesus says, "You are not far from the kingdom of God." There is even some blending with the account in Lk 10:25-29. In any case, on our hypothesis Mark clearly reveals a knowledge of the text of Luke when he takes the last two verses of Luke's version of the question on the resurrection (Lk 20:39-40) and incorporates them into the conclusion of the unit on the great commandment (Mk 12:32-34).

Mk 12:28. Mark omits Mt 22:34, which refers to the Pharisees and Sadducees. Instead, Mark connects this account with the previous one where the Lukan account has scribes who speak well of Jesus (Lk 20:39). Mark (12:28, cf. 32) chooses to feature one of these scribes who recognized that Jesus spoke well (καλῶς). Mark built his story as a dialogue between one of the scribes and Jesus. His use of the singular could also have been stimulated by the reference to the lawyer (νομικός) in Mt 22:35/Lk 10:25. For Mark, as noted above, the lawyers and scribes are practically coterminous. Hence he combined the common testimony in Matthew and Luke with respect to the use of νομικός and the reference to a scribe in Lk 20:39, resulting in "one of the scribes" (Mk 12:28).

Mk 12:29. In this verse Mark quotes the beginning of the Shema (Deut 6:4). His purpose is show his readers that Jesus honors the tradition of Israel. Such a demonstration was not necessary for Matthew, who wrote for an audience well versed in the traditional Jewish confessions.

Mk 12:30. In the current text of Nestle-Aland, Mark's version of Jesus' four-fold articulation of the demands of loving God agrees with Luke's except for their sequence (Lk 10:27). On this point Mark is closer to the text of Luke than Matthew, who has only a threefold reference to loving God with all one's strength (Mk 22:37). This shows Mark's awareness of the text of Luke as well as his main source, Matthew.

Mk 12:31. Mark asserts that the goal of the law is love for God and neighbor. On the other hand, for Matthew (Mt 22:40), love for God and neighbor can only be fully realized by keeping the other demands of the law—loving God and neighbors is only the doorway by which we enter into full obedience to the total demand of Torah. In keeping with his theological principle Mark substitutes the statement, "There is no other commandment greater than these," for Mt 22:40 (cf. Mk 12:31).

Mk 12:32-34. Mark has the scribe recapitulate the confession of monotheism and the two-fold demand of love of God and neighbor. Mark again may manifest knowledge of Luke who had revised the debate so that the scribe, rather than Jesus, stated these demands as a response to a counter question (Lk 10:27). In Mark, Jesus states the dual commandment (as in Matthew), then the scribe does so also (as in Luke). This recapitulation highlights the demand's importance for Mark. It will take the place of the burnt offerings and sacrifices in the temple (cf. Heb 9:11-10:18).

• Mk appears to blend the ending of the unit on the resurrection from Lk 20:39-40 with the ending of Matthew's account of the question of David's son (Mt 22:46), which is the next pericope in order in Matthew (See the electronic synopsis.). On the Two Gospel Hypothesis, Mk 12:32a drew on Lk 20:39, while Mk 12:34b is heavily dependent on Lk 20:40. Luke had already drawn on Mt 22:46, Matthew's unit on the question of David' son for Lk 20:40. Now Mark simply follows Luke. This not only brings the Matthean and Lukan accounts into some measure of harmony but it also provides a convenient stopping place for the various questions raised by leaders of the Jerusalem establishment. Now it is time for Jesus to give a response by setting forth his final verdict on the matter of his authority to teach in this manner.

¶ 68. Jesus Questions the Scribes' Claim That the Messiah is the Son of David

Mt 22:41-46 -------------------- Mk 12:35-37a <============ Lk 20:41-44

As Jesus was teaching in the temple, he asked, "How can the scribes say that the Messiah to come will be the *son* of David? David himself, inspired by the Holy Spirit, says in a psalm, 'The Lord said to my Lord, sit at my right hand while I put your enemies under your feet.' If David calls him 'Lord,' how can he be only his son?" No one answered Jesus.

General Observations. Mark has been carefully blending his sources' disparate accounts of Jesus' activity in Jerusalem during Jesus' final week of ministry. As we noted at the end of our discussion of the previous unit, Mark's redactional activity indicates that he has drawn upon Lk 20:40, the end of Luke's discussion with the Sadducees on the resurrection. This unit immediately precedes the Lukan account of the question of David's son (Lk 20:41-44). Mark follows the Lukan order to compose this pericope, blending elements from Mt 22:41-45. Mark had already used Mt 22:46 (or its close Lukan parallel) in the previous pericope, so he omits it from Mk 12:35-37.

Mk 12:35. Mark has just completed Jesus' dialogue with the friendly scribe. He carries over this thought by adding γραμματεῖς ("scribes") to Luke's indefinite question about David's son (Lk 20:41). This also provides a setting for the next unit where the scribes function as the subject (Mk 12:38). Since the scribes are teachers of the law, Mark may not see much difference between them and Matthew's Pharisees in Mt 22:41. The Markan linguistic characteristic, δέ/καί + ἀποκριθείς + a form of λέγω + dative, suggests Markan composition in Mk 12:35a (Peabody, *Mark as Composer*, 110, 70).

• The reference to teaching in the temple is a Markan addition designed to maintain continuity with the place of Jesus' teaching throughout the day (Mk 11:27; cf. 12:38; 13:1).

Mk 12:36-37a. The use of πνεῦμα + ἅγιον ("Holy Spirit") is Markan (Peabody, *Mark as Composer*, 3, 35).

• In Lk 20:43 Luke has ὑποπόδιον ("footstool"), which reflects the text of Ps 109:1 LXX. However, Matthew (Mt 22:44) has ὑποκάτω ("under, below"). Mark defers to Matthew.

• We have made the pericope break at Mk 12:37a. Mk 12:37b is included in the next pericope on the basis of source-critical conclusions discussed in the general observations there.

• The question about the Messiah being the son of David should be understood in the light of Mk 11:9-10. There the people expect the restoration of the kingdom of David with the coming of the Messiah. Jesus' response hints that the coming kingdom will be vastly different from King David's. In contrast to Matthew, Mark seems to have little at stake in the title, "Son of David." Mark is much more interested in the emphasis on a descendant of David being at God's right hand (i.e., Son of God). If Jesus is the one of whom Psalm 110 (109 LXX) speaks, then this again implies his coming exaltation/ resurrection, which, in turn, must be preceded by his death. So understood, this pericope functions as the answer to the earlier question on authority at Mk 11:27-33. Jesus can say what he has been saying about the temple because he is the Son of God.

SECTION TWO: WATCH. MK 12:37B-14:11.

This section is a self-contained unit. At its heart are Jesus' instructions warning his disciples about treacheries soon to come. As examples of the kind of conduct that he commends during the coming days, Mark prefaces and concludes Jesus' speech with accounts of women who act faithfully in the midst of great treachery.

¶ 69. Watch Out for the Scribes; Watch the Widow Who Gives Her Whole Life
Mt 23:1-36---------------->   Mk 12:37b-44   <========= Lk 20:45-21:4
(cf. Lk 11:37-12:3)

The large crowd listened to him joyfully. In his teaching, he said to them, "Watch out for the scribes who like to go around in their long robes, being greeted by people in the market square, and taking the best seats in the synagogue and seats of honor at feasts! They are the ones who rob widows of their possessions and yet offer long prayers for any occasion. In the day of judgment, they will receive greater punishment!" And he sat near the treasury box and watched people putting money into it. Rich people were putting in large amounts when up came a poor widow who put in the only two copper coins she had. Pointing her out to his disciples, Jesus said, "This poor widow has put in more than all of the rest put together. They gave out of their abundance while she gave out of her poverty everything she had, her whole life."

PART SIX. JESUS AND THE END OF THE TEMPLE ERA. MK 11:1-14:11

General Observations. Mark continues to follow the order of Luke (Lk 20:45-47; 21:1-4). Whether Luke regarded this passage as one or two literary units is not entirely clear. Mark, too, does nothing to link the two parts of the unit. Nevertheless, as we will show below, Mark carefully frames his version of Jesus' last eschatological discourse (Mk 13:1-37) with accounts of two women acting honorably in the context of betrayal by some male religious leaders (Mk 12:37b-44; 14:1-11). This framing is matched by the warning of Jesus to his disciples to be on the lookout for the appearance of similar acts of betrayal that may occur among his followers in coming days (Mk 13:9-13, esp. v. 12). Thus, on the grounds of our analysis of the literary structure of Mk 12:37b-14:11, it seems wise to understand Mk 12:37b-44 as one literary unit. Mark follows closely Luke's text, which we have noted is congruent at this point with his compositional purposes. There are also indications that Mark still has the text of Matthew in view. He has a demonstrated tendency to omit Matthew's lengthy discourses of Jesus. Mt 23:1-39 is one of these lengthy discourses. In addition, the content of Mt 23:1-29 was radically edited and utilized very differently by Luke. This makes the two contexts in Matthew and Luke difficult to conflate. Therefore, Mark omits both. Nevertheless, there are echoes of Matt 23:6-7 in Lk 20:46. Mark may have seen this. Along with echoing Mt 23:1 in Mk 12:37b, Mark gives occasional intimations of an acquaintance with the text of Mt 23.

Mk 12:37b. The reference to the ὄχλος ("crowd") echoes Mt 23:1. Thus, although Mark is not following the Matthean order he still leaves redactional evidence of his knowledge of Matthew's text.

• The expression καί + ἡδέως + αὐτοῦ + ἤκουεν appears here and at Mk 6:20 (Peabody, *Mark as Composer*, 157, 87). In both cases, it has no parallel in either Matthew or Luke. The expression, πολὺς ὄχλος in Mk 12:37b (cf. Mt 23:1, τοῖς ὄχλοις, and Lk 20:45, Ἀκούοντος δὲ παντὸς τοῦ λαοῦ) is consistent with the view that Mark combined the texts of Matthew and Luke and added an overlay that reflects the hand of the author.

Mk 12:38a. The phrase, καί + ἔλεγεν + ἐν τῇ διδαχῇ αὐτοῦ + 2d person plural present imperative, occurs twice in Mark (Mk 4:2; 12:38). At Mk 4:2 this expression helps to introduce the parables discourse and here it is used to anticipate the eschatological discourse. This phrase is probably Markan composition. Here it supplements the texts of Matthew and Luke.

Mk 12:38b-40. Βλέπετε ἀπό in the sense of "take heed" or "discern" will become characteristic of this unit.[6]

• Mark follows Lk 20:46-47 almost word for word in Mk 12:38b-40, with the exception of φιλούντων (Lk 20:46).

• In our judgment, Mk 12:40 is not parallel to Mt 23:14. We view Mt 23:14 as a scribal harmonization with the text of Luke 20:47.

• If the readings of D, W, f^{13}, 28 and 565 are more original, then Mark added to the indictment of the scribes that they devour the houses of *orphans* as well those of widows which Mark otherwise drew from Lk 20:47. Mark is highlighting Jesus' critique of the Jerusalem authorities by making more explicit the earlier charge that the leadership had abused its stewardship of the temple (Mk 11:17). If this reading is moe original, then Mark would have even been prepared to add new charges, i.e., that the scribes allowed the appropriation of the property of the downtrodden in order to maintain the temple's operation. In this way, Mark would have expanded upon his anti-temple and temple leadership theme.

Mk 12:41. Still within the temple precincts (Mk 12:35), Jesus is now seated opposite one of the chests of the temple treasury. Here he observes the process of financing the institution that he has denounced. The collocation καὶ καθίσας to begin a sentence diverges from Mark's source (Lk 21:1) but is characteristic of Markan composition (Mk 9:35; 12:41; cf. 13:3; see Peabody, *Mark as Composer,* 206, 101).

• Also, κατέναντι ("opposite") appears in a similar construction at Mk 13:3. This appears to be Markan composition.

Mk 12:42. In contrast to Luke, Mark highlights the actions of the *one* poor widow vis-a-vis the *many* rich men (Mk 12:41). Thus, Mark sharpens the distinction between the offering of the widow and the others. In the light of Mark's use of two stories about women to frame his eschatological discourse, this note about "a poor widow" may also foreshadow Jesus' words at Mk 14:7, "The poor you always have with you and, whenever you wish, you may do good to them, but you do not always have me." The unique Markan gloss, "and, whenever you wish, you may do good to them," also betrays

---

[6] Timothy J. Geddert, *Watchwords: Mark 13 in Markan Eschatology* JSNTSS 26 (Sheffield: JSOT Press, 1989), 82-87.

the secondary character of Mark's text when compared to the parallel at Mt 26:11 and John 12:8. Both of these other versions of the logion lack this gloss, which breaks the synonymous parallelism of the saying and which is thus better preserved in Matthew and John.

• In accordance with his style, Mark translates foreign words, like λεπτόν, for his readers (Peabody, *Mark as Composer,* 103, 68). Often these translations, making use of the formula ὅ ἐστιν or ὅ ἐστιν μεθερμηνευόμενον, have no parallel in the text of Matthew or Luke (e.g., Mk 5:41, ὅ ἐστιν μεθερμηνευόμενον cf. Mt 9:25 NP and Lk 8:54 NP).

Mk 12:43-44. Mark continues to follow Luke's account as his basic source. He introduces Jesus' comment about the poor widow with the construction καὶ προσκαλεσάμενος τοὺς μαθητὰς αὐτοῦ ("and having summoned his disciples"). This linguistic construction is characteristic of Markan composition (Peabody, *Mark as Composer,* 107, 69). It reinforces the importance of the word of Jesus about the poor widow for Mark's readers (cf. the use of ἀμήν in Mk 12:43, in place of ἀληθῶς in Lk 21:3.)

• Mark intends a close link between this reference to a poor widow (χήρα) and the reference earlier in the pericope to the widows harassed by the scribes (Mk 12:40). The poor widow is the paradigmatic contrast to the greed of the temple leadership. There are literary links between the action of the poor widow and the unnamed woman who anoints Jesus later (Mk 14:3-9). Both, out of their poverty, are still capable of amazing expressions of sacrificial love. In the presence of the great wealth of the temple, their gifts seem to be somewhat inconsequential. Yet their actions represent the kind of committed expressions of faith that will be the essence of the temple's replacement.

• Mark's phraseology ὅλον τὸν βίον αὐτῆς ("everything that sustained her life") represents a Markan intensification of Lk 21:4.

Excursus 12: Mark 12:41-44 as Secondary to Luke 21:1-4

It has never been difficult to find evidence to show that the text of Mark is secondary to Matthew. Most commentators on the Gospel of Mark, even those assuming Markan priority, take note of such passages. On the other hand, it has been more difficult to find evidence that Mark is also secondary to Luke. This book breaks new ground by drawing attention to places where Mark is secondary to the text of Luke. This is possible through the identification of Lukan literary characteristics that show up in Markan parallels; they can be most easily explained by Mark having copied Luke.

It is also now possible to identify literary characteristics of Mark that are absent from both Matthew and Luke. These can be most easily explained as coming from the compositional activity of the author of Mark as he drew upon the texts of Matthew and Luke in writing his Gospel.

However, even before this information was available, it was possible to demonstrate that Mark was secondary to Luke in some cases. Luke 21:1-4 is a case in point.

As was noted in *Beyond the Q Impasse,* the text here shows no evidence of Lukan composition apart from the use of τίς with a noun, not followed by a genitive (Lk 21:2), a linguistic characteristic of Luke. This story is, therefore, identifiable as tradition inserted into his Gospel account by the evangelist.[7] In its original form, this story was an anecdote about Jesus and what he had to say about a poor widow who cast two very small coins into the temple treasury.

> "Looking up, Jesus saw rich people casting their gifts into the Temple treasury. And he saw a needy widow casting in two very small coins. And he said, "Truly I say unto you, this poor widow cast in more than all of them.""

Verse 4 is what the rhetoricians termed an *aitia* or "reason." It was one of the standard acceptable additions to an anecdote of this kind. Its purpose was to explain the general principle inculcated in the story. Thus, vs. 4 begins with a post positive explanatory γάρ and reads as follows, "For all those others gave into the treasury out of their superabundance, but she, with less than enough, gave all that she had to sustain her." This *aitia* opened up the possibility for the rhetorician or preacher to comment on the topic of sacrificial giving, in the power and with the authority of the one who had spoken these life-giving words.

A developed and expanded version of this anecdote with its added *aitia* is found in the Gospel of Mark (12:41-44). There is, for example, a three-fold repetition of the term for "temple treasury" (see Mk 12:41a, 41b, and 43). Translators sometimes obscure this example of the repetitive style of Mark by using different words to translate the same Greek term.

The Markan introduction to this story adds the detail that he "called his disciples to him" (12:43). This is a literary effort at verisimilitude, adding nothing essential to the story. The clearest sign, however, of the secondary character of the Markan form of this tradition, as compared to that of

---

[7] McNicol et al., *Beyond the Q Impasse,* 257.

Luke, is found in the interpretative gloss added to v. 42, in which it is explained to Mark's readers that the two lepta amounted to a *quadrans* in Roman coinage.

The overall economy of language in the Lukan form of this story is a consideration favoring its originality. In general, it is more difficult to repeat a story in all its essentials in fewer words, than the other way around. The Lukan text preserves the story in all its essentials. The Markan text was clearly restructured for its intended readers, who presumably could benefit from knowing the value of a lepton in Roman coinage. As an expanded form of the text found in Luke, it is clearly secondary.

¶ 70. Jesus Warns That the Temple Will Be Destroyed
Mt 24:1-3 ==========>   Mk 13:1-4   <=========Lk 21:5-7

While he is walking out of the temple, one of his disciples says to him, "Teacher! Look at the amazing stones and incredible buildings!" But Jesus said to him, "See these huge buildings? Not one stone will remain upon another! It will all be torn down!" And after he had gone outside Jerusalem over to the Mount of Olives and sat down in full view of the temple across the valley, when they were alone Peter and James and John and Andrew asked him, "Tell us when all this will happen and what the signs will be when these things are to be accomplished."

General Observations. Mark has been focusing on the text of Luke and now comes to a pericope that sets the stage for Luke's version of the last eschatological discourse (Lk 21:5-7/Mt 23:1-3). Mark omits the polemic of Jesus against the Pharisees (Mt 23:1-39), which is not in the same order in Luke (cf. Lk 11:37-12:3/Mt 23:1-2, 4, 6-7, 13, 23, 25-27, 29-32, 34-36; Lk 13:34-35/Mt 23:37-39). Now with Luke and Matthew back together in the same sequence of pericopae Mark composes 13:1-4 using Matthew and Luke as sources. As will be noted below, Mark unites their texts creatively utilizing conflation and other characteristic compositional techniques.

Mk 13:1-2. Mark opens the pericope with a genitive absolute (cf. Mk 13:3). At this point, Mark is closer to Matthew's account of Jesus leaving the temple. The depiction of Jesus' departure is reinforced in Mk 13:3 (Mt 24:3), where he sits on the Mount of Olives κατέναντι τοῦ ἱεροῦ ("opposite the temple"). This labored description of Jesus leaving the temple and deliberately taking a seat directly opposite it deepens Matthew's explanation (Mt 24:3). It functions to provide an indisputable basis for the word of doom spoken against the temple. Matthew ("the disciples") and Luke ("certain ones") do not actually agree as to who made the remark about the grandeur of the temple (Mt 24:1/Lk 21:5). Mark describes the questioner as "one of the disciples." This use of εἷς with the partitive genitive is a recurrent Markan linguistic characteristic (Peabody, *Mark as Composer,* 136, 82). In its equivocation, it serves to unite Matthew and Luke's account.

• Mark has the phraseology ποταποὶ λίθοι καὶ ποταποὶ οἰκοδομαί ("what [huge] stones and what [marvelous] buildings"). This represents conflation. Mark draws λίθος from Lk 21:5 and οἰκόδομος from Mt 24:1.

• The use of ποταπός as a synonymous or duplicate expression is also characteristic of Mark's compositional procedure.

Mk 13:3-4. The combination of Peter, James, John, and Andrew as the ones who put the question to Jesus about "when will these things take place" is characteristic of Mark. All four different references to Andrew in the Synoptics are in Mark (Mk 1:16, 29, 3:17; 13:3).

• The composition of Mk 13:4, a crucial verse, appears to be another instance of Markan conflation. Mark takes ὅταν μέλλῃ ταῦτα from Lk 21:7 while drawing συντελεῖσθαι πάντα from Mt 24:3. The result is a blended version of the two accounts. Matthew 24:3, with its use of epexegetical καί, links the end of the temple closely to the parousia at the end of the age. Luke 21:7 understands the question of the disciples as only having to do with the end of the temple. Mark's blending of the two accounts has the disciples request *both* the time of the end of the temple *and* a sign when these catastrophic events will take place. Both questions are answered concurrently in Mk 13:5-23. But Mark was careful to separate these issues from his later comments on the end time (Mk 13:24-27, 32-37). Thus, even on the crucial issue of the eschatological timetable, Mark has both creatively blended the text of Matthew and Luke and made his own theological statement.

¶ 71. The First Signs of the Coming Judgment Day

Mt 24:4-8 ==========>   Mk 13:5-8   <========== Lk 21:8-11

Jesus said, "Be careful. Don't be fooled by appearances. Many will come claiming to speak in my name, saying, 'I'm the one!' Many will be misled. You will hear of wars and rumors of wars, don't be alarmed. They must occur and they are only the beginning. Nation will rise up against nation, kingdom against kingdom, there will be earthquakes in various places, famines—these will be the first 'labor pains.'"

General Observations. In the opening segments of his version of the Eschatological Discourse Mark follows the common order of Matthew and Luke. Mark adheres to the wording of Matthew more closely, but from time to time he blends phraseology from Luke into his account. The opening segment of the speech on the coming of religious deceivers in Mk 13:5-6 is also found in Mk 13:21-23. In Mk 13:5-6 there is a warning against being deceived replete with injunctions to "take heed" or "discern". A similar warning is sounded in Mk 13:21-23. Mk 13:23 ends with the admonition, "Take heed, I have told you all things." Thus Mk 13:5-6 and 21-23 delimit an *inclusio* around a series of prophetic announcements concerning various horrors that will take place in the next generation, i.e., the generation that concludes with the destruction of the temple in Jerusalem.

Mk 13:5. Mark opens his version of the Eschatological Discourse with a construction of ἤρξατο plus the infinitive, against the common testimony of Matthew and Luke (εἶπεν). This is a linguistic characteristic of Mark. The construction ἤρξατο/ἤρξαντο plus the infinitive is found 26 times in Mark.

Mk 13:6. In the current Nestle-Aland text the only divergence from Matthew is that Mark omits ὁ χριστός ("the Messiah"). If Nestle-Aland is correct (W, Θ, and f^{13} have ὁ χριστός in Mk 13:6), it indicates that Mark reflects Lk 21:8 with this omission.

Mk 13:7-8. Here Mark conflates Matthew and Luke. Mark 13:7 draws ὅταν δὲ ἀκούσητε ("whenever you hear") from Lk 21:9 and καὶ ἀκοὰς πολέμων ("and rumors of wars") from Mt 24:6. This conflation and blending of the text of Matthew and Luke is typical of Mark's compositional procedure for the Eschatological Discourse.

• Mark's description, based upon Matthew, of political and ecological turbulence is an excellent retrospective review of the decade of the 60s in the Roman Empire. These historical events were well documented by Martin Hengel.[8]

• There is a note throughout that these "horrors" are preliminary events before a coming great crisis; ἀλλ᾽ οὔπω τὸ τέλος "but not yet the end." That statement and ἀρχὴ ὠδίνων ταῦτα ("these things are the first birth pangs") serve as preliminary indicators of the coming great crisis. The crisis appears to focus on the appearance of the "horrible desecration (descecrator?)" described in Mk 13:14.

---

[8] Martin Hengel, *Studies in the Gospel of Mark* (trans. John Bowden; Philadelphia: Fortress, 1985), 14-28.

¶ 72. Watch Out for Persecutions

(Mt 10:17-23a) =======>   Mk 13:9-13   <----------------- Lk 21:12-19

Mt 24:9-10, 13-14   (Lk 12:11-12)

"Be careful! They will haul you before councils and beat you in synagogues; you will stand before governors and kings because of me, it being necessary first to proclaim the gospel to them and all nations for a witness to them. When they bring you to trial, don't worry about what you will say. Say whatever is given to you to say in that hour; it is not you but the Holy Spirit speaking. Brother will turn his brother over to the authorities for execution; a father, his child; children will have their parents put to death. Everyone will hate you because of my name, but he who perseveres to the day of judgment will be saved."

General Observations. Compositionally, this unit presented one of the Mark's greatest challenges in his attempt to unite the texts of Matthew and Luke. On the Two Gospel Hypothesis, Mark has three diverse accounts of the persecution of the disciples Mt 24:9-14/Lk 21:12-19/Mt 10:17-22). Moreover, Luke did not utilize Mt 24:9-14 as his major source for the composition of Lk 21:12-19, but Mt 10:17-22.[9] Mark chose to follow the two most similar descriptions of the persecution of the disciples, Mt 10:17-22 and Lk 21:12-14, to compose Mk 13:9-13. He occasionally echoed material from Mt 24:9-14.

• If Matthew and Luke are using Mark independently, why do they at first agree with Mk 13:5-8 line by line, then suddenly diverge both in sequence and content at Mk 13:9-13, but, just as suddenly, come back together for Mk 13:14ff.? The complicated, but not convincing, literary strategies that would have been followed on this hypothesis have been discussed thoroughly by B. Reicke.[10] Readers are urged to ponder carefully Reicke's analysis. In our judgment this is one of the most difficult of all the pericopae to account for on the Two Document Hypothesis.

Mk 13:9. Mark signals the importance of this unit with his use of βλέπετε ("Take heed, discern!"). This is Markan redaction. Its occurrences at Mk 13:5, 9, 23, 33 come at key turning points in the Eschatological Discourse.

---

[9] Allan J. McNicol, *Jesus' Directions for the Future* (New Gospel Studies 9; Macon, Ga.: Mercer University Press, 1996), 169-74.

[10] "A Test of Synoptic Relationships: Matthew 10:17-23 and 24:9-14 with Parallels," in Farmer, ed., *New Synoptic Studies,* 209-22. Additional helpful discussion on this matter may be found in C. S. Mann, *Mark,* 505-10, 516-20; and McNicol, *Jesus' Directions for the Future,* 169-174. Cf. McNicol et al., "Composition of the Synoptic Eschatological Discourse," in Dungan, ed., *Interrelations,* 188-93.

• For παραδώσουσιν ὑμᾶς ("They will betray you") Mark used Mt 10:17. Mark also indicated his acquaintance with Mt 24:9-14 by using 24:14 in the course of his composition of Mk 13:9-13.

• The disciples will confront both the Jewish and Gentile legal systems. They are to give testimony (μαρτύριον) by speaking the truth to these authorities in keeping with the mandates of the gospel.

Mk 13:10. "This saying is an enigma," says Morna Hooker, speaking as an advocate of the Two Document Hypothesis.[11] On that hypothesis, Mk 13:10 is a strange intrusion into the flow of the narrative between Mk 13:9 and 11. However, on the Two Gospel Hypothesis, Mark encountered a doublet at Mt 10:18 and Mt 24:14-15 about the testimony to all the Gentiles, so he adds as supplement in Mk 13:10 by conflating Mt 10:18 with Mt 24:14 on testifying on behalf of the gospel before the authorities. Indeed not only will this testimony be before the Jewish and Gentile courts but the announcement of the gospel will become widespread among all Gentiles. Mark takes this from Mt 24:14 and cleverly redacts Mt 24:14 to make this point. The redactional use of πρῶτον ("first") highlights Mark's point that this must take place before the end. Thus, we agree with those who would punctuate Mk 13:9-10 as one sentence.[12]

Mk 13:11-12. Here Mark follows very closely the terminology of Mt 10:19-21. For Mark, sufferings, treacheries, and betrayals by one's family are a necessary consequence of the proclamation of the gospel that will precede the appearance of the horrible desecration.

Mk 13:13. This verse is an exact repetition of Mt 10:22, 24:9b, and Lk 21:17. The significant, concurrent testimony serves as the perfect vehicle to bring Mark back into sequence with Mt 24 and Lk 21. By combining this with the common thought of Lk 21:19 and the Matthean doublet (Mt 10:22b and 24:13), Mark is able to bring closure to his call for faithful discipleship in the face of treachery by means of the phrase, ὁ δὲ ὑπομείνας εἰς τέλος οὗτος σωθήσεται ("the one enduring (persecutions) to the end will be saved"). Mark has carefully framed the Eschatological Discourse with accounts of two women who show great faithfulness amid treachery; similarly, in the heart of the discourse, the disciples are urged to show great faithfulness in the face of persecution.

---

[11] Hooker, *Mark*, 310.

[12] See G. D. Kilpatrick, "The Gentile Mission in Matthew and Mark 13:10-11," in *Studies in the Gospels,* ed. D. E. Nineham, 145-158.

This seems to be a deliberate literary strategy of Mark based on his sources in Matthew and Luke. On the other hand, as Bo Reicke has demonstrated, it is impossible on the basis of the Two Document Hypothesis to explain Mark's relationship to Matthew and Luke in this case.

¶ 73. The Great Crisis: The Appearance of the Horrible Desecration

Mt 24:15-25 ========> Mark 13:14-23 <----------------- Lk 21:20-24

(Lk 17:21, 23-24, 31, 37d-e)

"Now, when you see the Horrible Desecration standing where it should not be let the reader understand," Jesus continues, "and let the populace in Judea head for the hills. Indeed, it will be such a moment of crisis that you must not follow usual conventions with respect to going on a journey because of the need to leave suddenly. Of course, it will be a terrible time for pregnant women. Pray that it will not be in winter for these will be perilous times far beyond previous human experience. Only the elect of the Lord can survive that day! Do not believe it if anyone says the Messiah is there. It is no surprise that false messiahs and prophets will proliferate. Do not be deceived. When it happens, remember that you have heard this all earlier from me."

General Observations. Mark has now rejoined the common sequence of Mt 24:15-22 and Lk 21:20-24. However, the Matthean and Lukan versions of this event differ greatly. About the only common feature between the two accounts is that the historical locale is Judea. Matthew describes a crisis emerging with the appearance of the Horrible Desecration in the temple (Mt 24:15). Luke, clearly writing post 70 CE, focuses upon Jerusalem being surrounded by the Roman armies. Finally, the critical time hinted at since Mk 13:5 (cf. 13:7, 8) has arrived: the horrible desecration (Mk 13:14). There are three things for the disciples to do: (1) leave, if they are in Judea, (2) pray that the days may be shortened, and (3) not be deceived by spurious religious claims. As is clear from the synopsis, Mark cautiously follows the wording of Matthew, often overlapping where Luke agrees with Matthew. Mark tends to omit those sections of Luke that lack concurrent testimony with Matthew (Lk 21:20, 21b-22, 23b-24). It is noticeable that Mark omits all references to Jerusalem or the temple. However, oddly, he does maintain a reference to Judea, which is the minimal geographical locator for the events described. Mark's apparent ambiguity as to the locale of the horrible desecration is understandable. Although the Eschatological Discourse was precipitated by Jesus' announcement of the end of the temple (Mk 13:2-4) Mark is saying that the place of safety (ϵἰς τὰ ὄρη) during the *crisis* in Judea is to be understood metaphorically. The appearance of the horrible desecration is an indication that Judea no longer counts as a center of worship.

There is no value in being there physically. Figuratively, "to go to the hills" may mean to find shelter and safety in the community's relationship to its Lord.

Mk 13:14. Mark opens with the construction ὅταν δὲ Ἴδητε ("whenever you see"). This is found in Mt 24:15 and Lk 21:20, and indicates that Mark is back in step with the combined text of Matthew and Luke.

• Mark's omissions of the reference to Daniel in Mt 24:15 and to the soldiers surrounding Jerusalem in Lk 21:20 are significant. Likewise, if the text is correct, Mark's strange use of the masculine participle ἐστηκότα ("standing") with a neuter noun is most striking.[13] It is as though the horrible desecration described by Daniel has now become a person, or, at least, has been personified. Traditionally, the horrible desecration was thought to appear in Jerusalem (Dan 11:31; 12:11; 1 Macc 1:54). Mark does not care for the Jerusalem temple; but he would not have appreciated the erection of the Roman standards and recognition of Titus as Imperator that replaced it. To him that would be demonic power personified. Mark's readers are called to discern the realities of this situation and find their place of safety elsewhere (i.e., in the new community of faith).

Mk 13:15-18. These verses are very close to Mt 24:17-20. But another indication that Mark is writing for a predominantly Gentile-Christian readership is the omission of the reference to the Sabbath in Mt 24:20.

Mk 13:19-22. Mark makes only slight editorial changes in his text vis-a-vis that of Matthew. He takes the plural αἱ ἡμέραι ἐκεῖναι ("those days") in Mt 24:22 and makes it the subject of the sentence on the depth of the horrors (Mk 13:19-20). He thus creates an agreement against the text of Mt 24:21 and Lk 21:23, which have the singular verb ἔσται.

• In Mk 13:19, the use of a verb with a cognate noun with a relative pronoun (as in ἀπ' ἀρχῆς κτίσεως ἣν ἔκτισεν ὁ Θεός, "from the beginning of creation which God created") is a technique Mark employs to construct dualistic expressions (cf. Peabody, *Mark as Composer,* 169, 91). Similarly, in Mk 13:20 Mark has τοὺς ἐκλεκτούς οὓς ἐξελέξατο ("the chosen ones whom he chose").

---

[13] See McNicol, *Jesus' Directions for the Future,* 176-77, for a discussion of the textual problems.

Mk 13:23. Mark builds upon Mt 24:25 here. "Pay close attention" (βλέπετε) forms an *inclusio* around this segment of Jesus' eschatological instructions to the disciples (Mk 13:5, 23 cf. 13:9). After Jesus' momentous announcement in Mk 13:2 that the temple would be destroyed, the disciples ask two specific questions: (1) When will this be? (2) What will be the signal of it (Mk 13:4)? The first question is now answered with a description of the "horrors" of the decades culminating in the events of 70 CE. The second question is answered specifically in the occurrence of the great crisis of the horrible desecration set forth in Mk 13:14. The latter is a definite reference to the destruction of Jerusalem and the personified evil in the imperial power that overthrew it, the impact of which still existed at the time of the composition of Mark's Gospel. That is the distinguishing indicator. These events precipitated a great crisis for the church (Mk 13:15-23). Now, in retrospect, for those who live in the aftermath of this reality (Mk 13:24a), Mark has rehearsed how Jesus spoke prophetically of these times: "I have told you of all these things ahead of time" (Mk 13:23b).

¶ 74. The Coming of the Son of Man

Mt 24:29b-31 =========>   Mk 13:24-27   ------------------- Lk 21:25-28

"Sometime after the great crisis emerges, which I have just finished explaining," Jesus says, "there will be a great cosmic upheaval. At this time, the Son of Man will appear coming on the clouds in a great show of great power. The Son of Man will send forth his angels and he will gather the elect from everywhere."

General Observations. In the recitation of the eschatological scenario, Mark has reached the time of the composition of his Gospel. Mark is ready for Jesus to speak about events beyond the time of the initial crisis related to the time of the horrible desecration. Matthew has some terminology on the parousia of the Son of Man that is not paralleled in Lk 21 but occurs in Lk 17 (Mt 24:26-28/Lk 17:23-24,37). Since the coming of the Son of Man will also be the subject of the next pericope in Matthew, and the parallel does occur in the same narrative sequence in Luke, Mark prefers to incorporate the latter unit (Mt 24:29-31 and Lk 21:25-28) into his composition. Mark follows Luke in not allowing any material to intrude between the discussion about the crisis in Judea and the coming of the Son of Man. Thus, Mark omits Mt 24:26-28.

Mk 13:24. One of the most important elements of Mark's redaction in the whole of the Gospel occurs in Mk 13:24a: ἀλλὰ ἐν ἐκείναις ταῖς ἡμέραις μετὰ τὴν θλῖψιν ἐκείνην ("but in those days after that great crisis"). This is a critical alteration of the Matthean words "immediately after the crisis" (Mt 24:29). Matthew views the crisis of the horrible desecration and the parousia of the Son of Man as practically coterminous events (Mt 24:29 εὐθέως "immediately"). Mark, writing some time later, allows for an indeterminate interlude of delay between the time of the horrible desecration and the coming of the Son of Man. Hence Mark omits εὐθέως in spite of his preference for its cognates elsewhere. This provides a strong redactional indication that, for Mark, the coming of the Son of Man is in the indeterminate future. This is not as clear in Matthew and Luke.[14]

• The collocation ἐν ἐκείναις ταῖς ἡμέραις is a Markan linguistic feature. The terminology, however, is derived from Matthew (cf. Mt 24:19, 22, 29).

Mk 13:25-27. A possible blending of Matthew and Luke occurs in Mk 13:25a with Mark's use of ἔσονται (Lk 21:25a) and πίπτοντες (πεσοῦνται in Mt 24:29).

• The Markan omission of any references to signs (Mt 24:30; Lk 21:25a) is striking. In both Luke and Matthew, the signs appear in the cosmos. For Mark, false messiahs and false prophets will do signs on earth during the great crisis in their attempt to deceive the elect. But for Mark the true signal or sign that answers the question of the disciples (Mk 13:4) is the horrible desecration (Mk 13:14). Mark is not interested in turbulence in the cosmos as a sign.

• The Western text (D) has the Son of Man coming upon the clouds. If this is the correct reading it would conform to the text of Mt 24:30 (but cf. Lk 21:27). In any case, Mark's wording throughout is close to the text of Matthew.

¶ 75. The Parable of the Fig Tree

Mt 24:32-35 ============> Mk 13:28-31 <============ Lk 21:29-32

Jesus beckons his audience to take note of the fig tree and learn a lesson from it. "When the sap fills its branches and foliage begins to appear you know that summer is near." He goes on to say, "Likewise when the things that I am talking about burst forth you should know that it is close at hand. All of these things will take place within the span of a generation. What I say is true. Heaven and earth may pass away but my words will abide always."

General Observations. Mark is following the common sequence of Matthew and Luke. The next unit in both Matthew and Luke, after the description of the coming of the Son

---

[14] See McNicol, *Jesus' Directions for the Future,* 136-41.

of Man, is the Parable of the Fig Tree. Mark followed the concurrent testimony of Matthew and Luke. Therefore, he omitted Lk 21:28 that has no parallel in Matthew, and now utilizes the pericope on the fig tree. Redactional changes, even though minimal, are significant (see below). Mark concludes the pericope with a 'this generation' saying (Mk 13:30), and the 'heaven and earth' saying (Mk 13:31). Both of these sayings occur in the same order in Mt 24:34-35 and Lk 21:32-33 and seem to comprise a consistent thought unit. Mark tends to be closer to Matthean wording in this pericope than to Luke (cf. Mk 13:28). This was also observable in the previous pericope.

Mk 13:28-32. It is noticeable that Mark makes an interesting blend of Matthew and Luke with respect to the use of the critical phraseology ταῦτα ("these things") from Luke and πάντα ταῦτα ("all these things") from Mt. Mt 24:33, 34 has the phraseology πάντα ταῦτα twice. Lk 21:31 has ταῦτα γινόμενα, and πάντα γένηται in Lk 21:32. On the other hand, Mark has a blend of Matthew and Luke: ταῦτα γινόμενα in Mk 13:29, which parallels Lk 21:31, and ταῦτα πάντα γένηται in Mk 13:30, which parallels Mt 24:34.

• Another instance of conflation can be noted in the manner Mark has blended from Matthew and Luke different forms of γίνομαι ("to become").[15] A table is reproduced below:

Mt 24:32//Mk 13:28----->	γένηται	
	γινόμενα	<--------Mk 13:29//Lk 21:31
Mt 24:34//Mk 13:30----->	γένηται	<--------Mk 13:30//Lk 21:32

• By omitting the reference to the kingdom of God as near in Lk 21:31, Mark seems to move away from the idea that the image of the fig tree budding, putting on leaves, and coming to harvest in a determined but relatively short time period is to be connected with the events culminating in the coming of the Son of Man (Mk 13:24-27). Starting with the reference to the question about "these things" in Mk 13:4, for Mark "these things" point to the time of the first generation, which culminated in the destruction of the temple and the emergence of the horrible desecration in Mk 13:5-23 (cf. Mk 13:30). Matters pertaining to the coming of the Son of Man are discussed later in Mk 13:32-37.

• A significant agreement between Matthew and Luke against Mark is created at Mk 13:30 and parallels. There, Mark has created μέχρις οὖ as opposed to ἕως ἄν in Mt 24:34/Lk 21:32.

---

[15] McNicol, *Jesus' Directions for the Future,* 184.

• Mk 13:30 is one of three examples of prophetic sayings in Mark that share a common and complex literary structure (cf. Mk 9:1 and 14:25). All three of these Markan examples have parallels in both Matthew and Luke. Matthew and Luke, however, record not only the examples with Markan parallels, but also other examples of this prophetic sayings formula that have no Markan parallel (Mt 5:18NP; Mt 5:26//Lk 12:59; Mt 10:23NP; Mt 16:28//Mk9:1//Lk 9:27; Mt 23:39//Lk 13:35; Mt 24:24//Mk 13:30//Lk 21:32; Mt 26:29//Mk 14:25//Lk 22:16 and 18). This evidence supports the view that Mark is literarily dependent upon both Matthew and Luke,[16] for Mark appears to have preserved in a fragmentary way a complex literary structure broadly represented in his sources.

¶ 76. The Call to Vigilance

Mt 24:37-25:30=========>	Mk 13:32-37	<=========== Lk 21:33-36
(esp. Mt 24:36, 42-43; Mt 25:5, 12-15)		(esp. Lk 12:37a, 38a, 41, 44)

Finally, still seated on the Mount of Olives, Jesus draws his long discourse to a close. "Now concerning the precise time of the culmination of things [which you remember I have discussed] no one knows. Take heed, watch, for you do not know the time. It is similar to the situation of a doorkeeper. The master has gone away. The doorkeeper and the servants do not know when the master will come back. All that the doorkeeper knows is that he needs to be awake when the master comes — otherwise there will be trouble! As the doorkeeper must always be alert and awake, so my disciples must be ready during the four watches of the night less coming suddenly I find you sleeping. What I say to you I say to all, watch!"

General Observations. Throughout the Eschatological Discourse Mark has built a common text from Matthew and Luke, generally preferring those passages where the two agreed in order. We noted one exception to this phenomenon. At Mk 13:9-13, Mark diverged from the text of both Matthew and Luke only to resume following them again at Mk 13:14 (see above for our explanation of Mark's editorial policy on the Two Gospel Hypothesis). Here the phenomenon is repeated. The texts of Matthew and Luke differ from Mark significantly at Mk 13:33-37. However, the common narrative order is picked up by Mark at Mk 14:1. On the Two Document Hypothesis the overall macro-phenomenon is difficult to explain. That is, according to the Two Document Hypothesis, Matthew and Luke have followed Mark independently, reproducing their narrative accounts in the same sequence as Mark except in two pericopae where they both move

---

[16] For the entirety of this argument, see David Peabody, "A Pre-Markan Prophetic Sayings Tradition and the Synoptic Problem," *JBL* 97(1978): 391-409.

away from Mk 13 *at the same time* to use other source-material and then, at the same time, return to the same sequence. Can this compositional procedure be accounted for as sheer coincidence? Furthermore, the composition of Mark is difficult to explain on this hypothesis because it appears to echo other material in both Matthew and Luke. Indeed, exegetes advocating the Two Document Hypothesis are required to supply complicated theories of Mark-Q overlaps to account for the text of Mark at this point.[17] But on the Two Gospel Hypothesis, a more credible and less complex alternative explanation is available. Mark is ready to end his account of the Eschatological Discourse. Closure is indicated by a large *inclusio* delimited by Mk 13:4 and 13:37: εἰπὸν ἡμῖν ("say to us") in Mk 13:4, and ὃ δὲ ὑμῖν λέγω, πᾶσιν λέγω ("what I say to you I say to all") in 13:37. In keeping with his earlier summaries (Mk 3:7-8; 4:33-35; 9:49-50), Mark is brief. The endings of the Eschatological Discourse in Mt 24:36-25:46 and Lk 21:34-36 are very different in length and content. It would be impossible to blend these satisfactorily.

• In a manner similar to his procedure at Mk 13:9-13, Mark could have observed that Luke drew material from Matthew to establish a concurrent account of the eschatological teaching of Jesus (Mt 24:42-46/Lk 12:37-46). Drawing from this body of eschatological material, Mark composed his summary by blending together terminology from the text of both Matthew and Luke. Thus, he created a summary that emphasizes the message of his sources; i.e., the need to watch intently and constantly [or] with unbroken attention for the coming of the Lord.

Mk 13:32. This verse sets the tone for Mark's summary. Mark has just said that the events of the horrible desecration (Mk 13:5-23) will take place in one generation (cf. Mk 13:30). But with respect to the coming of the Son of Man (Mk 13:24-27) it will be very different. No one knows that particular time or day. Mark follows Mt 24:36 in order to create the setting for the highlight of his summary: the call "to watch" (cf. Acts 1:7-11).

Mk 13:33-34. This is the first of the two Markan summary couplets. It begins with a warning call (βλέπετε, ἀγρυπνεῖτε) and ends with a similar injunction (γρηγορῇ). For his composition of Mk 13:33-34 Mark cleverly blends material from Lk 21:34-36 (ἀγρυπνεῖν, καιρός) with echoes of terminology drawn from Mt 24:42 and 25:13-15 (see the synopsis).

---

[17] For an overview of some recent critical discussion on this issue see McNicol, *Jesus' Directions for the Future*, 187.

• The reference to the doorkeeper (θυρωρός) in Mk 13:34 is Markan redaction. This must have been important enough for Mark to cause him to shift the number from the plural references to the servants earlier in the verse to the singular reference to the doorkeeper later in the verse. This may be explained in the following way. Mk 12:38-14:11 is a literary unit. It is framed by the examples of the two women who keep faith in the presence of treachery. In Mk 13:9-13, the disciples also were urged to keep faith amid treachery. Now, by utilizing *synecdoche*, Mark lifts up an ideal disciple, the doorkeeper, as a model of the one who is faithful in keeping watch.

• Mk 13:34 not only echoes material on "watching" from Mt 25, but also the Lukan material on slaves waiting for the master in Lk 12:36-37a. Mark will make additional use of this material in the next verse. Mark, in his abbreviated account, may have had an additional theological reason for moving from the Matthean version of the Parable of the Chief Servant and Slaves (Mt 24:45-51) to the Lukan accounts of Servants Preparing for the Return of the Lord and the Chief Servant and Slaves (Lk 12:35-38; 42-46). Matthew's account ends with great violence, "weeping and gnashing of teeth" (Mt 24:51). On the Two Gospel Hypothesis, Mark always omits this terminology when he finds it in Matthew.

Mk 13:35-37. This is a second and final warning in the call to vigilance. Mark starts the unit by redacting Mt 24:42, the same verse he echoed in Mk 13:33b, (see the synopsis). Mark's redaction features the Roman four night watch scheme (cf. Mk 6:48).

• The concern to detail carefully the watches of the night may not only have come from the source material in Mt 24:43 and Lk 12:37b-38. It may also anticipate the fateful evening before Jesus' death when the disciples would go through their first major trial (cf. evening, Mk 14:17a; midnight, Mk 14:30(?); cockcrow, Mk 14:68(var.), 72; early, [πρωΐ] Mk 15:1; "coming, he may find you sleeping" (cf. Mk 14.37, 40; cf. Peabody, *Mark as Composer*, table 241, 110; 52, 49). Being faithful during the watches of the night functions as a metaphor for faithfulness in the time of trial both in the passion story and for the future course of the church.

• Mk 13:36-37 not only constitutes the end of the *inclusio* (Mk 13:5a, 37) but represents a final amalgamation of stock material on watching drawn from both Matthew (25:5, 12-13) and Luke (Lk 21:34, αἰφνίδιος = ἐξαίφνης in Mk 13:36). In Lk 12:41-42, Peter is depicted as asking Jesus a question. Could Mark have intended the metaphor of the doorkeeper (Mk 13:34-35) to be the answer to Peter's question (Lk 12:41, 44; cf. Mk 13:3)?[18]

¶ 77. In the Presence of Treachery, Another Woman Expresses Extraordinary Generosity
Mt 26:1-16 =======>   Mk 14:1-11   <------------------ Lk 22:1-6
                                                               (cf. Lk 7:36-50)

The full impact of Jesus' harsh teaching against the temple leaders begins to come home. Passover is approaching. The temple priests and teachers of the law make a determination that it will be necessary, under very careful circumstances, to seize Jesus and kill him. But there is considerable concern. The city is full of pilgrims and such a precipitous action may elicit a counter-response from the people.

Jesus is spending the day at Bethany in the house of Simon the Leper. While Jesus is sitting at table, in the presence of many men, a woman unobtrusively enters with a jar of expensive nard. To the astonishment of the onlookers she breaks the jar and allows the expensive ointment to pour out over Jesus' head as a kind of bizarre anointing. The onlookers are offended because of the expense involved. Couldn't the ointment be sold and given to the poor? "Leave her alone," Jesus replies, as if to say these are extraordinary times. "She has done a good work for me. The poor are always around. This woman gives what she has. In anticipation of my death, she anoints my body. It is the gospel being enacted. Wherever the gospel will go people will speak about this as her memorial."

Meanwhile, one of the chosen twelve, Judas Iscariot, makes himself available to the temple leadership. He knows of Jesus' whereabouts and indicates a willingness to divulge to them that important information. When they hear this they are glad and resolve to give him money. Judas bides his time.

General Observations. Throughout the unit Mark follows the order of the Matthean account. Mark utilizes some material from Luke in the verses about the plot against Jesus (Mk 14:1-2) and Judas (Mk 14:10-11). These topics are in the same order in Matthew and Luke.

• In keeping with our suggestion that Mark frames his version of the Eschatological Discourse with two accounts of women who show extraordinary generosity in the face of treachery, we now come to the end of this section and the closing member of both the *inclusio* and the part. A plot is instigated to destroy Jesus. Immediately after the account

---

[18] See McNicol, *Jesus' Directions for the Future*, 185-91, for additional details on the composition of this unit. See Mk 13:37//Lk 12:41-42 in Synopsis ¶ 76.

of a widow giving "all that she had, even her whole life," Mark provided a brief scene to set the stage for the Eschatological Discourse (Mk 13:1-4). Similarly, after the Eschatological Discourse, before the anonymous woman shows her great generosity by anointing Jesus with the expensive ointment, Mark provides a brief setting that functions to put the anointing incident in context (Mk 14:1-2).

• The Lukan and Matthean versions of the story of Jesus' anointing are rather different and appear in different literary contexts. Matthew and Luke both follow their respective accounts of Jesus' last eschatological discourse with a reference to a plot to kill Jesus (Mt 26:2-5; Lk 22:1-2). Matthew then has the account of the anointing of Jesus at Bethany (Mt 26:6-13); but Luke had already narrated a similar incident in Lk 7:36-50 and so omitted Matthew's account of the anointing at Bethany and went directly to Judas' betrayal (Mt 26:14-16; Lk 22:3-6). Mark follows the Matthean order throughout.

Mk 14:1-2. Having had Jesus conclude a second lengthy day of teaching in the temple precincts (Mk 11:20-13:37), Mark now begins to unfold several events that are the logical outcome of what has happened in the past several days.

• The account of the plot against Jesus is much more brief in Luke than in Matthew. Mark follows Luke in being relatively brief.

• Mark omits Mt 26:1. No parallel exists in Luke. Matthew 26:1 reminds the reader that the Eschatological Discourse was spoken to the disciples. If the Nestle-Aland text is correct, Mark will create a setting for the next pericope that does not feature the disciples (cf. Mt 26:1 and Mk 14:1). However, there is considerable doubt about this (see below).

• In the description of Passover, Mark blends the accounts in Matthew and Luke. Mark has Matthew's reference to the anticipated Passover coming "in or after two days"; but he also includes Luke's reference to it being the Feast of Unleavened Bread (Lk 22:1). In our view, the awkwardness of this construction is caused by the strained blending of the two accounts and Mark's need to furnish temporal markers.

Mk 14:3. Mark's reference to Bethany is noteworthy for its dependence on Matthew. The parallel to this pericope in Luke is elsewhere. The last Markan reference to Bethany was at Mk 11:12. As is characteristic of Mark, he uses vivid descriptive language to expand Matthew's account of the woman's act of pouring the ointment on Jesus.

Mk 14:4-5. If the Nestle-Aland text is correct, Mark has made a major editorial change from Matthew in these verses. There the disciples chide Jesus for allowing the lavish act of the woman to take place. In Mark, "certain ones" do the chiding. However, W, 788, and f^{13} have "certain disciples." The matter is of some consequence because Mark reads either "certain ones" or "certain disciples" who "scold the woman harshly (ἐνεβριμῶντο αὐτῇ cf. Peabody, *Mark as Composer,* 65, 53). Most commentators take the references to the disciples in the textual tradition to be a later accommodation to Matthew. There may be another explanation. It is a known *Tendenz* of Mark to denigrate the disciples. Perhaps later editors of the text of Mark have been offended by this description of the action of men who would later be the apostles and thus omitted "disciples."

• At least one prominent advocate of the Two Document Hypothesis has argued that the evaluation of the "myrrh/spikenard" in Mark at "more than 300 denarii" is a later development of the original tradition when Mark's text is compared with the parallels at Mt 26:9 and Jn 12:5.[19]

Mk 14:6-9. The Greek of Mk 14:8 is stilted and has led advocates of Markan priority to argue that it was improved by Matthew (cf. Mt 26:12). More than likely, on our hypothesis, the Markan alterations of Matthew at Mk 13:8 have been made to supply more conformity with the opening member of the *inclusio*, the story of the poor widow in Mk 12:44. In both cases, Mark wishes to emphasize that the women generously gave all they had (cf. ὃ ἔσχεν ἐποίησεν in Mk 14:8, and πάντα ὅσα εἶχεν in Mk 12:44). As such, these women become models of ideal discipleship for Mark (cf. Lk 8:1-3).

• The sacrificial action of the woman constitutes an anointing of Jesus' body in anticipation of his death. Thus, Mark, like Matthew, ties this action to the account of Jesus' death. Such an astonishing act will become part and parcel of the account of the gospel itself. Hence the gnomic expression that it will never be forgotten.

Mk 14:10-11. Juxtaposed to this expression of devotion by the woman is the perfidy of the action of Judas. Mark omits the explanation of the motivation by Satan from Lk 22:3 and any motivation of greed for money founded in prophecy (cf. Mt 26:15). For Mark,

---

[19] Raymond Brown, *The Gospel According to John* (AB 29; Garden City, N.Y.: Doubleday and Company, 1966), 451-52.

Judas' action is "unadorned treachery."[20] The plot to destroy Jesus is now ready to get underway. The outcome will unfold in the next section.

Summary

At the end of part 5, blind Bartimaeus confessed Jesus as the son of David, and began to follow him humbly along the way—a way that would lead to crucifixion. Part 6 then opens with Jesus entering the holy city in the presence of crowds. These crowds attempted to connect his entrance with the restoration of the glory of the Davidic kingdom (Mk 11:9-10).

Part 6 guides the readers to a redefinition of the nature of the kingdom that Jesus is bringing. The kingdom will not take the form of a restoration of the glory of David's kingdom, but will be much more in keeping with the action of following Jesus along the way as outlined in part 5. The temple, as well as those directly associated with its operation, has outlived its time of usefulness. The temple will be replaced by a people of faith, forgiveness, and prayer (Mk 11:12-13:2, esp. 11:20-25). The new community of faith will supersede the cult of burnt offerings and sacrifices (Mk 11:32-34).

On the Mount of Olives Jesus gave further instruction to a core of his closest disciples. He told them that the road of discipleship would be paved both with future distress and treachery within the faith community (Mk 13:9-13). This is coterminous with the coming of the kingdom. The disciples needed to understand this.

No one knows when the end of the age will come. What is important for the present is to watch and persist in discipleship. These words are no sooner out of the mouth of Jesus than Judas begins to execute an act of grave treachery; he will betray Jesus to the outraged temple authorities (Mk 14:1-2; 10-11).

---

[20] Mann, *Mark*, 559.

JESUS' PASSION, DEATH AND RESURRECTION

Overview

Near the end of the Eschatological Discourse Jesus uttered a strong warning to his disciples, "Watch therefore—for you do not know when the master of the house will come, in the evening, or at midnight, or at cockcrow, or in the morning—lest he come suddenly and find you asleep" (Mk 13:35-36a). In that context Jesus was speaking about the coming of the Son of Man at the final consummation. But his warning also serves as an anticipation of the events that will engulf the disciples over the next several days. The details of the four watches provide key elements within the story line of Jesus' last night, the narration of which constitutes the first of three sections of this part (Mk 14:12-72).

The three dramatic sections of this part are as follows: (1) Jesus' last night, which culminates in his arrest and preliminary trial before the temple authorities (Mk 14:12-72); (2) a day of judgment and execution before Pilate (Mk 15:1-47); and (3) Jesus' resurrection and commission to take the gospel to the whole world (16:1-8[9-20]). All three of these sections include elements of tension which contrast Jesus' faithfulness and his disciples' struggle, and failure, to be faithful. Only in the last section, as a result of God's action in Jesus' martyrdom and resurrection, is the tension resolved. The disciples return to faith.

Throughout the part, Jesus' prophecies and their precise fulfillment underscore the tension between Jesus' faithfulness and the disciples' lack of faith. The earlier Passion Predictions (Mk 8:31; 9:30-32; 10:32-34) are supplemented (Mk 14:18-21; 27-31; 43-50) to emphasize for the reader that it was God's purpose that Jesus would be abandoned by his disciples and die alone in incredible suffering. Mark pictures in minute detail the failure of Peter, even after the first cock crow, to heed the warning of Jesus that before the cock crows twice he would deny him three times. By the end of the first section the disciples have failed to watch through the night and have abandoned Jesus, fulfilling his prophecy completely.

In the second section, with its account of Jesus' trial and crucifixion by the Romans, Jesus' prophetic utterances continue to be fulfilled. Now, apparently even abandoned by God, Jesus dies alone, a victim of terrible violence.

The reader is then brought to section three where, just as Jesus predicted, after his death he is vindicated in three days. In the longer ending, the disciples finally come to faith and are commanded and empowered to proclaim the gospel to the whole world. God's promises to bring his kingdom have not been thwarted (Mk 1:15). Contrary to the expectations of both the authorities and the disciples it was necessary that the Messiah be crucified. But through the resurrection, God was able to reverse the blindness and hardness of heart of the disciples and set them on a different course. In the end they begin to function as the foundation of a new community that takes the place of the temple establishment. By following the crucified Messiah as a community of faith, forgiveness, and prayer they paradoxically become the pillars of the kingdom. The secret of this kingdom (Mk 4:10-12) is now evident. The kingdom both in its inauguration with Jesus and its continual coming in the life of the community emerges through death and resurrection. This is the gospel they are to embody and proclaim to the whole world.

SECTION ONE: A NIGHT BEFORE THE JERUSALEM RELIGIOUS AUTHORITIES. MK 14:12-72

¶ 78. Jesus Sends Two Disciples to Prepare for the Passover Meal

Mt 26:17-19 ==========>   Mk 14:12-16   <===========Lk 22:7-13

On the first day of Passover, Jesus' disciples said to him, "Where do you want us to go prepare the Passover meal for you?" And sending two of his disciples, he said, "Go into Jerusalem. A man will meet you carrying a jar of water. He will take you to a certain person's house. Say to him, 'Where is the guest room where our teacher and his disciples may eat the Passover?' He will show you a large upper room already well furnished." The disciples set out and it happened just as Jesus had said. And so they prepared for the Passover meal.

> *General Observations.* Mark continues to follow the common order of Matthew and Luke. In the previous pericope (Mk 14:1-11) Mark was following Matthew but incorporated material from Luke at the beginning and end of the unit. In this pericope, Mark is again following Matthew, but depends upon Luke for the essential structure of the account, especially the parts involving the story of the water-carrier and the meeting with the householder.

• Mk 11:1-7 and 14:12-16 are strikingly similar in structure. The most notable features include the use of "just as he said" (Mk 11:6/Mk 14:16) and the almost identical phrasing of the extended account about the sending of the two disciples. In addition, the story of the preparation for Jesus' triumphal entry and this story of the preparation for Passover share at least 26 words in common, most of them in exactly the same grammatical form and in the same order (Peabody, *Mark as Composer,* 229, 106). Either Mark wants to remind the reader here of a very similar prophecy and fulfillment story earlier, or he remembers the earlier story so well that it colors his telling of this account. Both accounts occur at the beginning of crucial points of the Markan Passion Narrative (Mk 11:1-7 begins our part 6 and this pericope begins our part 7). What Mark seems to be saying by such close attention to detail is that everything that will take place in this special time, down to the smallest item, happens in keeping with God's purposes.

Mk 14:12. Mark begins the story by blending elements from Matthew and Luke. Specifically, in Mk 14:12, τῇ δὲ πρώτῃ τῶν ἀζύμων from Matthew and ἦλθεν δὲ ἡμέρα τῶν ἀζύμων from Luke become καὶ τῇ πρώτῃ ἡμέρᾳ τῶν ἀζύμων in Mark.

• In conformity with the anonymity of the two disciples in the closely parallel account in Mk 11:2, Mark omits the Lukan identification of these disciples as Peter and John (cf. Lk 22:8).

Mk 14:13-16. The repetition of εἰς τὴν πόλιν in Mk 14:13 and Mk 14:16 further illustrates Mark's penchant for repeating the same phrasing (dualistic expressions) within a relatively limited literary context.

• The eschatological reference "my time is near" in Mt 26:18 is omitted by Mark. For Matthew the death and resurrection of Jesus is the decisive transition to the new age (cf. Mt 27:51-53). Matthew stresses that the time of the new age is near. Mark does not operate with this level of eschatological intensity. Instead Mark stresses that even in minute events everything taking place in the last week of Jesus' life occurs fully within God's purposes. Thus, for example, in Mk 11:2-6′ Mark stated that the two disciples would mysteriously discover a colt. They were to bring the colt back to the Lord. On this colt Jesus would make his important entrance to the city. Similarly, in this pericope, the two disciples are instructed to follow a man carrying a jar of water. This man will lead them to the place where the teacher will enter to celebrate his very significant last Passover.

¶ **79. At Passover, Jesus Predicts His Betrayal and Death**

Mt 26:20-29=========>   Mk 14:17-25   <--------- Lk 22:14-23, 28

(Mt 19:28)   (I Cor 11:23-24)

When evening had come Jesus arrived at the room and began the meal. While he eats with his disciples he makes several dramatic announcements. "One of those here at the table will betray me," he says. The disciples are dumbfounded. One by one they ask, "Is it I?" He tells them that indeed, it is one of them who is dipping with him into the dish. Jesus states that this act of betrayal is connected with the predestined fate of the Son of Man. As for the betrayer himself, "It would be better if that man had never been born," Jesus says.

While still at the table Jesus made another dramatic announcement. He took bread, gave thanks, broke it and gave it to the disciples. He said, "Take, this is my body." Upon taking a cup, and giving thanks, he also gave it to the disciples and they all drank from it. Then he said to them, "This is my blood of the covenant, which is poured out on behalf of the many. Truly I say to you, under no circumstances will I drink of the product of the vine until that day when I drink it new in the kingdom of God."

> ***General Observations.*** For this account, Mark continues to follow the common order of Matthew and Luke, but returns to his more usual practice of generally preferring the wording of Matthew. This feature of Markan composition is especially noticeable throughout the Passion Narrative. Matthew's version of the betrayal and Passover meal is straightforward and uncomplicated. Luke's version includes a speech of Jesus at the end of the meal that centers on a call for humility on the part of the disciples and somewhat blurs the focus on Jesus' impending death. Mark has omitted from Matthew and Luke a number of Jesus' earlier speeches, and he does so here.
>
> • There are major text-critical issues to be resolved with regard to the Lukan version of Last Supper.[1] This makes it difficult to know for certain what text of Luke Mark might have been reading.
>
> **Mk 14:17.** Mark generally follows the wording of Matthew in this verse. He follows a common linguistic preference in the use of ἔρχομαι for Mt's ἀνάκειμαι (cf. Mt 26:20).

---

[1] See the team discussion on this matter in McNicol et al., *Beyond the Q Impasse*, 283-84.

Also δώδεκα used absolutely of Jesus' disciples is a linguistic characteristic of Mark (Peabody, *Mark as Composer,* 102, 68; 231, 107).

Mk 14:18. The addition of ὁ ἐσθίων μετ' ἐμοῦ in this verse may have been influenced by the appearance of φαγεῖν μετ' ὑμῶν in Lk 22:15 (cf. φάγω in Lk 22:16). Or, it may echo Ps 41:9 (40:10 LXX), which was used in early Christian tradition to describe the betrayer (John 13:18).

Mk 14:19. Mark's change of εἷς ἕκαστος in Mt 26:22 to εἷς κατὰ εἷς, if it is not an idiom, may be a combination of a Markan preference for duplication used distributively (cf. Mk 6:7, 39-40 ; cf. Peabody, *Mark as Composer,* 152, 186) and the distributive use of κατά (cf. Mk 6:40; 13:8; and 14:49).

Mk 14:20. Mark's supplementary description of Judas as "one of the Twelve" is more specific than the parallel in Mt 26:23. It appears to be a Markan duplicate expression (Mk 14:17, 20, τῶν δώδεκα cf. Mk 14:18, 20, εἷς). It is thoroughly in keeping with Markan style and is a good example of a change or supplement of a source that conforms to the style of the author.

• The absence of the words "hand" and "betrays me" from Mk 14:20 (cf. Mt 26:23//Lk 22:21) is an agreement of Matthew and Luke against Mark.

Mk 14:21-22. Mark omits Mt 26:25. The readers of Mark are presumed to know the identity of Jesus' betrayer (cf. Mk 3:19; 14:10).

EXCURSUS 13: THE SECONDARY CHARACTER OF MARK TO MATTHEW IN THE ACCOUNT OF THE LAST SUPPER
THE APPROACH OF ADVOCATES OF MARKAN PRIORITY

Many who favor Markan priority assert that, if there is one place in the Passion Narrative where Matthew is dependent upon Mark, it is in account of the Last Supper (Mt 26:26-29/Mk 14:22-25).[2]

---

[2] Advocates of the Two Gospel Hypothesis have given a lengthy explanation for the composition of Lk 22:15-20 based on Matt 25:26-29. See McNicol et al., *Beyond the Q Impasse,* 279-84. There it is stated that besides using Matthew, Luke utilized traditions about the supper known by Paul, which were probably in use in the churches founded by him. On the Two Gospel Hypothesis, as is typical of the Passion Account, Mark follows

Although the wording of Matthew and Mark is very close in this passage, it is argued that, in those places where the wording of Matthew differs from Mark, the differences are to be explained as the result of later developments in the Eucharistic liturgy in Matthew's community.[3] Since Mark's text is viewed as less developed liturgically, it is claimed that Mark is earlier.

Frequently cited evidence of liturgical development in Matthew's community would include the following: First, Matthew parallels Jesus' command to drink the cup with Jesus' statement, "Take, eat [φάγετε]" the bread (Mt 26:26) rather than the simple "Take" of Mk 14:22. Second, Mark describes the giving of the cup to the disciples in his narrative with the words καὶ ἔπιον ἐξ αὐτοῦ πάντες ("and all drank from it"), whereas Matthew records similar words in the imperative, in direct speech, πίετε ἐξ αὐτοῦ πάντες "All of you, drink from it" (Mk 14:23/Mt 26:27). Supposedly, the direct speech is more liturgical and, therefore, later. Third and finally, Matthew adds a reference to "the forgiveness of sins" after the cup saying. (Mt 26:28, cf. the absence of this detail from Mk 14:24). These are the three prime examples that have been set forth to support the claim that the Markan account of the words of institution is earlier than the similar account in Matthew on the grounds that the Markan form is less liturgically developed.[4]

A RESPONSE FROM THE PERSPECTIVE OF THE TWO GOSPEL HYPOTHESIS

In a situation where two texts, very similar in wording, are being compared, arguments about stylistic preferences may appear reversible or inconclusive.[5] If Mark used Matthew, Mark should have

---

Matthew closely but blends Matthew's text with that of Luke in several places (καὶ ἔδωκεν αὐτοῖς, Lk 22:19/Mk 14:22; use of ὑπέρ in Lk 22:20/Mk 14:24; and kingdom of God in Lk 22:18/Mk 14:25 for "kingdom of my Father" in Mt 26:29 are particular cases in point). Also, it is noticeable that the phraseology [καὶ] ἔδωκεν αὐτοῖς is used with respect to both the bread and the cup by Mark (Mk 14:22, 23). On the Two Gospel Hypothesis Mark draws the first usage from Luke (Lk 22:19), the second from Matthew (Mt 26:27).

[3] Typical of those making this claim is I. H. Marshall, *Last Supper and Lord's Supper* (Grand Rapids, Mich.: Eerdmans, 1980), 161; "The point [that Matthew is dependent upon Mark] appears to be uncontested. It is true that some recent scholars defend the general priority of Matthew over against Mark, but to the best of my knowledge none of them has examined this particular passage in detail in order to demonstrate that Matthew was here the source for Mark." Since Marshall's writing, W. R. Farmer, *The Gospel of Jesus: The Pastoral Relevance of the Synoptic Problem* (Louisville, Ky.: Westminster/John Knox, 1994), 52-63, has set out some contours for an explanation of Mark's secondary character at this point. Farmer, however, did not address the compositional questions in detail.

[4] This has been elaborated by Rudolf Pesch, *Das Abendmahl und Jesus Todesverständnis* (Freiburg: Herder, 1978). Pesch viewed this unit in Mark as being an integral part of a Passion Account that served as the sub-strata of later developments in the gospel tradition.

[5] According to Donald Senior, *The Passion Narrative According to Matthew: A Redactional Study* (BETL 39; Leuven: Leuven University Press, 1982), 76-86, Mark 14:22-26 has 77 words of which 66 are exactly paralleled in Mt 25:26-29. Senior accounts for the other changes between Matthew and Mark primarily on the basis of Matthean stylistic preferences. His line of argumentation proceeds from the presupposition, presumed on other grounds, that Matthew is using Mark.

made changes in keeping with his stylistic preferences. Something comparable, but from the opposite perspective, might be claimed by advocates of Markan priority. However, since the two texts under comparison are so similar, there is little opportunity for significant differences to be observed. Therefore, since arguments based upon patterns of shared and distinctive linguistic usage may be inconclusive when this particular literary context is taken alone, the view that Matthew's account of the Last Supper is later because it is more developed liturgically becomes more significant to some advocates of Markan priority.

We believe, however, that another approach is less speculative than this argument from alleged "liturgical development." After all, we know and can say nothing about such alleged liturgical developments in the early Christian communities of the first century, apart from evidence provided by the texts of the Gospels themselves and therefore theories of development which *presuppose* a particular solution to the Synoptic Problem.

Our alternative approach begins with two basic observations. First, we note that the Matthean account of the Last Supper reflects themes proper to Matthew throughout that Gospel. Second, although Mark's parallel text is often similar, sometimes identical, to the wording of Matthew, it lacks some of the elements that provide for the sophisticated pattern of inter-textuality noted in Matthew. Therefore, since Mark preserves fragmentarily Matthew's pattern of theological argumentation, Mark is secondary. We turn now to more detailed observations on which to base our argument.[6]

First we observe that Matthew gave a special emphasis to his account of Jesus' preparing to keep the Passover. This would not be just another Passover celebration, or even Jesus' last meal on earth, but a meal where Jesus and his disciples proleptically celebrate the new covenant. According to Matthew, Jesus had twice previously celebrated such anticipatory meals of the new era (Mt 14:13-21 and 15:32-39). Now the time ($\kappa\alpha\iota\rho\delta\varsigma$) of the new eschatological era is at hand (Mt 26:18; no parallel in Mark). Jesus eats this meal in anticipation of what it will be like to enter into "the banquet of the kingdom of my Father" (Mt 26:29). Thus, this meal is both the climax of Jesus' earthly mission and the beginning of the transition into the new age (cf. Mt 26:29). Since it is such a crucial time, Matthew interweaves into his account subtle inter-textual references and echoes, several of which on the Two Gospel Hypothesis are omitted by Mark.

For Matthew, what comes to a climax at the Last Supper is the unfolding of the mission of the

---

[6] Other similar cases would be Mark's redaction regarding the tradition of the elders (Mk 7:1-23/Matt 15:1-20) and Matthew's parable unit (Mk 4:1-34/ Matt 13:1-35)

Servant-Messiah who will bring about the forgiveness of sins. In Matthew, that is implicit already with the giving of Jesus' name (Yeshua; Mt 1:21). Then, in Mt 8:17, his mission is seen as continuing the work of the Servant, prominent in Isaiah. Fulfilling the role of the Servant, Israel (Isa 42:1-4), Jesus' life is characterized by withdrawal and vulnerability as he prepares to take on the role of "a ransom" for his people (Mt 12:15-21; 20:28). Now, at the Last Supper, the final step is taken.

According to Isa 53:10, the Servant had to become an offering for sin. Thus, according to Matthew, Jesus shares the paradigmatic meal of the kingdom and entreats his disciples to eat (φάγετε) and drink (πίετε) in the realization that he is the Servant. In keeping with his style, Matthew uses direct speech.[7] Yet his point is that the disciples were to come to the realization that, in keeping with the scriptures, Jesus[8] was the Servant destined to inaugurate the New Covenant.

This brings us to the crucial verse, Mt 26:28. Matthew now has Jesus speak of the cup as "the blood of the [new] covenant."[9] Here Matthew utilizes the text of Jer 31:31. Then Matthew links Jesus and his mission with the words from Isa 53:10-12 by the direct allusion to his life being poured out "for many for the forgiveness of sins," περὶ πολλῶν εἰς ἄφεσιν ἁμαρτιῶν.[10] The use of περὶ with the Greek word for sin is a direct reference to Isa 53:10. By utilizing the preposition ὑπέρ rather than περί, Mark's text is further removed from Isa 53. It may reflect his dependence upon Lk 22:20 on the Two Gospel Hypothesis (cf. Mk 14:24), but in any case it is a fragmentary preservation of the tight web of Matthean Servant theology.

The reference to "forgiveness of sins" also becomes crucial for Matthew because it is featured in both Isa 53:10-12 and Jer 31:34=Jer 38:34 LXX, the two scriptural texts that undergird the whole of Matthew's version of the cup saying. Again, Mark's text lacks this detail, and thus Mark accidentally or intentionally blurs the sophisticated theological argument. More than likely Mark simply didn't see the pattern of scripture connections in the text.[11]

---

[7] cf. N. A. Dahl, "Die Passionsgeschichte bei Matthäus," *NTS*, 2 (1955-56): 17-32; see especially Appendix 1.

[8] Matthew's use of Ἰησοῦς (Matt 26:26) is characteristic of the author of the First Gospel. There is no reference to Jesus (the one who will save the people from their sins) in the parallel in Mk 14:22.

[9] There is much to commend the acceptance of καινῆς in this reading. Only the major Egyptian witnesses omit it. And the omission of καινῆς due to homeoteleuton with Mt 26:29 is just as likely as its addition as a harmonization with Lk 22:20.

[10] Even the reference to ἐχυννόμενον has an inter-textual connection in Matthew (Matt 23:35; cf. Lk 11:50-51) but not in Mark. This text seems to be part of a wider pattern of argumentation in Matthew where he is contending that the blood of the innocent shed earlier in Israel culminates in the pouring out of the life of the rightous one (Mt 27:19).

[11] Several other differences between Mt 26:29 and Mk 14:25 not yet noted (addition of οὐκέτι and omissions of ἀπ' ἄρτι and μεθ' ὑμῶν) do not materially affect our argumentation.

We conclude, therefore, that the critical words of institution in Mt 26:28, in their present form, do not represent Matthean additions to Mark which were occasioned by a more developed form of the eucharistic liturgy in Matthew's community. On the contrary, they are integral elements of a sophisticated account of the climax of Jesus' ministry, as interpreted through the image of Isa 53 and collateral passages. On the Two Gospel Hypothesis, Mark, in the process of blending the accounts of the Last Supper from Matthew and Luke, omitted several of the details that are required to communicate all of the nuances of Matthew's exegesis. Thereby the secondary character of Mark's text to that of Matthew becomes apparent.

¶ 80. Jesus Predicts His Resurrection Appearance in Galilee and Peter's Denial

Mt 26:30-35=========>   Mk 14:26-31   <--------------Lk 22:31-34, 39

At the end of the supper, they sang a hymn and went out of Jerusalem to the Mount of Olives. Jesus again said to them, "You will all desert me, for Scripture says, 'I will strike the shepherd and the sheep will be scattered.' But after I am raised up, I will go before you to Galilee." Peter said, "Even though the rest all desert you, I will not!" Jesus said to him, "Peter, I tell you that before the cock crows twice *you* will deny three times that you know me!" But Peter vehemently insisted, "If I must die with you, I will never deny knowing you!" And all the others said the same.

General Observations. Mark continues to follow the common order of Matthew and Luke, preferring the wording of Matthew. Only the word, σήμερον, in Mk 14:30//Lk 22:34, provides any substantive hint that Mark paid attention to Luke's version of this story. However, in order to move forward in both Matthew and Luke, Mark did have to omit the dialogue among the disciples about who is greater (Lk 22:24-27) and Jesus' response to it (Lk 22:28-30). Mark's omission of these materials may be explained by the fact that Matthew has no parallel to them *in this context* (cf. Mt 26:35-36). Since Mark is following the order and wording of Matthew, it would have been natural for him to move forward from Mt 26:29 to Mt 26:30 without adopting any of the intervening material from Luke. This, in fact, seems to be precisely what Mark has done (Mt 26:30//Mk 14:26). He utilized Mt 26:30//Mk 14:26 as a transition sentence to bring Jesus to the Garden of Gethsemane, as did Matthew. On the other hand, Luke gets Jesus to the Mount of Olives at Lk 22:39, through the unit on purse, bag, and sword (Lk 22:35-38). Since Mark omits Lk 22:35-38, he unites the text of Matthew and Luke.

Alternatively, Mark's stress on watches of the night may have left him no room for a dialogue on greatness, so he omitted it. Either explanation is possible.

Also, Mark might have considered this second debate about greatness in Luke to be redundant and/or unnecessary for his fast moving narrative, particularly since Mark had already utilized the similar material from Lk 9:46-48 at Mk 9:33-37 (cf. Mt 17:34, 18:1-4). Furthermore, part of Jesus' response in Lk 22:25-30 is found in a completely different literary context in Mt 19:28 (cf. esp. Lk 22:28-30). That may also help explain why neither Mt 19:28 nor Lk 22:28-30 finds any place in Mark's account.

• This pericope continues to ratchet up the rhetoric of prediction and fulfillment. Only Mark tells us before the cock will crow *twice* Peter will deny Jesus *three* times. As these predictions come to pass when the account unfolds, the reader gains added confidence that the predicted vindication (i.e., Mk 14:28) will also come to pass.

Mk 14:27. Mark abbreviates Matthew's version of Jesus' saying, Πάντες ὑμεῖς σκανδαλισθήσεσθε ἐν ἐμοὶ ἐν τῇ νυκτὶ ταύτῃ to a simpler, Πάντες σκανδαλισθήσεσθε. Mark universalized Jesus' teaching about those who would fall away (Mt 26:31) by omitting part of the subject in Matthew, ὑμεῖς, and by omitting the limiting time reference, ἐν τῇ νυκτὶ ταύτῃ. The problem of apostasy in the faith community appears to be a major issue at the time of the composition of Mark (cf. Mk 10:30; 13:9-13). Mark also makes this prophecy less specific by omitting the type of stumbling (i.e., "over Jesus"; ἐν ἐμοί). Mark's subsequent omission of ἐν σοί from Mt 26:33 at Mk 14:29 is consistent with these changes to Mt 26:31 in Mk 14:27.

• The text of the quotation from Zech 13:7 is worded slightly differently in Mark and Matthew. Neither is exactly in accord with the extant text of the LXX. The Matthean phrase τὰ πρόβατα τῆς ποίμνης may be a free rendering of either the LXX or a Hebrew original. The verb in both Matthew and Mark is altered to the future rather than the imperative, as is entirely fitting here.[12]

• Although it is unusual for Mark to include fulfillment citations from the Scripture, in this case the quotation functions as a prophecy on the lips of Jesus, paraphrasing the Scripture, speaking about the perfidy of the disciples. The quotation is integral to the

---

[12] See Krister Stendahl, *The School of St. Matthew* (Philadelphia: Fortress, 1968), 80-82.

story instead of a supplement intended for the reader. It continues to accent the fact that Jesus had spoken beforehand of all that would take place. This prophecy will be fulfilled in the disciples' abandonment in Mk 14:50.

Mk 14:28. Mark also heightens the contrast between the time of stumbling and the time when Jesus will precede his followers into Galilee after the resurrection by altering Matthew's δέ into the stronger adversative, ἀλλά.

• A third-century papyrus fragment, (Fayyum fragment) omits the whole of Mk 14:28. The verse is attested in other manuscripts of Mark. A scribe may have omitted it because it interrupts the flow of the narrative, more so in Mark than in Matthew because the phrase "because of me" in Mt 26:31 gives an antecedent for the "I" in Mt 26:32. Mark's abbreviation of Matthew, including the omission of ἐν ἐμοί from Mt 26:31 at Mk 14:27, probably created some of the awkwardness of Mark's text. The text-critical issue has some bearing on the Synoptic Problem. If Mark were the first Gospel to be written, Mk 16:7 most probably alludes retrospectively to Mk 14:28. However, if Mk 14:28 were not in the first texts of Mark, obviously one would need to look elsewhere for one or more "earlier" literary contexts where Jesus would have told his disciples that "he would precede them into Galilee" *and* "there they would see him" (Mk 16:7; cf. Mt 26:32 and 28:7, 10). However, it is not certain whether the Fayyum fragment is even from the text of Mark. The matter is important and warrants further investigation. Until the textual issue is settled, we will not attempt to substantiate our thesis on the basis of this verse.

• The vocabulary item σκανδαλίζω appears fourteen times in Matthew, eight times in Mark, and four times in Luke. Every time it appears in Mark and Luke, it is in parallel with a usage in Matthew. It is unquestionably a linguistic characteristic of Matthew. It appears twice in a dualistic expression in Mt 26:33, the parallel to Mk 14:29. The single occurrence in Mark indicates fragmentary usage derived from Matthew.

Mk 14:30. Only Mark has Jesus predict Peter's denial *three times* before the cock crows *twice* (δίς). When this prophecy is fulfilled in Mk 14:70, again only Mark refers to a second cock crow following Peter's denial. Mark's addition of "two" makes the prophecy more specific and, therefore, more impressive when it is fulfilled. This is a colorful detail missing from Matthew and Luke. Its insertion appears to intensify the wretchedness of Peter's betrayal.

• The double expression σήμερον and ταύτῃ τῇ νυκτί is characteristic of Mark, even if the two expressions, taken together, are intended to specify the night that begins the Jewish day. Noticeably, Matthew has ταύτῃ τῇ νυκτί and Luke has σήμερον so that Mark's phrase looks like conflation. On the alternative Two Document Hypothesis, Matthew and Luke would again have managed to divide Mark's double expression neatly between them, even though, according to this hypothesis, they were working independently.

Mk 14:31. One of Mark's supplements to Matthew in this verse, ἐκπερισσῶς, is found in Mark but nowhere else in the NT. At least one other compound of περισσῶς, ὑπερπερισσῶς, is also unique to Mark among NT authors (cf. Peabody, *Mark as Composer,* 176, 93). Mark tends to prefer compound words, and this is typical of his composition.

• Mark again universalizes the Matthean parallel at Mt 26:35 by omitting part of the subject, this time, οἱ μαθηταί, thus leaving the subject as πάντες ("everyone"). The resultant Markan text affirms that everyone, not just every one of the disciples, was saying, "If it is necessary for me to die with you, I will certainly not deny you." It is more difficult to imagine a later Christian author limiting such a universal affirmation (Two Document Hypothesis) than it is to imagine a later author universalizing a more limited affirmation (Two Gospel Hypothesis).

¶ 81. While Jesus Prays Three Times in Gethsemane, Three Disciples Fail to "Watch" Three Times

Mt 26:36-46 ========>	Mk 14:32-42	<------------------ Lk 22:40-46

And they went to a place called Gethsemane and he said to his disciples, "Sit here while I pray." He took Peter, James, and John with him and, being dismayed and in agony, he said to them, "My soul is sorrowful unto death. Stay here and keep guard." Going off a little way, he fell to the ground and prayed that this hour would pass from him, saying, "Abba, Father, all things are possible to you; remove this cup from me. Yet not what I will but what you will." Yet, after all this, when he comes back he finds them sleeping and says to Peter, "Simon, are you sleeping? Are you not strong enough to watch one hour? Watch and pray that you not be tempted—the spirit is willing but the flesh is weak." So he goes and prays again saying the same words as before. Again he returns and finds them sleeping. Their eyes were heavy. They didn't know how to answer him. And he comes back a third time and says to them, "Are you still sleeping and resting? Enough. The hour is come: the Son of Man is delivered into the hands of sinners. Get up. Let us go. Behold, he who betrays me is here."

General Observations: Mark continues to follow the order and wording of Matthew. However, there are a few touches in the Markan account that may derive from Luke (e.g., "take . . . from me," in Lk 22:42//Mk 14:36; "sleep," in Lk 22:46//Mk 14:37; and perhaps, "on the ground," in Lk 22:44; cf. Mk 14:35).

• The heart of this scene in Matthew is a complex three-fold literary structure. In our synopsis, the three basic parts of this structure are labeled A, B, and C. Within each of these three parts are six moments. In Matthew each of the parts repeat these six moments in basically the same order. These six moments are as follows:

➢ Jesus goes away from Peter and the sons of Zebedee to another place in the garden.

➢ He prays.

➢ He comes back.

➢ He finds the disciples.

➢ They are asleep.

➢ Jesus admonishes or speaks to them.

The whole of the literary unit is characterized by an ironic development. Specifically, at the close of parts A and B, Jesus chastises his disciples for falling asleep and admonishes them to "watch and pray" lest they come into temptation. However, by the time part C is concluded, Jesus has either become exasperated or filled with pity for his disciples, because this time he admonishes his disciples to sleep and rest, for "the [eschatological] hour" has come.

• Luke's version of this story (Lk 22:40-46) is so abbreviated that only elements of part A remain. Parts B and C are missing completely.

• Mark shares much of this three-part complex structure with Matthew. However, some pieces of the Matthean structure are missing in Mark. As a result there are a number of non-sequiturs in the Markan narrative, such as Jesus leaving the disciples twice but returning three times. This has led commentators who hold vastly different source theories than the research team to conclude that Mark is conflating and "has combined two versions of the story."[13] Therefore, once again, Mark can be said to represent the fragmentary preservation of a literary structure more clearly presented in Matthew. This constitutes further evidence that Mark's text is secondary to Matthew (cf. Mk 7:1-20, Mk 10:1-12, 17-22). Mark has fashioned a different structure and purpose for his narrative than that of Matthew's careful three part structure. As in a number of other units (including the Eschatological Discourse) Jesus carefully separates a few close disciples (here Peter, James, and John) from the others (Mk 14:33). He then charges them, as in Mk 13:33-37, to "watch" (γρηγορεῖτε Mk 14:34). Subsequently, he goes away alone in agonizing prayer (Mk 14:35-36). When he returns to the three (not "the disciples," as in Matthew) Jesus finds them asleep. Again, as in earlier instances when they are given special glimpses of divine glory, the constant weariness and sleep of the disciples indicates that they do not understand (Mk 14:37-42: cf. Mk 5:37-43; 9:2-8; esp. 9:6 as compared with 14:40). In the darkness of the night the disciples fail to comprehend the gravity of what is taking place. They fail to keep watch for the master (cf. Mk 13:33-37). Despite claims of fidelity their failure to understand will result in their abandonment of Jesus. Thus, for Mark, the Gethsemane incident is primarily about the failure of Peter, James, and John to understand what was happening.

Mk 14:32. Mark omits μετ'αὐτῶν in Mt 26:36 but, perhaps to emphasize Jesus' relationship with Peter, James, and John, adds μετ'αὐτοῦ at Mk 14:33.

• Although it is somewhat unusual for Matthew to use αὐτοῦ to mean "here," in accord with classical Greek usage (Mt 26:36), it would not be unusual to find Mark changing such classical usage to the synonymous and more commonly used word, ὧδε, as he has done here on the Two Gospel Hypothesis.

• Mark's omission of [οὖ] ἀπελθὼν ἐκεῖ from Mt 26:36 results in the removal of words that anticipate the repeated uses of compounds of ἐλθὼν that help to structure the whole pericope (cf. προελθὼν, Mt 26:39//Mk 14:35; ἀπελθὼν, Mt 26:42//Mk 14:39; and ἀπελθὼν, Mt 26:44NP). Here is further evidence, in the prelude to the story, that Mark is not aware of, nor concerned to preserve, the subtle elements of the literary structure present in Matthew.

---

[13] Hooker, *Mark,* 346; also Werner H. Kelber "The Hour of the Son of Man and the Temptation of the Disciples," in Werner H. Kelber, ed., *The Passion in Mark* (Philadelphia: Fortress Press, 1976), 41.

Mk 14:33-34. Matthew's reference to "the two sons of Zebedee" agrees with the earlier story about them at Mt 20:20-21. Similarly, Mark's more explicit reference to "James and John" here conforms more with Mark's version of that story in Mk 10:35. The depiction of Jesus going apart to a small group to give esoteric teaching is characteristic of Mark and often functions as part of his overlay (cf. Peabody, *Mark as Composer*, 21-23, 41.)

• The compound verb, ἐκθαμβέω, is found four times in Mark, but nowhere else in the NT (Mk 9:15; 14:33; 16:5-6bis). Again the use of compounds is typically Markan. The verb found in the Matthean parallel, λυπέω, which Mark, on the Two Gospel Hypothesis, altered to ἐκθαμβέω here, is characteristic of Matthew. Matthew uses this verb six times (Mt 14:9; 17:23; 18:31; 19:22; 26:22, 37); Mark, only uses it twice, both times in parallel with Matthew (Mk 10:22//Mt 19:22 and Mk 14:19//Mt 26:22). Again the pattern of appearances of the verb λυπέω in Matthew and Mark support Mark's literary dependence upon Matthew.

• Mark's alteration of the Matthean τότε to καί is consistent with generally recognized Markan usage.

Mk 14:35-36. Mark's addition in Mk 14:35b, "and prayed that if it were possible that this hour might be removed for him," echoes Mt 26:39, 42. It indicates that Mark wishes to emphasize the personal struggle Jesus was facing. Mark may also underscore the perfidy of Jesus' closest disciples who, despite Jesus' trauma, still abandon him.

• Mark's addition of the Aramaic, ἀββά, in Mk 14:36 to its Greek equivalent, ὁ πατήρ/πατέρ, also found in Matthew and Luke, may reflect his penchant for adding Aramaic-sounding words to his version of the gospel. This Aramaic address followed immediately by ὁ πατήρ, is found in only three NT contexts: Rom 8:15; Gal 4:6; and Mk 14:36. Matthew and Luke agree on the vocative, πατέρ (Mt 26:39//Lk 22:42 and Mt 26:42), while Mark agrees with Paul in using the definite article with the nominative, ὁ πατήρ.

Mk 14:37. The Markan supplement here, "Simon, are you *asleep?*" (Mk 14:37b, cf. Lk 22:46 and Mt 26:40) focuses specific attention on Peter and heightens his guilt.

• Note that Mark's version of Jesus' statement is couched in the second person singular. The parallels in Matthew and Luke are couched in the plural. Since Peter has been given great privileges his failure to understand is astonishing. The reader is being prepared for Peter's betrayal.

Mk 14:40. The wording of Mk 14:40b (cf. Mk 9:6) is unique to Mark. This sentence is part of the Markan overlay that highlights the failure of even the inner circle of the disciples to understand (cf. Mk 9:6).

• Mark has omitted Mt 26:44. As noted above, by omitting the reference to Jesus going away a third time Mark breaks the very compact and carefully structured account of Jesus going three times to his disciples. If Matthew has deliberately structured the careful threefold pattern, Mark has preserved it fragmentarily, and is thus secondary.

¶ 82. Jesus Is Arrested; Disciples Flee

Mt 26:47-56=========>   Mk 14:43-52   <----------------- Lk 22:47-53

And immediately, while he was still speaking, Judas arrived with a crowd sent by the chief priests and scribes and elders. They were carrying swords and clubs. The betrayer had given them a signal saying, "The one I kiss is he; seize him and take him away bound." Coming forward Judas greets Jesus, "Rabbi!" and kisses him. The crowd laid their hands on him and seized him. Someone drew his sword and struck the slave of the high priest and cut off his ear. Jesus answers and says, "Have you come out to catch a thief with these swords and clubs? Every day I was with you in the temple teaching and you did not seize me then. Nevertheless, let the Scripture be fulfilled." All of his disciples fled into the night. But a certain young man was following him wearing nothing but linen cloth. They seized him but he slipped out of the cloth and escaped.

General Observations. Mark again follows the common sequence of Matthew and Luke but, as usual in the Passion Narrative, strongly prefers the wording of Matthew. Parallels with Luke are sparse (cf. Mk 14:47//Lk 22:50 and Mk 14:49//Lk 22:53).

• Mark omits most of Mt 26:52-54, Jesus' reaction to the cutting off of the ear of the high priest's servant. Mark may omit this reply by Jesus because it could be understood as triumphalist. It is not in keeping with Jesus' forthcoming abandonment and his death in powerlessness. Another possible reason for this omission is the absence of a parallel in Luke.

Mk 14:43. Mark describes the turbulent arrest scene with some unique details. "Scribes" come out along with the chief priests and elders described in Matthew. This grouping of scribes, chief priests, and elders (or chief priests and scribes) is typical of Markan composition (cf. Peabody, *Mark as Composer,* 97, 107).

Mk 14:44. Mark's supplementary καὶ ἀπάγετε ἀσφαλῶς stresses that nothing was left to chance with respect to taking Jesus into custody. The climax of the passion episode is coming with speed and certainty.

Mk 14:45. Faced with the very different remarks of Jesus in Mt 26:50 and Lk 22:48, Mark omits any reply by Jesus.

Mk 14:47. Mark follows Luke's inclination to separate the person who cuts off the high priest's slave's ear from Jesus' circle: Matthew's "one of those with Jesus" becomes in Luke "one of them," which in turn becomes Mark's "one of the bystanders" (NJB). Thus it seems that Mark is saying that it was one of the armed mob, not one of those with Jesus, who took violent action. This is one of the few instances in this pericope where Mark seems to follow Luke.

• Mark utilizes παρίστημι five times in the Passion Narrative. It is also characteristic of Mark to use it in special constructions (cf. Peabody, *Mark as Composer,* 194, 99;136, 82).

Mk 14:49. The construction ἤμην πρὸς ὑμᾶς probably echoes ὄντος μου μεθ' ὑμῶν in Lk 22:53. The description of Jesus teaching daily in the temple during the passion week echoes Luke (Lk 19:47; 21:37; cf. 20:1).[14]

• The reference to the abandonment of the disciples as the fulfillment of scripture is important even though Mark omits the more specific Matthean "prophets" (Mt 26:56). For Mark, the emphasis on the disciples' apostasy is not just to fulfill the scripture (Zech 13:7) but also to fulfill Jesus' own word (Mk 14:29-31).

Mk 14:51-52. Mark inserts a reference to a mysterious young man (νεανίσκος) who flees, naked, leaving Jesus in the clutches of his enemies (cf. the description of the

---

[14] McNicol et al., *Beyond the Q Impasse,* 250.

νεανίσκος at the empty tomb; Mk 16:5). Speculation about this "young man" seems futile. What is paramount in this pericope is that Jesus was totally abandoned. Any discussion on the elaboration on "the young man" in the writings of Clement of Alexandria must await the "rediscovery" of the relevant manuscript. In the text as it stands the emphasis is on the abandonment of Jesus, an image burned into the early church's imagination by this unique reference.

¶ 83. The High Priest Questions Jesus; Peter Denies Him
Mt 26:57-75=========>   Mk 14:53-72   <--------- Lk 22:54-71

And they took Jesus away to the high priest. All the chief priests and elders and scribes began to come together as well. Peter was following at a distance until he came right into the courtyard of the high priest where he sat down with the guards and warmed himself at their fire. Now the chief priest and the whole Sanhedrin were trying to get testimony so that they could kill him. But it did not agree. Many people did come forward with false testimony against him, saying, "We heard him say, 'I will destroy this temple that is made with human hands and in three days I will build another not made with human hands.'" But still they could not get their testimonies to agree. And the high priest stood up before everyone and demanded of Jesus, "Have you no answer to make? What are these people saying about you?" But he was silent and said nothing. Again the high priest asked him saying, "Are you the Christ, the Son of the Blessed?" And Jesus said, "I am, and you will see the Son of Man seated at the right hand of Power and coming with the clouds of heaven!" And the high priest ripped his garments and said, "Why do we need witnesses? You have heard his blasphemy! What is your decision?" And they all condemned him to die. Some began to spit on him and to cover his face and strike him, saying, "Prophesy!" And the guards seized him with a series of slaps around the face.

Meanwhile, Peter was out in the courtyard. One of the servants of the high priest came and, spotting Peter warming himself by the fire, said, "Aren't you also with that Nazarene, Jesus?" But he denied it saying, "I don't understand a word you are saying!" He went outside to the outer courtyard and a cock crowed. The same servant saw him again and began to say to those standing there, "He is one of them!" But he denied it again and after a bit the bystanders repeated it, saying to Peter, "Yes you are one of them for you are a Galilean!" Peter started to curse and then he swore that he did not know this man. Immediately a cock crowed a second time. Then Peter remembered what Jesus had said, "Before the cock crows twice you will deny me three times." And Peter wept.

General Observations. Matthew and Luke have different orders of events within this literary unit. In Matthew Jesus is brought during the night and interrogated (Mt 26:57-68). Almost simultaneously Peter undergoes a three-fold interrogation of his own from various accusers: first, a maid (Mt 26:69); second, a *different* maid (Mt 26:71); and finally a group of bystanders who identify Peter as an accomplice of Jesus by his speech (Mt 26:73). Unlike Jesus, who remains faithful and who refuses to swear, Peter takes an oath that he is not a follower of Jesus (Mt 26:74). By the time the cock crows he has denied Jesus three times (Mt 26:75).

• Luke has re-arranged Matthew's account considerably. Luke has Jesus detained at the high priest's house at night. But while Jesus is suffering a violent beating from the underlings of the high priest (Lk 22:63-65), Peter, warming himself by the fire, suffering no violence, denies Jesus (Lk 22:54b-62). Unlike Matthew it is only *after* Peter's denial, ending with a riveting look from Jesus the next morning, that Jesus is brought to trial before the Jerusalem council of elders (Lk 22:66-71). Faced with a contradictory series of events in Matthew and Luke, Mark chooses to follow the Matthean order with its more structured account of the denial of Peter. Nevertheless, Mark occasionally blends into his narrative details from Luke. These include the reference to τὸ φῶς "fire" (Mk 14:54//Lk 22:56), the blindfolding of Jesus (Mk 14:65//Lk 22:64), the identification of Peter as a Galilean (Mk 14:70//Lk 22:59), and the use of ὡς εἶπεν αὐτῷ to reinforce Peter's remembrance of what Jesus had said (Mk 14:72//Lk 22:61).

• Taking up the essential outline of Matthew's detailed account, Mark manages to put his emphasis on the denial of Peter. He did this by having Jesus predict earlier that Peter would deny him *three times before the cock crows twice*. The point is obvious. After the first cock crow Peter had the opportunity to remember what Jesus had said and mend his ways. Yet, despite the poignant warning of the first cock crow, Peter goes on in the same pattern of denial, totally oblivious to what Jesus had said. Peter's denial thus becomes an amazing act of cowardice on the part of a key member of Jesus' inner circle. Jesus had already condemned the leaders of the temple in Jerusalem for their betrayal of God's purposes (Mk 11:12-19; 12:9-12). Now a chosen leader of Jesus' new spiritual community, in the hour of trial, fares no better than the old leaders. Mark is warning *his* readers to be aware of treachery even at the highest levels of the *new* faith community. You may expect it to come. Yet, in this cauldron of faithlessness, Mark's message is that one is called upon to be faithful (Mk 13:9-13, 33-37). Despite betrayal and treachery, the secret kingdom of faith, forgiveness, and prayer will become manifest and the gospel will be taken to the whole world.

Mk 14:53. Mark continues to use "chief priests, elders, and scribes" to describe the Jerusalem Jewish leadership (cf. the discussion on Mk 14:43). Here is another parallel with Luke (Lk 22:66).

Mk 14:54. The word θερμαίνω occurs five times in the NT: twice in Mark, twice in John, and once in James. The occurrences in Mark and John are in the same scene, namely where Peter is warming himself in the courtyard of the high priest's house. Mark employs this detail just before his version of the trial before the Sanhedrin (Mk 14:54b) and shortly thereafter (Mk 14:67), where it helps return the reader to the scene focusing on Peter.

• The word for "fire" that Mark chooses is not πῦρ, but τὸ φῶς, which appears in the parallel context at Lk 22:56. On the Two Gospel Hypothesis, Mark probably adopted this term from Luke. As noted above, in spite of Mark's heavy dependence upon the text of Matthew, this seems to be good evidence that Mark also knows the Lukan parallel to this sequence of stories.

Mk 14:55-59. For the first stage of the trial before the Sanhedrin, Mark gives his version of how the charges were brought against Jesus. Luke does not have an account of the charges brought against Jesus before the Jerusalem Jewish leadership. Mark, is therefore wholly dependent on Matthew. Matthew did not think the proceedings were fair but was prepared to say that the hearing had some semblance of legitimacy (Mt 26:59-61). In keeping with normal Jewish procedure two witnesses testify. They say that Jesus is *capable* of claiming the messianic ability to destroy the temple and to build another in three days (Mt 26:60-61). But Mark focuses on the total injustice of the matter. Witnesses do not agree (Mk 14:56, 59; cf. Peabody, *Mark as Composer*, 246, 112). The old temple is described pejoratively as "handmade" (cf. Acts 7:41, 48; 17:24; which in turn draws on a long tradition in Judaism indicating illegitimacy).[15] For Mark the scene is total chaos. Mark wants to depict this hearing before what he considers illegitimate temple authorities in the worst possible light.

---

[15] Donald Juel, *Messiah and Temple* (SBLDS 31; Missoula, Mont.: Scholars Press, 1977), 143-57.

Mk 14:60-62. Mark has carefully edited the part of the story that recounts the questioning by the high priest.

• The addition of οὐκ ἀπεκρίνατο οὐδέν in Mk 14:61 provides for a dualistic expression with similar words in Mk 14:60. This is characteristic of Markan composition.

• The question as to why Jesus did not answer his accusers presumes the consistency of the charge of the two witnesses in Matthew; Jesus could not plausibly respond to people who did not agree. This appears to reflect Markan dependence on Matthew.[16]

• Mark has also introduced a πάλιν used retrospectively to unite two verses within a pericope in Mk 14:61. This is also is characteristic of Markan composition.

• Mark has chosen to omit the Jewish oath formula from Mt 26:63. In light of Mt 5:33-37 it is ironic that Jesus was put under oath. Matthew does not have Jesus violate his teaching against oath taking. He has Jesus respond to the question about his messiahship with the retort "the words are your own" (Mt 26:64).

• Luke divided and separated the double question in Mt 26:63, "Are you the Christ" and "Are you Son of God." Luke moved the question about the Son of God three verses later (Lk 22:70) and put Jesus' reply in the second person plural, addressed to πάντες ("everyone"). In Matthew, Jesus answered the double question with the words, "You (the high priest) say so." In Luke, Jesus answered the second part of the double question with the words, "All of you say that I am." Mark has Jesus answer the double question simply with the words, "I am." Although Mark may have gotten the affirmation, "I am," from Lk 22:70, his omission of the words, "you say," whether singular or plural, makes this a striking difference in Mark's version compared to both Matthew and Luke. Although the demonic forces have confessed Jesus as "Son of God" (Mk 3:11), his disciples have not. Here, for the first and only time in the Markan narrative, Jesus openly states his claim to messiahship. Even here it is in response to a question. For Mark it is important that Jesus state openly who he is at this point. This is so because

---

[16] Cf. Hooker, *Mark,* 359, who, presuming Markan priority, awkwardly posits that the idea of the witnesses not agreeing comes into Mark at a later stage.

this claim of Jesus is the basis for his crucifixion. Ironically, it will constitute the central revelation that the crucified messiah is the Son of God.

• Mark's substitution of "Son of the Blessed One" for "Son of God" in Matthew 26:63 may simply reflect Mark's desire to postpone the use of the title "Son of God" for the climactic dramatic moment at the foot of the cross, when the centurion confesses Jesus as the "Son of God." It also may reflect (as when he uses Aramaic words) an effort to give apparent historical authenticity by using a circumlocution for the divine name.

• Mark omits the references to the present enthronement of the Son of Man in Mt 26:64 (ἀπ' ἄρτι) and Lk 22:69 (ἀπὸ τοῦ νυν). For Mark the days after the cross are not triumphal manifestations of the kingdom. The kingdom will only come for those who have eyes to see it. Thus, for Mark, the powerful manifestation of the Son will be at the parousia (Mk 13:24-27) not "from now on."

• Because Luke radically restructured Mt 26:63-64, Mark, in attempting to blend Matthew and Luke, has omitted at least ten words of agreement between them in this context (e.g., εἰ, a form of λέγω, ἡμῖν, a form of αὐτός, ὑμῖν, a form of λέγω, ἀπὸ τοῦ νῦν/ἀπ' ἄρτι, Θεοῦ, you say). Without resort to a Q overlap, which would require Q to contain a passion narrative, this is difficult to explain on the Two Document Hypothesis.

Mk 14:63-64. Because Jesus replied in the affirmative to the question "Are you the Son of the Blessed One," the council has no hesitancy at that moment (in contrast to Mt 26:66) in condemning Jesus (κατέκριναν) as worthy of death.

Mk: 14:65 Jesus is mocked by a series of taunts. Luke, in order to make more sense of the taunting command and question, "Prophesy! Who is the one who struck you?" added the detail that Jesus was blindfolded. Mark adopts the blindfold from Luke, but oddly omits the question which brought the blindfold into the scene in the first place, τίς ἐστιν ὁ παίσας σε; In doing so, Mark creates a famous agreement of Matthew and Luke against Mark. It is very difficult to understand how both Matthew and Luke could have independently added this very unusual and specific sentence at this precise point.

And if Mark is prior and not conflating, why does he include the blindfold without the accompanying question?[17]

• Mark continues to make a precise connection between prophecy and fulfillment. Matthew has no prediction of Jesus being spat upon, although it happens twice in the Passion Account (Mt 26:67; 27:30). Luke has a prediction of it but no fulfillment (Lk 18:32). Mark has both prediction (Mk 10:34) and a fulfillment, first before the Jerusalem religious authorities, then the Roman soldiers (Mk 14:65; 15:69). Ironically, at the very moment that Jesus is being beaten for speaking falsely one of his most specific predictions is coming true.

Mk 14:66-67. Mark adds to the text of Matthew by drawing imagery from Luke about the fire in the courtyard in Mk 14:67. On the Two Gospel Hypothesis Mark drew the reference to the fire, τὸ φῶς, at Mk 14:54 from Lk 22:56 (see above). Now Mark returns to Lk 22:56 to frame the description of the maid seeing Peter (ἰδοῦσα τόν Πέτρον in Mark, ἰδοῦσα δὲ αὐτόν in Lk 22:56; cf. ἰδὼν αὐτόν in Lk 22:58). Mark connects Mk 14:54 and 67 with the use of θερμαίνομαι in both passages. None of this is in Matthew. Once again, on the Two Gospel Hypothesis, Mark supplements the major source (Matthew), with material drawn from Luke.

• The maid identifies Jesus, somewhat implausibly, as the Nazarene (Mk 14:67; cf. Mk 1:23). This is a distinct difference from the identification of Jesus in Mt 26:69 as a Galilean. (But see Mt 26:71 where Jesus is described as being from Nazareth.) Nazarene is clearly pejorative and may represent a term of contempt used for followers of Jesus at the time of the composition of Mark.

Mk 14:68 With the two-fold statement that he did now know Jesus (οἶδα and ἐπίσταμαι) Mark deepens the betrayal of Peter. At that very moment the cock crows

---

[17] The literature on this subject is immense. The classic article on this subject is Michael Goulder, "A House Built on Sand," in *Luke: A New Paradigm.* 2 vols. (JSNTS 20; Sheffield: Sheffield Academic Press, 1989), 1:3-26, esp. 6-11, and echoed in "Luke's Knowledge of Matthew" in Strecker, ed., *Minor Agreements*, 153-55. The authoritative statement of the Two Document Hypothesis partisans on the issue is that of F. Neirynck, *Evangelica II 1982-1991: Collected Essays* (BETL 99; Peeters: Leuven University Press, 1991), 95-138 and 27-28; also C. M. Tuckett, "The Minor Agreements and Textual Criticism," in Strecker, ed., *Minor Agreements*, 135-41. See also Farmer, *Gospel of Jesus*, 134-36, for a recent analysis of this problem by those who hold the Two Gospel Hypothesis.

(Mk 14:68). Yet, even after this, Peter does not choose to hear what Jesus said earlier and will not have enough self-transcendence to turn from his course of denial.

Mk 14:69-70 Unlike Matthew (Mt 26:71) and Luke (Lk 22:58), in Mark it is the same maid who identifies Peter a second time. In order to tie together the second and third identifications of Peter as Jesus' follower Mark uses his characteristic πάλιν retrospective (Peabody, *Mark as Composer,* 95, 183).

• The use of παρίστημι (see above 14:47) is a linguistic characteristic of Mark-especialy in the Passion Narrative. Here it is also used as a characteristic dualistic expression. It is striking that there is no parallel to this dualism in either Matthew or Luke. It is much more reasonable to view this as Markan composition rather than Matthew and Luke independently omitting or editing both instances from Mark.

Mk 14:71-72 Mark brings his account to a crescendo with his depiction of the cock crowing the second time, in precise fulfillment of Jesus' earlier prophecy (Mk 14:30). On the Two Gospel Hypothesis Mark adds the second cock crow and δίς, "twice." The textual tradition of much of this has been disputed but, given the fact that it fits perfectly with the Markan tendency to give greater precision to the prophecies of Jesus, the team tends to believe it is genuine.[18]

• There is another striking agreement of Matthew and Luke against Mark at the very end of the story of Peter's denial in Mk 14:72. This agreement involves five words in Matthew and Luke: καὶ ἐξελθὼν ἔξω ἔκλαυσεν πικρῶς. It is difficult to see how Matthew and Luke could have used Mark's καὶ ἐπιβαλὼν ἔκλαιεν to arrive independently at the same construction.

---

[18] A fair assessment of the textual evidence is given by Markus Öhler, "Der Zweimalige Hahnschrei der Markus passion: Zur Textüberlieferung von Mk 14, 30. 68. 72 *ZNW* 85 (1994): 145-50. Öhler sees it all as genuine except 14:68.

¶ 84. Pilate Questions Jesus

Mt 27:1-2; 11-14======>   Mk 15:1-5   <---------- Lk 22:66, 23:1-7

Early in the morning all of the chief priests, elders, scribes, and the Sanhedrin held counsel, bound Jesus, and eventually gave him over to Pilate. So Pilate asked him, "Are you really the King of the Jews?" Jesus responds, "You are the one saying so." The chief priests began to accuse him of many other things. So again Pilate asks, "See how many charges they bring against you! Have you nothing to say?" Jesus refuses to speak. Pilate was amazed.

General Observations. Mark continues to follow the order and wording of Matthew but incorporates some key details from Luke, indicating a literary connection between Mark and Luke.

• Within this pericope, Mark evinces a series of omissions from the Passion Narrative in Matthew. A number of the omitted scenes focus on matters of special concern to a Christian-Jewish reader (e.g., Mt 27:52-53). Here Mark omits Matthew's digression about Judas' death (Mt 27:3-10), possibly because it is inconsistent with key elements of the Acts account which, on the Two Gospel Hypothesis, Mark may possess. Moreover, the parenthetical nature of this Matthean story is fairly clear. In Mt 27:2 and 11 the chief priests and elders are with Pilate the governor, but in the interlude explaining the death of Judas they are in the temple (Mt 27:3-10). Matthew's interest in the fate of Judas seems to be connected with a theme of the blood guilt of the leaders of Jerusalem for Jesus' wrongful death, a theme which he develops throughout the Passion Account (cf. Mt 23:35; 27:3-10; 24-25). Luke either omits the theme or removes this material from a direct connection with the death of Jesus. Mark does not appear to be interested in the ultimate fate of Judas. It was predicted earlier that Judas would be the betrayer (Mk 3:14; cf. Mk 14:21). He fulfilled this prediction exactly (Mk 14:10, 43). The reader knows that. This ends the matter as far as Mark is concerned.

• Mark has portrayed the scene before Pilate in such a way that it now reads more like a replay of the comparable "trial" before the Sanhedrin (Mk 14:60-64; cf. Mk 15:1-5). This editorial work is similar to the modifications of his sources which he made in the story of the preparation for the triumphal entry (Mk 11:1-7) and the story of the preparation for Passover (Mk 14:12-16; cf. Peabody, *Mark as Composer,* 248, 112).

• Whether we read ποιήσαντες or ἑτοιμάσαντες in Mk 15:1 it is clear that Mark is saying that a second meeting of the Sanhedrin was convened and some kind of a decision was reached to hand Jesus over to be punished by the Gentiles. This obviously puts the narrative in some kind of tension with Mk 14:64 where another judgment was made against Jesus. Matthew appears to understand that the court proceedings before the Sanhedrin went on all night. Matthew joins the phraseology "worthy of death" (Mt 26:66) with similar terminology "resulting in the death decision" in Mt 27:1. But Mark, perhaps drawing on Lk 22:66, where Luke has a daylight meeting of the Sanhedrin, somewhat awkwardly unites the two accounts in Matthew and Luke. The evening meeting comes from Matthew. The daylight meeting appears to come from Luke. It is noticeable that only Mark and Luke refer both to the convening of the Sanhedrin and the presence of the scribes. On the other hand, only Matthew and Mark refer to the time as a συμβούλιον ("meeting"). This seems to be an important instance of the pattern of alternating Markan agreement with Matthew and Luke in wording within a pericope (verse!).

Mk 15:1. Mark begins the paragraph with a characteristic Καὶ εὐθὺς instead of Matthew's Πρωΐας δέ.

• With the use of πρωΐ Mark continues his pattern of careful chronology of the passion account (cf. Mk 13:35NP; Mk 15:1//Mt 27:1).

• To the "chief priests and elders" noted by Matthew, Mark as Luke (see above) adds the "scribes." This is consistent with Markan usage (Peabody, *Mark as Composer,* 87, 97).

Mk 15:2. For some reason Mark omits the Matthean references to Pilate as governor (Mt 27:2, 11, cf. Mt 27:14, 17, 21, 27) Mark only refers to "governors" in Mk 13:9. Luke also omits any reference to Pilate as a governor in his Passion Narrative. Is this another indication of Mark's dependence on Luke?

Mk 15:3. Mark states that the chief priests brought πολλά "many things" against Jesus. Matthew has no parallel. Luke spells out the charges against Jesus at considerable length (Lk 23:4-5). On the Two Gospel Hypothesis the Markan πολλά may well be an echo of Lk 23:4-5.

Mk 15:4-5. The Matthean scene presupposes Isa 53:7, where the Servant is silent before his accusers, and Isa 52:14-15, where the activities of the Servant cause kings to be "amazed" (Mt 27:12-14). Here Mark follows the terminology of Matthew. But elsewhere in the Gospel Matthew's theology of the Servant is much more developed. Not much on the issue of literary dependence can be concluded from this except to say that this is additional evidence that the Servant theme is important for Matthew and this is one case where Mark overlaps.

• Mark utilizes πάλιν retrospective in Mk 15:4 to refer back to the previous question of Pilate. This accords with Markan style (cf. Peabody, *Mark as Composer,* 183, 95).

• Mark follows Matthew in having Pilate be puzzled at Jesus' silence rather than declare his innocence, as in Lk 23:4. It is unusual that Mark omits the adverb λίαν from Mt 27:14 since it is the kind of graphic touch which Mark often prefers.

• This is the place where Luke had Jesus' appearance before Herod. As Mark had omitted the extraneous story of Judas' death (Mt 27:3-10), now he chooses to omit the extraneous scene before Herod (Lk 23:8-12). That scene was part of the Lukan stress on the innocence of Jesus, a theme which is not developed in Mark.

¶ 85. Pilate Frees Barabbas and Condemns Jesus, "King of the Jews"
Mt 27:15-26=========>   Mk 15:6-15   <----------------- Lk 23:13-25

At the festival Pilate was accustomed to release one prisoner chosen by the people. Now there was among those in prison a rebel who had committed murder during the revolt, named Barabbas. A crowd appears and begins to ask Pilate to allow release as he usually did. "Do you want me to release the King of the Jews?" Pilate says. He knew it was out of envy that the high priests had handed Jesus over. But the chief priests incited the crowd to demand Barabbas instead. Pilate asks again, "What should I do with the King of the Jews?" "Crucify him!" They shouted. "Why, what evil has he done?" asked Pilate. Still they shouted all the more, "Crucify him!" So Pilate, wishing to satisfy the crowd, releases Barabbas. In the meanwhile Jesus is whipped and delivered up for crucifixion.

General Observations. Mark continues to follow Matthew for his narrative. He draws very little terminology from Luke in this unit. But, even here, there is at least one striking agreement of Mark with Luke. This is Luke's terminology for the revolutionary activity of Barabbas. Twice in Lk 23:19 and 23:25 Luke uses forms of φόνος and στάσις to describe the activities of Barabbas as a revolutionary. Mark uses similar terminology at Mk 15:7. None of this is in Matthew. On the Two Gospel Hypothesis this is a clear indicator of a literary connection between Mark and Luke.

• Mark's version focuses attention on the contrast between the cowardice of the cynical Roman magistrate and Jesus' astonishing bravery. To provide this careful focus Mark omits Matthew's anecdotes about Pilate's wife's dream (Mt 27:19), the washing of Pilate's hands (Mt 27:24), and the acceptance of guilt by the crowd (Mt 27:25). Matthew places the blame and guilt for the death of Jesus on the leaders of the temple community in Jerusalem and the crowd which followed them. While Matthew is not exactly enamored of the governor, his listing of Pilate's wife's expression of Jesus' innocence and the governor's own self-exculpation makes it clear that Matthew believes the ultimate blame for the killing of Jesus rests with the temple authorities and the crowd. Mark is more ambivalent. The Jerusalem leaders handed over one of their own to a Gentile (Mk 15:1). They and their sympathizers prefer that a guilty revolutionary be freed and the innocent Jesus be put to death (Mk 15:6-15). But in the face of the mob, Pilate, the Roman official, has only one desire: to placate (Mk 15:15). As a public official (cf. Mk 13:9-13) Pilate could not bring himself to declare Jesus innocent. Ultimately he acts with cowardice and treachery. This is part and parcel of the continuing Markan pattern of the total abandonment of Jesus during Passion Week.

Mk 15:6-7. Although it does not have strong textual support commentators tend to believe that the parallel reference in Mt 15:16-17 to Jesus Barabbas is the more original name of Barabbas. Thus, strong Markan priorists concede that, in this instance, Mark is secondary to Matthew.[19]

• As noted above, Mark, drawing from Lk 21:19, 25, has deepened the guilt of Barabbas. He is no longer a "notorious prisoner" (Mt 27:16). He has "committed murder in the insurrection." Although the terminology is drawn from Luke, this is also a typical example of Markan vivid description.

Mk 15:8. This verse is Markan composition. Mark 15:8 includes the use of ἄρχομαι + the infinitive (ἤρξατο αἰτεῖσθαι) which is characteristic of Mark (Peabody, *Mark as Composer*, 67, 54).

---

[19] Dahl, "Die Passionsgeschichte bei Matthäus," 49.

• The antecedent to ὄχλος, "the crowd," is unclear. Perhaps Mark drew this reference from Lk 23:4 (ὄχλους). There Pilate addresses the crowds and the high priests. Or it may have came from a similar context in Mt 27:20. Some take the crowds to be partisans of Barabbas demanding his release.[20] This probably goes too far. Following Matthew, but without the legal precision about false witnesses, Mark is probably saying that the people, incited by the temple leaders, despise Jesus to such an extent that they are even prepared to see an innocent man suffer and set a guilty man free.

Mk 15:9. Mark focuses upon the identification of Jesus as "King of the Jews" by changing Matthew's more circumspect phrase, "who is said to be the Messiah" to a direct "King of the Jews" (Mk 15:12/Mt 27:22). This is not only Markan verisimilitude (Pilate would have had no problem asking Jesus whether he proposed to be a king and take the place of Caesar) but it also has theological overtones. For Mark, ironically, Jesus is truly a king. Already he was anointed by a poor woman (Mk 14:8). Jesus' kingship will be shown in his capacity to gain the allegiance of his subjects by the courageous decision to go to the cross. Thus, when it comes to the crucifixion narrative, "King of the Jews" is critical to Mark. Mark shares the title "King of the Jews" with Matthew every time it appears (cf. Mt 27:29//Mk 15:18; Mt 27:37// Mk 15:26) in addition to his unique references in the passion account.

Mk 15:12. Once again πάλιν retrospective occurs uniting two verses within a pericope, (cf. Mk 15:9). Indeed, the entire introduction for Mk 15:12 includes characteristic Markan phrasing: ὁ δὲ Πιλᾶτος πάλιν ἀποκριθεὶς ἔλεγεν αὐτοῖς (cf. Peabody, *Mark as Composer*, 110, 70).

Mk 15:13-14. The use of πάλιν in Mk 15:13 is unique for Mark. Here, it has to be prospective rather than retrospective (cf. Mk 15:13-14).

• Luke makes use of a compound of κράζω relatively early in this literary context (Lk 23:18), while Matthew uses a form of κράζω later (Mt 27:23). Mark adopts both and brings a grammatical conformity to the two usages (See ἔκραξαν in Mk 15:13 and14).

Mk 15:15. Luke and Mark have omitted the scene where Pilate washes his hands (Mt 27:24-25), so they provide a rationale for Pilate's decision and bring closure to this

---

[20] Hooker, *Mark*, 369.

pericope by narrating the release of Barabbas and handing over Jesus to be crucified. Hence, Mark follows Luke more closely here.

¶ 86. Soldiers Mock Jesus as "King of the Jews"

Mt 27:27-32=========>   Mk 15:16-21   <---------------- Lk 23:26-32

The soldiers lead Jesus into the enclosed courtyard known as the Praetorium before the entire battalion. They put a purple robe on him and fashion a crown out of thorns for his head. They begin to salute him, "Hail, King of the Jews!" Then they hit him about the head with a reed, spit upon him, and kneel in mock homage in front of him. When they are done they put his own cloak back on him and take him out for crucifixion. They compel a by-stander, one Simon from Cyrene (the father of Rufus and Alexander), to carry his cross.

General Observations. Mark follows Matthew closely for this story, but, again, there are hints in Mark's account of Simon from Cyrene that he was also aware of the text of Luke (cf. ἀπήγαγον αὐτόν in Mk 15:16//Lk 23:26 and τινα . . . ἐρχόμενον ἀπ' ἀγροῦ in Mk 15:21//Lk 23:26). Luke, possibly for apologetic purposes, omitted the account of the callous taunting and brutality of the Roman soldiers. As is well known, in Luke-Acts Roman soldiers are presented in a remarkably favorable light. But Mark has no problem including the Matthean account of the taunting because it fits well into his overall theme of the humiliated and rejected Christ (King).

• At the end of this story, Mark omits the reference to the daughters of Jerusalem in Lk 23:27-31. For Mark the destruction of the holy city is well in the past and further reflection upon it would not be relevant for his predominantly Gentile Christian audience.

Mk 15:16. Mark inserts the reference to the αὐλή (courtyard), then takes the opportunity to insert, "which means," as a formula for translation. These additions, although awkward, conform to Markan style (Peabody, *Mark as Composer,* 103, 68).

• Mark follows Mt 27:27 in saying that the whole battalion, ὅλην τὴν σπεῖραν, was gathered even though the existence of such a large group is improbable. It is a touch probably derived from the application of Psalm 22 to the crucifixion (Ps 22:16, "a company of evildoers encircle me"). The account of the crucifixion in Matthew and Mark is strongly interwoven with allusions to Ps 22. This motif probably developed early in Christian tradition. Allusions to Ps 22 are more developed in Matthew than in

309

Mark; thus we have another instance of a Matthean theme only fragmentarily preserved in Mark.

Mk 15:17-20. Matthew has provided an internally consistent and realistic picture of the mockery of Jesus by the soldiers. For instance, Matthew has Jesus undressed by the soldiers. The cloak they place on him is scarlet, in conformity with a soldiers' garb. The Markan change to purple (the emperor's color) is clearly Mark's attempt to highlight the kingship theme. In Matthew the soldiers not only plait a crown of thorns and place it on Jesus' head, but also insert a reed scepter into his hand. Once "the king" is appropriately attired, on their knees the soldiers "Hail him as King." Then they begin to beat and mock him. This is a realistic description of a display of crude and brutal military power by an occupying force. As noted above, Mark has elevated Jesus to a mock imperial figure, changing the color of the robe from scarlet to purple. On the other hand, by eliminating the reed scepter, Mark has omitted a key feature of the regalia of the emperor. Furthermore, with this omission Mark does not prepare as well as Matthew for the later appearance of the reed scepter. Matthew depicts the soldiers kneeling and hailing him as king in all of his regal attire. Mark somewhat awkwardly delays the soldiers bending their knees and worshipping the divine emperor until after the beating and spitting has begun. Furthermore, Matthew had clearly described the removal of Jesus' own clothes by the soldiers at the outset of this scene, and the replacement of them at the end. Mark, in agreement with Matthew, records the replacement of Jesus' own clothes without having adopted the account of their removal at the beginning of the scene. In sum, Mark's editing has heightened the theme of both the kingship of Jesus and his humiliation, but, somewhat clumsily, has not given the same attention as Matthew to the function of the details of the account. It is possible to argue that Matthew has straightened out Mark's "clumsy account," but it is more likely that Mark has substituted an emphasis on certain theological points at the expense of an inner consistency of details.

Mk 15:21. Mark has added to the description of Simon of Cyrene, "the father of Alexander and Rufus." This is consistent with his tendency to add colorful detail. Perhaps the two were known to the original readers of Mark, but that is beyond our capacity to assert as historical fact.

¶ 87. Roman Officials Crucify the "King of the Jews" between Two Thieves

Mt 27:33-44==========>   Mk 15:22-32   <------------------ Lk 23:33-43

They bring Jesus to the place of a skull: Golgotha. They offer to give him a sedative of wine mixed with myrrh; but he refuses it.

They crucify him and decide by lot who would receive the various parts of his clothing. This took place at 9 a.m. in the morning. Written on his inscription was the charge, "the King of the Jews". With him, one on the right the other on the left, they crucify two bandits.

Those who pass by revile him, shake their heads and exclaim, "Oh, you who would destroy the temple and build it in three days, come down and save yourself!" The chief priests and scribes likewise mock him. They say, "He claims to save others but he cannot save himself! Let the messiah, the king of Israel, come down from the cross now, that we may see and believe." And those who were crucified with him joined the chorus of mockery.

General Observations. Mark's account of the crucifixion of Jesus parallels Matthew closely, but differs in some significant details. At some points Mark prefers to follow Luke. An example of a Markan alteration of the Matthean text is Mk 15:23, where Jesus refuses a sedative. In Matthew Jesus tastes wine mingled with *gall* and then refuses to drink more (Mt 27:34). Also, Mark has "and there was an inscription (ἐπιγραφή)," drawn from Luke (Mk 15:26/Lk 23:38). Mark occasionally omits from Matthew (e.g., Mt 27:43), and inserts some details of his own (cf. the reference to Jesus' crucifixion at the third hour in Mk 15:25).

• In editing the crucifixion account Mark maintains his focus on the total abasement and powerless suffering of the Messiah, the Son of God. By refusing to take the sedative Jesus chooses not to short-circuit in any way this process of humiliation. Jesus endures to the bitter end. For three hours (from 9:00 o'clock to noon) Jesus is taunted, first by the passersby, then by the chief priests and scribes, and finally by the bandits. Jesus has walked the way of bitter rejection until the last.

Mk 15:22. Mark slightly modifies Matthew and Luke by using a different and characteristically Markan translation formula, ὅ ἐστιν μεθερμηνευόμενον (cf. Mk 5:41 and 15:34), versus simply ὅ ἐστιν... λεγόμενος in Matthew and τὸν καλούμενον in Luke. The use of καλούμενος conforms with Lukan literary style and λεγόμενος conforms with Matthean literary style, although μεθερμηνευόμενον does occur once in Mt 1:23.

Mk 15:23. Mark has the soldiers offer Jesus myrrhed wine where Matthew has wine mixed with gall. Originality here is hotly debated. Matthew 27:34 (cf. *Gospel of Peter,* 5:16; *Barnabas,* 7:3,5) is much closer to Ps 69:22 (LXX 68:22). The precision of the Psalm allusion appears to favor Matthean originality. On the other hand myrrhed wine was a delicacy in Roman culture, and although out of place in this context, it may represent some kind of a subtle taunt, as if to say, "The King of the Jews needs a drink fit for a King!" This is an intriguing detail, but it suggests little about the direction of literary dependence between Matthew and Mark.

Mk 15:24. Mark's explanation of the casting of lots for the clothes of Jesus, "to decide what each should take (ἐπ' αὐτὰ τίς τί ἄρῃ)," is absent from both Matthew and Luke. Both Matthew and Luke refer to Ps 22:19 (Ps 21:19 LXX) for the matter of casting lots over Jesus' clothes. But the Markan explanation as to how this was done constitutes a significant addition to the text. In our judgment it is more probable that Mark added this detail than that both Matthew and Luke, independently, chose to omit it. This constitutes a rather significant Markan addition.

Mk 15:25. Mark is the only one to give a time, "the third hour," for this part of the story. This continues Mark's concern to provide significant temporal markers during the last days of Jesus' life (see the chart above in the overview of part 6). Whether this time scheme is historical or not is debated, since Mark could not have derived this temporal note from Matthew or Luke or even from John. Matthew 27:45 may imply that the darkness descended shortly after Jesus was placed on the cross and that he was crucified at noon. By way of contrast, Mark's three-hour span from the time of the crucifixion to the descent of darkness seems odd. The early trial, Pilate's conviction, Jesus' beating, etc., were compressed between the first to third hour of the morning. Mark's text accentuates the mocking of Jesus by implying that nothing else significant took place over a span of three hours from 9:00 a.m. until noon. This time frame seems to have been constructed for theological purposes, and would appear to be secondary.

• Mark omits Matthew's description of the soldiers sitting down and keeping watch at the crucifixion site (Mt 27:36). Mark may have thought that this casual comment about the ordinariness of the scene is out of place in the description of a scene of unspeakable brutality.

Mk 15:26. As noted above, Mark's terminology for the inscription is dependent upon Luke. Luke states that the inscription is on Jesus (Lk 23:38). Matthew notes that it is above Jesus' head (Mt 27:37). Mark simply chooses not to say where the inscription is placed.

Mk 15:27. The second reference to a crucifixion (cf. Mk 15:24) has been a source of mystification to scholars. However, this is probably a use of epexegetical καί. In Mark 15:24 the crucifixion of Jesus is described. Then in Mk 15:27 Mark wishes to add, "and in addition they crucified with Jesus the two bandits."

• The reference to the two bandits being placed on the right and the left appears to be an echo of the story of the question of James and John (Mk 10:39). If so, now the meaning of Jesus' answer to their question has become evident. To share the glory of Jesus one must first share his fate.

Mk 15:28. If the text is genuine it is drawn from Lk 22:37, which is not in sequence with Mark. In Luke, the use of Is 53:12, "numbered with the transgressors," makes perfectly good sense. This is a prophecy of the very near arrest of Jesus as a criminal (Lk 22:52) and his eventual crucifixion between two criminals (Lk 23:32).[21] Mark does not usually introduce echoes of scripture with a formula quotation such as, "the scripture was fulfilled saying." Thus it is more than likely that this text entered into the tradition of Byzantine witnesses of the text of Mark sometime in the early centuries through the influence of Lk 22:37. We are inclined not to accept it as original.

Mk 15:29-32. Mark's version of the mocking of the bystanders is similar to that of Matthew in that it echoes Ps 22, but Mark makes a significant change by omitting both of Matthew's references to mockery for pretending to be the Son of God (Mt 27:40,43). This is probably another instance where Mark chooses to give a simple, realistic description of what took place at Golgotha rather than point to its ultimate significance in Christian confessional terminology as Matthew often does (cf. Mt 16:16//Mk 8:29). In any case Mark will bring in the confession of Jesus as the Son of God at Mk 15:39.

---

[21] See McNicol et al., *Beyond the Q Impasse,* 287.

This comes when Jesus is hanging upon the cross; it is the ultimate climax of his basic thematic and theological argument about Jesus.

• Mark adopts "in three days" from Mt 27:40. (Contrast Mark's distinctive "after three days" in his three passion prediction passages.) Mark's purpose here is to get the reader to recall the original charge before the Jerusalem temple authorities in Mk 14:58. Mark desires his readers to understand the irony of that charge. Jesus is being ridiculed for the apparently preposterous claim rumored at his trial that he would be the agent of the destruction and rebuilding of the temple in three days. Now, as he hangs on the cross the taunts rain down. Yet, there is deep irony to the reader, who knows the story of the empty tomb after "three days." The mockers are unwittingly speaking the truth. In the span of three days God will begin a new spiritual community that will function as a replacement for the outmoded physical temple in Jerusalem. A new temple will emerge in three days.

Mk 15:31. Mark adds πρὸς ἀλλήλους to the chief priests' mocking in Mt 27:41. This phrase is characteristic of Mark (Peabody, *Mark as Composer.* 128, 78). Perhaps it also functions (if somewhat awkwardly) as the Markan reference to the elders which, on the Two Gospel Hypothesis, he would have seen in Mt 24:41. In any case, Mark usually refers to the Jerusalem authorities as the chief priests, scribes, and elders, but sometimes simply as chief priest and scribes (Mk 11:18; 14:1; cf. Peabody, *Mark as Composer,* 187, 97).

Mk 15:32. The central thread of the Markan Passion Account is the rejection and total abasement of the King of the Jews by his own people. Mark highlights this by conflating Luke and Matthew at this point. To describe the taunt of the crowd, Mark draws from Lk 23:32 the reference to "Christ" (ὁ Χριστός). On the other hand, he draws "The King of Israel" (ὁ βασιλεὺς 'Ισραήλ) from Mt 27:42. The one who was asked earlier whether he was the Messiah, the Son of the Blessed One, now is taunted for what seemed to be a preposterous answer. But again, there is great irony; the taunts speak the truth. He is the Messiah, albeit a crucified one. And shortly, in his dying gasp, he will be confessed as the Son of the Blessed One (=Son of God; cf. Mk 15:39). Thus, through a daring conflation, Mark has highlighted his central Christological claim that Jesus, the crucified Messiah, is truly the King of Israel (i.e., Son of God).

• Mark omits Mt 27:43. This omission is crucial, because Mt 27:43 is an allusion to Ps 22:8 (21:9 LXX) and has strong echoes of Is 52:13-53:12 and Wisdom 2:10-20, featuring Jesus as the just and obedient Son. It is usually argued that Mark incorporated a pre-Markan interpretation of Ps 22 into his passion narrative to give structure to his account, and that Matthew, following Mark closely, simply includes the Ps 22 material in his narrative. But here, it is Matthew who has the Ps 22 material and not Mark. While it is possible to argue that Matthew saw the Ps 22 theme in Mark and supplemented it, it is much more likely that Matthew either copied it from his tradition or interwove it into his account himself. Then Mark, unaware of the connections to the Psalm, preserved fragments of the allusions to Ps 22 in his account.

¶ 88. Jesus Dies; A Centurion Confesses Him as "Son of God"

Mt 27:45-56========>   Mk 15:33-41   <======= Lk. 23:44-49

At noon darkness falls upon the whole land and lasts until three in the afternoon. Finally Jesus vents a loud cry, "*Eloi, Eloi, lemma sabachthani.*" It means, "My God, my God, why have you forsaken me?"

Misunderstanding and confusion continue to reign. Some of those nearby say, "He is calling for Elijah." Someone runs and dips a sponge with sour wine, puts it on a reed and gives it to him to drink, remarking, "Let us see if Elijah will come to rescue him."

But Jesus lets out another loud scream and dies. The curtain of the holy of holies is ripped into two parts from top to bottom. The Roman centurion, standing opposite him, seeing the manner of Jesus' death, can only blurt out, 'Truly, this man was God's son.'

Meanwhile, some women were viewing all of this from some distance. These women included Mary Magdalene, Mary the mother of James the younger and Joses, and Salome. These were the women who were accustomed to follow and provide help for Jesus in Galilee. Also, a number of other women were there who had come up to Jerusalem with Jesus.

General Observations. Mark continues to follow Matthew closely. There is some occasional blending with Luke, the most important instance being the terminology for Jesus' mode of death (ἐξέπνευσεν Mk 15:37// Lk 23:46). Mark also omits key phraseology from both Matthew and Luke. The most critical omission is Matthew's account of the earthquake at the death of Jesus (Mt 27:51b-53). In Matthew, the death of Jesus inaugurated a series of apocalyptic type events that came to culmination in the response of the centurion and those with him. Upon seeing those extraordinary things they confess Jesus as God's son. Mark wishes to place Jesus' death in another context where the apocalyptic signs are unimportant. For Mark Jesus dies abandoned and rejected. And yet, paradoxically, it is precisely this total weakness that Jesus manifests in his death that exhibits his real power. It is here that most truly Jesus' life is the gospel that calls upon one to lose one's life in order to save it (Mk 1:1; 8:35-37). Throughout Mark there is a major emphasis on "seeing" the kingdom. Immediately before his death those who taunted him claimed that they would only see and believe if he would come down from the cross (Mk 15:30, 32). Now the centurion sees that precisely in Jesus' defeat he has become the victor.[22] At the climactic point in his account the Roman officer is the vehicle for speaking both the secret of the kingdom and a central truth of the gospel.

Mk 15:33. Mark's statement about darkness coming over the land is fairly close to Matthew and Luke. The only significant difference is that Mark uses γενομένης in a time construction. This is a linguistic characteristic of Mk (cf. Peabody, *Mark as Composer,* 45, 47).

Mk 15:34. Mark attempts to render Jesus' last cry (already in Matthew) from Ps 22:1 into his own version of Aramaic. However, in the process, he creates a difficulty with the subsequent reference to Elijah (Mk 15:35b), which cannot be derived from the Aramaic, "Eloi" (cf. Matthew's Hebrew, "Eli"). These words from the cross bring to conclusion Mark's theme of the abandonment of Jesus.

• Again, Mark's ὅ ἐστιν μεθερμηνευόμενον is characteristic (Peabody, *Mark as Composer,* 130, 68).

• Matthew's account of the cry of forsakenness from the cross is part of his wider understanding of Jesus' death as God's just and obedient Son (cf. Mt 27:43 and our comments on Mk 15:32 above). Even though Jesus dies in agony with the words of Ps 22:1 on his lips, the echoes of the Psalm point the reader forward to the vindication expressed in Ps 22:22-31. In Mark, the emphasis on the faith of Jesus is not so clear.[23]

---

[22] Timothy J. Geddert, *Watchwords: Mark 13 in Markan Eschatology* (JSNTSS 26; Sheffield: JSOT Press, 1989), 154.

[23] Contra Donald Senior, *The Passion of Jesus in the Gospel of Mark* (Collegeville, Minn.: Liturgical Press, 1984), 123-24.

Mark wishes to emphasize the theme of abandonment and rejection. Jesus maintains until the end a clear sense of doing the will of God (Mk 14:32-42). In that sense his trust never falters. But, at the same time, the description of Jesus' agonizing cries in Mk 15:34, 37 seems to suggest that Mark wishes to portray that, in the end, Jesus would die alone, even abandoned by God.

Mk 15:35-36. The theme of abandonment is continued with the taunt about Elijah. Earlier, the Markan reader has been told that Elijah (in the form of John the Baptist) has come and suffered martyrdom (Mk 9:8-13). John never accomplished the restoration expected with the return of Elijah. There we are also told that a similar fate of martyrdom will befall Jesus (Mk 9:12). Now it has come to pass. Once again a prophecy of Jesus has been fulfilled. But Mk 9:8-13 also intimates that Jesus will bring the restoration promised by the return of Elijah. At first the occurrence of this restoration does not seem promising as Jesus is taunted with the remark, "Let us see if Elijah will come to rescue him." But this will not be the last word on the matter.

Mk 15:37. The description of Jesus' death is surprising. Note the use of ἐξέπνευσεν here (borrowed from Lk 23:46, where it is a distinctive characteristic of Luke's story) and its addition by Mark at Mk 15:39. This creates a Markan dualistic expression and underscores the startling nature of the Markan description of Jesus' death. Literally, Jesus gives a loud scream and expires. He dies in total ignominy. Mark has carefully constructed this stark description by conflating Matthew and Luke. Theologically, his view of Jesus' death is very different from Matthew and Luke. In Matthew Jesus dies as God's rejected Messiah who will return in triumph. In Luke, Jesus dies in quiet trust, giving back his spirit to God. But in Mark Jesus dies alone, rejected and abandoned.

In keeping with his theological emphasis (see above) Mark omits most of Lk 23:46b.

Mk 15:38. The word ἐσχίσθη for the tearing of the temple curtain reminds the reader of the baptism scene where Mark used a form of the same word, against Matthew and Luke, to describe the tearing/opening of the heavens. Here the curtain veiling the most sacred site of the presence of God is ripped in two just as the firmament dividing the divine world from the human world was also rent at Jesus' baptism. If this use of language by Mark is not accidental (Mt 27:51 has the same terminology), Mark has drawn attention to the relationship between the first event in Jesus' public ministry, his baptism, and the last event, his death. For Mark, the tearing of the temple veil indicates the end of the process inaugurated by Jesus' critique of the temple in Mk 11:11-26. The old temple has outlived its usefulness in God's purposes. The new temple made up of a community of faith, forgiveness, and prayer will now be open to all nations (cf. Mk 11:17, 22-26). Consequently the confession of Jesus as the Son of God by a Gentile (in the next verse) can hardly be accidental.

Mk 15:39. Mark's κεντυρίων (Mk 15:39, 44, 45) is a loan-word used here against the common testimony of Matthew and Luke (τὸ ἑκατοντάρχης). There are only three occurrences in the NT. The Latinism is typical of Mark and may have been more compatible for a Roman audience.

• The appearance of ἑκατοντάρχης as an agreement between Mt and Lk against Mk is the first of a sequence of these agreements in Mt 27:54-55//Lk 23:47.

EXCURSUS 14: THE "MINOR AGREEMENT" OF MATTHEW AND LUKE AGAINST MARK AT
MATTHEW 27:54-55//LUKE 23:47-48 (CF. MARK 15:39)

Synopsis ¶ 88, partial
Coding
Solid Underlining = Verbatim Agreements
Dashed Underlining = Partial Agreement, e. g., Same Lexeme, Different Form
Plain Text with Underlining= Mt//Mk//Lk Agreements
Bold Text with Underlining= Mt//Lk Agreements Against Mk
Italics with Underlining= Mk//Lk Agreements Against Mt
Plain Text with Double Underlining=Mt//Mk Agreements Against Lk
No Underlining=No Agreement with either of the other two gospels

27:54 Ὁ δὲ	15:39 Ἰδὼν δὲ	23:47 Ἰδὼν δὲ
ἑκατόνταρχος	ὁ κεντυρίων	ὁ ἑκατοντάρχης
	ὁ παρεστηκὼς	
	ἐξ ἐναντίας αὐτοῦ ὅτι	
	οὕτως ἐξέπνευσεν	τὸ γενόμενον
		ἐδόξαζεν τὸν θεὸν
	εἶπεν, Ἀληθῶς	λέγων, Ὄντως
	οὗτος ὁ ἄνθρωπος	ὁ ἄνθρωπος οὗτος
	υἱὸς θεοῦ ἦν.	δίκαιος ἦν.
καὶ		23:48 καὶ πάντες
οἱ μετ' αὐτοῦ τηροῦντες		οἱ συμπαραγενόμενοι

τὸν Ἰησοῦν

ἰδό**ντες** τὸν σεισμὸν
καὶ **τὰ γενόμενα**
ἐφοβήθησαν σφόδρα,

λέγοντες, Ἀληθῶς
θεοῦ υἱὸς ἦν οὗτος.

ὄχλοι
ἐπὶ **τὴν** θεωρίαν
ταύτην,
θεωρήσα**ντες**
τὰ γενόμενα,
τύπτοντες τὰ στήθη
ὑπέστρεφον.

Heretofore, the most striking minor agreement of Matthew and Luke against Mark within the passion narrative was believed to be the "positive agreement" at Mk 14:65, i. e. the "addition" of τίς ἐστιν ὁ παίσας σε; found at Mt 26:68//Lk 22:64 in parallel with Mk 14:65. Although this is a striking verbatim agreement (5 words in exactly the same grammatical form in exactly the same order), the evidence provided by the parallels to Mk 15:39 presents an equally striking set of agreements that includes not only several verbatim agreements in order, but also an equally impressive number of agreements in grammar and syntax in order, where synonyms are used or even where the vocabulary items may differ more significantly. Such agreements in grammar and syntax would seem to be even less likely to have been introduced by scribes seeking to harmonize the texts of Luke and Matthew than the verbatim agreements in Mt 26:68//Lk 22:64 (contra Mk 14:65) may have been.

All of the literary features in the list below appear in a range of one or two verses in the synoptics within the larger context of "triple tradition" material in the passion narrative. Although there are many so-called "minor agreements" of Matthew and Luke against Mark, even within the passion narrative, there is rarely such a striking set of agreements as this one.

The following list includes both "positive" and "negative" agreements. Positive agreements against Mark in Matthew and Luke may be defined either as changes or supplements to the text of Mark on the Two Document Hypothesis or as Markan omissions of material common to Matthew and Luke on the Two Gospel Hypothesis. "Negative agreements" may be defined either as common omissions from the text of Mark by Matthew and Luke on the Two Document Hypothesis or as distinctive Markan supplements to the texts of both Matthew and Luke on the Two Gospel Hypothesis. Other source hypotheses, of course, would have different explanations of these data within the synoptic gospels. For instance, these data might be explained on the Farrer-Goulder hypothesis as the result of Luke preferring a few details from the parallel text of Matthew while basically following the order, content and wording of the text of Mark.

COMPOSITIONAL ANALYSIS OF MARK ON THE TWO GOSPEL HYPOTHESIS

Here is a description of this particular network of agreements of Matthew and Luke against Mark at Mk 15:39 and parallels. With the exception of number three in the list of eight items below, all of the following "minor agreements" in Matthew and Luke against Mark appear in the same sequence.

➤ Mark and Luke both begin their parallel verses (Mk 15:39//Lk 23:47-48) with the words, ἰδὼν δέ. . . . After this, Matthew and Luke begin to agree against Mark in the following ways.

➤ Mt 27:54, ὁ ἑκατόνταρχος//Lk 23:47, ὁ ἑκατόνταρχης used as the subject of a sentence. Contrast Mark's transliterated Latin equivalent, ὁ κεντυρίων, used in the same way.

➤ Mt 27: 54//Lk 23:47. The "omission" of the description of the centurion in Mk 15:39 as ὁ παρεστηκὼς ἐξ ἐναντίας αὐτοῦ ὅτι οὕτως ἐξέπνευσεν Although a couple of comparable words, εἱστήκεισαν and αὐτῷ, do appear in Luke 23:49, they are used in a syntactical construction to express content that is considerably different from this clause in Mark 15:39.

➤ Mt 27:54, λέγοντες//Lk 23:47, λέγων. The use of the nominative masculine present active participle of λέγω to introduce the words of confession about Jesus. Contrast Mark's use of the 3rd singular aorist active indicative, εἶπεν, for the same purpose. This is the only element in this set of "minor agreements" that does not appear in the same order in Matthew and Luke.

➤ Mt 27:54, καὶ οἱ . . . τηροῦντες//Lk 23:48, καὶ . . . οἱ συμπαραγενόμενοι. καί + οἱ + a nominative masculine plural participle used either to introduce the second subject of the sentence or the subject of a second sentence.

➤ Mt 27:54, μετ᾿//Lk 23:48, συμ. . ., a preposition meaning "with" either standing alone or attached as a prefix in a compound verb, in the attributive position between the definite article, οἱ, and the expressed nominative plural subject of the sentence/clause and used to modify that subject.

➤ Mt 27:54, τὸν Ἰησοῦν//Lk 23:48, τὴν θεωρίαν ταύτην, the definite article in the accusative singular followed immediately by an accusative reference to Jesus or "this sight," referring to the events surrounding his crucifixion.

➤ Mt 27:54, ἰδόντες //Lk 23:48, θεωρήσαντες, a second nominative masculine plural participle, this time more specifically in the aorist active, of a verb meaning "to see," also used to modify the plural subject of the sentence.

➤ Mt 27:54, τὰ γενόμενα//Lk 23:48, τὰ γενόμενα, used as the direct object of this second participle.

In the case of this set of agreements of Matthew and Luke against Mark, it is much more likely that Luke first edited Matthew and that Mark subsequently edited both Matthew and Luke (Two Gospel Hypothesis) than that the texts of Matthew and Luke would accidentally come to contain such an ordered set of agreements against Mark as the result of their independent editing of Mark (Two Document Hypothesis).

Of course, if an advocate of the Two Document Hypothesis were to appeal to a Mark-Q overlap to explain this set of data, then one would have to conclude, against the current critical opinion of those who advance the Q hypothesis, that Q did have a passion narrative. In fact, these data would provide some significant evidence that Q even included the very scene of Jesus' crucifixion.

- In contrast to the taunters at the cross who do not "see" (Mk 15:32, 36), this Gentile "sees" that Jesus is the Son of God. Literally speaking, given what happened immediately beforehand with Jesus dying in ignominy, and without the earthquake as in Matthew, the episode is implausible. Some have even wondered whether the confession of the centurion was still another expression of contempt for Jesus ("Some Son of God!"). But for Mark, the confession is theological. He wants the reader to understand that the true Son of God, the subject of the Gospel, is a crucified Messiah. By omitting the parallel references to Son of God in Mt 27:40, 43 Mark has carefully prepared the way for the appropriate context for this striking confession of Jesus as Son of God: the suffering Son of God dying on the cross. As the one who serves as the prototype of gospel reality, Jesus must first die before he will be raised in glory.

- The reference to Jesus as this "man" (οὗτος ὁ ἄνθρωπος) on the Two Gospel Hypothesis reflects Markan dependence on Luke (cf. Lk 23:47).

Mk 15:40. The list of women watching from afar differs slightly from that of Matthew. Mark has James the younger for James, Joses for Joseph, and Salome in place of the mother of the sons of Zebedee (cf. Peabody, *Mark as Composer*, 250, 113). Such differences in detail with reference to the women around Jesus are typical of the author of Mark.

- Mark's name for one of the women, Σαλώμη, is found only in this Gospel. This seems to be Mark's identification of the mother of the sons of Zebedee.

Mk 15:41. Mark follows the testimony that the women were followers of Jesus from Galilee, but adds that "many other women went up with him into Jerusalem." Mark depicts these women, even in Jerusalem, as the most faithful witnesses. Like those women whose stories were used by Mark to frame his version of Jesus' last eschatological discourse, these, too, were models of faithfulness (cf. Mk 12:37b-44; 14:1-11).

¶ 89. Joseph of Arimathea Buries Jesus

Mt 27:57-61 ========>   Mk 15:42-47   <======== Lk 23:5056

Evening had come. In the parlance of the Jews it was "Preparation," the day before the Sabbath. Joseph of Arimathea, a prominent member of the Council, expecting the coming of the kingdom of God, summons up his courage and goes to Pilate with a request for Jesus' body. Pilate is somewhat surprised that Jesus had already died. Before doing anything he determines whether it is true that Jesus had died. Then, after hearing the truth from the centurion, he hands the body over to Joseph. Thereupon, Joseph of Arimathea purchases linen cloth, takes Jesus down from the cross and wraps the body in the cloth. He places Jesus in a tomb cut out of rock and rolls a stone across the entrance to the tomb. Ever faithful, Mary Magdalene and Mary, the mother of Jesus, watch intently where Jesus was laid.

General Observations. This unit is substantially different in its use of source tradition from those units that immediately precede it. Mark appears to blend considerable material from both Matthew and Luke. However, what is most striking is the amount of phraseology Mark has added, especially to his Matthean source. Mark's account of the Joseph of Arimathea episode is more expansive. Mark gives us additional details about what happened immediately after Jesus died. These details center on Pilate's determination that Jesus had actually died. For Mark, Joseph of Arimathea is pictured as summoning enough courage to ask Pilate for Jesus' body (Mk 15:43). Then Mark, perhaps for apologetic purposes (refuting ancient swoon theories?), has Pilate go through a detailed process of certification to determine whether Jesus had died (Mk 15:44-45a). The account of this process is unique to Mark.

• Throughout the unit the emphasis is on the determination of the reality of Jesus' death (Mk 15:44, 45). In his own way Joseph of Arimathea is also drawn to Jesus in his death. He asks for Jesus' body (Mk 15:43; cf. Mt 27:58; Lk 23:52), receives it (Mk 14:45// Mt 27:58), goes to the trouble of buying a cloth and wrapping it around Jesus' body (Mk 15:46a) and placing the body in a tomb (Mk 15:46b//Mt 27:60//Lk 23:53).

• Mark omits the Matthean story of the guard at the tomb (Mt 27:62-66). It might be suggested that the Markan account of the certification of the death of Jesus is the apologetic equivalent of the Matthean story about the posting of a guard at the tomb. But it is more likely that the author of Matthew has his own reasons for including this detail. It seems clear that both accounts were constructed for apologetic purposes.

Perhaps another indicator that Mark knew this Matthean passage is that Mt 27:63 has μετὰ τρεῖς ἡμέρας to describe the resurrection of Jesus. Mark uses the same formulation in 8:31; 9:31; 10:34.

Mk 15:42. Mark again is careful to provide a time indicator (καὶ ἤδη ὀψίας γενομένης), primarily dependent upon Mt 27:57. However, throughout the passion account and especially during Jesus' last day, Mark, more than the other synoptics, has consistently punctuated his account with time intervals (cf. Mk 13:35-36; 14:7, etc., for the last night of Jesus' death; 15:1, 25, 33, 34 for his last day). If one follows the sequence, it appears that Mark is attempting to tell the reader that after Jesus' death at 3:00 p.m. the day was about to end.[24]

• The explanatory note that it is Preparation (Παρασκευή) is awkward for the modern reader, especially since it is followed by an additional note that it was the day before the Sabbath.[25] Mark's terminology may reflect Lk 23:54 (cf. Mt 27:62), but it seems clear that his language suggests that the day was rapidly drawing to a close. As darkness falls the Sabbath begins. It seems that Mark wishes to explain to a Gentile reader why there was so much haste to bury Jesus. The Sabbath is a holy day, which precludes burial. Therefore the burial must be done quickly.

Mk 15:43. On our hypothesis Mark is clearly dependent upon Lk 23:50 with his use of βουλευτής "council."

• Mark's omission of most of Lk 23:51 is typical of a tendency to omit lengthy Lukan supplements to Matthew in the Passion Narrative.

Mk 15:46. Only Mark refers to the purchase of the linen cloth. If Jesus died at 3:00 p.m., it stretches credulity that all of the action described in Mk 15:43b-46 could have taken place before the beginning of the Sabbath at sundown. Again, as we have seen with regard to the whole of the Markan crucifixion account, it is an expression of a careful theological agenda rather than an actual description of what happened.

---

[24] Raymond E. Brown, *The Death of the Messiah: A Commentary on the Passion Narratives in the Four Gospels.* 2 vols. (New York: Doubleday, 1994), 2:1211, notes at Mt 14:15, and 20:8 have been similarly taken to mean later afternoon.

[25] Josephus, *Ant.,* 16.6.2; cf. John 19:14, 31, 42.

• Notice again the parallel between Mark and Luke with the use of καθελών (Mk 15:46//Lk 23:53).

• Mark's word for "wrap" (ἐνειλέω) differs from that of Matthew and Luke (Mt 27:59//Lk 23:53), who use ἐντυλίσσω (cf. Jn 20:7). This is a major agreement of Matthew and Luke against Mark.

Mk 15:47. Matthew 27:61 has the women sitting opposite the tomb. Luke 23:55 has the women follow and see the tomb and how the body was laid. Mark 15:47 only has the women see where the body was laid. It is an uncharacteristic abbreviation by Mark. Either he felt that getting them to this new tomb was unnecessary for his story, or Matthew and Luke saw the omission and corrected it. In our view, the former explanation is simplest.

SECTION THREE: THE EMPTY TOMB AND ITS CONSEQUENCES

¶ 90. Women Find Jesus' Tomb Is Empty; He Has Been Raised

Mt 28:1-8 ==========>   Mk 16:1-8   <========== Lk 24:19

After the Sabbath, Mary Magdalene, Mary the mother of James, and Salome bought spices in order to anoint Jesus. Very early on the morning on the first day of the week, just at sunrise, they arrive at the tomb. They began to say to one another, "Who can help us by moving the stone at the door of the tomb. Looking up they see that the stone had been moved. (It was a very large one.)

After entering the tomb they see a young man sitting in the right section of the tomb dressed in a white robe. They were astonished. He says to them, "Cease being alarmed. You are looking for Jesus of Nazareth who was crucified. He is raised. He is not here! Take a look at the place where they laid him! You go, tell his disciples and Peter that he goes before you into Galilee. There you will see him just as he told you."

They get outside and flee from the tomb in fear and confusion. They did not speak to anyone for they were afraid.

General Observations. In the previous pericope about the burial of Jesus Mark drew from Matthew and Luke, and also composed freely (Mk 15:42-47). Mark seems to follow a similar procedure in this pericope. However, by primarily following Luke in the first part of the pericope and then primarily switching to Matthew in the second part, Mark has given us a striking instance of the pattern of alternating agreement between Luke and Matthew. This is especially evident in the story line. In Luke and Mark the women come to the tomb with spices very early on the first day of the week (Lk 24:1//Mk 16:1-3). The women find the tomb open and they go inside to look for Jesus' body (Lk 24:2-3//Mk 16:4-5a). In Luke the women encounter two angelic figures (Lk 24:4; cf. 24:23). In Mark they encounter the νεανίσκος (youth or angel, Mk 16:5b). At this point Mark begins the shift toward Matthew. The response of the youth/angel to the women in Mk 16:6-7 is very close linguistically to the response of the angel to the women in Mt 28:5-7. Thus, on the Two Gospel Hypothesis, Mark has primarily followed Luke in the first part of this pericope (Mk 16:1-5a), and Matthew in the latter part (Mk 16:5b-8). These verses constitute another example of the pattern of alternating Markan agreement with Matthew and Luke within a pericope.

• The pericope is transitional. In the previous verses Mark emphasized that the crucified Jesus was dead when he was placed in the tomb. Now the tomb is found to be empty and the youth/angel announces that Jesus is raised. But the reader is still left in a situation of suspense. Nothing is resolved. The women are terrified and in fear. They flee the scene. The same verb (φεύγω) is used to describe their flight as was used to describe the earlier abandonment by both the disciples and the young man (Mk 14:50, 52). The women are supposed to inform the disciples about the empty tomb. The promise is that the disciples will see Jesus in Galilee (Mk 16:7). But until an actual appearance of Jesus the confession that Jesus is the crucified and risen Son of God has not reached closure.

Mk 16:1-2. Mark and Luke claim that the women come to the tomb to anoint the body. In Matthew the women come simply to see the tomb. Matthew does not have an account of the anointing of Jesus' body. The Matthean account is more congruent with Jewish practices in antiquity. He simply announces that the women go to "see" the tomb (Mt 28:1). This seems to allude to the Jewish practice recorded in *Semahot* 8:1 which presupposes inspection of the tomb for three days after burial to insure that the buried person was not alive. It is also interesting to observe that there is no evidence from extant Jewish sources for anointing a body after burial.[26] Furthermore, it is worth noting that, according to the Mishna (Sabbath 23:5), which may well preserve earlier tradition,

---

[26] See T.W Longstaff, "The Women of the Tomb: Matthew 28:1 Re-Examined," *NTS* 27 (1981): 277-82.

it is explicitly permissible to prepare a body for burial, including washing and anointing it, on the Sabbath, a point that those unfamiliar with Jewish burial practices may not have appreciated.

• Mark basically follows Luke while blending in the names of the women from Matthew in this verse (Mt 28:1, but cf. the names of the women later in Lk 24:10).

• Mark creates his temporal setting by drawing terminology from Luke: "on the first day of the week." Mark reads the Lukan ὄρθρου βαθέως and writes "after sunrise" (ἀνατείλαντος τοῦ ἡλίου, cf. Mk 16:2).

Mk 16:3. This verse is a Markan suppplement to Matthew and Luke. Mark anticipates the subsequent narrative and introduces further uses of the vocabulary, ἀποκυλίω and μνημεῖον, thus producing duplicate expresssions in Mk 16:3-5. Mark's use of μνημεῖον here, however, is a triplet (Mk 16:2, 3, and 5). As he often does, Mark expands his narrative with additional details and vivid descriptions (cf. the next verse, Mk 16:4, for the comment on the size of the stone: "for it was exceedingly great"). This detail creates some awkwardness in the narrative flow. After the women had already taken the trouble to buy the spices and are making the journey to the tomb, only then do they become concerned about how they may gain entrance to the tomb. Yet, in the story-world that Mark has created, such awkwardness is acceptable.

• The use of the reflexive pronoun (πρὸς ἑαυτάς) is typical of Markan composition (Peabody, *Mark as Composer,* 37, 45).

Mk 16:4. There appears to be another instance of alternating Markan agreement between Matthew and Luke in Mk 16:4. On the Two Gospel Hypothesis Mark draws his use of θεωρέω from Mt 28:1 and his use of the perfect passive of ἀποκυλίω from Lk 24:2 (cf. ἀπεκύλισεν, Mt 28:2).

Mk 16:5. Curiously, the description of the young man in 16:5 (Καὶ . . . νεανίσκος . . . περιβεβλημένον . . . ὁ δέ) is nearly identical to the description of the mysterious young man in 14:51 (Καὶ νεανίσκος . . . περιβεβλημένος . . . καὶ . . . ὁ δέ). This certainly suggests that the author of the Gospel is responsible for at least one of the descriptions, if not both. The announcement to the women is made by an angel in Matthew and two men in Luke (afterwards called "angels" in Lk 24:23). Mark's use of νεανίσκος not only "sidesteps" the conflict, but has about it a certain degree of irony. The young man who had abandoned Jesus is now the first to announce his victory over death. In turn, his announcement will cause the women "to flee." But, in the end, they too must come to faith—as the longer ending intimates (cf. Mk 16:10).

Mk 16:6-7. The advice of the youth/angel to "go tell the disciples that *you will see him* in Galilee *as he told you*" is not attributed to Jesus in the earlier prediction in Mk 14:28//Mt 26:32. So, in the story line of Mark, there was no earlier prediction. However, in Mt 28:7 this announcement is made and repeated in Mt 28:10. Thus, the youth's/angel's command in Mark presupposes that Mark was following the narrative flow of Matthew in order for the text of Mark to be comprehensible.[27]

• Mark's demonstrable penchant for precise fulfillment of Jesus' prophecies would seem to require the fulfillment of this prophecy with some account of one or more subsequent appearances of the resurrected Jesus to his disciples.

• The command to speak to Peter is one of the substantial differences between Mk 16:6-7 and Mt 28:6-7. The note, "and to Peter," reads like a gloss on the parallel text in Matthew. In our previous study of Luke, the team argued that Lk 24:12, with its reference to Peter running to the empty tomb, was part of the genuine text of Luke.[28] If Mark knew this story about Peter running to the empty tomb in Luke or John 20:2-10, that may explain why Mark has supplemented the texts of Matthew and Luke here with the phrase "and to Peter." This editorial supplement is consistent with Markan dependence on Luke.

Mk 16:8. The famous ending of the Gospel remains baffling. Manuscript evidence exists both for the text ending at Mk 16:8 and for Mk 16:9-20. If Mark ends at 16:8 and it is the complete text of the oldest Gospel, then is problematic. The women do not tell anyone about the empty tomb. Then no one finds out about it. Then how does Mark know? Moreover, the book ends with the post-positive conjunction γάρ. Though there have been numerous attempts to explain the text as it stands, we find it difficult to believe that any writer, even Mark, would have ended in this way. Thus we favor some

---

[27] William R. Farmer, "Notes for a Compositional Analysis on the Griesbach Hypothesis of the Empty Tomb Stories in the Synoptic Gospels," in *Occasional Notes on Some Points of Interest in New Testament Studies,* privately published pamphlet (August 1980), 7-14.

[28] McNicol et al., *Beyond the Q Impasse,* 311.

version of a *lost ending* solution. Certainly, on our hypothesis, had he known both Matthew and Luke it is difficult to think that he would have omitted all reference to the appearances of the risen Christ.

EXCURSUS 15: THE LAST TWELVE VERSES OF MARK

Did Mark end at Mk 16:8? Or did it end at Mk 16:20, so that the absence of these twelve verses in some manuscripts is due to scribal omission? These are some of the most vexed and disputed questions of Gospel studies. The most recent scholarly monograph on the subject went beyond 500 pages.[29] And this represents only the tip of the iceberg with respect to scholarly production on the issue during the last couple of centuries.

In the space allowable for an excursus on this subject we can do little more than set out our perspective. In this excursus we will focus on two points. First, the case for acceptance of the genuineness of the last twelve verses of Mark is much stronger than is usually thought. Second, valid critical concerns nevertheless remain about the connection of these twelve verses to the rest of Mk.

DID MARK END AT MARK 16:8?

In his magisterial book, *The Text of the New Testament*, Bruce Metzger finds himself convinced on critical grounds that the original text of Mark ends at 16:8.[30] But then he goes on to express what many believe, "But did Mark intend to conclude his Gospel with the melancholy statement that the women were afraid (ἐφοβοῦντο γάρ)? Despite the arguments which several modern scholars have urged in support of such a view, the present writer cannot believe that the note of fear would have been regarded as an appropriate conclusion to an account of the Evangel or Good News."[31]

In our judgment Metzger understates the sense of *uneasiness* that the reader has when he or she is left with the narrative account awkwardly interrupted and unfinished at Mk 16:8.

---

[29] James A. Kelhoffer, *Miracle and Mission: The Authentication of Missionaries and Their Message in the Longer Ending of Mark* (WUNT 2.112; Tübingen: Mohr Siebeck, 2000).

[30] Bruce M. Metzger, *The Text of the New Testament: Its Transmission, Corruption, and Restoration* (London/New York: Oxford University Press, 1964), 228.

[31] Ibid., 228. There are isolated instances of this phraseology ending paragraphs in Greek literature. Mark is not an elegant author and it is not incomprehensible that grammatically he could have composed a paragraph ending in ἐφοβοῦντο γάρ. What is difficult to accept is that Mark, a non-stylist, writing to a nonliterary Christian audience, would be so sophisticated in his narrative craft as to construct an account showing how everything that Jesus had predicted came to pass, but when it came to seeing Jesus as risen, he left that entirely to the imagination of the reader. That is the difficulty with accepting the view that Mark ended at 16:8.

As we have argued in this book, the plot line in Mark revolves around the tension between Jesus and his disciples. Jesus chooses the disciples, gives them the secret of the kingdom, and commissions them to carry out his mission (Mk 4:11; 6:7-13). They are the recipients of the message that he must first be crucified and die before he will be raised and vindicated at the right hand of God (cf. Mk 8:31; 9:9, 33; 10:33-34; 14:28, 62). Jesus' vindication by resurrection from the dead is foreshadowed in numerous other places (see, e.g., our discussion on Mk 5:35-43; 9:14-29). Throughout the Passion Narrative, Mark goes out of his way to say that nothing occurs accidentally, but happens in keeping with the previously announced word of Jesus or scripture. What Jesus has spoken, including the defection of the disciples, does take place (Mk 14:37-50). But, in the narrative flow of Mark, all of this would be to no avail if the greatest promise of all, the resurrection of Jesus and its attendant acceptance by the disciples were not stated. A recent writer says, "Either Jesus and the disciples do reconcile, and hence God does have the final word even over human fallibility or obduracy, or God's promises cannot ultimately be trusted."[32]

A resolution of some kind between Jesus and the disciples is demanded by the logic of the narrative. The idea that Mark ends with ἐφοβοῦντο γάρ, the women in panic and fear, is difficult to accept.

This view is strengthened if one reads Mark on the basis of the Two Gospel Hypothesis. Advocates of Markan priority frequently assert that this sense of incompleteness was apparent to Matthew and Luke, who readily solved the difficulties by furnishing their respective accounts of the resurrection appearances. But, on the Two Gospel Hypothesis, this solution is not an option. If Mark (and his readership) were aware of the tradition of the appearances of Jesus after his death, and these were recorded in other narratives, what reason would there be for Mark to conclude with an account of the fear and panic of Jesus' followers? Thus, we take a position with Bultmann and many others that the text of Mark must have continued beyond Mk 16:8; and most likely would have concluded with a Galilean appearance and reconciliation with the eleven.[33]

---

[32] James Hansen, "The Disciples in Mark's Gospel: Beyond the Pastoral/Polemical Debate," *Horizons in Biblical Theology* 20 (1998): 129.

[33] On the matter of the Galilean appearance see below. Cf. R. Bultmann, *History of the Synoptic Tradition*, 284-86. Of course we are aware of the many interpretations that Galilee is merely a metaphor for Mark and that the disciples will only "see" Jesus when they begin to follow his teachings and manner of life that had their origin there. If this means that Mark is saying that discipleship entails a cross before a crown there is something to this. But, again, it is scarcely plausible to read the promise to see him given at the empty tomb in Mk 16:8, as only applicable to discipleship and entirely devoid of an expectation of encountering the risen Christ.

There are only three Greek manuscripts of Mark (Vaticanus, Sinaiticus, and 304, a twelfth century commentary on Matthew and Mark) which end at Mk 16:8.[34] On the other hand, the number of Greek manuscripts that include Mk 16:9-20 is substantial.

It is true that the longer ending of Mark 16:9-20 is found in 99 percent of the Greek manuscripts as well as the rest of the tradition, enjoying over a period of centuries practically an official ecclesiastical sanction as a genuine part of the Gospel of Mark.[35]

Such widespread evidence for inclusion of the "longer ending" in the Greek manuscripts, by and large, is matched in the versions, in patristic quotations, and lectionaries.[36] Especially noteworthy is the witness of two second-century church fathers. Justin Martyr (*Apol.*, i. 45), though not referring directly to Mark, appears to reflect Mark's influence (ἐξελθόντες πανταχοῦ ἐκήρυξαν cf. Mk 16:20 ἐξελθόντες ἐκήρυξαν πανταχοῦ). Irenaeus (*Haer.* 3.10.5) quotes Mk 16:19 as from the Gospel of Mark.[37] When one considers that the textual attestation for Mark's Gospel is much less in the early centuries of the Common Era than for the other Gospels the evidence for the acceptance of the "longer ending" of Mark from the mid-second century onward is quite extraordinary. Usually this amount of attestation would carry the day for the acceptance of a text such as Mk 16:9-20 as genuine.

What is especially interesting is that there is no clear evidence that any manuscript of Mark was known to circulate in the second and third centuries *without* the "longer ending."[38] Thus, we see that,

---

[34] D.C. Parker, *The Living Text of the Gospels* (Cambridge: Cambridge University Press. 1997), 125.

[35] Kurt Aland and Barbara Aland, *The Text of the New Testament: An Introduction of the Critical Editions and to the Theory and Practice of Modern Textual Criticism* (rev. and enl. 2d ed.; trans. E. F. Rhodes; Grand Rapids, Mich.: Eerdmans, 1987), 292.

[36] A still very useful list of the data including material on other forms and combinations of the ending is that of J. K. Elliott, "The Text and Language of the Endings to Mark's Gospel," *TZ* 27 (1971): 255-62. This is reprinted in J. K. Elliott, *The Language and Style of the Gospel of Mark: An Edition of C. H. Turner's "Notes on Marcan Usage" Together with Other Comparable Studies* (NovTest Sup 71; Leiden: Brill, 1993), 203-11. As is well known, W. R. Farmer, *The Last Twelve Verses of Mark* (SNTSMS 25; Cambridge: Cambridge University Press, 1974) has argued that most of the versions without the longer ending can be traced to an Alexandrian text type.

[37] Kelhoffer, *Miracle and Mission,* considers the *terminus ante quem* of the longer ending to be 140 CE.

[38] As noted by Parker, *The Living Text*, 136-37, the failure of Clement of Alexandria and Origen to quote from the longer ending when they discuss resurrection appearances cannot be construed as evidence that these authors had texts with the shorter ending. This is a very dangerous use of the argument from silence. The same should be said for Parker's claim that, since 𝔓[75] (an early third-century manuscript) is of the Alexandrian text type, and since the major Alexandrian manuscripts (Vaticanus and Sinaiticus) end at Mk 16:8, scholars should conclude that the ending of Mark at Mk 16:8 can be verified from 𝔓[75]. The fact is, however, that 𝔓[75] contains

based on the manuscript evidence, the issue of the authenticity of the "longer ending" must center upon what happened in the late first/early second centuries and what happened in the fourth and fifth centuries. We will note the latter issue first.

ORIGIN OF VATICANUS AND SINAITICUS

Recent research on the origins of Sinaiticus and Vaticanus throw important light on the history of transmission of these two manuscripts.[39] Skeat argues from the available evidence that both manuscripts were produced as part of Eusebius' response to the request of Constantine in 330 CE for copies of the Christian Scriptures for churches in Constantinople.[40] Sinaiticus was produced first, but its format was unsuitable for church use.[41] On the other hand, Vaticanus most probably was sent to Constantinople where it was used for many centuries.[42] The basic point of this argumentation is that if Vaticanus and Sinaiticus came from the same scriptorium, they cannot be cited as independent witnesses of an earlier text type that ends at Mk 16:8.

We do not know the basis for the omission of the verses after Mk 16:8 in Sinaiticus and Vaticanus. Was it done on the grounds of linguistic characteristics or for some other philological reasons? Was it done for political reasons? (The claims of Mk 16:17-18 would hardly sit well among the literate classes who were being co-opted in Constantine's policy of Christianization of the Empire!) Or were there already manuscripts of Mark that ended at Mk 16:8? And why at Mark 16:8 anyway?

Light may be shed on the latter question by an obscure work attributed to Eusebius.[43] In his

---

fragmentary texts only from Luke and John. To appeal to a papyrus in which Mark is not even extant is to build conjecture upon conjecture.

[39] Here we are accepting as authoritative the significant article of T. C. Skeat, "The Codex Sinaiticus, the Codex Vaticanus, and Constantine," *JTS* 50 pt 2 (1999): 583-625.

[40] Ibid., 604-9.

[41] Ibid., 604-19.

[42] Ibid., 619-22.

[43] We refer to the fragments of a manuscript found in the Vatican in the nineteenth century and edited by Cardinal Angelo Mai. In these fragments, an abridged version of a larger work, there are several questions on the death and the resurrection addressed to someone called Marinus. One of these questions posits a problem raised with respect to perceived differences in the timing of the resurrection between Mt 28:1 and Mk 16: 9. The exact reference is *Quaestiones ad Marinum*, Mai, NPB, 4, 255-57. The Greek and Latin texts of the *ad Marinum* were published by Cardinal Angelo Mai, *Scriptorum Veterum Nova Collectio e Vaticani Codicibus* (Rome. Typis Vaticanis, 1825), 1 61-82. Mai published a revised edition of the *ad Marinum* in idem, *Novae patrum bibliothecae* (Rome: Typis Sacri Concilii propagando christiano nomini, 1844-1905 [Vol.4,1847]), 4.255-268=J.-P. Migne, PG 22.937-953.

response to the question on alleged discrepancies in the Gospels with respect to the time of the appearance of Jesus to Mary Magdalene, the writer argues that Mark ended at Mk 16:8 and that the "longer ending" is a spurious reading. Therefore, one would not have to deal with the Mary Magdalene passage in Mk 16:9-11. Indeed, the writer refers to manuscripts that end at Mk 16:8 as "the accurate copies" (ἀκριβής). Then, with respect to copies that end at Mk 16:8 he goes on to say, "For at those words [the last words of Mk 16:8], in almost all copies of the Gospel of Mark, comes the end."

We wonder on what basis could an author make such a statement? We have observed that no manuscript of Mark from the second and third centuries is known to exist without the longer ending. If Eusebius were the author of this tractate (and that is by no means certain) he would have known of the existence of the copies sent to Constantinople that do not have the longer ending. But this would only be a small sampling of the extant manuscripts on Mark. All of the evidence in the later Greek Manuscript tradition as well as the versions point to a preference for retaining the longer ending. The issue is very complex and cannot be addressed adequately in a short excursus but we may tentatively suggest that the reference to the "accurate copies" refers to a critically constructed text in keeping with the canons of ancient textual criticism. In other words, competent scholars associated with Eusebius had some questions with reference to the authenticy of Mk 16:9-20. They even produced manuscripts ending at Mk 16:8. But at the same time, they could not deny that in many parts of the empire Mk 16:9-20 was the received text. This hypothesis can be strengthened by noting that Jerome recapitulates both a similar tradition found in the Greek text attributed to Eusebius and a similar response with respect to the manuscript tradition.[44] Nevertheless, he includes Mk 16:9-20 (the received text?) in his Latin translation of the New Testament and treats these verses as part of the Gospel in his *Commentary on Mark*.[45]

Thus, we tentatively conclude that some scholars in the Christian community in the early fourth century, on critical grounds, began to reject the authenticity of Mk 16:9-20. We are unclear as to the precise basis for their conclusion.[46] But it renders plausible what happened. While the received text

---

[44] Jerome, *Epist.* 120.3 (PL 22.980-1006).

[45] PL 30.642-44. Also, it is on a critical basis that the author of the scholium to the later *Commentary on Mark* by Victor of Antioch concludes that Mark should end at Mk 16:8. On the other hand when Augustine, who stated that these verses were read publicly at Easter in the churches of Africa, did his *Harmony of the Gospels* (3.65-86) he lists Mark's account of the post-resurrection appearances of Jesus along with those of Matthew, Luke, and John.

[46] As the Mai Fragments and Jerome note, it may have been precipitated by attacks on the discrepancies in the Gospels with respect to the resurrection appearances—although, no doubt, this was not the entire story; cf. David L. Dungan, *A History of the Synoptic Problem*: *The Canon, the Text, the Composition, and the Interpretation of the Gospels*, Anchor Bible Reference Library (New York: Doubleday, 1999), 98-111.

remained popular, some manuscripts and versions emerged with the ending at Mk 16:8, while, in certain quarters, various alternative endings began to emerge.

THE "LONGER ENDING" IN THE EARLIEST YEARS OF THE TRANSMISSION OF MARK

As noted above, we have reason to believe that as early as Eusebius some scholars of the church were raising critical questions about the originality of Mk 16:9-20. What might have caused these scholars to be suspicious about the "longer ending" of Mark?

Three points come readily to mind. First, there is the issue of the composition of Mk 16:9-20, which appears to be heavily dependent upon Matthew, Luke, and perhaps John. Second, there is the issue of grammatical style and linguistic characteristics. Some have argued that the literary features of the "longer ending" are not Markan. Third, some argue that it is not an appropriate vehicle to complete the story line of the rest of the Gospel. We will summarize *seriatim* the present state of this discussion.

First, we regard Mk 16:9-20 as a conflation of Matthew and Luke with some blending either from John or a tradition behind John. This has been demonstrated in detail in the recent dissertation of Kelhoffer.[47] This is an important finding. However, this conclusion must be weighed judiciously with respect to the authenticity of these verses. On the Two Gospel Hypothesis Kelhoffer's conclusion is what one would expect if this composition came from the hand of the author of Mark. On the other hand, a disciple of the evangelist may have imitated Markan style. The genuineness of Mk 16:9-20 must be substantiated on the basis of additional considerations, rather than merely showing it is a conflation of Matthew and Luke.[48]

Second, there is the issue of the style and linguistic characteristics of Mk 16:9-20. Here, again, we believe the answer may be somewhat inconclusive. According to Gould there are 163 words in this passage, and of these, 19 words and two phrases are distinctive, not occurring elsewhere in the Gospel.[49] To this it is often added that there are some astonishing instances of new vocabulary for

---

[47] Kelhoffer, *Miracle and Mission*, 1-156.

[48] On the other hand, Kelhoffer's conclusion is devastating for those who hold the Two Document Hypothesis and wish to sustain the authenticity of Mk 16:9-20. One must either give up the priority of Mark or claim that Mk 16:9-20 is a forgery. Kelhoffer, *Miracle and Mission*, 150-54, is a classic case in point. He will not forsake the priority of Mark, and so he argues that Mk 16:9-20 was a forgery compiled sometime in the first decades of the second century.

[49] E. P. Gould, *A Critical and Exegetical Commentary on the Gospel According to St. Mark* (New York: Charles Scribner's Press, 1896), 303.

Mark (πορεύομαι three times, ἀπιστέω two times, etc.). What is not always noted is that certain characteristic Markan terminology continues in the longer ending (e.g., εὐαγγέλιον used absolutely and synonyms). What is also not noted is that throughout Mark in other units *hapax legomena* and idiosyncratic terminology are relatively plentiful. The issue is whether Mk 16:9-20 is quantitatively different from the rest of Mark in the use of this new terminology. We do not believe the case has been made that it is.[50]

Third, there is the issue as to whether Mk 16:9-20 is an appropriate ending to the Markan story line. Here, we believe there is a considerable problem. Throughout the Markan account of the Passion Narrative we have noted time and time again that Mark has carefully argued, sometimes painstakingly, that Jesus' predictions are fulfilled. This is not only a narrative device. Fulfillment of Jesus' prophecies is theologically crucial to Mark. If this is the case, why does Mark have Jesus predict (twice) he will be reconciled with the disciples in Galilee (Mk 14:28, 16:7) but offers no proof of fulfillment? Furthermore, Mark says that the women are to tell Peter that Jesus is risen, but they do not do so (Mk 16:7) if Mark ended at Mk 16:8. In our judgment this raises a serious question about the authenticity of this ending. In a very fundamental way the longer ending in its present form does not complete the Markan story line in a fully satisfactory manner either.

CONCLUSION

Our brief overview concludes that very early in the Christian movement (after several decades of the second century) Mk 16:9-20 was part of the received text of the second Gospel. As Mark made its way into lectionaries and key commentaries and became firmly entrenched as a vital part of the Christian canon, the "longer ending" was used regularly in the Easter season. There were doubters, even in antiquity, as to the authenticity of Mk 16:9-20. Doubts centered on apparent discrepancies between its account of the resurrection appearances and those of the other Gospels. In our judgment, a key discrepancy was that the promise of reunion with the disciples in Galilee did not take place. One can only speculate as to what happened in the early days of the publication of Mark. Perhaps Mark did produce a text (now lost) that spoke about reconciliation in Galilee but it failed to resolve the differences between Matthew and Luke with respect to the locale of the resurrection appearances and so was replaced with the present longer ending (Mk 16:9-20). Because of the presence of Markan linguistic characteristics within Mk 16:9-20 in a proportion comparable to that found in Mk 1:1-16:8, it is reasonable to conclude that this subsequent revision (Mk 16:9-20) made use of much of the text that

---

[50] See the commentary below, where this will be taken up in detail.

the author of Mk 1:1-16:8 composed, as well as Matthew and Luke. This would seem to be a more plausible scenario than the later production of a second century forgery.[51] In any case, Mk 16:9-20 became part of the generally received text and was accepted as canonical by the church.

¶ 91. Jesus Appears to His Followers after the Resurrection

Mt 28:10-11, 18-19--------->	Mk 16:9-20	<===== Lk 24:9-13, 36-37, 46-47
(Jn 20:1, 16-19)		(Lk 10:17, 19)
(Jn 21:1)		(Lk 8:2-3)

After rising early on the first day of the week, Jesus appeared first to Mary Magdalene from whom he had cast out seven demons. Although she reported this to Jesus' sad and weeping disciples, they would not believe her. So, after this, he appeared again in another form, this time to two male disciples while they were walking in a field. These two also reported the appearance of the resurrected Jesus, but again the eleven disciples would not believe. Finally, on a third occasion, Jesus appeared directly to the eleven while they were reclining at table. He upbraided them for the lack of faith and hardness of heart they displayed in not trusting these others who had seen him earlier. Nevertheless, Jesus said to them, "Go into the whole world. Preach the gospel to all creation, for whoever believes and is baptized will be saved, but whoever does not believe will be condemned. And these will be the accompanying signs for those who do believe. They will cast out demons in my name, speak new languages, pick up snakes in their hands, even drink deadly poison, but not be harmed. By the touch of the disciples, the sick will become well."

The Lord Jesus, after he had said these things to them, was taken up into heaven and sat at the right hand of God. Subsequently, the disciples went out and preached everywhere, having been empowered by the Lord who confirmed the word they preached with accompanying signs.

General Observations. Mk 16:9-20 consists of four elements: the report of Mary Magdalene (Mk 16:9-11); an appearance of Jesus to two disciples (Mk 16:12-13); an appearance of Jesus and commissioning of the eleven (Mk 16:14-18); the ascension and summary of apostolic activity (Mk 16:19-20). Whatever the actual circumstances of the publication of this unit, it is clear that its author follows a similar *procedure* of

---

[51] The longer a manuscript is in circulation the more difficult it would be to attach a forgery to it without other copies circulating without the forgery. It is remembered that the textual "fruit salad" of endings begins to emerge about the time of Constantine.

composition as the author of Mk 1:1-16:8. That is, the author composes by drawing heavily from similar contextual material in Matthew and Luke. The only difference may be that in Mk 16:9-20 the influence of John is more pervasive. The author of the "longer ending" may have drawn upon "appearance traditions" in John or a source behind it to compose a unified narrative emphasizing the movement of the disciples from unbelief to belief. It is clear that the author of Mk 16:9-20 followed in chronological sequence the basic text of Lk 24, blending into it terminology drawn from Mt 28 and thematic elements from John, especially the movement from unbelief to belief. Already in Mk 16:1-8 there is heavy dependence on Lk 24:1-9. Mark 16:9 continues the use of Lk 24:1-11/Lk 8:2, supplementing it with an echo of Mt 28:1 and Jn 20:1. For Mk 16:10-11 the author continues to work in the context of Lk 24:10-12, but clearly supplements his composition with material drawn from Mt 28:10-11. The second appearance account (Mk 16:12-13) is a drastic abbreviation of Lk 24:13-35. For the third appearance and the commissioning of the Twelve (Mk 16:14-18) the text of Luke continues to be followed (Lk 24:36-49 supplemented by Lk 10:17, 19), but here as well there is blending with the Great Commission narrative in Mt 28:16-20. Finally, the author clearly depends upon Luke (Lk 24:50-53/Acts 1:2-11) for the composition of Mk 16:19-20. The unit seems to divide in two. There are two appearances of Jesus characterized by unbelief (16:9-13). This is followed by another appearance of Jesus where the disciples are upbraided for their unbelief and then commissioned to proclaim the good news (Mk 16:14-18). A brief epilogue (Mk 16:19-20) concludes the narrative account.

Thus the author of Mk 16:9-20 has spliced into a unified narrative the Matthean and Lukan accounts of the appearances of Jesus after his death. The theological import begins to emerge. After several failures to believe that Jesus was alive, the disciples come to faith. Their sight mutates into belief. The crucified Jesus is the risen Lord who is now to be proclaimed to the world (Mk 16:15-16). The same power present in the mission of Jesus can be recapitulated by the disciples in their mission. Finally, albeit uneasily, Jesus and the disciples are reconciled. The kingdom has come in the community of believers that has replaced the temple. God's promises have not been thwarted through unbelief.

• Mk 16:9-20 is similar to earlier summaries in Mk 9:33-50 and Mk 13:33-37. As in this pericope, both Mk 9:33-50 and 13:33-37 represent summaries of longer units in Matthew and Luke. Thus, the almost frantic pace here is not without precedent.[52]

Mk 16:9. Ἀναστάς is unusual here because an active participle use of ἀνίστημι is not used to describe the resurrection anywhere else in the Gospels.[53] However, Mark does use this form of the participle in other contexts earlier in his narrative and the same verb is used several times in connection with the passion predictions (Mk 8:31 etc., cf. Lk 24:12 with respect to Peter running to the tomb). Also, it is noticeable that in the pericope on the epileptic boy (a unit we identified as foreshadowing resurrection) ἀνίστημι is used with ἐγείρω (Mk 8:27). This is precisely what occurs in Mk 16:6, 9.

• The words "early" (πρωΐ) and "on the first day of the week" (πρώτῃ σαββάτου) repeat motifs that introduced the empty tomb story at Mk 16:2 (cf. Mk 16:1). These kinds of repetitions, particularly in retrospective passages, are consistent with the style of Mark.

• The repetition of πρώτῃ/ πρῶτον is consistent with the usage of the author of Mark in his preference for repetition within a limited literary context.

• The use of πρῶτον seems to be a major structural feature of the first part of the pericope (Mk 16:9-13). This is followed in Mk 16:14 with the use of Ὕστερον to structure the second part of the unit.

• The word φαίνω occurs in a different usage ("seemed") in Lk 24:11. But Lk 24:11 is a close contextual parallel (cf. the use of ἀπιστέω in Mk 16:11) and is immediately preceded by a reference to Mary Magdalene (Lk 24:10). The reference to Mary Magdalene, in turn, is conflated by Mark with another reference in Lk to her activities

---

[52] Kelhoffer, *Miracle and Mission*, 169, employs the image of the difference between a jogger (Luke) and the athlete who runs a hundred yard sprint (Mark).

[53] Kelhoffer, *Miracle and Mission*, 67, concludes that the use of ἀναστάς in this verse is clear evidence of the work of a forger, mainly because there is no participial usage of ἀνίστημι in the Gospels or Acts with respect to the resurrection. In our judgment Kelhoffer sets a far too demanding standard for what could be genuinely Markan composition and thus stretches the linguistic evidence in order to warrant his claim (cf. Peabody, *Mark as Composer*, 52, 49).

(Lk 8:2). Indeed the linguistic parallels between Mk 16:9 and Lk 8:2 are quite striking.[54]

• The "casting out" of demons rather than the "coming out" of demons is consistent with demonstrable Markan stylistic preferences (cf. Peabody, *Mark as Composer,* 49, 48; 62, 52; 211, 102).

Mk 16:10-11. The author of the longer ending has been working in the context of Lk 24:10-12 for the composition of Mk 16:9. The failure of the disciples to believe is echoed in Lk 24:11 with the same verb (ἀπιστέω) which is used in Mk 16:11.

•The author of Mk 16:9-10 has clearly blended Lk 24:11 with echoes of Matthean terminology. Noteworthy is the use of ἀπαγγέλλω from Mt 28:10. In the next verse from the bribing of the soldiers pericope (Mt 28:11-15), Mk 16:10 and Mt 28:11 are parallel in the use of πορεύομαι, ἀπαγγέλλω, and γίνομαι in the same order! Clearly, the author is developing the response to Mary Magdalene that he draws from Lk 24:10-12. He has supplemented this with terminology drawn from Mt 28:10-11.

• The use of the participial form of πορεύομαι is often cited as one of the strongest linguistic arguments for an author other than the author of Mark.[55] Mark does not use πορεύομαι at all in 1:1-16:8 (Mk 9:30 is probably a compound form), but this verb occurs three times in a participial form in the longer ending. It is good evidence in favor of a different author for the longer ending. But it may be argued that the author of the long ending drew πορεύομαι from Mt 28:11 in the first place and, finding it a "pleasing expression," used it again in Mk 16:12, 15.

• The construction τοῖς μετ' αὐτοῦ γενομένοις to refer to the disciples is similar to the unique Markan terminology μετ' αὐτοῦ in the call of the Twelve passage in Mk 3:14 (cf. Peabody, *Mark as Composer,* 58-59, 50). This usage conforms to Markan style.

---

[54] Kelhoffer, *Miracle and Mission*, 70, has a very instructive table.

[55] J. K. Elliott, "The Text and Language of the Endings to Mark's Gospel" in *The Language and Style of the Gospel of Mark: An Edition of C. H. Turner's "Notes on Marcan Usage" Together with Other Comparable Studies* (NovTSup 71; Leiden: Brill, 1993), 203-11, esp. 206-7.

• The use of θεάσαι twice (Mk 16:11, 14), and forms of πιστεύω (seven times in the long ending) reflects important teminology for the author of Mk 16:9-20. This author clearly wishes to highlight the movement from "unfaith" to faith. Through a series of appearances of Jesus faith ultimately comes to the disciples. Thus the frequent use of cognates of πιστεύω, in particular, are fully understandable in this context.

Mk 16:12-13. This unit continues to follow the text of Lk 24, which serves as the major source for Mk 16:9-20. Mark 16:12-13 is an extreme abbreviation of the Emmaus story in Lk 24:13-35. Particularly striking are parallel references to the "two of them" in Mk 16:12 and at the beginning of the unit in Lk 24:13, and the cognate references in the form of an announcement to others of what had happened (ἀπήγγειλαν τοῖς λοιποῖς, Mk 16:13//αὐτοὶ ἐξηγοῦντο, Lk 24:35).

• The clause μετὰ ταῦτα + the third singular aorist of φανερόω with Jesus as the subject may link Mk 16:12 to Jn 21:1. However, it is also noticeable that the use of μετά (Mk 16:12) seems to be an appropriate counterpoint to the use of πρῶτον in Mk 16:9 to complete the first segment of the pericope. And μετά also performs a similar function for the second segment of the pericope (ὕστερον [Mk 16:14] and μετὰ [Mk 16:19]). Thus there is a distinct possibility that this is a compositional feature of the author of Mk 16:12-13. This is substantiated by the fact that μετὰ δὲ ταῦτα is an unusual construction only occurring at Lk 10.1, 18.4, and Jn 19:38.[56]

• The second use of πορεύομαι (πορευομένοις εἰς ἀγρόν) may be derived from a similar participial usage in Lk 24:13. It is not clear why the writer uses "field" instead of the Lukan "village" as the destination of the two. Ἀγρός is a linguistic characteristic of Mark. But could it be that the author of Mk 16:12 drew upon the Matthean account of the death of Judas (Mt 27:7, 8, 10)? This unit has not been used earlier in Mark. Thus, in the longer ending, we may have distinct echoes of two units in the Matthean Passion Account not used previously by Mark: the bribing of the soldiers (Mt 28:11-15), and the Death of Judas (Mt 27:3-10).

Mk 16:14. This is the opening verse of the second segment of Mk 16:9-20. It appears to be an attempt to focus upon the strong reference to the unbelief of the disciples at the outset of the critical appearance and commissioning scene (Lk 26:36-43//Mt 28:17).

---

[56] Kellhoffer, *Miracle and Mission*, 84.

• The author of the long ending emphasizes the "hard-heartedness" of the disciples, a theme that is central to Mark (Mk 6:52; 8:17; 10:5 cf. Peabody, *Mark as Composer,* 166, 91). The phrasing is somewhat different in most of Mk 1:1-16:8; but note σκληροκαρδία in Mk 10:5.

• Clearly, there is an awkward shift from the stinging critique of the disciples' unbelief in Mk 16:14 to the commissioning scene in Mk 16:15. Missing are the beautiful Lukan accounts of dawning belief. This awkward shift between Mk 16:14 and 15 is similar to that between Mk 16:8 and 9. A partial explanation may be that it is a function of the process of abbreviation.

Mk 16:15-16. The author continues to follow the order of Luke but now draws heavily on the terminology of Mt 28:18-20.

• The use of καὶ εἶπεν αὐτοῖς is probably drawn from Lk 24:46. However, the terminology is also Markan (cf. Mk 1:17; 2:19; 4:40; 9:29: 10:14:14:24).

• Πορευθέντες is derived from Mt 28:19. However, the subsequent usage of κηρύξατε may be derived from Lk 24:47. This would then be another instance of alternating Markan agreement between Matthew and Luke in one verse. In any case κηρύσσω is not unknown to Mark (12 times in Mk 1:1 to 16:8) and it is used earlier in Mark in connection with a proclamation to the whole creation (cf. Mark 14:9; Peabody, *Mark as Composer,* 242, 110).

• The reference to the connection between baptism and salvation underscores an earlier emphasis in Mark on the importance of both baptism and the Lord's Supper (see our discussion on Mk 10:39).

• Εὐαγγέλιον used in an absolute sense is characteristic of Mark.[57] Now that the disciples "see" or believe that the crucified Lord is the risen Christ they are charged to proclaim this "gospel" (cf. Peabody, *Mark as Composer,* 11 and 14, 38).

Mk 16:17-18. The author now lists five signs that will attend those who believe the gospel. Here σημεῖον is unusual for Mark. In Mk 1:1-16:8 the point is made repeatedly

---

[57] Farmer, *The Last Twelve Verses,* 94-96.

that beyond the preaching and work of Jesus there will be no additional sign of the coming of the kingdom (Mk 8:11-12; 13:4). Indeed it is the false prophets who give signs (Mk 13:22). The appearance of signs as a kind of *inclusio* to the last verses of the passage (Mk 16:17, 20) clearly reflects the influence of John (cf. Jn 20:30). The author is not interested in incorporating the sophisticated nuances of the functions of "signs" in John but, perhaps noting the connection between signs and belief in Jn 20:30-31, takes the opportunity to incorporate his list of powers and wonders as part of his unifying the appearance traditions in the Gospels. These "signs" would emerge among those who believed. Already in Mark Jesus is viewed as one who did mighty deeds by the power of the Spirit. And he commissioned the disciples to carry on this mission (Mk 6:12-13). Now, upon their return to faith the full force of these powers will burst forth. We will discuss these five signs *seriatim.*

• The specific idea of "casting out demons in Jesus' name" is found in Mk 9:33-42, which deals more generally with "acting in the name" (see esp. Mk 9:38-39//Lk 8:49-50, Peabody, *Mark as Composer,* 210, 102). Although less impressive than the evidence which supports the parallel between Mk 9:38-39 and Lk 8:49-50 in that context, there is good evidence that Mk 16:17-18 is parallel to Lk 10:17-20 (see esp. Lk 10:17, 19). Mark 16:17-18 and Lk 10:17, 19 share at least ten words. Many of these words appear in the same order in Mark and Luke. Six of the ten are in exactly the same grammatical form. The author of Mk 16:9-20 may have considerably rewritten the material from Lk 10:17-20 in accord with his own literary purposes, but the similarities between them in content, wording, and grammar are still clearly demonstrable. Many of the ideas found in Mk 16:17-20 are also present in Acts 4:29-32a, e.g., "speaking the word," "stretching out the hand to heal," "signs performed in the name of Jesus," and "believers." In short, Mark 16:17-20 seems to reflect many ideas that were important to the author of Luke-Acts.

• Although "speaking in *new* tongues" or some kind of ecstatic speech is found only here in the NT, the idea of "speaking in tongues" is found both in Acts 2:4, 11; 10:46; and 19:6 and in Paul's correspondence with the Corinthians (1 Cor 12:30; 13:1, 14:2, 4, 5, 6, 13, 18, 23, 27, 39). Clearly this was a well known communal phenomenon in early Christianity.

• "Picking up snakes in one's hands without being harmed" does not appear specifically in the NT, but the idea of touching snakes without being harmed is also found in Lk 10:17, already noted as a probable parallel to Mk 16:18 (cf. Acts 28:1-10).

• There is no parallel to this dominical affirmation anywhere else in the canonical Gospels. However Eusebius (*Hist. eccl.,* 3.39) refers to an incident in Hierapolis where Papias learned from the daughters of Philip about a certain Justus surnamed Barsabas who drank poison but suffered no harm. Such accounts are widely found in early Christian apocryphal literature.[58]

• "Touching the sick and healing them" is rather common in the Gospels, but the word used for "the sick" in Mk 16:18, ἀρρώστος, occurs only five times in the NT (Mt 14:14; 1 Cor 11:30; and three times in Mark: Mk 6:5; 6:13; and 16:18). In fact, the wording of Mk 6:5 is so similar to what is found in Mk 16:18 that one could argue that these two verses came from the same hand or that the author of Mk 16:8 deliberately followed Mk 6:5 (Peabody, *Mark as Composer,* 151, 86, cf. 139, 83).

Mk 16:19-20. Following the sequence in Lk 24, the author now rewrites Lk 24:50-53 and possibly the parallel passages in Acts (cf. Acts 1:2-11; 7:55-56) to finish his account. His obvious purpose is to paraphrase the generalized beliefs current in early Christianity, as expressed in Luke-Acts, that Jesus ascended to the right hand of God and his mission continued in the work of the disciples. Mark 16:19-20 thus serves as an epilogue, not only to the longer ending, but to the entire Gospel.

• The epilogue is constructed in the form of a ὁ μέν . . . δέ construction. In Mk 16:19 the subject is the Lord Jesus. In Mk 16:20 the subject is ἐκεῖνοι (the disciples). Also, worthy of note is the construction μετὰ τὸ λαλῆσαι. This construction complements the use of ὕστερον in Mk 16:14 in the same way μετὰ δὲ ταῦτα (Mk 16:12) complements πρῶτον in Mk 16:9. This attention to literary detail indicates that the long ending was the work of a single author.

• The use of ἀναλαμβάνω to describe the ascension is very pronounced in Acts (Acts 1:2, 11, 22). The synonym ἀναφέρω is found in Lk 24:51. The text of Lk 24:51-53 is

---

[58] Kellhoffer, *Miracle and Mission,* 417-63.

questionable and we cannot be certain what Lukan account of the ascension was available to the author.

- The "word" used absolutely is characteristic of Markan usage (Peabody, *Mark as Composer*, 69, 55).[59] Throughout Mark it is a synonym for the gospel. Thus the longer ending concludes as Mark began with a reference to the gospel (Mk 1:1). The account of the Son of God who would be brutalized and crucified before being exalted functions as both a paradigm and prerequisite for insight for all later seekers of the kingdom.

Summary

Mark's rendering of the gospel has now run its full course. Fault lines which emerged earlier in the narrative between Jesus and the disciples break wide open in this part and by the end take on a totally new configuration. Jesus has asked his disciples to stand firm and watch (Mk 13:33-37). But their pattern of failure to understand continues and finally they abandon him (Mk 14:50). On the other hand, despite total rejection, Jesus holds fast to his commitment. He dies in total humiliation and degradation.

Yet this is not the end of the story. As Jesus dies the curtain veiling the divine presence in the temple is ripped from top to bottom. The confession of a Gentile that the crucified Jesus was the Son of God is an ironic sign that a new temple not made with hands, in the form of a community of faithful people, has replaced the old temple. To enter it one must follow the way pioneered by Jesus.

And, at the very end, in the longer ending[60] even the disciples come to see and believe. Despite their obduracy and lack of faith God has fulfilled his promises in the resurrection of Jesus. Despite apparent marginalization God has brought his kingdom through a crucified Messiah. He has kept his promises. For Mark, this is the gospel.

---

[59] Farmer, *The Last Twelve Verses*, 100-102.
[60] We struggled with this but tentatively agree that something like this must be what the author of Mark intended, even if we do not have the original ending of Mark.

CONCLUSION

The task of studying the Gospel of Mark from the perspective of the Two Gospel Hypothesis has concerned some members of our research team for decades. However, when the decision was made in 1991 to postpone further work on Mark until we had completed our work on Luke's use of Matthew (1996), it had important consequences. The experience of working together on Luke over six years forged both a working style and a working team. Therefore, by the time the team, now enhanced by the addition of Thomas R. W. Longstaff, returned to its work on Mark, our collaborative process had been well refined.

When we returned to our work on Mark, it was also with an awareness that is shared by only a few of the best source critics of the Gospels; namely, that the classical arguments for the priority of Mark, especially as these were expressed by B. H. Streeter, are either deeply flawed or completely reversible. Here we have attempted to show that it is, at the very least, critically defensible to read Mark as the last and not the first of the Synoptic Gospels to be written and as a careful conflation of Matthew and Luke with Mark's own perspectives providing a distinctive overlay on his Gospel's narrative. In this sense, this book has met a modest goal set by the team at the inception of this project.

As this work neared completion, however, all of us were acutely aware that it still represents a beginning, rather than an end. It is a venture into a way of viewing Mark that has rarely been systematically pursued by NT scholars in the last century, but it is a view of Mark that is fundamental to a revised perspective on the development of the Synoptic Gospels and for a renewed understanding of the development of early Christian history and thought. Nevertheless, along the way some things have fallen into place that will surely advance the discussion of the Synoptic Problem. These would include the following.

First, Peabody and Longstaff have now produced a new research tool that provides the scholar and the student, for the first time, a complete color-coded, electronic synopsis of Mark and its parallels from the perspective of the Two Gospel Hypothesis. Whatever else may result from this study, this synopsis provides a significantly more detailed and focused presentation of the synoptic data in support of Mark's use of Matthew and Luke than we have had heretofore.

Furthermore, one of the many discoveries made in the course of developing this Markan synopsis, was that Mark took into account both of Luke's first two long sermons of Jesus in structuring his Gospel. This discovery represents an important step forward in understanding synoptic relationships. At Mk 1:21-22, although the author of Mark chose to omit the specific content of both the Sermon on the Mount in Matthew and the contextually parallel sermon in Nazareth in Luke, he clearly acknowledged that Jesus delivered a sermon at this point in the common sequence of events, as these are related by Matthew and Luke. He makes explicit use of redactional material from Mt 7:28-29 (cf. Lk 4:31-32). Then, when Mark subsequently reached the Sermon on the Plain while telling his own story of the life of Jesus (Mk 3:19//Lk 6:20-7:1), in a consistent and complementary manner, he also omitted its content and returned to follow Matthew at precisely the point where he had last made use of that Gospel.

These insights go a long way toward answering some longstanding questions about where, in Mark's sequence of events, the synopsis maker should place Matthew's Sermon on the Mount and Luke's Sermon on the Plain. The answers now appear to be as follows. First, in spite of their very similar content, these two sermons should be placed at different points in the Markan order of pericopae in a synopsis. The Sermon on the Mount should be placed so that it concludes at Mk 1:21-22 and Luke's Sermon in Nazareth should be placed in the same contextual parallel with the Sermon on the Mount at Mk 1:21-22. The Sermon on the Plain should be placed, contextually, between Mk 3:19 and Mk 3:20. On the other hand, the similar content of the Sermon on the Mount in Matthew and the Sermon on the Plain in Luke surely warrants a display of the verbal parallels within these two sermons, in spite of the fact that they should appear in different contextual parallels when compared to Mark's sequence of pericopae.

Second, most of us knew of several instances of the curious alternation of wording from Matthew and Luke within individual pericopae in Mark, but none of us were fully aware of the amount of such material until this study. In case after case, Mark's sentences or paragraphs reveal an alternation of a word or phrase found in Matthew with one found in Luke. In any individual case, or even in a few cases, one might argue that Matthew and Luke independently, and accidentally divided the wording of their Markan source neatly between them. But there are so many instances of such alternation of agreement that Mark's conflation of words and phrases from Matthew and Luke, clearly explains the data far better than does their independent use of Mark.

Third, perhaps the most striking discovery along the way was the extent and networked character of what we came to call the Markan overlay. Not only does Mark have some linguistic, structural, and theological elements that are never found in the other two Synoptic Gospels (πάλιν used retrospectively uniting two or more separated pericopae, τὸ εὐαγγέλιον used absolutely, etc.), but there are many other features of Mark that provide threads for the network we have called the Markan overlay, even though some of these threads are not wholly absent from the parallel texts of Matthew and Luke.

If this special layer of Markan material is extracted from Mark, Mark's story becomes incoherent. Therefore, neither an Ur-Markus nor a Deutero-Markus best accounts for this network of distinctively Markan material. The Markan overlay is a linguistic, stylistic, and thematic unity which is interwoven throughout the Markan Gospel. Most of this material would be attributed to the author of Mark on any analysis, so this allows us to ask again, from the perspective of the Two Source Hypothesis as classically stated by Streeter, "How did Matthew and Luke, while making independent use of Mark, manage to agree in omitting so much of the Markan overlay?" It is far more likely that we see in this overlay the compositional and theological work that this author, Mark, added to his newly edited form of the Gospel, one that he composed primarily by drawing together material from his predecessors, Matthew and Luke.

Anyone who studies the new Markan synopsis, who considers the extensive evidence of Mark's alternating use of Matthew and Luke, not only in terms of the overall order of pericopae, but in terms of the order of words and phrases within pericopae as well, and who also considers the broad and integrated character of the Markan overlay will be led to agree that the Gospel of Mark is not the earliest, primitive Gospel, but the last of the synoptics to be composed. That conclusion, admittedly, has far-reaching consequences for understanding Jesus, the Gospels, and early Christian history. It establishes a new agenda for New Testament scholarship which will require both the refinement of this study and the pursuit of those consequences which it entails.

Finally, we would add that even though the critical evidence, on balance, best supports the view that Mark is the third of the synoptics and that this evangelist carefully combined material drawn from Matthew and Luke, overlaid with editorial work that reflects his own distinctive perspectives, we do not believe that accepting this source-critical and compositional view of Mark's literary history provides any reason to denigrate or devalue Mark's form of the Gospel. It may be true that Mark will not be of great value in reconstructing the words and deeds of the historical Jesus or even the ideas and activities of the very earliest Christian communities, but Mark is a valuable Gospel nonetheless. Mark's concentrated focus on Christian faith as centered in the crucified and risen Christ and his corollary focus on the martyrs' way of Christian discipleship is not only fully in harmony with elements of Pauline theology, but it is an important focus that the vast majority of Christians throughout the centuries have claimed as authentic. Mark's story of Jesus, one of more actions than of long speeches, also provides a healthy counterpoint, within the Christian canon, to the Gospels of Matthew and John, each of which contains a number of long discourses of Jesus. It also provides an important counter to a modern tendency, manifested in the work of some contemporary scholars of the New Testament and Jesus, toward a reduction of Jesus' life and message to a collection of wisdom sayings.

But most of all, Mark's Gospel maintains its value, even as a carefully edited conflation of Matthew and Luke with its own distinctive perspective, because this evangelist is clearly the best storyteller among the Gospel writers. Although Mark's Greek literary style may lack sophistication or even adequate control of the Greek language at times, particularly when compared with Luke, Mark knows how to spin a story and it is that feature, above all, that has won his Gospel a place in the canon and in the hearts and minds of generations of readers. The dramatic Markan story of Jesus, the crucified Son of God, has been and remains, on the Two Gospel Hypothesis, a remarkable treasure of the historic Christian community of faith.

APPENDIX 1: THE MESSIANIC SECRET IN MARK

Allan J. McNicol

A century has now gone by since William Wrede wrote his pivotal work on the messianic secret.[1] Since its publication this work has remained a towering presence in Markan studies. A basic reason for its popularity in scholarly lore can be found in its proposal. Wrede argued that Mark focused upon several features of the *received* traditions of Jesus' deeds and teaching of an esoteric nature and consciously included them in his Gospel as part of a unified configuration which he called the "messianic secret." Thus, Wrede concluded that there was at least one significant element of the text of Mark that had undergone direct editorial activity by the author of Mark.

The insight that the received Jesus tradition may have undergone editorial development, coming as it did at the beginning of the twentieth century, presaged not only the era of form criticism, but a growing focus on Mark as a compiler, editor, or composer in his own right. This development remains a central feature in Markan studies to this day.

Under the general rubric of messianic secret Wrede highlighted several significant characteristics of the Markan narrative. Chief among these were:

➢ Jesus' commands of silence to both the demonic forces and to humans who were healed.

➢ Jesus' esoteric teaching to small selected groups apart from crowds.

➢ Jesus' parables, given not only to provide insight to his followers but to confuse outsiders.

➢ The disciples portrayed as dull and hard of heart with respect to understanding Jesus' identity and nature of his mission.

All of these features were thought to contribute to one unified configuration. As far as we know Wrede was the first to hypothesize that these characteristics of the narrative were all created by the author of Mark as a unified motif: the messianic secret.

Wrede viewed the messianic secret as the answer to a dilemma that he believed had emerged in early Christianity. The dilemma had to do with the tension between, on the one hand, the traditions about a non-messianic Jesus becoming Messiah at his resurrection and, on the other hand, the belief, developing in the ensuing decades after the resurrection, that Jesus' life was a revelation of his

---

[1] William Wrede, *Das Messiasgeheimnis in den Evangelien* (Göttingen: Vandenhoeck und Reprecht, 1901); ET *The Messianic Secret* (trans. J. C. G. Greig; Cambridge and London: James Clarke & Co. Ltd. 1971).

ministry as the Son of God. Wrede's genius was to propose that Mark solved the problem by combining the two traditions in a special way. Wrede read Mark as saying that throughout Jesus' ministry various hints emerged as to his divine status. But any overt claim that he was the Messiah or Son of God had to be hushed up until after his resurrection (Mk 9:9). This, in essence, is how Wrede understood Mark's creation of the messianic secret.

Variations of this hypothesis are well traveled among Markan priorists. But how does one view Wrede's conclusion if Mark is using Matthew and Luke as sources? Without the priority of Mark it is doubtful whether one could arrive at anything like Wrede's proposal for a unified secrecy configuration in Mark. This is so for two reasons. First, on the thesis that Mark is following Matthew and Luke, Mark is using accounts that, at best, are only dimly aware of the so-called earliest Christology that Wrede thought shone through such passages as Rom 1:4 and Acts 2:36. In fact, both Matthew and Luke portray Jesus as Son of God and a messianic figure *from his birth*. Second, although many features of what Wrede identified as the messianic secret are present in Matthew and Luke, the way these materials function there precludes any notion that Matthew and Luke were aware of them as a unified motif. And, if this is true for Matthew and Luke, it is likely that these elements, which appear in Mark, *also* do not constitute a unified configuration.

Now, there is no question that some of the literary features that Wrede identified as elements of the messianic secret are present in Mark. But it is questionable whether anything approximating what Wrede claimed as the essential components of the messianic secret ever existed as a unified concept in the mind of the final editor of Mark. If it had, Mark would have been far more consistent in his application of these features.[2] Thus, if these features are explicable on other grounds it is more economical to accept these grounds as an explanation than to *add* the complicating factor of a unified secrecy motif.

Essentially these features coalesce into two areas. First, since Mark was utilizing Matthew and Luke as his primary sources much of what Wrede considered messianic secret terminology was, in actuality, fragmentary preservation of the text of Matthew and Luke. Second, to the extent that Mark does utilize such terminology, he does so in the interest of his theological agenda. That is, it contributes to his argument that the only appropriate confession of Jesus is as the crucified Son of God. This explains why throughout Mark some, including those in the unseen world (both divine and

---

[2] Wrede himself conceded that Mark was not a work of consistent application of the secrecy motif. See Heiki Räisänen, *The Messianic Secret in Mark* (trans. Christopher Tuckett; Edinburgh: T&T Clark 1990), 71-75, for references to those who have made similar observations. It is noteworthy that in healing passages such as Mk 2:1-12; 3:1-6; 5:25-34; 7:24-30; 9:14-27; and 10:46-52 there is no prohibition to silence. If the secrecy motif is a signature of Mark he is hardly consistent.

demonic), perceive that Jesus has divine status; but it is only when the centurion sees him as the suffering *crucified* Son of God that humans can understand his Sonship and confess it appropriately.

Through the lens of the Two Gospel Hypothesis we now propose to make some brief observations on the major literary features of the material which Wrede thought constituted a unified configuration.[3] We believe that the reasons for their presence in Mark can be elucidated without resorting to the Wrede hypothesis.

JESUS COMMANDS BOTH DEMONIC POWERS AND HUMANS TO BE SILENT

There is no reference in Matthew to a demonic power recognizing Jesus and being asked to be silent.[4] Several commands for humans to be silent after healings do appear (Matt 8:4: 9:30; 12:16). However, Matthew connects the first instance with the need to hasten to fulfill an obligation to the Mosaic law and the latter instance with the fulfillment of a prophecy from Isaiah (Matt 12:17, 19). It is true that in Mt 9:30 there is a command to silence after the healing of the two blind men. But it is noticeable that this prohibition functions to demonstrate that Jesus' glory cannot be kept hidden (Mt 9:21). At the end of Jesus' revelatory ministry, when a similar incident occurs, Jesus gives no such prohibition (Matt 20:29-34).[5] In Mt 16:20 and 17:9 Jesus does give a definite command for silence. But here it is addressed to the disciples. In keeping with the word on Jesus' sonship in Mt 11:25-26 and 14:33 the point is that just as "pearls are not to be thrown before swine," so the truth about Jesus' nature must not be spread abroad indiscriminately but must be revealed at the appropriate time.

Luke has several instances of Jesus rebuking the demons or commanding them to be silent (Lk 4:35; 4:41; 8:29), and he has some instances in which persons healed by Jesus are commanded to be silent (Lk 5:14; 8:56). In respect to the former it is widely accepted that these situations are understood to be part of the wider motif of Luke's view of the Holy Spirit. Jesus' whole ministry is undergirded with the power of the Holy Spirit. Evil can be identified and rebuked by the Spirit. With respect to the latter, the first usage is paralleled in Matthew (Matt 8:4/Lk 5:14). The second usage (Lk 8:56) occurs in a passage that is an early foreshadowing of the resurrection. Luke is consistent in indicating that there is confusion on the matter of resurrection until Jesus explains it from the scriptures at the end of the Gospel (Lk 24:19-27; 44-49; cf. Lk 9:21, 36).

---

[3] Neil Elliott, "The Silence of the Messiah: The Function of Messianic Secret Motifs across the Synoptics," *SBL Seminar Papers*, 1993 (SBLSP 32; Atlanta, Georgia: Scholars Press, 1979), 607-10 has a succinct listing of literary motifs which we will basically follow. This seems to be a well-established reading of Wrede.

[4] Elliott, "The Silence of the Messiah," 610.

[5] Elliott, "Silence of the Messiah," 610. Indeed, Räisänen, *Messianic Secret in Mark*, 242, claims that this is the core of Mark's messianic secret teaching. Yet, as noted above, on the Two Gospel Hypothesis little of it is strictly Markan.

In Mark there is only one clearly substantiated instance, *beyond* Matthew and Luke, where Jesus commands either the demons or a human to be silent. This is Mk 7:36, where the charge comes after Jesus had earlier taken the deaf and speech impaired man aside alone (Mk 7:33). Mark 3:12 is sometimes called a unique Marcan passage. But, on the Two Gospel Hypothesis, it is paralleled with Mt 12:16 and possibly Lk 4:41. Interestingly enough, in Matthew's first instance of the healing of the two blind men there is a prohibition against speaking out (Mt 9:30); likewise, in Mark's first healing of the blind man there is a prohibition against returning to the village (Mk 8:26).[6] Thus, on the Two Gospel Hypothesis, Mark essentially reproduces what was in his sources. Why he does so ought to be explained. But it is readily apparent that it is a gross overstatement to say that the silence motif is a major feature distinguishing Mark from Matthew or Luke.

OTHER SUPPOSED FEATURES OF THE MESSIANIC SECRET

With respect to the other features of Mark which Wrede lumped into the configuration of the messianic secret we need only speak briefly.

There are a number of instances where Jesus either deliberately conceals himself or goes with a small group (often into a house) and gives esoteric teaching (e.g., Mk 1:24, 35; 4:10; 5:38, 40; 7:17, 24; 10:10; 13:3). What is striking about this is that certain elements of this literary feature probably do represent Markan editorial overlay on his source material (cf. Peabody, *Mark as Composer*, 76, 122; 41, 22-23; 158 Table M). But what is more significant is the reason Mark prefers this image. The point is that despite Jesus' proclivity to give esoteric instruction to selected groups this is only a temporary curtailment of the truth about him coming to light.[7] Thus the motif of esoteric teaching seems part of a wider theme of Jesus' hidden glory that breaks out from time to time, but will only fully emerge at the cross/resurrection. This is a far cry from Wrede's understanding that this functioned as part of a complex discussion of Christology in the early church.

Moreover, a similar point can be made with respect to the theory on parables (Mk 4:12). As we note in our critical comments there, the mystery of the kingdom is that there are those who grasp as "the word" or "gospel" that Jesus' life ending in underserved suffering is the essence of the way of the kingdom. Why some do and some do not grasp this point is governed by the mysterious purpose of God (Mk 4.11-12). But, again, it is a stretch to connect the material on the purpose of parables in Mark with a larger complex of the secret.[8]

---

[6] The additional statement "not to speak to anyone" is not found in the best tradition of the Egyptian manuscripts or D. As in Mt 20:29-34, Mark has a second healing of the blind (Bartimaeus: Mk 10:46-52). It is interesting to note that in this second account in both Matthew and Mark there is no prohibition of speaking out.

[7] Räisänen, *Messianic Secret in Mark*, 166, has noted this point when he says, "Jesus *could* not remain hidden. His glory breaks through irresistibly and the needy will not remain without help.

[8] As Räisänen, *Messianic Secret in Mark*, 143, notes, "But even so, the connection with the Messianic Secret is at

Finally, there is the incomprehension of the disciples with respect to Jesus' mission. There is no question that in a number of places Mark has accented his source material and taken the misperception of the disciples to a new level. For example, both in Mk 6:52 and 8:17 we learn about the hardening of the hearts of the disciples. There is no parallel in Matthew and Luke.

However, the issue is whether the messianic secret is the appropriate "house" for this feature of Mark, or whether there is another more plausible explanation for such an emphasis. We believe that explanation can be found in the Markan editorial attempt to underscore the problematic nature of the disciples' faith while they were with Jesus and the deeper level of insight they were given as a result of Jesus' death and resurrection. This explanation is congruent with the intra-textual logic of the narrative of Mark and has the advantage of not requiring an explanation drawn from a hypothetical view of the development of Christology in the ancient church as opposed to the inner logic of the text.

ANOTHER EXPLANATION

For the past century Wrede's tortured attempt to combine several varied themes in Mark into a unified complex called the messianic secret, has continued to haunt NT Studies like a ghost.[9] At least in the form that Wrede brought it to light, it is time to put this ghost to rest.

This does not mean that the rich lode of literary and theological themes that Wrede mined in Mark should be forgotten. These features, along with others, constitute part of the wide panorama of the Markan narrative world. Although the Wrede synthesis is implausible, especially on the Two Gospel Hypothesis, it is still possible to see that some of the features which Wrede isolated function as a coherent part of the Markan literary strategy.

For Mark, at the outset, Jesus is openly declared (at least to his readers) as the Son of God (Mk 1:1, 11). Until he is later confessed by Peter (Mk 8:29), Jesus does many acts of power that are congruent with this claim. Observers sense a special significance to Jesus' life (cf. Mk 1:45; 2:11; 4:41; 5:20).

But, even with these epiphanies, there is an equally significant feature of Jesus' withdrawal and concealment throughout his ministry. With this motif Mark is preparing the reader for a different understanding of Son of God than one which was common in the Greco-Roman world. In so doing, Mark utilizes themes from his sources and, in some instances (e.g., esoteric teaching given to a select group) extends these themes in the interest of making the point that Jesus' ministry was enveloped in

---

least a loose one. The Parable Theory cannot be made the cornerstone of that theory [i.e., Messianic Secret]."

[9] Cf. the collection of essays of famous scholars, *The Messianic Secret* (IRT 1; ed. Christopher Tuckett; Philadelphia and London: Fortress/SPCK, 1983).

mystery. Some of these themes, such as the call for silence, parables as vehicles of mystery, and the hardening of the hearts of the disciples, were used as building blocks by Wrede for his unlikely hypothesis. It is much more reasonable to see these features simply as part of Mark's strategy of explaining that it was in the divine purpose that the Son of God who manifested himself in power in Galilee must inaugurate God's kingdom not by mighty deeds but through the way of the cross. If after all, everyone had recognized who Jesus really was, who would have crucified him?

This theme is driven home in the latter part of Mark, by the esoteric teachings on the death and resurrection of the Son of Man (for Mark a divine figure), in the passion predictions (Mk 8:31; 9:30-32; 10:33-34), and finally in the revelation of the crucified Son of God at the cross (Mk 15:39). It is very noticeable that after Mk 8:31, the only call for silence serves to highlight this point (Mk 9:9). For Mark, this was "the word" or "gospel" he attempted to set forth. It was not his intent to create a secret motif to solve a problem of early Christian Christology.

APPENDIX 2: THE LINGUISTIC ARGUMENT AND THE SYNOPTIC PROBLEM:

Common Vocabulary Items and Selected Phrases As Indicators of the Direction of Literary Dependence Between Synoptic Gospels

David Barrett Peabody

In recent years, the value of the "linguistic argument" for solving the Synoptic Problem has been questioned. We believe, however, that the doubt that has been cast upon the value of this argument is not appropriate, at least as it has been constructed and used by some scholars. One of these scholars whose work we believe to be worth revisiting, restudying and even adopting for current use is Eduard Zeller.[1]

Each word or phrase in each of the lists that conclude this article is believed to meet Eduard Zeller's stringent criteria, outlined already in 1843, as a direction indicator of literary dependence between any two of the Synoptic Gospels.[2] With regard to these criteria, Zeller wrote,

> If we then pursue this connection [among the synoptic gospels] more precisely, a relationship among these writings comes to light also with respect to the vocabulary --- which is the only respect which can be taken into consideration here --- which is similar to what can also be demonstrated from a consideration of their contents, in spite of the most recently revived preference for Mark. That is, Luke has the most of that which is peculiar; Mark has the least. However, with respect to what is common the greatest originality seems to lie on the side of Matthew. The least, on the side of Mark. However, isolated exceptions always provide something unsteadying in this relationship. With regard to what is common, certainly it is often difficult to decide to whom an expression may have belonged originally. If a word is found in all the gospels with equal frequency or in all of them with equal rarity or even in one gospel, but not in the same narrative context as another gospel, then there is no criterion for making this decision. On the other hand, the circumstance may be discovered not too infrequently that the one evangelist uses

---

[1] The lists that conclude this article represent limited expansions and refinements of lists made by Eduard Zeller in his article, "Studien zur neutestamentlichen Theologie. 4. Vergleichende Uebersicht über den Wörtervorrath der sämmtlichen neutestamentlichen Schriftsteller." *Theologische Jahrbücher* (Tübingen, 1843): 443–543, especially 527–37.

[2] See Peabody's discussions of Zeller's method for making linguistic characteristics of the Synoptic Gospels of service in solving the Synoptic Problem and Peabody's work with these representative samplings of relevant data in *Mark as Composer* (Macon, Ga.: Mercer University Press, 1987), 168–71, and in "Chapters in the History of the Linguistic Argument for Solving the Synoptic Problem: The Nineteenth Century in Context," in *Jesus, the Gospels and the Church: Essays in Honor of William R. Farmer* (ed. E. P. Sanders, Macon, Ga.: Mercer University Press, 1987), 47-68, esp. 61-67.

an expression *only*[3] in such narrative contexts where another evangelist also has it, while the latter, by contrast, uses the same expression also in yet further literary contexts for which the first provides no parallel. In this situation, it is probable that the expression belonged to the characteristic vocabulary of the second evangelist, and, should such cases be repeated a number of times in a manner such that the greater originality of expression falls to one and the same evangelist in all or in the majority of cases, then we would be justified in assuming that he had been the source from which the other had drawn.[4]

When Zeller applied his method for making shared vocabulary items and selected phrases of each of the Synoptic Gospels of service in solving the Synoptic Problem, the data support the following conclusions, which have also been used to name the tables below.

Table 1 - Luke Depends on Mark. (51 items support this conclusion)

Table 2 - Luke Depends on Matthew. (40 supportive items)

Table 3 - Mark Depends on Luke (134 supportive items)

Table 4 - Mark Depends on Matthew (194 supportive items)

Table 5 - Matthew Depends on Luke (58 supportive items)

Table 6 - Matthew Depends on Mark (82 supportive items)

As may be seen from this abstract of his work, Zeller called attention to data that could be taken to support every possible direction of literary dependence between the Synoptic Gospels. He, therefore, advocated a method whereby these data would be "weighed" in drawing conclusions about the dominant direction of literary dependence between any two of these Gospels.

Since Zeller had to place some data on both sides of the scale, Zeller's argument as a whole cannot be said to provide "one-way" evidence. However, the evidence provided by any particular linguistic characteristic may be said to provide a "one-way" indicator of literary dependence, at least when Zeller's most basic criteria are applied, as distinguished from the subsidiary considerations he used to explain anomalous data. In any case, Zeller talked about weighing the relevant evidence and, keeping with this metaphor, unless the scale is perfectly and equally balanced, the more weighty evidence can only tip the balance of a scale in one way.

---

[3] Italics added.
[4] See Zeller, "Wortervorrath," 527–28; ET in Peabody, "Chapters," 62.

The Lighter Side of the Scale	The Heavier Side of the Scale
82 Matthew Depends on Mark	Mark Depends on Matthew 194
51 Luke Depends on Mark	Mark Depends on Luke 134
40 Luke Depends on Matthew	Matthew Depends on Luke 58

As indicated in the graphic display above, there is more than twice the amount of this type of linguistic evidence weighing in favor of Matthew's priority to Mark (194 items in table 4) than there is comparable evidence that would weigh in the direction of Mark's priority to Matthew (82 items in table 6). In balance, therefore, Zeller concluded that these data supported the view that Mark was literarily dependent upon Matthew.

Something comparable is true about the weight of the evidence when the vocabulary common to Luke and Mark is considered. Specifically, there is more than twice as much evidence indicating Mark's literary dependence upon Luke (134 items in table 3) as there is comparable evidence indicating Luke's literary dependence upon Mark (51 items in table 1).

Zeller, therefore, concluded from both of these sets of data that Mark's use of both Matthew and Luke, which accords with the Griesbach Hypothesis, was much more likely than Markan priority to either Matthew or Luke. In fact, based upon these data alone, it appeared to be more than twice as likely that Mark was literarily dependent upon both Matthew and Luke than that either Matthew or Luke was literarily dependent upon Mark.

Once he had drawn his primary conclusions from the simple weight of the literary evidence in comparing the vocabulary and selected phrases shared by Mark and Matthew and Mark and Luke, Zeller also provided secondary explanations for those data that were anomalous for his more weighty conclusion that the Griesbach hypothesis best explained these data.

For example, Zeller felt constrained to provide an explanation of the 82 items in table 6, on the lighter side of the scale, which seemed to support Mark's priority to Matthew and were, therefore, anomalous for the Griesbach Hypothesis, and an explanation of the 51 items in Table 1 that seemed to support Mark's priority to Luke, as well as an explanation for the imbalance of the raw data, with respect to the Griesbach hypothesis, when he compared the vocabulary and selected phrases shared by Matthew and Luke.[5]

---

[5] See, Zeller, "Wortervorrath," 531–32; cf. Peabody, "Chapters," 64.

With reference to those words and phrases that seemed to argue for Matthew's literary dependence upon Mark (82 items), Zeller responded with the following words.

> But even the words which were cited first [in favor of Mark's priority to Matthew] can prove nothing against the greater originality of Matthew; not only because their number stands in hardly any proportion to those cited for Matthew, but also because one may discover also something which is very noteworthy, [namely, that] almost none of the expressions in Mark's list would be designated as favorite words of the author on the basis of the frequency with which they are repeated like these in Matthew: ἀναχωρεῖν, ἀποδιδόναι, γέεννα, εἰσέρχεσθαι εἰς τὴν ζωήν, θησαυρός, καλεῖν, κόσμος, μισθός, ναί, ὅμοιος and ὅπως, ὄχλοι, ὁ πατὴρ ὁ ἐν τοῖς οὐρανοῖς (ὁ οὐράνιος), πονηρός, πρόβατον, προφήτης, προσφέρειν, πρόσωπον, υἱὸς Δαυίδ. Moreover, on this ground too they cannot be used as an appeal against the general canon that we are employing here. That a copyist, who is not entirely dependent [upon his source(s) may find isolated expressions in his original which are otherwise already current with him and which he, therefore, also employs where they are lacking in the original comes as no surprise. However, if this [disproportionate] relation takes place not simply in isolated cases, if it is extended to quite an overburdening proportion of the points of literary contact [between two evangelists], if a long list of favorite expressions of one author are supposed to have been borrowed from a few scattered expressions of another, then one would probably call this a reversal of the natural connection between cause and effect and a forced labeling of something as earlier which shows off its [literary] dependence in all places.[6]

When Zeller compared the vocabulary and selected phrases shared by Matthew and Luke, however, even the raw data were problematic for the Griesbach hypothesis. Specifically, the data slightly supported Matthew's literary dependence upon Luke (58 items in table 5) more than Luke's priority to Matthew (40 items in table 2).

In response to this anomaly for the Griesbach hypothesis, Zeller first admitted that "[t]he lexical relationship of Mt and Lk provides a less decisive indication (Merkmale) [of literary dependence.]"[7] Then, after presenting all of the relevant evidence, Zeller wrote in more detail.

> Nevertheless, a comparison of the data cited above [comparing the vocabularies and selected phrases common to Matthew and Luke] also speaks this time for the greater originality of Matthew. Generally, Luke has a much richer vocabulary than Mt, and so it cannot appear strange, even in the case when the presentation of the first Evangelist is the older one, many a word in him

---

[6] Zeller, "Wortervorrath," 531–32.
[7] Ibid., 533.

[Matthew], which the former one [Luke] used, at the same time is to be met with as his [Matthew's] original property. Furthermore, however, this also must come into consideration: that Luke, to conclude from his own parts of his presentation in individual pericopae (like Lk 1-2, Acts 3-4, 10:1-11:18, chapter 13f.) not seldom has made himself dependent even on the expression of his sources; so, even in a longer pursuit with the writing of Mt, an individual part could go over from the latter [Mt] into his own [Luke's] linguistic usage. Finally, the main thing is that the expressions by which Luke has the advantage over Mt are, for our question, not of the same weight as those which seem to have belonged to the original linguistic treasury of Mt. The latter are, for the most part, termini technici, keywords of the proclamation of the gospel by which the maxims are naturally stitched together, the πατήρ ἐν τοῖς οὐρανοῖς, the υἱὸς Δαυίδ, the one who proclaims him, the ὑποκριταὶ, the γεννήματα ἐχιδνῶν, the ὀλιγόπιστοι, the σκάνδαλα, against which he struggles, the βρυγμός τῶν ὀδόντων, the one who has converted the unbelievers, or characteristic turns of phrase, like the frequent διὰ τοῦτο, the solemn ἀμὴν λέγω ὑμῖν. On the other hand, among the words which Matthew could have borrowed from Lk, no such significance and not so close a connection with the content of the gospel narrative can be demonstrated. Now, if expressions precisely of the first kind are all clues to the original property of the first Evangelist, then all probability is at hand, that even the solemn presentation of those [same] expressions [in Luke] are to be found in him [Matthew] in their greatest originality.[8]

Later in the history of the application of this linguistic argument, however, when H. J. Holtzmann misunderstood Zeller's method for making the linguistic characteristics of the several evangelists of service in solving the Synoptic Problem and utilized Zeller's secondary explanations of the evidence on the lighter side of his scale in support of Holtzmann's Two Source Theory, academic "slippage" took place in the discussion of the linguistic argument for solving the Synoptic Problem that has yet to be fully recognized and corrected.

For instance, Holtzmann assumed that a simple analysis of comparative frequency of vocabulary items and selected phrases between two Gospels was telling evidence of literary dependence and many scholars have followed him in this mistake. It would seem that Holtzmann and his followers did not pay sufficient attention to Zeller's use of the word only in the excerpt from his work quoted in English translation above. Clearly, Zeller had more stringent criteria than simple comparative frequency of occurrence of words and phrases. He made use of more refined linguistic evidence in his more sophisticated and balanced argument for determining the more probable direction of literary dependence between any two of the Synoptic Gospels.

---

[8] Ibid., 535–36.

THE LINGUISTIC ARGUMENT AND THE SYNOPTIC PROBLEM

What follows below are twelve tables of data drawn from Zeller's article of 1843. To enhance the usefulness of these tables, the data within them have been sorted in two ways.

First, the words and phrases have been sorted alphabetically (tables 1a, 2a, 3a, etc.) The "a" stands for "alphabetical" sorting. Then, these same data are presented in descending order of frequency in which these words and phrases appear in the "dominant" or "non-dependent" Gospel (tables 1f, 2f, 3f, etc.). The "f" stands for sorting by descending order of "frequency." To illustrate this second sorting arrangement, the first word in table 1f is καθεύδειν which appears 8 times in Mark and only 2 times in Luke, both in parallel with Markan usages of this same word. The second word in table 1f is πέραν, which occurs 7 times in Mark and only 1 time in Luke in a passage paralleled by a Markan usage, etc.

Table 1a. Words and Phrases That Suggest		
Luke Depends on Mark – Alphabetical Sorting		
Word or Phrase Occurrences	Occurrences in Mark	Occurrences in Luke
ἅλας	3	2
ἁλιεύς	2	1
ἅλυσις	3	1
Ἀλφαῖος	2	1
Ἀνδρέας	4	1
ἀποκαθίσταναι	3	1
ἀποκεφαλίζειν	2	1
βαραββᾶς	3	1
βασανίζειν	2	1
βλασφημία	3	1
γαζοφυλακεῖον	3	1
γρηγορεῖν	6	1
δαιμονίζεσθαι	4	1
διδαχή	5	1
ἐκπνεῖν	2	1
ἐμπτύειν	3	1
ἔναντος	2	1
Ζεβεδαῖος	4	1
Ἡρωδίας	3	1
θανατοῦν	2	1
ἰσχύς	2	1
καθεύδειν	8	2
κάμηλος	2	1
καρποφορεῖν	2	1
κατέναντι	3	1
κλάσμα	4	1
κύκλῳ	3	1
λεγιών	2	1
λευκός	2	1
μαρτυρία	3	1

μνῆμα	4	3
νυμφίος	3	2
ξηραίνειν	6	1
πεδή	2	1
πειράζειν	4	2
πεντακισχίλιοι	2	1
πέραν	7	1
περιβλέπεσθαι	6	1
περίλυπος	2	1
πλανᾶν	4	1
σίδων	3	1
σπαράσσειν	2	1
σταχύς	3	1
στρωννύειν	2	1
συνακολουθεῖν	2	1
συνέδριον	3	1
τιμᾶν	3	1
τολμᾶν	2	1
φιμοῦν	2	1
ψευδομαρτυρεῖν	3	1
ὠφελεῖν	3	1

Table 1f. Words and Phrases That Suggest Luke Depends on Mark - Frequency Sort		
Word or Phrase	Occurrences in Mark	Occurrences in Luke
καθεύδειν	8	2
πέραν	7	1
γρηγορεῖν	6	1
ξηραίνειν	6	1
περιβλέπεσθαι	6	1
διδαχή	5	1
Ἀνδρέας	4	1
δαιμονίζεσθαι	4	1
Ζεβεδαῖος	4	1
κλάσμα	4	1
μνῆμα	4	3
πειράζειν	4	2
πλανᾶν	4	1
ἅλας	3	2
ἅλυσις	3	1
ἀποκαθίσταναι	3	1
βαραββᾶς	3	1
βλασφημία	3	1
γαζοφυλακεῖον	3	1
ἐμπτύειν	3	1
Ἡρῳδίας	3	1
κατέναντι	3	1
κύκλῳ	3	1
μαρτυρία	3	1

νυμφίος	3	2
σίδων	3	1
στάχυς	3	1
συνέδριον	3	1
τιμᾶν	3	1
ψευδομαρτυρεῖν	3	1
ὠφελεῖν	3	1
ἁλιεύς	2	1
Ἀλφαῖος	2	1
ἀποκεφαλίζειν	2	1
βασανίζειν	2	1
ἐκπνεῖν	2	1
ἔναντος	2	1
θανατοῦν	2	1
ἰσχύς	2	1
κάμηλος	2	1
καρποφορεῖν	2	1
λεγιών	2	1
λευκός	2	1
πεδή	2	1
πεντακισχίλιοι	2	1
περίλυπος	2	1
σπαράσσειν	2	1
στρωννύειν	2	1
συνακολουθεῖν	2	1
τολμᾶν	2	1
ψιμοῦν	2	1

Table 2a. Words and Phrases that Suggest Luke Depends on Matthew - Alphabetical Sort		
Word or Phrase	Occurrences in Matthew	Occurrences in Luke
ἀμὴν λέγω ὑμῖν	31	3
ἀνάπαυσις	2	1
βασανίζειν	3	1
βόθυνος	2	1
γέεννα	7	1
γεννήματα ἐχιδνῶν	3	1
δαιμονίζεσθαι	7	1
διὰ τοῦτο to begin a sentence	11	4
ἐγερθείς as a colorful addition to a verb of motion	ca. 8-10	2
ἐκεῖ ἔσται ὁ κλαυθμὸς καὶ ὁ βρυγμὸς τῶν ὀδόντων	5	1
ἔνδυμα	7	1
ἔνεκεν	6	2-5
ζύμη	5	2
θανατοῦν	3	1
θέρισμος	6	3
θησαυρός	8	4

καθεύδειν	7	2
κακῶς ἔχειν	5	2
κάλαμος	5	1
ἀπὸ καταβολῆς κόσμου	2	1
κατακρίνειν	4	2
κερδαίνειν	6	1
κλάδος	3	1
κράσπεδον	3	1
κρίσις	12	4
νυμφίος	7	2
ξηραίνειν	3	1
ὀλιγόπιστοι	4	1
ὁ πατὴρ ὁ οὐράνιος	5	0
ὁ πατὴρ ὁ ἐν οὐρανοῖς	12	1
ποσάκις	2	1
πρόβατον	11	2
σαπρός	5	2
σκάνδαλον	5	1
σκανδαλίζεσθαι	14	2
συλλέγειν	7	1
υἱὸς Δαυίδ	9	3
ὑποκριτής	14	2
φιλεῖν	5	2
φωτεινός	2 (2 contexts)	3 (1 Context)
χόρτος	3	1

Table 2f. Words and Phrases that Suggest Luke Depends on Matthew - Frequency Sort		
Word or Phrase	**Occurrences in Matthew**	**Occurrences in Luke**
ἀμὴν λέγω ὑμῖν	31	3
σκανδαλίζεσθαι	14	2
ὑποκριτής	14	2
ὁ πατὴρ ὁ οὐράνιος	5	0
ὁ πατὴρ ὁ ἐν οὐρανοῖς	12	1
κρίσις	12	4
διὰ τοῦτο to begin a sentence	11	4
πρόβατον	11	2
υἱὸς Δαυίδ	9	3
ἐγερθείς as a colorful addition to a verb of motion	ca. 8-10	2
θησαυρός	8	4
γέεννα	7	1
δαιμονίζεσθαι	7	1
ἔνδυμα	7	1
συλλέγειν	7	1
καθεύδειν	7	2
νυμφίος	7	2
κερδαίνειν	6	1
ἔνεκεν	6	2-5

θέρισμος	6	3
ἐκεῖ ἔσται ὁ κλαυθμὸς καὶ ὁ βρυγμὸς τῶν ὀδόντων	5	1
κάλαμος	5	1
ζύμη	5	2
φιλεῖν	5	2
σκάνδαλον	5	1
κακῶς ἔχειν	5	2
σαπρός	5	2
ὀλιγόπιστοι	4	1
κατακρίνειν	4	2
βασανίζειν	3	1
γεννήματα ἐχιδνῶν	3	1
θανατοῦν	3	1
κλάδος	3	1
κράσπεδον	3	1
ξηραίνειν	3	1
χόρτος	3	1
ἀνάπαυσις	2	1
βόθυνος	2	1
ἀπὸ καταβολῆς κόσμου	2	1
ποσάκις	2	1
φωτεινός	2 (2 contexts)	3 (1 Context)

Table 3a. Words and Phrases that Suggest Mark Depends on Luke - Alphabetical Sort		
Word or Phrase	**Occurrences in Mark**	**Occurrences in Luke**
Ἀβραάμ	1	15
ἀγαθός	4	16
αἷμα	3	8
ἄκανθαι	3	4
ἀμπελών	5	7
ἀνακλίνειν	1	3
ἀνάστασις	2	6
ἄπιστος	1	2
ἀποδημεῖν	1	2
ἀποδιδόναι	1	8
ἀπόστολος	1	6
ἀργύριον	1	4
ἄρχων	1	8
ἄρωμα	1	2
ἀσπασμός	1	5
ἀφαιρεῖν	1	4
ἄφεσις	2	5
βαστάζειν	1	5
βάτος	1	2
βεελζεβούλ	1	3
βίος	1	4
βόσκειν	2	3

Γαλιλαῖος	1	5
γαμίζειν	1	3
γαστήρ	1	2
Γερασηνός	1	2
γονεῖς	1	6
δεικνύναι	2	4
δέχεσθαι	6	16
διαθήκη	1	2
διαμερίζειν	1	6
διάνοια	1	2
διεγείρειν	1	2
δοξάζειν	1	9
δῶμα	1	3
ἐγγύς	2	3
εἰρήνη	1	13
ἕκτος	1	3
ἐκχύνεσθαι	1	3
ἐντρέπειν	1	3
ἐπίβλημα	1	2
ἐπισκιάζειν	1	2
ἔτος	2	15
εὐδοκεῖν	1	2
εὐθύς adjective	1	2
εὔκοπος	2	3
ἐχθρός	1	8
ζῆν	3	6
ἡγεμών	1	2
θηλάζειν	1	2
θησαυρός	1	4
θύειν	1	4
Ἰακώβ	1	4
ἱερεύς	2	5
Ἰσαάκ	1	3
καθαρισμός	1	2
Καῖσαρ	4	7
κατάλυμα	1	2
κατασκευάζειν	1	2
καταφιλεῖν	1	3
κατεσθίω	1	3
κενός	1	3
κλαίειν	4	11
κληρονομεῖν	1	2
κληρονομία	1	2
κόκκος	1	2
κρίμα	1	3
κρυπτός	1	2
κωλύειν	3	6
λέπρα	1	2
λεπτόν	1	2
Λευί	1	4
λίμος	1	4

λυχνία	1	2
λύχνος	1	6
μακρός	1	3
μάρτυς	1	2
μέριμνα	1	2
μετάνοια	1	5
μέτρον	1	2
μισεῖν	1	7
μοιχεύειν	1	3
νέος	2	7
νόσος	1	4
ξηρός	1	3
οἰκοδεσπότης	1	4
ὁμοιοῦν	1	3
ὄπισθεν	1	2
οὔ	1	2
οὐαί	2	15
παλαιός	3	5
παρατηρεῖν	1	3
πάσχα	5	7
πατάσσειν	1	2
πειρασμός	1	6
πενθερά	1	3
πεντήκοντα	1	3
περισσεύειν	1	4
περίχωρος	1	5
πετεινόν	2	4
πήρα	1	4
πίστις	5	11
πλείων, πλεῖον	1	9
πλούσιος	2	11
πρό	1	7
προφήτης	6	29
προσδέχεσθαι	1	5
προσφέρειν	3	4
προστιθέναι	1	7
πρωτοκαθεδρία	1	2
πρωτοκλισία	1	3
πυρετός	1	2
ῥύσις	1	2
σαλεύειν	1	4
σεαυτοῦ	3	6
σήμερον	1	11
σίναπι	1	2
σκηνή	1	2
σκότος	1	4
σκύλλειν	1	2
στάσις	1	2
συλλαλεῖν	1	3
συλλαμβάνειν	1	7
τράχηλος	1	2

ὑπαντᾶν	1	2
ὑπέρ	2	5
ὑπόδημα	1	4
ὕψιστος	2	7
φυλάσσειν	1	6
φυτεύειν	1	4
φῶς	1	7
χάρα	1	8
χηρά	3	9
ὦ	1	2

Table 3f. Words and Phrases that Suggest Mark Depends on Luke - Frequency Sort		
Word or Phrase	Occurrences in Mark	Occurrences in Luke
προφήτης	6	29
ἀγαθός	4	16
δέχεσθαι	6	16
Ἀβραάμ	1	15
ἔτος	2	15
οὐαί	2	15
εἰρήνη	1	13
σήμερον	1	11
πλούσιος	2	11
κλαίειν	4	11
πίστις	5	11
δοξάζειν	1	9
πλείων, πλεῖον	1	9
χηρά	3	9
ἀποδιδόναι	1	8
ἄρχων	1	8
ἐχθρός	1	8
χάρα	1	8
αἷμα	3	8
μισεῖν	1	7
πρό	1	7
προστιθέναι	1	7
συλλαμβάνειν	1	7
φῶς	1	7
νέος	2	7
ὕψιστος	2	7
Καῖσαρ	4	7
ἀμπελών	5	7
πάσχα	5	7
ἀπόστολος	1	6
γονεῖς	1	6
διαμερίζειν	1	6
λύχνος	1	6
πειρασμός	1	6
φυλάσσειν	1	6

ἀνάστασις	2	6
ζῆν	3	6
κωλύειν	3	6
σεαυτοῦ	3	6
ἀσπασμός	1	5
βαστάζειν	1	5
Γαλιλαῖος	1	5
μετάνοια	1	5
περίχωρος	1	5
προσδέχεσθαι	1	5
ἄφεσις	2	5
ἱερεύς	2	5
ὑπέρ	2	5
παλαιός	3	5
ἀργύριον	1	4
ἀφαιρεῖν	1	4
βίος	1	4
θησαυρός	1	4
θύειν	1	4
Ἰακώβ	1	4
Λευί	1	4
λίμος	1	4
νόσος	1	4
οἰκοδεσπότης	1	4
περισσεύειν	1	4
πήρα	1	4
σαλεύειν	1	4
σκότος	1	4
ὑπόδημα	1	4
φυτεύειν	1	4
δεικνύναι	2	4
πετεινόν	2	4
ἄκανθαι	3	4
προσφέρειν	3	4
ἀνακλίνειν	1	3
βεελζεβούλ	1	3
γαμίζειν	1	3
δῶμα	1	3
ἕκτος	1	3
ἐκχύνεσθαι	1	3
ἐντρέπειν	1	3
Ἰσαάκ	1	3
καταφιλεῖν	1	3
κατεσθίω	1	3
κενός	1	3
κρίμα	1	3
μακρός	1	3
μοιχεύειν	1	3
ξηρός	1	3
ὁμοιοῦν	1	3
παρατηρεῖν	1	3

πενθερά	1	3
πεντήκοντα	1	3
πρωτοκλισία	1	3
συλλαλεῖν	1	3
βόσκειν	2	3
ἐγγύς	2	3
εὔκοπος	2	3
ἄπιστος	1	2
ἀποδημεῖν	1	2
ἄρωμα	1	2
βάτος	1	2
γαστήρ	1	2
Γερασηνός	1	2
διαθήκη	1	2
διάνοια	1	2
διεγείρειν	1	2
ἐπίβλημα	1	2
ἐπισκιάζειν	1	2
εὐδοκεῖν	1	2
εὐθύς adjective	1	2
ἡγεμών	1	2
θηλάζειν	1	2
καθαρισμός	1	2
κατάλυμα	1	2
κατασκευάζειν	1	2
κληρονομεῖν	1	2
κληρονομία	1	2
κόκκος	1	2
κρυπτός	1	2
λέπρα	1	2
λεπτόν	1	2
λυχνία	1	2
μάρτυς	1	2
μέριμνα	1	2
μέτρον	1	2
ὄπισθεν	1	2
οὔ	1	2
πατάσσειν	1	2
πρωτοκαθεδρία	1	2
πυρετός	1	2
ῥύσις	1	2
σίναπι	1	2
σκηνή	1	2
σκύλλειν	1	2
στάσις	1	2
τράχηλος	1	2
ὑπαντᾶν	1	2
ὦ	1	2

Table 4a. Words and Phrases That Suggest Mark Depends on Matthew - Alphabetical Sort		
Word or Phrase	**Occurrences in Mark**	**Occurrences in Matthew**
Ἀβραάμ	1	7
ἄγγελος	6	20
ἀγέλη	2	3
αἰτία	1	3
αἰών	4	8
ἄκανθαι	3	5
ἀληθῶς	2	3
ἀναγινώσκειν	4	7
ἀνακεῖσθαι	3	5
ἀνακλίνειν	1	2
ἀνάστασις	2	4
ἀναχωρεῖν	1	10
ἀντί	1	5
ἀποδημεῖν	1	3
ἀποδιδόναι	1	18
ἀποστάσιον	1	2
ἀπώλεια	1	2
ἀργύριον	1	9
ἀρνεῖσθαι	2	4
ἄρχων	1	5
ἀσθενής	1	3
ἀστήρ	1	5
βαπτιστής	2	7
βαραββᾶς	3	5
βασανίζειν	2	3
βεεζεβούλ	1	3
βλασφημία	3	4
γαμίζειν	1	3
γαστήρ	1	3
γεννᾶν	1	45
γεωργός	5	6
γωνία	1	2
Δαυίδ	7	17
δέκα	1	3
διακονεῖν	5	6
διάκονος	2	3
διακρίνειν	1	2
διασκορπίζειν	1	3
δοξάζειν	1	4
δοῦλος	5	30
δῶμα	1	2
δῶρον	1	9
ἐγγίζειν	3	7
ἐγγύς	2	3
ἕκαστος	1	4
ἐκδιδόναι	1	2
ἐκδύειν	1	2

ἐκλεκτός	3	4
ἐκτείνειν	3	6
ἔκτος	1	2
ἐκχύνεσθαι	1	2
ἐμπαίζειν	3	5
ἔνατος	2	3
ἔξεστι	6	9
ἐξομολογεῖν	1	2
ἐργάζεσθαι	1	4
εὐδοκεῖν	1	3
εὐώνυμος	2	5
ἐχθρός	1	7
ἕως = conjunction	15	48
ζῆν	3	6
ἡγεμών	1	10
Ἠσαΐας	2	6
θάνατος	6	7
θανατοῦν	2	3
θέλημα	1	6
θερισμός	1	6
θηλάζειν	1	2
θησαυρός	1	9
θλῖψις	3	4
θρίξ	1	3
Ἰακώβ	1	6
ἰδού	7	62
ἱερεύς	2	3
Ἰορδάνης	4	6
Ἰουδαία	4	8
Ἰούδας	4	10
Ἰσαάκ	1	4
καθέδρα	1	2
κακῶς	4	7
κάλαμος	2	5
κάμηλος	2	3
καταλύειν	3	5
καταμαρτυρεῖν	1	2
καταρτίζειν	1	2
κερδαίνειν	1	6
κῆνσος	1	3
κινεῖν	1	2
κλέπτειν	1	5
κοιλία	1	3
κόκκος	1	2
κόπτειν	1	3
κόσμος	3	8
κράσπεδον	1	3
κρυπτός	1	5
κυλλός	1	3
κῦμα	1	2
λαός	2	14

λεπρός	2	4
λευκός	2	3
λῃστής	3	4
λυπεῖν	2	6
λύχνος	1	2
Μαθθαῖος	1	2
μανθάνειν	1	3
Μαρία	8	11
μάρτυς	1	2
μαστιγοῦν	1	3
μάχαιρα	3	7
μέν	6	20
μένειν	2	3
μετάνοια	1	2
μέτρον	1	2
μισεῖν	1	5
μισθός	1	10
μοιχεύειν	1	4
μύλος	1	2
ναί	1	9
νοεῖν	3	4
νόσος	1	5
νυμφών	1	2
οἰκοδομεῖν	4	8
ὁμοιοῦν	1	8
ὀνειδίζειν	2	3
ὄπισθεν	1	2
ὅπως	1	17
ὅρκος	1	4
ὀρύσσειν	1	2
ὀρχεῖσθαι	1	2
οὔ	1	4
οὐαί	2	12
οὖν	5	57
παράπτωμα	1	2
πατάσσειν	1	2
πεινᾶν	2	9
πειράζειν	4	6
πειρασμός	1	2
πενθερά	1	2
πέντε	3	12
περιάγειν	1	3
πετεινόν	2	4
πέτρα	1	5
πιπράσκειν	1	3
πληροῦν	2	16
πόθεν	3	5
ποῖος	4	7
ποιμήν	2	3
πορνεία	1	3
ποταμός	1	3

ποτίζειν	2	5
πρίν	2	3
πρό	1	5
πρόβατον	2	11
προστιθέναι	1	2
πρόσωπον	3	10
προτάσσειν	1	2
προφητεύειν	2	4
πωλεῖν	3	6
Σαδδουκαῖοι	1	7
σαλεύειν	1	2
σάρξ	4	5
σεαυτοῦ	3	5
σεισμός	1	4
σημεῖον	7	13
σίναπι	1	2
σῖτος	1	4
σκότος	1	6
σοφία	1	3
σταυρός	4	5
στρατιώτης	1	3
συκῆ	4	5
συμβούλιον	2	5
ταράσσειν	1	2
τιμᾶν	3	6
τρεῖς, τρία	7	12
τριάκοντα	2	5
τύπτειν	1	2
ὑπαντᾶν	1	2
ὑπόδημα	1	2
ὑποκριτής	1	13
ὑπομένειν	1	2
ὑψηλός	1	2
φιλεῖν	1	5
φονεύειν	1	5
φυλακή	3	10
φυτεύειν	1	2
χαρά	1	6
χειμών	1	2
χόρτος	2	3
χωλός	1	5
χωρίς	1	3
ψευδοπροφήτης	1	3
ὦ	1	2
ὡσαννά	2	3

Table 4f. Words and Phrases That Suggest Mark Depends on Matthew - Frequency Sort		
Word or Phrase	**Occurrences in Mark**	**Occurrences in Matthew**
ἰδού	7	62
οὖν	5	57
ἕως = conjunction	15	48
γεννᾶν	1	45
δοῦλος	5	30
ἄγγελος	6	20
μέν	6	20
ἀποδιδόναι	1	18
ὅπως	1	17
Δαυίδ	7	17
πληροῦν	2	16
λαός	2	14
ὑποκριτής	1	13
σημεῖον	7	13
οὐαί	2	12
πέντε	3	12
τρεῖς, τρία	7	12
πρόβατον	2	11
Μαρία	8	11
ἀναχωρεῖν	1	10
ἡγεμών	1	10
μισθός	1	10
πρόσωπον	3	10
φυλακή	3	10
Ἰούδας	4	10
ἀργύριον	1	9
δῶρον	1	9
θησαυρός	1	9
ναί	1	9
πεινᾶν	2	9
ἔζωιι	6	9
ὁμοιοῦν	1	8
κόσμος	3	8
αἰών	4	8
Ἰουδαία	4	8
οἰκοδομεῖν	4	8
Ἀβραάμ	1	7
ἐχθρός	1	7
Σαδδουκαῖοι	1	7
βαπτιστής	2	7
ἐγγίζειν	3	7
μάχαιρα	3	7
ἀναγινώσκειν	4	7
κακῶς	4	7
ποῖος	4	7
θάνατος	6	7

θέλημα	1	6
θερισμός	1	6
Ἰακώβ	1	6
κερδαίνειν	1	6
σκότος	1	6
χαρά	1	6
Ἠσαΐας	2	6
λυπεῖν	2	6
ἐκτείνειν	3	6
ζῆν	3	6
πωλεῖν	3	6
τιμᾶν	3	6
Ἰορδάνης	4	6
πειράζειν	4	6
γεωργός	5	6
διακονεῖν	5	6
ἀντί	1	5
ἄρχων	1	5
ἀστήρ	1	5
κλέπτειν	1	5
κρυπτός	1	5
μισεῖν	1	5
νόσος	1	5
πέτρα	1	5
πρό	1	5
φιλεῖν	1	5
φονεύειν	1	5
χωλός	1	5
εὐώνυμος	2	5
κάλαμος	2	5
ποτίζειν	2	5
συμβούλιον	2	5
τριάκοντα	2	5
ἄκανθαι	3	5
ἀνακεῖσθαι	3	5
βαραββᾶς	3	5
ἐμπαίζειν	3	5
καταλύειν	3	5
πόθεν	3	5
σεαυτοῦ	3	5
σάρξ	4	5
σταυρός	4	5
συκῆ	4	5
δοξάζειν	1	4
ἕκαστος	1	4
ἐργάζεσθαι	1	4
Ἰσαάκ	1	4
μοιχεύειν	1	4
ὅρκος	1	4
οὖ	1	4
σεισμός	1	4

σῖτος	1	4
ἀνάστασις	2	4
ἀρνεῖσθαι	2	4
λεπρός	2	4
πετεινόν	2	4
προφητεύειν	2	4
βλασφημία	3	4
ἐκλεκτός	3	4
θλῖψις	3	4
λῃστής	3	4
νοεῖν	3	4
αἰτία	1	3
ἀποδημεῖν	1	3
ἀσθενής	1	3
βεελζεβούλ	1	3
γαμίζειν	1	3
γαστήρ	1	3
δέκα	1	3
διασκορπίζειν	1	3
εὐδοκεῖν	1	3
θρίξ	1	3
κῆνσος	1	3
κοιλία	1	3
κόπτειν	1	3
κράσπεδον	1	3
κυλλός	1	3
μανθάνειν	1	3
μαστιγοῦν	1	3
περιάγειν	1	3
πιπράσκειν	1	3
πορνεία	1	3
ποταμός	1	3
σοφία	1	3
στρατιώτης	1	3
χωρίς	1	3
ψευδοπροφήτης	1	3
ἀγέλη	2	3
ἀληθῶς	2	3
βασανίζειν	2	3
διάκονος	2	3
ἐγγύς	2	3
ἔνατος	2	3
θανατοῦν	2	3
ἱερεύς	2	3
κάμηλος	2	3
λευκός	2	3
μένειν	2	3
ὀνειδίζειν	2	3
ποιμήν	2	3
πρίν	2	3
χόρτος	2	3

ὡσαννά	2	3
ἀνακλίνειν	1	2
ἀποστάσιον	1	2
ἀπώλεια	1	2
γωνία	1	2
διακρίνειν	1	2
δῶμα	1	2
ἐκδιδόναι	1	2
ἐκδύειν	1	2
ἕκτος	1	2
ἐκχύνεσθαι	1	2
ἐξομολογεῖν	1	2
θηλάζειν	1	2
καθέδρα	1	2
καταμαρτυρεῖν	1	2
καταρτίζειν	1	2
κινεῖν	1	2
κόκκος	1	2
κῦμα	1	2
λύχνος	1	2
Μαθθαῖος	1	2
μάρτυς	1	2
μετάνοια	1	2
μέτρον	1	2
μύλος	1	2
νυμφῶν	1	2
ὄπισθεν	1	2
ὀρύσσειν	1	2
ὀρχεῖσθαι	1	2
παράπτωμα	1	2
πατάσσειν	1	2
πειρασμός	1	2
πενθερά	1	2
προστιθέναι	1	2
προτάσσειν	1	2
σαλεύειν	1	2
σίναπι	1	2
ταράσσειν	1	2
τύπτειν	1	2
ὑπαντᾶν	1	2
ὑπόδημα	1	2
ὑπομένειν	1	2
ὑψηλός	1	2
φυτεύειν	1	2
χειμών	1	2
ὤ	1	2

Table 5a. Words and Phrases that Suggest Matthew Depends on Luke - Alphabetical Sort			
Word or Phrase	Occurrences in Luke	Occurrences in Acts	Occurrences in Matthew
ἀκριβῶς	1	5	1
ἀλείφειν	3		1
ἀλώπηξ	2		1
ἀναβλέπειν	7	5	3
ἀνάγειν	3	17	1
ἀναπίπτειν	4		1
ἀποδεκατοῦν	2		1
ἀποπνίγειν	2		1
ἄριστον	2		1
ἀσπασμός	5		1
αὐξάνειν	4	4	2
ἀφαιρεῖν	4		1
ἄχρι	4	16	ca. 1-2
γονεῖς	6		1
δάκτυλος	3		1
δεῖπνον	5		1
δεῖσθαι	8	7	1
δέρειν	5	3	1
διαθήκη	2	2	1
διαλογίζεσθαι	6		3
διαμερίζειν	6		1
διέρχεσθαι	10	20	ca. 1-2
δῶμα	3	1	2
εἰρήνη	13	7	4
ἐντρέπεσθαι	3		1
ἐπιδιδόναι	6	2	2
ἔτος	15	11	1
εὐαγγελίζομαι	10	15	1
ἡλικία	3		1
ἱερεύς	6	4	3
Ἰερουσαλήμ	26		1
καταργεῖν	1	4	1
καταφάγειν	3		2
καταφιλεῖν	3	1	1
κλαίειν	10	2-3	2
κλίνειν	4		1
κονιόρτος	2	2	1
μακρόθεν	4		2
μακρός	3		1
μαρτυρεῖν	1	11	1
νομικός	6		1
παριστάναι transitive	3	13	1

πειρασμός	6	1	2
περίλυπος	1-2		1
πετείνα	4	2	4
πήρα	4		1
προσδοκᾶν	6	5	2
προστιθέναι	7	6	2
προσφωνεῖν	4	2	1
πρωτοκαθεδρία	2		1
πρωτοκλισία	3		1
σαροῦν	2		1
συλλαμβάνω	7	4	1
ὃν τρόπον	1	4	1
ὑπέρ + genitive	3	7	1
ὑποδεικνύναι	3	2	1
ὑψοῦν	5	3	1

Table 5f. Words and Phrases that Suggest Matthew Depends on Luke - Frequency Sort			
Word or Phrase	Occurrences in Luke	Occurrences in Acts	Occurrences in Matthew
Ἰερουσαλήμ	26		1
ἔτος	15	11	1
εὐαγγελίζομαι	10	15	1
εἰρήνη	13	7	4
διέρχεσθαι	10	20	ca. 1-2
κλαίειν	10	2-3	2
δεῖσθαι	8	7	1
προστιθέναι	7	6	2
ἀναβλέπειν	7	5	3
συλλαμβάνω	7	4	1
γονεῖς	6		1
διαμερίζειν	6		1
νομικός	6		1
προσδοκᾶν	6	5	2
ἐπιδιδόναι	6	2	2
πειρασμός	6	1	2
ἱερεύς	6	4	3
διαλογίζεσθαι	6		3
ἀσπασμός	5		1
δέρειν	5	3	1
ὑψοῦν	5	3	1
δεῖπνον	5		1
ἄχρι	4	16	ca. 1-2
κατανοεῖν	4	4	1
προσφωνεῖν	4	2	1
ἀναπίπτειν	4		1
ἀφαιρεῖν	4		1
κλίνειν	4		1

Word or Phrase			
πήρα	4		1
αὐξάνειν	4	4	2
μακρόθεν	4		2
πετείνα	4	2	4
ἀνάγειν	3	17	1
παριστάναι transitive	3	13	1
ὑπέρ + genitive	3	7	1
ὑποδεικνύναι	3	2	1
καταφιλεῖν	3	1	1
ἀλείφειν	3		1
δάκτυλος	3		1
ἐντρέπεσθαι	3		1
ἡλικία	3		1
μακρός	3		1
πρωτοκλισία	3		1
δῶμα	3	1	2
καταφάγειν	3		2
διαθήκη	2	2	1
κονιόρτος	2	2	1
ἀλώπηξ	2		1
ἀποδεκατοῦν	2		1
ἀποπνίγειν	2		1
ἄριστον	2		1
πρωτοκαθεδρία	2		1
σαροῦν	2		1
περίλυπος	1-2		1
μαρτυρεῖν	1	11	1
ἀκριβῶς	1	5	1
ὃν τρόπον	1	4	1

Table 6a. Words and Phrases Which Suggest Matthew Depends on Mark - Alphabetical Sort		
Word or Phrase	**Occurrences in Mark**	**Occurrences in Matthew**
ἀδελφή	5	3
ἄζυμος	2	1
ἀλάβαστρον	2	1
ἅλας	3	2
ἀλήθεια	3	1
Ἀλφαῖος	2	1
ἀναπίπτειν	2	1
Ἀνδρέας	4	2
ἀπιστία	3	1
ἀποδοκιμάζειν	2	1
ἀποκαταστῆναι	3	2
ἀποκεφαλίζειν	2	1
Βηθανία	4	2
δεῖπνον	2	1
Δεκάπολις	2	1
δερεῖν	3	1

διαλογίζεσθαι	7	3
διωγμός	2	1
δόλος	2	1
δυνατός	5	3
εἰσπορεύεσθαι	8	1
ἐναντίος	2	1
ἐπιγραφή	2	1
ἐπιτιμᾶν	9	6
ἔσω	2	1
ἔτος	2	1
εὐθύς	42	7
Ἡρωδιάς	3	2
Ἡρωδιανοί	2	1
θεωρεῖν	7	2
ἰατρός	2	1
Ἰεριχώ	2	1
Ἰάκωβος	15	6
καθώς	8	3
κακολογεῖν	2	1
κἄν	3	2
καρποφορεῖν	2	1
κατηγορεῖν	3	2
κλάσμα	4	2
κοπάζειν	2	1
κοράσιον	5	3
κωλύειν	3	1
Μαγδαληνή	4	3
μακρόθεν	5	2
μέλει	2	1
μερίζειν	4	3
μηκέτι	4	1
μύρον	3	2
ξηραίνειν	6	3
οἰκοδομή	2	1
οἶνος	5	4
οἷος	2	1
οὐκέτι	7	2
οὔπω	4	2
παράδοσις	5	3
παραπορεύεσθαι	4	1
παιδίσκη	2	1
περίλυπος	2	1
περισσῶς	2	1
πλήρωμα	3	1
πολλάκις	2	1
προέρχομαι	2	1
Σίμων	11	9
σίνδων	3	1
σιωπᾶν	5	2
σκεῦος	2	1
σκληροκαρδία	2	1

σταχύς	3	1
συμπνίγειν	2	1
τέσσαρες	2	1
τολμᾶν	2	1
ὑπακούειν	2	1
ὑποκάτω	3	1
ὕψιστος	2	1
φανερός	3	1
φόνος	2	1
φύλλον	3	2
φωνεῖν	9	5
χαλκός	2	1
ψευδομαρτυρεῖν	3	1

Table 6f. Words and Phrases Which Suggest Matthew Depends on Mark - Frequency Sort		
Word or Phrase	Occurrences in Mark	Occurrences in Matthew
εὐθύς	42	7
Ἰάκωβος	15	6
Σίμων	11	9
φωνεῖν	9	5
ἐπιτιμᾶν	9	6
εἰσπορεύεσθαι	8	1
καθώς	8	3
θεωρεῖν	7	2
οὐκέτι	7	2
διαλογίζεσθαι	7	3
ζηταίνειν	6	3
μακρόθεν	5	2
σιωπᾶν	5	2
ἀδελφή	5	3
δυνατός	5	3
κοράσιον	5	3
παράδοσις	5	3
οἶνος	5	4
παραπορεύεσθαι	4	1
μηκέτι	4	1
Ἀνδρέας	4	2
Βηθανία	4	2
κλάσμα	4	2
οὔπω	4	2
Μαγδαληνή	4	3
μερίζειν	4	3
σίνδων	3	1
ἀλήθεια	3	1
ἀπιστία	3	1
δερεῖν	3	1
κωλύειν	3	1
πλήρωμα	3	1

σταχύς	3	1
ὑποκάτω	3	1
φανερός	3	1
ψευδομαρτυρεῖν	3	1
ἅλας	3	2
ἀποκαταστῆναι	3	2
Ἡρωδιάς	3	2
κἄν	3	2
κατηγορεῖν	3	2
μύρον	3	2
φύλλον	3	2
ἄζυμος	2	1
ἀλάβαστρον	2	1
Ἀλφαῖος	2	1
ἀναπίπτειν	2	1
ἀποδοκιμάζειν	2	1
ἀποκεφαλίζειν	2	1
δεῖπνον	2	1
Δεκάπολις	2	1
διωγμός	2	1
δόλος	2	1
ἐναντίος	2	1
ἐπιγραφή	2	1
ἔσω	2	1
ἔτος	2	1
Ἡρωδιανοί	2	1
ἰατρός	2	1
Ἰεριχώ	2	1
κακολογεῖν	2	1
καρποφορεῖν	2	1
κοπάζειν	2	1
μέλει	2	1
οἰκοδομή	2	1
οἷος	2	1
παιδίσκη	2	1
περίλυπος	2	1
περισσῶς	2	1
πολλάκις	2	1
προέρχομαι	2	1
σκεῦος	2	1
σκληροκαρδία	2	1
συμπνίγειν	2	1
τέσσαρες	2	1
τολμᾶν	2	1
ὑπακούειν	2	1
ὕψιστος	2	1
φόνος	2	1
χαλκός	2	1

APPENDIX 3: MORE STRUCTURAL AND LINGUISTIC ELEMENTS OF THE MARKAN OVERLAY

David Barrett Peabody

Most, if not all, critical scholars agree that the author or redactor of Mark who provided quite a number of demonstrable thematic emphases within this Gospel also provided its current integrated and unified structure. Mark's most significant structural feature is composed of fifteen instances of πάλιν (again) used retrospectively uniting two or more separated pericopae.[1] This compositional feature is unique to Mark among the Synoptics, but common in John.[2] With its aid Mark depicts Jesus as repeatedly entering Capernaum,[3] which Mark may have viewed as the home base for Jesus' adult ministry in Galilee. With πάλιν Mark also depicts Jesus as repeatedly appearing and/or teaching by the sea,[4] in a synagogue,[5] or in a house.[6] Great crowds follow him time and again.[7] In some cases these crowds are so large that they interrupt the normal course of human activity,[8] such as eating a meal[9] or gaining entrance to the house.[10] Nevertheless, Jesus repeatedly demonstrates his power to summon these crowds, as he does with his own closest disciples whom the author of Mark typically describes as "the twelve."[11]

On four occasions Mark distinctively describes Jesus as withdrawing from the crowds, usually into a house, where his disciples question him about some immediately previous public teaching or healing and Jesus provides them with esoteric teaching on the same topic.[12]

Time and again, Jesus embarks in a boat and crosses to "the other side" of the Sea of Galilee.[13] Finally, toward the end of his Gospel, Mark introduces πάλιν one last time to underscore the three times that Jesus entered the city of Jerusalem and its temple during the last week of his earthly life.[14]

---

[1] Peabody, *Mark as Composer* 70, 56-57.

[2] For examples of this same type of structural use of πάλιν in John, see, e.g., Jn 4:3 (cf. Jn 1:43), Jn 4:46 (cf. Jn 2:1), Jn 4:54 (cf. Jn 2:11), Jn 6:15 (cf. Jn 6:3), Jn 8:2 (cf. Jn 7:14), etc.

[3] Peabody, *Mark as Composer*, 27, 42.

[4] Ibid., 15, 39.

[5] Ibid., 28, 42.

[6] Ibid., 42, 47.

[7] Ibid., C, 150; E, 152; I, 155.

[8] Ibid., 68, 54;

[9] Ibid., 105, 69.

[10] Ibid., 47, 48

[11] Ibid., 107, 69; 102, 68.

[12] See Mk 4:10-11a (different from Mt 13:10-11a//Lk 8:9-10a), Mk 7:17-18a (different from Mt 15:12-15; Lk, no parallel), Mk 9:28-29a (different from Mt 17:19-20a, cf. Lk 17:5-6a) , Mk 10:10 (supplementary to Mt 19:7; Lk, no parallel). Cf. Peabody, *Mark as Composer*, M, 158.

[13] Peabody, *Mark as Composer*, 123, 76.

[14] Ibid., 221, 104. A full discussion of Mark's use of πάλιν may be found in Ibid., 115-47. Also see Table 70, pp. 56-57. Cf. Table 183, p. 95, which displays another type of retrospective usage of πάλιν and is therefore to be

Of these fifteen uses of πάλιν, which provide basic structure for a major part of Mk (i.e., Mk 1:16 -13:1 and which integrate separated literary contexts within it, *not one ever appears in the parallels in either Matthew or Luke*.[15] It seems incredible that the authors of Matthew and Luke, if they were making independent use of Mark as most advocates of the Two Document Hypothesis would have it, could have managed to omit all fifteen instances of this most important structural feature of Mark while adopting many, if not all, of the elements that Mark uses in conjunction with πάλιν.

On the other hand, this evidence is entirely consistent with the Two Gospel Hypothesis. If Mark indeed was composed by conflating the text of Matthew and Luke, then the hand of the author of Mark would most likely appear in those passages that represent supplements and consistent alterations of Matthew and Luke. And that is just what we find.

In addition to πάλιν used retrospectively uniting two or more separated pericopae, Mark demonstrates his interest in retrospection in other ways. For instance, πάλιν is also frequently used retrospectively to unite two verses within a pericope.[16] Mark also uses the phrases, "just as he said" [17] and, "Peter remembered"[18] to call his readers' attention to earlier literary contexts. Finally, Mark also utilizes entire pericopae for the purpose of promoting retrospection to one or more earlier pericopae. For instance, Mk 6:1-6a looks back upon the whole of Mk 3:20-5:43. Mark 8:14-21 looks back at least to Mk 6:30-44 and Mk 8:1-10, if not to further literary contexts between these two (e.g., Mk 6:52). In short, retrospection is a major structural feature of the Gospel of Mark and a clear preference of the author for structuring his narrative. However, some of these other literary features are distinctive, rather than unique, to Mark. That is, not every member of every category represents a Markan supplement to the texts of Matthew and Luke, although at least one member in every category represents Markan editing of Matthew or Luke or, frequently, their common testimony.

Complementary to Mark's use of retrospection is a somewhat less pronounced but still significant use of prospection or foreshadowing. The clearest examples of prospection are, of course, provided by the three Passion Prediction passages (Mk 8:27, 30-32a; 9:30-32, and 10:32-34) and their

---

distinguished from table 70. A slightly revised, English version of table 70 from Peabody, *Mark as Composer* has been provided in this book as Appendix 4.

[15] See the uniquely Markan uses of πάλιν at Mk 2:1, 13; 3:1, 20; 4:1, 5:21; 7:14, 31; 8:1, 13; 10:1 (bis), 10, 32; 11:27. C. Clifton Black fundamentally misrepresents Peabody's claims about this recurrent literary feature of Mark's text in *The Disciples according to Mark: Markan Redaction in Current Debate* (JSNTSS 27; Sheffield: JSOT, 1989), 212-18. For instance, Black claims that this usage occurs 52 times in Mark, rather than the 15 times it actually does occur (p. 213). In fact, πάλιν itself only occurs 28 times in Mark. Black compounded this and other mistakes by repeating some of them in his review of Peabody, *Mark as Composer* in *JAAR* 57 (Winter 1989): 421. A more accurate review that includes a number of corrections to Black's reading was subsequently provided by S. Johnson Samuel in the *Bangalore Theological Forum* 22 (1990): 45-63.

[16] Peabody, *Mark as Composer*, 183, 95.

[17] Ibid., 230, 107.

[18] Ibid., 233, 108.

fulfillment in the Passion Narrative (Mk 14-16). Mark's overlay here, as noted above, includes the affirmation that the resurrection will take place "after three days."[19]

Other, perhaps less obvious, examples of Mark's use of the literary technique of prospection and its subcategories, foreshadowing and prophecy-fulfillment, would include the following:[20]

First, Mark summarily describes Jesus as modeling ministry by "preaching and casting out demons" (Mk 1:39). Then he calls all twelve of his closest disciples "in order that he might send them out to preach and to have authority to cast out demons" (Mk 3:14-15). Subsequently Mark depicts the twelve as fulfilling Jesus' intention for them when "they preached and cast out demons" (Mk 6:12-13).[21] This Markan theme is also found in the disputed last twelve verses (Mk 16:15, 17).

Second, Mark anticipates a scene where Jesus is depicted as teaching in a boat by depicting the readying of that boat slightly earlier in his narrative (Mk 4:1, cf. Mk 3:9).[22]

Third, only Mark has Jesus prophesy Peter's triple denial before the cock would crow "twice" (Mk 14:30, cf. Mk 14:72).[23]

Fourth, Mark has rewritten the common testimony of Matthew and Luke, in order to enhance the similarity between the preparations made for Jesus' triumphal entry and for the Last Supper (Mk 11:1-10 and Mk 14:12-16; cf. Mt 21:1-9//Lk 19:28-40 and Mt 26:17-19//Lk 22:7-13).[24] In this case, the Two Document Hypothesis would have Matthew and Luke making independent use of Mark and yet managing to split Mark's language between them and, at the same time, sometimes accidentally agreeing in making the same changes to Mark's text. But according to the Two Gospel Hypothesis, Mark incorporated most of the common testimony of Matthew and Luke, changing a few elements of it, sometimes drawing material from them alternately, while overwriting the whole of both scenes in accord with his own stylistic preferences. Mark does something similar with the burial scenes of John the Baptist and Jesus (Mk 6:29//Mt 14:12 and Mk 15:45-46//Mt:27:59-60, cf. Lk 23:53, 55).[25]

---

[19] See n. 39 above.
[20] Peabody, *Mark as Composer,* 184, 96.
[21] Cf. Mk 6:7, where Jesus commissions "the twelve," sends them out two by two, and gives them "authority over the unclean spirits."
[22] *Mark as Composer* 96, 67
[23] Ibid., 233, 108.
[24] Ibid., 229, 106.
[25] Ibid., 158, 87.

Fifth and finally, there is even a singular but potentially prospective usage of πάλιν at Mk 15:13 (cf. Mk 15:14).[26]

As is well known, Mark utilizes καὶ εὐθύς as an introductory or connecting formula. This element of the Markan overlay provides an immediacy or sense of urgency to the Markan narrative.[27] Other, somewhat more complex introductory or linking formulae in Mark would include:

➤ Καὶ + a verb of motion + εἰς Καφαρναούμ to introduce a pericope[28]

➤ Καί + a form of συνάγω + πρός[29]

➤ καί + verb of motion + εἰς + name of place + εἰς + name of place[30]

➤ καί + historic present of verb of motion + πρὸς αὐτόν [= Ἰησοῦν][31]

➤ καὶ ἔλεγεν αὐτοῖς as a linking and/or introductory formula[32]

➤ καί + ἔρχεται/ἔρχονται + εἰς + name of place + καί[33]

➤ Καὶ προσκαλεσάμενος τὸν ὄχλον/τοὺς μαθητάς/ αὐτούς + 3rd singular of λέγω + αὐτοῖς[34]

➤ καὶ ἤρξατο διδάσκειν[35]

➤ καὶ ἐδίδασκεν καὶ ἔλεγεν αὐτοῖς[36]

➤ καί + ἔλεγεν + ἐν τῇ διδαχῇ αὐτοῦ[37]

➤ Καὶ ὅτε + verb + phrase meaning "privately" + [ἐπ]ηρώτων αὐτόν + phrase meaning "disciples" + accusative of ἡ παραβολή + καί + 3rd singular of λέγω + αὐτοῖς[38]

➤ Καί + ἦλθόν εἰς + καί + genitive absolute using the personal pronoun and ἐξέρχομαι to begin a new sentence + ἐκ τοῦ πλοίου εὐθύς[39]

➤ Καί + participle of διαπεράω to introduce a section[40]

➤ ὁ δὲ Ἰησοῦς[41]

---

[26] See the discussion in Ibid., 146-47.

[27] Ibid., 5, 36. Mark uses εὐθύς 42 times. Thirty-five of these are preceded by καί; twenty-six have no words intervening between καί and εὐθύς. There are no occurrences of εὐθύς in Mt without a parallel in Mk, although Mt does include occurrences of εὐθέως apart from a parallel in Mk. Luke also includes uses of εὐθύς/εὐθέως apart from a Markan parallel.

[28] Peabody, *Mark as Composer* 27, 42.

[29] Ibid., 48, 48.

[30] Ibid., 61, 51.

[31] Ibid., 63, 53.

[32] Ibid., 89, 64.

[33] Ibid., 106, 69.

[34] Ibid., 107, 69.

[35] Ibid., 111, 70.

[36] Ibid., 115, 71.

[37] Cf. ibid., 117, 72.

[38] Ibid., 120, 75.

[39] Ibid., 129, 78.

[40] Ibid., 134, 79.

[41] Ibid., 146, 85.

➤ καί + 3rd Singular of διαστέλλω + αὐτοῖς + ἵνα + a negative[42]

➤ Καί [δια]γενομένου σαββάτου to begin a sentence[43]

➤ καί + a form of ἐμβαίνω + [εἰς τὸ πλοῖον] + a verb of motion + εἰς τὸ πέραν[44]

➤ Καί ἔρχονται εἰς + name of city. καί τo introduce a section of the gospel[45]

➤ καί + genitive absolute + εἰς + name of place + "disciples" + κατ' ἰδίαν + a form of ἐπερωτάω + αὐτόν[46]

➤ Καὶ καθίσας to begin a sentence[47]

➤ καί + a verb of summoning + τοὺς δώδεκα + 3rd singular of λέγω + αὐτοῖς[48]

➤ Καί + a form of [προσ]έρχομαι + "opponents of Jesus" + ἐπηρώτων αὐτόν[49]

➤ Καί ἐκπορευομένου αὐτοῦ to introduce a section[50]

➤ Καί + participle + εἰς + 3rd singular of ἐπερωτάω + αὐτόν[51]

➤ ἦσαν/ἦν γάρ to introduce a parenthetical comment.[52] Like Mark's preference for quoting non-Greek words followed by a formula introducing a translation, parenthetical comments beginning with ἦσαν/ἦν γάρ clearly represent Markan glosses. Inasmuch as glosses are generally recognized by text-critics as secondary features of a text, these two categories of evidence from the Markan overlay demonstrate the "secondary" nature of Mark's text.

Other Selected Linguistic Elements of the Markan Overlay

➤ κηρύσσειν + εὐαγγέλιον[53]

➤ ὁ καιρός used absolutely[54]

➤ Mark depicts Simon Peter, James, John and Andrew as an inner core of *four* of Jesus' closest disciples.[55] Matthew and Luke tend to depict such an inner core as consisting of only three disciples: Peter, James and John.

---

[42] Ibid., 147, 85.

[43] Ibid., 148, 85.

[44] Ibid., 165, 90.

[45] Ibid., 182, 94.

[46] Ibid., 204, 101.

[47] Ibid., 206, 101.

[48] Ibid., 207, 101.

[49] Ibid., 214, 103.

[50] Ibid., 217, 103.

[51] Ibid., 218, 103.

[52] Ibid., 18, 40. Mk 1:16//Mt 4:18; Mk 1:22//Mt 7:29 cf. Lk 4:32; Mk 2:15NP, cf. Lk 5:29; Mk 5:42NP, cf. Lk 8:42; Mk 6:31NP; Mk 6:48//Mt 14:24; Mk 10:22//Mt 19:22, cf. Lk 18:23 same construction, diff. vocabulary; Mk 14:40//Mt 26:43; Mk 16:4NP, cf. Mt 28:2, cf. Lk 24:2.

[53] Peabody, *Mark as Composer*, 11, 38. Mk 1:14, cf. Mt κηρύσσειν w/o εὐαγγέλιον; Mk 13:10//Mt 24:14; Mk 14:9//Mt 26:13; Mk 16:15//κηρύσσειν w/o εὐαγγέλιον in Lk 24:47

[54] Peabody, *Mark as Composer*, 12, 38. Mt 1:15NP, cf. Mt 4:17; Mt 13:33 cf. Lk 21:36, anarthrous καιρός

[55] Cf. Peabody, *Mark as Composer*, 21, 41. The occurrence at Mk 13:3 is a Markan alteration of Mt 24:3, οἱ μαθηταί Lk 21:7 is different. At Mk 1:29 the author adds the names of James, John, and Andrew to that of Simon/Peter as found in the parallels at Mt 8:14 and Lk 4:38. The other two Markan occurrences of these four

>   ἐν τῷ πλοίῳ[56]

>   The motif of people running to Jesus.[57]

>   Having "unclean spirits" as a preferred Markan description of people who were possessed by demonic powers.[58]

The following were also listed, by means of partial quotations with chapter and verse references, by Sir John Hawkins,[59] as examples of "the transference and repetition of formulas" that are "peculiar to Mark." The descriptions below, however, are from *Mark as Composer*.

>   "Crowds" + negative + φαγεῖν. The motif of not being able to eat because of the crowd.[60]

>   καί + ἔλεγεν + ἐν τῇ διδαχῇ αὐτοῦ + 2nd person plural present imperative.[61]

>   καί + ἡδέως + αὐτοῦ + ἤκουεν[62]

>   Καί + a negative + ἤθελεν + a form of γινώσκω[63]

>   οὐ[κ] + ἤδει[σαν] + τί + 3rd person aorist passive subjunctive of ἀποκρίνομαι[64]

>   καὶ ἐναγκαλισάμενος + accusative of αὐτός[65]

---

names found together both have a parallels in Matthew or Matthew//Luke (Mk 1:16-20//Mt 4:18-20; Mt 10:2-4//Lk 6:14-16//Mk 3:16-18).

[56] Peabody, *Mark as Composer*, 26, 42. Mark uses this phrase six times; Matthew, twice: once with a Markan parallel and once without. Luke never uses this phrase in the Gospel, but there are two occurrences in Acts (Acts 27:31, 37). See Mk 1:19//Mt 4:21 cf. Lk 5:10, Mk 1:20NP, cf. Mt 4:22, τὸ πλοῖον, cf. Lk 5:11, τὰ πλοῖα; Mk 4:36, cf. Mt 8:23, εἰς τὸ πλοῖον, cf. Lk 8:22, εἰς πλοῖον; Mk [5:21NP], cf. Mt 9:18, cf. Lk8:40; Mk 6:32//Mt 14:13, ἐν πλοίῳ, cf. Lk 9:10; Mk 8:14NP, cf. Mt 16:5; Mt 14:33, cf. Mk 6:52.

[57] Details about use of this motif in all three Synoptic Gospels are included in our discussion of Mk 6:55 below.

[58] Peabody, *Mark as Composer* 33, 44. cf. 32, 44.

[59] Rev. Sir John C. Hawkins, *Horae Synopticae: Contributions to the Study of the Synoptic Problem* (Oxford: Clarendon, 1909), 169. With one exception (noted), we have added the references to parallels in Matthew and Luke in the next six footnotes. This is a good example of differences in detail in parallels that one might see when consulting different synopses.

[60] Mk 3:20NP and Mk 6:31NP; cf. Peabody, *Mark as Composer*, 105, 69.

[61] Mk 4:2 (cf. Mt 13:3 and Lk 8:4) and Mk 12:38 (cf. Mt 23:1-2 and Lk 20:45-46); cf. Peabody, *Mark as Composer* 117, 72.

[62] Mk 6:20NP and Mk 12:37 (cf. Mt 23:1 and Lk 20:45); cf. Peabody, *Mark as Composer*, 157, 87.

[63] Mk 7:24NP (cf. Mt 15:21) and Mk 9:30NP (cf. Mt 17:22 and Lk 9:43); cf. Peabody, *Mark as Composer*, 173, 92.

[64] Mk 9:6NP (cf. Lk 9:33) and Mk 14:40NP (cf. Mt 26:43). In this case, Hawkins himself also calls attention to the partial parallel to Mk 9:6 in Lk 9:33. Cf. Peabody, *Mark as Composer*, 197, 99.

[65] Mk 9:36NP (cf. Mt 18:2 and Lk 9:47) and Mk 10:16NP (cf. Mt 19:15 and Lk 18:17); cf. Peabody, *Mark as Composer*, 209, 102.

APPENDIX 4: THE GREEK WORD, "AGAIN," (πάλιν) USED
RETROSPECTIVELY TO UNITE TWO OR MORE SEPARATED PERICOPES
[*Mark as Composer*, 70, 56-57, revised and in English Translation]
David Barrett Peabody

Sets of Verses in Mark	A summary description of those elements between or among separated pericopes to which the Greek word for "again" calls attention, followed by synoptic displays of the relevant evidence.

Set 1	Jesus repeatedly goes into Capernaum.
1:21	And they enter into Capernaum
2:1	And after going again into Capernaum

Set 2	Jesus repeatedly appears beside the sea.
1:16	And going along beside the sea of Galilee he saw Simon and Andrew
2.13-14	And he went out again beside the sea... And going along he saw Levi...

Set 3	Jesus repeatedly goes into Capernaum and repeatedly enters a synagogue.
1:21	And they enter into Capernaum and immediately on the Sabbath, after entering into the synagogue, he was teaching.
2:1	And after going again into Capernaum
3:1	And he entered again into the synagogue.

Set 4-6	Jesus repeatedly enters a house and repeatedly appears by the sea and crowds repeatedly gather around him.
1:45	and they were coming toward him from everywhere so that no longer
2:1-2	And after going again he is in a house. And were brought many, so that no longer...
2:13	And he came out again beside the sea and all the crowd was coming toward him,...
3:7-10	And... toward the sea; and a great multitude...came toward him so that...
3.20	And he comes into a house; and (there) gathers again [the] crowd, so that not...

Set 7	Jesus repeatedly appears beside the sea of Galilee.
1:16	And... beside the sea...
2:13	And again beside the sea; and all the crowd was coming toward him, and he was teaching them.
4:1-2	And again beside the sea; and (there) was gathering toward him a great crowd...and he was teaching them

Set 8a	Jesus repeatedly crosses to the other side of the Sea of Galilee.
4:35-36	And...let us go through to the other side. And after leaving the crowd...as he was in the boat,...
5:1	And they came to the other side...
5:21	And...[in the boat] again to the other side (there) was gathered a great crowd...and he was beside the sea.

Set 8b	Jesus repeatedly enters a house, appears beside the sea, crowds gather around him and he goes to the other side.
1:45	and they were coming toward him from everywhere so that no longer...
2:1-2	And after entering <u>again</u> he is in a house. And were brought many, so that no longer...
2:13	And he came out <u>again</u> beside the sea and all the crowd was coming toward him,...
3:7-10	And... toward the sea; and a great multitude... came toward him... so that...
3:20	And he comes into a house; and (there) comes together <u>again</u> [the] crowd, so that not...
4:1-2	And <u>again</u> beside the sea and (there) was gathering toward him a great crowd, so that...
5:21	And... <u>again</u> into the other side (there) was coming a great crowd upon him, and he was beside the sea.

Set 9	Jesus repeatedly summons crowds and speaks to them.
3:20	and (there) was coming <u>again</u> [the] crowd...3:23 and after summoning them he was saying to them,...
7:14	And after summoning <u>again</u> the crowd he was saying to them,...

Set 10	Jesus goes in and out of the regions of Tyre.
7:24	Furthermore, from there, after he rose up, he went away into the regions of Tyre.
7:31	And <u>again</u>, after he went out of the regions of Tyre...

Set 11	Huge crowds repeatedly gather and Jesus feeds them.
6:34	And after he went out, he saw a great crowd...+ Feeding of the 5000.
8:1	In those days <u>again</u> when there was a great crowd...+ Feeding of the 4000.

Set 12a	Jesus repeatedly embarks in a boat and goes away.
8:10	And immediately, after embarking into the boat...he went to the districts of Damanutha.
8:13	And after leaving them, after <u>again</u> embarking [into the boat] he went away to the other side.

Set 12b	Jesus repeatedly embarks in a boat and goes to the other side of the Sea of Galilee.
6:45	And immediately he compelled his disciples to embark into the boat and to proceed to the other side...
8:13	And after he left them, after <u>again</u> embarking [into the boat] he went away to the other side

Set 13	Crowds repeatedly gather around Jesus <u>and</u> Jesus repeatedly teaches them.
2:13	and all the crowd was coming toward him, and he was teaching them.
4:1-2	and (there) was gathered toward him a great crowd, and he was teaching them
10:1	and (there) were <u>again</u> crowds walking toward him, and, as he was accustomed, <u>again</u> he was teaching them.

Set 14	When Jesus is traveling in the vacinity of Judea and beyond the Jordan crowds repeatedly come to him.
3:7-8	And...he withdrew... from Judea...and beyond the Jordan... a great multitude... came toward
10:1	And...he comes into the regions of Judea [and] beyond the Jordan...and (there) were <u>again</u> crowds walking toward

Set 15	Jesus repeatedly withdraws, usually into a house, where his disciples question him about his previous public teaching/healing.
4:10	And when he happened to be alone, they were asking him with the twelve...
7:17	And when he came into a house away from the crowd his disciples were putting questions to him
9:28	And after he went into a house his disciples privately were putting questions to him;
10:10	And into the home <u>again</u> his disciples, concerning this, were putting questions to him.

SOME USES OF THE GREEK WORD FOR "AGAIN" USED RETROSPECTIVELY

Set 16	Jesus repeatedly calls "the twelve" in order to commission them or to speak with them.
3:13-15	and he calls forth…and made "twelve"…in order that he might send them…
6:7	And he calls forth the twelve and began to send them…
9:35	And after he sat down he summoned the twelve and says to them;…
10:32	And after he had <u>again</u> taken aside the twelve, he began to say to them…

Set 17	Jesus repeatedly anticipates or actually does come into Jerusalem. After entering the city, he repeatedly goes into the temple.
10:32a	Furthermore, they were…, going up to Jerusalem, and…
10:33a	… "Look, we are going up to Jerusalem, and…
11:1a	And when they drew near to Jerusalem to Bethphage and Bethany…
11:11a	And he went to Jerusalem into the temple;…
11:15	And he comes to Jerusalem. And after he had come into the temple…
11:27	And he comes <u>again</u> to Jerusalem. And in the temple…

BIBLIOGRAPHY

Aland, Barbara, Kurt Aland, Johannes Karavidopoulos, Carlo M. Martini, and Bruce M. Metzger. *The Greek New Testament*. 4th ed. Stuttgart: Deutsche Bibelgesellschaft, 1983.

Aland, Kurt, and Barbara Aland. *The Text of the New Testament: An Introduction of the Critical Editions and to the Theory and Practice of Modern Textual Criticism*. 2d ed. Translated by E. F. Rhodes. Grand Rapids: Eerdmans, 1987.

Bacon, Benjamin Wisner. *Is Mark a Roman Gospel? HTS* 7. Cambridge, Mass.: Harvard University Press, 1919. Repr., New York: Kraus Reprint, 1969.

Bauckham, R. "Jesus and the Wild Animals (Mark 1:13): A Christological Image for an Ecological Age." Pages 3-21 in *Jesus of Nazareth, Lord and Christ: Essays on the Historical Jesus and New Testament Christology*. Edited by Joel B. Green and Max Turner. Grand Rapids: Eerdmans, 1994.

Beare, F. W. Review of W. R. Farmer, *The Synoptic Problem. JBL* 84 (1965): 295-97.

Bellinzoni, Arthur J. *The Sayings of Jesus in the Writings of Justin Martyr*. NovTSup 17. Leiden: E. J. Brill, 1967.

Benoit, Pierre, and M. -É. Boismard. *Synopses des quatre Evangiles en français. avec parallèles des apocryphes et des Pères*. 3 vols. Paris: Editions du Cerf, 1965-1972; 2d ed., et corrigée par P. Sandevoir, 1972, 2 vols.

Black, C. Clifton. *The Disciples according to Mark: Markan Redaction in Current Debate*. JSNTSS 27. Sheffield: JSOT, 1989.

———. "Review of David Barrett Peabody, *Mark as Composer*." *JAAR* 57 (Winter 1989): 421.

Boismard, Marie-Émile. "Introduction au premier récit de la multiplication des pains." Pages 244-53 in *The Interrelations of the Gospels: A Symposium led by M.É. Boismard — W. R. Farmer — F. Neirynck*. Edited by David L. Dungan. Leuven: University Press/Peeters 1990.

———. *L'Evangile de Marc sa prehistoire*. Études bibliques, nouv. ser. 26. Paris: Libraire Lecoffre, 1994.

Brown, Raymond E. *The Death of the Messiah: A Commentary on the Passion Narratives in the Four Gospels*. 2 vols. New York: Doubleday, 1994.

———. *The Gospel According to John*. AB 29. Garden City, N.Y.: Doubleday and Company, 1966.

———. *An Introduction to the New Testament*. New York: Doubleday, 1997.

Bultmann, Rudolf. *The History of the Synoptic Tradition*. Rev. ed. Translated by John Marsh. Oxford: Blackwell, 1963. Pbk. ed., New York: Harper & Row, 1976.

BIBLIOGRAPHY

Burton, Ernest DeWitt. *Some Principles of Literary Criticism and their Application to the Synoptic Problem.* Decennial Publications of the University of Chicago, Vol. 5. Chicago: University of Chicago Press, repr. 1904.

Büsching, Anton Friedrich. *Die vier Evangelisten mit ihren eigenen Worten zusammengesetzt und mit Erklärungen versehen.* Hamburg, 1766.

Butler, B. C. "St. Luke's Debt to St. Matthew." *HTR* 32 (October 1939): 237-308.

————. *The Originality of St. Matthew.* Cambridge University Press, 1951.

Campbell, Colin. *The First Three Gospels in Greek: Arranged in Parallel Columns.* Glasgow: Hugh Hopkins, 1882. 2d ed., London, Edinburgh and Oxford: Williams and Northgate, 1899. 3d ed., Edinburgh and London: Oliver and Boyd, 1918.

Campenhausen, Hans von. *The Formation of the Christian Bible.* Philadelphia: Fortress Press, 1972.

Carlson, Steven C. "Clement of Alexandria on the 'Order' of the Gospels." *NTS* 47/1 (January 2001): 118-25.

Cartlidge, David R., and David L. Dungan. *Documents for the Study of the Gospels.* 2d ed. Minneapolis: Fortress, 1994.

Chapman, Dom John. *Matthew, Mark and Luke: A Study in the Order and Interrelation of the Synoptic Gospels.* Edited with an introduction and some additional matter by John M. T. Barton. London: Longmans, Green, 1937.

Cope, Lamar. "The Death of John the Baptist in the Gospel of Matthew, or The Case of the Confusing Conjunction." *CBQ* 38/4 (1976): 515-19.

————. *Matthew: A Scribe Trained for the Kingdom of Heaven.* CBQMS 5. Washington: The Catholic Biblical Association of America, 1976.

Corley, Bruce C., ed. *Colloquy on New Testament Studies: A Time for Reappraisal and Fresh Approaches.* Macon, Ga.: Mercer, 1983.

Dahl, Nils A. "Die Passionsgeschichte bei Matthäus." *NTS* 2 (1955-56): 17-32.

————. "The Purpose of Mark's Gospel." Pages 52-66 in *Jesus in the Memory of the Early Church.* Minneapolis: Augsburg Publishing House, 1976.

Derrenbacker, Robert A. "Review of *Beyond the Q Impasse: Luke's Use of Matthew.*" *Toronto Journal of Theology* 14/1 (1998): 4pp. Online: http://www.bham.ac.uk/theology/synoptic-l/derrenba.htm.

Donahue, John. "Windows and Mirrors: The Setting of Mark's Gospel." *CBQ* 57 (1995): 25.

Donaldson, Terence L. *Jesus on the Mountain: A Study in Matthean Theology.* JSNTSS 8. Sheffield: JSOT Press, 1985.

Downing, F. Gerald. "Compositional Conventions and the Synoptic Problem." *JBL* 107 (1988): 69-85.

―――. "Redaction Criticism: Josephus' Antiquities and the Synoptic Problem I." *JSNT* 8 (1980): 46-65.

―――. "Redaction Criticism: Josephus' Antiquities and the Synoptic Problem II." *JSNT* 9 (1980): 29-48.

Drury, John H. *Luke.* The J. B. Phillips' Commentaries. London & Glasgow: Collins, 1973.

―――. *The Parables in the Gospels: A History and Allegory.* London: SPCK, 1985.

―――. *Tradition and Design in Luke's Gospel.* London: Darton, Longman and Todd, 1976.

Dungan, David L. *A History of the Synoptic Problem: The Canon, the Text, the Composition, and the Interpretation of the Gospels.* Anchor Bible Reference Library. New York: Doubleday, 1999.

―――, ed. *The Interrelations of the Gospels: A Symposium Led by M. É. Boismard — W. R. Farmer — F. Neirynck, Jerusalem 1984.* BETL 95. Leuven: Uitgeverij Peeters, 1990.

―――. "Mark—the Abridgement of Matthew and Luke." In *Jesus and Man's Hope.* Edited by Donald Miller. 2 vols. Pittsburgh: Perspective Books, 1970.

―――. "The Purpose and Provenance of the Gospel of Mark According to the 'Two-Gospel' (Griesbach) Hypothesis." Pages 151-52 in *Colloquy on New Testament Studies: A Time for Reappraisal and Fresh Approaches.* Edited by Bruce C. Corley. Macon, Ga.: Mercer, 1983.

―――. "Review of Dom John Bernard Orchard, *A Synopsis of the Four Gospels in Greek.*" *Biblica* 59 (1978): 584-87.

―――. *The Sayings of Jesus in the Churches of Paul.* Philadelphia: Fortress, 1971.

―――. "Synopses of the Future." *Biblica* 66 (1985): 457-92.

―――. "Theory of Synopsis Construction." *Biblica* 61 (1980): 305-29.

Eichhorn, J. G. *Einleitung in das Neue Testament.* 2 vols. Leipzig: Weidmann, 1820.

Elliott, J. K. "The Text and Language of the Endings to Mark's Gospel." TZ 27 (1971): 255-62. Repr., J. K. Elliott. Pages 203-11 in *The Language and Style of the Gospel of Mark: An Edition of C.H. Turner's "Notes on Marcan Usage" Together with Other Comparable Studies.* NovTSup 71. Leiden: Brill, 1993.

Elliott, Neil. "The Silence of the Messiah: The Function of Messianic Secret Motifs across the Synoptics." Pages 604-22 in *SBL Seminar Papers 1993.* SBLSP 32. Atlanta: Scholars Press, 1979.

BIBLIOGRAPHY

Ennulat, Andreas. *Die "Minor Agreements": Untersuchungen zu einer offenen Frage des synoptischen Problems.* Tübingen: Mohr/Siebeck, 1994.

Enslin, Morton Scott. *Christian Beginnings.* Harper Torchbooks: Cloister Library TB 6. 2 vols. New York: Harper & Brothers, 1938.

Evanson, Edward. *The Dissonance of the Four Generally Received Evangelists and the Evidence of Their Respective Authenticity Examined.* Ipswich: G. Jermyn, 1792.

Farmer, William R., ed. *Anti-Judaism and the Gospels.* Harrisburg, Pa.: Trinity Press International, 1999.

————. "Certain Results Reached by Sir John C. Hawkins and C. F. Burney which make more sense if Luke knew Matthew, and Mark knew Matthew and Luke." Pages 75-98 in *Synoptic Studies.* JSNTSS 7. Edited by C. M. Tuckett. Sheffield: Sheffield Academic Press, 1984.

————. *The Gospel of Jesus: The Pastoral Relevance of the Synoptic Problem.* Louisville, Ky.: Westminster/John Knox, 1994.

————, gen. ed. *The International Bible Commentary.* Collegeville, Minn.: Liturgical, 1998.

————. "Kritik der Markushypothese." *ThZ* 34 (1978): 172-74.

————. *The Last Twelve Verses of Mark.* SNTSMS 25. Cambridge: Cambridge University Press, 1974.

————. "The Minor Agreements of Matthew and Luke against Mark and the Two-Gospel Hypothesis." Pages 163-208 in *Minor Agreements: Symposium Göttingen 1991.* Göttinger Theologische Arbeiten 50. Edited by Georg Strecker. Göttingen: Vandenhoeck & Ruprecht, 1993.

————, et al. "Narrative Outline of the Markan Composition According to the Two Gospel Hypothesis." Pages 212-39 in *SBL 1990 Seminar Papers.* SBLSP 29. Edited by David J. Lull. Atlanta: Society of Biblical Literature, 1990.

————, ed. *New Synoptic Studies: The Cambridge Gospel Conference and Beyond.* Macon, Ga.: Mercer University Press, 1983.

————. "Notes for a Compositional Analysis on the Griesbach Hypothesis of the Empty Tomb Stories in the Synoptic Gospels." Pages 7-14 in *Occasional Notes on Some Points of Interest in New Testament Studies.* Privately published pamphlet. August 1980.

————. "The Present State of the Synoptic Problem." Pages 11-36 in *Literary Studies in Luke-Acts. Essays in Honor of Joseph B. Tyson.* Edited by Richard P. Thompson and Thomas E. Phillips. Macon, Ga.: Mercer University Press, 1998.

———. "Redaction Criticism and the Synoptic Problem." Pages 1:239-50 in *The Society of Biblical Literature One Hundred Seventh Annual Meeting Seminar Papers — 28-31 October 1971 Regency Hyatt House — Atlanta, Ga.* 2 vols. Atlanta: Society of Biblical Literature, 1971.

———. "Reply to Michael Goulder." Pages 105-9 in *Synoptic Studies: The Ampleforth Conferences of 1982 and 1983.* JSNTSS 7. Edited by C. M. Tuckett. Sheffield: JSOT Press, 1984.

———. "State *Interesse* and Marcan Primacy." Pages 15-49 in *Biblical Studies and the Shifting of Paradigms 1850-1914.* Edited by Henning Graf Reventlow and William Farmer. Sheffield: Sheffield Academic Press, 1995.

———. "The Stoldt-Conzelmann Controversy: A Review Article." *Perspectives in Religious Studies* 7 (1980): 152-62.

———. *Synopticon: The Verbal Agreement Between the Greek texts of Matthew, Mark, and Luke Contextually Exhibited.* London: Cambridge University Press, 1969.

———. *The Synoptic Problem: A Critical Analysis.* New York: MacMillan, 1964. Repr., Dillsboro, N.C.: Western North Carolina Press, 1976.

Farrer, Austin. "On Dispensing with Q." Pages 55-88 in *Studies in the Gospels: Essays in Memory of R. H. Lightfoot.* Edited by Dennis E. Nineham. Oxford: Basil Blackwell, 1955. Repr. on pages 321-56 in *The Two-Source Hypothesis: A Critical Appraisal.* Edited by Arthur J. Bellinzoni, Jr. Macon, Ga.: Mercer University Press, 1985.

Feine, P., J. Behm, and rev. W. G. Kümmel. *Introduction to the New Testament.* 14th ed. Translated by H. C. Kee. Nashville: Abingdon, 1966.

Franklin, Eric. *Luke. Interpreter of Paul, Critic of Matthew.* JSNTSup 92. Sheffield: Sheffield Academic Press, 1994.

Friedrichsen, Timothy A. "Critical Observations on a Team Effort: *Beyond the Q Impasse: Luke's Use of Matthew.*" 38pp. Online: http://www.bham.ac.uk/theology/synoptic-l/#articles.

Frye, Roland Mushat. "The Synoptic Problems and Analogies in Other Literatures." Pages 261-30 in *The Relationships Among the Gospels: An Interdisciplinary Dialogue.* TUMSR 5. Edited by William O. Walker, Jr. San Antonio: Trinity University Press, 1978.

Fuchs, Albert. "Die 'Seesturmperikope' Mk 4,35-41 parr im Wandel der urkirchlichen Verkündigung." Pages 65-92 in *Minor Agreements: Symposium Göttingen 1991.* Edited by Georg Strecker. Göttingen: Vandenhoeck & Ruprecht, 1993.

Fuller, Reginald H., E. P. Sanders, and Thomas R. W. Longstaff. "The Synoptic Problem: After Ten Years." *PSThJ* 28/2 (1975): 63-74.

Funk, Robert, Roy Hoover, and the Jesus Seminar. *The Five Gospels: The Search for the Authentic Words of Jesus.* New York: Macmillan, 1993.

Gamba, Giussepe Giov. "A Further Reexamination of Evidence from the Early Tradition," Pages 17-35 in *New Synoptic Studies:The Cambridge Gospel Conference and Beyond.* Edited by William R. Farmer. Macon, Ga.: Mercer University Press, 1983.

Geddert, Timothy J. *Watchwords: Mark 13 in Markan Eschatology.* JSNTSS 26. Sheffield: Sheffield Academic Press, 1989.

Gerhardsson, Birger. *Memory and Manuscript: Oral Tradition and Written Transmission in Rabbinic Judaism and Early Christianity.* Acta Seminarii Neotestamentici Upsaliensis 22. Translated by Eric J. Sharpe. Lund: C. W. K. Gleerup, 1964.

———. *Tradition and Transmission in Early Christianity.* Coniectanea Neotestamentica 20. Lund: C. W. K. Gleerup, 1964.

Gieseler, Johann Carl Ludwig. *Historisch-kritischer Versuch über die Entstehung und die frühesten Schicksale der schriftlichen Evangelien.* Leipzig: W. Engleman, 1818.

Goodacre, Mark S. "'*Beyond the Q Impasse'* or Down a Blind Alley?" *JSNT* 76 (1999): 35-52.

———. *The Case Against Q: Studies in Markan Priority and the Synoptic Problem.* Harrisburg, Pa.: Trinity Press International, 2001.

———. "Fatigue in the Synoptics." *NTS* 44 (1998): 45-58.

———. *Goulder and the Gospels: An Examination of a New Paradigm.* JSNTSS 133. Sheffield: Sheffield Academic Press, 1996.

Gould, E. P. *A Critical and Exegetical Commentary on the Gospel According to St. Mark.* New York: Charles Scribner's Press, 1896.

Goulder, Michael D. *Luke: A New Paradigm.* 2 vols. JSNTSS 20. Sheffield: Sheffield Academic Press, 1989.

———. "Some Observations on Professor Farmer's 'Certain Results...'." Pages 99-104 in *Synoptic Studies: The Ampleforth Conferences of 1982 and 1983.* JSNTSS 7. Edited by C. M. Tuckett. Sheffield: JSOT Press, 1984.

Green, H. Benedict. "The Credibility of Luke's Transformation of Matthew." In *Synoptic Studies: The Ampleforth Conferences of 1982 and 1983.* JSNTSup 7. Edited by C. M. Tuckett. Sheffield: JSOT Press, 1984.

Griesbach, Johann Jakob. "Marcus totum libellum suum, si viginti et quatuor circiter commata, quae de sua penu addidit, excipias, de quibus posthaec dicetur, e Matthaei et Lucae commentariis" *Io. Iac. Griesbachii theol. D. et Prof Primar in academia Jenensi commentatio qua Marci Evangelium totum e Matthaei et Lucae commentariis decerptum esse monstratur, scripta nomine Academiae Jenensis (1789, 1790) jam recognita multisque augmentis locupletata.* Repr. On pages 74-102 in *J. J. Griesbach: Synoptic and text-critical studies 1776-1976.* Edited by Bernard Orchard and Thomas R. W. Longstaff. Translated on pages 103-35 by Bernard Orchard. Cambridge: Cambridge University Press, 1978.

Gundry, Robert H. *Mark: A Commentary on His Apology for the Cross.* Grand Rapids: Eerdmans, 1993.

Hanson, James. "The Disciples in Mark's Gospel: Beyond the Pastoral/Polemical Debate." *Horizons in Biblical Theology* 20 (1998): 129.

Hawkins, F. *Horae Synopticae: Contributions to the Study of the Synoptic Problem.* Oxford: Clarendon Press, 1899. 2d rev. and suppl., 1909. Repr., 1968.

Head, Peter M. *Christology and the Synoptic Problem: An Argument for Markan Priority.* SNTSMS 94. Cambridge: Cambridge University Press, 1997.

Hengel, Martin. *Studies in the Gospel of Mark.* Translated by John Bowden. Philadelphia: Fortress, 1985.

Herder, Johann Gottfried. "Regel der Zusammenstimmung unser Evangelien, aus ihrer Entstehung und Ordnung." Pages 17:169-232 in his *Sammtliche Werke zur Religion und Theologie.* Stuttgart, Tübingen: J. G. Cotta, 1830.

———. *Vom Erlöser der Menschen, nach unsern drei ersten Evangelien.* Riga: J. F. Hartknoch, 1796. Herder's *Christliche Schriften* 2; *Von gotes Sohn, der Welt Heiland, nach Johannes Evangelium. Nebst einer Regel der Zusammenstimmung unserer Evangelien aus ihrer Entstehung und Ordnung.* Riga: J. F. Hartknoch, 1797. Herder's *Christliche Schriften* 3.

Hooker, Morna D. *The Gospel According to Saint Mark.* Black's New Testament Commentary 2. Peabody, Mass.: Hendrickson, 1991.

Howard, Robert Paul. *The Markan Idiographs: What Do They Imply?* MA Thesis. Oxford, Ohio: Miami University, 1984.

Iersel, Bas M. F. van. *Mark: A Reader-Response Commentary.* JSNTSS 164. Sheffield: Sheffield Academic Press, 1998.

Ingolfsland, Dennis. "Review of *Beyond the Q Impasse.*" *Christian Library Journal* (March 1997): 71-72.

Jackson, Samuel Macauley, et al., eds. *The New Schaff-Herzog Encyclopedia of Religious Knowledge.* 13 vols. New York, London: Funk & Wagnalls, 1908-1914. Repr., Grand Rapids: Baker Book House, 1950.

Jacobsen, Arland. *The First Gospel.* Missoula, Mont.: Polebridge, 1992.

Jameson, H. G. *The Origin of the Synoptic Gospels: A Revision of the Synoptic Problem.* Oxford: Blackwell, 1922.

Jeremias, Joachim. *New Testament Theology: The Proclamation of Jesus.* Translated by John Bowden. New York: Scribner's, 1971.

BIBLIOGRAPHY

Jervell, Jacob. *The Theology of the Acts of the Apostles.* NTT. New York: Cambridge University Press, 1996.

Juel, Donald. *Messiah and Temple.* SBLDS 31. Missoula, Mont.: Scholars Press, 1977.

Kelber, Werner H., ed. *The Passion in Mark.* Philadelphia: Fortress Press, 1976.

————. *The Oral and Written Gospel: The Hermeneutics of Speaking and Writing in the Synoptic Tradition, Mark, Paul, and Q.* Philadelphia: Fortress, 1983.

————. *The Passion in Mark: Studies on Mark 14-16.* Philadelphia: Fortress, 1976.

Kelhoffer, James A. *Miracle and Mission: The Authentication of Missionaries and their Message in the Longer Ending of Mark.* WUNT 2.112. Tübingen: Mohr Siebeck, 2000.

Kennedy, George. "Classical and Christian Source Criticism." Pages 147-52 in *The Relationship Among the Gospels: An Interdisciplinary Dialogue.* Edited by William O. Walker, Jr. San Antonio: Trinity University Press, 1978.

Kilpatrick, G. D. "The Gentile Mission in Matthew and Mark 13:10-11." Pages 145-58 in *Studies in the Gospels: Essays in Memory of R. H. Lightfoot.* Edited by D. E. Nineham. Oxford: Blackwell, 1955.

Kloppenborg Verbin, John S. *Excavating Q: The History and Setting of the Sayings Gospel.* Minneapolis: Augsburg Fortress; Edinburgh: T&T Clark, 2000.

Kloppenborg, John S. "The Sayings Gospel Q and the Quest of the Historical Jesus." *HTR* 89/4 (1996): 307-44.

————, ed. *The Shape of Q: Signal Essays on the Sayings Source.* Minneapolis: Fortress, 1994.

————. "Review of *Beyond the Q Impasse.*" *CBQ* 61 (1999): 370-72.

————. "The Theological Stakes in the Synoptic Problem." Pages 93-120 in *The Four Gospels 1992: Festschrift Frans Neirynck.* 3 vols. BETL 100. Edited by F. van Segbroeck, et al. Leuven: Leuven University Press/Uitgeverij Peeters, 1992.

Koester, Helmut. "History and Development of Mark's Gospel (From Mark to *Secret Mark* and "Canonical Mark")." Pages 35-57 in *Colloquy on New Testament Studies: A Time for Reappraisal and Fresh Approaches.* Edited by Bruce C. Corley. Macon, Ga.: Mercer, 1983.

Koppe, J. B. *Marcus non epitomator Matthaei* Programme University of Göttingen. Helmstadii, 1782. Repr. in *Sylloge commentationum theologicarum.* Edited by D. J. Pott and G. A. Ruperti. 8 vols. Helmstadt, Germany: C. G. Fleckeisen, 1800-1807.

Kümmel, W.G. *The New Testament, the History of the Investigation of Its Problems.* Translated by H. C. Kee. Nashville: Abingdon, 1972.

Lachs, Samuel Tobias. *A Rabbinic Commentary on the New Testament: The Gospels of Matthew, Mark, and Luke.* Hoboken, N.J.: KTAV; New York: Anti-Defamation League of B'Nai Brith, 1987.

Lampe, G. W. H. "St. Peter's Denial and the Treatment of the *Lapsi.*" Pages 113-21 in *The Heritage of the Early Church: Essays in Honor of G.V. Florovsky. Orientalia Christiana Analecta* 195. Edited by D. Neiman and M. Schatkin. Rome: Pontifical Oriental Institute, 1973.

Léon-Dufour, Xavier. "Les évangiles synoptiques." Pages 2:143-334 in *Introduction à la Bible.* 2 vols. Edited by André Robert and André Feuillet. Tournai: Desclée, 1957, 1959. Repr. On pages 139-324 in *Introduction to the New Testament.* Translated by Patrick W. Skehan. New York: Desclée, 1965.

Levine, Amy-Jill. *The Social and Ethnic Dimensions of Matthean Salvation History.* Studies in the Bible and Early Christianity 14. Lewiston: Edwin Mellen Press, 1988.

Linnemann, Eta. *Is There a Synoptic Problem? Rethinking the Literary Dependence of the First Three Gospels.* Translated by Robert W. Yarbrough. Grand Rapids: Baker, 1992.

Longstaff, Thomas R. W. "Crisis and Christology: The Theology of Mark." Pages 373-92 in *New Synoptic Studies: The Cambridge Gospel Conference and Beyond.* Edited by William R. Farmer. Macon, Ga.: Mercer University Press, 1983.

———. "The Minor Agreements: An Examination of the Basic Argument." *CBQ* 37/2 (April 1975): 184-92.

———. "Order in the Synoptic Gospels: A Response." *The Second Century* 6/2 (1986): 98-106.

———. *Evidence of Conflation in Mark? A Study in the Synoptic Problem.* SBLDS 28. Missoula, Mont.: Scholars Press, 1977.

———. and Page A. Thomas, eds., *The Synoptic Problem: A Bibliography, 1716–1988.* New Gospel Studies 4. Macon, Ga.: Mercer, 1988.

———. "The Women of the Tomb: Matthew 28:1 Re-Examined." *NTS* 27/2 (1981): 277-82.

Lummis, E. *How Luke Was Written.* Cambridge: University Press, 1915.

Mack, Burton. *Q --- The Lost Gospel.* San Francisco: HarperSan Francisco, 1993.

Mann, C. S. *Mark: A New Translation with Introduction and Commentary.* AB 27. Garden City, N.Y.: Doubleday, 1986.

Marshall, I. H. *Last Supper and Lord's Supper.* Grand Rapids: Eerdmans, 1980.

Marxsen, Willi. *Mark the Evangelist.* Translated by R. Harrisville. Nashville: Abingdon, 1969.

McNicol, Allan J., with David L. Dungan and David B. Peabody, eds. *Beyond the Q Impasse: Luke's Use of Matthew, A Demonstration by the Research Team of the International Institute for [Renewal] of Gospel Studies.* Valley Forge, Pa.: Trinity Press International, 1996.

McNicol, Allan J. "The Composition of the Synoptic Eschatological Discourse." Pages 157-300 in *The Interrelations of the Gospels: A Symposium Led by M. É. Boismard — W. R. Farmer — F. Neirynck, Jerusalem 1984.* BETL 95. Edited by David L. Dungan. Leuven: Uitgeverij Peeters, 1990.

————. *Jesus' Directions for the Future: A Source and Redaction-History Study of the Use of the Eschatological Traditions in Paul and in the Synoptic Accounts of Jesus' Last Eschatological Discourse.* New Gospel Studies 9. Macon, Ga.: Mercer University Press, 1996.

Meier, John. "The Historical Jesus and the Historical Herodians." *JBL* 119/4 (2000): 740-46.

Meijboom, H. U. *A History and Critique of the Origin of the Marcan Hypothesis 1835-1866.* New Gospel Studies 8. Translated by John J. Kiwiet. Leuven: Peeters; Macon, Ga.: Mercer University Press, 1992.

Metzger, Bruce M. *The Text of the New Testament: Its Transmission, Corruption, and Restoration.* London/New York: Oxford University Press, 1964.

————. *A Textual Commentary on the Greek New Testament: A Companion Volume to the United Bible Societies' Greek New Testament (third edition).* London/New York: United Bible Societies, 1971.

Moffatt, James. *Introduction to the Literature of the New Testament.* New York: Scribner's; Edinburgh: T&T Clark, 1911.

————. *Introduction to the New Testament.* Edinburgh: T&T Clark, 1918.

Moule, C. F. D. *Birth of the New Testament.* 3d ed. San Francisco: Harper and Row, 1981.

————. *An Idiom-Book of New Testament Greek.* 2d ed. Cambridge: Cambridge University Press, 1959.

Neirynck, Frans. "Duality in Mark." *ETL* 47/3-4 (Dec. 1971): 394-463.

————. *Duality in Mark: Contributions to the Study of the Markan Redaction.* BETL 31. Leuven: Leuven University Press, 1972; 2d ed., 1988, with supplementary notes.

————. "Duplicate Expressions in the Gospel of Mark." *ETL* 48/1 (Jan-March, 1972): 150-209.

————. *Evangelica II: 1982-1991 Collected Essays.* BETL 99. Leuven: Leuven University Press, 1991.

————. "The Griesbach Hypothesis: The Phenomenon of Order." *ETL* 58 (1982):114.

————, in collaboration with Theo Hansen and Frans van Segbroeck. *The Minor Agreements of Matthew and Luke against Mark with a cumulative list.* BETL 37. Leuven: Leuven University Press, 1974.

————. "Q: From Source to Gospel." *ETL* 71 (1995): 421-30.

————. "Synoptic Problem." Pages 845-48 in *The Interpreter's Dictionary of the Bible.* Supplementary Volume. Nashville, Abingdon, 1976.

————. "Synoptic Problem." Pages 587-95 in *The New Jerome Biblical Commentary.* Edited by Raymond E. Brown, Joseph A. Fitzmyer, and Roland E. Murphy. Englewood Cliffs, N.J.: Prentice-Hall, 1990.

————. "The Two-Source Hypothesis Textual Discussion. Matthew 4:23-5:2 and the Matthean Composition of 4:23-11:1." Pages 23-46 in *The Interrelations of the Gospels: A Symposium Led by M. É. Boismard --- W. R. Farmer --- F. Neirynck, Jerusalem 1984.* BETL 95. Edited by David L. Dungan. Leuven: Uitgeverij Peeters, 1990.

Neville, David J. *Arguments from Order in Synoptic Source Criticism: A History and Critique.* New Gospel Studies 7. Macon, Ga.: Mercer University Press, 1994.

Nineham, Dennis E. *Studies in the Gospels: Essay in Memory of R. H. Lightfoot.* Oxford: Blackwell, 1955.

Öhler, Markus. "Der Zweimalige Hahnschrei der Markuspassion: Zur Textüberlieferung von Mk 14, 30. 68. 72." *ZNW* 85 (1994): 145-150.

Orchard, Bernard, and Thomas R. W. Longstaff, eds., *J. J. Griesbach: Synoptic and Text-Critical Studies 1776-1976.* SNTSMS 34. Cambridge: The University Press, 1978.

Orchard, Bernard, and Harold Riley. *The Order of the Synoptics: Why Three Synoptic Gospels?* Macon, Ga.: Mercer University Press, 1987.

Orchard, Bernard. "Part Two: "The Historical Tradition." Pages 111-226 in *The Order of the Synoptics: Why Three Synoptic Gospels?* Edited by Bernard Orchard and Harold Riley. Macon, Ga.: Mercer University Press, 1987.

Orchard, John Bernard. *A Synopsis of the Four Gospels in Greek Arranged According to the Two-Gospel Hypothesis.* Macon, Ga.: Mercer University Press; Edinburgh: T&T Clark, 1983.

Pagels, Elaine. *Adam, Eve, and the Serpent.* New York: Random House, 1988.

Painter, John. "When is a House not Home? Disciples and Family in Mark 3.13-35." *NTS* 45/4 (October 1999): 498-513.

Parker, D.C. *The Living Text of the Gospels.* Cambridge: Cambridge University Press: 1997.

Parker, Pierson. "The Posteriority of Mark." Pages 67-142 in *New Synoptic Studies: The Cambridge Gospel Conference and Beyond.* Edited by W. R. Farmer. Macon, Ga.: Mercer University Press, 1983.

Peabody, David Barrett. "Augustine and the Augustinian Hypothesis: A Reexamination of Augustine's Thought in *de consensu evangelistarum.*" Pages 37-66 in *New Synoptic Studies: The Cambridge Gospel Conference and Beyond.* Edited by W. R. Farmer. Macon, Ga.: Mercer University Press, 1983.

————. "Chapters in the History of the Linguistic Argument for Solving the Synoptic Problem: The Nineteenth Century in Context." Pages 47-68 in *Jesus, the Gospels, and the Church. Essays in Honor of William R. Farmer.* Edited by E. P. Sanders. Macon, Ga.: Mercer University Press, 1987.

————. "Farmer, William Reuben (1921-)." Pages 1:385-86 in *Dictionary of Biblical Interpretation.* 2 vols. Edited by John H. Hayes. Nashville: Abingdon, 1999.

————. "Griesbach, Johann Jakob (1745-1812)." Pages 319-25 in *Historical Handbook of Major Biblical Interpreters.* Edited by Donald K. McKim. Downers Grove, Ill.: Intervarsity, 1998.

————. "H. J. Holtzmann and His European Colleagues: Aspects of the Nineteenth-Century European Discussion of Gospel Origins." Pages 50-131 in *Biblical Studies and the Shifting of Paradigms: 1850-1914.* JSOTSS 192. Edited by Henning Graf Reventlow and William Farmer. Sheffield: Sheffield Academic Press, 1995.

————. "The Late Secondary Redaction of Mark's Gospel and the Griesbach Hypothesis. A Response to Helmut Koester." Pages 87-132 in *Colloquy on New Testament Studies: A Time for Reappraisal and Fresh Approaches.* Edited by Bruce C. Corley. Macon, Ga.: Mercer, 1983.

————. "Luke's Sequential Use of the Sayings of Jesus from Matthew's Great Discourses: A Chapter in the Source-Critical Analysis of Luke on the Two-Gospel (Neo-Griesbach) Hypothesis." Pages 37-58 in *Literary Studies in Luke-Acts: Essays in Honor of Joseph B. Tyson.* Edited by Richard P. Thompson and Thomas E. Phillips. Macon, Ga.: Mercer University Press, 1998

————. *Mark as Composer.* New Gospel Studies 1. Macon, Ga.: Mercer University Press, 1987.

————. "A Pre-Markan Prophetic Sayings Tradition and the Synoptic Problem." *JBL* 97 (1978): 391-409.

Peabody, David Barrett, and Thomas R. W. Longstaff. *A Synopsis of Mark: A Synopsis of the First Three Gospels Showing the Parallels to the Markan Text.* CD-ROM. Distributed by Trinity Press International of Harrisburg, Pa., 2002.

Peabody, David B. "Repeated Language in Matthew: Clues to the Order and Composition of Luke and Mark." Pages 647-86 in *Society of Biblical Literature 1991 Seminar Papers.* SBLSP 30. Edited by Eugene H. Lovering, Jr. Atlanta: Scholars Press, 1991.

―――. "Response to the Multi-Stage Hypothesis." Pages 217-30 in *The Interrelations of the Gospels: A Symposium Led by M. É. Boismard ― W. R. Farmer ― F. Neirynck, Jerusalem 1984.* BETL 95. Edited by David L. Dungan. Leuven: Uitgeverij Peeters, 1990.

Peabody, D. B., and B. Reicke. "Synoptic Problem." Pages 2:517-24 in *Dictionary of Biblical Interpretation.* 2 vols. Edited by John H. Hayes. Nashville: Abingdon, 1999.

Pesch, Rudolf. *Das Abendmahl und Jesus Todesverständnis.* Freiburg: Herder, 1978.

Petersen, William L. *Tatian's Diatessaron: Its Creation, Dissemination, Significance, & History in Scholarship.* Supplements to Vigiliae Christianae 25. Leiden: Brill, 1994.

Räisänen, Heiki. *Das "Messiasgeheimnis" im Markusevangelium.* Helsinki: Lansi-Suomi, 1976. ET, *The Messianic Secret in Mark.* Translated by Christopher Tuckett. Edinburgh: T&T Clark, 1990.

―――. "The 'Messianic Secret' in Mark's Gospel." Pages 132-40 in *The Messianic Secret.* Issues in Religion and Theology 1. Translated and edited by Christopher Tuckett. London: SPCK, 1983; Philadelphia: Fortress, 1983.

Reicke, Bo. *The Roots of the Synoptic Gospels.* Philadelphia: Fortress, 1986.

―――. "A Test of Synoptic Relationships: Matthew 10:17-23 and 24:9-14 with Parallels." Pages 209-22 in *New Synoptic Studies: The Cambridge Gospel Conference and Beyond.* Edited by W. R. Farmer. Macon, Ga.: Mercer University Press, 1983.

Riesenfeld, Harald. *The Gospel Tradition and Its Beginnings: A Study in the Limits of "Formgeschichte." An Address Delivered at the Opening Session of the Congress on the Four Gospels in 1957, in the Examination Schools, Oxford, on 16 September 1957.* London: A. R. Mowbray, 1957; repr., 1961.

Rist, John M. *On the Independence of Matthew and Mark.* SNTSMS 32. Cambridge: Cambridge University Press, 1978.

Robinson, James M., Paul Hoffmann, and John S. Kloppenborg, eds. *The Critical Edition of Q: Synopsis Including the Gospels of Matthew and Luke, Mark and Thomas with English, German and French translations of Q and Thomas.* Minneapolis: Fortress; Leuven: Peeters, 2000.

Robinson, James M. "The Sayings Gospel 'Q.'" Pages 1:361-88 in *The Four Gospels: 1992 Festschrift Frans Neirynck.* 3 vols. Edited by F. van Segbroeck et al. Louvain: Leuven University Press, 1992.

Rolland, Philippe. "A New Look at the Synoptic Question." *European Journal of Theology* 8/2 (1999): 133-44.

―――. *Les premiers évangiles: un nouveau regard sur le probléme synoptique.* Lectio Divina 116. Paris: Cerf, 1984.

BIBLIOGRAPHY

Ropes, James Hardy. *The Synoptic Gospels.* Cambridge, Mass.: Harvard University Press, 1934. Repr. with a new preface by David E. Nineham. London: Oxford University Press, 1960.

Samuel, S. Johnson. "Review of David Barrett Peabody, *Mark as Composer.*" *Bangalore Theological Forum* 22 (1990): 45-63.

Sanday, William, ed. *Studies in the Synoptic Gospels: By Members of the University of Oxford.* Oxford: Clarendon Press, 1911.

Sanders, E. P. *Jewish Law from Jesus to the Mishnah.* London: SCM; Philadelphia: Trinity Press International, 1990.

Sanders, E. P. and Margaret Davies. *Studying the Synoptic Gospels.* London: SCM; Philadelphia: Trinity Press International, 1989.

Sanders, E. P. *The Tendencies of the Synoptic Tradition.* SNTSMS 9. Cambridge: The University Press, 1969.

Schleiermacher, Friedrich Daniel Ernst. *A Critical Essay on the Gospel of St. Luke: With an introduction by the translator, containing an account of the controversy respecting the origin of the three first Gospels since Bishop Marsh's dissertation.* ET by Connop Thirwall. *Über die Schriften des Lucas, ein kritischer Versuch.* Berlin: G. Riemer, 1817. London: J. Taylor, 1825.

Schulze, Johann Daniel. "Über den schriftstellerischen Charakter und Werth des Evangelisten Markus. Ein Beitrag zur Specialhermeneutik des N. T." In *Analekten für das Studium der exegetischen und systematischen Theologie.* Edited by Carl August Gottlieb Keil und Heinrich Gottlieb Tzschirner. Leipzig. J. A. Barth, 1812-22. "Erster Abschnitt." 2/2 (1814): 104-51. "Zweiter Abschnitt. Erster Halfte." 2/3 (1815): 69-132. "Zweiter Abschnitt. Zweiter Halfte." 3/1 (1816): 88-127.

Segbroeck, Frans van, et al. *The Four Gospels 1992: Festschrift Frans Neirynck.* 3 vols. BETL 100. Leuven: Leuven University Press/Uitgeverij Peeters, 1992.

Seim, Turid Karlsen. *The Double Message: Patterns of Gender in Luke-Acts.* Edinburgh: T&T Clark, 1994.

Senior, Donald. *The Passion of Jesus in the Gospel of Mark.* Collegeville, Minn.: Liturgical Press, 1984.

―――. *The Passion Narrative According to Matthew: A Redactional Study.* BETL 39. Leuven: Leuven University Press, 1982.

Shepherd, Tom. *Markan Sandwich Stories: Narration, Definition and Function.* Andrews University Seminary Doctoral Dissertation Series 18. Grand Rapids: Andrews University Press, 1993.

Skeat, T. C. "The Codex Sinaiticus, the Codex Vaticanus, and Constantine." *JTS* 50 pt 2 (1999): 583-625.

Stein, Robert H. *The Synoptic Problem: An Introduction.* Grand Rapids: Baker, 1987.

Stendahl, Krister. *The School of St. Matthew.* Philadelphia: Fortress Press, 1968.

Stoldt, Hans-Herbert. *Geschichte und Kritik der Markus-hypothese.* Göttingen: Vandenhoeck & Ruprecht, 1977. 2d ed., Giessen: Brunen, 1986. ET of first edition, *History and Criticism of the Marcan Hypothesis.* Translated and edited by Donald J. Niewyk. Macon, Ga.: Mercer University Press; Edinburgh: T&T Clark, 1980).

————. "Reflections on Legitimacy and Limits of Theological Criticism by Hans-Herbert Stoldt." English translation by Virgil Howard. *PSTJ* (Summer 1980): 49-54.

Storr, Gottlob C. *Ueber den Zweck der evangelischen Geschichte und der Briefe Johannis.* Tübingen, J. F. Heerbrandt, 1786.

Strecker, Georg. *Minor Agreements: Symposium Göttingen 1991.* Göttinger Theologische Arbeiten 50. Göttingen: Vandenhoeck & Ruprecht, 1993.

Streeter, Burnett Hillman. *The Four Gospels: A Study of Origins, Treating of the Manuscript Tradition, Sources, Authorship, and Dates.* London: Macmillan 1924.

Streeter, B. H. "V. St. Mark's Knowledge and Use of Q." Pages 166-83 in *Studies in the Synoptic Gospels: By Members of the University of Oxford.* Edited by W. Sanday. Oxford: Clarendon Press, 1911.

Stroth, Friedrich Andreas. "Von Interpolationem im Evangelium Matthaei." In *Repertorium für biblische und morgenlandische Literatur* 9 (1781): 99-156.

Styler, G. "The Priority of Mark." In *The Birth of the New Testament.* Edited by C.F.D. Moule. 2d. ed. San Francisco: Harper & Row, 1962.

Swanson, Reuben, ed. *New Testament Greek Manuscripts: Variant Readings Arranged in Horizontal Line Against Codex Vaticanus, Matthew.* Sheffield: Sheffield Academic Press; Pasadena, Calif.: William Carey International University Press, 1995.

————, ed. *New Testament Greek Manuscripts: Variant Readings Arranged in Horizontal Line Against Codex Vaticanus, Mark.* Sheffield: Sheffield Academic Press; Pasadena, Calif.: William Carey International University Press, 1995.

————, ed. *New Testament Greek Manuscripts: Variant Readings Arranged in Horizontal Line Against Codex Vaticanus, Luke.* Sheffield: Sheffield Academic Press; Pasadena, Calif.: William Carey International University Press, 1995.

Taylor, Vincent. *The Gospel According to Mark.* 2d ed. New York: Macmillan, 1966. Repr., Grand Rapids: Baker, 1981.

Thompson, Richard P., and Thomas E. Phillips. *Literary Studies in Luke-Acts: Essays in Honor of Joseph B. Tyson.* Macon, Ga.: Mercer University Press, 1998.

BIBLIOGRAPHY

Tuckett, Christopher M. "Jesus and the Gospels." Pages 8:71-86 in *The New Interpreter's Bible.* 12 proposed vols. Edited by Leander Keck et al. Nashville: Abingdon Press, 1995.

———. "The Minor Agreements and Textual Criticism." Pages 135-41 in *Minor Agreements: Symposium Göttingen 1991.* Göttinger Theologische Arbeiten 50. Edited by Georg Strecker. Göttingen: Vandenhoeck & Ruprecht, 1993.

———. "Review of Allan J. McNicol, et al., *Beyond the Q Impasse.*" *JBL* 117/2 (Summer 1998): 363-65.Online: http://www.bookreviews.org/bookdetail.asp?TitleId=2355&CodePage=2355

———. *The Revival of the Griesbach Hypothesis: An Analysis and Appraisal.* SNTSMS 44. Cambridge/New York: Cambridge University Press, 1983.

———, ed. *Synoptic Studies: The Ampleforth Conferences of 1982 and 1983.* JSNTSS 7. Sheffield: JSOT Press, 1984.

Vaganay, Léon. *Le problème synoptique—une hypothèse de travail Bibliothèque de théologie.* série 3: Théologie biblique 1. Tournai: Desclée, 1954.

Walker, Jr., William O., ed. *The Relationship Among the Gospels: An Interdisciplinary Dialogue.* TUMSR 5. San Antonio: Trinity University Press, 1978.

Wansborough, Henry, ed. *Jesus and the Oral Gospel Tradition.* JSNTSS 64. Sheffield: JSOT Press, 1991.

Wrede, William. *Das Messiasgeheimnis in den Evangelien: Zugleich ein Beitrag zum Verständnis des Markusevangeliums.* Göttingen: Vandenhoeck & Ruprecht, 1963. English translation by J. C. G. Grieg. *The Messianic Secret.* Cambridge: James Clark & Co., 1971.

Zeller, Eduard. "Studien zur neutestamentlichen theologie 4: Vergleichende Übersicht uber den Wörtervorrath der neutestamentlichen Schriftsteller." *Theologische Jahrbücher* 2 (1843): 443-543.

INDEX OF NAMES

SELECTED SCRIPTURE INDEX

SELECTED SUBJECT INDEX